STATISTICAL ANALYSIS
FOR BUSINESS DECISIONS

STATISTICAL
FOR BUSINESS

McGRAW-HILL

New York   St. Louis   San Francisco   Auckland
Mexico   Montreal   New Delhi   Panama   Pa

ANALYSIS
DECISIONS

Paul Jedamus
College of Business and Administration
University of Colorado

Robert Frame
School of Business Administration
Southern Methodist University

Robert Taylor
College of Business and Administration
University of Colorado

BOOK COMPANY

Düsseldorf   Johannesburg   Kuala Lumpur   London
São Paulo   Singapore   Sydney   Tokyo   Toronto

STATISTICAL ANALYSIS FOR BUSINESS DECISIONS

34567890 DODO 7987

Library of Congress Cataloging in Publication Data

Jedamus, Paul, date
    Statistical analysis for business decisions.

    Includes index.
    1. Statistical decision. I. Frame, Robert, joint
author. II. Taylor, Robert, date   joint author.
III. Title.
HD69.D4J43   658.4'03   75-20762
ISBN 0-07-032302-X

This book was set in Times Roman.
The editors were William J. Kane and Shelly Levine Langman;
the designer was Scott Chelius;
the production supervisor was Charles Hess.
New drawings were done by Eric G. Hieber Associates Inc.
R. R. Donnelley & Sons Company was printer and binder.

CONTENTS

CONTENTS

PREFACE

This book has grown out of our experience in teaching business statistics, a course that is all too often regarded by students as an ordeal to be endured or as an imposing hurdle, difficult to cross but meaningless in relation to other business subjects studied. We have found, however, that the subject matter of such a course can prove both interesting and relevant when cast in the context of concrete business decision problems. Furthermore, we have found that even difficult content can be readily mastered by most students when the material is presented to them in small "bites" which identify specific learning objectives and provide a feedback mechanism for measuring the student's progress toward them. We have therefore designed a basic book in business statistics which combines the more positive features of programmed learning—i.e., carefully stated learning objectives and frequent reinforcement and feedback—with an informal style that is more interesting and readable than many of the highly structured programmed texts available. To these ends, this book incorporates the following principal features:

Division of the materials into a number of small, self-contained segments covering particular topics. Each of the 23 *modules* (which are roughly equivalent to chapters in a conventional textbook) is further divided into a number of *sections*, which each have specific learning objectives.

General learning objectives are presented at the beginning of each module, and *specific learning objectives* are provided in advance of each section. These specific objectives clearly define what a student is expected to learn from a given segment of material and are stated in terms that enable him to determine whether he has achieved them.

Review exercises to be worked by the student are found at the end of each section. Answers follow each exercise, enabling students to check their solutions and measure their own progress toward the stated learning objectives for that section. These self-correcting exercises reinforce student learning and provide a clear indication of when it may be necessary to restudy previous material before proceeding to the next learning step.

A large collection of unanswered *questions* and *problems* is provided at the end of each module to test the student's ability to integrate important concepts and apply them to realistic business problems. Complete solutions are contained in an *Instructor's Manual*.

Intuitive explanations of important principles are substituted for mathematical proofs wherever possible. The mathematical sophistication required of the student is minimal, only occasionally at the level of elementary algebra.

Difficult concepts are presented in an informal but straightforward style and illustrated by simple, concrete examples drawn from business situations.

Classical statistics and decision theory are integrated with "modern" Bayesian concepts by emphasizing the combined use of information in the form of historical data, subjective judgments, and sample results in business decision-making situations.

The book can be used in a variety of ways and for a variety of different purposes. For example, the authors use it as the basic text for a two-semester sequence in quantitative analysis that includes conventional topics in business statistics but places considerable emphasis on statistical inference and decision theory. Students also learn computer programming in this course sequence, and although computers are neither covered in this book nor necessary preparation for it, a number of the end-of-module problems can serve as student programming exercises or as vehicles for the illustration and use of library programs. (These are identified in the Instructor's Manual).

For a shorter course, many of the modules can be omitted conveniently. Modules 15–18 deal with special topics that are not required preparation for the following modules. Some instructors may prefer to omit portions of Modules 19–23, which deal with the use of subjective probabilities and Bayesian methods in solving decision problems. On the other hand, an instructor wishing to emphasize decision theory and the Bayesian approach could omit any of the material in the first 9 modules (or in Modules 15–18) without loss of continuity.

Contributions of students and colleagues to the preparation of this book are too numerous to acknowledge here. We cannot begin to identify the source of all the ideas and criticisms that influenced the final product. Naturally, we must take responsibility for any errors, omissions, or inconsistencies.

Paul Jedamus
Robert Frame
Robert Taylor

STATISTICAL ANALYSIS
FOR BUSINESS DECISIONS

MODULE 1
INTRODUCTION

General learning objectives

Your general learning objectives for this module are to be able to:

1. Define the term *statistics* both in its singular and plural meanings
2. Identify major areas to be covered in this book

INTRODUCTION

To most students, the study of statistics is a mystery. We'd like to keep it that way.

Look at the elements common to most murder mysteries. There is a lot at stake, and decisions must continually be made in the light of incomplete or even confusing information. The level of tension—even fear—is high. From an abundance of data, facts must be ascertained and sifted for clues. The clues are analyzed in a logical, systematic way, leading to a conclusion, or at least a hypothesis about the guilty person. Often the hypothesis is tested by setting up a carefully structured situation, and appropriate action is taken to solve the mystery.

A business decision maker is confronted with much the same situation. Important problems must be solved, where the stakes are high. Information is incomplete and confusing. People who have the ability to identify relevant facts and the skill to analyze the problem have a higher than average probability of reaching a successful solution. The process is exciting, and resolution of the problem is satisfying.

Your situation as a student of statistics isn't very different. We hope to relieve some of the tension and fear but preserve the other characteristics of the mystery. Careful sifting of information, identifying fruitful methods of analysis, and tracing a logical path to the solution of a problem will all be part of the process. It can be both exciting and rewarding.

STATISTICS AND BUSINESS DECISIONS

Statistics (plural) are numerical data that serve as a record of the past. Statistics (singular) is the collection, analysis, and interpretation of numerical data. Statistics (singular) is also a process for making informed business decisions. Let's examine each of these definitions in more detail.

Statistics as numerical data can be dry bits of irrelevant trivia or interesting clues to future performance, depending upon their nature and their meaning to the person using them. Casualty lists of Civil War battles, for example, are grim reminders of the magnitude of human suffering and the folly of war, but they are of interest mainly to the historian since they provide few clues that relate to the future. Similarly, the record of bank failures in the depression of the 1930s may provide a measure of the

3

weakness of a past economic system but little useful information to guide current economic policy. Both the latest report of stock market transactions and the profit and loss statement of General Motors may be boring statistics to the average English professor but interesting or even exciting to an investor. The difference, of course, is how knowledgeable the reader is about the statistics and how meaningful they may be with respect to future decisions of the reader.

A considerable body of knowledge has been accumulated dealing with the collection, analysis, and interpretation of numerical data for business use. This process— the study of statistics—is demanding and requires considerable training and experience. It involves the use of a scientific process to decide what data need to be collected, how they are to be obtained and analyzed, and how the outcome of the analysis bears upon the problem that initiated the effort. This process is problem-oriented and forward-looking. Its foundation is mathematics, particularly probability theory; its methodology is scientific; and its focus is on problem solving.

In recent years, particularly since World War II, tremendous strides have been made in developing more powerful statistical techniques for the analysis of business problems. These new techniques, incorporated with the accumulated knowledge of the past, constitute a large part of the framework of business decision theory, to which this book is an introduction. You'll find that studying statistics is demanding, but more important, it should be interesting and perhaps even exciting because its focus will be on developing your capacity to make better-informed business decisions —and this is the stuff that turns management trainees into corporate executives.

ORGANIZATION OF THE BOOK

The contents of this book can be divided into three clearly defined areas:

1. Information analysis
2. Statistical inference
3. Decision analysis

The general content of each of these areas will be discussed briefly.

INFORMATION ANALYSIS

The area incorporating information analysis includes the first nine modules of this book, essentially covering data collection, presentation, and analysis, descriptive statistics, index numbers, time-series analysis, the analysis of association, and forecasting. Most of this material is not difficult, either conceptually or computationally. It forms a "least common denominator" for effective understanding of the business scene.

The place of this material in statistics courses has had an interesting history. For years, it formed the core of most introductory business statistics courses. Then, around the time of World War II, it was overshadowed by the great development in the theory and application of techniques of statistical estimation and inference. Still later, in the early 1960s, decision analysis was developed and almost immediately became widely used in business.

Since statistical inference and decision analysis are both important and conceptually difficult, most recent texts emphasized them, and relegated information analysis to cursory treatment at the beginning of a text or to a collection of miscellaneous topics at the end.

As a consequence, employers were discovering that while students knew some fairly sophisticated statistical techniques, they didn't "know the territory." The terms "t test," "variance ratio," and "beta coefficient" were in their vocabulary, but they didn't know what GNP meant (to say nothing of its current level) or how to construct a simple price index, calculate a rate of increase, or measure seasonal variation.

The modules on information analysis are designed to fill this gap. Among other things, you'll learn where to go to get business information, how to use it to measure changes in business activity, and how, with a little luck, to make reasonable estimates of the shape of the future.

STATISTICAL INFERENCE

When confronted with uncertainty, scientists usually resort to experimentation. They formulate some basic notion, called a *hypothesis*, about the behavior of the phenomenon under consideration and design an experiment whose results will either confirm or refute the hypothesis. (It may, of course, prove to be inconclusive.) Usually the experiment cannot encompass every possible case involving the subject being investigated, so sampling must be used. The same situation holds in business. Does a manufactured product meet specifications? Will customers accept a new product? Is brand A really better? Will a new inventory policy reduce total inventory costs? To answer these questions, an investigator must design an experiment that involves basing a conclusion about the characteristic being studied upon evidence obtained from a sample.

This is no simple matter because even the most carefully selected samples will not have exactly the same characteristics as the larger set of items from which the samples were obtained, and no two samples will be likely to be exactly the same. Therefore you must use rather sophisticated statistical techniques to measure sampling error and to guard against arriving at a false conclusion about the hypothesis in question.

Problems like these have typically been approached using a methodology known as classical *statistical inference*, or hypothesis testing. This methodology forms a conceptual basis for much of the quantitative analysis done in market research, production, inventory, and quality control, the testing and evaluation of personnel, the application of sampling to auditing, and many other business applications.

Modules 10 to 18 are related to this area. Module 10 develops concepts of probability which you'll use throughout the remainder of the book. Modules 11 to 14 develop the reasoning behind statistical inference, and answer questions you may have about how large samples should be and how to measure the chances you're taking of making a mistake when estimating values from samples. Modules 15 to 18 develop special applications, including estimating the values of a variable (such as the price of a stock) on the basis of other variables (such as the company's sales, profits, and dividends) and how sample surveys are designed, conducted, and interpreted.

DECISION ANALYSIS

Decisions play an important role in your everyday life. When to get up, what to order for lunch, or whether or not to study tonight, are the sorts of decisions you must make daily. Of course not all decisions are trivial. Many involve millions of dollars or even life and death. Indeed decision making may constitute one of the highest forms of human activity. Psychologists tell us of a universal desire to avoid making decisions whenever possible, and there is abundant evidence that those who are willing to perform this activity and perform it well are among the best-paid members of society.

Why is such a premium placed on the willingness and ability to make decisions? Perhaps it is because the decision maker always runs the risk of being wrong. By its very nature, making a decision involves choosing between a number of possible courses of action that could be taken. After the decision has been made and action taken, time and hindsight may show that a better choice among the alternatives could have been made. You are rarely sure, at the time you make it, what all the ramifications of a particular decision may be. There is always the chance that a well-thought-out decision may produce unfortunate—even disastrous—results. Even a truly superior decision maker lives with the knowledge that some decisions will, in retrospect, prove costly.

But can you really characterize a particular decision as "good" or "bad" depending solely on how things finally work out? The decision to repair the motor of an old car may seem perfectly sound to you in the light of an anticipated trip and the car's generally sound condition, at least at the time the decision is made. If the car is totally wrecked in an accident a week after the repair is made, you may lose all the money invested in the repair, but can you fault yourself with a "bad" decision? If you make an investment that appears highly speculative with very little chance of working out well, can you credit yourself with a "good" decision if it brings returns beyond your expectations? In one sense you may answer these questions yes, in another, no.

The ambiguity here can be resolved by recognizing that there is a difference between the merit of the alternative chosen (viewed from an after-the-fact perspective) and the merit of the method or procedure used to select that alternative. While you can never be sure that a particular decision will turn out well, you owe it to yourself to be sure that the *method* used to make the decision was the best available.

From the 1940s these problems were approached from the standpoint of a methodology known as *classical statistical inference*. This method attacks the problem by explicitly measuring the risks of sampling errors using probability and statistical theory and by incorporating these risks into the formulation of appropriate decision rules.

In the early 1960s this methodology was extended by enabling the decision maker to bring to bear on the problem not only the evidence obtained from sampling but also from accumulated past experience. Further, the costs as well as the probabilities of possible errors in interpreting the sample were systematically incorporated into the process of formulating decision rules. This extension of classical analysis is called *decision analysis* or *Bayesian analysis*.

This book views Bayesian analysis as a logical and fruitful extension of classical analysis and attempts to integrate these concepts into a unified and consistent theory for making business decisions under uncertainty. Modules 19 to 23 develop the rationale of Bayesian decision analysis.

MATHEMATICS OR MANAGEMENT?

In the modules that follow, you'll find neither a treatise on mathematical statistics nor a cookbook compendium of formulas for all occasions. To be an intelligent user of the statistical method and to form a base from which you may become a proficient practitioner, you need to obtain a firm grasp of the logic behind the process you are learning to apply. In a sense, then, the book becomes an exercise in applied logic more than in applied mathematics. While formulas and techniques are important, they should be understood for what they are—a means of transition between a nonmathematical process of applied logic and solutions to practical problems in applied decision making.

The world of business is extremely complex. To make a mathematical model that exactly described all the variables and interrelationships in even a small part of such a system would match in complexity the mathematics involved, say, in putting a man on the moon. Therefore it is obvious that the models of the business world you'll be using in an introduction to statistical analysis for business will be very much simplified versions of the real thing. Nevertheless, all the models of business situations used will bear a resemblance to the real world. Some will be general enough so that solutions derived from them will represent a significant improvement over solutions that are now commonly applied every day in business practice.

HOW TO USE THE BOOK

This book is divided into *learning modules*, which are subdivided into single-concept sections. A "learning module" might be just a fancy name for a chapter, but there's more to it than that. Each module begins with a set of *general learning objectives*, and each section begins with a set of specific action-oriented *learning objectives*. You don't have to read a module and then ask: What am I supposed to get out of this material? You are told in advance what you should master, in very specific terms.

At the end of each section, you'll find a set of *review exercises* (in addition to the end-of-chapter problems). These exercises, closely tied to the learning objectives, are designed so that you can quickly and accurately check to see that you understand the material in the section before continuing. Use them to your advantage.

REVIEW EXERCISES 1

1. Statistics:
   a. Is the collection, analysis, and interpretation of numerical data.
   b. Is a process for making informed business decisions.
   c. Are numerical data.
   d. All the above.
2. Match the definitions with the major areas they represent:

a. The process of formulating and testing hypotheses based on sample information	(1) Decision analysis
	(2) Statistical inference
b. The process of the collection, analysis, and interpretation of numerical data	(3) Information analysis
c. The process of combining sample evidence with past experience to arrive at a course of action	

Answers 1

1. d   2. a. 2; *b.* 3; *c.* 1

Questions and Problems

1.1. Important decisions that don't work out well usually attract lots of attention, like Ford's decision to build the Edsel. Can you think of other now infamous decisions in business or politics that hindsight has shown to be bloopers? Are these necessarily "bad" decisions? Explain.

1.2. What factors do you consider in deciding whether to take along a raincoat or an umbrella? Have you ever been drenched from a failure to take either? Or have you lugged both along on what turned out to be a hot, sunny day? Should the blame be placed with the decision-making process you used, or did a sound decision simply go awry?

1.3. Give some examples of some situations you have faced involving decision making under uncertainty. Identify the source of the uncertainty in each situation.

1.4. Give two examples of business decisions that would be made under uncertainty.

1.5. Find a list of statistics (from a newspaper, periodical, or book) that might be of interest to a businessperson and describe a situation in which such statistics might be useful in making a business decision.

1.6. State a hypothesis that a businessperson might make relative to the operation of a business. Outline in general terms a possible method that might be used to test the hypothesis.

1.7. A supermarket chain is considering building a store in a new suburb. Make a list of factors that the decision makers would be likely to consider in deciding whether or not to build. For each factor identify pertinent statistics they might want to obtain, and state whether or not uncertainty would be involved in obtaining them.

1.8. The corner newsboy may appear to have an environment free of the stresses of executive decision making. The economics of his business are indeed simple. Suppose he buys papers for 7 cents each and sells them for 10 cents. However, if he has only one opportunity at the start of his day to purchase his inventory of newspapers, he *does* have to decide how many to try to sell.

    a. Is this decision making under uncertainty?

    b. What factors should be considered in making this decision?

    c. What (if anything) complicates this seemingly simple decision situation?

MODULE 2
DATA, INFORMATION, AND DECISIONS

General learning objectives

Your general learning objectives for this module are to be able to:

1. Explain the nature and use of data, and why the way a problem is stated and the kind of data gathered affect solutions and decisions
2. Describe how data are used to record, report, control, and decide
3. Recognize common sources of errors that can occur in your own statistical analyses or those of others

Section 2.A
How Data Affect Decisions

Learning objective

Your learning objective for this section is to be able to distinguish between numbers and the things that numbers represent.

Man seems to have an insatiable desire to count, measure, and compare. Show a man a mountain, and he asks: How high is it? Show him two, and he asks: Which one is higher?

It has often been said that measurement is the beginning of understanding. The process of counting, measuring, and comparing is fundamental to scientific progress. Progress itself presumes measurement and comparison of where you are with where you were.

That business decisions are affected by the collection and analysis of data hardly needs elaboration. In contemplating an investment, an analyst would study the history of a company's stock prices, earnings, profits, cash flow, capital position, debt-equity ratio, liquidity, price-earnings ratio, and many other statistics which reflect the company's strengths and weaknesses. In planning and pricing programs, TV executives rely heavily on audience ratings of competing programs. Economic policy is both determined and evaluated on the basis of changes in the consumer price index.

We could go on and on. It's probably safe to say that without the process of quantification and measurement the economy would grind to a rapid halt. If you doubt this, try a microexample. See if you can get through a day without using numbers—no measurement of time, money, distance, etc!

In the remainder of this section, you'll study some examples of things people quantify and how the process of quantification affects their decisions.

EXAMPLE 1: GRADES

Stripped to its essentials, the objective of a higher education is to learn something. Reduced to an absurdity, the objective of a higher education is to accumulate enough credits (120) with a high enough grade-point average (2.0) to get a college degree (1).

This numbers game originated in a sincere attempt to validate the breadth and depth of the collegiate experience but is perverted by many faculty and students alike to the point where a crucial switch takes place. The accumulation of numbers, rather

12

than measuring the progress a student is making toward an education, *becomes* an education. The numbers are mistaken for the real thing.

Statisticians call things like credit hours and grade-point averages *surrogates*, where a surrogate is essentially something measurable (credit hours) that is substituted for something else that is not measurable (an education). Maximization of the surrogate, it is then assumed, leads to maximization of the attribute the surrogate measures. Maybe it does and maybe it doesn't. Has it so far in your education? If not, is it the fault of the system, or yours?

EXAMPLE 2: CARS

The number of cars on our streets and highways at any one time is a *datum*. A datum is a statistician's way of saying "a numerical fact." The number of cars, whatever it is, is simply a description of a physical presence of that many cars. The number as such is amoral and neutral, but the presence it measures is not. To some the number of cars measures progress, affluence, and freedom. To others the same number measures pollution and materialism. Numbers in the abstract are neutral, but our reaction to numbers in the real world is often emotional.

EXAMPLE 3: GNP

Gross national product (GNP) is an aggregate which measures the production of goods and services in a nation. It is obtained by adding expenditures for final products and services for the economy. The use of final products eliminates double counting. For example, expenditures for steel and glass by automobile manufacturers to make cars are not counted because they are included in the final purchase price of the car.

National goals for the economy are usually stated in terms of expected levels of GNP or rates of growth of GNP adjusted for changes in the value of the dollar. The assumption implicit in stating goals this way is that growth in GNP is commensurate with growth in national well-being.

However, GNP is inflated by factors that no one would construe as being to the benefit of the nation. A natural disaster adds to GNP. An extensive and severe earthquake, for example, could entail the expenditure of billions of dollars for emergency services and rebuilding, which would all add to GNP, while the nation would have suffered a huge social loss in the form of death, suffering, and the depletion of natural resources. Another example is the untold waste of money and resources generated by car accidents. Medical bills, litigation fees, and replacement of property all add to GNP, but all are measures of a social tragedy.

On the other hand, GNP does not include many social costs. The depletion of irreplaceable natural resources is often not measured adequately by customary accounting procedures which would ultimately reflect in GNP. An industry that was a big polluter would reflect real social costs only if it cleaned up the pollution and if those costs were reflected in the cost of their product to the consumer. GNP, then, includes some socially undesirable costs and excludes others. Rather than assuming that whatever makes GNP bigger makes the country better, we need a compilation you might call gross social product, which would measure the changes in the nation's quality of life. Economists, statisticians, and others are well aware of this need and are hard at work attempting to devise meaningful statistics. The task is incredibly difficult. Can you imagine some of the things you would have to consider in such an effort? Remember that even if such a measure were devised, it would still be just a number. It would be a *measure* of quality, not quality itself.

These examples should illustrate that people not only use data to make decisions but that the decisions they make are often affected by the nature of the data they collect.

REVIEW EXERCISES 2.A

1. Accumulation of credit hours is:
    a. The same as an education.
    b. A surrogate for an education.
    c. A surrogate for a grade-point average.
    d. None of the above.
2. Numbers are often emotional: true or false?

Answers 2.A

1. b. An education is a qualitative concept that is very difficult to measure. The accumulation of credit hours is a surrogate that represents an education and can be quantified, but it is by no means the *same* as an education.
2. False; numbers can't be emotional. However, the things numbers represent can evoke all sorts of emotional responses in people.

Section 2.B
The Uses of Numbers

Learning objectives

Your learning objectives for this section are to be able to:

1. Differentiate between recording, reporting, controlling, and deciding
2. Differentiate between primary and secondary data
3. Distinguish between data and information
4. Explain what is meant by "control by exception"
5. Identify the key elements involved in decision making under uncertainty

---

Business uses numbers in four ways: to *record*, to *report*, to *control*, and to *decide*. A *record* is one or more numbers that is kept, presumably because it may be of interest at some future date, either as an identifier (such as a social security number) or as a piece of information (such as your gross earnings last year). A *report* is a compilation of records organized to facilitate comparison and understanding. Records and reports are useful when they assist people in controlling activities and making decisions. In this context, "control" means the guidance of a *process* toward specific objectives, while "decide" is a broader term that includes controlling. "Control" can be thought of as short-run and operational, such as the control of quality of automobiles on an assembly line, while "decide" is longer-run and related to policy, as in the decision of an automobile manufacturer to introduce a new product. Each of these functions will be elaborated upon throughout this book, and each will be commented upon briefly below.

RECORDING

It's hard to believe the volume and variety of records kept in an economy. Massive files on individuals are maintained by employers, lenders, credit bureaus, and governmental units including school systems, city, county, and state agencies, the Internal Revenue Service, the Bureau of the Census, the Social Security Administration, Selective Service, the FBI, and countless other agencies.

Data on consumers' financial, educational, and personal characteristics, how they spend their time and money, their preferences regarding consumer goods, TV programs, and political candidates are collected, maintained, and evaluated.

The college or university you are attending has records—probably duplicated in five or six places from professors' offices to central administrative files—concerning every course you have taken, when and where you took it, and the grade you received, along with many descriptors such as your sex, age, marital status, and parents' income and occupation. These data are recorded and preserved indefinitely for good reason: you'd be pretty unhappy if you couldn't get a transcript or proof of your graduation.

A recent calculation suggests adopting a new unit of classification for the amount of data kept by the federal government, the *stadium*. Translating the billions of documents into millions of cubic feet and figuring the cubic feet in a typical professional football stadium, the analyst found that the documents would fill four or five stadia from bottom to top.

Impractical though it is, this calculation illustrates the magnitude of the problem and suggests that before you keep any record you should carefully consider whether it should be kept, in what form it should be kept, and how long it should be kept.

Primary data and information systems. Data collected and used by the same individual or agency are called *primary data*. You collect and maintain data about your personal affairs, from your shoe size to your checkbook balance. Companies

15

and governmental agencies do the same thing many times over, covering every aspect of their operation.

Data can be collected in a number of ways. Most data are derived through the routine recording of the on-going process of the operation of the business. For example, as raw materials are ordered, received, and used, they generate data. The labor and material put into a product are routinely recorded. The number of units produced, inventoried, and sold constitute still more data. Other important sources of primary data are censuses, surveys, and experiments.

Data and information are not synonymous. Data become information only when they are useful and available. This implies the organization of data files and efficient means of data retrieval. Data can be stored on pieces of paper in folders in file cabinets, on microfilm, punched cards, or computer tape, in a computer memory, or in someone's head. Most organizations use all the storage devices mentioned above; some use many more. The same datum can be stored in many different places or in just one place.

How data files are created, maintained, accessed, merged, and purged constitutes a field called *information systems*. To define the data requirements of an organization and then organize appropriate files that produce data with speed commensurate with their importance, all at as low a cost as possible, is no simple feat. A feel for the magnitude of even the most simple system is provided in the problems at the end of this module.

Secondary data and sources of information. Data collected by one agency and used by another are called *secondary data* by the user. It is probably safe to say that no student, businessman, or organization can work effectively without a system for identifying and using secondary data. You could hardly invest without knowledge about stock prices, corporate earnings, and profits, all of which are secondary data.

You would probably learn very little by reading a list of sources of data categorized by type without some specific objective. Instead of classifying sources of data here we provided you with such a list at the end of this module, to use in conjunction with the end-of-module problems. This should give you a feeling for how important and useful a knowledge of secondary data sources can be.

Secondary as well as primary data may be included in an organization's information system. Most of the information in the system of an investment counseling firm, for example, would come from individual companies, the Securities and Exchange Commission, and the stock exchanges.

REPORTING

Most people think of reports as neatly bound documents which summarize and perhaps interpret information. There are many reports like this, and their uses are many and varied. There are annual reports to the stockholders, the President's Economic Report to the Nation, and environmental impact reports, to mention a few.

Table 2.1 / Population including Armed Forces abroad by age groups, July 1 of selected years, 1960–1975 (Thousands)

Age	1960	1970	1975 projected*
Under 5	20,364	17,184	19,706
5–13	32,985	36,615	33,177
14–17	11,211	15,902	16,792
18–21	9,550	14,540	16,346
22–24	6,572	10,082	11,368
25–34	22,911	25,278	31,180
35–44	24,223	23,126	22,751
45–54	20,581	23,269	23,603
55–64	15,627	18,648	19,779
65 and over	16,659	20,156	21,859
Total	180,684	204,800	216,561

*From Series D, one of the lower-range projections of the Bureau of Census, based on extrapolation of the 1970 Census.
Source: Bureau of the Census, excerpted from S. Lees Booth, *1972 Finance Facts Yearbook*, National Consumer Finance Association.

Our use of the term "report" is in one sense more restrictive than the one commonly used, and in another sense more inclusive. We'll consider only reports that relate to numbers of records and their interpretation—book reports don't count. We'll consider a report to be any compilation of records identified or organized to facilitate understanding. It doesn't have to contain prose or have a cover. It doesn't even have to be printed or typed. A grade school report card is a report in this sense. So is a college transcript. So is a display on a computer terminal of an airline which shows the number of seats on a particular flight available at that moment. The following tables and charts are all reports in this broad sense.

Table 2.1 is a typical two-way cross-classification table, in this case comparing *age* distribution of population over *time*. The table is good because it is easy to understand. It does have two flaws, though, that make interpretation difficult. First, the age groupings are not constant. For example, the group 14 to 17 covers 4 years, 22 to 24 covers 3 years, and 55 to 64 covers 10 years. This makes it hard to tell which age grouping has the greatest population density. The figure 6572 for the 22 to 24 age group in 1960 is smaller than any of the others, but is it smaller because there are really fewer people *per year* in that group or just because it spans only 3 years? Dividing 6572 by 3, you would find a population density of 2191 per year for the 22 to 24 age group. When this is compared with 15,627/10 = 1563 for the 55 to 64 age group, you can see that the population density in the older age group is considerably less than that of the younger. The absolute number in the older group was larger just because it covered a bigger span of years.

A second difficulty in interpreting Table 2.1 arises because absolute values are difficult to compare. A column showing what *percentage* each age group is of the total for each year would help. Looking at the original data and comparing the

17

Table 2.2 / Extensions, repayments, and net changes in outstanding consumer installment credit, by type and holder, 1970 and 1971 (Millions of dollars)

	Extensions		Repayments		Net change	
	1970	1971	1970	1971	1970	1971
Total installment credit	104,130	117,638	101,138	109,254	2992	8383
Commercial banks	39,136	45,099	37,961	41,018	1590	4081
Finance companies	29,662	32,036	29,858	31,019	−611	1017
Other financial lenders	14,619	17,312	13,516	15,388	1103	1924
Retail outlets	20,713	23,191	19,803	21,829	910	1362
Automobile paper	29,831	34,638	30,943	31,818	−1112	2820
Commercial banks	17,002	19,865	17,671	18,130	−384	1735
Purchased	(10,491)	(11,641)	(11,127)	(11,071)	(−351)	(570)
Direct	(6,511)	(8,224)	(6,544)	(7,059)	(−33)	(1165)
Finance companies	7,839	8,878	8,666	8,540	−1112	338

Source: Federal Reserve Board, from S. Lees Booth, *1972 Finance Facts Yearbook*, National Consumer Finance Association.

change in the 18 to 21 age group from 1960 to 1975 (9550 to 16,346) with the corresponding change for the 65 and over group (16,659 to 21,859) doesn't tell you much. Percentage columns would show that the 18 to 21 age group constituted 5.3 percent of the total in 1960 and 7.5 percent in 1975, while the 65 and over group changed from 9.2 percent of the total to 10.1 percent.

Table 2.2 is part of an excellent *triple* cross-classification table. A table like this is not compiled without considerable effort. There are many possible arrangements for the data. Usually the analyst places the most important category down the left margin, the next most important category across the top, and the third most important as a subset of the second. In Table 2.2 the analyst also included Net Change columns to facilitate comparison of Extensions and Repayments. Judicious use was also made of parentheses and underlinings to make it easy to tell which numbers are sub-components and which are totals.

A table like this conveys a great deal of information in a small amount of space. Accomplishing this task without confusing the reader is a high art.

Charts as well as tables can be used for reporting. A few examples of good and bad charts are shown in Figs. 2.1 to 2.4.

Do you see the difference between the first two charts? They both use areas to show magnitudes, but Fig. 2.1 is hard to understand while Fig. 2.2 is easy. The problem with Fig. 2.1 is scaling. First, it's hard to tell just what area to equate with the total of 208 million. It may seem at first glance that it is the area of the entire large rectangle, but further inspection shows that it's the sum of all of the little rectangles. But that's not the biggest problem. It's very hard to compare areas when both the height and width vary. The rectangle representing the 30 million housewives not in the labor force is no doubt 50 percent larger than the one representing 20 million retired, but you'd never guess it from a visual comparison.

18

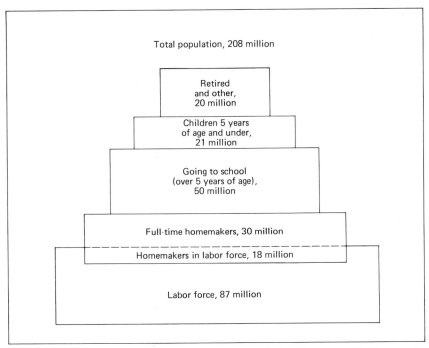

Fig. 2.1 / Population of the United States, January 1972. (Source: *1972 Finance Fact Yearbook*.)

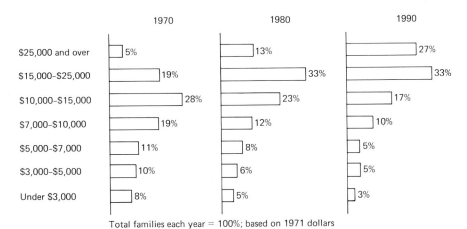

Total families each year = 100%; based on 1971 dollars

Fig. 2.2 / The changing pyramid of income distribution. (Source: The Conference Board, from *1972 Finance Fact Yearbook*.)

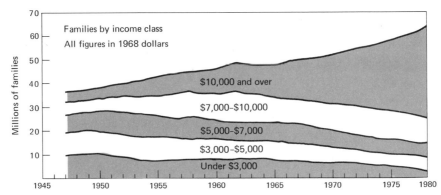

Fig. 2.3 / Changing income distribution, 1947–1980. (Source: The Conference Board, from *1972 Finance Fact Yearbook.*)

Figure 2.2 is easy to follow. The reason is that the heights of *all* the bars are the same, so their relative sizes can be compared easily and accurately by looking at their widths. As a consequence, the chart graphically shows the anticipated change in income distribution.

Charts that compare sizes using cubes or figures like little men or tanks or battleships of varied size are generally still more misleading since few people can relate accurately the relative magnitude of volumes or areas of irregular shapes. Watch out for them!

Figure 2.3 shows a *time series*, where an income-distribution pattern is graphed over time. It is a good chart. Without a lot of detail it shows clearly that the proportion of families with incomes of $10,000 and over has grown rapidly and is expected to continue to grow both in absolute magnitude and as a proportion of the total number of families. Further, the scales are clearly labeled, the shading makes it easy to follow the different income categories, and the information that figures are in 1968 dollars is clearly stated.

We'll make extensive use of tables and charts in the modules on time-series analysis and forecasting. The few provided here should illustrate that tables and charts are excellent means of reporting if they're carefully thought out but can be misleading if they aren't.

CONTROLLING

One of the chief functions of business management is controlling the operation of the organization. Control is exercised in many ways, of course, some having nothing to do with numbers. In this brief introduction we'll focus on two examples of controlling using numbers, both illustrating control by exception.

Control by exception: budgeting. You've used the principle of control by exception many times in your daily activities, probably without consciously recognizing it. When you drive a car, for example, you come to expect certain things. The

Table 2.3 / Expenditure analysis

Category	Expenditures		Budget calendar year
	To July 1	Year ago to July 1	
A	120	122	150
B	120	50	100
C	120	110	240

temperature gauge is usually at a certain normal operating level, and the car at a certain speed exhibits a variety of sounds—the hum of the tires, the engine noise, etc., that are characteristic of that speed. If all these things continue to operate in normal fashion, you proceed with little concern. If the temperature gauge suddenly rose dramatically, if the tires started thumping, or if some other event occurred, your attention and concern would immediately be focused on that event, and you'd take whatever action you felt appropriate to get things back to normal. Another more dramatic example would be your immediate concern if for no apparent reason your heart started beating at twice its normal rate and your chest hurt.

Good managers are as adept at recognizing exceptional conditions in the operation of a business as you'd be in the two examples above. One way this is done is to compare operating statistics with anticipated goals or norms. Table 2.3 shows a firm's current expenditures, expenditures for the same date for the previous calendar year, and the budget expenditures for the entire calendar year for three categories of expenditures. Which items would you question?

Expenditures for item C aren't exceptional. The amount spent to date is about the same as last year, and exactly half of the budgeted funds were spent in the first 6 months of the year. Expenditures for item A are running 85 percent of the total yearly budget in the first 6 months, but the amount spent is almost exactly what it was last year at the same time. This could indicate that there is a strong seasonal variation in category A and that you'd ordinarily expect to spend most of the budgeted amount in the first half of the year. Item B may well be worth more attention. Last year to July 1 exactly half of (this year's) budgeted amount was spent, but this year by July 1 the expenditures are 20 percent over the budget for the entire year.

An alert manager will know the kind of variations to expect from year to year around the norms and thus he can tell which items to worry about and which not to. Some items might be exceptional but not by an amount large enough to be worth investigating. The manager must judge the significance of an exception, as well as its occurrence.

Control by exception: quality control. Figure 2.4 illustrates another control device, a quality-control chart. Each dot on this chart represents the average quality of a sample taken from a process at a particular time. The principle involved is simple: if the average falls between the limits, you should judge the process in control and not worry about it. If the average falls outside either limit, as in the ninth period, the process is to be judged out of control and appropriate action should

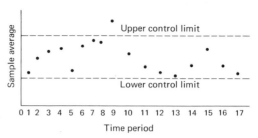

Fig. 2.4 / Quality-control chart.

be taken. While the use of a chart such as this is simple, the reasoning behind its construction is complex and will be given very careful consideration in Module 12.

DECIDING

Top managers are paid high salaries for taking the responsibility of making decisions. Such decisions always involve the future and therefore always involve uncertainty. Even though the future is no more predictable now than before, modern executives can rely on increasingly sophisticated statistical techniques to help them make good decisions under uncertainty.

Consider deciding whether or not to market a new product. You want to market the product if it'll make money but not otherwise. The basic source of uncertainty is how many consumers will buy the product. If this uncertainty can be quantified in the form of a *probability distribution,* and if the costs of making mistakes can be predicted, the best course of action can be determined.[1] Further, you might be surer of the market for the product if you sampled in a test market. Sampling reduces uncertainty but also costs money. Statistical analysis can help to decide whether or not sampling is likely to be profitable and, having sampled, how to use the information obtained. A product-development example is used in Module 19 to illustrate this process of decision making under uncertainty.

REVIEW EXERCISES 2.B

1. Which one of the terms "record," "report," "control," or "decide," applies to each of the statements below?
   a. The guidance of a process toward specific objectives.
   b. One or more numbers kept for use at a future date.
   c. Judging long-run alternatives.
   d. A compilation of records used to facilitate understanding.

---

[1] A probability distribution is a listing of all of the values a variable can have together with how likely each is. Two general kinds of mistakes would be to introduce the product if it would lose money or not to introduce it if it would make money. The cost of either of these mistakes is a function of the amount of product demand.

2. Which statements below are true?
   a. Primary data are the most important data.
   b. Primary data are collected by the user.
   c. Secondary data are collected by someone other than the user.
   d. Secondary data aren't very important.
3. Which of these statements are true?
   a. All data are bits of information.
   b. Only useful and available data are information.
   c. Someone could have lots of data and little information.
4. Two types of control processes are control through _____ and _____ control. They are both examples of control by _____.
5. Two key elements in decision making under uncertainty are the calculation of the _____ of errors and formulating a _____ for the source of uncertainty. The process of _____ can help in finding the optimal decision under uncertainty.

Answers 2.B

1. a. control, *b.* record, *c.* decide, *d.* report   *2. a.* F, *b.* T, *c.* T, *d.* F   *3. a.* F, *b.* T, *c.* T   *4.* budgeting, quality, exception   *5.* costs, probability distribution, sampling

---

Section 2.C

Sources of Errors and Data Preparation

Learning objectives

Your learning objectives for this section are to be able to:

1. Recognize a phony or spurious statistic when you see one
2. Describe the major kinds of nonsampling errors
3. Describe what is meant by sampling error
4. Identify the key elements in data preparation

SOURCES OF ERRORS AND DATA PREPARATION

The most refined statistical analyses may be worthless if the data on which the analyses were performed are of poor quality. Even if the data are a reasonable representation of the phenomena they measure, the statistical process itself may generate errors. This section deals with the recognition of possible errors in data, the importance of understanding the nature and limitation of the data you use, the necessity for careful preparation of data before analysis, and the errors that can result from sampling. This process will rely heavily on information described in an excellent and thorough presentation of the subject by Oskar Morgenstern.[1]

PHONY OR SPURIOUS STATISTICS

Phony or spurious statistics can be classified under three headings: meaningless statistics, unknowable statistics, and irrelevant statistics. You've had wide experience with all three. See if these examples sound familiar.

Daniel Seligman[2] defines a meaningless statistic as one that uses undefined terms or ambiguous thought so that the exact meaning of the statistic is unclear. A beautiful example cited by Seligman is the statement by Mayor Wagner of New York that overall cleanliness of the streets (of New York City) had risen to 85 percent in 1960—up from 56 percent in 1950. Try to picture an 85 percent clean street; how many abandoned cars, discarded mattresses, and turned-over trash cans are left?

An unknowable statistic is one whose meaning is perfectly clear but which no one would be able to measure. Sieloff in *Statistics in Action* discusses measures that are both meaningless and unknowable with reference to the wastes of our society. Traffic jams cost the nation 5 million dollars in 1956 (or 5 billion dollars if one reads the next sentence in the article). The statistic is just as good at 5 million or 5 billion dollars because it's meaningless anyway. What constitutes a traffic jam? How would you measure the cost? The loss of gasoline? Gasoline plus wear on the car? Lost time from gainful work?

You can add almost indefinitely to the list of national losses—losses from organized crime, unorganized crime, frauds, worthless health and nutritional programs, fires, accidents, hurricanes, strikes, sit-ins, and dog bites to name a few. If all the wastes published somewhere were added, the sum would probably come close to the gross national product; Sieloff gets up to 25 percent of GNP without attempting to compile an exhaustive list.

Morgenstern cites other kinds of irrelevant or specious statistics, such as the use of a price index whose composition is outmoded, or the aggregate of "profits" for many companies which all use different definitions and methods to arrive at their figures for profits.

---

[1] Oskar Morgenstern, *On the Accuracy of Economic Observation*, Princeton University Press, 2d ed., Princeton, N.J., 1963.

[2] Daniel Seligman, We're Drowning in Phony Statistics, *Fortune*, November 1961, reprinted in Theodore J. Sieloff (ed.), *Statistics in Action*, Lansford, San Jose, Calif., 1963.

NONSAMPLING ERRORS

Morgenstern cites a number of reasons for the presence of errors in statistics that do not arise from the process of sampling. These include outright lies, lack of trained observers, problems of handling masses of data, problems of classification and definition, inherent weaknesses in the instruments used for data collection, and lack of comparability over time. We'll discuss each of these briefly.

Lies and falsification.   You would be naïve to believe that the reporting of economic data was free of falsification. Many income tax returns for both individuals and companies are deliberately understated. Deliberate misstatements about sales, profits, and other financial figures are often made because companies do not want to divulge information to competitors. Another equally serious problem arises from falsification made not in an effort to deceive but simply because it is easier to make up figures than to derive them from actual measurement.

Lack of trained observers.   Most observations in the physical sciences are made by trained observers under carefully controlled conditions. This is not true in the gathering of economic and business data, where very few observations are made using the scientific method. Most business observations are simply records accumulated in the course of the operation of the business. Tabulations of such observations are subject to a whole series of human errors; the more hands the data pass through, the greater the possibility of error.

Masses of data.   No matter how careful the count, it is physically impossible to determine the exact size of any large population. Morgenstern points out that a careful study showed that the 1950 U.S. census was about 5 million people short, including the entire population of some 26 cities of 5000 or more people in Connecticut. This understated population figure was then used to generate more statistics like per capita income.

Large counts, totaling in the millions or even billions and accumulated through complicated and diffused reporting processes, are often reported to a degree of accuracy that is impossible to obtain.

Figures for GNP are reported to the nearest $1000, yet Morgenstern estimates that they are accurate only within 10 to 15 percent, which would amount to about 100 billion dollars! In spite of this level of possible error, changes of as little as 1 or 2 billion dollars are often heralded as signs that the nation is on the road to recovery or that it is slipping into a recession.

Similarly, changes in the consumer price index of a few tenths of a percent are taken as indications that we are winning or losing the battle against inflation, when vagaries from month to month in the collection and reporting process can be expected to exceed that amount often.

Classification and definition of data.   It is difficult to achieve meaningful statistics when they are collected from varied sources because of differences in definitions. Take the seemingly simple case of finding out how many students there are attending colleges in the United States. You first have to define a college: does it include proprietary institutions? Correspondence institutions? Then you have to define a student. Full-time only? If so, what is full-time? If not, do you count part-time students the same as full-time? What about correspondence students? Extension-center students? Noncredit students in special programs?

These and similar questions make it easy to see that as statistics on students are collected for institutions throughout the nation, there are bound to be discrepancies from college to college in spite of how carefully the collecting agency defines its terms. Most of these discrepancies are not intentional but occur because the reporter at an institution is careless or because the definitions asked for cannot be reported without extra cost because they are too different from the categories the institution routinely uses.

The situation is no less complicated in business. Consider the difficulties involved in classifying General Motors, which not only makes cars, but also jet engines, diesel locomotives, power generators, and many other products in addition to operating as a finance company. If you report General Motors as an automobile manufacturer, you are overstating the case for autos and ignoring everything else.

If General Motors is that much of a problem, imagine the great statistical difficulties in arriving at valid financial figures for the United States automobile industry. These difficulties do not mean that such tasks should not be attempted or that they are so inaccurate that they become meaningless if attempted. They do point out that very careful work is required and that even at best the figures are approximations.

Errors of instruments.   Whatever "instrument" is used to record or collect data, it is subject to error. The most common instrument is people. Morgenstern describes a series of errors in the 1950 census that came to light because some of the results were less than believable. There seemed to be a disproportionately high number of widowed 14-year-old boys. The number of 13- to 15-year-olds in the first and second grades looked large. The number of husbands living with their wives was different from the number of wives living with their husbands. It turned out that there was in fact a whole series of keypunch errors, where values were consistently punched in the wrong fields, making, for example, "head of household" read "white," "wife" read "Negro," and "child" read "Indian." The scary part of this illustration is that if some of the errors hadn't been obvious, they could have gone undetected and the figures could have been used indefinitely.

Another way people contribute to the generation of errors is in the design, administration, and response to questionnaires. Questionnaires are tricky. It's easy to use terms that are meaningful to the writer but meaningless to the responder. It's easy to carry through all sorts of personal biases, undetected, from the writer to the questions. The sociologist phrases questions the way a sociologist thinks, and this may be quite different from the way the respondent thinks.

There are mechanical as well as human sources of error in processing data. Calculators as well as operators make mistakes, and those which aren't obvious are seldom discovered. Nor are computers infallible. Assuming proper programming on the part of the user, there are still two kinds of errors a computer can make and both are very hard to discover. The first of these is in the system's software. Even though these kinds of errors are human rather than mechanical, they are not the user's fault but the system's. The second error is caused by roundoff in complex, lengthy series of calculations. These are not errors in a technical sense; the computer operates as it was designed to. However, the accumulation of tiny roundoffs over thousands of calculations can count up to substantial errors that may not cancel out and are hard to determine.

Factor of time.   In the physical sciences investigators can often control an experiment so that they can duplicate the circumstances under which the experiment was conducted. This enables them to obtain many sets of data and to increase the chances of measuring the phenomenon accurately. Typically social scientists have no such option since control of complex social systems is not feasible. They usually record what happens rather than conducting an experiment, and they have just one chance, since the event will never happen again. Political pollsters can assess the sentiment of voters only once at any given time; they can't make either time or people's attitudes stand still while they take another sample.

A statistician making a price index has only one opportunity at any one time. It's very hard in repeated samplings over time to tell how much of the observed change is really caused by a change in prices and how much is caused by vagaries in the reporting system.

DATA PREPARATION

The subject of how to prepare data before analysis is extensive. It can be summarized under three headings: (1) ask the right questions; (2) define the data needs; (3) understand the data—what they measure and what their limitations are.

One of the biggest problems in statistical analysis is that of correctly identifying the problem to be solved. In our personal lives we are often incapable of identifying our problems correctly. We think that if we had more money, a different job, or something else, life would be better, only to discover upon achieving these ends that they were really not the problem. Businesses have the same difficulty. Wishful thinking and lack of careful analysis can lead a company to spend a great deal of money trying to solve a problem that is unimportant or misses the basic issue.

Once the problem has been identified, it should be possible to envision an appropriate method of analysis and to specify its data requirements. This process is not as simple as it seems. Business executives are often guilty of wanting to use a previously successful technique on a new problem for which it is not appropriate or of "not trusting" the statistician or management scientist who recommends a method

27

with which the executives are not familiar. It is also tempting (and very wasteful) to formulate a problem in terms of existing data because they are available even though they are not appropriate.

Often before data can be useful they need to be adjusted in some way. In a recent study, it was reported that the University of Colorado had the highest monthly theft loss of the Big Eight institutions. This might be true or might not: the losses were reported in some institutions for as few as 5 months, in others for 12 months. The monthly average was found by dividing the total loss by the period over which the records were kept. Since this period varied among institutions, the average figure would be meaningful only if there were no seasonal variation, which is doubtful. Further, average loss figures should probably have been adjusted for the size of the institution; we might expect larger institutions to incur a greater absolute amount of loss than smaller institutions.

Another example of adjustment of data occurs in using income statistics which should be deflated by a price index before being used to show a person's affluence at one time vs. another. Of course, you'd have to decide what price index would be most appropriate for a given comparison.

The accuracy of the original data is also very important in its interpretation. As mentioned before, you're hardly justified in writing a headline COST OF LIVING DROPS if the consumer price index goes down 0.1 percent from one month to the next because the accuracy with which the index is computed could well vary by more than that amount from month to month purely by chance. Identifying the proper way to adjust data before it can be interpreted is a very important part of data analysis.

SAMPLING ERROR

The errors discussed above were a consequence of the reporting process. These errors could occur whether you were taking a census or a sample.[1] Another source of error is strictly the consequence of the sampling process. *Sampling error* occurs because no sample is a microcosm of the population from which the sample is drawn.

Individual samples differ from each other and from the population they come from. In order to make statistical inferences about a population from a sample, the nature of sampling error or variation must be known. Let's see if you can get an idea about sampling error from the following illustration.

Assume that you're drawing samples from a population consisting of half red balls and half white balls. After mixing the balls and drawing one, you record the color and return it before sampling again. You realize that you would not always expect to get exactly 50 percent red balls in any sample you drew using this method. No sample consisting of an odd number of balls could have 50 percent red. Further, you'd probably believe that the larger the sample, the more likely it would be for the

---

[1] In a census, the characteristics of the entire population or set in question are enumerated. In a sample, the characteristics of a subset of the population are enumerated.

proportion of red balls to be close to 50 percent. Getting 1 red ball and 4 white in a sample of 5 might not surprise you much, but getting 200 red and 800 white in a sample set of 1000 would. In other words, you'd expect the sampling error to become smaller as the sample size increased.

Now stop a minute and think of what you'd expect if the population consisted of 1 red ball in every 1000 rather than half red and half white. What would you expect in a sample of 5 balls? A sample of 1000 balls? The answers you are likely to give are these. In a sample of 5 balls you would expect 0 red balls. In fact, you would probably be quite surprised if you got anything but 0 red balls from a sample of 5. You would probably expect 1 red ball from the sample of 1000. You wouldn't be greatly surprised if you got 0 red or even 2 red, but you wouldn't expect much more variation than that. The phenomenon you're contemplating here is caused by the fact that the variability in the sample is a function of the proportion of red balls in the population as well as the size of the sample.

Thus you could conclude that the proportion of red balls in a sample *as a consequence of the sampling process* would be an inverse function of the size of the sample and a direct function of the variability of the population.

You'll find that without specific measures of sampling error it'll be impossible to infer the characteristics of a population from a sample. You'll spend a good deal of time in later modules measuring sampling variation of the sort you've speculated about here.

REVIEW EXERCISES 2.C

1. Which statement below is phony or unknowable?
  a. Americans waste 10 billion dollars per year day-dreaming on company time.
  b. Eighty-five percent of all Americans over the age of 50 are overweight.
2. Sampling errors in statistical investigations are:
  a. Inevitable.
  b. Measurable.
  c. Controllable.
  d. All the above.
3. Name six kinds of nonsampling errors that could occur in statistical investigations.
4. Name the three key elements in data preparation.

Answers 2.C

1. a. Statement *b* could be verified by sampling; statement *a* couldn't.
2. d. Sampling errors come about because of chance variation in samples. Sampling errors are inevitable, but their size can be measured and controlled.
3. falsification, lack of trained observers, large counts, differences in definition and classification, measuring instruments, factor of time.
4. ask the right question, define data needs, understand the data

Section 2.D
Summary

The subject of this module is the use of numerical data in reporting, recording, controlling, and making business decisions.

In discussing recording, a distinction was made between primary and secondary data. Primary data are collected by the same agency that uses them, while secondary data are obtained by the user from another source. The need for an information system was discussed. Sources of secondary business and economic data are described at the end of this module.

The reporting function was illustrated through the use of a three-dimensional table, a triple cross-classification table, several charts, and a time-series graph. Examples of control were given with reference to budgeting and quality control. The notion of the use of probability distributions for making decisions under uncertainty was discussed.

Sources of errors in the use of data were discussed under the headings of spurious statistics, nonsampling errors, and sampling errors. Spurious statistics were described as meaningless, unknowable, or irrelevant—the sort of data that convinces the unsophisticated but turns off the knowledgeable because they are meant to impress rather than inform. Nonsampling errors are errors people make in collecting and analyzing data, as distinguished from the chance errors which occur in the process of sampling. Nonsampling errors can be caused deliberately or inadvertently, through lack of training or carelessness in defining, classifying, or tabulating data. Sampling errors arise in the process of attempting to assess the characteristics of a population on the basis of a sample. Fortunately, if sampling is done correctly, the extent of sampling error can be measured for many types of decision problems.

The importance of careful preparation of data was discussed in terms of identifying the problem, defining data requirements, and understanding the nature and limitations of the data.

This has been a very simple module—no formulas, no mathematics (which the rest of the book will occasionally include). Reading this module should have made you think more carefully than you did before about data, their uses, and the problems associated with their uses.

SECONDARY SOURCES OF BUSINESS STATISTICS

These sources constitute only a very small proportion of the thousands of documents produced by government and private sources, but they cover a wide range of subjects and will usually provide the information you need.

A. U.S. government
  1. General: These documents provide statistics on population, labor force, production, wages, profits, finance, and many other essential topics.
    a. *Statistical Abstract of the United States*, U.S. Bureau of the Census

  b. *Historical Statistics of the United States*, U.S. Bureau of the Census
  c. *Survey of Current Business*, U.S. Department of Commerce
  d. *Federal Reserve Bulletin*, Board of Governors, Federal Reserve System
  e. *Business Cycle Developments*, U.S. Bureau of the Census
  f. *Economic Indicators*, Council of Economic Advisers
  g. *Current Population Reports*, U.S. Bureau of the Census
  h. *Monthly Labor Review*, Bureau of Labor Statistics
  i. *Economic Report of the President*, Council of Economic Advisers
  j. *The Budget of the U.S. Government*, Bureau of the Budget
  k. *Historical Chart Book*, Federal Reserve System
  l. *Federal Reserve Monthly Chart Book*, Federal Reserve System
2. Specific: These documents provide information about specific segments or aspects of the economy.
  a. *Summary of Employment and Unemployment Statistics*, Bureau of Labor Statistics
  b. *Monthly Vital Statistics Report*, U.S. Department of Health, Education, and Welfare
  c. *Health, Education, and Welfare Indicators*, U.S. Department of Health, Education, and Welfare
  d. *Current Retail Sales*, U.S. Bureau of the Census
  e. *Current Retail Trade Reports*, U.S. Bureau of the Census
  f. *Mineral Yearbook*, U.S. Bureau of Mines
  g. *Statistical Summary*, U.S. Department of Agriculture
  h. *Agricultural Statistics*, U.S. Department of Agriculture
  i. *Current Industrial Reports*, U.S. Bureau of the Census
  j. *Statistical Bulletin*, Securities and Exchange Commission
  k. *Statistics of Income*, Internal Revenue Service
  l. *Quarterly Financial Reports of Manufacturing Corporations*, Federal Trade Commission and Securities and Exchange Commission
  m. *Statistics of Electric Utilities in the United States*, Federal Power Commission
  n. *Transportation Statistics in the United States*, Interstate Commerce Commission
  o. *Statistical Handbook of Aviation*, Federal Aviation Agency
  p. *Statistics of Communications Common Carriers*, Federal Trade Commission
B. Private
  1. *Fact Book*, Institute of Life Insurance
  2. *Fact Book*, Investment Company Institute
  3. *Ward's Automotive Report*, Ward's
  4. *Automobile Facts and Figures*, Automobile Manufacturers' Association
  5. *Survey of Consumer Finances*, University of Michigan Survey Research Center
  6. *Monthly New Business Incorporations*, Dun & Bradstreet
  7. *Monthly Business Failures*, Dun & Bradstreet
  8. *Standard and Poor's Industry Surveys*, Standard and Poor's
  9. *The Outlook*, Standard and Poor's
  10. *Security Price Index Record*, Standard and Poor's
  11. *The Wall Street Journal*, Dow-Jones
  12. *Business Week*, McGraw-Hill
  13. *Moody's Investor's Service*, Moody's
  14. *Stock Survey*, Moody's
C. International
  1. *Statistical Yearbook*, United Nations

31

2. *International Financial Statistics*, International Monetary Fund
3. *General Statistics*, Organization for Economic Cooperation and Development
4. *Main Economic Indicators*, Organization for Economic Cooperation and Development
5. *General Statistical Bulletin*, European Economic Community
6. *Canadian Statistical Review*, Dominion Bureau of Statistics

NOTES ON "SOURCES OF SOURCES"

To obtain sources of both government and private statistics, see:

1. Justine Farr Rodriguez, Sources of Statistics, chap. 5 in W. S. Butler and R. A. Kavesh (eds.), *How Business Economists Forecast*, Prentice-Hall, Englewood Cliffs, N.J., 1966.
2. Paul Wasserman, Eleanor Allen, Charlotte Georgi, and Janice McLean, *Statistics Sources*, 3d ed., Gale Research Co., Detroit, 1971.
3. Paul Wasserman, et al., *Encyclopedia of Business Information Sources*, 2 vols., Gale Research Co., Detroit, 1970.
4. Margaret Fisk (ed.), *Encyclopedia of Associations*, 8th ed., Gale Research Co., Detroit, 1973.

Questions and Problems

2.1. From *Ward's Automotive Reports:*
  a. Find the total number of passenger cars sold in the United States each year for the past 5 years.
  b. Calculate for each year the percentage of the cars in part *a* that were made in the United States and the percentage that were made abroad.
  c. From your general knowledge of economic conditions, can you think of any factors that could explain the changes in percent of United States-made cars sold in the United States over this period?
2.2. From the *Statistical Abstract of the United States*, find the United States population by decades from 1860 to 1970.
  a. Plot these data on arithmetic paper.
  b. Calculate the rate of increase for each decade by taking, for example
$$(\text{pop. } 1870/\text{pop. } 1860 - 1)100.$$
  c. Assume that the company for which you work has the following growth pattern from 1900 to 1970:

Year	Sales, thousands	Year	Sales, thousands
1900	$1200	1940	$1430
1910	1260	1950	1573
1920	1336	1960	1668
1930	1402	1970	1851

Calculate the rate of increase for each decade for your company. Plot the rate of growth for the United States population and the rate of growth for your company on the same arithmetic grid. What conclusions can you come to with respect to your company's growth?

2.3. How many students attend your institution? You should have some trouble answering this question because there are lots of ways to count students.
  a. Describe some of the *definitional* problems you might encounter in attempting to count students.
  b. What do you think is the best way to count students? Why?

2.4. To give you some insight into the problems of creating and maintaining an information system, consider the minimal system that a college needs solely to keep track of students.
  a. Identify the major categories or *files* that must be kept.
  b. List some of the relevant statistics you'd keep in each file.
  c. Code each of these statistics, using P for permanent, unchanging data, C for data that could change, and A for data that must be updated *and* accumulated.
  d. Describe some of the problems you might encounter in creating, maintaining, and coordinating these files.

2.5. Assume that sailing is your hobby and that over the past 7 years you have designed and developed a unique sailboat, on which you hold several patents. Your goal is to produce the boat and eventually make some money. Before this year, the operation was a typical garage production and cigar box accounting operation. Now, though, you have a going concern; you've incorporated, rented production and office space, and have subcontractors and sales agents lined up. You also decide that you need to replace the cigar box with an information system.
  a. Identify the major files you'd organize for such a system.
  b. List some of the components of each file (without going into such details as complete accounting or inventory control systems).

2.6. In J. M. Tanur, et al. (eds.), *Statistics: A Guide to the Unknown*, Holden-Day, San Francisco, 1972, choose one of the essays classified under Available Data, on page xvi. Write a summary of the article, including a discussion of how it relates to the sources and use of secondary data.

2.7. Find an example of a misleading graph or chart from a current newspaper, magazine, or book. Explain why you believe it to be misleading and how you would correct it to present the same data in an accurate manner.

2.8. Find the table Employment in Nonagricultural Establishments, by Industry Division, from the *Survey of Current Business* or the *Federal Reserve Bulletin*. Using these data for the past 7 years:
  a. Make a table which shows not only the *number* of persons employed by category but also the *percentage* of total nonagricultural employment for each category.
  b. Make a graph or chart showing the percentages by category over this period.
  c. On the basis of your table and chart, interpret the changes that have occurred in nonagricultural employment. Were these changes more evident from the table or from the chart?

2.9. Urban planners and businessmen frequently work with a statistic called a *housing unit*.
  a. What problems could you encounter in defining exactly what is meant by a housing unit?
  b. How would you define this measure?

2.10. Find data on the GNP for the past 5 years, measured in billions of dollars and in billions of 1958 dollars.

    a. Plot both these series on the same arithmetic chart.

    b. What do the changes in these series tell you about the United States economy over this period?

2.11. For each of the statements below, indicate why the statistic involved is either meaningless or misleading:

    a. His punting average last season was a mediocre 42 yards.

    b. During President Flinches' tenure, the university grew from 7000 to 20,000 students.

    c. During his presidency, company sales increased from 1 billion to 1.5 billion dollars per year.

    d. The super radial 226 is guaranteed to give you up to 40,000 miles of service.

2.12. Find an article in a current newspaper or magazine which apparently involves the use of a meaningless statistic, a misleading statistic, or an error in the presentation or interpretation of statistics. Explain the reason for your conclusion.

2.13. Find an article in which something big is made of an insignificant statistic, such as "The rate of increase in inflation slowed last month by one-tenth of 1 percent," where the change in question could have been caused by measurement error but is interpreted as a hard and significant fact.

2.14. "More accidents occur on straight stretches of road than on curves." "More people are killed in accidents in their homes than anywhere else." "Raw materials inventories increased in value from $250,000 to $287,000 over the last 6 months."

    a. Why could each of the statements above be misleading because the data were not properly adjusted? What adjustment would make each more meaningful?

    b. Think of three other examples where statements could be misinterpreted because the data were not properly adjusted.

2.15. To illustrate the concept of sampling error, perform the following experiment:

    1. Toss a coin 20 times and record the number of heads.

    2. Repeat this process 9 more times.

    3. Make a distribution of the *proportion* of heads for the 10 samples, plotting the proportion on the horizontal axis, and the frequency of its occurrence on the vertical axis.

    4. Treat the 10 samples of 20 each, above, as 5 samples of 40 each, by combining the first and second, third and fourth, etc.

    5. Make a distribution of the proportion of heads for the 5 samples of size 40.

    a. What principles about sampling error does the experiment above illustrate?

    b. Why is the concept of sampling error important in business decision making?

2.16. For the past five summers you have had the same job. The hourly rate at which you were paid each summer was:

Year	1970	1971	1972	1973	1974
Hourly rate, $	1.50	1.60	1.90	2.25	2.50

Looking back, you feel that your wage increases have been satisfactory, but you've hardly saved any more money the last summer than the first. You believe that the cost of living might have something to do with your lack of progress and decide to *deflate* your summer wage rate for each year by dividing the wages by an appropriate price index. Your only notable expenses were for food and rent, but since you have no record of what you've spent, you decide to use national statistics on consumer prices for these items as a deflator. Further, you figure that you spent twice as much for food as for rent, so you want to weight the food index twice as much as the rent index.

a. Find the appropriate food and rent consumer price indexes from the *Survey of Current Business* or the *Federal Reserve Bulletin*.

b. Combine these indexes into a single index, giving food double weight.

c. Deflate your hourly wage rate by the composite price index for each year.

d. On the basis of the deflated wage rates, how much have your hourly earnings increased over the past five summers?

MODULE 3
SUMMARIZING DATA—
DESCRIPTIVE STATISTICS

This module is devoted to an explanation of some statistical measures that are used to summarize or *describe* sets of numbers. Study of these *descriptive statistics* is justified on two grounds. (1) You'll use descriptive measures to summarize masses of unwieldy data. Actually you've probably done this many times in the past. You may have asked about the "average" and "range" of grades on a test to get an idea of how well you did or what average mileage you could expect from various kinds of cars. (2) You'll need to be able to calculate some descriptive measures in order to use the methods of statistical inference and decision analysis you'll encounter later in the course.

General learning objectives

Your general learning objectives in this module are to be able to:

1. Calculate several measures of location: the arithmetic mean, the median, and the mode
2. Calculate several measures of dispersion: the range, the mean deviation, and the standard deviation
3. Make point estimates of means and standard deviations of populations from sample data
4. Construct frequency distributions and calculate descriptive measures from them
5. Plot frequency polygons and relative frequency distributions and calculate a measure of skewness

Section 3.A
Measures of Location

Learning objectives

Your learning objectives for this section are to be able to:

1. Define the mean, median, and mode
2. Calculate these measures for a population
3. Explain the uses and limitations of these measures

A *measure of location* is a single value that characterizes one particular point in an *array*, or listing of values in numerical order. This point may be the *center of gravity*, called the *arithmetic mean* (or *average*), the middle value, called the *median*, or the most frequently occurring value, the *mode*. Any of these points describes the *central tendency* of the array and may be important to a decision maker. For example, the median station on an assembly line might represent the optimum location for a service facility, while a retailer would want to stock more modal size dresses than any other size.

THE ARITHMETIC MEAN

The arithmetic mean is the most commonly used of several *calculated averages* whose values depend on the size of *every* number in the group from which they are calculated.[1] From here on, the word "mean," used without any qualifying adjective, will refer to the *arithmetic mean*.

---

[1] Three other calculated averages are the geometric, quadratic, and harmonic means. Formulas for these means are

$$\text{Geometric mean} = N\text{th root of product of } N \text{ numbers}$$

$$= \text{antilog } \frac{\sum \log X}{N}$$

$$\text{Quadratic mean} = \text{root mean square} = \sqrt{\frac{\sum X^2}{N}}$$

$$\text{Harmonic mean} = \text{reciprocal of mean of reciprocals}$$

$$= \frac{1}{[\sum (1/X)]/N}$$

You learned long ago how to calculate the arithmetic mean by adding the values to be considered and dividing by the number of values. Before formalizing this calculation in a formula, we must distinguish between a population and a sample. A *population* is defined as *all* the elements in the set under consideration, while a *sample* is a subset of a population.

When studying statistical inference and decision analysis in later modules, you'll have to distinguish carefully between measures calculated from a population and the same measures calculated from a sample. Therefore the mean of a *population* will be designated by μ (lowercase Greek mu), while the mean of a *sample* will be designated by a Latin letter with a bar over it ($\overline{X}$ for a group of X's, or $\overline{Y}$ for a group of Y's).

When this convention is used, the formula for a population mean is

$$\mu_X = \frac{\sum\limits_{i=1}^{N} X_i}{N}$$

where X_i = value of variable X
N = number of items in population

The symbol $\sum$ (uppercase Greek sigma) means "the sum of," so $\sum_{i=1}^{N}$ means the sum of the values of X from the first through the Nth.

In this book you'll always sum values through the entire group being considered, rather than taking partial sums, so the notation in the formula can be simplified by omitting the subscripts and superscripts and expressing the formula as

$$\mu_X = \frac{\sum X}{N}$$

To illustrate the calculation and characteristics of the mean, look at the salaries of the top executives of the ABC Corporation in Table 3.1. The sum of the salaries of the six executives making up this population is 948 and the mean salary is 158 (both in thousands). Column 3 shows that the sum of the deviations from the mean is equal

Table 3.1 / Annual salaries of top executives, ABC Corporation (Thousands of dollars)

(1) Officer	(2) Salary X	(3) $X - \mu_X$	(4) $(X - \mu_X)^2$
President	400	+242	58,564
Executive vice president	150	−8	64
Vice president marketing	120	−38	1,444
Vice president production	120	−38	1,444
Secretary	80	−78	6,084
Treasurer	78	−80	6,400
Sum	948	0	74,000

$$\mu_X = \frac{\sum X}{N} = \frac{948}{6} = 158$$

40

to zero, an important characteristic that defines the mean as the center of gravity of the distribution.

Another important characteristic of the mean that isn't true for other measures of location is that since $\mu = \sum X/N$, $N\mu = \sum X$. This enables you to calculate the total when the mean is known. A third important characteristic of the mean is that the sum of the *squares* of the deviations between the mean and each of the values is a minimum, or the smallest sum you could get by adding squared deviations between the original values and *any* number. For example, the sum of the squared deviations in column 4 of Table 3.1 is 74,000 (thousand). If you're skeptical that this is truly a minimum, try taking squared deviations about 150 or 100 or any other value that appeals to you and see for yourself. You'll make use of this important characteristic of the mean when you calculate the standard deviation later in this module.

Being a calculated average, the mean is affected by extremes. This is evident in Table 3.1, where the president's high salary pulls the mean up to a value higher than *any* of the *other* five salaries. Thus while the mean of 158 (thousand) may be very useful for some purposes, it is really not a very good typical value for this array of salaries.

FRACTILES

Unlike the mean, which was a *calculated* measure, a fractile is a *positional* measure. Specifically, a fractile is the value of a number which falls a given proportion of the way through an array. The .33 fractile is the number such that one-third of the numbers in the array are equal to it or less while two-thirds of the numbers are equal to it or greater. Remember that the executive salaries in Table 3.1 are in an array from highest to lowest. Therefore, the .33 fractile is any value between 80 and 120, since one-third of the values are 80 or less while two-thirds are 120 or more.

You'll often want to use a single value for a fractile rather than a range of possible values. In that case, you'd simply take the midpoint of the possible values for that fractile (or 100 for the executive salaries in the example above).

THE MEDIAN

The value of the *middle* number in an array is called the *median* (Md). The median is then another name for the .50 fractile. The median executive's salary in Table 3.1 is 120 (thousand), since that is the value of both of the numbers in the middle of the array.

Being a measure of position, the median is not affected by extremes. The median would not be changed if the president's salary in Table 3.1 had been $500,000, $200,000 or any other value greater than $120,000.

Another important characteristic of the median is that the sum of the *absolute* deviations between it and the original values is a minimum. The sum of the absolute differences between 120 and each of the X values in column 2 of Table 3.1 is 392.

41

This sum is smaller than that of absolute deviations calculated from any other value. For example, you might note that by adding the deviations from the mean in column 3, *disregarding signs*, you'd get a sum of 484. You'll make use of this characteristic of the median soon in calculating the mean deviation, a measure of dispersion.

THE MODE

Another commonly used positional measure of central tendency is the *mode*. The mode is simply the value in a set of numbers that occurs most frequently. In Table 3.1 the modal value is 120. Although particular sets of data may have no mode or more than one mode, they typically have but one, which occurs near the middle of an array of the values. Sets of data having more than one mode are likely to be mixtures of different populations which should be separated. An array of the weights of college students would be bimodal because there would be a modal weight for women and a larger one for men. Since it may make little sense to talk about a typical weight of college students without specifying sex, separate listings should be made for each sex.

Like the median, the mode is unaffected by extremes, though the extreme value *could* be the modal value of an array. This could happen, for example, if someone gave a test so easy that more students got 100 than any other value. If a more difficult test were given to the same group, the modal value would probably fall toward the middle of the array since the new test would discriminate between students of varied abilities who all got 100 on the previous test.

REVIEW EXERCISES 3.A

1. Identify the measure or measures of location described below:
  a. The value of the middle number in an array.
  b. The sum of the values divided by their number.
  c. The most frequently occurring value in a series.
  d. A calculated average.
  e. A positional average.
  f. The measure about which the absolute deviations are a minimum.
  g. The measure about which the sum of the deviations adds to zero.
  h. The measure about which the sum of the squares of the deviations are a minimum.
2. For the numbers 3, 8, 2, 10, 10, 8, 5, 6, 5, 12, 8:
  a. Calculate the arithmetic mean.
  b. Calculate the median.
  c. Calculate the mode.

Answers 3.A

1. a. median; *b.* mean; *c.* mode; *d.* arithmetic mean (or quadratic, geometric, or harmonic mean); *e.* median or mode; *f.* median; *g.* mean; *h.* mean   *2. a.* 7; *b.* 8; *c.* 8.

Section 3.B
Measures of Dispersion

Learning objectives

Your learning objectives for this section are to be able to:

1. Define the range, mean deviation, variance, and standard deviation
2. Calculate these measures
3. Explain their uses and limitations

The measures described in Sec. 3.A were measures of location. In providing one *point* in a set of values, they showed nothing about the uniformity or spread of those values which may also be important.

Structural-steel beams are expected not only to have a high average strength but also to be uniformly strong. Likewise, you probably wouldn't be impressed by the quality of a pair of shoes if the left one wore out in 2 weeks and the right one lasted 10 years, even though their average length of life would be high. Measures of *dispersion* are designed to show the spread or *variation* that exist in sets of values.

THE RANGE

The *range* is the difference between the largest and the smallest values in a set of numbers. Although it is a simple measure of dispersion to calculate and to understand, its use is limited because by definition it is calculated using the extreme values, and, as you know, extremes can be very misleading.

THE MEAN DEVIATION

A better measure of dispersion, called the *mean deviation*, can be calculated by averaging the *absolute differences* between the values in a set and their median. Since the sum of the absolute deviations is a minimum about the median, use of the median as a central value is preferred in calculating this measure. The usual formula for the mean deviation is

$$\text{Mean deviation} = \frac{\sum |X - \text{Md}_x|}{N}$$

43

Referring back to the data of Table 3.1, you'll remember that $\sum |X - Md_x| = 392$, so the mean deviation is $392/6 = 65.3$. This is the mean (or average) absolute deviation between the individual salaries and their median (measured in thousands, as are all the data in Table 3.1).

THE VARIANCE

Instead of summing the absolute deviations, as in calculating the mean deviation, you could deal with the problem of positive and negative deviations canceling each other in another way. If you *squared* each of the $X - \mu_x$ values, both positive and negative deviations would result in positive squared deviations. The *variance* is obtained by taking the mean of the squared deviations between the values and their mean. The formula for the variance of a population is

$$\text{Variance}_x = \frac{\sum (X - \mu_x)^2}{N}$$

Deviations are taken from the mean rather than the median because the sum of the *squared* deviations about the mean is a minimum.

The variance of the executives' salaries in Table 3.1 is $74{,}000/6 = 12{,}333$.

The variance might seem to be a rather strange method for measuring dispersion since its units are in terms of squared errors. However, the variance is an extremely powerful measure of dispersion. It is useful in many kinds of statistical analyses because it has a property no other measure of dispersion has. The variance of a sum of independent variables is the sum of the variances of the individual variables. Thus var $(X + Y + Z) =$ var $X +$ var $Y +$ var Z, where X, Y, and Z are independent random variables.[1]

THE STANDARD DEVIATION

While the variance is widely used, an even more common measure of dispersion is the positive *square root of the variance*, called the *standard deviation*. It has the advantage of being expressed in the same units as the data from which it was computed. Whereas the variance in the executives' salaries was 12,333 *thousands of dollars squared*, which makes interpretation difficult, the standard deviation equals $\sqrt{12{,}333}$, or 111, *in thousands of dollars.*

---

[1] A random variable can be defined as any quantity which has a definite value corresponding to every possible event, such as the demand for a product. Independent random variables are random variables which are neither directly nor indirectly related.

The formula for the standard deviation of a population is symbolized by the lowercase Greek sigma σ and is

$$\sigma_X = \sqrt{\frac{\sum (X - \mu_X)^2}{N}}$$

REVIEW EXERCISES 3.B

1. Identify each of the following measures of dispersion:
   a. The difference between the highest and lowest values in a population.
   b. The mean of the squared differences between the values and their mean.
   c. The square root of the answer to part b.
   d. The mean of the absolute deviations between the values and their median.
2. For the values 2, 4, 15, 8, and 6, calculate:
   a. The range.
   b. The mean deviation.
   c. The variance.
   d. The standard deviation.

Answers 3.B

1. a. range; b. variance; c. standard deviation; d. mean deviation

2.

X	$\|X - Md\|$	$X - \mu_X$	$(X - \mu_X)^2$
2	4	-5	25
4	2	-3	9
6	0	-1	1
8	2	$+1$	1
15	9	$+8$	64
35	17	0	100

$$Md = \text{middle value in the array} = 6$$

$$\mu_X = \frac{\sum X}{N} = \frac{35}{5} = 7$$

a. $\text{Range}_X = \text{highest} - \text{lowest} = 15 - 2 = 13$

b. $\text{Mean deviation}_X = \frac{\sum |X - Md|}{N} = \frac{17}{5} = 3.40$

c. $\text{var } X = \frac{\sum (X - \mu_X)^2}{N} = \frac{100}{5} = 20$

d. $\sigma_X = \sqrt{\frac{\sum (X - \mu_X)^2}{N}} = \sqrt{\frac{100}{5}} = 4.47$

Section 3.C

Point Estimates of Population Parameters from Sample Statistics

Learning objectives

Your learning objectives for this section are to be able to:

1. Define the terms simple random sample, parameter, statistic, point estimate, and unbiased estimator
2. Make point estimates of population means, variances, and standard deviations from random samples

If you could always get descriptive measures for whole populations, many of your statistical problems would be over. The trouble is that in business and many other fields it is usually impossible or impractical to measure every item in the population. Market researchers or political pollsters can specify a population as all the people or families in the United States, but they could hardly interview them all to find out how they felt about a product or a president. They'd have to resort to sampling from the population and estimating the characteristics, or *parameters*, of the population from the corresponding characteristics, or *statistics*, of the sample. Much of the remainder of this book is devoted to this process of estimation. However, at this point all you have to know is how to make the best single or *point* estimate of a *population* mean, variance, or standard deviation from *sample* data.

POINT ESTIMATE OF A POPULATION MEAN

The mean of a random sample is called an *unbiased point estimator* of the mean of the population. A random sample, about which you'll hear much more later, is a sample obtained in such a way that each possible combination of items that could make up a given size sample has an equal chance of being selected. The word "unbiased" refers to the fact that the mean of all of the *possible* sample means that could be taken from a population using a certain size sample would be equal to the mean of the population itself. That is, even though any particular sample mean is likely to be different from the population mean, it is no more likely to be above the

46

population mean than below it. This fact makes estimation of the population mean from a sample very simple. All you have to do is to get the mean of the sample and you have the best point estimate of the mean of the population. Thus

$$\overline{X} = \frac{\sum X}{n}$$

where $\overline{X}$ = mean of sample
n (lowercase) = size of sample

POINT ESTIMATE OF A POPULATION VARIANCE AND STANDARD DEVIATION

It would be nice if the variance of a sample were an unbiased estimator of the variance of the population, but it isn't. The variances of all of the possible random samples of a certain size that could be taken from a given population would average somewhat *less* than the population variance. You might suspect this would be true since you know that squared deviations from the mean are greatly affected by extremes and that the most extreme values in the population would be unlikely to be included in any particular sample.

In order to make an *unbiased* estimate of a population variance from a sample you must divide $\sum (X - \overline{X})^2$ by $n - 1$, rather than by n, the sample size.[1]

Thus while the variance and standard deviation of a sample would be found by

$$\text{Sample variance} = \frac{\sum (X - \overline{X})^2}{n}$$

$$\text{Sample standard deviation} = \sqrt{\frac{\sum (X - \overline{X})^2}{n}}$$

the unbiased point estimates of the variance and standard deviation of a *population* made *from* a sample are found by

$$\text{Estimate of population variance from sample} = s_x{}^2 = \frac{\sum (X - \overline{X})^2}{n - 1}$$

---

[1] The $n - 1$ used here represents the number of *degrees of freedom* involved in estimating the variance. Of the total number of values in the sample, only $n - 1$ are free to vary. One degree of freedom is lost when the mean is used in the calculation of the squared errors, for if the mean of a group of values is specified, only $n - 1$ of those values can vary without changing the mean. For example, if you were asked to list five values whose mean was 10, you could assign any value to the first four numbers, but you would have no freedom concerning the fifth.

$$\text{Estimate of population standard deviation from sample} = s_X = \sqrt{\frac{\sum (X - \bar{X})^2}{n - 1}}$$

The most common reason for using sample data is to estimate population parameters, so you'll use these latter formulas frequently. Note that s_X refers to such an estimate, not to the standard deviation of the sample itself.

REVIEW EXERCISES 3.C

1. Define:
   a. A random sample.
   b. A parameter.
   c. A statistic.
   d. A point estimate.
   e. An unbiased estimate.
2. A random sample of size 5 produces the values 4, 10, 9, 15, 2.
   a. Estimate the population mean.
   b. Estimate the population standard deviation.

Answers 3.C

1. a. a sample taken in such a way that each possible combination of items that could make up a given size sample has an equal chance of being selected
   b. a characteristic of a population
   c. a characteristic of a sample
   d. the best *single* estimate of a population parameter
   e. one for which the mean of all possible estimates is equal to the population parameter being estimated

2.

X	$X - \bar{X}$	$(X - \bar{X})^2$
4	−4	16
10	+2	4
9	+1	1
15	+7	49
2	−6	36
40	0	106

a. $\bar{X} = \dfrac{\sum X}{n} = \dfrac{40}{5} = 8$

b. $s_X = \sqrt{\dfrac{\sum (X - \bar{X})^2}{n - 1}} = \sqrt{\dfrac{106}{4}} = 5.1$

Section 3.D
Descriptive Measures for Frequency Distributions

Learning objectives

Your learning objective for this section is to be able to construct frequency distributions from ungrouped data, and use them to calculate descriptive measures.

SUMMARIZING DATA

Masses of raw data in themselves convey little useful information. While business decision makers may be vitally interested in the kind of people who buy their product, a listing from a gigantic computer file containing each customer's income, age, family size, and a bewildering variety of other information might be of little value. Without further analysis, the sheer volume of the data could be overwhelming. The decision makers would probably find themselves in that familiar position of being unable to see the forest for the trees.

The fact is that data must be summarized in some way to provide for meaningful interpretation or use in the decision process. Questions concerning the income level of customers (which might be relevant for advertising decisions) would not be answered best by a complete listing of the income of each customer. Even if such a listing could be obtained, which is doubtful, it would be expensive. Besides, a lengthy list of exact dollar incomes is not what decision makers are really looking for in their effort to zero in on the crucial variables in their problems. Actually faced with such a list, they would certainly attempt some means of summarizing the data, perhaps describing the entire list with one or two numbers that identify its salient characteristics. Here, you'll study some methods of classifying large quantities of data and computing those measures you learned earlier in this module.

FREQUENCY DISTRIBUTIONS

When dealing with a large number of values, it is often convenient and more meaningful for presentation to group them, counting the number of values that fall within arbitrary limits or classes. Such a grouping is called a *frequency distribution*.

49

SELECTION OF CLASSES AND DEFINITION OF CLASS LIMITS

The selection of appropriate classes for a frequency distribution is an art. If you choose too many classes, the pattern of distribution of the values is obscured and little time is saved in calculating summary measures. If you choose too few classes, the calculation of summary measures from the distribution will probably be in error. A satisfactory number of classes is usually between 8 and 20.

Table 3.2 illustrates some possible choices of class limits for a sample of 100 individual sales of gasoline at a service station. One point should be noted with respect to the third and most reasonable of these distributions. Since cash sales are discrete observations and the classes are nonoverlapping, the midvalues are (.50 + 1.49)/2 or $.995, $1.995, $2.995, etc.[1] This makes the midvalues very close to round dollar figures of $1, $2, $3, etc. This was done intentionally because people tend to round to even dollar amounts of gas rather than filling up the tank. If these even dollar amounts of concentration were placed, say, at the lower limits of the classes rather than at the midvalues, the midvalues would not be representative of the bulk of the values in a class. This would misrepresent the actual data and lead to

---

[1] Since the penny is the smallest unit in United States currency, it is impossible to pay for gas in units of less than 1 cent. One could pay either $5.25 or $5.26, for example, but nothing in between. Since possible gas sales in cash must move in *discrete* steps (1 cent in this case), the variable "cash sales" is called a *discrete* variable, and measurements of gas sales are discrete observations.

The actual amount of gas delivered to a tank is not limited in this way. Gas delivered can be measured in smaller and smaller units: gallons, hundredths of a gallon, thousandths of a gallon, etc. Thus gas delivered can be considered a *continuous* variable, since between any pair of numbers measuring gas delivered, it would be possible to have another number. *Measurements* of gas delivered would be discrete variables with units depending on the accuracy of the measuring device, but gas *delivered* (at least down the individual molecules) would be continuous.

In this book we'll use the convention of coding frequency distributions for discrete variables as in Table 3.2, for example:

Children per family, U.S.

Limits	0–2	3–5	6–8	. . .
Midvalues	1	4	7	. . .

For continuous variables (or discrete variables where the unit of measurement is very small compared to the magnitude of the variable) we'll use the following convention:

Time to perform a task, seconds

From	Up to	Midvalues
1000	2000	1500
2000	3000	2500
3000	4000	3500
. . . .	. . . .	. . . .

Here "up to" means "up to but *not* including," so the classes do not overlap.

Table 3.2 / Sales of gasoline

Too few classes		Too many classes		A reasonable number of classes	
Class limits	Fre-quency	Class limits	Fre-quency	Class limits	Fre-quency
$ 0–$4.99	55	$1.00–$1.09	1	$0.50–$1.49	4
5.00– 9.99	45	1.10– 1.19	0	1.50– 2.49	9
	100	1.20– 1.29	1	2.50– 3.49	17
		.	.	3.50– 4.49	25
		.	.	4.50– 5.49	19
		.	.	5.50– 6.49	12
		.	.	6.50– 7.49	7
		9.70– 9.79	0	7.50– 8.49	4
		9.80– 9.89	1	8.50– 9.49	2
		9.90– 9.99	0	9.50–10.49	1
			100		100

inaccurate computations of descriptive measures, since these measures will be calcu-lated using the assumption that the midpoint is typical of the values in that class. You must be careful, then, both about the number of classes you choose and about the limits of these classes. If there are regular points of concentration in the values, these points should be made midvalues of the classes.

You'll note that in each of the three distributions in Table 3.2, the span of the classes, or *class interval*, was kept constant. The first distribution had a class interval of $5, the second one of $.10, and the third one of $1. Unless there is some special reason for doing otherwise, frequency distributions should have a constant class interval.

THE ARITHMETIC MEAN: GROUPED DATA

Assume that through a questionnaire you obtained expenditures on transportation during the past academic year from a random sample of 2000 college freshmen. The results of the sample are summarized in the frequency distribution of Table 3.3.

In estimating the mean of the sample (and of the population from which the sample was drawn), you could assume that the mean of all values in a class corresponds to the class midvalue. That is, the 25 students who spent between $50 and $149 had a mean expenditure of $99.50, and so on. If this assumption were true, then the midvalue of each class times the frequency of that class would exactly equal the sum of the values in that class. Although this assumption is not likely to be true for any one class, if you use enough classes and choose the limits carefully, errors should average out over all the classes. To find the mean, then, simply multiply each midvalue by the number of values in that class, sum these products for all classes,

51

Table 3.3 / Expenditures by freshmen for transportation

Expenditures	Number of students
$ 50–$149	25
150– 249	130
250– 349	720
350– 449	530
450– 549	365
550– 649	135
650– 749	75
750– 849	20
	2000

and divide by the total number of values in the distribution (the sum of the frequency column):

$$\bar{X} = \frac{\sum f\text{MV}}{n}$$

Calculations to find the mean of the student transportation expenditures are shown in Table 3.4. A short method that saves effort and time in calculating the mean for grouped data is shown in Sec. 3.F.

THE STANDARD DEVIATION: GROUPED DATA

When the arithmetic mean is known (again it is assumed that the midvalue of a class is equal to the mean of the values in that class), the calculation of the standard deviation for grouped data is straightforward. The sum of the squared deviations for

Table 3.4 / Calculation of the mean, transportation expenditures

Expenditures	Midvalues (MV)	Number of students f	Sum of expenditures for any class fMV
$ 50–$149	$ 99.50	25	$ 2,487.50
150– 249	199.50	130	25,935.00
250– 349	299.50	720	215,640.00
350– 449	399.50	530	211,735.00
450– 549	499.50	365	182,317.50
550– 649	599.50	135	80,932.50
650– 749	699.50	75	52,462.50
750– 849	799.50	20	15,990.00
		2000	$787,500.00

$$\bar{X} = \frac{\sum f\text{MV}}{n} = \frac{787,500}{2000} = \$393.75 \approx \$394 \text{ to nearest dollar}$$

Table 3.5 / Calculation of the standard deviation, transportation expenditures

Expenditures	Midvalue (MV)	Number of students f	$MV - \bar{X}$	$(MV - \bar{X})^2$	$f(MV - \bar{X})^2$
$ 50–$149	$ 99.50	25	$-294.50	$ 86,730.25	$2,168,256.25
150– 249	199.50	130	-194.50	37,830.25	4,917,932.50
250– 349	299.50	720	-94.50	8,930.25	6,429.780.00
350– 449	399.50	530	5.50	30.25	16,032.50
450– 549	499.50	365	105.50	11,130.25	4,062,541.25
550– 649	599.50	135	205.50	42,230.25	5,701,083.75
650– 749	699.50	75	305.50	93,330.25	6,999,768.75
750– 849	799.50	20	405.50	164,430.25	3,288,605.00
		2000			$33,584,000.00

$$s_X = \sqrt{\frac{\sum f(MV - \bar{X})^2}{n - 1}} = \sqrt{\frac{33,584,000}{1999}} = \sqrt{16,800} = 129.6 \approx \$130 \text{ to nearest dollar}$$

the entire distribution, $\sum f(MV - \bar{X})^2$, would equal $\sum (X - \bar{X})^2$, and the standard deviation of the population from which this sample was drawn would be estimated by

$$s_X = \sqrt{\frac{\sum f(MV - \bar{X})^2}{n - 1}}$$

Table 3.5 illustrates the calculation of the standard deviation for the transportation expenditures. Note that after the squared difference between the midvalue and the mean is obtained for each class, each of these squared values must be weighted by the frequency of its class before taking the sum.

As might be expected, there is also a less time-consuming way of obtaining this result, shown in Sec. 3.F.

THE MEDIAN

The median must be estimated when using a frequency distribution, because the exact value of every number is lost in the process of summarizing the data. The median is estimated by finding the class that contains the middle number of the distribution and interpolating arithmetically within that class to estimate its value. Calculations to obtain the median for the student transportation expenditures are shown in Table 3.6.

At first glance, these calculations are not obvious, so let's go through the process step by step. With 2000 ungrouped but arranged values, the median would be found by averaging the values of the two numbers in the 1000 and 1001 positions. For a frequency distribution, we'll assume that the values are spread evenly throughout each class, so that the mean of the numbers in the 1000 and 1001 position would be exactly halfway between them, or in the 1000.5th position. Generalized, this means that for

53

Table 3.6 / Calculation of the median, transportation expenditures

Expenditures	Number of students f	Cumulative frequency
$ 50–$149	25	25
150– 249	130	155
250– 349	720	875
350– 449	530	1405
450– 549	365	1770
550– 649	135	1905
650– 749	75	1980
750– 849	20	2000
	2000	

$$\text{Median} = 350 + \frac{1000.5 - 875}{530} \times 100 = \$374$$

distributions of *discrete* values, the position of the median would be found by taking $(n + 1)/2$, in this case $(2000 + 1)/2 = 1000.5$.[1]

Looking at the cumulative-frequency column in Table 3.6, we observe that the 1000.5th value must fall in the fourth class and have a value between 350 and 449. In fact, the 1000.5th number in the entire distribution must be the 125.5th number in the class from 350 to 499, since $1000.5 - 875 = 125.5$. If the numbers are spread evenly throughout the class, the 125.5th number would fall $125.5/530 = .2367$ of the distance through the class. Since the class interval is 100, this means that the median must have a value of $350 + .2367(100) = \$374$.

Formalizing this reasoning, we define the median for grouped data as

$$\text{Md} = L_{\text{Md}} + p(i)$$

where L_{Md} = lower limit of class containing median value

p = proportion of way through that class to point where median number is located

i = class interval

Other fractile values are estimated in a similar manner, by interpolating to find the value of the number at the desired fractile position.

THE MODE: GROUPED DATA

The mode can also be approximated from a frequency distribution. It is often assumed that the mode occurs at the midvalue of the class containing the greatest number of values. A more satisfactory estimate of the mode can be obtained by adjusting for

---

[1] For a distribution of *continuous* values, the middle value is located using $n/2$, rather than $(n + 1)/2$.

the drop-off in frequency on either side of the modal class (the class containing the greatest number of values) by using the formula

$$\text{Mode} = L_{\text{Mod}} + \frac{\Delta_1}{\Delta_1 + \Delta_2} i$$

where L_{Mod} = lower limit of modal class
Δ_1 = difference between frequency of modal class and frequency of class adjacent to modal class having values smaller than those of modal class
Δ_2 = difference between frequency of modal class and frequency of class adjacent to modal class having values larger than those of modal class
i = class interval

For the transportation expenditures, the mode is then

$$250 + \frac{720 - 130}{(720 - 130) + (720 - 530)} \times 100 = \$326$$

REVIEW EXERCISES 3.D

1. For the frequency distribution of the sample below:

Values	Frequency
2–4	4
5–7	10
8–10	6
11–13	2
	22

a. Estimate the population mean.
b. Estimate the population median.
c. Estimate the population mode.
d. Estimate the population standard deviation.

Answers 3.D

1.

Values	Frequency	MV	fMV	Cumulative frequency	$X - \bar{X}$	$(X - \bar{X})^2$	$f(X - \bar{X})^2$
2–4	4	3	12	4	−3.82	14.59	58.37
5–7	10	6	60	14	−.82	.67	6.72
8–10	6	9	54	20	2.18	4.75	28.51
11–13	2	12	24	22	5.18	26.83	53.66
	22		150				147.26

a. $\bar{X} = \dfrac{\sum f\text{MV}}{n} = \dfrac{150}{22} = 6.82$

b. The value of the $(22 + 1)/2 = 11.5$th number is the median value.

$$\text{Md} = L_{\text{Md}} + p(i) = 5 + \frac{7.5}{10} \times 3 = 7.25$$

c. $\text{Mo} = L_{\text{Mod}} + \dfrac{\Delta_1}{\Delta_1 + \Delta_2}\, i = 5 + \dfrac{10 - 4}{(10 - 4) + (10 - 6)} \times 3 = 6.80$

d. $s_X = \sqrt{\dfrac{\sum f(X - \bar{X})^2}{n - 1}} = \sqrt{\dfrac{147.26}{21}} = 2.65$

Section 3.E

Frequency Polygons, Relative Frequency Distributions, and Skewness

Learning objectives

Your learning objectives for this section are to be able to:

1. Plot frequency polygons
2. Calculate a measure of skewness
3. Calculate relative frequency distributions

FREQUENCY POLYGONS

It is often instructive to graph a particular frequency distribution to obtain a better understanding of its general characteristics. A frequency polygon is one such graph. To graph a frequency polygon, plot the frequency of a class on the Y axis and plot the midvalue of the class on the X axis. The frequency polygon for the transportation expenditures is shown in Fig. 3.1.

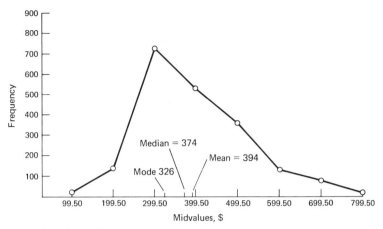

Fig. 3.1 / Frequency polygon for transportation expenditures.

SKEWNESS

The mean, the median, and the mode, as calculated earlier, are shown in the frequency polygon of Fig. 3.1. Note that since the distribution tails off farther on the right than on the left, i.e., there are more extreme values to the right than to the left, the mean is farther to the right than the median and the mode. The mean will always be farther toward the extremes of distribution than the median or mode because every value is used in its calculation, while the median and the mode are determined by considering the position rather than the value of every number.

Skewness, a statistical property describing lack of symmetry, can therefore be measured by comparing the arithmetic mean of a distribution with its median. A common formula for skewness is

$$\text{Skewness} = \frac{3(\overline{X} - \text{Md})}{\text{standard deviation}}$$

If the distribution had extremes on the left rather than on the right, the mean would be smaller than the median and skewness would be negative. If the distribution were symmetrical, the mean and the median would be equal and the skewness would be zero.

For the student-transportation-expenditure example

$$\text{Skewness} = \frac{3(394 - 374)}{130} = +.46$$

57

Note that since the unit of measurement (dollars in this case) appears in both the numerator and denominator of the ratio above, it cancels and skewness becomes a dimensionless value.

There are other more precise methods of measuring skewness, but the one shown above is sufficient for a rough comparison of the symmetry of various distributions.

RELATIVE FREQUENCY DISTRIBUTIONS

To form a relative frequency distribution, merely express the frequency of each class as a proportion of the total frequency. This relationship is illustrated for the transportation expenditures in Table 3.7, where the first two columns constitute a frequency distribution and the first and third columns constitute a relative frequency distribution.

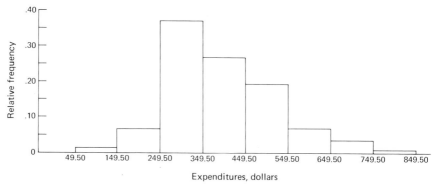

Fig. 3.2 / Plot of relative frequency distribution for transportation expenditures.

Relative frequency distributions can be graphed as bar charts by plotting class limits on the X axis and the relative frequency in each class on the Y axis. Figure 3.2 is a graph of the relative frequency distribution of Table 3.7. Since expenditures

Table 3.7 / Frequency distribution and relative frequency distribution, transportation expenditures

Expenditures	Number of students f	Relative frequency
$ 50–$149	25	.0125
150– 249	130	.0650
250– 349	720	.3600
350– 449	530	.2650
450– 549	365	.1825
550– 649	135	.0675
650– 749	75	.0375
750– 849	20	.0100
	2000	1.0000

were rounded to the nearest dollar, the class 50 to 149 starts at 49.50 and goes to 149.50. The next class starts at 149.50, etc., so there are no little $1 gaps between the bars. The relative frequency for the first class of .0125 is plotted in the Y axis as a horizontal line across the first class interval.[1]

REVIEW EXERCISES 3.E

1. The distribution below represents purchases made by a random sample of 30 customers in a supermarket:

Limits	Frequency
$ 0–$ 9.99	5
10– 19.99	9
20– 29.99	11
30– 39.99	3
40– 49.99	2
	30

a. Calculate the relative frequency distribution.
b. Plot the frequency polygon.
c. Using 5, 15, 25, etc., to represent midvalues, make a point estimate of the population skewness.

Answers 3.E

1.a.

Values	Relative frequency
$ 0–$ 9.99	.17
10– 19.99	.30
20– 29.99	.36
30– 39.99	.10
40– 49.99	.07
	1.00

b.

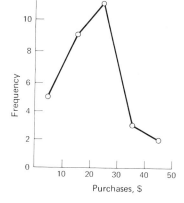

---

[1] A *histogram* could be made from Table 3.7 by plotting the relative frequency *per unit of width* on the Y axis; rather than just the relative frequency. Thus, the height of the bar for the first class would be $.0125/(149.50 - 49.50) = .000125$. A histogram is useful because the area under the entire graph is made equal to 1.000, and the area of each bar represents the *probability* of an occurrence in each class. One definition of probability is "long-run relative frequency under a constant-cause system." Probabilities will be discussed in detail in Module 10.

c.

Limits	MV	Fre-quency	fMV	Cumulative frequency	MV $-$ $\bar{X}$	(MV $-$ $\bar{X}$)²	f(MV $-$ $\bar{X}$)²
$ 0–$ 9.99	5	5	25	5	-16	256	1280
10– 19.99	15	9	135	14	-6	36	324
20– 29.99	25	11	275	25	4	16	176
30– 39.99	35	3	105	28	14	196	588
40– 49.99	45	2	90	30	24	576	1152
		30	630				3520

$$\bar{X} = \frac{630}{30} = 21 \qquad\qquad s_X = \sqrt{\frac{3520}{29}} = 11.02$$

$$Md = 20 + \left(\frac{1.5}{11}\right) 10 = 21.36 \qquad SK = \frac{3(21 - 21.36)}{11.02} = -.10$$

Section 3.F
Short Method for Calculating the Arithmetic Mean and Standard Deviation

While the techniques for calculating the mean and standard deviation shown in previous sections are basic, they are often cumbersome. This section develops short methods for calculating these measures.

Learning objectives

Your learning objectives for this section are to be able to:

1. Calculate the mean by the short method for both ungrouped and grouped data
2. Calculate the standard deviation by the short method for both ungrouped and grouped data

UNGROUPED DATA

Mean. Since the sum of the deviations about the mean is equal to 0, you can obtain the mean by *estimating* its value and correcting the estimate by the average amount that the deviations about the estimate differ from 0. The formula for this calculation is

$$\bar{X} = EM + \frac{\sum (X - EM)}{n}$$

where EM is the estimated mean.

Standard deviation.   To arrive at a short-cut formula for the standard deviation for ungrouped data, you can simplify the expression $\sum (X - \bar{X})^2$:

$$\sum (X - \bar{X})^2 = \sum (X^2 - 2\bar{X}X + \bar{X}^2) = \sum X^2 - 2\bar{X} \sum X + n\bar{X}^2$$

$$= \sum X^2 - 2\bar{X} \sum X + n\bar{X} \frac{\sum X}{n} = \sum X^2 - \bar{X} \sum X$$

$$= \sum X^2 - \frac{(\sum X)^2}{n}$$

Thus the formula

$$s_X = \sqrt{\frac{\sum (X - \bar{X})^2}{n - 1}}$$

reduces to

$$s_X = \sqrt{\frac{\sum X^2 - (\sum X)^2/n}{n - 1}}$$

While this formula looks more complicated than the original one, it often simplifies computations since it involves only the sum of the original values and the sum of their squares.

GROUPED DATA

The short formulas for grouped data are derived from those for ungrouped data. They make use of deviations from an assumed mean, where the deviations are expressed in units of class intervals.

Assume for the moment that after having looked at the transportation expenditure data of Table 3.3, you estimated the arithmetic mean as $399.50 (it's most convenient to use some midvalue as the assumed mean) and coded the differences between this assumed mean and the other midvalues by expressing them in terms of *class-interval* units. The data needed for the calculation of the mean and the standard deviation are shown in Table 3.8.

If the estimated mean were in fact the mean of the sample, the sum of the *fd* column would be 0. Therefore the mean is found by adjusting the estimated mean

Table 3.8 / Calculation of the mean and standard deviation, transportation expenditures

Expenditures	Midvalue (MV)	Coded midvalue d	Number of students f	fd	fd²
$ 50–$149	$ 99.50	−3	25	−75	225
150– 249	199.50	−2	130	−260	520
250– 349	299.50	−1	720	−720	720
350– 449	399.50	0	530	0	0
450– 549	499.50	+1	365	365	365
550– 649	599.50	+2	135	270	540
650– 749	699.50	+3	75	225	675
750– 849	799.50	+4	20	80	320
			2000	−115	3365

by the average of the weighted deviations fd times the class interval i, using the formula

$$\overline{X} = \text{EM} + \sum \frac{fd}{n} i$$

Substituting the appropriate values from Table 3.8 gives

$$\overline{X} = \text{EM} + \sum \frac{fd}{n} i = 399.50 - \left(\frac{115}{2000} \times 100\right) = \$393.75$$

$$= \$394 \text{ to the nearest dollar}$$

For the data of Table 3.8 the standard deviation of the population is then estimated as

$$s_X = 100 \sqrt{\frac{3365 - (-115^2)/2000}{1999}} = \$129$$

It is easy to see that this computation is much simpler than the long method shown in Table 3.5. The only difference is rounding error (and the short formula contains less rounding error than the long one).

REVIEW EXERCISES 3.F

1. Estimate the mean and standard deviation of the population from which the following values were selected at random: 2, 3, 7, 8, and 12.
2. Estimate the mean and standard deviation of the population from the sample shown below:

Values	Frequency
2–3	4
4–5	6
6–7	9
8–9	4
10–11	3
	26

Answers 3.F

1.

X	$X - 7$	X^2
2	−5	4
3	−4	9
7	0	49
8	+1	64
12	+5	144
32	−3	270

$$\bar{X} = 7 - \tfrac{3}{5} = 6.4$$

$$s_X = \sqrt{\frac{270 - (32^2)/5}{4}} = 4.04$$

2.

Values	Frequency	d	fd	fd^2
2–3	4	−2	−8	16
4–5	6	−1	−6	6
6–7	9	0	0	0
8–9	4	+1	4	4
10–11	3	+2	6	12
	26		−4	38

$$\bar{X} = 6.5 - \tfrac{4}{26}(2) = 6.2$$

$$s_X = 2\sqrt{\frac{38 - (-4^2)/26}{25}} = 2.4$$

Questions and Problems

3.1. There are many silly stories about statistics—like the one about the nonswimming statistician who drowned wading across a stream that had an average depth of 3 ft, or about the new convoy commander during World War II who ordered his ships to proceed at the median of the maximum speeds of the ships in the convoy, or the golfer who always hooked or sliced and therefore whose average drive was straight down the fairway. What important point do all these stories illustrate?

3.2. A sample of five college professors, drawn at random from a list maintained by a national professional association, had total incomes last year as follows:

A	B	C	D	E
$8700	$12,300	$14,600	$11,800	$87,100

a. Compute the mean income from this sample.

b. What is the median income for these values?

c. Explain the reason for the sizable differences between $\bar{X}$ and the median. Which is more "typical" of the data?

d. Compute s_X and s_X^2 for these data.

3.3. *a.* Find the mean and the variance of a population consisting of the five numbers 10, 12, 14, 16, and 18.

b. Subtract 4 from each of the values given above and find the mean and variance of the population.

c. Divide each of the original five values in part *a* by 2 and find the mean and variance of the population.

d. Can you make any generalizations based on your experience in completing parts *a, b,* and *c?*

3.4. *a.* If the two values 144 and 152 are added to a sample of size 98, the mean of all 100 values is 50. What was the mean of the original 98 values?

b. What simple but important characteristic of the mean is illustrated by the computation in part *a?*

3.5. One of the best ways of making sure you understand something is to explain it to someone else.

a. Explain, step by step, in the language of a person who knows no statistics, exactly how to calculate the standard deviation of a set of numbers.

b. Make up a demonstration problem involving five numbers in which the mean and standard deviation both come out whole numbers (integers).

3.6. *a.* Show that the variance of a population σ_X^2 can be calculated by an alternative formula that does not involve deviations around the mean. Specifically, prove that

$$\sigma_X^2 = \frac{\sum (X - \mu)^2}{N} = \frac{\sum X^2}{N} - \left(\frac{\sum X}{N}\right)^2$$

b. Under what circumstances would this alternative formula prove more convenient to use?

3.7. Explain why the sample variance $\sum (X - \bar{X})^2/n$ tends to underestimate the population variance σ_X^2. Unless you are equipped to do this job mathematically, you may want to use data like those in Prob. 3.2 to show that squared deviations around the sample mean total less than squared deviations around any other value. (Suppose for example, that the *population mean* μ_X for the data in Prob. 3.2 were $12,500.)

3.8. If you were to make a frequency distribution of the heights (or weights) of all college students in the United States, you'd probably obtain a bimodal distribution. On the other hand, if you made a frequency distribution of IQs of all college students, you could expect to obtain a distribution with a single mode.

a. How do you explain the difference between these two distributions?

b. How might you want to modify the distribution of heights so that it made more sense?

3.9. Files of a life insurance company show the following data on mortgages owned:

Mortgage balance outstanding	Number of mortgages	Mortgage balance outstanding	Number of mortgages
$ 0–$ 3,999	2	$24,000–$27,999	20
4,000– 7,999	14	28,000– 31,999	7
8,000– 11,999	17	32,000– 35,999	2
12,000– 15,999	29	36,000– 39,999	0
16,000– 19,999	50	40,000– 43,999	0
20,000– 23,999	41	44,000– 47,999	1

a. Compute the arithmetic mean mortgage balance outstanding.

b. Estimate the median balance.

c. Twenty-five percent of the mortgages are less than _____.

d. Estimate the mode of the distribution.

e. Compute the standard deviation of this distribution.

f. Compute the skewness of this distribution.

3.10. Assume that you are an accountant with a mail-order firm. You are asked to make an investigation of errors in billing. After laboriously going over a large number of orders, you arrive at the following distribution of errors:

Size of error	Number of errors
$ 0–$ 3.99	36
4.00– 7.99	14
8.00– 11.99	6
12.00– 15.99	3
16.00– 19.99	1
	60

a. Calculate the arithmetic mean size of error.

b. Calculate the median size of error.

c. For this problem, do you think the mean or the median represents the best measure of location? Explain.

d. Calculate the standard deviation of the distribution.

e. Calculate a measure of skewness for the distribution.

3.11. A children's photographer can't be sure what number of pictures or what dollar sales of pictures each sitting will produce. From 60 appointments during 1 week's operation, the following dollar sales resulted:

$	$	$	$	$	$
6	19	0	16	16	12
9	12.50	0	64	13	6
0	10	19	6	10	26
6	15	26	32.50	25	8
50	16	22	16	0	0
20	22	42	26	0	20
16	15	72	16	16	13
70	17.50	44	39	18	0
0	22	0	23	6	27
76	11	20	5	10	14

a. Calculate the arithmetic mean sale per sitting, using the ungrouped data.

b. Obtain the median, using ungrouped data.

c. Obtain the mode, using ungrouped data.

d. Calculate the variance, using ungrouped data.

e. Calculate the standard deviation, using ungrouped data.

f. Group these data into a frequency distribution, using at least six class intervals.

g. Repeat parts *a* through *e* for the grouped data.

h. Explain why each answer in part *g* differs from its counterpart in parts *a* through *e*.

i. In this module, a long and a short method were used to calculate means and standard deviations. Would the answers obtained by the shorter method differ from those obtained using the longer method?

j. Confirm your answer to part *i* by actually performing the calculations by the alternative method from the one you used in parts *a* and *e*.

3.12. You operate a small retail store, and have tabulated the amounts of credit sales for a typical day. These sales are as follows:

$	$	$	$	$	$
27.42	21.04	18.93	27.80	15.23	5.23
44.08	38.92	29.37	15.82	24.16	26.12
14.73	11.32	7.60	20.17	34.28	29.26
45.45	18.70	41.82	36.03	8.30	47.46
17.38	28.76	23.75	27.18	21.32	13.46
29.00	3.20	24.82	48.92	40.37	41.26
25.14	16.47	12.13	30.00	31.26	21.63
22.45	31.82	42.60	32.04	10.27	22.04
35.27	21.24	26.50	19.90	27.13	25.92
24.95	24.87	34.08	37.26	22.34	25.25

For these values, ungrouped, calculate:

a. The arithmetic mean.

b. The median.

c. The mode.

d. The standard deviation.

Group the data in five classes, from 0 to $9.99, $10.00 to $19.99, etc. From the grouped data calculate:

e. The arithmetic mean by the long method.

f. The arithmetic mean by the short method (coding from an assumed mean).

g. The median.

h. The mode.

i. The standard deviation by the long method.

j. The standard deviation by the short method.

3.13. The following distribution shows the width of slots that have been cut in pieces of aluminum used in a precise assembly.

Width of slot, in		Number of pieces
From	Up to, but not including	
.1100	.1110	40
.1110	.1120	65
.1120	.1130	122
.1130	.1140	183
.1140	.1150	165
.1150	.1160	142
.1160	.1170	57
.1170	.1180	26
		800

  a. Find the arithmetic mean of the distribution.
  b. Find the median.
  c. Find the standard deviation.
  d. Plot a frequency polygon of the distribution.
  e. What percent of the pieces would be rejected if tolerance limits were set by accepting any piece that was within ± 2 standard deviations from the mean?

3.14. The New York Stock Exchange Index represents the average price of a share traded on the Exchange. Suppose the computer that normally takes care of this sort of thing breaks down and you're asked to compute the index based on today's closing prices. Without even an adding machine, the problem appears almost insurmountable.
  a. How might you compute the index?
  b. If you decide to use a frequency distribution, how wide should the class intervals be? On what does your answer depend?
  c. How would you select class limits? Will it make any difference in your computation of the average?
  d. Try your approach on actual data by using those stocks beginning with the letter A from the financial section of a recent newspaper. (It might be interesting to compare your mean with the actual value for all stocks traded that day.)

3.15. a. Why are so many distributions of importance in business positively skewed?
  b. Give an example drawn from a business context of a distribution you would expect to be *negatively* skewed.

MODULE 4
INDEX NUMBERS— CONSTRUCTION

The measurement of change is an obsession of an industrial society. Though perhaps unfortunate, this statement is nevertheless true and easily justified. In a society where nothing is static, rapid and accurate assessment of change is prerequisite to making informed decisions.

Index numbers are probably the most widely used means of measuring change in business activity. An index number is simply the expression of the size of a variable as a percent of a base variable. If your pay for a part-time job was $1.85 per hour in 1972, $2.15 in 1973, and $2.50 in 1974, the corresponding index numbers with 1972 as a base would be 1.85/1.85 = 100, 2.15/1.85 = 116, and 2.50/1.85 = 135.

Complex index numbers, which combine many variables into one number, represent a much more powerful tool than the simple index described above. Probably the most widely known complex index number is the consumer price index (CPI). The CPI compares the current price of a collection of consumer goods and services purchased by urban wage earners and clerical workers with the price of the same collection at a base time period.

Trying to visualize changes in consumer prices without constructing an index would be almost impossible. Consumers buy thousands of different goods and services in varying quantities from cottage cheese to Cadillacs, and they buy these products from many outlets at varying prices. An index number which summarizes these prices is a very valuable tool.

This tool is not obtained without thought and effort. There is no way to keep track of everything everyone buys. Therefore, a representative sample of commodities priced over a representative sample of outlets must be obtained and combined into one number using representative weights.

Index numbers don't have to relate to prices. You'll study price, quantity, value, and quality indexes in this module. You'll also discover that there are two basic ways to construct index numbers, the method of aggregates and the method of relatives, both of which will be employed using different weighting schemes.

General learning objective

Your general learning objective for this module is to be able to construct and interpret price, quantity, value, and quality index numbers, both aggregate and relative.

Section 4.A
Price Index Numbers

Learning objective

Your learning objective for this section is to be able to construct aggregate and relative price index numbers, both unweighted and weighted, using either base-year or given-year weights.

Simple index numbers are constructed from a single series by taking the ratio of each value in the series to a particular value chosen as the base and multiplying by 100. Table 4.1 shows the price of regular gasoline at a certain gas station over a 9-month period and an index of those prices using the September 1972 price as a base.

Table 4.1 / Price of gasoline

Date	Price, cents per gallon	Index, Sept. 1 $= 100$
Sept. 1, 1972	27	$\frac{27}{27}(100) = 100$
Oct. 1	28	$\frac{28}{27}(100) = 104$
Nov. 1	30	$\frac{30}{27}(100) = 111$
Dec. 1	31	$\frac{31}{27}(100) = 115$
Jan. 1, 1973	32	$\frac{32}{27}(100) = 119$
Feb. 1	34	$\frac{34}{27}(100) = 126$
March 1	36	$\frac{36}{27}(100) = 133$
Apr. 1	38	$\frac{38}{27}(100) = 141$
May 1	40	$\frac{40}{27}(100) = 148$

Studying the magnitude of price *changes* is facilitated by using index numbers. This is shown by comparing the two series in Table 4.2 that are part of the *Business Week* index. Here automobile production is in the number of units, while intercity truck tonnage is expressed as an index number.

You can easily see that truck tonnage increased by 18 percent since 1967, but the extent of change since 1967 in automobile production isn't very obvious. However, you get no idea of the absolute magnitude of truck tonnage when you look at the index.

Now let's turn to the construction of a *complex* index number, which involves several variables. Suppose you want to make an index-number series showing the

Table 4.2 / Comparison of automobile production and intercity truck tonnage

	Automobiles	Truck tonnage
Latest week	209,094	118
Previous week	217,462	118
Month ago	215,327	111
Year ago	183,265	113
1967 average	142,438	100

Source: *Business Week*, June 2, 1973.

changes in the price of your breakfast. Every day your spartan breakfast consists of one cup of coffee, a 6-oz glass of orange juice made from frozen concentrate, a bowl of cereal, and a 6-oz glass of milk.

UNWEIGHTED AGGREGATE OF PRICES

The most straightforward index you could construct would be based on the *market-basket* approach. You could price the four commodities in the quantities you usually buy them and compare the aggregate prices over time. Table 4.3 shows the prices of a 2-lb can of coffee, a 6-oz can of frozen orange juice, a box of cereal, and a quart of milk.

Table 4.3 / Breakfast price index, unweighted aggregate

	1970	1971	1972	1973
Coffee	$1.50	$1.59	$1.70	$1.87
Orange juice	.20	.22	.25	.30
Cereal	.40	.43	.48	.53
Milk	.25	.25	.26	.28
Total	$2.35	$2.49	$2.69	$2.98
Unweighted aggregate, 1970 = 100	100	106.0	114.5	126.8

This small basket of groceries cost $2.35 in 1970, $2.49 in 1971, etc. To make a price index, choose one of the years as the base and express the prices in the other years as a percentage of that base. The unweighted aggregate index with 1970 as a base is shown in the bottom line of Table 4.3. The formula for an unweighted aggregate price index is

$$\text{Unweighted price aggregate} = \frac{\sum p_n}{\sum p_0} \times 100$$

where p_0 = prices of commodities in base period
p_n = prices of commodities in period for which index is computed

72

WEIGHTED AGGREGATE, BASE-YEAR WEIGHTS

An unweighted price aggregate is easy to understand but is not very satisfactory. Its limitations can easily be seen by visualizing the calculation of an index for all food prices. With an unweighted aggregate index, changes in the price of rarely purchased items would be just as important as changes in those consumed in great quantities. This situation can be corrected through the use of weights. The most obvious weights to use for a price series are the quantities consumed.

To adjust your index of breakfast prices by incorporating quantities, you calculate that you use .22 can of coffee per week, 1.75 cans of orange juice, .70 box of cereal, and 1.31 qt of milk. Using these weights, you calculate the revised index in Table 4.4.

Table 4.4 / Breakfast price index, weighted aggregate, base-year weights

	Quantity q_0	1970		1971		1972		1973	
		p_0	$p_0 q_0$	p_n	$p_n q_0$	p_n	$p_n q_0$	p_n	$p_n q_0$
Coffee	.22	1.50	.3300	1.59	.3498	1.70	.3740	1.87	.4114
Orange juice	1.75	.20	.3500	.22	.3850	.25	.4375	.30	.5250
Cereal	.70	.40	.2800	.43	.3010	.48	.3360	.53	.3710
Milk	1.31	.25	.3275	.25	.3275	.26	.3406	.28	.3668
Sum			1.2875		1.3633		1.4881		1.6742
Index, 1970 = 100			100		105.9		115.6		130.0

The formula used is

$$\text{Weighted aggregate index, base-year weights} = \frac{\sum p_n q_0}{\sum p_0 q_0} \times 100$$

where the q_0's are the weights, in this case, the quantities consumed. The term "base-year weights" means that the same set of weights is used for all time periods. This form of index number is logical, easily interpreted, and widely used. It is often called *Laspeyres' method*. The base for the quantity weights does not have to be the same year used as a base for the index, although it often is in practice.

WEIGHTED AGGREGATE, GIVEN-YEAR WEIGHTS

You might not be happy with the use of base-year weights if the relative amounts of the various components consumed varied considerably from period to period. In such cases, a weighted aggregate index with *given-year* weights can be calculated by using new quantity weights for each period.

Let's assume you ate the original quantities for breakfast until 1973, when you became conscious of the rapid inflation and decided you could get by with less orange juice. You therefore cut your consumption of orange juice in half, resulting in a quantity weight of .875 for orange juice, while all other weights remain as they were. Since the quantities for 1971 and 1972 were the same as for 1970, the indexes for those

73

years remain the same as before, but the values for 1973 would now be calculated as in Table 4.5.

Table 4.5 / Weighted aggregate, given-year weights (1973 only)

	Quantity q_n	1970		1973	
		p_0	$p_0 q_n$	p_n	$p_n q_n$
Coffee	.22	1.50	.3300	1.87	.4114
Orange juice	.875	.20	.1750	.30	.2625
Cereal	.70	.40	.2800	.53	.3710
Milk	1.31	.25	.3275	.28	.3668
Sum			1.1125		1.4117
Index, 1970 = 100			100		126.9

The appropriate formula for this method, called *Paasche's method*, is

$$\text{Weighted aggregate, given-year weights} = \frac{\sum p_n q_n}{\sum p_0 q_n} \times 100$$

where the q_n's are quantity weights for each year. Note that these weights are applied to the base year as well as to the other years. If you'd used the new weights for 1973 but the old weights for 1970, the index for 1973 would have been $(1.4117/1.2875)(100) = 109.6$ rather than the correct value of 126.9. The 109.6 is wrong because it reflects not only the increase in prices between 1970 and 1973 but also the decrease in quantities consumed, and the objective here was to construct a *price* index.

There are two problems with the use of given-year weights. Given-year weights are difficult to interpret. While you can compare any one year with the base year, it is not possible to relate consecutive indexes to each other. Technically, you can relate any year only to the base year and not to any other year.

There is also a practical problem in using given-year weights. A new set of weights must be calculated for each *time* period. In any real problem the collection of quantities is a formidable task. While prices for a food-price index could be obtained and verified relatively easily, it would require extensive effort to obtain the quantities of each commodity sold. Further, since the quantities have to be applied to the base year as well as to the given year, much more calculation is necessary. For these reasons most indexes use base-year weights. Periodically, as consumer preferences change, new weights are calculated and applied to the series.

UNWEIGHTED AVERAGE OF PRICE RELATIVES

Aggregate indexes show price changes through time for a quantity of goods—the market-basket approach. A conceptually different approach to the construction of index numbers is the averaging of price relatives. Using this method, you calculate the relative change in the price of *each commodity* from its base-period price and then obtain the index by averaging these price relatives for each period. This technique

Table 4.6 / Unweighted average of price relatives

	1970		1971		1972		1973	
	p_0	Relative $= \dfrac{p_0}{p_0}$	p_n	Relative $= \dfrac{p_n}{p_0}$	p_n	Relative $= \dfrac{p_n}{p_0}$	p_n	Relative $= \dfrac{p_n}{p_0}$
Coffee	1.50	1.00	1.59	1.060	1.70	1.133	1.87	1.247
Orange juice	.20	1.00	.22	1.100	.25	1.250	.30	1.500
Cereal	.40	1.00	.43	1.075	.48	1.200	.53	1.325
Milk	.25	1.00	.25	1.000	.26	1.040	.28	1.120
Sum		4.00		4.235		4.623		5.192
Index		100		105.9		115.6		129.8

is applied to the breakfast example in Table 4.6. The appropriate formula is

$$\text{Unweighted average of price relatives} = \frac{\sum (p_n/p_0)}{I} (100)$$

where p_0 = price of item in base period

p_n = price in period for which index is being calculated

I = number of items

A relative index is interpreted quite differently from an aggregate index. For example, the 129.8 for 1973 in Table 4.6 no longer represents the change in the price of the entire breakfast: it now represents the average of the changes in the prices for all items included in the breakfast.

An unweighted relative index is subject to the same criticism as is an unweighted aggregate index, namely that the quantities consumed are not considered.

WEIGHTED AVERAGE OF PRICE RELATIVES

The use of pure *quantity* weights for a relative price index is illogical. The quantities used are expressed in many units, and these units cannot be added. Adding was all right for an aggregate index because it involved the price of a "basket" of goods. Even though there was a can of orange juice and a box of cereal in the basket, it was the price of the entire basket that was compared over time. With a relative index the weight would consist of cans added to boxes, which is illogical.

For this reason *value* weights are applied to relative indexes. Value weights are found by multiplying the price per unit of each good by the quantity used. Thus in adding the weights, one adds

$$(\$/\text{can})(\text{cans}) + (\$/\text{box})(\text{boxes})$$

which means one is legitimately adding dollars to dollars. Table 4.7 illustrates the calculation of a weighted relative index. The formula appropriate to this calculation is

$$\text{Weighted average of price relatives, base-year value weights} = \frac{\sum [(p_n/p_0)(100 p_0 q_0)]}{\sum p_0 q_0}$$

where p_n/p_0 = price relatives

$p_0 q_0$ = base-year value weights

Table 4.7 / Weighted average of price relatives, base-year weights

	1970	1971	1972	1973
	Price relatives 1970 = 100			
	$\frac{p_0}{p_0} \times 100$	$\frac{p_n}{p_0} \times 100$	$\frac{p_n}{p_0} \times 100$	$\frac{p_n}{p_0} \times 100$
Coffee	100	106.0	113.33	124.7
Orange juice	100	110.0	125.00	150.0
Cereal	100	107.5	120.00	132.5
Milk	100	100.0	104.00	112.0

	Price relatives × value weights			
	Value weights $p_0 q_0$	$\frac{p_0}{p_0} \times 100 p_0 q_0$	$\frac{p_n}{p_0} \times 100 p_0 q_0$	$\frac{p_n}{p_0} \times 100 p_0 q_0$	$\frac{p_n}{p_0} \times 100 p_0 q_0$
Coffee	.3300	33.00	34.98	37.40	41.15
Orange juice	.3500	35.00	38.50	43.75	52.50
Cereal	.2800	28.00	30.10	33.60	37.10
Milk	.3275	32.75	32.75	34.06	36.68
Sum	1.2875	128.75	136.33	148.81	167.43
Index		100	105.9	115.6	130.0

If you have a good memory and are observant, you should make a discovery when looking over Table 4.7. The final indexes are exactly the same as those derived from the weighted aggregate of prices using base-year quantity weights. You can prove that these two indexes are the same by canceling the p_0 from the numerator and the denominator of the upper part of the relative index formula:

Relative index, value weights = aggregate index, base-year quantity weights

$$\frac{\sum [(p_n/p_0)(100 p_0 q_0)]}{\sum p_0 q_0} = \frac{\sum (p_n q_0)(100)}{\sum p_0 q_0}$$

You may wonder why anyone would go to the extra bother of calculating a relative index when the same result could be obtained with less effort using the aggregate index. The answer is that in using the relative index you can observe the relative price changes in the *individual components* as well as their composite change.

You could also weight price relatives by using given-year value weights rather than base-year weights. The resulting formula is

Weighted average of price relatives, given year value weights $= \dfrac{\sum [(p_n/p_0)(100 p_n q_n)]}{\sum p_n q_n}$

The index numbers resulting from the use of this formula are subject to the same conceptual difficulties encountered when given-year weights were applied to aggregates. Also, relative indexes with given-year weights do not correspond to any aggregate index. For these reasons relative indexes with given-year weights are seldom used.

REVIEW EXERCISES 4.A

Let's say that you have two hobbies, skiing and sailing. You are interested in the price changes involved in *participating* in these sports. These prices include gas used to get to the site of the sport, lift tickets, and entrance fees to the lake. These costs per trip for 1970 and 1973 were:

	1970	1973
Ski	$15	$20
Sail	5	8

1. The index for an unweighted aggregate for 1973 is _____, and for an unweighted relative for 1973 is _____, both on a 1970 base.

2. Say that in 1970 you went skiing 20 times and sailing 80 times. The index for a weighted price aggregate for 1973 with 1970 base-year quantity weights is _____ and for a weighted relative for 1973 with 1970 base-year quantity weights is _____.

3. Say that 1973 was a bad year for skiing but a good year for sailing, so you skied 10 times and sailed 90 times. The index for a weighted price aggregate for 1973 with given-year quantity weights is _____ and for a weighted relative index with given-year quantity weights is _____.

4. The weighted relative price index for 1973 using 1970 base-year *value* weights is _____. This is the same value as you got when you calculated the _____ index in an exercise above.

Answers 4.A

1. 140, 147

	1970		1973	
	$	Relative	$	Relative
Ski	15	1.00	20	1.333
Sail	5	1.00	8	1.600
	20	2.00	28	2.933
Unweighted aggregate	$\left(\frac{20}{20}\right)(100) = 100$		$\left(\frac{28}{20}\right)(100) = 140$	
Unweighted average of relatives	$\left(\frac{2.00}{2}\right)(100) = 100$		$\left(\frac{2.933}{2}\right)(100) = 147$	

2. 149, 155

		1970		1973	
	Weight	$	$ × weight	$	$ × weight
Ski	20	15	300	20	400
Sail	80	5	400	8	640
	100		700		1040
Weighted aggregate, base-year quantity weights		$\left(\frac{700}{700}\right)(100) = 100$		$\left(\frac{1040}{700}\right)(100) = 149$	

77

	Weights	\$	1970 Relative	1970 Weight × relative	\$	1973 Relative	1973 Weight × relative
Ski	20	15	1.00	20.00	20	1.333	26.66
Sail	80	5	1.00	80.00	8	1.600	128.00
	100			100.00			154.66
Weighted relative, base-year quantity weights		$\left(\dfrac{100}{100}\right)(100) = 100$			$\left(\dfrac{154.66}{100}\right)(100) = 155$		

3. 153, 157

	1970 Weight	1970 \$	1970 \$ × weight	1973 Weight	1973 \$	1973 \$ × weight
Ski	10	15	150	10	20	200
Sail	90	5	450	90	8	720
	100		600	100		920
Weighted aggregate, given-year quantity weights	$\left(\dfrac{600}{600}\right)(100) = 100$			$\left(\dfrac{920}{600}\right)(100) = 153$		

	1970 Weight	1970 \$	1970 Relative	1970 Weight × relative	1973 Weight	1973 \$	1973 Relative	1973 Weight × relative
Ski	10	15	1.00	10.00	10	20	1.333	13.33
Sail	90	5	1.00	90.00	90	8	1.600	144.00
	100			100.00	100			157.33
Weighted relative, given-year quantity weights		$\left(\dfrac{100}{100}\right)(100) = 100$				$\left(\dfrac{157.33}{100}\right)(100) = 157$		

4. 149, weighted aggregate, base-year quantity weights

	1970 Weight	1970 \$	1970 Value = weight × \$	1970 \$	1970 100 × relative	1970 Value × 100 × relative	1973 \$	1973 100 × relative	1973 Value × 100 × relative
Ski	20	15	300	15	100	30,000	20	133.3	39,990
Sail	80	5	400	5	100	40,000	8	160.0	64,000
			700			70,000			103,990
Weighted relative, base-year value weights	$\dfrac{70,000}{700} = 100$					$\dfrac{103,990}{700} = 149$			

Section 4.B
Quantity Index Numbers

Learning objectives

Your learning objectives for this section are to be able to:

1. Differentiate between price indexes and quantity indexes
2. Construct aggregate and relative quantity indexes, both unweighted and weighted

Quantity index-number series, though not as common as price indexes, are often used when it is important to show changes in the *volume* of an activity. Exactly the same techniques that were used for price indexes can be applied to the construction of quantity indexes. Where it was logical to use either quantity or value weights for a price index, it becomes equally logical to use either price or value weights for a quantity index. Therefore any price-index formula can be converted into the equivalent quantity-index formula simply by interchanging the p's and q's. Table 4.8 summarizes these relationships for the most commonly used indexes.

The use of the four quantity index-number formulas is illustrated in Table 4.9. Hypothetical data for metal production are used in order to emphasize the characteristics of each index. The symbols S, A, C, and M will be used to identify the four metals.

The unweighted aggregate index stays at 100 for all three periods because the changes in the production of metal S are exactly offset by the changes in metal M. While it is technically correct that no overall change in the quantity of production

Table 4.8 / Summary of index-number formulas

	Price index	Quantity index
Unweighted aggregate	$\dfrac{\sum p_n}{\sum p_0} \times 100$	$\dfrac{\sum q_n}{\sum q_0} \times 100$
Weighted aggregate, base-year weights	$\dfrac{\sum p_n q_0}{\sum p_0 q_0} \times 100$	$\dfrac{\sum q_n p_0}{\sum q_0 p_0} \times 100$
Unweighted average of relatives	$\dfrac{\sum [(p_n/p_0)(100)]}{I}$	$\dfrac{\sum [(q_n/q_0)(100)]}{I}$
Weighted average of relatives, base year value weights	$\dfrac{\sum [(p_n/p_0)(100 p_0 q_0)]}{\sum p_0 q_0}$	$\dfrac{\sum [(q_n/q_0)(100 q_0 p_0)]}{\sum q_0 p_0}$

79

Table 4.9 / Calculation of quantity index numbers of metal production
(q's in thousands of tons)

		Year 0	Year 1	Year 2
Metal	p_0, per ton	q_0	q_1	q_2
S	$ 2	3000	3004	2992
A	8	400	400	400
C	12	80	80	80
M	50	8	4	16
Sum		3488	3488	3488

$$\text{Unweighted aggregate index} = \frac{\sum q_n}{\sum q_0} \times 100$$

Index	100	100	100

Metal	$q_0 p_0$	$q_1 p_0$	$q_2 p_0$
S	6,000	6,008	5,984
A	3,200	3,200	3,200
C	960	960	960
M	400	200	800
Sum	10,560	10,368	10,944

$$\text{Weighted aggregate index, base-year price weights} = \frac{\sum q_n p_0}{\sum q_0 p_0} \times 100$$

Index	100	98.2	103.6

Metal	$\dfrac{q_0}{q_0}$	$\dfrac{q_1}{q_0}$	$\dfrac{q_2}{q_0}$
S	1.00	1.001	.997
A	1.00	1.000	1.000
C	1.00	1.000	1.000
M	1.00	.500	2.000
Sum	4.00	3.501	4.997

$$\text{Unweighted average of relatives} = \frac{\sum (q_n/q_0)(100)}{I}$$

Index	100	87.5	124.9

Metal	$\dfrac{q_0}{q_0}(q_0 p_0)(100)$	$\dfrac{q_1}{q_0}(q_0 p_0)(100)$	$\dfrac{q_2}{q_0}(q_0 p_0)(100)$
S	600,000	600,600	598,200
A	320,000	320,000	320,000
C	96,000	96,000	96,000
M	40,000	20,000	80,000
Sum	1,056,000	1,036,600	1,094,200

$$\text{Weighted average of relatives, base-year value weights} = \frac{\sum [(q_n/q_0)(100 q_0 p_0)]}{\sum q_0 p_0}$$

Index	100	98.2	103.6

occurred, the results of the unweighted aggregate index are not completely satisfactory because they do not take into account the relative worth of the various metals. A change of 4000 tons in metal S is insignificant, but the same change in metal M is, since metal M costs 25 times as much as metal S.

The unweighted relative index changes drastically from period to period because the change of 4000 tons is a very small amount relative to the quantity of metal S but a very large amount relative to the quantity of metal M. Though the resulting index is perhaps unduly affected by the relative changes in metal M, the components of the index show exactly what happened to the relative quantities of each metal.

The weighted aggregate index takes the relative worth of the metals into account by weighting the quantities produced by their prices. Note that since base-year prices were used, the prices themselves were assumed to remain constant from period to period. The index changes from period to period reflect changes in *quantities* produced (weighted by what each metal is worth).

The weighted average of relatives index using base-year *value* of production weights combines the advantages of the weighted aggregate and unweighted relative indexes. The final index is exactly the same as the weighted aggregate, although relative changes in the quantity of each component are now readily apparent from the q_n/q_0 ratios. (These ratios are shown in the section of Table 4.9 on unweighted average of relatives but are an integral part of the calculation of the weighted average of relatives.)

REVIEW EXERCISES 4.B

1. To change any price-index formula to the corresponding quantity-index formula, simply interchange the _____'s and the _____'s.

Suppose that you work at a sports shop and note that in 1970 you sold 5 pairs of cross-country skis at \$30 per pair and 100 pairs of downhill skis at \$150 per pair. By 1973 your sales had increased to 30 cross-country skis and 110 downhill.

2. An unweighted aggregate *quantity* index would have a value of _____ for 1973, while an unweighted relative *quantity* index would have a value of _____ for 1973, where 1970 is used as the base in both cases.

3. A weighted aggregate *quantity* index using 1970 *price* weights and a 1970 base, would have a value of _____ in 1973.

4. A weighted relative *quantity* index using 1970 *value* weights and a 1970 base would have a value of _____ in 1973.

Answers 4.B

1. *p*'s and *q*'s

2. 133, 355

	1970		1973	
	q	Relative	*q*	Relative
Cross-country	5	1.00	30	6.00
Downhill	100	1.00	110	1.10
	105	2.00	140	7.10
Unweighted aggregate	$\left(\dfrac{105}{105}\right)(100) = 100$		$\left(\dfrac{140}{105}\right)(100) = 133$	
Unweighted relative	$\left(\dfrac{2.00}{2}\right)(100) = 100$		$\left(\dfrac{7.10}{2}\right)(100) = 355$	

3. 115

		1970			1973	
	Price	*q*	*q* × price		*q*	*q* × price
Cross-country	30	5	150		30	900
Downhill	150	100	15,000		110	16,500
			15,150			17,400
Weighted aggregate, base-year *price* weights		$\left(\dfrac{15,150}{15,150}\right)(100) = 100$			$\left(\dfrac{17,400}{15,150}\right)(100) = 115$	

4. 115

		1970			1973		
	p × *q* = value	*q*	Relative	Relative × value × 100	*q*	Relative	Relative × value × 100
Cross-country	30 × 5 = 150	5	1.00	15,000	30	6.00	90,000
Downhill	150 × 100 = 15,000	100	1.00	1,500,000	110	1.10	1,650,000
	15,150			1,515,000			1,740,000
Weighted relative, base-year *value* weights		$\dfrac{1,515,000}{15,150} = 100$			$\dfrac{1,740,000}{1,515,000} = 115$		

Section 4.C
Value Index Numbers

Learning objectives

Your learning objective for this section is to be able to compute a value index, either aggregate or relative.

Sometimes the combination of changes in price *and* quantity is more meaningful than the change in either taken alone. Such is the case with earnings. A high hourly wage is certainly nicer than a low one, but it doesn't mean much if you work only a few hours. Conversely, working long hours is worthwhile only if the amount paid per hour is significant. In a case like this, a *value* index might be appropriate.

Consider the data in Table 4.10 pertaining to the hours worked and the wages paid in three industries.

Table 4.10 / Calculation of value index numbers

(Hours worked and wages paid in three industries)

Industry	Year 1			Year 2		
	p_0, \$/h	q_0, h/wk	p_0q_0, \$/wk	p_n, \$/h	q_n, h/wk	p_nq_n, \$/wk
A	10	20	200	9	30	270
B	5	40	200	5	42	210
C	2	50	100	2	45	90
Sum			500			570

$$\text{Aggregate value index} = \frac{\sum p_nq_n}{\sum p_0q_0} \times 100$$

Index	100	114

Industry	$\dfrac{p_0q_0}{p_0q_0} \times 100$	$\dfrac{p_0q_0}{p_0q_0} \times 100p_0q_0$	$\dfrac{p_nq_n}{p_0q_0} \times 100$	$\dfrac{p_nq_n}{p_0q_0} \times 100p_0q_0$
A	100	20,000	135	27,000
B	100	20,000	105	21,000
C	100	10,000	90	9,000
Sum		50,000		57,000

$$\text{Relative value index} = \frac{\sum [(p_nq_n/p_0q_0)(100p_0q_0)]}{\sum p_0q_0}$$

Index	100	114

The formulas for an aggregate value index and a relative value index having value weights result in the same number since the term $p_0 q_0$ can be canceled from the numerator of the relative formula. With either the aggregate value index or the relative value index using value weights, the take-home pay in the example increased 14 percent from year 1 to year 2.

REVIEW EXERCISES 4.C

1. For the ski problem in the review exercise for Sec. 4.B, assume that in 1973 the prices changed to $40 and $170 for cross-country and downhill skis. The aggregate *value* index for 1973 with 1970 as the base year is _____.

2. For the data above, the relative *value* index for 1973 with 1970 as the base year is

_____

Answers 4.C

1. 131

	1970			1973		
	p_0	q_0	$p_0 q_0$	p_n	q_n	$p_n q_n$
Cross-country	30	5	150	40	30	1,200
Downhill	150	100	15,000	170	110	18,700
			15,150			19,900
Aggregate value index	$\left(\dfrac{15,150}{15,150}\right)(100) = 100$			$\left(\dfrac{19,900}{15,150}\right)(100) = 131$		

2. 131

	1970				
	p_0	q_0	$p_0 q_0$	Relative	Relative $\times$ $p_0 q_0$ $\times$ 100
Cross-country	30	5	150	1.00	15,000
Downhill	150	100	15,000	1.00	1,500,000
			15,150		1,515,000

$$\text{Relative } value \text{ index } \frac{1,515,000}{15,150} = 100$$

	1973				
	p_n	q_n	$p_n q_n$	Relative	Relative $\times$ $p_0 q_0$ $\times$ 100
Cross-country	40	30	1,200	8.00	120,000
Downhill	170	110	18,700	1.247	1,870,000
			19,900		1,990,000

$$\text{Relative } value \text{ index } \frac{1,990,000}{15,150} = 131$$

Section 4.D
Quality Index Numbers

Learning objectives

Your learning objectives for this section are to be able to:

1. Describe the nature and use of a quality index
2. Identify some difficulties encountered in constructing quality indexes

Though index numbers composed of prices and/or quantities are most useful in measuring changes in economic and business activity, index numbers reflecting changes or differences in other attributes are used in many other fields. Textbooks relating to social measurement include dozens of sociometric scales or indexes.[1] However, since these indexes are not necessarily concerned with changes over time and do not compare attributes with base-period values, they do not conform to our definition of index numbers. Though many of them, such as indexes of morale, job satisfaction, and leadership, are relevant to business, they won't be discussed here.

What we want to discuss are the opportunities and pitfalls in the measurement of *quality*. Let's consider a performance index of passenger-tire quality. To build such an index you would first have to list what you considered to be important attributes of tire quality. Let's assume that you decide that mileage, blowout resistance, traction, and noise are a sufficient set of attributes.

Now you'd have to find a way to measure each attribute. Obtaining measurements would involve statistical sampling and all the problems inherent in that process. (These problems are the subject of future modules.) At this point we'll assume that you've obtained representative measurements for each of the attributes, as summarized in Table 4.11.

Before constructing an index, you've got to take care of an important point. Mileage is measured on a scale where the better the tire, the greater the mileage. The other three attributes are measured on scales such that the better the tire, the *smaller* the value. In order to make a meaningful index, the values will have to be converted to consistent scales. Since it's logical to want the index to be greater for better tires, we'll convert the three "lower is better" scales by using their reciprocals. The converted table together with the calculation of a *relative* index is shown in Table 4.12.

---

[1] See Delbert C. Miller, *Handbook of Research Design and Social Measurement*, McKay Company, New York, 1970, for many examples.

Table 4.11 / Attributes of tire quality

Attribute	Brand		
	A	B	C
Mileage, thousands of miles of tread wear	15	20	30
Blowout resistance, failures per 1000 tires on an impact test	10	8	5
Traction, feet to stop on dry pavement at 50 mi/h	500	480	550
Noise, decibels inside car at 50 mi/h on concrete pavement	20	24	16

A relative index is much more appropriate than an aggregate because of the large differences in the size of the numbers, as well as the problem of interpreting the meaning of the mixed dimensions in an aggregate index.

To this point, you might think that this index was very objective. However, there is a subjective factor buried in the index. Brand C tire can be judged 54 percent better than brand A only if you give *equal* weight to all the attributes. If you were interested only in economy and safety, for example, the factor of noise could be eliminated. If that were done, the indexes would read 100, 121, and 164 rather than 100, 111, and 154. Thus the feelings of different people regarding the importance of the different attributes would result in different values for an index.

This problem is universal in attempting to develop quality indexes. No simple weighting scheme will suffice because different people would want to use different weights. In measuring the quality of a corporation, for example, you might decide to rate corporations on the basis of their treatment of stockholders, employees, customers, and society in general. None of these attributes can be measured on a machine like mileage, so measurement problems would be great. Further, not everyone would agree to the inclusion of all these attributes, to say nothing of their relative importance.

Quality indexes become even more value-laden when they are used to measure desirability rather than performance. In the tire example above people might argue

Table 4.12 / Index of tire quality

Attribute	Brand					
	A		B		C	
	Value	Relative	Value	Relative	Value	Relative
Mileage	15.0	1.00	20.0	1.33	30.0	2.00
Blowout resistance	.10	1.00	.125	1.25	.200	2.00
Traction	.00200	1.00	.00208	1.04	.00182	.91
Noise	.05	1.00	.0417	.83	.0625	1.25
Sum of relatives		4.00		4.45		6.16
Index		100		111		154

 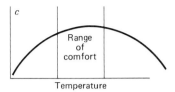

Figure 4.1 / Desirability curves.

about the relative importance of the components, but no one would argue about the *direction* of change that was desirable. The more mileage the better, the less noise the better. Other things (such as price) being equal, twice the mileage means twice as good. Such a scaling of desirability might be graphed as a straight line, as in Fig. 4.1*a*, where desirability increases in proportion to mileage.

Other attributes could be related to desirability in the form of a curve. A pollution-vs.-desirability curve might look like Fig. 4.1*b*. Here an increase in pollution at a low level would not decrease desirability very much, but the same increase at a higher level might become intolerable.

In other cases some middle zone might represent the most desirable level. In an index of the quality of a city, both low and high extremes of temperature would be undesirable. Such a curve is shown in Fig. 4.1*c*. While individuals might associate different temperatures with different degrees of desirability, the general pattern would be consistent among all people. Too cold and too hot both represent undesirable attributes.

The value problem becomes more difficult when different people view opposite directions of change as desirable. Some communities strive for as little income dispersion among the population as possible by excluding low-income families. Others attempt to increase the variability in income dispersion by making the community attractive to all income levels. These two attitudes would produce different desirability curves for the same attribute as shown in Fig. 4.2.

If some people in a city hold to one of these curves and some to the other, things might really get interesting for the city government.

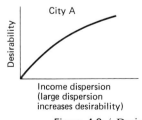 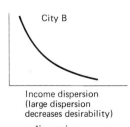

Figure 4.2 / Desirability vs. income dispersion.

The Midwest Research Institute has published an index of rating comparing the quality of life in various states. Separate ratings were prepared for such factors as

1. Living conditions
   a. Marriage and divorce rates
   b. Poverty and crime levels
   c. Living costs
   d. Weather
   e. Accident and death rates
2. Individual status
   a. Employment rates
   b. Financial independence
   c. Mobility of residents
3. Economic status
   a. Personal income
   b. Employment
   c. Commercial bank assets
4. Education
   a. Public school enrollment
   b. Attendance records
   c. Number of college students
   d. Pupil-teacher ratios
5. Health and welfare
   a. Ratio of doctors, nurses, dentists, and lawyers to population
   b. Expenditures on social benefits
6. Government
   a. Number and quality of employees and teachers
   b. Efficiency of revenue raising
   c. Reductions in crime
   d. Increases in job placement and size of voting population

A composite rating was then prepared from these components.[1]

Think about the attributes listed above and whether you agree that they measure quality of life. What changes would *you* want to make in these measures? A little such examination should convince you that the construction of quality indexes is very difficult.

In spite of formidable problems, though, emphasis on the environment, corporate responsibility, and the quality of life can be expected to focus much attention on quality indexes in the future.

---

[1] Further information is available from Midwest Research Institute, 425 Volker Boulevard, Kansas City, Mo, 64110.

REVIEW EXERCISES 4.D

1. True or false: a quality index:
  a. Is a price or quantity index of high quality.
  b. Is an index of the quality of a product, place, organization, or life.
  c. Is used to measure how people feel or are affected by changes in their environment.
2. Difficulties in constructing a quality index include:
  a. The choice of components of the index. .
  b. Deciding on the relative importance of the components.
  c. Knowing whether a given change in a component would be desirable or undesirable.
  d. Taking into account that one man's meat is another man's poison.
  e. All the above.

Answers 4.D

1. a. F; *b.* T; *c.* T   *2. e.*

Questions and Problems

4.1. A dairy prices the components involved in producing ½ gal of homogenized milk (excluding labor, overhead, and profit) as:

	1974	1962
Milk	$.46000	$.30913
Container	.03033	.02457
Machine rental	.00300	.00300
Plant loss	.00727	.00500

  a. Calculate an unweighted aggregate price index, using 1962 as the base.
  b. Calculate an unweighted average of relatives price index, using 1962 as the base.
  c. Which of these index numbers do you think is better? Why?

4.2. Costs for a nonresident student at the University of Colorado are shown below:

	Academic year		
	1974–1975	1973–1974	1972–1973
Tuition	$1908	$1758	$1412
Fees	162	113	111
Room and board (minimum)	1236	1086	950

  a. Calculate an unweighted aggregate price index, using 1972–1973 as the base.
  b. Calculate an unweighted average of relatives price index, using 1972–1973 as the base.
  c. Which index number do you think is better? Why?

4.3. Records of a manufacturer of sleeping bags show the following statistics for major components of a certain style bag:

	1974	1971	Quantity per bag
Prime goose down	$10/lb	$8/lb	$2\frac{1}{2}$ lb
Ripstop nylon	0.765/yd	0.670/yd	9 yd
Zipper	1.257	1.020	1

a. Calculate a weighted aggregate price index, with 1971 as the base, using quantity weights.

b. Calculate a weighted average of relatives price index, with 1971 as the base, using quantity weights.

c. Calculate a weighted average of relatives price index, with 1971 as the base, using value weights.

d. Which of the index numbers above do you prefer? Why?

4.4. Suppose that the sleeping bag prices quoted in Prob. 4.4 are accurate but that in 1971 it took $3\frac{1}{2}$ lb of down to make a bag. In 1974 improved design and technology enabled the company to reduce the down content per bag to $2\frac{1}{2}$ lb, with no loss in insulating qualities.

a. Calculate a weighted aggregate price index with base-year quantity weights.

b. Calculate a weighted aggregate price index with given-year quantity weights (express weights in their absolute values).

c. Calculate a weighted aggregate price index with given year quantity weights (express weights as percentage of total weight for each year).

d. Calculate a weighted average of relatives price index with base-year quantity weights.

e. Calculate a weighted average of relatives price index with given-year quantity weights.

f. Calculate a weighted average of relatives price index with given-year value weights.

g. How do you explain the differences in the indexes calculated above?

h. Which of the indexes above do you prefer? Why?

4.5. Assume that you are hired by an M.B.A. of 10 years ago, who is now the president of a paving company. He provides you with the following statistics on producing asphalt paving (AC oil and aggregate are the only materials in the blacktop):

	1974	1972
AC oil at plant, per ton	$85	$25
$\frac{3}{4}$-in graded aggregate, per ton	$2	$1.70
Processing costs per ton of blacktop	$2	$1.75
Indirect costs, % of materials and processing costs	18	18
Profit margin, % of materials and processing costs	15	15

Blacktop consists of 6 percent oil and 94 percent aggregate (by weight).

a. Construct what you consider to be the best price index to show the change in the customer's price of blacktop.

b. Explain why you think the index you chose in part a is better than all the other types of index you could have made.

4.6. As a manufacturer of industrial paints, you are trying to explain to a purchasing agent of a large company why your prices have risen so much in the past few years. You compile the following data:

	Cost			Paint, parts by weight*
	1974	1972	1970	
Barrel†	$15.04	$9.50	$8.50	
Solvent,‡ per gal	.38	.19	.16	$\frac{1}{8}$
Alkyd resin, per lb	.34	.12	.10	$\frac{3}{8}$
Extender, per lb	.04	.028	.02	$\frac{1}{4}$
Prime pigment, per lb	.72	.30	.27	$\frac{1}{4}$

*Paint weighs 10 lb/gal.
†Paint is sold to the customer in 55-gal barrels, which are not returned.
‡Solvent weighs 6.6 lb/gal.

Using as weights the number of pounds of each component in a 55-gal barrel (and a weight of 1 for one barrel), calculate:

a. A weighted aggregate price index with 1970 as the base, using quantity weights.

b. A weighted average of relatives price index with 1970 as a base, using quantity weights.

c. A weighted average of relatives price index with 1970 as a base, using value weights.

d. Which of the above indexes do you prefer? Why?

4.7. The prices below show the costs of the major components of a 1.5-lb loaf of home-made bread.

	Cost, cents	
	1974	1972
Milk	7.50	6 23
Sugar	1.50	.84
Margarine	3.75	2.51
Flour	27.50	12.10

a. Calculate an unweighted aggregate price index, with 1972 as the base.

b. Calculate an unweighted average of price relatives index with 1972 as the base.

c. Though we called the values above unweighted, in what sense are the indexes weighted?

d. Which of the price indexes above do you prefer? Why?

4.8. You gather the data below to construct a United States production index:

	Week of Mar. 11	
	1974	1973
Steel, thousands of tons	2,839	2,977
Autos, units	126,152	210,188
Electric power, millions of kilowatt hours	34,314	33,552
Crude oil refinery runs, daily average, thousands of barrels	11,037	12,341

a. Construct an unweighted aggregate quantity index.

b. Construct an unweighted relative quantity index.

c. Change the units in which autos are measured from single units to thousands of units and recompute part *a* and *b*.

d. What do these calculations illustrate about aggregate and relative indexes?

e. Which of the above indexes do you prefer for this problem? Why?

4.9. The following data show the number (in thousands) of private housing starts in the United States, classified by single and multiple units.

	1 unit	2 or more units
1967	844	448
1968	899	608
1969	811	656
1970	813	661
1971	1151	901
1972	1309	1047

Source: Economic Indicators, March 1973.

a. Construct two quantity index-number series, one for single-unit housing, and one for multiple-unit housing, both with 1967 as a base.

b. Comment on the relative growth in single- and multiple-unit housing since 1967.

4.10. The following data show average weekly hours worked and average gross hourly earnings for 1950 to 1970 by type of industry:

Year	Average weekly hours worked			Average gross hourly earnings		
	Mfrg	Constr	Retail	Mfrg	Constr	Retail
1950	40.5	37.4	40.4	1.440	1.863	.983
1955	40.7	37.1	39.0	1.860	2.450	1.250
1960	39.7	36.7	38.0	2.260	3.080	1.520
1965	41.2	37.4	36.6	2.610	3.700	1.820
1970	39.8	37.4	33.8	3.360	5.240	2.440

a. Construct a relative value index for this series.

b. On the basis of total weekly earnings, in what industry would you have preferred to work? What figures did you look at to tell?

c. On the basis of relative increase in earnings, in what industry would you have preferred to work? What figures did you look at to tell?

d. Overall, by what percent did earnings increase from 1950 to 1970?

4.11. You work for a mining company and have collected the following data showing the prices and quantities produced for two different grades of ore that you mine in two locations:

Grade	1970		1974	
	Price per ton	Tons	Price per ton	Tons
High	$3.00	50,000	$5.50	30,000
Low	1.50	200,000	2.00	300,000

a. Construct a relative value index for ore production, using 1970 as the base.
b. Interpret your results.

4.12. A substitute for ordinary gas for use in cars comes on the market. Cars need no modification to use the new product. The products have the following characteristics:

	Pollution index*	Price per gallon	Mileage, mi/gal
Gas	50	$.60	20
New product	30	.30	10

*Measured on a scale from 0 to 100, where the higher the number, the greater the pollution.

Make a quality index in which *economy* and *environmental benefits* (low pollution) are given equal weight. Use regular gas as the base for the index. Construct the index so that the better the product, the higher the index.

4.13. You've graduated and are trying to decide what job to take. (You can already tell that things are bad: if they were good, you'd be deciding which position to accept.) You narrow the field down to two. Both are desirable, and you find it hard to make a choice, so you decide to quantify your feelings by making a quality index.

You know that the four attributes that really count with you are the environment (location, etc.), initial salary, opportunity for advancement, and type of work. Further, you feel that of these, initial salary ranks lowest, opportunity for advancement counts 50 percent more than salary, environment twice as much as salary, and type of work 3 times as much as salary. You need a scale for ranking everything but salary, so you rank the others on a scale from 0 to 100, where 0 means the worst of all possible situations (not just the ones you're considering) and 100 means the best of all possible situations.

You summarize these data as follows:

Attribute	Weight	Job 1	Job 2
Environment	2	60	70
Salary	1	$11,000	$12,500
Opportunity for advancement	1.5	40	50
Type of work	3	80	50

Make a weighted relative quality index to help you decide which job to take.

4.14. Describe and compare the advantages and disadvantages of aggregate vs. relative index numbers.

4.15. Of all the price indexes you have learned to construct, describe which you think is the best overall. Defend your choice.

MODULE 5
INDEX NUMBERS—PROBLEMS, EXAMPLES, AND USES

General learning objectives

Your general learning objectives for this module are to be able to:

1. Recognize and solve problems involved in constructing index-number series
2. Describe some common index-number series and their uses

Section 5.A

Problems in the Construction and Use of Index Numbers

Learning objectives

Your learning objectives for this section are to be able to:
1. Explain why it is necessary to use sampling in constructing most index-number series
2. Differentiate between a judgment sample and a random sample
3. Explain why:
   a. Every index-number formula makes an assumption about the weights or relative importance of the component
   b. There are many variations of basic index-number formulas
4. Describe the problems that arise in building an index-number series because of changes over time in:
   a. The relative importance of components
   b. The quality of components
5. Determine a suitable base period for an index-number series
6. Splice an index-number series

SAMPLING

The requirement of timeliness at reasonable cost makes sampling a necessity for all but the most trivial index-number series. The easiest way to visualize the necessity of sampling and its problems is to consider a specific situation. Suppose you were asked to construct a food-price index in your community. How would you proceed? Your first concern would probably be which items to price. There are thousands of items in any store, so many that the task of complete enumeration would be impossible. You would have to select a manageable number of items, hoping they were ones that made up the bulk of the purchases of the consumers. Here you would run into trouble on two counts. (1) Just what are these items? You might have to send questionnaires to consumers or audit selected stores' sales to find out. (2) Just what consumers are you talking about? Babies, college students, and septuagenarians have different tastes and consumption patterns, so you'd better define carefully the group you plan to construct the index for.

Once you'd resolved all these problems, you'd have to get the prices of the items you chose. How would you pick the stores to include? What kind of stores—supermarkets? Neighborhood stores? Specialty stores? Drugstores? Theaters? Street vendors? Some of each? How many? In proportion to total sales? You'd probably resolve this problem by taking a carefully thought-out judgment sample.

A *judgment sample* is one based on considered opinion regarding its representativeness rather than on the concepts of randomness and probability. It's important to make a distinction between judgment and random or probability samples here, because the techniques of statistical inference, which you'll learn later, can be applied only to probability samples. This means that the conclusions based on judgment samples cannot be used to make scientifically based generalizations about the population from which the sample was taken. Thus the consumer price index, which is based on a judgment sample, technically should not be used to generalize about the cost of living of United States citizens or even all urban wage earners and clerical workers (though it often is because nothing better is available).

You still haven't answered all the questions regarding the food-price index. You'd also have to consider how and when to measure the prices of the commodities you selected. It would be great to price them all at the same time, but that would require a large staff. You'd also have to confront the problems of weights, changes in product mix, and changes in product quality, all of which have sampling implications.

CHOICE OF WEIGHTS AND INDEX-NUMBER FORMULAS

We have already developed some two dozen formulas for index numbers. Considering only price indexes, for example, we've identified and discussed 10 formulas. Even so, we have only scratched the surface. Some 168 different formulas for index numbers have been devised. Here we'll consider only a few variations of the basic formulas already developed. When we averaged price relatives, we used an arithmetic mean, but we could have used any of several other types of averages. For example, the *geometric mean* is often used to average relatives. The geometric mean is the n root of the product of n numbers, and it gives *proportionate* changes equal weight rather than giving equal *amounts* of change equal weight, as the arithmetic mean does. To illustrate the difference, consider the example in Table 5.1.

The arithmetic mean of the relatives in Table 5.1 shows that prices increased by 25 percent from 1960 to 1970. But what if you had made 1970 the base for the same index (Table 5.2)? Now prices are 25 percent higher in 1960 than in 1970! The

Table 5.1

	1960		1970	
	Price/lb	Relative × 100	Price/lb	Relative × 100
Product A	$.30	100	$.60	200
Product B	.30	100	.15	50
Index		100		125

Table 5.2

	1960		1970	
	Price/lb	Relative × 100	Price/lb	Relative × 100
Product A	$.30	50	$.60	100
Product B	.30	200	.15	100
Index		125		100

reason for this strange state of affairs is that in both cases there was an underlying assumption about weights. In the first case you can see that in 1960 you could buy $3\frac{1}{3}$ lb of product A for $1 and $3\frac{1}{3}$ lb of product B for $1. In arithmetically averaging the relatives for 1970, we assumed that these same quantities of A and B would be bought. That is, $3\frac{1}{3}$ lb of product A would now cost $2 while $3\frac{1}{3}$ lb of product B would now cost $.50, for an average cost of $1.25 for $3\frac{1}{3}$ lb. In calculating the index using a 1970 base, we assumed that the weights to apply to 1960 were $1\frac{2}{3}$ lb of product A and $6\frac{2}{3}$ lb of product B. Application of these weights to 1960 resulted in the inconsistency of the prices apparently going up in either direction in time. This inconsistency is corrected by using the geometric mean of the relatives rather than the arithmetic mean. Regardless of which year is the base, the index is 100 for *both* years since $\sqrt{100(100)} = 100$ and $\sqrt{200(50)} = 100$.

From this illustration perhaps you can begin to see that each index-number formula you can devise reflects an underlying reality in a somewhat different way. For example, we've assumed that the demand for any good is inelastic and that goods are not substitutes for each other. Neither of these assumptions is likely to be true in reality. If there were perfect elasticity, you'd halve consumption if a product doubled in price and double consumption if a product's price were halved. But this would mean that the total quantity of goods would change from period to period. If goods were perfect substitutes, any difference in price would drive the more expensive product out of the market completely. Reality lies somewhere between the poles of perfect inelasticity and perfect elasticity or nonsubstitutability and complete substitutability. Some index-number formulas reflect one situation more realistically, some another.

Much work has been done in an attempt to cope with these problems.[1] Irving Fisher developed an "ideal" index number formula by taking the geometric mean of Laspeyres' formula (which uses base-year quantity weights) and Paasche's (which uses given-year quantity weights):

$$\text{Fisher's ideal} = \sqrt{\frac{\sum p_n q_0 \ \sum p_n q_n}{\sum p_0 q_0 \ \sum p_0 q_n}} \times 100$$

---

[1] See F. Croxton, D. Cowden, and S. Klein, *Applied General Statistics*, 3d ed., chap. 17, Prentice-Hall, Englewood Cliffs, N.J., 1967, for an excellent discussion.

Fisher considered this formula ideal because it met a *time-reversal test* and a *factor-reversal test*, both measures of the logical consistency of index numbers. However, its precise meaning is very hard to comprehend, and its use has not been widespread. In general one can say that since all index-number formulas involve implicit or explicit assumptions about the way people behave, and since more complex formulas are both more difficult to compute and explain, most widely used index numbers are of the relatively uncomplicated sort described in preceding sections.

CHANGES IN PRODUCT MIX AND CHARACTERISTICS

As mentioned above, there is a complex, little-understood relationship between the price of commodities and the substitution of one commodity for another because of these price changes. Thus the concept of a basket of goods becomes dynamic rather than static; the contents of the basket changes for other reasons too. Changes in people's real incomes and living habits affect their consumption. Over the years in the United States people have generally decreased their per capita consumption of meat. Part of this might be a consequence of price changes, but it also reflects a change in tastes. Increased consumption of wine and decreased consumption of bourbon per capita is another example. When such changes in preference occur, new base-year quantity weights must be calculated.

Newly developed products also change the contents of the market basket. The development of television and miniaturized calculators are cases in point. As the use of a new product becomes widespread, logic dictates its inclusion in the index, just as obsolete products must be dropped. Those responsible for the construction of the index must make considered judgments of when to add and drop components. While these judgments are never completely objective, they may be a consequence of surveys of consumer expenditures or other factual data.

It's even more difficult to cope with changes in product quality. Today's cars are surely not the same as yesterday's, nor are the tires on which they run. A color TV today is a very different product from one 10 years ago. The same thing is true of many other products you think of as unchanging. A box of strawberries, tomatoes, or apples is very different from one of 30 years ago. The quality of meat has changed. Milk is now homogenized and vitaminized. Two-by-fours actually used to measure 2 by 4 in. Today a two-by-four looks like a large toothpick. In fact, it's rather hard to think of products which have not changed. Even the so-called "free" goods like air and water are no longer free and are often of dubious quality.

The Bureau of Labor Statistics tries to cope with these problems by describing the goods and services that enter into their indexes in great detail. Items to be priced must meet fixed specifications to ensure that no price changes are due to quality changes. However these valiant attempts, though important and necessary, are really in a lost cause. Products *do* change, and we must attempt to assess that part of the price change (if any) attributable to the quality change. The difficulty of such a procedure can easily be seen in the case of desk (or hand) calculators. Here, the use of transistors and integrated circuits made possible the introduction of products vastly superior to older types at prices some 70 percent *less* than comparable models. Stop and think how you'd cope with that problem!

The objective of this section is not to provide a set of answers or guidelines, since each case must be considered individually. The construction of valid, reliable index-number series is a difficult art, not a science, which requires not only the application of fixed formulas but also the exercise of considerable judgment.

THE CHOICE OF A BASE PERIOD; SPLICING INDEXES

The base period for an index is by definition the period from which all changes are measured. The value of the index at the base period is always 100. While the base of a price index, for example, could be the prices of the commodities on a particular day, averages over longer periods of from 1 to several years are usually used. The reason for this is to average out any random fluctuations which might have occurred at any given time. Furthermore, it makes sense to select a typical period. You wouldn't choose the peak of a prosperity or the depth of a depression as a base period.

Most indexes in the United States have tended to move upward over the past 50 years as a consequence of economic policy and natural development, but due to the statistical characteristics of most indexes, errors are likely to be magnified as the index itself becomes larger. Therefore the base years of continuing economic indexes are updated from time to time. In the recent past, the CPI was calculated on a 1947–1949 base, then on a 1957–1959 base. Now, it is reported on a 1967 base.

Two methods are available for converting index-number series from one base to another. One is to recalculate the entire series using the new base. This is a very complex, expensive task and would require knowledge of all the original statistics. A much easier method is known as *splicing the index*. An index series is spliced by dividing each value of the series on the old base by the value of the old series for the new base year and multiplying by 100.

Table 5.3 illustrates the splicing of a series formerly reported on a 1968 base to a 1971 base. Each of the values in the old base was divided by 120, the value of the

Table 5.3 / Splicing an index-number series

| | Value | | Splicing factor | Spliced index, 1971 base |
	1968 base	1971 base		
1968	100		$\frac{100}{120} \times (100)$	83
1969	108		$\frac{108}{120} \times (100)$	90
1970	112		$\frac{112}{120} \times (100)$	93
1971	120	100	$\frac{120}{120} \times (100)$	100
1972		104		104
1973		110		110

old series for the current base year, and multiplied by 100, to change the old values to the new base. If the series did not overlap, it would be impossible to make the conversion.

The results obtained by shifting the base this way will be identical with the results obtained by recalculation *only* if the series had been constructed by the methods of unweighted aggregates, weighted aggregates with base-year weights, or weighted average of relatives with base-year value weights. The technique is often applied to indexes calculated by other methods, however, because the errors involved are usually small.

REVIEW EXERCISES 5.A

1. True or false:
  a. Sampling is usually necessary in the construction of index-number series because there are too many items to enumerate.
  b. Conclusions based on random samples can be used to make scientifically founded generalizations about population characteristics.
  c. Most widely used index-number series are based on random sampling.
  d. A sample based on careful selection rather than randomization is called a judgment sample.
  e. If you don't use *good* judgment, an index computed from a judgment sample could be misleading.
2. True or false:
  a. An unweighted average of relatives index contains implicit weights because if the arithmetic mean is used, it gives equal weight to equal *amounts* of change, while if the geometric mean is used, it gives equal weight to *proportionate* changes.
  b. You've studied all the variations of index numbers possible in this module.
  c. Most of the widely used index-number series are very complex theoretically.
  d. All index-number formulas involve implicit or explicit assumptions about the way people behave.
3. All the situations below pose problems in maintaining a consistent index-number series. For each problem, write "can handle" for those that can be taken care of, though with difficulty. Write "essentially can't" for those for which there is no clear-cut solution.
  a. A new product takes over a large market share.
  b. An old product becomes unimportant.
  c. Consumers substitute one product for another.
  d. A product improves in quality and its price rises.
  e. A product improves in quality and its price drops.
4. A good period to choose as the base for an index-number series would be:
  a. The bottom of a depression, because it represents a "floor" from which the index will rise.
  b. A middle point between a business peak and trough, so the series will fluctuate around 100.
  c. A point long ago, so the series has continuity.
  d. An average of several adjacent years, so the base is "typical."

5. Splice the two index-number series below, using 1968 as the base.

1966	100	
1967	110	
1968	120	100
1969		105
1970		110

Answers 5.A

1. a. T; *b.* T; *c.* F; *d.* T; *e.* T   *2. a.* T; *b.* F; *c.* F; *d.* T   *3. a.* can handle, *b.* can handle, *c.* can handle, *d.* can handle, *e.* essentially can't   *4. b* and *d*

5. 1966	83
1967	92
1968	100
1969	105
1970	110

Section 5.B
Examples of Index-Number Series

Learning objectives

Your learning objective for this section is to be able to describe in general how the wholesale price index and the consumer price index are constructed, what their major components are, and how they have changed in recent years.

To help you develop a further appreciation for the complexities of index-number construction we'll examine in some detail the development of the two most important price series, the wholesale price index (WPI) and the consumer price index (CPI).[1]

The WPI, which measures the price level of goods including imports at their first level of transaction in the United States, is the oldest continuous price index in the

---

[1] Much of this discussion is based on Jan M. Bechter and Margaret S. Pickett, The Wholesale and Consumer Price Indexes: What's the Connection, *Monthly Review*, Federal Reserve Bank of Kansas City, June 1973, pp. 3–9.

United States. When it was first developed in 1902 to measure the effect of tariff laws, it was an unweighted relative index of some 250 commodities. Currently the WPI is a weighted index consisting of some 2200 commodities at several stages of production. The commodity groupings together with their patterns of change are shown in Table 5.4.

Table 5.4 / Wholesale price index, 1967 = 100*

	1960	1972	April 1973
All commodities	94.9	119.1	130.7
Farm products	97.2	125.0	160.6
Processed foods and feeds	89.5	120.8	139.8
Industrial commodities	95.3	117.9	124.4
Textile products and apparel	99.5	113.6	120.8
Hides, shoes, and leather products	90.8	131.3	145.0
Fuels and related products and power	96.1	118.6	131.8
Chemicals and allied products	101.8	104.2	107.7
Rubber and plastics products	103.1	109.3	110.6
Lumber and wood products	95.3	144.3	182.0
Pulp, paper, and allied products	98.1	113.4	119.8
Metals and metal products	92.4	123.5	130.5
Machinery and equipment	92.0	117.9	120.8
Furniture and household products	99.0	111.4	114.1
Nonmetallic mineral products	97.2	126.1	130.0
Transportation equipment		113.8	114.9†
Miscellaneous products	93.0	114.6	118.6

* *Source:* Bureau of Labor Statistics.
† For transportation equipment, December 1968 = 100, not available earlier.

Weights for the composite indexes are value weights for sales in a particular year. Data for these weights are obtained from the Census of Manufacturers of the Bureau of Census, from the Bureau of Mines, and from the Department of Agriculture. These weights change as new data from these sources become available.

Price information for the series is obtained primarily from questionnaires sent directly to the producers and typically represent prices (less discounts) of these producers on the fifteenth of each month. Some published (secondary) data are also used.

The CPI was first published in 1919 to study inflationary tendencies during World War I under the awesome title Index of Change in Prices of Goods and Services Purchased by City Wage Earners and Clerical Workers' Families to Maintain Their Level of Living. Somehow the acronym ICPGSPCWECWFTMLL never caught on, and the series was renamed the Consumer Price Index for Urban Wage Earners and Clerical Workers. It is important to remember that the series does apply only to the prices paid by those persons rather than all the people in the United States, as is often assumed.

The task of compiling the CPI is formidable. In order to determine the goods and services which urban workers buy, the Consumer Expenditures Survey is conducted every 10 years. The 400 items selected to constitute the index include the most common categories of expenditures plus a sampling of other items. Value weights for items are also derived from the Consumer Expenditures Survey. Trained representatives from the Bureau of Labor Statistics, equipped with detailed descriptions of items to be priced to ensure as much compatibility among areas and over time as possible, collect most of the price data by visiting 18,000 retail stores and source outlets in 56 cities. Weights to be assigned each city are constructed from census data in proportion to the size of its working population. Rental rates are obtained through questionnaires sent to 40,000 renters. Other data are obtained from a multitude of governmental and private sources. A notion of major categories of the CPI and their recent changes can be obtained from Table 5.5.

Table 5.5 / Consumer price index, 1967 = 100*

	1960	1972	March 1973
All items	88.7	125.3	129.8
Food	88.0	123.5	134.5
Housing	90.2	129.2	132.3
Rent	91.7	119.2	122.6
Home ownership	86.3	140.1	143.2
Fuel oil and coal	89.2	118.5	127.8
Gas and electricity	98.6	120.5	125.0
Furnishings and operation	93.8	121.0	123 0
Apparel and upkeep	89.6	122.3	124.8
Transportation	89.6	119.9	121.5
Health and recreation	85.1	126.1	128.6
Medical care	79.1	132.5	135.8
Personal care	90.1	119.8	123.1
Reading and recreation	87.3	122.8	124.5
Other goods and services	87.8	125.5	127.6

* *Source:* Bureau of Labor Statistics.

REVIEW EXERCISES 5.B

1. The wholesale price index is a (weighted; unweighted) relative index of (220; 2,200; 22,000) commodities, which measures the price level of goods (including; excluding) imports at their first level of transaction in the United States.

2. *a.* Name the three major components of the WPI.
  b. Which of these increased fastest from 1960 to 1972?
  c. By what percent did it increase?

3. The CPI applies to prices paid by all consumers in the United States: true or false?

4. The CPI consists of (400; 4000; 40,000) items. Prices are collected from (180; 1800; 18,000) retail outlets in (5; 56; 560) cities, as well as from many other sources.

5. *a.* Name the five major components of the CPI.
  b. Which of these increased fastest from 1960 to 1972?
  c. By what percent did it increase?

Answers 5.B

1. weighted, 2200, including
2. a. farm products, processed foods and feeds, industrial commodities; *b.* processed foods and feeds; *c.* 35 percent
3. false
4. 400, 18,000, 56
5. a. food, housing, apparel and upkeep, transportation, and health and recreation; *b.* health and recreation; *c.* 48 percent

Section 5.C
Uses of Index Numbers

Learning objective

Your learning objective for this section is to be able to adjust dollar series to take into account changes in the value of the dollar.

All index numbers measure change, and the measurement and understanding of change is one of the most important tasks of businesspeople and economists. Comparison of various index-number series facilitates an understanding of the complex interrelationships of components of the economy.

Most index numbers are averages, and averages are effective means of condensing much information into a single, salient number. The ability to see at a glance what has happened to wholesale prices, consumer prices, or some other measure of price, quantity, value, or quality is a great asset. Without index numbers you might sense inflation, for example, but wouldn't be able to measure it, and you wouldn't have any means of judging whether anti-inflationary measures were effective.

Index numbers may serve as indicators of the future as well as measures of the past and present. Patterns of change can be extrapolated (though not without pitfalls), and lead-lag relationships between series may be helpful in forecasting. For example, the WPI is often used to estimate the direction of future changes in consumer prices.

Price indexes are often used to estimate changes in costs. The changes in an appropriate price index of construction products can be used to adjust cost estimates in the building of such long-term projects as highways, dams, or nuclear power plants. In a similar fashion changes in the CPI can be used to estimate future changes in wage and salary costs. In many industries, in fact, future wage rates are directly tied to changes in the CPI, through cost-of-living clauses in wage contracts.

Finally, price indexes are often used to adjust current dollar values to "real" dollar values. To see how this is done, consider the following example. The annual salary of an M.B.A. in a middle management position with a large company is summarized in the first two columns of Table 5.6. While his increases in income seem rather high,

Table 5.6 / Income, actual and real, manager with M.B.A.

Year	Income	CPI, 1967 = 100	Income, constant 1967 dollars
1960	$12,000	88.7	$13,529
1965	15,000	94.5	15,873
1970	18,000	116.3	15,477
1972	20,000	125.3	15,962

the manager has a disquieting feeling that he's not getting anywhere, so he decides to convert his income into "real" dollars by adjusting for changes in the cost of living. The CPI isn't exactly what he'd like to use as a deflator, but he knows that since no CPI is available for middle managers it's the best he can do. He therefore gets the statistics for CPI shown in the third column of Table 5.6 and arrives at his income in constant 1967 dollars by dividing his actual salary for each year by the corresponding CPI figure. This conversion confirms his suspicions. He hasn't gained much in real dollars over the entire 12-year period, and for the past 7 years his income has been practically constant.

Another way of arriving at the same conclusion is to observe that between 1960 and 1972 the CPI increased by a factor of 1.41. This same rate of increase applied to the $12,000 salary in 1960 shows that to just keep up with the cost of living his salary in 1972 would have to be $12,000(1.41) = $16,920.

The CPI isn't always the best or most appropriate deflator. For other types of problems the WPI or some other index specifically tailored to the series being studied should be used.

REVIEW EXERCISE 5.C

1. Your father and your older brother are having a discussion about incomes. Your father says that your brother, who took a job in 1972 for $9500, is earning far more than he deserves. He cites the fact that back in 1945 when he was the same age as your brother is now he was earning only $4200 for the same type of work. You know that the CPI was 53.9 in 1945 and 125.3 in 1972 (both on a 1967 base). Is your father's point valid?

Answers 5.C

1. Your brother might be earning more than he deserves, but in terms of the value of the dollar alone, your father was better off. You can prove this two ways:
   a. Your father's 1945 salary converted to 1972 dollars is $4200(125.3/53.9) = $9764 compared to your brother's $9500.
   b. Converting salaries to constant 1967 dollars, your father was making $4200/.539 = $7792 while your brother made $9500/1.253 = $7582.

Questions and Problems

5.1. The data below are price indexes for two categories of consumer prices, rent and medical care, each on a 1967 base.

  a. Compare the changes in these indexes from 1941 to 1973. Which series showed the greatest increase over this period?

  b. Recalculate the indexes by shifting the base period from 1967 = 100 to 1941 = 100.

  c. Does changing the base help you in comparing the changes in the two series? How?

Year	Rent index (1967 = 100)	Medical-care index (1967 = 100)
1941	57.2	37.0
1945	58.8	42.1
1960	91.7	79.1
1965	96.9	89.5
1970	110.1	120.6
1973	124.2	137.7

5.2. The WPI (1967 = 100) is shown below for a number of years:

Year	WPI	Detail, Feb. 1973–Feb. 1974		Year	WPI	Detail, Feb. 1973–Feb. 1974	
		Month	WPI			Month	WPI
1960	94.9	Feb. 1973	126.9	1967	100.0	Sept.	140.2
1961	94.5	March	129.7	1968	102.5	Oct.	139.5
1962	94.8	April	130.7	1969	106.5	Nov.	141.8
1963	94.5	May	133.5	1970	110.4	Dec.	145.3
1964	94.7	June	136.7	1971	113.9	Jan. 1974	150.4
1965	96.6	July	134.9	1972	119.1	Feb. 1974	152.7
1966	99.8	Aug.	142.7	1973	135.5		

  a. By how many points did the WPI increase over the last reported 12 months, February 1973 to February 1974?

  b. How does this change compare with the change from 1960 through 1972?

  c. Do you think that the Bureau of Labor Statistics might be justified in shifting the base of the WPI from 1967 = 100 to 1973 = 100? Why or why not?

5.3. The table below shows GNP in current dollars and in constant (1958) dollars, along with the CPI on a 1967 base. The constant-dollar series for GNP was obtained by the Bureau of Labor Statistics by adjusting each of the components of GNP in current dollars by an appropriate price index and aggregating these adjusted values. Dividing the current-dollar GNP by the constant-dollar GNP produces an index called the *implicit price deflator*.

Using the data provided, calculate the implicit price deflator for the years shown and compare it with the CPI for those years. (Be sure to make the bases of the two series comparable before comparing the series.)

| Year | GNP (billions) | | CPI 1967 = 100 |
	Current dollars	Constant 1958 dollars	
1958			86.6
1969	930.3	725.6	109.8
1970	977.1	722.5	116.3
1971	1055.5	745.4	121.3
1972	1155.2	790.7	125.3
1973	1289.1	837.4	133.1

5.4. Do you think it would be more valid to compare changes over a long period of time for a *raw-materials* price index or for a *consumer* price index? Why?

5.5. The two most recent periods that have been used by the Bureau of Labor Statistics as the base for index number series are the 1957–1959 average and 1967. What makes these years particularly suited for bases for index numbers?

5.6. A. J. Johnson Company won a contract in 1969 to do the framing for a large dam. The job started in January 1970 and lasted exactly 4 years. All the costs in the contract were fixed, except for the prices of lumber and labor. The costs of lumber and labor were calculated at 6 million dollars each (in 1969 prices), spread evenly over the 4-year period, plus a 3 percent inflation escalator per year for both lumber and labor.

At the end of the job, Johnson knows very well that his profit was really cut by inflation and asks you to figure out exactly how much the inflation cost him. You know that the price he pays for lumber is reflected very well in the wholesale price index for lumber and related products and that his wage increases were tied to the national CPI. You therefore collect the following information:

	1969	1970	1971	1972	1973
WPI, lumber, 1967 = 100	125.3	113.7	127.0	144.3	177.2
CPI, 1967 = 100	109.8	116.3	121.3	125.3	133.1

a. Calculate how much Johnson's contract had provided for the entire job.

b. Calculate how much Johnson actually paid for lumber and labor for the job.

c. How much did inflation cost Johnson?

5.7. Suppose that the base academic-year salary for a beginning assistant professor at a certain university was $5500 in 1960 and that by 1973 the base salary had increased to $12,800. In 1960 the CPI was 88.7, while in 1973 it was 133.1. How much better off, if at all, was a new assistant professor appointed in 1973 compared with one appointed in 1960?

5.8. The data below show personal income in the United States and the CPI from 1969–1973.

a. Deflate the personal-income figures by the CPI.

b. Calculate the percentage increase in personal income from 1969 to 1973 using the original personal-income figures and using the deflated figures.

c. Interpret the figures you obtained in part *b.*

Year	Personal income (billions)	CPI (1967 = 100)
1969	$ 750.9	109.8
1970	808.3	116.3
1971	863.5	121.3
1972	939.2	125.3
1973	1035.4	133.1

5.9. To get an idea of the problems involved in building an index-number series, describe the procedure you would use to gather the data to make an index of milk prices (to the consumer) in the town where you live. Be specific enough so that someone working for you could gather the necessary data by following your step-by-step instructions.

5.10. Find the latest available data on the WPI. Compare changes in the index for farm products with the index for industrial commodities from 1967 to the present. Over the past 12 months, which changed the most, farm prices or industrial commodity prices?

MODULE 6
MEASURING CHANGE—
TIME-SERIES TREND

We can be certain about one thing in life: nothing stays the same.

In times past whole centuries could be characterized, for better or worse, by the words "continuity" and "stability." A young gentleman farmer in seventeenth-century England knew his future by looking at his past. He would live where and how his father and grandfather had lived, as would his sons and grandsons. Life was less pleasant but no less certain for the laborer and tradesman of the time.

Today's most appropriate descriptors are "discontinuity" and "change" rather than "continuity" and "stability." The tempo of life is undeniably faster now than it was even a decade ago. Some product lines go through the whole cycle of development, test marketing, production, and withdrawal from the market in less time than it took to get them to the market a few years ago.

A textbook[1] published in 1969 stated that uncertain though life was, there were some things of which the "average American" could be certain, including:

1. Where he'll be working and what he'll be earning in 5 years.
2. When the children will go to college and roughly how much it'll cost.
3. When the mortgage on the house will be paid.
4. When he'll retire, and how much he'll have to live on.
5. Approximately how long he'll live.
6. What political system he'll live under, and how he'll vote on most issues.
7. The major international actors, which ones will be strongest, richest, or most threatening.

How many of these can you be certain of today?

Until recently it was generally assumed that *growth* was good and more growth was better. "Either grow or stagnate" was the slogan of many a chamber of commerce. Now, some cities, states, and regions are searching for ways to control and limit growth rather than promote it.

In an environment like this, the description of growth and change has become crucial for the planning of business and government. In this module you'll learn how to measure amounts and rates of change and how to identify and describe long-term patterns of change called *secular trends.*

You might expect that in addition to long-term trends there'd be shorter-term fluctuations about the trend. These shorter variations may be due to seasonal variation, the business cycle, or many other causes (some known but most unknown) called *irregular variation.* In the next module you'll learn some techniques for identifying and measuring these shorter-term fluctuations. For the moment let's concentrate on the secular trend.

The secular trend is caused by basic factors underlying the series in question. Trends of most business series you're likely to encounter are upward. One obvious reason for this is survival. Companies or industries having sustained downward trends usually aren't around very long. The upward movement of most successful business in the United States is largely explained by expansion of the population and the benefits of technological innovations. Other factors such as merger, acquisition, or the quality of management dictate the long-run course of individual businesses.

General learning objectives

Your general learning objectives for this module are to be able to:

1. Identify series whose trends change by constant amounts (arithmetic trends) or by constant rates (geometric trends)
2. Find the constants in equations describing linear, geometric, and parabolic trends by the method of least squares
3. Fit and use trends for modified exponential, logistic, and Gompertz growth curves

---

[1] Robert U. Ayres, *Technological Forecasting and Long Range Planning,* McGraw-Hill, New York, 1969.

Section 6.A

Amounts of Change

Learning objectives

Your learning objectives for this section are to be able to:

1. Describe an arithmetic trend mathematically
2. Find the equation for a linear trend using the method of semiaverages

A series that changes by constant amounts is called an *arithmetic progression*. Its formula is $Y_c = a + bX$, where Y_c is the computed value of the dependent variable, such as sales, which is being measured over time, X is time, the independent variable, and a, the Y_c intercept at the origin, and b, the slope or change in Y_c per unit change in X, are constants.

In describing a time-series trend you must always specify what point in time is being used as the origin and in what units of time the slope is being expressed. Thus the line $Y_c = 50 + 5X$ (origin 1960, $\Delta X = 1$ year) means that the value of Y_c is 50 in the year 1960 and that the Y_c value changes by $+5$ units each year. Thus successive Y_c values would be 50 in 1960, 55 in 1961, 60 in 1962, etc. Note that the *first difference* of an arithmetic progression, the difference in Y_c between successive years, is its slope, or the constant b.

It would be a rare business time series that formed a perfect arithmetic progression over time. The expression $Y_c = a + bX$ refers only to a linear secular-trend fit to the actual data. The actual data could be expected to include seasonal, cyclical, and irregular variation as well as a trend.

Many statistical series have essentially linear trends over long periods of time. Three such series are graphed in Fig. 6.1: government securities held by nonfinancial public from 1952 to 1972, time and savings deposits from 1952 to 1972, and public debt held by mutual savings banks, 1952 to 1972. Note that while the general pattern of movement of each series is essentially linear, the degree of variation about the trend differs considerably from series to series.

If you wanted to *fit* a linear trend, that is, to find the specific constants a and b that describe the best trend equation for any of the series in Fig. 6.1, you could choose from a variety of methods. The simplest method would be to eyeball a straight line through the data, trying visually to equate areas above and below the line. While some people become very adept at this procedure, it isn't very good because such a line is subjective and has no specific mathematical relationship to the values in the series.

113

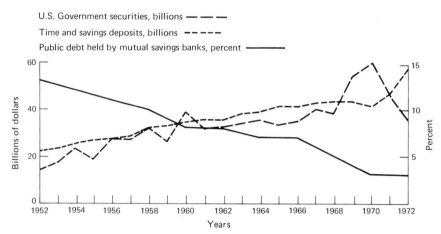

U.S. Government securities, billions — — —
Time and savings deposits, billions — — — — —
Public debt held by mutual savings banks, percent ————

Figure 6.1 / Series exhibiting linear trends. (*Historical Chart Book 1972.*)

The *method of semiaverages* is a very simple objective method for fitting a linear trend. With this technique the data are divided into halves, and the arithmetic mean of X and Y for each half of the data is plotted. A straight line drawn through these points must go through the mean of Y at the mean of X for all the data. This makes the sum of the deviations between the Y values and their corresponding Y_c values equal to zero, while the slope is pinned down by forcing the line to go through the semiaverage points. This technique is illustrated in Table 6.1.

Table 6.1 / Fitting a linear trend by semiaverages

Time	Y	Mean
1960	97	
1962	126	$\dfrac{360}{3} = 120$
1964	137	
1966	163	
1968	174	$\dfrac{540}{3} = 180$
1970	203	

The semiaverage values, 120 in 1962 and 180 in 1968, provide two points on the line of semiaverages. Using the first point as the origin sets a at 120. The slope b is found by dividing the increase from 1962 to 1968 by the number of years between these points: $b = (180 - 120)/6 = 10$. The equation is then $Y_c = 120 + 10X$, origin 1962, $\Delta X = 1$ year.

Using this equation, you could calculate Y_c values by substituting the appropriate value for X and solving the equation. Since the origin is 1962, the appropriate X value for 1960 is -2. For 1962 it is 0, for 1964 it is $+2$, etc. When you substitute in the equation, the Y_c values from 1960 to 1970 are 100, 120, 140, 160, 180, and 200. Note that the mean of these values, 150, is the same as that of the original Y values (the line does go through the mean of the system) and that the sum of the $Y - Y_c$ values, $97 - 100$, $126 - 120$, etc., is equal to zero.

There are more sophisticated methods for fitting trends, in particular the method of least squares, discussed later in this module. The method of semiaverages, however, is a simple method worth remembering.

The concept of linearity is important not only because many real-world trends are linear but also because many trends that are nonlinear can be treated as linear trends for purposes of analysis by making appropriate transformations. You'll soon apply a logarithmic transformation to convert a geometric progression into a linear model. Other types of transformations that are widely used are reciprocals and differences.

REVIEW EXERCISES 6.A

1. What is the general form of the equation for a linear trend? Identify each of the symbols.
2. Fit a line of semiaverages to the data below. Calculate the Y_c values, and show that the sum of the $Y - Y_c$ values equals zero.

X	1945	1950	1955	1960	1965	1970
Y	100	125	135	160	185	195

Answers 6.A

1. $Y_c = a + bX$ (origin ___, $\Delta X =$ ___), where Y_c represents the trend values, a is the Y_c value at the origin, b is the slope of the trend $\Delta Y/\Delta X$, and X is time.
2. $Y_c = 120 + 4X$ (origin 1950, $\Delta X = 1$ year).

Section 6.B

Rates of Change

Learning objectives

Your learning objectives for this section are to be able to:

1. State what is meant by the expression *exponential growth*
2. Describe some national statistical series that have exhibited exponential growth
3. Use semilog paper to see if a series is changing at a constant rate and determine that rate

The basic process of change in life is essentially exponential. A cell divides and each resulting cell divides, producing a series 1, 2, 4, 8, 16, 32, 64, . . . that doubles with each generation. Such a series is called a *geometric* or *exponential series*. Its chief characteristic is that the *ratio* of each value to its predecessor is a constant. In this case the constant is 2, that is, $2/1 = 2$, $4/2 = 2$, etc.

The equation for a geometric progression is an exponential of the form $Y_c = ab^X$, where a is the Y_c value at the origin and b is the ratio of change.[1] Thus the series above is described by the equation $Y_c = 1(2^X)$.

Exponential growth—or growth at a constant rate—is pervasive in business as well as in nature. The well-known formula for compound interest is exponential. More basically, many business and economic series are geometric because the two factors influencing their trends, population and productivity, have long-term exponential trends themselves. United States population had an average growth rate from 1900 to 1970 of about 1.3 percent per year, just a little more than the world growth rate of 1.2 percent per year. Productivity, measured by output per man-hour, grew at an average rate of about 1.5 percent per year from 1900 to 1930 and at 3.5 percent per year from 1930 to 1970. The combination of these two factors has a pervasive influence on most aggregate statistics for the United States. Among the many series exhibiting exponential growth are GNP in constant dollars, personal consumption expenditures, industrial production, corporate security issues, assets of life insurance companies, and residential construction. Naturally many corporate series exhibit exponential growth as well.

A basic contradiction inherent in exponential growth leads to the possibility of serious error in its use to describe trends. Though many series have trends that have been essentially exponential over many years, such growth is impossible in the long run. The reason for this is that regardless of the rate of increase, any geometric series eventually becomes asymptotic to a vertical line. It is easy to maintain exponential growth when the numbers are small, but sooner or later continued growth at the same rate becomes absurd. The population of Boulder, Colorado, has roughly doubled each 10 years for the past 30 years. This is equivalent to an annual rate of growth of 7.2 percent. If this rate were to continue in the future, Boulder's population would be 640,000 by the year 2000; 20,400,000 by 2050; and 652,800,000 by 2100.

It has been claimed by many people that the growth of knowledge has about the same 10-year doubling time exhibited by Boulder's population.[2] This may currently be true. If it were to continue in the future, though, we could expect great things. Fifty years from now we would collectively know 32 times as much as we do now. In 100 years we would know a little over 1000 times as much. But after 500 more years at that same rate, we would be approximately 1 million *billion* times smarter than we are now. Even admitting that mankind isn't too bright at the moment, that's quite a bit to expect in a mere 500 years.

---

[1] For future reference, remember that $b^X = 1$ when $X = 0$.

[2] Though "growth of knowledge" may be an example of the kind of "unknowable" statistic identified in Module 2, attempts have been made to measure it through surrogates such as the number of research articles published per year in scholarly journals.

One more example. About 10 years ago the total United States annual sales of recreational vehicles was about 60,000 units. The industry grew at a rate of about 20 percent per year to a value of 375,000 per year in 1972. Projected at that same rate, the sales would be estimated at 2.3 million 10 years from now, and 14.5 million in 20 years. Perhaps basing their estimates on these heady figures, recreational vehicle manufacturers seemed amazed in 1973 when actual sales fell far below their anticipated volume.[1]

The reason exponential growth cannot continue indefinitely is that it is always subject to limiting factors. These factors impose barriers or critical levels beyond which growth either stops or proceeds at a much slower pace. Boulder's growth rate has already been blunted by the general decline in the birth rate, by planning decisions relative to industrial location, by setting fees for extension of utility services at actual cost, and by zoning and building requirements. The ultimate limiting factor is probably the water supply, which imposes a critical level beyond which further growth is essentially impossible.

Limiting factors for the recreational vehicles are even more obvious. New products typically go through a stage of slow development followed by a very rapid expansion once the product catches on. This stage, especially if the economic climate is favorable, gives the impression of almost insatiable demand as the backlog of effective demand is met. In fact, production and distribution capabilities rather than demand often determine sales at this stage. Once the initial pool of people having the means and the desire for a recreational vehicle is satisfied, further growth would proceed at a much slower pace contingent upon population growth, increases in disposable income, and replacement demand.

As mentioned earlier, the equation for a series that changes at a constant rate is $Y_c = ab^X$. Computation of rates of change and fitting of geometric equations is greatly facilitated by the use of logs.

Expressed in logs,

$$Y_c = ab^X$$

becomes $$\log Y_c = \log a + (\log b)X$$

This last expression is linear. The logs of a geometric series change by constant amounts. Note, for example, that the logs of the series 2, 4, 8, 16, 32 are 0.3010, 0.6020, 0.9030, 1.2040, and 1.5050 and the *first differences* of the logs are constant. Thus the equation for this series could be written either as $Y_c = 2(2^X)$ or $\log Y_c = 0.3010 + 0.3010X$, using logs and the form for a straight line.

An easy way to see if the trend of a series can be approximated by a geometric progression is to plot the data on a semilog chart, where the Y axis is scaled in proportion to logarithmic values. A geometric progression will graph as a straight line on such a grid. Figure 6.2 shows two graphs of GNP. Figure 6.2a is on an arithmetic scale, and Fig. 6.2b is on a semilog scale. While the exact nature of the

---

[1] Sales were far under projections *before* the energy crisis precipitated by the Arab-Israeli War.

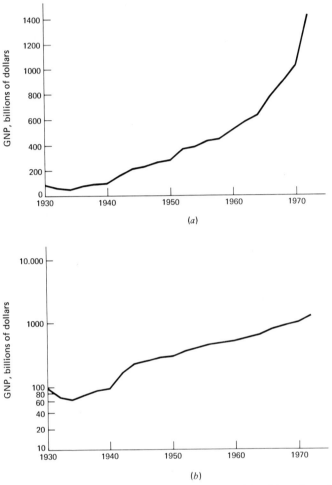

Figure 6.2 / Gross national product, 1930–1972: (*a*) arithmetic scale; (*b*) logarithmic scale. (*Department of Commerce.*)

trend is difficult to judge on inspection of Fig. 6.2*a*, it is easy to see from Fig. 6.2*b* that the trend is geometric, since the data fluctuate about a straight line on the semilog scale.

If you wanted to determine the trend equation and the rate of change for GNP by inspection, you'd draw your estimate of the best-fitting straight line through the data of Fig. 6.2*b*. Choosing two points near either end of the series, say 103 billion dollars in 1929 and 1152 billion dollars in 1972, you'd then find the logarithmic change per year. Since the log of 1152 is 3.0615 and that of 103 is 2.0128, the logarithmic change per year is $(3.0615 - 2.0128)/43 = 0.0243$.

With 1929 as the origin, the trend equation could be expressed as

$$\log Y_c = 2.0128 + 0.0243X \qquad \text{origin 1929, } \Delta X = 1 \text{ year}$$

or
$$Y_c = 103(1.058^X)$$

where $b = 1.058$ is the antilog of 0.0243. The rate of increase per year is $(b - 1)(100) =$ 5.8 percent per year.

If a series were *decreasing* geometrically, its trend on semilog paper would be linear with a *negative* slope. This situation is illustrated by the holdings of U.S. Government securities by life insurance companies from 1945 to 1970. The trend value for 1945 was 20 billion dollars, and for 1970 it was 4 billion dollars. Thus the logarithmic change per year was $(0.6020 - 1.3010)/25 = -0.0280$ per year. The antilog of -0.0280 is .9376. Remember that this is obtained by subtracting 0.0280 from 10.0000 $- 10$ to obtain a log with a positive mantissa, namely 9.9720 $- 10$, and then looking up the antilog.

The equation for the trend is

$$\log Y_c = 1.3010 - 0.028X \qquad \text{origin 1945, } \Delta X = 1 \text{ year}$$

or
$$Y_c = 20(.9376^X)$$

The rate of *decrease* is $(b - 1)(100) = -6.24$ percent per year.

REVIEW EXERCISES 6.B

1. Exponential growth:
   a. Is described by the equation $Y_c = ab^X$.
   b. Is described by the equation $\log Y_c = \log a + (\log b)X$.
   c. Cannot continue forever.
   d. Has a constant rate of increase.
   e. All the above.
2. Name three series mentioned in this section which exhibit exponential growth.
3. a. Plot the data shown on the semilog grid provided.

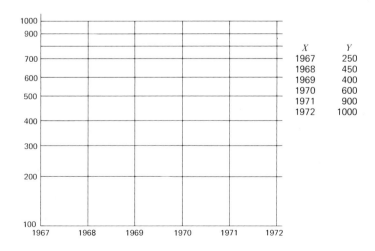

X	Y
1967	250
1968	450
1969	400
1970	600
1971	900
1972	1000

b. Do you think the *trend* could be exponential? Why?

c. Draw a straight line through the points.

d. What is the equation for the trend you have drawn? (Use 1967 as the origin with $\Delta X = 1$ year.)

e. What is the rate of increase for your line?

Answers 6.B

1. *e*

2. Any three of these: United States population, output per man hour, GNP (constant dollars), personal consumption expenditures, industrial production, corporate security issues, assets of life insurance companies, residential construction

3. *a.* no answer

   b. Yes; the data fluctuate around a straight line on the semilog grid.

   c. no answer

   d. When we did it, we got $\log Y_c = 2.4771 + 0.1046X$ or $Y_c = 300(1.272^X)$ both with origin 1967, $\Delta X = 1$ year. (Your answer'll be somewhat different.)

   e. We got 27.2 percent increase per year (your answer should be close to this).

Section 6.C
Least-Squares Trends

Learning objectives

Your learning objectives for this section are to be able to:

1. Describe the characteristics and limitations of the least-squares method for fitting trend lines
2. Fit linear, geometric, and parabolic trends using the method of least squares

---

THE LEAST-SQUARES METHOD

Linear. The trend equations you have learned so far have been determined by inspection or by semiaverages. We now consider a method that is less subjective and has better mathematical properties than either of these, the method of *least squares*. Consider the three linear trend lines representing the data in Fig. 6.3. All three lines

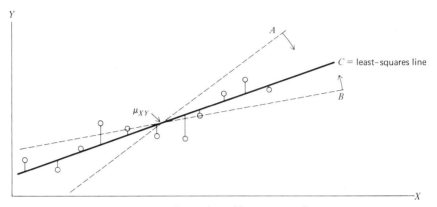

Figure 6.3 / Illustration of least-squares line.

go through the point μ_{XY}, the mean of the system, but the two dashed lines A and B don't fit the data as well as the solid line C. If you measured for each data point the difference between the Y value and the corresponding Y_c value on the trend line, the sums of those $Y - Y_c$ values would be zero for all three lines since they all go through the mean of the system and the positive and negative deviations from the trend line would cancel out. However, if you squared each of these differences and then summed the squares, the two dashed lines would have large squared errors, line A because its slope was too steep compared to the original data and line B because its slope was too small. Line C would have a much smaller squared error than either line A or line B. Now there must be one straight line that has a smaller squared error than *any* other line for a given set of data. This line is called the line of *least squares*.

The trick, of course, is to figure out how to get this one unique line from all the many possibilities. This turns out to be easy; just solve the following set of *normal equations* for a and b:[1]

$$\sum Y = Na + b \sum X$$
$$\sum XY = a \sum X + b \sum X^2$$

The solution of these equations to find the constants a and b will be illustrated with hypothetical data using a very short time span to make the procedure easy to follow.

---

[1] For those who are interested we give the derivation of these equations. We want to minimize $\sum (Y - Y_c)^2$, where $Y_c = a + bX$. Expanding gives

$$\sum (Y - Y_c)^2 = \sum (Y^2 - 2YY_c + Y_c^2) = \text{min}$$

Substituting $a + bX$ for Y_c leads to

$$\sum [Y^2 - 2Y(a + bX) + (a + bX)^2] = \text{min}$$

Simplifying and clearing, we have

Table 6.2

X'	Y	X	XY	X^2	Y_c	$Y - Y_c$
1967	1010	0	0	0	1002	+ 8
1968	1125	1	1,125	1	1101	+24
1969	1170	2	2,340	4	1200	−30
1970	1275	3	3,825	9	1298	−23
1971	1394	4	5,576	16	1397	− 3
1972	1520	5	7,600	25	1496	+24
	7494	15	20,466	55		0

$$\sum Y = Na + b \sum X$$
$$\sum XY = a \sum X + b \sum X^2$$
$$7494 = 6a + 15b \tag{6.1}$$
$$20{,}466 = 15a + 55b \tag{6.2}$$

Multiplying Eq. (6.1) by −5 and Eq. (6.2) by 2 gives

$$-37{,}470 = -30a - 75b$$
$$\underline{40{,}932 = 30a + 110b}$$

Summing
$$3{,}462 = \phantom{-30a + {}} 35b$$
$$b = 98.91$$

Substituting in (6.1)

$$7494 = 6a + 15(98.91) \qquad\qquad a = 1001.7$$
$$Y_c = 1001.7 + 98.91X \qquad \text{origin 1967, } \Delta X = 1 \text{ year}$$

The data above represent the number of cars sold per year by a local car dealer. Upon plotting these data you decide that the trend can be described adequately by a straight line. Choosing to use 1967 as the origin and to express the slope in terms of change per year, you proceed to fit a linear least-squares trend as shown in Table 6.2.

As a check you could calculate the Y_c values for all the years and plot the trend along with the original data. This plot is shown in Fig. 6.4. Note that the trend fits

---

or
$$\sum [Y^2 - 2aY - 2bXY + a^2 + 2abX + b^2X^2] = \min$$
$$\sum Y^2 - 2a \sum Y - 2b \sum XY + Na^2 + 2ab \sum X + b^2 \sum X^2 = \min$$

Taking the partial derivative with respect to a and setting the expression equal to zero, we get

or
$$-2 \sum Y + 2Na + 2b \sum X = 0$$
$$\sum Y = Na + b \sum X \qquad \text{first normal equation}$$

Taking the partial derivative with respect to b and setting the expression equal to zero, we get

or
$$-2 \sum XY + 2a \sum X + 2b \sum X^2 = 0$$
$$\sum XY = a \sum X + b \sum X^2 \qquad \text{second normal equation}$$

122

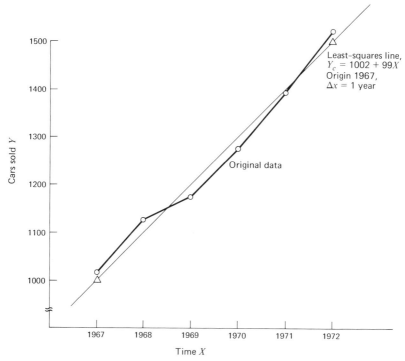

Figure 6.4 / Linear least-squares trend, car-sales data.

the data well. You could also calculate $\sum (Y - Y_c)$ and note that the sum of these deviations equals zero, as it should.

This solution didn't take very long, but you may wonder how much time would be involved if the problem were a real one covering a long time. Since you can put the origin any place you want, you might decide that you'd put it at the midpoint of the data (so that $\sum X = 0$) rather than at the first year. That should simplify the solution of the normal equations. You do this, as shown in Table 6.3, noting that you must be very careful about how you specify the ΔX units. If the origin is placed at the midvalue in time (January 1970, assuming that the original data points were plotted at the middle of their respective years), the time interval between July 1969 and January 1970 is -1 *half year*, while the time between July 1968 and January 1970 is -3 *half years*. You record the proper deviations from the origin in the X column, and proceed to solve for a and b (Table 6.3).

Since there is only one linear least-squares line for any given set of data, this equation must describe exactly the same line you found before. You can prove this by calculating the Y_c values from each of the equations and observing that they described exactly the same line. Another proof is to restate the present equation in terms of the origin and ΔX units of the original equation. This is accomplished by moving the origin back 5 half years (the X value for 1967 is -5) and doubling the

Table 6.3

X'	Y	X	XY	X^2
1967	1010	-5	-5050	25
1968	1125	-3	-3375	9
1969	1170	-1	-1170	1
1970	1275	$+1$	1275	1
1971	1394	$+3$	4182	9
1972	1520	$+5$	7600	25
	7494	0	3462	70

$$\sum Y = Na + b \sum X$$
$$\sum XY = a \sum X + \sum bX^2$$

$$7494 = 6a + 0 \qquad\qquad a = 1249$$
$$3462 = 0 + 70b \qquad\qquad b = 49.46$$

$$Y_c = 1249 + 49.46X \qquad \text{origin January 1970, } \Delta X = \tfrac{1}{2} \text{ year}$$

slope (from half to whole years). Upon substituting $2X - 5$ for X, the calculations are

$$Y_c = 1249 + 49.46(2X - 5)$$
$$= 1249 + 98.92X - 247.30$$
$$= 1001.7 + 98.92X \qquad \text{origin 1967, } \Delta X = 1 \text{ year}$$

Since the solution is always simpler when $\sum X = 0$, that method is usually preferred. If the equation is wanted in other terms, the transformation illustrated above can be made.

Geometric. We have already noted that the logarithmic form of a geometric progression is a straight line. It is very easy, then, to solve for a geometric least-squares trend by fitting a linear trend to the *logs* of the Y values. In this case the normal equations become

$$\sum \log Y = N \log a + (\log b) \sum X$$
$$\sum (X \log Y) = \log a \sum X + (\log b) \sum X^2$$

The process of fitting this type of least-squares trend is illustrated in Table 6.4.

Graphs of the original values and the trend line are shown on an arithmetic scale in Fig. 6.5a and on a semilog scale in Fig. 6.5b.

Second-degree parabola. A trend expressed as a second-degree parabola has the form $Y_c = a + bX + cX^2$. This is like the basic form equation for a straight line, except that a squared term, cX^2, has been added. The chief characteristic of a second-degree parabola is that its *second* difference is a constant, so that its first difference forms a straight line. The series in Table 6.5 illustrates this characteristic.

Table 6.4 / Manufacturer's shipments, 1964–1972

(Shipments in billions of dollars)

X'	Y	X	$\log Y$	$X \log Y$	X^2	$\log Y_c$	Y_c
1964	39	-4	1.591	-6.364	16	1.602	40
1965	43	-3	1.633	-4.899	9	1.627	42
1966	45	-2	1.653	-3.306	4	1.652	45
1967	49	-1	1.690	-1.690	1	1.677	47
1968	52	0	1.716	0	0	1.701	50
1969	53	1	1.724	1.724	1	1.726	53
1970	52	2	1.716	3.432	4	1.751	56
1971	58	3	1.763	5.289	9	1.776	60
1972	67	4	1.826	7.304	16	1.801	63
			15.312	1.490	60		

$$\sum \log Y = N \log a + \log b \sum X$$
$$\sum X \log Y = \log a \sum X + \log b \sum X^2$$

$$15.312 = 9 \log a \qquad \log a = 1.7013$$
$$1.490 = 60 \log b \qquad \log b = 0.0248$$
$$\log Y_c = 1.7013 + 0.0248X \qquad \text{origin 1968, } \Delta X = 1 \text{ year}$$

or

$$Y_c = 50(1.059)^X$$

Source: Department of Commerce.

A parabolic trend can have one of four shapes, depending upon the sign of the *b* and *c* values in the equation. The four typical curves are shown in Fig. 6.6, together with the corresponding signs of the constants.

To fit a parabolic trend by least squares requires the use of *three* normal equations,

Table 6.5

Y	First difference	Second difference
2		
	2	
4		2
	4	
8		2
	6	
14		2
	8	
22		2
	10	
32		2
	12	
44		

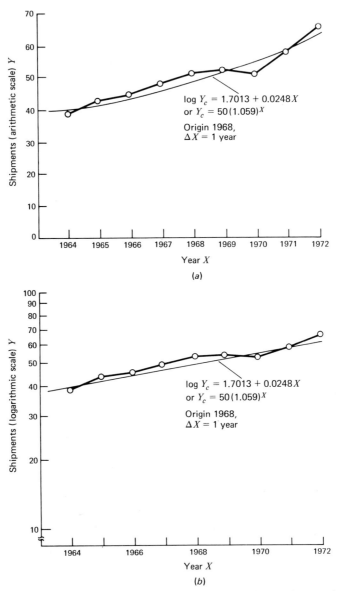

Figure 6.5 / Geometric least-squares trend, manufacturers' shipments in billions of dollars, 1964–1972. (*a*) Arithmetic scale; (*b*) geometric scale.

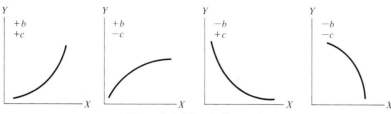

Figure 6.6 / Parabolic trends.

since three constants are to be determined. These equations are derived exactly like those for a straight line, and are

$$\sum Y = Na + b \sum X + c \sum X^2$$
$$\sum (XY) = a \sum X + b \sum X^2 + c \sum X^3$$
$$\sum (X^2Y) = a \sum X^2 + b \sum X^3 + c \sum X^4$$

The application of these equations is shown in Table 6.6. If you wanted to move

Table 6.6 / Ratio of consumer installment credit to income, 1945–1970

(Consumer installment credit as a percentage of income)

X'	Y	X	XY	X^2	X^2Y	X^4	Y_c	$Y - Y_c$
1945	3.38	-5	-16.90	25	84.50	625	4.11	$-.73$
1950	11.01	-3	-33.03	9	99.09	81	9.82	$+1.19$
1955	14.38	-1	-14.38	1	14.38	1	13.76	$+.62$
1960	14.32	$+1$	14.32	1	14.32	1	15.95	-1.63
1965	16.69	$+3$	50.07	9	150.21	81	16.37	$+.32$
1970	15.27	$+5$	76.35	25	381.75	625	15.03	$+.24$
	75.05	0	$+76.43$	70	744.25	1414		$-.01$

$$\sum Y = Na + b \sum X + c \sum X^2$$
$$\sum (XY) = a \sum X + b \sum X^2 + c \sum X^3$$
$$\sum (X^2Y) = a \sum X^2 + b \sum X^3 + c \sum X^4$$

$$75.05 = 6a + 0 + 70c \qquad\qquad (6.3)$$
$$76.43 = 0 + 70b + 0 \qquad b = 1.092 \qquad (6.4)$$
$$744.25 = 70a + 0 + 1414c \qquad\qquad (6.5)$$

Eq. (6.3) × 20.2 $1516.01 = 121.20a + 1414c$

Eq. (6.5) × (−1) $-744.25 = -70.00a - 1414c$

Summing $771.76 = 51.20a \qquad a = 15.073$

Substituting in Eq. (6.3) gives

$$75.05 = 6(15.073) + 70c$$
$$c = -.22$$
$$Y_c = 15.073 + 1.092X - .22X^2 \qquad \text{origin Jan. 1958, } \Delta X = 2\tfrac{1}{2} \text{ years}$$

Source: Federal Reserve Chart Book, 1972.

127

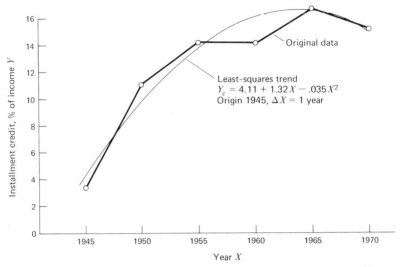

Figure 6.7 / Parabolic trend, consumer installment credit as a percentage of income, 1945–1970.

the base to 1945 and change the time units to 1 year, you'd substitute $(X/2.5) - 5$ for X as follows:

$$Y_c = 15.073 + 1.092[(X/2.5) - 5] - .22[(X/2.5) - 5]^2$$

Simplifying gives

$$Y_c = 4.113 + 1.317X - 0.035X^2 \qquad \text{origin 1945, } \Delta X = 1 \text{ year}$$

A plot of the original data and the trend line is shown in Fig. 6.7.

Note that the high point of the parabolic trend was reached in 1965. Values for succeeding years would become smaller and smaller. While extrapolation for a few years might yield credible values, trend values far in the future would not only become implausible but even impossible. By the year 2000 the ratio would be -30 percent, an obviously impossible figure. Thus, just as with a straight-line or geometric progression, extrapolation of a parabola can be extended beyond the point of reason.

The technique for fitting parabolic trends can be applied to parabolas beyond the second degree. For example, a fourth-degree parabola

$$Y_c = a + bX + cX^2 + dX^3 + eX^4$$

requires the solution of five normal equations, one for each constant. Parabolas beyond the third degree are seldom used in trend analysis since they tend to be overinfluenced by past random movements.

REVIEW EXERCISES 6.C

1. A line of least squares:
  a. Makes the sum of the $Y - Y_c$ values equal zero.
  b. Makes the number of data points above the line equal to the number below it.
  c. Makes $\sum (Y - Y_c)^2$ a minimum.
  d. Goes through $\bar{X}$ at $\bar{Y}$.
  e. All the above.
2. A line of least squares:
  a. Is reproducible: two people using the same method would get the same answer.
  b. Can be safely extrapolated far into the future.
  c. Can be used to fit many different kinds of trends.
  d. All the above.
3. You can derive the following values from the data given:

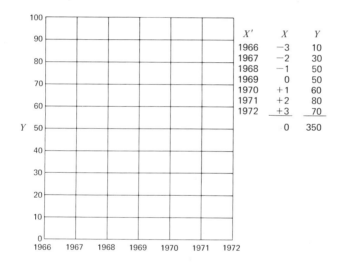

X'	X	Y
1966	−3	10
1967	−2	30
1968	−1	50
1969	0	50
1970	+1	60
1971	+2	80
1972	+3	70
	0	350

$$N = 7 \qquad\qquad \sum Y = 350$$
$$\sum X = 0 \qquad\qquad \sum XY = 290$$
$$\sum X^2 = 28 \qquad\qquad \sum X^2 Y = 1270$$
$$\sum X^3 = 0 \qquad\qquad \sum \log Y = 11.4015$$
$$\sum X^4 = 196 \qquad\qquad \sum X \log Y = 3.4665$$

a. Plot the original data on the grid.
b. Using the values given, find the equations for the following least-squares lines:
  (1) Straight line: $Y_c = a + bX$
  (2) Second-degree parabola: $Y_c = a + bX + cX^2$
  (3) Geometric progression: $\log Y_c = \log a + (\log b)X$
c. Which of the lines above do you think best fits the data?

Answers 6.C

1. a, c, and *d*   *2. a* and *c*
3. a. no answer
   b. (1) $Y_c = 50 + 10.36X$
      (2) $Y_c = 56.2 + 10.36X - 1.55X^2$
      (3) $\log Y_c = 1.6287 + 0.1238X$
      all with origin 1969, $\Delta X = 1$ year
   c. The second-degree parabola fits best. You can tell this by looking at the plot of the original data, by plotting the Y_c values from the equations, or by calculating the $\sum (Y - Y_c)^2$ values for each type of line. If you did calculate $\sum (Y - Y_c)^2$, you'd get about 200 for the second-degree parabola, 400 for the straight line, and 1400 for the geometric progression.

Section 6.D
Growth Curves

Learning objectives

Your learning objectives for this section are to be able to:

1. State the general equations for modified exponential, logistic, and Gompertz curves
2. Explain the uses and limitations of growth curves

Over the long run, many time series go through three stages of growth: (1) a slow period of development, followed by (2) a period of rapid expansion, and then (3) a tapering off at maturity. This characteristic S shape was first observed in the study of population statistics but is also characteristic of many business series, such as sales of color TVs, skimobiles, and computers. The growth in sales of color TV sets, for example, was small over a long period while transmission facilities and reception capabilities were being developed. As transmission and reception problems were solved, sales expanded at a very rapid rate to fill a new market. Once the primary market was satisfied, future growth in sales slowed to a steady rate determined primarily by population growth and replacement needs.

You'll learn how to fit three types of growth curves, the modified exponential, the Gompertz, and the logistic. The discussion is limited to the versions of these curves that approach an upper limit, or asymptote, as time progresses.

130

MODIFIED EXPONENTIAL

A modified exponential series is one which has a constant percentage decrease in a positive amount of growth. Its equation is $Y_c = K + ab^X$, where K is the asymptote, or limit, a is the difference between the Y_c value when $X = 0$ and the asymptote K, and b is the ratio between successive *increments* of growth. For a trend which approaches an upper limit, a will always be negative and b less than 1.

The constants in a modified exponential trend won't be found by least squares but by a simpler method in which the fitted trend will pass through the mean of each third of the original data. The equations which accomplish this objective are

$$b = \sqrt[n]{\frac{\sum_3 Y - \sum_2 Y}{\sum_2 Y - \sum_1 Y}} \qquad a = (\sum_2 Y - \sum_1 Y)\frac{b-1}{(b^n-1)^2}$$

$$K = \frac{1}{n}\left(\sum_1 Y - \frac{b^n-1}{b-1}a\right)$$

where the sums of the successive thirds of the Y values are represented by $\sum_1 Y$, $\sum_2 Y$, and $\sum_3 Y$, respectively, and n is the number of observations in each third of the data.

To illustrate how the process of fitting works, we'll generate data from a specific modified exponential equation, $Y_c = 100 - 70(.80^X)$ and then use the formulas to reproduce the constants K, a, and b. The calculations are shown in Table 6.7, and the trend line is plotted in Fig. 6.8.

Note that the asymptote $K = 100$ and that a is the distance the Y_c value is below K when $X = 0$ ($30 - 100 = -70$). The meaning of b is shown by taking the ratios of the successive first differences, which equal .8. This is the rate of decrease in the amount of increase.

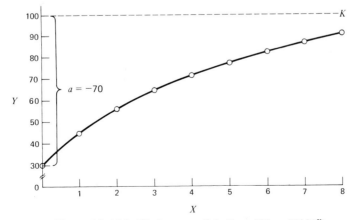

Figure 6.8 / Modified exponential, $Y_c = 100 - 70(.80^X)$.

Table 6.7

X	Y	First difference	Ratio of successive first differences b
0	30.00		
1	44.0 $\sum_1 Y = 129.20$	14.00	
2	55.20	11.20	$\dfrac{11.20}{14.00} = .8$
3	64.16	8.96	$\dfrac{8.96}{11.20} = .8$
4	71.33 $\sum_2 Y = 212.55$	7.17	$\dfrac{7.17}{8.96} = .8$
5	77.06	5.73	$\dfrac{5.73}{7.17} = .8$
6	81.65	4.59	$\dfrac{4.59}{5.73} = .8$
7	85.32 $\sum_3 Y = 255.23$	3.67	$\dfrac{3.67}{4.59} = .8$
8	88.26	2.94	$\dfrac{2.94}{3.67} = .8$

$$b = \sqrt[n]{\frac{\sum_3 Y - \sum_2 Y}{\sum_2 Y - \sum_1 Y}} = \sqrt[3]{\frac{255.23 - 212.55}{212.55 - 129.20}} = .80$$

$$a = (\sum_2 Y - \sum_1 Y)\frac{b - 1}{(b^n - 1)^2} = (212.55 - 129.20)\frac{.80 - 1}{(.80^3 - 1)^2} = -70$$

$$K = \frac{1}{n}\left(\sum_1 Y - \frac{b^n - 1}{b - 1}a\right) = \frac{1}{3}\left[129.20 - \frac{.8^3 - 1}{.8 - 1}(-70)\right] = 100$$

$Y_c = 100 - 70(.80^X)$ \quad origin year 0, $\Delta X = 1$ year

All the Y_c values for the equation above coincide with the Y values because the data were generated from the equation. In any real series the Y and Y_c points would differ, but the sums of the Y and the Y_c values would be equal for each third of the data.

LOGISTIC

The logistic is a symmetrical S-shaped growth curve whose lower limit approaches zero and whose upper limit approaches the value of $1/K$. The logistic is simply a modified exponential of the *reciprocals* of the original data. Its formula is

$$\frac{1}{Y_c} = K + ab^X$$

Table 6.8 / Mortgage debt (all types of properties), 1945–1970

Year	Y_A (billions)	$Y = \dfrac{1}{Y_A}$
1945	35.5	.028169
1950	72.8	.013736 $\sum_1 Y = .041905$
1955	129.9	.007698
1960	206.8	.004836 $\sum_2 Y = .012534$
1965	325.8	.003069
1970	451.7	.002214 $\sum_3 Y = .005283$

$$b = \sqrt[n]{\frac{\sum_3 Y - \sum_2 Y}{\sum_2 Y - \sum_1 Y}} = \sqrt{\frac{.005283 - .012534}{.012534 - .041905}} = .4969$$

$$a = \left(\sum_2 Y - \sum_1 Y\right)\frac{b-1}{(b^n-1)^2} = (.012534 - .041905)\frac{.4969 - 1}{(.4969^2 - 1)^2} = .02605$$

$$K = \frac{1}{n}\left(\sum_1 Y - \frac{b^n-1}{b-1}a\right) = \frac{1}{2}\left(.041905 - \frac{.4969^2 - 1}{.4969 - 1}.02605\right) = .001455$$

$$\frac{1}{Y_c} = .001455 + .02605(.4969)^x \qquad \text{origin 1945, } \Delta X = 5 \text{ years}$$

Source: Economic Report of the President, January 1973, p. 264.

Table 6.9 / Calculation of Y_c values, mortgage debt

X	$(.4969)^x$	$.02605(.4969)^x$	$\dfrac{1}{Y_c} = .001455 + .02605(.4969)^x$	Check $\sum$	Y_c
0	1.00000	.02605	.027505	.041900	36.4
1	.49690	.012940	.014395		69.5
2	.24690	.006432	.007887	.012538	126.8
3	.12268	.003196	.004651		215.0
4	.06096	.001588	.003043	.005287	328.6
5	.03029	.000789	.002244		445.6

where all the constants have the same meaning (with respect to the reciprocals of the Y values) as for the modified exponential.

The logistic curve will be illustrated using mortgage debt from 1945 to 1970 (Table 6.8). The actual data are labeled Y_A. The reciprocals of the Y_A values are labeled Y, and the modified exponential is fitted to these reciprocals, again by dividing the data into thirds.

To find Y_c values, simply substitute values of X in the last equation in Table 6.8. Note that the check sum figures in Table 6.9 are equal within rounding error to the

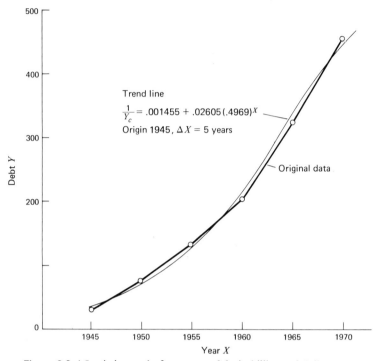

Figure 6.9 / Logistic trend of mortgage debt in billions of dollars, 1945–1970.

sums of the thirds shown earlier. A graph of the actual data and the trend equation is shown in Fig. 6.9.

GOMPERTZ CURVE

The Gompertz curve, like the logistic, is an S-shaped growth curve, but its point of inflection is the geometric mean of the Y values rather than the arithmetic mean, as with the logistic. Its equation is

$$Y_c = Ka^{b^x}$$

When this equation is expressed in logs as $\log Y_c = \log K + (\log a)b^x$, it is evident that the constants can be found by fitting a modified exponential to the *logarithms* of the Y values. This process is illustrated using hypothetical data for the share of the market captured by a firm from 1947 through 1970 (Table 6.10). Calculated values for the years 1945 to 1980 are derived in Table 6.11.

The fitted trend describes the original data very well, as you might expect since the original data were made up. That is only part of the reason for using this example, though. It is clear that the company's market share can at most approach but never

Table 6.10 / Gompertz curve, market share

Year	Market share Y_A, %	$Y = \log Y_A$	
1945	2	0.301	$\sum_1 Y = 0.903$
1950	4	0.602	
1955	8	0.903	$\sum_2 Y = 2.049$
1960	14	1.146	
1965	20	1.301	$\sum_3 Y = 2.778$
1970	30	1.477	

$$b = \sqrt[n]{\frac{\sum_3 Y - \sum_2 Y}{\sum_2 Y - \sum_1 Y}} = \sqrt{\frac{2.778 - 2.049}{2.049 - 0.903}} = .7977$$

$$a = (\sum_2 Y - \sum_1 Y)\frac{b - 1}{(b^n - 1)^2} = (2.049 - .903)\frac{.7977 - 1}{(.7977^2 - 1)^2} = -1.751$$

$$K = \frac{1}{n}\left(\sum_1 Y - \frac{b^n - 1}{b - 1}a\right) = \frac{1}{2}\left[.903 - \frac{.7977^2 - 1}{.7977 - 1}(-1.751)\right] = 2.026$$

$\log Y_c = 2.026 - 1.751(.7977^X)$ origin 1945, $\Delta X = 5$ years

exceed 100 percent. The log K value in our problem is 2.026, and its antilog K, the asymptote, is 106.2. This is an impossible value. The trouble here is that the method wasn't smart enough to know anything about the critical level appropriate for the problem. In using formulas for growth curves, you can't expect the method to identify critical levels, since they are exogenous to the data. If such a level exists, you must adjust the fitted curve to approach that level rather than the one determined by K.

It might, though, be quite reasonable to obtain several future trend values by extrapolation. The values of 38 and 46 obtained for 1975 and 1980 might be very logical.

Table 6.11 / Calculation of Y_c values, market share

Year	X	$.7977^X$	$-1.751(.7977^X)$	$\log Y_c = 2.026 - 1.751(.7977^X)$	Check $\sum$	Y_c
1945	0	1.000	-1.751	0.275	.904	2
1950	1	.7977	-1.397	0.629		4
1955	2	.6363	-1.114	0.912	2.049	8
1960	3	.5076	- .889	1.137		14
1965	4	.4049	- .709	1.317	2.777	21
1970	5	.3230	- .566	1.460		29
1975	6	.2577	- .451	1.575		38
1980	7	.2056	- .360	1.666		46

Many people might be tempted to describe the trend of the series above using a geometric progression. Actually such a line fits the past data quite well. If such a curve were extrapolated, however, you'd obtain market shares of 60 percent for 1975 and 103 percent for 1980, which clearly are unreasonable. You don't have to pursue the literature of business too far to find companies that have based estimates of the future on the extrapolation of geometric progressions rather than more plausible growth curves.

REVIEW EXERCISES 6.D

1. What are the equations for modified exponential, logistic, and Gompertz trends?
2. A logistic trend is obtained by fitting a modified exponential to the _____
   of the original data, while a Gompertz trend is obtained by fitting a modified exponential to the _____ of the original data.
3. The asymptote for a growth curve may not reflect the critical level of the data being analyzed because:
   a. The historical data may not approach close enough to the critical level to reflect it.
   b. The critical level is often exogenous to the historical data: it is caused by outside factors that may not show in past data.
   c. Both the above.

Answers 6.D

1. Modified exponential: $Y_c = K + ab^X$
   Logistic: $1/Y_c = K + ab^X$
   Gompertz: $Y_c = Ka^{b^X}$ or $\log Y_c = \log K + (\log a)b^X$
2. reciprocals, logarithms   3. c

Questions and Problems

6.1. For the data on civilian labor force below:
   a. Plot the data on an arithmetic chart.
   b. Find the equation for a linear trend fit by inspection.
   c. Find the equation for a linear trend fit by semiaverages.
   d. Plot the trend lines found in parts b and c on the graph of the original data.

Year	Civilian labor force, millions	Year	Civilian labor force, millions
1968	78.7	1971	84.1
1969	80.7	1972	86.5
1970	82.7	1973	88.7

6.2. Find the equation for a linear trend fit to the civilian labor force data of Prob. 6.1, using the method of least squares.
6.3. The index of industrial production for the United States has increased nearly

geometrically from a value of about 39 in 1947 to a value of about 110 in 1971 (with 1967 = 100). Calculate the rate of increase per year for this series.

6.4. Assume that a business series *decreased* geometrically from a value of 110 in 1947 to a value of 39 in 1971.

a. Calculate the rate of decrease per year for this series.

b. If you solved Prob. 6.3, you should have found that industrial production increased at a rate of 4.4 percent per year from 1947 to 1971. Since the numbers involved were just the same as for this problem (but reversed), why isn't your answer to part *a*, above, a *decrease* of 4.4 percent per year?

6.5. The data below show GNP from 1961 through 1973. For these data:

a. Plot the data on both arithmetic and semilog charts.

b. Find the equation for a geometric trend fit to the data by least squares.

c. Plot the trend found in part *b* on the charts you made in part *a*.

d. Use the trend equation to estimate GNP for 1978. Do you think the value is reasonable?

Year	GNP, billions	Year	GNP, billions	Year	GNP, billions
1961	$520	1966	$750	1971	$1056
1962	560	1967	794	1972	1155
1963	590	1968	864	1973	1289
1964	632	1969	930		
1965	685	1970	977		

6.6. For the GNP data of Prob. 6.5:

a. Plot the data on an arithmetic chart.

b. Find the equation for a second-degree parabola fitted to the data by least squares.

c. Plot the trend found in part *b* on the chart you made in part *a*.

d. Use the trend equation to estimate GNP for 1978.

6.7. A town has doubled in population every 10 years for the past 50 years. Its present population is 100,000.

a. Find the rate per year at which the town has been growing.

b. Determine the trend equation for the town's growth.

c. Assuming that the growth continues at the same rate as in the past, use the equation in part *b* to calculate the town's size 50 years from now; 100 years from now.

d. What does this problem illustrate?

6.8. Find a *Historical Chart Book* (published annually by the Board of Governors of the Federal Reserve System) or a *Monthly Chart Book* (published monthly by the same agency). Page through the book and find:

a. Five series that can be described well by a *linear* trend.

b. Five series that can be described well by a *geometric* trend.

6.9. The sales of a company from 1967 to 1973 are shown below. Find the equation for the line of least squares which *best describes* these data.

Year	Sales, thousands	Year	Sales, thousands
1967	$10,000	1971	$12,864
1968	10,650	1972	13,700
1969	11,342	1973	14,591
1970	12,079		

6.10. For the data below:
  a. Graph the data on an arithmetic chart.
  b. Calculate the equation for a least-squares second-degree parabola.
  c. Graph the trend on the chart you made in part a.

Year	Profit	Year	Profit
1962	$24,000	1968	$107,000
1964	65,000	1970	117,000
1966	89,000	1972	125,000

6.11. Corporate profits before taxes are shown below from 1930 to 1970.

Year	Corporate profits, billions	Year	Corporate profits, billions	Year	Corporate profits, billions
1930	$ 4.1	1945	$20.0	1960	$49.7
1935	3.8	1950	42.6	1965	78.4
1940	10.0	1955	48.4	1970	75.4

  a. Calculate the equation for a logistic growth curve fit to these data.
  b. Plot the original data and the logistic trend on arithmetic paper.
  c. From what has happened in the economy since 1970, do you think that this curve would describe the future course of corporate profits well? Why or why not?
6.12. Refer to the data on corporate profits in Prob. 6.11.
  a. Calculate the equation for a Gompertz growth curve fitted to these data.
  b. Plot the original data and the Gompertz trend on arithmetic paper.
  c. Answer part c of Prob. 6.11 with reference to the Gompertz trend.
6.13. a. How do you find the asymptote (the limit that the series approaches) for a modified exponential trend? A logistic trend? A Gompertz trend?
  b. Why is it often the case that the asymptote calculated for a growth curve will not be a good predictor of the real limit of the series being measured?
6.14. Define the secular trend. What are some of the factors influencing the secular trend of most business and economic series in the United States? Why is the trend of most of these series rising? Find some examples of secular trends which are *falling* and see if you can explain why.
6.15. The data below are for the ratio of profits after federal income taxes to stockholders' equity (as a percent) for tobacco manufacturers from 1952 to 1971.

Year	Profit/equity, %	Year	Profit/equity, %	Year	Profit/equity, %
1952	8.4	1959	13.4	1966	14.1
1953	9.4	1960	13.4	1967	14.4
1954	10.2	1961	13.6	1968	14.4
1955	11.4	1962	13.1	1969	14.5
1956	11.7	1963	13.4	1970	15.7
1957	12.5	1964	13.4	1971	15.8
1958	13.5	1965	13.5		

  a. Graph these data on an arithmetic grid.
  b. Calculate the equation for a linear trend fit to these data by the least-squares method.
  c. Graph the trend you found on the graph of the original data.

MODULE 7
TIME-SERIES ANALYSIS—
SEASONAL, CYCLICAL, AND
IRREGULAR

General learning objectives

Your general learning objectives for this module are to be able to

1. Identify typical causes of seasonal variation and of the business cycle
2. Measure the reliability of a seasonal index and identify changing seasonal patterns
3. Complete the process of classical decomposition of a time series by measuring and isolating the trend, cycle, seasonal, and irregular movements

In the last module you were concerned with describing the *secular trend* of a business series, i.e., the long-term general direction in which the series was moving. In this module you'll learn to measure and analyze the shorter fluctuations about the secular trend. These fluctuations will be broken down into three components: seasonal variation, the business cycle, and irregular or random movements. Division of a time series into the trend T, seasonal S, cyclical C, and irregular I components is called *classical time-series decomposition.*

Fluctuations in any time series are caused by a multitude of factors, some known and many unknown. The *TSCI* model is just one way of looking at the resultant of all of these forces. Like most time-series analysis techniques, it may appear objective but in fact is subjective, depending upon the judgment of the analyst.

Here, for example, we'll assume that the four components are related in multiplicative fashion, which means that the series can be described as $T \times C \times S \times I$. We make this assumption because it usually leads to more satisfactory results than other possibilities such as $T + S + C + I$ or $T \times C + S + I$.

Section 7.A
Seasonal Variation

Learning objectives

Your learning objectives for this section are to be able to:

1. Calculate an index of seasonal variation using the method of ratios of data to moving average
2. Describe what is meant by spurious seasonal variation
3. Measure the reliability of a seasonal pattern and identify changing seasonal patterns
4. Adjust data for seasonal variation and incorporate seasonal variation in the planning process

Seasonal variation is a pattern of change in a time series that repeats itself in the same general fashion year after year and thus has a *period* of exactly 1 year. Seasonal variation may be caused by weather and the customs or institutions of societies. For example, seasonal variation in food production, transportation, skiing, and swimming are directly related to the weather. Other seasonal activities such as public school attendance and its many related activities were originally due to the weather, since farm children had to work at home during the summer months, but now are adhered to primarily out of custom. Business activity stemming from the Christmas and Easter seasons is related not to the weather but to the customs surrounding the celebration of those holidays.

There are many other types of periodic variations, all shorter in duration than the seasonal. Traffic on a city street shows regular patterns by hours of the day, days of the week, and months of the year, as would the number of shoppers in a supermarket or depositors at a bank. The business cycle, which you'll study later in this module, is longer in duration and is *not* periodic in the same sense as the seasonal because its swings are not constant and its amplitude fluctuates widely from cycle to cycle.

Seasonal variation is an expensive nuisance for most companies. Swings in sales through the year generate production, investment, and cash-flow problems that wouldn't be present if there weren't any seasonal variation. In order to cope effectively with seasonal variation a company must first be able to measure it and then to plan for it. The method of *ratios of data to moving average*, which you'll learn here, is widely used to measure seasonal variation.

141

Table 7.1

X	$\dfrac{\sum X}{n}$	Moving average
3		
2	9/3	3
4	12/3	4
6	15/3	5
5		

CALCULATION OF SEASONAL INDEX BY METHOD OF RATIOS OF DATA TO MOVING AVERAGE

Moving averages are often used to *smooth* time series. To calculate an nth-period moving average, the arithmetic mean of the first n values is calculated. The first value, X_1, is dropped and a new value, X_{n+1}, is added, and a new mean is found. This process is repeated for the entire series. The resulting means or *moving averages* smooth the data by averaging out extreme values. The larger the value of n, the more smoothing takes place. A three-period moving average is shown for the series in Table 7.1.

Since seasonal variation has a period of exactly 1 year, any yearly average can contain no seasonal variation. If all you knew was that the sales of a company averaged 1 million dollars per month for a year, you would have no idea of the variation in sales *within* that year. Thus the seasonal could be eliminated from monthly data by taking a 12-month moving average or from quarterly data by taking a 4-quarter moving average.

Calculating a moving average over the period of a year has no effect on the trend and little effect on the business cycle since both these movements last longer than a year. Irregular movements are often short-run, most lasting considerably less than a year. Therefore, a yearly moving average would smooth the irregular component considerably but not remove it entirely. Thus if the original data contain all the components *TSCI*, a yearly moving average of these data could be said to contain *TCi*, where *i* indicates in a qualitative sense that the irregular has been partly removed. The *TCi* values are called *deseasonalized* data. Deseasonalized series are used extensively in business analysis because it is much easier to see whether the trend and business cycle are meeting expectations *after* the seasonal variation has been eliminated and the irregular smoothed.

The method of ratios of data to moving average is used to calculate an index of seasonal variation as follows:

1. Calculate a moving average of the original *TSCI* data using a period of 1 year. Assure that the moving average points correspond in time to the original data points by *centering* the moving average. *This produces deseasonalized data TCi.*

142

2. Take the ratio of each original data point to its corresponding moving average. *This isolates the seasonal and some irregular*

$$\frac{TSCI}{TCi} = Si$$

3. Arrange the *Si* values, called *specific seasonal values*, in columns for each month or quarter and calculate the median value for each period. *This separates S from i.*
4. Divide the *S* value for each period by the mean of the *S* values for the entire year and multiply by 100. *This produces the seasonal index.*

The calculation of a seasonal index will be clearer when illustrated. Let's calculate such an index using data on new housing starts (private) in the United States from 1960 to 1972 (Table 7.2). The data are in thousands of units. Quarterly data are used here to reduce the number of calculations. Ordinarily seasonal indexes are found by month rather than by quarter.

There are several points worth noting in Table 7.2. The first moving total in column 3, 1237, is obtained by adding the first four figures in column 2. This figure is placed between II and III since that is the midvalue of the four original numbers. The next moving total in column 3, 1223, is the sum of the second through fifth values in column 2, etc. Before you calculate the moving average, *center* the moving total by taking a two-period moving total of the values in column 3. Thus the first figure in column 4, 2460, is the sum of 1237 and 1223. It is placed between them in time, centering back on the third quarter of 1960. The four-quarter moving average centered in column 5 is then obtained by dividing the figures in column 4 by 8, since two 4-quarter totals (or eight individual values) were added to get the centered moving totals. The original values in column 1 can now be divided by the moving average values in column 5 since they correspond in time. Thus 333/307.5 = 1.08, the ratio of data to moving average for the third quarter of 1960.

The other calculations are straightforward. The *Si* values are arranged in columns of quarters, and their median value, which represents a pure seasonal component, is found. These values are transformed into the seasonal index by expressing each as a percentage of their mean.

RELIABILITY OF A SEASONAL INDEX

The median values in Table 7.2 (.805, 1.200, 1.080, and .930) reflect the average seasonal value for each quarter over the entire period studied. Comparison of these *S* values with the *Si* values for each quarter provides a measure of the *reliability* of the seasonal index. If there were little dispersion of the *Si* values from their median value, the seasonal index for that period would be considered reliable and you might expect that future seasonals for that period would not be far from the seasonal index. But if there were wide dispersion of the *Si* values from their median, you'd still use

143

Table 7.2 / Calculation of seasonal index of private new housing starts, 1960–1972 (Thousands)

(1) Year and quarter	(2) Original data TSCI	(3) 4-quarter moving total	(4) 4-quarter moving total centered	(5) 4-quarter moving average TCi	(6) Ratios of data to moving average $\dfrac{TSCI}{TCi} = Si$
1960 I	265				
II	373				
		1237			
III	333		2460	307.5	1.08
		1223			
IV	266		2443	305.4	.87
		1220			
1961 I	251		2481	310.1	.81
		1261			
II	370		2565	320.6	1.15
		1304			
III	374		2629	328.6	1.14
		1325			
IV	309		2717	339.6	.91
		1392			
1962 I	272		2806	350.8	.78
		1414			
II	437		2867	358.4	1.22
		1453			
III	396		2926	365.8	1.08
		1473			
IV	348		2986	373.3	.93
		1513			
1963 I	292		3069	383.6	.76
		1556			
II	477		3142	392.8	1.21
		1586			
III	439		3210	401.3	1.09
		1624			
IV	378		3237	404.6	.93
		1613			
1964 I	330		3195	399.4	83
		1582			
II	466		3137	392.1	1.19
		1555			
III	408		3068	383.5	1.06
		1513			
IV	351		3026	378.3	.93
		1513			
1965 I	288		3018	377.3	.76
		1505			
II	466		3010	376.3	1.24
		1505			

Table 7.2 / Calculation of seasonal index of private new housing starts, 1960–1972—Continued
(Thousands)

(1) Year and quarter	(2) Original data $TSCI$	(3) 4-quarter moving total	(4) 4-quarter moving total centered	(5) 4-quarter moving average TCi	(6) Ratios of data to moving average $\dfrac{TSCI}{TCi} = Si$
III	400		3011	376.4	1.06
		1506			
IV	351		2956	369.5	.95
		1450			
1966 I	289		2801	350.1	.83
		1351			
II	410		2564	320.5	1.28
		1213			
III	301		2349	293.6	1.03
		1136			
IV	213		2233	279.1	.76
		1097			
1967 I	212		2267	283.4	.75
		1170			
II	371		2460	307.5	1.21
		1290			
III	374		2661	332.6	1.12
		1371			
IV	333		2812	351.5	.95
		1441			
1968 I	293		2919	364.9	.80
		1478			
II	441		2986	373.3	1.18
		1508			
III	411		3047	380.9	1.08
		1539			
IV	363		3099	387.4	.94
		1560			
1969 I	324		3088	386.0	.84
		1528			
II	462		2994	374.3	1.23
		1466			
III	379		2862	357.8	1.06
		1396			
IV	301		2718	339.8	.89
		1322			
1970 I	254		2666	333.3	.76
		1344			
II	388		2774	346.8	1.12
		1430			
III	401		2987	373.4	1.07
		1557			
IV	387		3320	415.0	.93
		1763			

Table 7.2 / Calculation of seasonal index of private new housing starts, 1960–1972—Continued
(Thousands)

(1) Year and quarter	(2) Original data TSCI	(3) 4-quarter moving total	(4) 4-quarter moving total centered	(5) 4-quarter moving average TCi	(6) Ratios of data to moving average $\dfrac{TSCI}{TCi} = Si$
1971 I	381		3698	462.3	.82
		1935			
II	594		3987	498.4	1.19
		2052			
III	573		4228	528.5	1.08
		2176			
IV	504		4419	552.4	.91
		2243			
1972 I	505		4551	568.9	.89
		2308			
II	661		4667	583.4	1.13
		2359			
III	638				
IV	555				

Si values from column 6

	I	II	III	IV
1960			1.08†	.87*
1961	.81	1.15*	1.14†	.91*
1962	.78*	1.22†	1.08	.93†
1963	.76*	1.21†	1.09†	.93†
1964	.83†	1.19*	1.06*	.93
1965	.76*	1.24†	1.06*	.95†
1966	.83†	1.28†	1.03*	.76*
1967	.75*	1.21	1.12†	.95†
1968	.80	1.18*	1.08	.94†
1969	.84†	1.23†	1.06*	.89*
1970	.76*	1.12*	1.07*	.93
1971	.82†	1.19	1.08†	.91*
1972	.89†	1.13*		
S	.805	1.200	1.080	.930 $\dfrac{\Sigma}{4} = \dfrac{4.015}{4} = 1.0037$
Seasonal index	80	119	108	93

* Lows.
† Highs.
Source: Federal Reserve Bulletin.

146

the seasonal index as a predictor of future seasonal values with the reservation that any particular future value might vary considerably from the seasonal index.

For the housing start data, the Si values show little dispersion in any quarter, and the seasonal indexes could be considered quite reliable. Other seasonal indexes might prove to be unreliable for all periods or reliable for some and unreliable for others. If a family used gas only for heating their house and kept the pilot light on during the summer months, they'd find the seasonal for August not only very low but also very reliable, since year after year the only gas used would be for the pilot light. The seasonal variation for November might be expected to be quite unreliable since the amount of heat needed would vary a great deal from the average from year to year depending on the weather.

CHANGING SEASONAL PATTERNS

Though seasonal patterns are usually consistent from year to year, there may be series for which the seasonal variation is changing. In almost all these cases the change is in the direction of smoothing the seasonal variation. You'd find, for example, that over the past 30 years the seasonal variation for passenger miles flown by airlines has risen for the winter months and fallen for the summer months. This means that the airlines are flying a greater *proportion* of their total miles in the winter now than they did before. Reasons for this shift are greater winter demand on the part of passengers, as well as technological improvements in navigational equipment, landing equipment, and airport construction which have permitted more extensive winter flying. The same leveling of seasonal variation would be apparent in other series such as expenditures for vacations (more people are taking winter vacations), construction activity, and the length of the football season. If you want a challenge, try to think of a seasonal that is becoming more accentuated through time rather than smoother! You won't find many, because smoothing seasonal variation pays but accentuating it doesn't.

To discover whether the seasonal variation for a series is changing or not, again you'd examine the Si values arranged in columns of months or quarters. If there's no change in the seasonal variation, these values will be randomly distributed about their median. If the seasonal's changing, there will be a concentration of low and high values at opposite ends of the series. In the housing-start data of Table 6.2, there wasn't any shift in the seasonal variation over time since the highs and lows of all the columns showed no pattern of change. If most of the lows in the first quarter had occurred in the early years and most of the highs in the later years, you might suspect that the seasonal variation for the first quarter was increasing over time. If the *proportion* of activity rises in one period, it must fall in another, so an increase in seasonal variation in one quarter must be accompanied by a falling seasonal variation for other quarters.

If the seasonal variation for a particular month or quarter isn't changing, a graph of the Si values for that period will fluctuate about a horizontal line, while if the seasonal is changing, the graph will exhibit a trend. This isn't the *secular* trend you

147

studied in Module 6, which was eliminated by taking the ratios of the data to the moving average. A company could be going broke, with a declining trend of sales, while its seasonal for January was increasing.

If a series does exhibit a changing seasonal, you'd use the median of a recent set of *Si* values to make the index rather than the median *Si* value for the entire period.

SPURIOUS SEASONAL VARIATION

Sometimes series can give the impression of having seasonal variation when in fact they don't. The most obvious illustration involves the seasonal for a continuous process. Papermaking machines are blocks long and very expensive to start and stop. If a particular machine were run 24 hours a day, 365 days a year, producing 10 rolls per day, there'd be no seasonal variation at all. However, if a seasonal index of production is made by the usual method, a small seasonal variation appears because not all months have the same number of days. The index for January would be 102 and for a non-leap-year February, it would be 92.[1] This *spurious* seasonal variation can be corrected by multiplying the index obtained for each month by the ratio "average number of days per month divided by actual number of days in that month."

The same problem appears when considering working-day variation per month where plants run a standard 5-day week, since some months have five weekends while others have four and months vary with respect to the number of days off for holidays. If you want to measure production on a *working-day* basis, you adjust by multiplying each index by the ratio "average number of working days per month divided by actual number of *working* days in that particular month."

USES OF SEASONAL INDEXES

Seasonal indexes are used both for *interpreting* existing data and for *planning* for future levels of activity.

As mentioned earlier, dividing by an appropriate seasonal index deseasonalizes data and makes it much easier to see changes that are taking place in the trend and the business cycle. Most of the series reported by the government such as GNP and national income are given in terms of *seasonally adjusted values at annual rates*. This adjustment is made by dividing the actual figure, say for a particular quarter, by the

---

[1] For January

$$\frac{31(10)}{365(10)/12} \times 100 = 102$$

For February

$$\frac{28(10)}{365(10)/12} \times 100 = 92$$

seasonal index for that quarter and multiplying by 4. Thus if the actual data gathered by the Bureau of Labor Statistics for the first quarter of a given year showed total GNP at 225 billion dollars and the seasonal index for that quarter was 75, the adjusted total would be $(225/.75)(4) = 1200$ billion, seasonally adjusted, annual rate. While it would be difficult for a layman to interpret the raw data, 225 billion, the 1200 figure is easy to compare with projections to see if GNP is running ahead or behind the anticipated level.

The use of seasonal indexes in planning can be illustrated by the following example. Suppose that a company's sales forecast for the coming year is 240,000 units. Without any knowledge of the seasonal demand for their product, it would be very difficult to assign reasonable sales quotas by months or quarters. However, if they knew that their seasonal indexes in the past had been 56 for January, 65 for February and 92 for March, they could easily establish quotas by first observing that if there were no seasonal variation, they would expect to sell $240,000/12 = 20,000$ units per month. In view of the seasonal variation this figure would be adjusted by multiplying it by the appropriate seasonal index. Thus the sales forecast would be:

January	$20,000(.56) = 11,200$ units
February	$20,000(.65) = 13,000$
March	$20,000(.92) = 18,400$
First quarter	42,600 units

REVIEW EXERCISES 7.A

1. Match the descriptions in the column on the left with the appropriate symbols or expressions on the right.

    a. Original data
    b. 12-month centered moving average of original data
    c. Ratios of original data to moving average
    d. Median ratio of data to moving average
    e. $\dfrac{\text{Sum of median ratios}}{12} \times 100$

    (1) TCi
    (2) Si
    (3) $TSCI$
    (4) Seasonal index
    (5) S

2. Arrange the steps below in the sequence necessary to calculate an index of seasonal variation. Eliminate all unnecessary or incorrect steps.

    a. Take a 12-month centered moving average of the original data.
    b. Fit a trend line to the centered 12-month moving average.
    c. Divide the trend values by the corresponding original values.
    d. Divide the original values by the corresponding centered 12-month moving-average values.
    e. Find the median of the ratios of data to moving average for each month.
    f. Divide each median value by the mean of its median values over the 12 months, and multiply each ratio by 100.

3. The seasonal index for a company's production was 85 for April. Adjust this index to account for spurious variation caused by the length of the month.

4. For which column of Si values below:
   a. Is the seasonal index unreliable?
   b. Is the seasonal variation increasing over time?

Column Jan. Si	Column Feb. Si	Column Jan. Si	Column Feb. Si
1.20	.32	1.46	.37
1.40	.31	1.25	.40
1.52	.35	1.50	.42
1.35	.38		

5. You forecast that your company sales will be 84 million dollars next year. You know that the seasonal indexes for sales are

Quarter	I	II	III	IV
Index	35	96	150	119

Determine your sales quotas for each quarter.

Answers 7.A

1. a. (3), b. (1), c. (2), d. (5), e. (4)   2. a, d, e, f   3. $85 \dfrac{30.417}{30} = 86.2$ 4. a. Jan.; b. Feb.   5. I = $7,350,000; II = $20,160,000; III = $31,500,000; IV = $24,990,000

Section 7.B

The Business Cycle and Irregular Movements

Learning objectives

Your learning objectives for this section are to be able to:

1. Define the business cycle
2. Identify some causes of the business cycle
3. Identify the steps used in classical time-series decomposition
4. Characterize and measure irregular variation

Business cycles are fluctuations in business activity which last from 1 to about 12 years and which vary considerably in amplitude. While they are persistent, occurring over and over, they are unlike seasonal variation in that neither their period nor amplitude is consistent. You could easily make an analogy between the "health" of the economy and your own health. Recessions can be compared to minor illnesses like colds or the flu. Depressions, lasting longer and being more severe, would be analogous to major illnesses. The great depression of the 1930s was like having several major illnesses, all with complications, at the same time. On the upswing too, periods of prosperity can be minor or major. Sometimes combinations of physical and psychological factors in the economy lead to sustained heady periods like those of the 1960s.

Some factors causing business cycles are endogenous, coming from within the business system. These include overaccumulation of inventories, the exploitation of particular natural resources, or technological innovations. Some factors are exogenous, coming from outside the system but affecting it. These include natural events such as droughts, political events such as wars, or social phenomena such as changes in birth rates.

MEASURING THE BUSINESS CYCLE AND IRREGULAR VARIATION—CLASSICAL METHOD

According to classical decomposition, the business cycle is measured as a residual; i.e., it is obtained by removing T, S, and I from the original data, leaving C. Once the seasonal variation has been measured and an appropriate trend line determined, S and T are removed by division. The irregular component is then smoothed using a short-period moving average, and the residual is the cycle, expressed as a ratio or index. This decomposition process will be illustrated by continuing the analysis of housing starts from which the seasonal variation was isolated.

In this analysis, the original data $TSCI$ are first divided by the seasonal index S, which was calculated in Table 7.2, giving deseasonalized data TCI. This process is shown in columns 2 to 4 of Table 7.3. The TCI values are then averaged for each year and graphed in Fig. 7.1. Inspection of this graph shows that a *linear* trend fits the data well, so a straight line of least squares is fitted to the TCI values, as shown in Table 7.4 and graphed in Fig. 7.1.[1]

Quarterly trend values are then calculated from the trend equation and entered as T in column 5 of Table 7.3. The TCI values are then divided by T, resulting in CI (column 6). The CI values are smoothed, using a 3-quarter moving average (column 7), which measures C. Finally, the CI values are divided by C, obtaining I (column 8). A graph of the cyclical and irregular values is shown in Fig. 7.2.

The cycle shown here is for the particular series being studied, namely housing

---

[1] This trend is almost identical to those which would be obtained by fitting a straight line either to the original quarterly data or to annual averages of the original data.

Table 7.3 / Time-series decomposition of private new housing starts, 1960–1972 (Thousands)

(1) Year and quarter	(2) TSCI	(3) S	(4) TCI	(5) T	(6) CI	(7) 3-month MA of CI = C	(8) $\dfrac{CI}{C} = I$
1960 I	265	80	331	298	1.11		
II	373	119	313	301	1.04	1.05	.99
III	333	108	308	305	1.01	.99	1.02
IV	266	93	286	308	.93	.98	.95
1961 I	251	80	314	311	1.01	.98	1.03
II	370	119	311	315	.99	1.03	.96
III	374	108	346	318	1.09	1.04	1.05
IV	309	93	332	322	1.03	1.06	.97
1962 I	272	80	340	325	1.05	1.07	.98
II	437	119	367	328	1.12	1.09	1.03
III	396	108	367	332	1.11	1.12	.99
IV	348	93	374	335	1.12	1.10	1.02
1963 I	292	80	365	338	1.08	1.12	.96
II	477	119	401	342	1.17	1.14	1.03
III	439	108	406	345	1.18	1.17	1.01
IV	378	93	406	348	1.17	1.17	1.00
1964 I	330	80	413	352	1.17	1.15	1.02
II	466	119	392	355	1.10	1.11	.99
III	408	108	378	359	1.05	1.06	.99
IV	351	93	377	362	1.04	1.03	1.01
1965 I	288	80	360	365	.99	1.03	.96
II	466	119	392	369	1.06	1.01	1.05
III	400	108	370	372	.99	1.02	.97
IV	351	93	377	375	1.01	.98	1.03
1966 I	289	80	361	379	.95	.95	1.00
II	410	119	345	382	.90	.86	1.05
III	301	108	279	386	.72	.74	.97
IV	213	93	229	389	.59	.66	.89
1967 I	212	80	265	392	.68	.69	.99
II	371	119	312	396	.79	.78	1.01
III	374	108	346	399	.87	.85	1.02
IV	333	93	358	402	.89	.89	1.00
1968 I	293	80	366	406	.90	.90	1.00
II	441	119	371	409	.91	.91	1.00
III	411	108	381	413	.92	.92	1.00
IV	363	93	390	416	.94	.94	1.00
1969 I	324	80	405	419	.97	.94	1.03
II	462	119	388	423	.92	.90	1.02
III	379	108	351	426	.82	.83	.99
IV	301	93	324	429	.76	.77	.99
1970 I	254	80	318	433	.73	.75	.97
II	388	119	326	436	.75	.78	.96
III	401	108	371	439	.85	.85	1.00
IV	387	93	416	443	.94	.95	.99
1971 I	381	80	476	446	1.07	1.04	1.03
II	594	119	499	450	1.11	1.12	.99
III	573	108	531	453	1.17	1.16	1.01
IV	504	93	542	456	1.19	1.24	.96
1972 I	505	80	631	460	1.37	1.25	1.10
II	661	119	555	463	1.20	1.28	.94
III	638	108	591	466	1.27	1.25	1.02
IV	555	93	597	470	1.27		

Table 7.4 / Calculation of linear trend of private new housing starts, 1960–1972 (Thousands)

Year	X	$TCI = Y$	XY	X^2
1960	-6	310	-1860	36
1961	-5	326	-1630	25
1962	-4	362	-1448	16
1963	-3	395	-1185	9
1964	-2	390	-780	4
1965	-1	375	-375	1
1966	0	304	0	0
1967	$+1$	320	320	1
1968	$+2$	377	754	4
1969	$+3$	367	1101	9
1970	$+4$	358	1432	16
1971	$+5$	512	2560	25
1972	$+6$	594	3564	36
	0	4990	2453	182

$$a = \frac{\sum Y}{N} = 383.85 \qquad b = \frac{\sum XY}{\sum X^2} = 13.48$$

$$Y_c = 383.85 + 13.48X \qquad \text{origin 1966,} \quad \Delta X = 1 \text{ year}$$

or $\quad Y_c = 297.92 + 3.37X \qquad \text{origin 1960 I,} \ \Delta X = 1 \text{ quarter}$

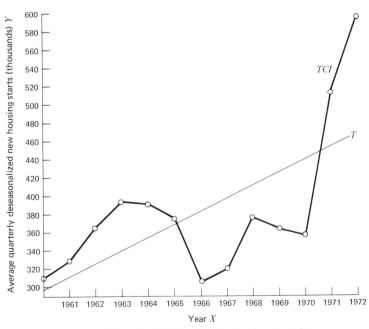

Figure 7.1 / Graph of *TCI* and *T* for housing-start data.

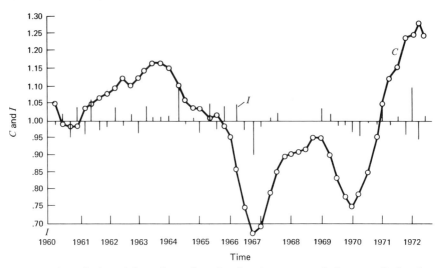

Figure 7.2 / Cyclical and irregular values for housing starts; circles = cyclical values; lines = irregular values.

starts. You shouldn't confuse this cycle or other specific business cycles with the business cycle for the aggregate of economic activity. The overall business cycle is made up of thousands of specific cycles encompassing the national economy. The National Bureau of Economic Research, which has devoted years of exceptional effort to the study of business cycles, has developed composite reference cycles from some 1000 deseasonalized individual and aggregate economic series. They then analyze the reference cycles in a systematic way to locate their peaks and troughs. Individual series can then be compared with the reference cycle. The cycles of some individual series show no correspondence to the reference cycle, while others show consistent leading, lagging, or coincident behavior. A list of indicators and their use in forecasting will be discussed in Module 9.

IRREGULAR VARIATION

Irregular variation is a catchall term for any movement that is not trend, seasonal, or cyclical. Irregular movements can be caused by many sorts of random circumstances such as strikes, fires, floods, the discovery of a new raw-material resource, a favorable (or unfavorable) tax ruling, or changes in the prime interest rate. It's important to analyze irregular variation because you may get some clues to how well the T, S, and C components have been removed and whether there are still some other components that should be analyzed.

If any definite pattern appeared when the irregular variation I was isolated, or if its magnitude was exceptionally large, further investigation would be warranted. This could occur, for example, if there were other cyclical types of swings besides the business cycle which appear in some series, if a bad-fitting trend line was used, or if the components would have been more appropriately treated as additive than as multiplicative.

In the housing-starts problem, the irregular values average 1.00, as one would expect. They occur in what appears to be a random fashion, showing no apparent relation to cyclical or seasonal activity. Most of the irregular movements are small with a high of 1.10 and a low of .89. For these reasons, the decomposition technique used in this example seemed reasonable, and further analysis was judged unnecessary.

REVIEW EXERCISES 7.B

1. The business cycle is defined as:
  a. Fluctuations in business activity which occur over and over but which have irregular periods and vary widely in amplitude from cycle to cycle.
  b. Fluctuations in business activity which have a regular period and amplitude like seasonal variation but which last longer than seasonal variation.
2. The factors listed below are all causes of business cycles. For each one, write En if it is an endogenous factor, and Ex if it is an exogenous factor.
  a. War.
  b. Drought.
  c. Inventory accumulation.
  d. Innovation.
  e. Birth-rate changes.
  f. Exploitation of natural resources.
3. The steps below describe the classical decomposition of a time series. Summarize each step with appropriate symbols or equations.
  a. Calculate a seasonal index and deseasonalize the original data by dividing it by the seasonal index.
  b. Fit a trend line to the deseasonalized data and find the Y_c values for each time period.
  c. Divide the deseasonalized data by the trend.
  d. Take a short period moving average of the resultant of step *c.*
  e. Divide the resultant of step *c* by the short period moving average from step *d.*
4. True or false: irregular variation is:
  a. Obtained by taking a short-period moving average of *CI* values.
  b. Isolated to help one tell if the decomposition technique followed has been reasonable and complete.
  c. Any variation in a time series other than *T*, *C*, and *S.*
  d. Usually short-run.
  e. Usually caused by many different factors, even in the same time series.

Answers 7.B

1. a   *2. a.* Ex; *b.* Ex; *c.* En; *d.* En; *e.* Ex; *f.* En   *3. a.* $TCSI/S = TCI$; *b.* $Y_c = T$; *c.* $TCI/T = CI$; *d.* Short-period moving average of $CI = C$; *e.* $CI/C = I$ *4. a.* F; *b.* T; *c.* T; *d.* T; *e.* T

Questions and Problems

7.1. Define seasonal variation. What are the principal causes of seasonal variation? Name 10 products, processes, or activities in business that exhibit strong seasonal variation; 5 that exhibit little seasonal variation; and 2 that might have no seasonal variation.

7.2. One way business has found to combat seasonal variation is to dovetail products that have opposite seasonal patterns but use the same facilities or skills. Two classic examples are the ice and fuel companies, and the Jantzen Company, which discovered that it could make swimming suits with the same materials and machines that it used to make sweaters. Describe some current examples of the dovetailing principle.

7.3. In preparing a report for the manager of a department store, you include statistics on last year's sales by months. Upon seeing them, the president says, "These figures confirm what I've been telling you; business is getting worse and worse." You protest that the figures look pretty good to you. The manager tells you to prepare an index of seasonal variation from past sales data and to deflate the actual sales by the index. The monthly sales and the index are shown below. Upon deflating, do you think the manager's pessimism is justified?

Month	Sales, thousands	Seasonal index	Month	Sales, thousands	Seasonal index
Jan.	56.2	51	July	85.4	96
Feb.	53.1	52	Aug.	77.4	90
Mar.	88.5	84	Sept.	92.2	101
Apr.	91.0	95	Oct.	101.4	118
May	101.6	110	Nov.	116.0	142
June	93.4	99	Dec.	130.2	162

7.4. Quarterly sales for Vervcraft Inc., a leisure-products company, are shown below.

Sales of Vervcraft, Inc.
(Millions)

Year	I	II	III	IV
1967	57	138	183	117
1968	70	175	193	110
1969	66	156	189	101
1970	51	139	175	146
1971	69	183	287	170
1972	101	234	226	161
1973	83	167	214	105
1974	43	115	198	137

Calculate an index of seasonal variation for Vervcraft, Inc., using the method of ratios of data to moving average.

7.5. Using the seasonal index calculated in Prob. 7.4, deseasonalize the sales of Vervcraft, Inc., presented in Prob. 7.4. Fit a linear least-squares trend to the quarterly deseasonalized data and calculate the trend values for each quarter from the least-squares equation.

7.6. Remove the trend from the deseasonalized sales of Vervcraft, Inc. in Prob. 7.5. Calculate the cyclical component by taking a 3-quarter moving average of the resulting *SI* values. (The cyclical values will be in the form of ratios fluctuating around a value of 1.0.) Obtain a measure of the irregular residuals (*I*) by dividing the *SI* values by the corresponding cyclical ratios.

7.7. A company's sales budget for a certain year is 54 million units. Their seasonal variation by quarters is

Quarter	I	II	III	IV
Variation	45	120	175	60

As the year progressed, their sales turned out to be 7 million for the first quarter and 18 million for the second.

a. Calculate their sales for the first two quarters *deseasonalized* at *annual rates*. Explain the meaning of these statistics.

b. Calculate the company's quarterly sales quotas for the year. After the first 2 quarters, by how much do their actual sales differ from budgeted sales? To what time-series components could you attribute this difference?

7.8. Define the business cycle. In classical time-series analyses, why is the cycle calculated as a residual? From your library, find the peaks and troughs of United States business cycles since 1948. From this history, can you make any generalizations about the length of upswings and downswings in the business cycle?

7.9. The data below illustrate (in exaggerated form) the way that ratios of data to moving average (*Si* values) for tourist expenditures in Colorado might look:

Year	I	II	III	IV
1965			1.90	.52
1966	.42	1.12	1.82	.54
1967	.40	1.10	1.86	.62
1968	.44	1.15	1.70	.58
1969	.50	1.13	1.72	.66
1970	.55	1.06	1.60	.65
1971	.65	1.10	1.64	.70
1972	.58	1.09	1.62	.72
1973	.72	1.07	1.50	.76
1974	.75	1.09		
Median	.55	1.10	1.70	.65

a. What does the variation *between* columns, as typified by the median values, represent?

b. What does the variation *within* columns represent?

c. Is there any evidence that the seasonal pattern for tourist expenditures is changing over time?

d. What do you think might cause a change in the seasonal pattern for these data?

e. Calculate an index of seasonal variation you'd be willing to use to forecast next year's quarterly tourist expenditures.

7.10. What is meant by the *reliability* of a seasonal index? How might the reliability of the seasonal for a particular quarter or month be assessed? Make three sketches showing:

a. The pattern of ratios of data to moving average you would expect for a typical quarter or month.

b. The pattern you would expect if the seasonal for that period were increasing over time.

c. The pattern you would expect if the seasonal were becoming more *reliable* over time.

7.11. A large camera company is putting a new camera on the market. They forecast sales to be 420,000 cameras for the first year, and on the basis of past experience with other cameras, they expect their seasonal index to be

Jan.	45	Apr.	87	July	143	Oct.	86
Feb.	40	May	95	Aug.	121	Nov.	130
Mar.	52	June	128	Sept.	94	Dec.	179

Because of the skills involved in making cameras, it is very difficult to vary production from month to month. The company therefore decides that it would be cheaper for them to gear production to a level rate of $420,000/12 = 35,000$ cameras per month and make up monthly differences out of inventory accumulated during the year.

a. They want to produce exactly their forecast demand for cameras and to have 35,000 available for sale Jan. 1. If inventory holding costs are 15 cents per camera per month, what is the total holding cost for the first year's sales?

b. Suppose that the problem is exactly the same as before, except that the company wants to take advantage of Christmas sales by having cameras available on Nov. 1. To just meet peak demand, how many cameras will they have to have available by Nov. 1? What will their inventory holding cost be for their first 12 months of *sales*?

7.12. Find quarterly statistics on GNP in billions of dollars and GNP in billions of 1958 dollars, both seasonally adjusted at annual rates for a recent year. Explain:

a. The significance of differences between quarterly values for each of the series.

b. The significance of differences between the two series for any given quarter.

7.13. The Jet Brush Company invented and developed an electric water-pulse toothbrush in the early 1960s. Since then they have grown rapidly as their sales expanded to a national market. Like many new companies, they really haven't taken time to analyze their past operations, responding more to the pressures of the moment. Now they have reached a level calling for more careful planning and analysis.

Here's where you come in. You get a summer job in their newly formed analysis department, and they present you with the record of their sales (in units) for the past 10 years shown below:

Year	I	II	III	IV
1965	1110	1952	2,578	3,249
1966	1429	2082	3,480	4,203
1967	2237	2871	4,811	6,593
1968	2585	3613	4,363	5,908
1969	2124	3000	3,906	4,702
1970	1886	2260	4,714	5,359
1971	2938	4724	7,256	8,738
1972	4555	6437	9,355	11,942
1973	4824	6565	10,568	10,220
1974	5297	6240	8,226	10,034

A quick glance at these data shows that there is a strong seasonal variation. Find the index of seasonal variation using the method of ratios of data to moving average.

7.14. Provided with the seasonal index for the Jet Brush data of Prob. 7.13, you decide to continue your analysis by finding an appropriate trend equation.

    a. Deseasonalize the original data using the index calculated in Prob. 7.13.

    b. Plot the deseasonalized data on arithmetic and semilog grids.

    c. Fit a geometric line of least squares to the deseasonalized data and calculate the trend values for each quarter.

7.15. Continuing the analysis of the Jet Brush data of Probs. 7.13 and 7.14, you decide to isolate the business cycle and irregular components.

    a. Divide the deseasonalized data from Prob. 7.13 by the corresponding trend values calculated in Prob. 7.14. Take a 3-quarter moving average of these data to isolate the cyclical relatives.

    b. Isolate the irregular relatives by dividing the deseasonalized, detrended *CI* values above by the 3-quarter moving average data *C.*

7.16. Having completed the time-series decomposition of the Jet Brush Company sales (Probs. 7.13 to 7.15), you proudly turn in your analysis to your boss. It consists of about 50 pages of data, computer output, and scratch paper, with not one word of text. Your boss looks through the pile for about 30 seconds and returns it to you, saying not too politely: "I don't want to wade through all this mess. I want a concise report of your analysis, including what you did, what you found, and what it means." Write such an analysis, including only relevant data and its interpretation.

MODULE 8
THE ANALYSIS OF ASSOCIATION

In Module 3 you learned some techniques of quantitative analysis by considering the mean and variance of distributions of *single variables*, such as income or sales. In Modules 6 and 7 you continued the analysis of single variables, but you analyzed them through time. Thus, you implicitly added a new variable (time) to the analysis and you examined the relationship between sales (or profits, etc.) and time.

In this module you'll see that the relationship between *any* two variables can be examined through the use of *association analysis*. Instead of studying only sales through time or income through time, you might want to consider the relationship *between* sales and income. In analyzing the relationship between these or other variables, you might be concerned with measuring the nature or *direction* of the relationship and the extent, or *degree*, of the relationship.

The data you might wish to analyze could consist of an entire population (such as the ages and incomes of all of the employees in a company) or only a sample (such as the ages and incomes of a sample of 100 employees), which you want to use to represent the entire population. No distinction will be made between these problems in this module. However, you should realize that there are special problems involved in using sample results to make inferences about populations, since it is unlikely that any one sample will correspond exactly to the population. A discussion of these concepts will be postponed until Module 14, after you have learned about sampling distributions and statistical inference.

General learning objectives

Your general learning objectives for this module are to be able to:

1. Solve least-squares equations for estimating the value of a variable through the use of another variable
2. Measure the total, explained, and unexplained variation and the standard error of estimate
3. Measure the extent and direction of the relationship between two variables, using the coefficient of determination, the covariance, and the coefficient of correlation

Section 8.A

The Linear Model of the Relationship between Two Variables

Learning objectives

Your learning objectives for this section are to be able to:

1. State the relationship between two variables in terms of a linear model
2. Define the various terms in the linear model

Suppose you were a manufacturer of farm tractors and were trying to develop an accurate means for estimating next year's sales. During your investigation you obtained a series of figures showing farm income for a number of years and the corresponding sales of tractors in the following year. These data are shown in Table 8.1 and are plotted as a *scatter diagram* in Fig. 8.1.

Table 8.1 / Farm income and tractor sales, 1963–1972

Year	Farm income preceding year X, billions	Tractor sales Y, units
1963	$37.8	23,000
1964	38.9	24,000
1965	39.1	27,000
1966	41.5	28,000
1967	46.5	33,000
1968	45.9	34,000
1969	47.8	31,000
1970	51.2	36,000
1971	54.2	37,000
1972	55.9	44,000

Looking at Fig. 8.1, you might note that the points are scattered along a reasonably straight line, so you could draw such a line and use it to express the general relationship between the two variables or to estimate sales on the basis of the prior year's income.

163

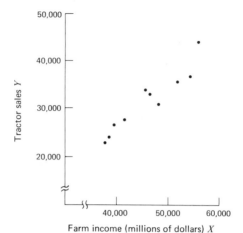

Figure 8.1 / Farm income vs. tractor sales the previous year, 1963–1972.

Realizing that different people would probably draw different lines and that a more objective method for finding the line is needed, so that everyone who uses the method will arrive at the same answer, you recall the line of *least squares*, which you used in trend analysis in Module 5.

All the *estimating equations* used in the analysis of association in this module (and later in regression analysis) will be least-squares lines. Such lines will be fitted using the same *normal equations* that were used in trend analysis.[1]

The formula for the least-squares line in association analysis is

$$\overline{Y}_X = a + bX$$

where $\overline{Y}_X$ = predicted value of *dependent* variable
X = value of *independent* variable

The dependent variable is the one that is to be predicted using the estimating equation, and it is usually measured on the vertical axis. The independent variable is the one that is used to predict the dependent variable (through the use of the estimating equation), and it is usually measured on the horizontal axis.

Remember from Module 5 that a is the Y intercept at the origin (where $X = 0$) and b is the slope (the change in Y per unit change in X).

---

[1] The symbols used will be different, however. In Module 5 you used Y_c to represent a value on the trend line. Here you'll use the symbol $\overline{Y}_X$ to represent a point on the estimating equation. The reason for the change in notation is that in time-series analysis there was only one Y value for any value of X, whereas in association there could be many Y values for any value of X. The mean of the Y values for a *given* value of X is represented by $\overline{Y}_X$, the *conditional* mean of Y, given X.

The relationship we originally observed between X and Y can now be expressed as a mathematical model that incorporates the least-squares equation. This model is expressed as

$$Y = a + bX + e$$

where e, the vertical deviation between a Y value and the corresponding $\overline{Y}_X$ value for any given value of X, represents the *error term*. This error term comes about because other factors besides X influence Y.[1] In our case we have assumed that tractor sales are related to farm income in the prior year, but it is apparent from Fig. 8.1 that there is some variation in sales caused by factors other than income since the Y values could not fall on *any* straight line drawn through them. Even if there were two years with the same farm income, you wouldn't expect tractor sales to be exactly the same in the following years. Thus for each value of farm income (or any independent variable X), you'd expect to find a *conditional distribution* of tractor sales (or any dependent variable Y). For example, there could be a number of years when farm income was 50 billion dollars and the range of the following year's tractor sales could be from 28,000 to 42,000 units. This conditional distribution might look like that shown in Fig. 8.2. Like any distribution, it has a mean $\overline{Y}_X$ and a standard deviation $s_{Y \cdot X}$. The subscripts contain X's to remind you that the distribution is conditional on a particular value of X.

The *mean* of the conditional distribution $\overline{Y}_X$ is simply the value computed from the least-squares equation at a particular value of X. You'll learn later in this module

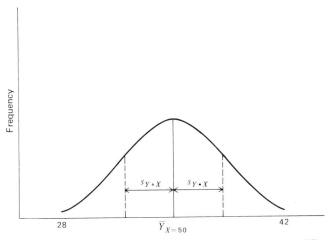

Figure 8.2 / Conditional distribution of Y given $X = 50$ billion dollars, tractor-sales data.

---

[1] If the only factor actually affecting Y were X, all Y values would be equal to their corresponding $\overline{Y}_X$ values, the error terms would all be zero, and you could make perfect estimates of Y using the equation $\overline{Y}_X = a + bX$.

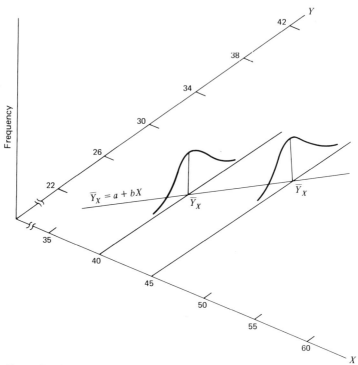

Figure 8.3 / Conditional distributions of Y; tractor sales Y vs. income X.

how to compute the conditional variance $s^2_{Y \cdot X}$ from the error terms. For the moment we'll assume that this variance is the same for all possible values of X. Figure 8.3 gives a three-dimensional view of the conditional distribution of Y at several X values, and you can see that while the mean $\bar{Y}_X$ changes, the conditional variance $s^2_{Y \cdot X}$, remains constant.

More restrictive assumptions will be added in Module 14, because as we move from description to statistical inference, we find that qualifications must be made on the model.

REVIEW EXERCISES 8.A

1. What is the mathematical model that represents sales as a linear function of income?
2. Draw a picture that illustrates the meaning of a, b, and e in the expression $Y = a + bX + e$.
3. In Exercise 1, which is the independent variable and which is the dependent variable?
4. What assumption is made about the variances of the conditional distributions in the linear model?
    a. They get larger as X gets larger.
    b. They are equal.
    c. No assumption is made.
5. $\bar{Y}_X$ is the conditional mean, or predicted value, from the linear model: true or false?
6. $s^2_{Y \cdot X}$ is the variance of Y values around $\bar{Y}$: true or false?

Answers 8.A

1. Sales $= a + b$ (income) or $\bar{Y}_X = a + bX$.

2.

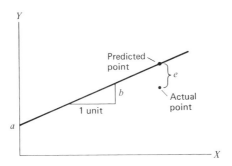

3. Sales is the dependent variable. Income is the independent variable.
4. b. They're equal.
5. true
6. False; $s_{Y \cdot X}^2$ is the variance of Y values around the predicted value $\bar{Y}_X$ from the estimating equation.

Section 8.B

Estimating the Model's Coefficients

Learning objectives

Your learning objectives for this section are to be able to:

1. Use the least-squares approach to estimate the coefficients of the linear model
2. Predict values through the use of the estimating equation

Before fitting a least-squares estimating equation to the tractor-sales–farm-income data, let's review the least-squares criterion developed in Module 5. A line of least squares is the line that minimizes the sum of the squared error terms for all the data points. Remember that an error term is the deviation between any Y value and its corresponding $\bar{Y}_X$ value.

Thus, solving for the error term in the equation

$$Y = a + bX + e$$

gives
$$e = Y - (a + bX) \quad \text{or} \quad e = Y - \bar{Y}_X$$

since
$$\bar{Y}_X = a + bX$$

Then, squaring the error term and summing over all the data points yields

$$\sum e^2 = \sum (Y - a - bX)^2$$

167

Table 8.2 / Computations for least-squares estimating equation, tractor-sales–farm-income data

Farm income preceding year X, millions	Tractor sales Y, number of units	XY	X^2
$37,800	23,000	869,400,000	1,428,840,000
38,900	24,000	933,600,000	1,513,210,000
39,100	27,000	1,055,700,000	1,528,810,000
41,500	28,000	1,162,000,000	1,722,250,000
46,500	33,000	1,534,500,000	2,162,250,000
45,900	34,000	1,560,600,000	2,106,810,000
47,800	31,000	1,481,800,000	2,284,840,000
51,200	36,000	1,843,200,000	2,621,440,000
54,200	37,000	2,005,400,000	2,937,640,000
55,900	44,000	2,459,600,000	3,124,810,000
$458,800	317,000	14,905,800,000	21,430,900,000

The calculus for finding the particular a and b values that minimize this squared error was developed in a footnote on page 121. The solution gave two *normal equations*

$$\sum Y = na + b \sum X \quad \text{and} \quad \sum XY = a \sum X + b \sum X^2$$

These sums are calculated for the tractor-sales–farm-income data in Table 8.2. Substituting in the normal equations gives

$$317,000 = 10a + 458,800b$$
$$14,905,800,000 = 458,800a + 21,430,900,000b$$

Solving these equations simultaneously for a and b, as in Module 5, you'd find that the least-squares estimating equation is

$$\bar{Y}_X = -11,854 + .94932X$$

ESTIMATING USING THE EQUATION

From this equation you might observe the danger of applying results out of the range of the independent variable. It says, for example, that if farm income were zero ($X = 0$), tractor sales would be a *negative* 11,854 units. Since negative sales are impossible, the equation clearly is *not* appropriate for a zero farm-income figure. In fact, the equation is strictly appropriate only for farm incomes within the range of the observed data (from 37,800 to 55,900), and caution should be used when substituting values of farm income far outside that range.

The second thing you can learn from this equation is that tractor sales may be expected (on the average) to go up by .94932 unit for each unit change in farm income.

Remember that farm income is in millions of dollars, so an increase of 1 million dollars in aggregate farm income could be expected to cause an increase in the company's tractor sales of approximately 1 unit.

Suppose that you wanted to predict next year's tractor sales for the company. Knowing the relationship that has existed in the past between farm income and tractor sales and assuming the same relationship will exist in the near future, you might be willing to use the estimating equation developed above. The only piece of information you'd need is this year's farm income. Of course, you could wait until February of next year to find out what farm income was for this year (that is when the figures will be published). However, since that may be too long to wait, you might have to use preliminary estimates of farm income for this year. The closer it is to the end of this year, the more accurate the estimates will be, and the more confidence you'll have in the estimates.

Suppose you expected farm income for this year to be 58,000 million dollars. Using the equation developed above, you'd predict next year's tractor sales to be

$$\overline{Y}_X = -11,854 + .94932(58,000) = 43,207 \text{ units}$$

Remember that the farther you extend beyond the range of observed values, the less likely your prediction will be correct, because it is possible that the linear estimating equation you are using is no longer valid. However, since the 58,000 farm-income figure is not far from the 55,900 maximum of the observed values, the assumption of continued linearity is probably not overtaxed.

SUMMARY

We initially posed the problem of having a plot of points showing the relationship between two variables and asked what the best-fitting straight line would be. The criterion chosen was to minimize the sum of the squared errors, and this resulted in the set of simultaneous equations

$$\sum Y = na + b \sum X$$
$$\sum XY = a \sum X + b \sum X^2$$

These can be solved for a and b in the equation for the straight line

$$\overline{Y}_X = a + bX$$

This equation can then be used for prediction purposes or simply to describe the nature of the relationship between the two variables. In prediction, the values of the independent variable X should not go far beyond the range of values used to estimate the equation.

169

REVIEW EXERCISES 8.B

1. What criterion was used to find the best-fitting straight line?
  a. Minimize the sum of the deviations around the line.
  b. Maximize the absolute squared deviation around the line.
  c. The line that best reproduces the normal equations.
  d. None of the above.
2. State the normal equations for estimating a linear relationship between two variables.
3. What is one major use of the estimating equation?
  a. Simply knowing what *a* and *b* are.
  b. Prediction.
  c. Being able to regress backward in time.
  d. All the above.

Answers 8.B

1. d. None of these. The criterion is least squares, to minimize the sum of the squared deviations around the estimating equation.
2. $\sum Y = na + b \sum X; \sum XY = a \sum X + b \sum X^2$ *3. b.* prediction

---

Section 8.C
Additional Considerations in the Analysis of Association

Learning objectives

Your learning objectives for this section are to be able to describe:

1. The results of switching the dependent and the independent variables
2. What happens when either or both of the axes are shifted before computing the equation
3. Two particular modifications so the linear model can be used to fit nonlinear situations

---

DIRECTIONALITY AND CAUSATION

In the problem involving tractor sales and farm income, there was no question which was to be the independent variable and which the dependent. You wanted to predict next year's tractor sales on the basis of this year's income, so you made income the independent variable X and sales the dependent variable Y. You'd hardly be interested in reversing the direction and attempting to predict last year's income on the basis of this year's sales!

Now let's consider a problem involving the relation between *employment* in a number of companies in a certain industry and the *output* of those companies. If you wanted to predict output on the basis of employment, the problem would be formulated using employment as the independent variable and output as the dependent variable. On the other hand, if you worked for the personnel department, you might just as logically want to predict employment based on expected output and therefore make output the independent variable and employment the dependent.

If you switched the roles of independent and dependent variables and recomputed a least-squares estimating equation, would you get the same line as before? The answer is generally no. In fact, the only case where you would obtain the same line is when all the *original* data points fall on a straight line and there is no error term.

Consider the data in Table 8.3, which shows employment and output for 10

Table 8.3 / Employment and output for 10 companies

Company	Employment	Output	Company	Employment	Output
A	100	500	F	420	2700
B	220	800	G	300	2800
C	120	1300	H	410	3500
D	240	1600	I	590	3800
E	350	2000	J	470	3900

companies. If you fitted two least-squares lines to these data, one using output as the dependent variable and the other using employment as the dependent variable, you'd get

$$\bar{E}_O = 59.108 + .1148O$$
$$\bar{O}_E = -21.6058 + 7.1789E$$

where O = output
E = employment

These lines are plotted in Fig. 8.4, and it is clear that they are different. This is because the line $\bar{E}_O = a + b(O)$ minimizes the *vertical* squared errors $\sum (E - \bar{E}_O)^2$, while the line $\bar{O}_E = a + b(E)$ minimizes the *horizontal* squared errors $\sum (O - \bar{O}_E)^2$. The only point the lines share is where they cross at the mean of output and employment.

When employment is the dependent variable, the a value of 59.108 is the employment level at zero output and the b value of .1148 is the required number of additional employees necessary for a unit increase in production. When output is the dependent variable, the a value of -21.6058 is the output level at zero employment and the b value shows that each added employee increases output by 7.1789 units.

It should now be clear that which variable is to be the independent and which the dependent must be specified *before* computing the estimating equation. You *cannot*

171

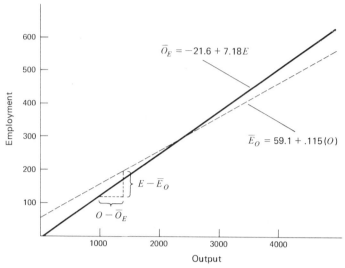

Figure 8.4 / Least-squares lines for employment vs. output.

estimate a value for output by substituting a value of employment in the equation $\bar{E}_O = a + bO$ and solving for O. In order to estimate O, you must use the equation $\bar{O}_E = a + bE$.

So far, nothing has been said about *causation*. If the estimating equations fit the data well, you can make accurate estimates of either variable in terms of the other as long as you use the appropriate equation. If two variables are causally related, you don't have to make the cause the independent variable and the effect the dependent. In fact, people often do just the opposite. For example, we estimate temperature on the basis of the height of a column of mercury, though it is clear that the temperature is the cause and the height of the column is the effect. You should not make any assumptions about causality on the basis of how you construct a particular estimating equation.

SHIFTING AXES AND CHANGING SCALE

Computing least-squares estimating equations can be simplified if the sum of the X values and the sum of the Y values can be made to add to zero. This can be accomplished by expressing the X and Y values as deviations from their arithmetic means. (Remember from Module 3 that one of the characteristics of the arithmetic mean is that the sum of the deviations between a set of numbers and their arithmetic mean is zero.)

172

Table 8.4 / Calculation of estimating equation using coded values, employment vs. output

(1) Company	(2) Employment Y	(3) Output X	(4) $Y' = Y - \bar{Y}$	(5) $X' = X - \bar{X}$	(6) $X'Y'$	(7) $(X')^2$
A	100	500	− 222	− 1790	397,380	3,204,100
B	220	800	− 102	− 1490	151,980	2,220,100
C	120	1,300	− 202	− 990	199,980	980,100
D	240	1,600	− 82	− 690	56,580	476,100
E	350	2,000	28	− 290	− 8,120	84,100
F	420	2,700	98	410	40,180	168,100
G	300	2,800	− 22	510	− 11,220	260,100
H	410	3,500	88	1210	106,480	1,464,100
I	590	3,800	268	1510	404,680	2,280,100
J	470	3,900	148	1610	238,280	2,592,100
	3220	22,900	0	0	1,576,200	13,729,000

$$\sum Y' = na + b \sum X' \qquad \sum X'Y' = a \sum X' + b \sum (X')^2$$
$$0 = na + 0 \qquad\qquad a = 0$$
$$1,576,200 = 0 + 13,729,000b \qquad b = .1148$$
$$\bar{Y}'_X = .1148X'$$

The employment-output data from Table 8.3 are shown in Table 8.4, together with the coded values and the sums necessary for the solution of the least-squares equation for estimating employment when output is known. The solution of the equation using the coded values is shown as part of Table 8.4. Note that since $\sum Y'$ and $\sum X'$ are both equal to zero, the solution for a and b is very easy. The estimating equation is

$$\bar{Y}'_X = .1148X'$$

where the primes on X' and $\bar{Y}'_X$ indicate that they are deviations from their respective means.

It can easily be shown that this equation represents exactly the same least-squares line that was calculated earlier. The equation above can be decoded by substituting the identities $\bar{Y}_X - \bar{Y}$ for $\bar{Y}'_X$ and $X - \bar{X}$ for X', as follows:

$$\bar{Y}_X - \bar{Y} = .1148(X - \bar{X})$$
$$\bar{Y}_X = \bar{Y} + .1148(X - \bar{X})$$
$$\bar{Y}_X = 322 + .1148(X - \bar{X})$$
$$\bar{Y}_X = 59.108 + .1148X$$

or
$$\bar{E}_O = 59.108 + .1148O$$

173

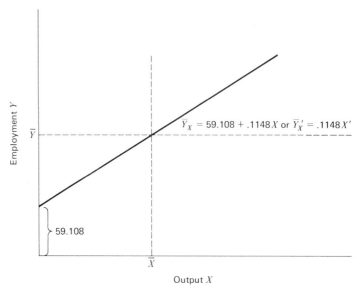

Figure 8.5 / Effect of coding in terms of deviations from mean X and mean Y for employment-output example.

Figure 8.5 shows what the coding accomplished. The axis was shifted so that instead of a being equal to 59.108 where $X = 0$, it is now equal to zero when the axis is placed at $(\overline{X}, \overline{Y})$. The slope, .1148, is of course unchanged by shifting the axis.

For some applications, other forms of transformation are desirable. One common application is to *standardize* the variables by expressing deviations from the means in terms of the respective standard deviations. The standardized values would then be

$$X' = \frac{X - \overline{X}}{s_X} \quad \text{and} \quad Y' = \frac{Y - \overline{Y}}{s_Y}$$

EXTENSIONS TO NONLINEAR MODELS

It is possible to use the least-squares procedure for other than linear models. For example, you might propose a parabolic relationship between variables (as was discussed in Module 6 for a time series). In this case, the model is

$$Y = a + bX + cX^2 + e$$

174

and the normal equations are

$$\sum Y = na + b \sum X + c \sum X^2$$
$$\sum XY = a \sum X + b \sum X^2 + c \sum X^3$$
$$\sum X^2 Y = a \sum X^2 + b \sum X^3 + c \sum X^4$$

The three equations could then be solved for the unknowns a, b, and c.

Higher-order polynomial models can be used, as well as other forms such as the exponential. In many such cases, the equation can be changed to linear form, say by using logs, and the normal equations applied to the transformed values. You may want to review the material in Module 6 to see how this was done.

REVIEW EXERCISES 8.C

1. For the employment-output example of Table 8.3, assume that the X and Y values for company J were $X = 3900$, $Y = 750$, rather than 3900 and 470.
   a. Plot the 10 points on a graph and indicate whether a straight line represents the true nature of the relationship.
   b. What factors could cause the relationship that you see?
   c. Propose an alternative to the linear model; i.e., what type of equation would you use?
   d. Going back to the original data, assume you liked the straight line you used to estimate output from employment but wanted to shift axes by taking deviations from the means. What would the new equation be? (Do this without going through all the computations again.)
2. A major caution in making predictions based on a least-squares estimating equation is that you should not predict with values of the independent variable that are far outside the range of values used to find the equation: true or false?
3. Reversing the roles of the dependent and independent variables:
   a. Doesn't change the estimating equation.
   b. Changes the estimating equation only in the sense that the intercept and slope coefficients are measured along a different axis.
   c. Creates an entirely new line.

Answers 8.C

1. a. The line appears to be curved, so a straight line doesn't seem appropriate.
   b. The curve becomes asymptotic near an output of 4500, indicating that the addition of more employees won't increase output, possibly because of restrictions on plant size. The shape of the curve indicates a decreasing marginal return from the addition of new employees (each one adds less to output).
   c. A better fit might be obtained with a quadratic equation $\bar{Y}_X = a + bX + cX^2$.
   d. Shifting along both axes, the equation would be $\bar{Y}_X' = 7.18X'$.
2. true
3. c. An entirely new line is created (unless the association is perfect).

175

Section 8.D

Variation, the Coefficients of Determination and Correlation, and Covariance

Learning objectives

Your learning objectives for this section are to be able to:

1. Calculate the standard error of estimate and the total, explained, and unexplained variations
2. Calculate and interpret the coefficient of determination
3. Calculate and interpret the covariance and the coefficient of correlation

Now that you've learned how to fit an estimating equation describing the association between two variables, you may ask: How *strong* is this association? In this section we'll develop three measures to answer this question: the coefficient of determination, the covariance, and the coefficient of correlation.

The need for a measure of the strength of the association between two variables is illustrated in the scatter diagrams of Fig. 8.6, where identical estimating equations might describe the association in the three cases but the strength of the association varies. In Fig. 8.6a, every data point falls on a straight line, indicating a perfect relationship between the two variables. Using an estimating equation, you could predict a value of Y through the use of X with absolute confidence. Figure 8.6b illustrates a strong but not perfect association. While the points would not all fall on the estimating equation, their scatter about it would be small. Figure 8.6c shows a very weak association; you'd have little confidence in predicting a Y value using an estimating equation.

THE STANDARD ERROR OF ESTIMATE AND THE COEFFICIENT OF DETERMINATION

Considering the scatter diagrams in Fig. 8.6, you must have been struck by the notion that the extent of the scatter of the data points about the estimating equation could provide a measure of the strength of the association. In fact, two measures, the *standard error of estimate* $s_{Y \cdot X}$ and the *coefficient of determination*, can be developed this way.

176

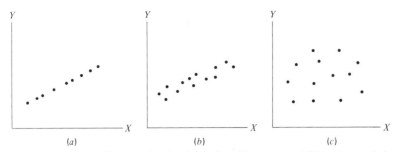

Figure 8.6 / Scatter diagrams showing (*a*) perfect, (*b*) strong, and (*c*) weak association between two variables.

As noted in Fig. 8.2, the standard error of estimate is the standard deviation of a set of Y values about their conditional mean $\overline{Y}_X$. Since we assumed that this standard deviation was the same for all conditional means, we can measure it using the squared error terms for all the data points. These $(Y - \overline{Y}_X)^2$ values are the same values that were minimized in developing the line of least squares. Thus, $\sum (Y - \overline{Y}_X)^2/n$ is $s_{Y \cdot X}^2$, the *conditional* variance, and its square root,

$$s_{Y \cdot X} = \sqrt{\frac{\sum (Y - \overline{Y}_X)^2}{n}}$$

is the *standard error of estimate.*

It is clear from Fig. 8.6 that with perfect association the standard error of estimate is zero, and as the association becomes weaker, the standard error of estimate becomes larger. In Fig. 8.6c, the standard error of estimate becomes as large as the standard deviation $\sqrt{\sum (Y - \overline{Y})^2/n}$, and there is no useful association at all.

Before defining the coefficient of determination, we must identify three types of squared errors, the total, the unexplained, and the explained variation, defined as

$$\text{Total variation} = \sum (Y - \overline{Y})^2$$
$$\text{Explained variation} = \sum (\overline{Y}_X - \overline{Y})^2$$
$$\text{Unexplained variation} = \sum (Y - \overline{Y}_X)^2$$

The meaning of these measures should become clear from Fig. 8.7, which shows the estimating equation for predicting the weight of male college students based on their height, the mean weight of all of the students, and the height and weight of one particular student. The *total variation* $\sum (Y - \overline{Y})^2$ is a measure of the squared error that would be involved in using the mean of Y as an estimator of the weight of a student picked from the group at random. For the particular point in the illustration,

177

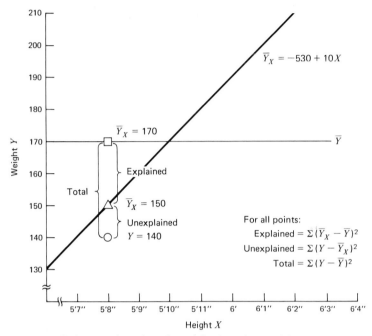

Figure 8.7 / The meaning of total, explained, and unexplained variation for height vs. weight.

this student weighed 140 lb, but if you knew nothing about his height, your best guess of his weight would be the mean of the group, or 170 lb. His contribution to the total variation would then be $(140 - 170)^2 = 900$.

The *explained variation*, $\sum (\bar{Y}_X - \bar{Y})^2$, is a measure of how much better you can predict using the estimating equation than using the mean of Y. If you'd been told that the student chosen at random was 5 ft 8 in tall and you had the estimating equation $\bar{Y}_X = -530 + 10X$, you'd predict that he weighs 150 lb. If someone asked why you predicted that he weighs 150 lb rather than the 170 lb you predicted before you knew his height, you'd say that the 20-lb difference was *explained* by the fact that he is shorter than average by 2 in and therefore is expected to weigh less than average by 20 lb.

The *unexplained variation*, $\sum (Y - \bar{Y}_X)^2$, is a measure of the residual error, or the amount of variation in weight that is *not* attributable to height. How would you explain the fact that the person in question weighed 10 lb less than he should for his height? You couldn't. It might be that his bones were smaller than average, that he didn't get enough to eat, or that he worried a lot, but with only the information at hand, you just don't know. (As you'll see in Module 16, if you could measure these other variables, you might be able to include them in the estimating equation and improve your predicting ability.)

178

The coefficient of determination r^2 is simply the ratio of the explained to the total variation.[1]

$$\text{Coefficient of determination} = r^2 = \frac{\text{explained variation}}{\text{total variation}}$$

$$= \frac{\sum (\bar{Y}_X - \bar{Y})^2}{\sum (Y - \bar{Y})^2}$$

Since the explained plus the unexplained variation equals the total variation, the coefficient of determination can also be expressed as

$$r^2 = 1 - \frac{\text{unexplained variation}}{\text{total variation}} = 1 - \frac{\sum (Y - \bar{Y}_X)^2}{\sum (Y - \bar{Y})^2}$$

Noting that $\sum (Y - \bar{Y}_X)^2$ is the numerator in the calculation of the standard error of estimate and that $\sum (Y - \bar{Y})^2$ is the numerator in the calculation of the standard deviation, we see that the last equation reduces to

$$r^2 = 1 - \frac{s_{Y \cdot X}^2}{s_Y^2}$$

This expression quantifies what we observed before, that the smaller the standard error of estimate, the stronger the extent of the association.

The coefficient of determination is interpreted in a very straightforward way. Multiplied by 100, it is simply the percent improvement in predicting ability that you obtain through the use of the estimating equation rather than the use of the mean.

Table 8.5 shows the calculations of the total, explained, and unexplained variations and the coefficient of determination for the output-employment example of Table 8.4.

COVARIANCE AND COEFFICIENT OF CORRELATION

The strength of the association between two variables can also be measured using *covariance* and the *coefficient of correlation*, which are closely related to the standard error of estimate and the coefficient of determination.

To illustrate the concept of covariance, consider the scatter diagrams in Fig. 8.8, which show the scatter of data points about dotted lines representing the mean of X and the mean of Y. In Fig. 8.8a, most of the data points fall in the first and third

---

[1] The symbol r^2 is used because the coefficient of determination is the square of the coefficient of correlation, which will be developed later.

Table 8.5 / Calculation of total, explained, and unexplained variation and the coefficient of determination, employment Y vs. output X

Co.	Employment Y	Output X	$Y - \bar{Y} = Y'$	Total variation $(Y')^2$	$\hat{Y}'_x$	$\hat{Y}'_x + \bar{Y} = \hat{Y}_x$	$Y - \hat{Y}_x$	Unexplained variation $(Y - \hat{Y}_x)^2$	$\hat{Y}_x - \bar{Y}$	Explained variation $(\hat{Y}_x - \bar{Y})^2$
A	100	500	−222	49,284	−205.5	116.5	−16.5	272	−205.5	42,230
B	220	800	−102	10,404	−171.1	150.9	+69.1	4,775	−171.1	29,275
C	120	1,300	−202	40,804	−113.7	208.3	−88.3	7,797	−113.7	12,928
D	240	1,600	− 82	6,724	− 79.2	242.8	− 2.8	8	− 79.2	6,273
E	350	2,000	28	784	− 33.3	288.7	+61.3	3,758	− 33.3	1,109
F	420	2,700	98	9,604	47.1	369.1	+50.9	2,591	+ 47.1	2,218
G	300	2,800	− 22	484	58.5	380.5	−80.5	6,480	+ 58.5	3,422
H	410	3,500	88	7,744	138.9	460.9	−50.9	2,591	+138.9	19,293
I	590	3,800	268	71,824	173.3	495.3	+94.7	8,968	+173.3	30,033
J	470	3,900	148	21,904	184.8	506.8	−36.8	1,354	+184.8	34,151
	3,220	22,900	0	219,560			0.0	38,594	0.0	180,932

Least-squares equation (from Table 8.4): $\hat{Y}'_x = .1148X'$

$$r^2 = \frac{\text{explained var}}{\text{total var}} = \frac{180,932}{219,560} = .82$$

or

$$r^2 = 1 - \frac{\text{unexplained var}}{\text{total var}} = 1 - \frac{38,594}{219,560} = .82$$

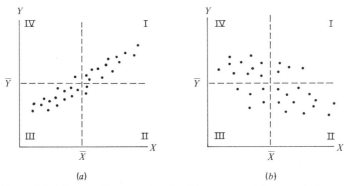

Figure 8.8 / Scatter diagrams showing (a) strong positive association and (b) weak negative association.

quadrants. If a data point falls above the mean of X, it usually falls above the mean of Y as well. If a point falls below the mean of X, it usually falls below the mean of Y. There are very few points in the second and fourth quadrants. Overall, the relationship seems high (because the points would show little dispersion about a line drawn through them) and positive (because high values of X tend to be associated with high values of Y and low values of X with low values of Y). In Figure 8.8b, most of the data points fall in the second and fourth quadrants. Negative deviations from the mean of X are generally associated with positive deviations from the mean of Y, and vice versa. The scatter shows that the association is not strong and that the relationship is negative, since low values of X are associated with high values of Y while high values of X are associated with low values of Y.

You could obtain a measure of the direction and strength of the relationship by computing the deviations of each point from the mean of X and the mean of Y, multiplying these paired deviations together, and finally adding the cross products of the deviations over all the points. This sum is exactly the same as the one you obtained when calculating the least-squares estimating equation using coded values (see the sum of column 6 in Table 8.4).

Dividing the sum of the cross products of X and Y, when expressed as deviations from their respective means, by n, the number of data points, produces a measure of association called the *covariance* (cov) between X and Y :

$$\text{cov}(X,Y) = \frac{\Sigma(X'Y')}{n}$$

Thus for the output-employment data of Table 8.4, the covariance is

$$\text{cov}(X,Y) = +\frac{1{,}576{,}200}{10} = 157{,}620$$

181

One problem with the covariance is that its value depends on the dimensions of the original data. For example, if output in Table 8.4 had been measured in hundreds of units rather than single units, the covariance would have been 1576.2 rather than 157,620.

A dimensionless value showing the extent and direction of the association can be obtained by dividing the covariance by the standard deviation of X and the standard deviation of Y. This value is the *coefficient of correlation*:

$$\text{Coefficient of correlation} = r = \frac{\text{cov }(X,Y)}{s_X s_Y} = \frac{\sum (X'Y')}{n s_X s_Y}$$

For the output-employment example of Table 8.4,

$$s_X = \sqrt{\frac{\sum (X')^2}{n}} = 1172 \qquad \text{and} \qquad s_Y = \sqrt{\frac{\sum (Y')^2}{n}} = 148.2$$

The coefficient of correlation is then

$$r = +\frac{157,620}{1172(148.2)} = +.91$$

The coefficient of correlation is a dimensionless value that shows the extent and direction of the association between two variables. It can vary between -1 (perfect negative correlation) and $+1$ (perfect positive correlation). A correlation coefficient of zero indicates total absence of correlation.

As mentioned earlier, the coefficient of determination is the square of the coefficient of correlation. Thus for the output-employment example,

$$\text{Coefficient of determination} = r^2 = .82$$
$$\text{Coefficient of correlation} = r = +.91$$

In obtaining the coefficient of correlation from the coefficient of determination, you'd attach to the square root of r^2 the sign of the slope in the estimating equation, which will always be the same as the sign of the covariance used to calculate the coefficient of correlation.

REVIEW EXERCISES 8.D

1. Draw a plot of points where the correlation is zero, and explain why.
2. Suppose you computed covariance, where one of the variables was scaled in thousands, and you wanted to recompute the covariance with the variable scaled in units. You could do this by:
   a. Dividing the original covariance by 1000.

b. Multiplying the original covariance by 1000^2.

c. Multiplying the original covariance by 1000.

d. Making no change at all.

3. The correlation coefficient will always lie between 0 and 1: true or false?

4. The correlation coefficient is the covariance divided by the product of the variances of the two variables: true or false?

5. The coefficient of determination is the square root of the correlation coefficient: true or false?

6. Residual error is:

a. The variance of the dependent variable.

b. The error explained by the estimating equation.

c. The sum of the squared error around the estimating equation.

7. Write the formulas for calculating the total, explained, and unexplained variations.

Answers 8.D

1. This is one possible plot. There is no correlation because you cannot predict Y any better by using $\bar{Y}_X = a + bX$ than by simply using $\bar{Y}$.

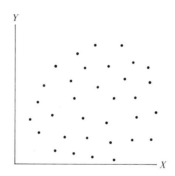

2. c. If one of the variables is multiplied by 1000, the covariance will also increase by 1000 (and so will the standard deviation of the variable, showing why scale cancels out when you use correlation).

3. False; it will lie between -1 and $+1$.

4. False; the correlation coefficient is the covariance divided by the product of the *standard deviations* of the two variables.

5. False; the coefficient of determination is the square (not the square root) of the correlation coefficient.

6. c

7. Total variation $= \sum (Y - \bar{Y})^2$; explained variation $= \sum (\bar{Y}_X - \bar{Y})^2$; unexplained variation $= \sum (Y - \bar{Y}_X)^2$

Questions and Problems

8.1. Assume that you work for a manufacturing company which purchased a new automatic machine with a variable output rate. In determining how fast to run the machine in normal operation, you need to know what the relationship is between the speed of the machine and the error rate in output. You set up an experiment where the machine is operated for two full days at each of several speeds within the operating range of the machine, and obtain the following sample data:

Speed of machine X, output per hour	Error rate Y, number of errors per 8-hour day	Speed of machine X, output per hour	Error rate Y, number of errors per 8-hour day
100	13	100	6
125	14	125	19
150	23	150	18
175	20	175	27
200	28	200	32

a. Plot these data on an arithmetic grid.

b. Compute the estimating equation $\bar{Y}_X = a + bX$, using the method of least squares, and plot it on the graph in part a.

c. Interpret the meaning of the coefficients a and b in the estimating equation as they relate to this problem.

d. Calculate the standard error of estimate.

e. Calculate the covariance between X and Y, the coefficient of correlation, and the coefficient of determination. Explain their meaning.

f. If you chose to run the machine at an output of 175 pieces per hour, how many errors would you expect in an 8-hour day?

8.2. As a trainee in the industrial management department of a manufacturing company, you're interested in the relationship between the level of background noise and work efficiency. On the basis of pretesting, you choose a sample of 10 supervisors who are equally adept at the task of scheduling jobs on machines in a job shop, and who are also generally equivalent in background, education, and other relevant variables. You place each person in a separate room with differing noise levels and give them all the same task to do. The respective noise levels for the 10 subjects and the length of time required to complete the task are:

Noise X, decibels	Time Y, min	Noise X, decibels	Time Y, min
0	11.5	0	9.5
20	12.5	20	13.0
40	14.0	40	16.0
60	20.0	60	19.5
80	28.5	80	27.5

a. Plot the data on an arithmetic grid.

b. Calculate the least-squares equation for estimating the time to complete the task on the basis of noise level and plot it on the graph made in part a.

c. Does the estimating equation fit the data well? Calculate the explained, unexplained, and total variation, and the coefficient of determination.

d. How long would it take a supervisor, located at a work station where the noise level was 30 decibels, to complete the task performed in the test above?

8.3. The S F Corporation is a firm whose major service is to maintain mailing lists and print mailing labels for their customers, generally specialized magazines with national distribution. The director of operations wants to determine the relationship between the cost of serving customers and the size of their mailing lists. The following information is collected from a random sampling of customers:

Average list size for period, X, names	Total cost of servicing for period, Y	Average list size for period, X, names	Total cost of servicing for period, Y
5,750	$5,270	45,230	$ 8,310
9,300	6,110	79,870	9,540
15,230	6,670	112,450	12,370
40,150	6,930	150,200	14,150

a. Plot the data on arithmetic paper.
b. Calculate the least-squares equation for estimating servicing cost based on list size and plot it on the grid in part a.
c. Explain the meaning of the coefficients a and b in the estimating equation.
d. If a new account with a 30,000-name mailing list became a customer, and the company wanted to make a 20 percent gross profit over estimated costs, what fee should they charge per period?

8.4. The food-service supervisor for a local conference facility has to plan food ordering several weeks in advance. In the past there has been a great deal of waste, since food was ordered for every registrant at each conference but many people did not eat at the facility. The supervisor asks you to examine the relationship between the number of meals served and the number of registrants for past conferences. You gather the following information on the last 12 conferences:

Registrants, X	Maximum servings at any one meal, Y	Registrants, X	Maximum servings at any one meal, Y
289	235	358	275
339	315	160	158
391	355	365	345
479	399	319	305
482	475	561	522
500	441	331	225

a. Plot the data on arithmetic paper.
b. Compute the least-squares equation for estimating the maximum number of meals based on the number of registrants, and plot it on the graph in part a.
c. Compute the standard error of estimate, the covariance, the coefficient of correlation, and the coefficient of determination. Explain the meaning of each of these measures.
d. A new conference has 575 registrants. What is the best estimate of the maximum servings at any one meal?

8.5. A bank in a medium-sized city perceived that the middle-income market segment in the city was not being served by any of the banks. Therefore, they restructured their services and promoted specifically to this middle-income group. After a year of the campaign they wanted to see how their bank was perceived by the various income groups within the city. They created a questionnaire, including two questions related to income and perception. The perception question was based on a simple 9-point scale:

How appealing is First State Bank to you?

Very appealing   (9) | (8) | (7) | (6) | (5) | (4) | (3) | (2) | (1)   Very unappealing

A random sample of 15 customers produced the following results:

Annual income, X	Appeal score, Y	Annual income, X	Appeal score, Y	Annual income, X	Appeal score, Y
$14,700	2	$ 8,300	8	$21,400	9
15,300	4	16,900	4	17,900	1
16,500	6	9,600	1	15,300	4
19,900	7	15,300	6	18,300	9
18,400	9	13,300	5	16,100	4

a. Plot the data on an arithmetic grid.

b. Compute the least-squares equation for estimating appeal score based on income and plot it on the graph in part a.

c. State what the estimating equation would be if you recoded both the X and Y values as deviations from their respective means. (You don't have to recompute the entire problem to answer this question.)

d. You aren't very pleased with the fit of the linear estimating equation calculated in part b, so you decide to fit a quadratic model to the data. Using the least-squares method, fit a line $\bar{Y}_X = a + bX + cX^2$ to the data. Graph this line on the grid in part a. (You may want to review Sec. 6.C before attempting this question.)

e. Calculate the standard error of estimate for the linear estimating equation and for the quadratic estimating equation. Which line do you believe describes the data better?

f. Estimate the rating a person would give the bank if their income were $15,000. Use the estimating equation with the smaller standard error of estimate to answer this question.

8.6. As a buyer in a large department store, you're planning the total amount of money to be spent on purchasing toys for the coming Christmas season. The wholesale firm from whom you purchase always makes a forecast of regional sales of toys for the coming season, and that forecast usually turns out to be accurate. You decide to relate your store's sales to the forecasts made by the wholesaler to see how good the relationship is. If the relationship is strong, you'll then use the forecast in planning your budget for the coming season. The data you collect are:

186

Regional forecast X, thousands	Store sales Y, thousands	Regional forecast X, thousands	Store sales Y, thousands
$2940	$144	$3050	$235
2970	175	2980	166
3000	200	2880	114
3040	220	2980	196
3040	246	2960	190

a. Plot these data on arithmetic paper.

b. Calculate the least-squares equation for estimating sales through the use of the regional forecast.

c. Explain the meaning of the coefficients a and b in the estimating equation.

d. Compute the covariance between X and Y, the coefficient of correlation and the coefficient of determination. Explain their meaning.

e. If the regional forecast for the coming season was 3.1 million dollars, what are the store's expected sales?

For Probs. 8.7 to 8.12 data will be summarized, rather than being given point by point. To facilitate calculations using these summarized data, remember that

$$\sum (X - \bar{X})^2 = \sum X^2 - \frac{(\sum X)^2}{n}$$

and

$$\sum [(X - \bar{X})(Y - \bar{Y})] = \sum XY - \frac{\sum X \sum Y}{n}$$

From these relationships it follows that

$$r_{XY} = \frac{\text{cov}(X,Y)}{\sqrt{s_X^2 s_Y^2}} = \frac{\sum [(X - \bar{X})(Y - \bar{Y})]}{\sqrt{\sum [X - \bar{X}]^2 \sum (Y - \bar{Y})^2}}$$

Also, since $\quad r_X{}^2{}_Y = \dfrac{\text{explained variation}}{\text{total variation}} = 1 - \dfrac{\text{unexplained variation}}{\text{total variation}}$

you can obtain the explained variation, the unexplained variation, and $s_{Y \cdot X}$, the standard error of estimate.

8.7. You've been hired to evaluate a firm's training program. To relate a measure of work performance on a 9-point scale Y to the length of each employee's training period in months X you obtain the following sample data:

$$\sum X = 191 \qquad \sum X^2 = 2107$$
$$\sum Y = 94 \qquad \sum Y^2 = 530$$
$$\sum XY = 1026 \qquad n = 20$$

a. Compute the least-squares equation for estimating performance on the basis of training.

b. Compute the coefficients of correlation and determination and explain their meaning.

c. Estimate the work performance measure for an employee who had 8 months of training.

8.8. You work for a local company that lays sod, and you want to be able to forecast sales. Homes are ready for sod approximately 4 months after the building permit is granted, so you gather a random sample of past monthly data on the number of building permits issued in units, X and relate them to the sales of your company 4 months later in thousands of dollars, Y, obtaining the following data:

$$\sum X = 4762 \qquad \sum X^2 = 394{,}909$$
$$\sum Y = 242 \qquad \sum Y^2 = 1058$$
$$\sum XY = 20{,}094 \qquad n = 60$$

a. Compute the least-squares equation for estimating sales through a knowledge of the number of building permits issued 4 months earlier.

b. Compute the covariance between X and Y, the coefficient of correlation and the coefficient of determination. Explain their meaning.

c. If 73 building permits were issued last April, what would you expect August sales to be?

8.9. You work for a large corporation and are worried because profitability has been declining. You decide to investigate the relationship between profitability and sales, so you measure profitability as a percent of sales, Y and sales in thousands of dollars, X and obtain the following data for the past 20 years:

$$\sum X = 5{,}024{,}269 \qquad \sum X^2 = 1{,}270{,}580{,}000{,}000$$
$$\sum Y = 233 \qquad \sum Y^2 = 2853$$
$$\sum XY = 57{,}989{,}332 \qquad n = 20$$

a. Calculate the least-squares equation for estimating profitability on the basis of sales.

b. Interpret the meaning of the coefficients a and b in the estimating equation.

c. Compute the coefficients of determination and correlation, and explain their meaning.

d. If next year's sales are estimated to be 200 million dollars, what would you expect profits to be, expressed both as a percentage of sales and a dollar amount?

8.10. You work in the personnel department of a large insurance company. A psychologist you know has developed a test which supposedly can predict a potential salesperson's selling ability. To see how well the test works, you give the test to a random sample of 80 salespeople, and obtain the following results, where X is the test score on a 100-point scale and Y is sales per year in tens of thousands of dollars:

$$\sum X = 5662 \qquad \sum X^2 = 406{,}472$$
$$\sum Y = 4044 \qquad \sum Y^2 = 242{,}344$$
$$\sum XY = 290{,}701 \qquad n = 80$$

a. Calculate the least-squares equation for estimating sales from test scores.
b. Calculate the coefficient of correlation and the coefficient of determination. Do you think the test is good? Why?
c. Calculate and interpret the standard error of estimate.
d. Calculate the least-squares equation for estimating test scores from sales, $\bar{X}_Y = a + bY$.
e. What test score would you predict for a salesperson who sold $600,000 of insurance last year? ($600,000 per year is 60 in the units of the problem.)
f. How much insurance would you expect would be sold by a salesperson who scored 75 on the test?

8.11. A computing center wanted to estimate Y, the actual running time in seconds of computing jobs submitted, based on X, the estimated running time in seconds stated by the individual submitting the job. They collected information at random from a recent batch of jobs and computed:

$$\sum X = 7109 \qquad \sum X^2 = 517,314$$
$$\sum Y = 3036 \qquad \sum Y^2 = 99,529$$
$$\sum XY = 222,562 \qquad n = 100$$

a. Calculate the least-squares estimating equation for predicting actual running time based on estimated running time.
b. Calculate the least-squares estimating equation for predicting a student's time estimate based on actual running time.
c. Calculate the coefficients of correlation and determination.
d. How long would you expect a job to run if the student's estimate was 35 seconds?
e. What do you think the estimate submitted by a student would be for a job that ran 30 seconds?
f. Why can't you use the equation calculated in part *a* to answer the question in part *e*?

8.12. An electronics firm wanted to determine the relationship between time to failure in days, Y and operating voltage, X of a piece of equipment advertised to be completely reliable at any operating voltage between 5 and 50 volts. They tested a sample of 30 parts, each at a different voltage, and measured the time to failure. The experiment resulted in these data:

$$\sum X = 776 \qquad \sum X^2 = 22,421$$
$$\sum Y = 2150 \qquad \sum Y^2 = 173,949$$
$$\sum XY = 50,496 \qquad n = 30$$

a. Compute the least-squares line $\bar{Y}_X = a + bX$.
b. Compute the least-squares line $\bar{X}_Y = a + bY$.
c. Interpret the meaning of the coefficients a and b in each of the equations calculated above.
d. If a piece of equipment failed after 65 days, at what voltage would you estimate it was operated?
e. If a piece of equipment was to be operated at 28 volts, how long would you expect it to operate before failure?

8.13. Explain the concept of total, explained, and unexplained variation. Use graphs to illustrate your answer. Relate these concepts to the coefficient of determination and the standard error of the estimate.

8.14. Prove that the short form for computing covariance (given in the note to Probs. 8.7 to 8.12) is correct.

8.15. Explain, in words and with graphs, the concept of a conditional distribution.

8.16. Return to Prob. 8.6 and assume that the *dependent* variable Y is exactly one-half of the stated value. Recompute parts a through d of that problem and compare your answer with the original results. What differences are there? Why?

8.17. Return to Prob. 8.6 and assume that the *independent* variable X is exactly one-half of the stated value. Recompute parts a through d of that problem and compare your answer with the original results. What differences are there? Why?

8.18. Describe, using formulas, the relationships that exist between the standard error of the estimate, the coefficient of determination, covariance, and the correlation coefficient.

8.19. Suppose that the relation between two variables could be described better with an exponential estimating equation, $\bar{Y}_X = ab^X$, than with a linear equation. Convert this equation to linear form and show the normal equations you could use to determine its coefficients. How would you interpret the coefficients of this linear estimating equation?

8.20. Fit a quadratic model to the data of Prob. 8.2 by finding the coefficients for the least-squares estimating equation $\bar{Y}_X = a + bX + cX^2$. Answer parts a through d in Prob. 8.2 for this new estimating equation.

MODULE 9
BUSINESS FORECASTING

Anticipation of the future is one of the activities that separates people from other animals. Everyone forecasts, from the aborigine hunter anticipating the movement of game with the change of the seasons to the corporate president planning the introduction of new products into new markets.

The need for forecasting has become more apparent as the tempo of change has accelerated. Fifty years ago most companies expected to be producing essentially the same product in the future as they had in the past. Today new demands and technology lead to products whose market dimensions are unknown but must be estimated.

The basis for forecasting depends on the nature of the process being forecast. If nothing changes, yesterday's fact becomes tomorrow's forecast. If the pattern of change is steady, the direction and magnitude of future changes can be extrapolated using past data. The past may be of little help in estimating the future if breakthroughs leading to discontinuities with the past are anticipated. Then instead of measuring a rate of change you'd attempt to answer questions like: What will life be like when . . . ? or What would life be like if . . . ?

This module will describe forecasting techniques that relate to all three of the situations above; the steady state, orderly change, and discontinuities. It will begin with the extension of techniques you've already learned in the modules on index numbers, classical time-series analysis, and association. Then it will describe a variety of other more complex methods.

General learning objectives

Your general learning objectives for this module are to be able to:

1. Make forecasts based upon classical time-series analysis
2. Forecast using exponential smoothing
3. Identify and describe more complex forecasting models

According to classical time-series analysis, trend, seasonal, cyclical, and irregular factors are constantly operating together to produce the specific level of the variable being studied at any time. It is the *relative importance* of these factors that leads to the distinction between short, intermediate, and long-run forecasts.

In short-run forecasting (periods of less than 1 month) the existence of periodic movements of short duration and irregular movements are dominant. The trend, cycle, and seasonal influences are irrelevant. Some short-term forecasts involve the identification of a regular periodic variation that is like seasonal variation but has a period of a day or a week rather than a year. Traffic on the street or in a retail store, for example, exhibits both daily and weekly periodic variation as well as a seasonal pattern. Such movements could be analyzed using the same method of ratios of data to moving average that you learned for seasonal variation, except that the period would be a day (by hours) or a week (by days). This index of variation could then be applied to estimates of daily (or weekly) volume that were obtained by short-term extrapolation, as explained below. Other series for which short-term forecasts are desired may not show periodic variation or any seasonal, cycle, or trend because the time interval is too short to identify any of these factors. The series then would consist of irregular variation around a process average. Such series can also be forecast using short-term extrapolation or by using exponential smoothing, discussed later in this module.

In intermediate forecasting (1 month to 2 years), seasonal and cyclical factors are dominant, with irregular factors of some importance and the trend less important. A variety of forecasting techniques will be described for estimating cyclical values. Among these are short-term extrapolation (again) and three techniques making use of business indicators: their qualitative use, their use in association, and their use in diffusion indexes. These techniques will be applied to seasonally adjusted values, which can be modified by the appropriate seasonal index, if necessary, to obtain forecasts which include seasonal variation.

In a long-run forecast (more than 2 years), trend factors are dominant, with the cycle playing a minor role and seasonal and irregular factors being ignored. In terms of classical time-series analysis, long-term forecasts will be made through trend extrapolation modified by limiting factors. Other more complex techniques will be discussed in the final section of this module.

You should realize that breaking down a continuum of possible forecasts into these three categories is arbitrary and an oversimplification and that all three stages blend into each other. Indeed, some authors use quite different definitions of short, intermediate, and long-term forecasts from those used here.

Section 9.A
Forecasting with Classical Time-Series Analysis— Naïve Extrapolation

Learning objective

Your learning objective for this section is to be able to forecast using *naïve extrapolation*.

Naïve extrapolation is a forecasting technique used to make short or intermediate forecasts. The simplest kind of naïve extrapolation uses the current value of a series as the forecast of its next value. Today's value is tomorrow's estimate. If you want to beat the record of the local weather forecaster, try this technique. If it's fair today, predict that tomorrow will be fair. If it's rainy today, predict rain for tomorrow. Obviously, when there is a change in the weather you'll miss completely, but since weather patterns usually persist for more than one day, you'll be right many more days than you'll be wrong.

Simple though this method is, its use is well founded in theory. Granger and Morgenstern have shown that stock market prices can be predicted better using this very naïve method than through any other method.[1]

Michael Prell, in a study of the accuracy of forecasts of interest rates over $3\frac{1}{2}$-year periods, showed that forecasts by about 30 "market professionals" were a little worse than the last-value method when predicting interest rates 6 months ahead and only slightly better than this simple naïve method when predicting 3 months ahead.[2]

Another naïve extrapolation method is to predict that the *change* that occurred between the last two periods of a series will persist between the last period and the next. This method is illustrated in Table 9.1, where the components of GNP for the third and fourth quarters of 1972 are used to predict the first-quarter values for 1973. The values in Table 9.1 are *seasonally adjusted at annual rates*. This means that the actual expenditures for a particular quarter were divided by the seasonal index for that quarter and multiplied by 4. This gives the *annual* amount which the expenditures

---

[1] Clive W. J. Granger and Oskar Morgenstern, *Predictability of Stock Market Prices*, Heath, Lexington, Mass., 1970.
[2] Michael J. Prell, How Well Do the Experts Forecast Interest Rates?, *Monthly Review* (Federal Reserve Bank of Kansas City), September–October 1973, pp. 2–13.

Table 9.1 / Naïve estimate of GNP for fourth quarter 1973
(Billions of dollars, seasonally adjusted values at annual rates)

	II 1973 actual	III 1973 actual	Change	IV 1973 Forecast	IV 1973 Actual	Error	% error
Personal consumption expenditures	(795.6)	(816.0)	(+20.4)	(836.4)	(825.2)	(+11.2)	(+ 1.4)
Durable goods	132.8	132.8	+ 0.0	132.8	125.6	+ 7.2	+ 5.7
Nondurable goods	330.3	341.6	+11.3	352.9	349.6	+ 3.3	+ 0.9
Services	332.6	341.6	+ 9.0	350.6	350.0	+ 0.6	+ 0.2
Gross private domestic investment	(198.2)	(202.0)	(+ 3.8)	(205.8)	(213.9)	(− 8.1)	(− 3.8)
Nonresidential structures	47.2	49.5	+ 2.3	51.8	51.7	+ 0.1	+ 0.2
Producers' durable equipment	86.9	88.6	+ 1.7	90.3	90.1	+ 0.2	+ 0.2
Residential structures	59.6	59.2	− 0.4	58.8	54.0	+ 4.8	+ 8.9
Change in business inventories	4.5	4.7	+ 0.2	4.9	18.0	− 13.1	− 72.8
Net export of goods and services	(2.8)	(7.6)	(+ 4.8)	(12.4)	(12.8)	(− 0.4)	(− 3.1)
Exports	97.2	104.5	+ 7.3	111.8	116.4	− 4.6	− 4.0
Imports	94.4	97.0	+ 2.6	99.6	103.6	− 4.0	− 3.9
Government purchase of goods and services	(275.3)	(279.0)	(+ 3.7)	(282.7)	(285.6)	(− 2.9)	(− 1.0)
National defense	74.2	74.2	+ 0.0	74.2	73.0	+ 1.2	+ 1.6
Other federal	33.1	32.7	− 0.4	32.3	33.8	− 1.5	− 4.4
State and local	168.0	172.2	+ 4.2	176.4	178.8	− 2.4	− 1.3
Gross national product	(1272.0)	(1304.5)	(+32.5)	(1337.0)	(1337.5)	(− 0.5)	<(− 0.1)

would reach if the economy kept operating through the year at the level implied by that particular quarter.

Looking at Table 9.1, you'll see that the forecast for total GNP could have been obtained by applying the change between GNP for the second quarter of 1973 and the third quarter of 1973 to obtain the estimate for the fourth quarter of 1973, as well as by adding the individual components [the forecast is 1304.5 + (1304.5 − 1272.0) = 1337.0]. What then, is the value of projecting all the components separately? The answer is that investigation of the detail gives you the opportunity to learn which components are most likely to cause a change in the total and to modify the naïve projection, if you choose to, on the basis of your current knowledge of the components.

If you looked carefully at a whole series of quarterly changes like those in Table 9.1, you might be able to generalize in a manner only hinted at by Table 9.1 alone. For example, you might find that (1) the most volatile components as a percentage of their base are the two *net* statistics *changes* in business inventories and *net* exports. Not only are the percentage errors likely to be large for these components, but their absolute errors contribute considerably to the total error. (2) The most volatile component of personal consumption expenditures is durable goods expenditure, both as a percentage of its base and in its absolute magnitude. Nondurable goods

196

expenditure is somewhat less volatile. Expenditure for services, though large in magnitude, is slow to change and easy to predict.

Observations like these enable you to identify stable components which can be forecast using the naïve method with relative confidence and unstable components for which more careful analysis is indicated.

You could further identify components, such as federal government expenditures, which you should be able to modify on the basis of current knowledge, since budgets and legislation often commit expenditures of known amounts to future periods.

Thus by carefully studying the components of GNP you should be able to modify the naïve projections on the basis of current knowledge or considered expectation. Even without such modification, GNP projections by quarters usually can be estimated with less than 1 percent error. When such modifications are made, the results are often excellent. Over a number of years the authors have found that students using this modified naïve method can obtain forecasts that are comparable to estimates made by complex models or panels of experts and often better.

REVIEW EXERCISES 9.A

1. Which is (are) the most important component(s) (*T, C, S,* or *I*) in the following type of forecasts?
  a. Short-term.
  b. Intermediate.
  c. Long-term.
2. It is helpful to forecast GNP by extrapolating its components rather than the total because:
  a. It focuses attention on crucial components.
  b. It leads to a better understanding of the total figure.
  c. It's more likely that you'll discover obvious inconsistencies.
  d. It's more accurate.
  e. All the above.

Answers 9.A

1. a. I; b. C, S; c. T   2. a, b, and *c*

Section 9.B

Forecasting with Classical Time-Series Analysis— Business Indicators

Learning objectives

Your learning objectives for this section are to be able to:

1. Identify important leading, coincident, and lagging cyclical business indicators
2. Use business indicators to forecast through:
   - *a.* Qualitative analysis
   - *b.* Association
   - *c.* Diffusion indexes

A business indicator is a business-related time series that is used to help assess the general state of the economy, particularly with reference to the business cycle.

For years, ever since governments and private organizations began to collect comprehensive statistics on business activity, economists have looked for series whose cyclical ups and downs (called *specific business cycles*) would give them some clue or *indication* of cyclical changes in overall business activity (called the *general, aggregate, or reference business cycle*). After investigating thousands of series, they found that there is no one series, not even a large aggregate like GNP, whose swings are perfectly correlated with the business cycles of the total economy. Through extensive effort the National Bureau for Economic Research narrowed the list to 80 series that exhibit the most consistent relationship with the general business cycle. These cyclical indicators are published monthly by the U.S. Department of Commerce in *Business Conditions Digest*, along with a "short list" of the 26 indicators judged to be most useful based on their consistency and timing. These indicators are divided into three categories: those which consistently *lead* the general business cycle, those which are nearly *coincident* with it, and those which consistently *lag* it. This short list is shown in Table 9.2.

The government also publishes *Economic Indicators* monthly. This document includes 37 indicators (which are further subdivided), under the general headings of (1) output, income, and spending, (2) employment, unemployment, and wages, (3) production and business activity, (4) prices, (5) money, credit, and securities markets, and (6) federal finance.

In this section three ways of using business indicators will be discussed: (1) their

Table 9.2 / NBER short list of cyclical indicators

Leading indicators:
    Average workweek, production workers, manufacturing (hours)
    Average weekly initial claims, state unemployment insurance (thousands, inverted scale)
    Net business formation (index, 1967 = 100)
    New orders, durable goods industries (billions of dollars)
    Contracts and orders, plant and equipment (billions of dollars)
    New building permits, private housing units (index, 1967 = 100)
    Change in book value, manufacturing and trade inventories (annual rate, billions of dollars)
    Industrial materials prices (index, 1967 = 100)
    Stock prices, 500 common stocks (index, 1941–1943 = 100)
    Corporate profits after taxes (annual rate, billions of dollars)
    Ratio, price to unit labor cost, manufacturing (index, 1967 = 100)
    Change in consumer installment debt (annual rate, billions of dollars)
Roughly coincident indicators:
    Personal income (annual rate, billions of dollars)
    GNP in current dollars (annual rate, billions of dollars)
    GNP in 1958 dollars (annual rate, billions of dollars)
    Industrial production (index, 1967 = 100)
    Manufacturing and trade sales (billions of dollars)
    Sales of retail stores (billions of dollars)
    Employees on nonagricultural payrolls (billions)
    Unemployment rate, total (percent, inverted)
Lagging indicators:
    Unemployment rate, persons unemployed 15 weeks and over (percent, inverted)
    Business expenditures, new plant and equipment (annual rate, billions of dollars)
    Book value, manufacturing and trade inventories (billions of dollars)
    Labor costs per unit of output, manufacturing (index, 1967 = 100)
    Commercial and industrial loans outstanding, weekly reporting large commercial banks (billions
      of dollars)
    Bank rates on short-term business loans (percent)

Source: Business Conditions Digest, U.S. Department of Commerce.

use in a qualitative sense, (2) their use in association analysis, and (3) their use in diffusion indexes to predict cyclical turning points.

QUALITATIVE FACTORS

In spite of the growing acceptance and use of sophisticated quantitative models, the *qualitative* analysis of business indicators is still the most widespread form of business forecasting.

The Federal Open Market Committee of the Federal Reserve Board is a powerful group whose actions have a pervasive effect on the nation's economic life. Their use of business indicators in determining policy directives is illustrated by their directive of Feb. 13, 1973:[1]

---

[1] Record of Policy Actions of the Federal Open Market Committee, *Federal Reserve Bulletin*, May 1973, pp. 350–351.

The information reviewed at this meeting suggests continued substantial growth in real output of goods and services in the current quarter, although at a rate less rapid than in the fourth quarter of 1972. The unemployment rate has declined slightly further. In recent months wage rates have increased at a relatively rapid pace, and unit labor costs turned up in the fourth quarter of 1972. The rise in consumer prices slowed in December when retail prices of foods changed little, but prices of foods and foodstuffs at earlier stages of distribution rose sharply in both December and January. The excess of U.S. merchandise imports over exports remained large in December. Heavy speculative movements out of dollars into German marks and some other currencies developed in late January and early February. On February 12 the government announced that the United States would devalue the dollar by 10 per cent.

The narrowly defined money stock changed little in January after having increased sharply in December, and growth over the 2 months combined was at an average annual rate of about 6½ per cent. Growth in the more broadly defined money stock slowed less abruptly from December to January as inflows of consumer-type time and savings deposits to banks accelerated. A sharp and pervasive increase has taken place in bank loans to businesses. In recent weeks market interest rates generally have risen further, with increases substantial for short-term rates and relatively moderate for long-term rates. Most recently, however, Treasury bill rates have moved back down under the influence of foreign official buying.

In light of the foregoing developments, it is the policy of the Federal Open Market Committee to foster financial conditions consonant with the aims of the economic stabilization program, including further abatement of inflationary pressures, sustainable growth in real output and employment, and progress toward equilibrium in the country's balance of payments.

To implement this policy, while taking account of possible domestic credit market and international developments, the Committee seeks to achieve bank reserve and money market conditions that will support somewhat slower growth in monetary aggregates over the months ahead than occurred on average in the past 6 months.

Another example of how analysts combine the use of indicators with their interpretation of current economic developments to predict the future can be shown by reading any Business Outlook section of *Business Week* magazine. The issue for Aug. 25, 1973 contains the following analysis:

Housing still up, but the decline is in the works   Housing bounced upward in July. New home starts rose to an annual rate of 2,176,000 units in the month, from June's 2,093,000.

There may be another month or two of the same. Backlogs of unused permits are still high. But then housing seems headed for a toboggan ride, even though there appears to be no general overbuilding of homes.

In the second quarter, the rental vacancy rate was 5.8%. That is up only a bit from the 5.4% of early 1970, when the housing boom began to roll.

And it is well under the 8%-plus, averaged throughout the first half of the 1960s.

. . . .

Mortgage rates at record highs   The National Assn. of Home Builders also takes a gloomy view of the future.

NAHB points out that the decline in funds in the mutual savings banks and the savings and loan companies has forced a suspension of most advance commitments for mortgages.

. . . .

Price indexes don't show the surge to come

The consumer price index rose only 0.2% in July—an annual rate of increase of less than 3%. In the previous half year, it rose at a rate of 8%.

But the price indexes for July hardly indicate the inflationary pressures still cooking in the economy. The slowing in prices was merely a temporary consequence of Freeze II.

The horrible surge in wholesale food prices in late summer will kick up the August consumer price index.

And for September, with the freeze ended, a whole raft of price boosts is waiting in the wings.

. . . .

There's a lot of life left in manufacturing

Economic activity is losing some of its fast forward speed; but there is plenty of zip still left in manufacturing.

Industrial production rose 0.7%, seasonally adjusted, in July—the largest gain since last February. In manufacturing, the monthly increase of 1.1% was the steepest advance since October.

While the gain in real gross national product (GNP adjusted for price change) is now figured to have been at an annual rate of only 2.4% in the second quarter, manufacturing output was clipping along at a rate of 6.9%.

That, of course, marks some slowing in the furious pace of production; in the first quarter, manufacturers were expanding output at a rate of 10%, and in last year's fourth quarter, the rate was $13\frac{1}{2}$%.

. . . .

Output checked by capacity

Capacity limitations are clearly keeping a rein on output. Industrial equipment, which has been the fastest area of growth, showed only a minor gain in July.

The slower pace is not owing to the diminished demand; new orders for machinery are setting new peaks each month, and backlogs are more than 30% higher than a year ago.

. . . .

Backlogs pile up in hard goods

New orders for hard goods declined $310-million in July, according to preliminary estimates.

But June's orders, which had previously been reported as flat, are now figured to have jumped $567-million.

Orders are still outpacing shipments; backlogs grew by $1.3-billion in July, bringing them to $99-billion. That is a thumping $23-billion increase over the year.

The process of forecasting through the use of indicators illustrated by the examples above can be found again and again in the practice of business. In all these cases, analysts look carefully at what they consider to be key indicators and then combine their judgment about the significance of the indicators with other factors in a qualitative manner to arrive at a forecast. They usually use gut feel rather than formal mathematical relationships. Though the forecasts obtained in this manner are only as good as the forecaster's judgment, you shouldn't underestimate the intuition of an experienced observer of the business scene; many successful businessmen are where they are now simply because of their highly developed feel for what the future holds.

201

ASSOCIATION

Business indicators can also be used as independent variables in forecasting through association analysis. One of the important uses for the analysis of association you studied in Module 8 is in forecasting. You already know the technique, but we'll expand the discussion a bit here to explain the use of autocorrelation and leading indicators in forecasting.

When the value of a variable is strongly associated with the value of that same variable at an earlier point in time, *autocorrelation* is said to exist. A simple example of the use of autocorrelation is in predicting the emergence of 17-year locusts based on their previous appearance. Since this insect's life cycle is perfectly regular, the emergence of a horde of locusts 17 years after their previous appearance is practically a certainty. Another example is new car sales, which are strongly affected by the number of cars sold 3 years earlier, since many people operate on a 3-year trade-in cycle.

In cases like these, the dependent variable is forecast by using its value at a previous time as the independent variable. This makes forecasting easy, because historical values of the independent variable are known and do not have to be forecast.

Another technique widely used in forecasting through association is that of using a leading indicator as the independent variable. This has the same advantage as autocorrelation; the present value of the independent variable can be used to forecast a future value of the dependent variable.

Changes in wholesale prices generally foreshadow changes in consumer prices for the same commodity. Therefore, particular consumer prices can often be forecast with accuracy by using the wholesale price of that commodity in a past period as the independent variable. The farm-income–tractor-sales example in Module 8 also made use of this principle, since this year's farm income was used to forecast next year's tractor sales. There are many other examples of foreshadowing indicators, such as spring rainfall being used to forecast summer crop yields or building permits issued being used to forecast construction activity several months later.

All the examples above involved leading indicators whose values were easily measured or were developed by a national agency such as the Bureau of Labor Statistics. Another technique for forecasting by association uses leading indicators in the form of surveys of consumers' or companies' expectations. In these cases data on expectations are obtained from sample surveys, the relationships between these expectations and later changes in the dependent variable are determined, and the estimating equation is used to predict outcomes based on expectations. The University of Michigan Survey Research Center and the U.S. Bureau of Census make surveys of consumers' plans to buy capital goods such as cars and houses. The Securities Exchange Commission and the National Industrial Conference Board make surveys of producers' expectations regarding capital expenditures. Once the relationship between the variable obtained in the survey and the dependent variable is determined, the values obtained from the survey can be used to forecast the dependent variable.

Association techniques can also be used even though the independent variable is not known but has to be forecast, since it may be easier to forecast the independent variable than it is to forecast the dependent variable directly, by other means. A company that can relate its sales to some aggregate economic measure can take advantage of other people's "expert" forecasts to make its own. The American Statistical Association, for example, surveys professional forecasters regarding aggregate economic statistics in the United States. A company that finds its sales are related to one of these statistics could then use the professionals' forecasts to make its own. Similarly, the U.S. Department of Agriculture publishes much information regarding crop expectations that could profitably be exploited by agribusinesses.

Before leaving the subject of association and its use in forecasting, the subject of data treatment should be considered. Sometimes you might want to find the association between two variables not in their raw form but after they had been adjusted statistically. As an example, consider the short-run relationship between the quantity of an agricultural product and its price. Suppose that you gathered statistics for a number of years on the quantity of green peas produced in a certain area and their price per pound. These series are graphed in Fig. 9.1.

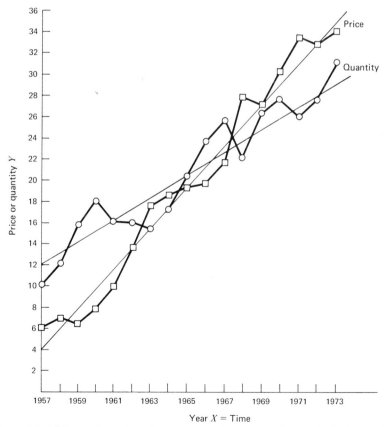

Figure 9.1 / Price and quantity of green peas; price per pound, quantity in thousands of tons.

If you determined the coefficient of correlation between the quantity and price data shown in Fig. 9.1, you'd find that $r = +.90$. This might be confusing, since your intuition may tell you that quantity and price should be *negatively* related; i.e., the *larger* the crop in a given year, the *lower* you'd expect the price to be.

The problem here is that in calculating the relationship, you correlated *long-run* price with *long-run* quantity. Over the 17 years the trends of both quantity and price increased, resulting in the positive correlation. What you really want to measure is the *short-run* relationship. To do this, you could calculate the trend for both quantity and price, remove that trend in each case by subtracting the Y from the Y_c values, and then find the association between the *deviations from the trends* for quantity and price.

If you completed all of these calculations, you'd find that the *short-run* correlation between quantity and price is $-.87$ and that the equation for estimating changes from trend of price on the basis of changes from trend of quantity is $\Delta P = -.77 \Delta Q$. In other words, an increase of 1000 tons of peas in a given year beyond its trend value will produce a decrease in price of -77 cents per pound below its trend value. Notice in Fig. 9.1 that in general, for years in which there was an increase in quantity above the trend, there was a decrease in price below the trend, and vice versa.

Removing the trend is by no means the only way you might want to treat or adjust data before studying association. Many times if data are expressed by dividing the values by their standard deviations before estimating one variable in terms of the other, the association is improved. In other cases, still other adjustments would be appropriate. Only by logic and experimentation can you tell what treatment will be most effective for a given problem.

DIFFUSION INDEXES

The simplest kind of diffusion index is a *percentage of indicators expanding*. To make such an index, choose a number of business indicators, perhaps around 50, and calculate the percentage of these indicators that is expanding for each period.

Diffusion indexes are used in an attempt to predict turning points in the business cycle. The rate of participation in business activity varies substantially among series during different phases of the business cycle. In the early phase of a business upswing, nearly all indicators are rising except for a few lagging indicators. As prosperity loses its momentum but before the peak of activity, some of the indicators that were previously rising start to turn down. By the time the peak is reached, about half of the indicators are still expanding while half are falling. After the peak, more and more of the indicators join the bandwagon and fall. However, the lowest point in terms of the percentage of indicators expanding is reached before the bottom of the depression. By the time the actual trough is reached, about half of the indicators are still going down but the other half are rising. There is an upsurge in the percentage expanding on the next upswing and the process repeats itself through the course of the next cycle.

The percent of indicators expanding, or *diffusion index*, gives a clue to when turning points in the business cycle are being reached. This is of particular importance because most other methods of forecasting which rely on past data project the direction of present change into the future and therefore almost always miss the turns, which are, of course, the crucially important points to forecast correctly.

Before calculating a diffusion index, you must decide which indicators to include. This sounds easy: simply pick indicators that conform to the cycle but lead it. But there are two problems: (1) no indicator has a perfect record of conformity to the business cycle and (2) leading indicators are notoriously volatile; they bounce around a lot. If only leading indicators were used, you might get many false signals for turns. For these reasons concurrent and sometimes even lagging indicators are included in the indicators since they are much less volatile. This decreases the lead time in forecasting turns but also decreases the number of false turns.

To illustrate the use of a diffusion index, suppose you'd chosen a list of 50 indicators and calculated the percentage of these indicators which were expanding every month for the past 11 years. Further, suppose that you'd graphed the percentage expanding against time and inserted the business-cycle peaks and troughs as determined by the National Bureau for Economic Research, with the results shown in Fig. 9.2.

Before making a forecast, look at the behavior of the index over these 11 years. The index crossed near the 50 percent line at each of the peaks and troughs. (The rate of expansion slows going toward the peak, as more and more indicators decline; when more than half the series are falling, the peak must have been passed.) This

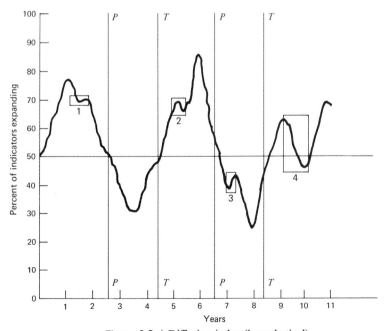

Figure 9.2 / Diffusion index (hypothetical).

205

can be expected almost by definition for any broad-based series. Further, turning points in the cycles would have been forecast correctly by turns in the index, with the possible exceptions of the areas noted by number. Area 1 would not likely have been misinterpreted as signaling a recovery since it occurred long before the series reached the 50-percent level. Likewise, area 2 would probably not have been interpreted as signaling a downturn since the movement was very short lived. Area 3 could well have been misinterpreted as signaling an upswing, since its rise from the previous level was considerable. Area 4 would certainly have been misinterpreted since what proved after the fact to be a false swing dropped below the 50-percent mark, apparently confirming a recession when one did not exist.

Now what would you predict for the future after time 11? The slight dip from the high of nearly 70 percent expanding might lead you to anticipate a peak. You'd be surer of your prediction if you waited a few more months to see if the decline continued. You can see the tradeoff though; in gaining confidence you lose valuable time.

More complex types of diffusion indexes can be constructed, which take into account how long particular series have been rising or falling or weight series by their relative importance, but they won't be discussed here.

The overall record of diffusion indexes has been spotty. For some periods they have predicted turning points quite accurately, while for others they haven't. In the absence of better methods for predicting turning points, however, they must be judged to be useful, especially if used in conjunction with the forecaster's knowledge of the current forces affecting the economy.[1]

REVIEW EXERCISES 9.B

1. Identify whether each of the following business indicators leads, is coincident with, or lags the general business cycle.
   a. Industrial materials prices.
   b. Unemployment rate, persons unemployed 15 weeks and over.
   c. Business expenditures, new plant and equipment.
   d. New building permits, private housing units.
   e. Stock prices, 500 common stocks.
   f. GNP in current dollars.
   g. Sales of retail stores.
   h. Contracts and orders, plant and equipment.
2. Which method [the use of (1) qualitative factors, (2) association, or (3) diffusion indexes] is described by each of the following statements?
   a. Uses a mixture of leading, coincident, and lagging indicators to help predict cyclical turning points.
   b. Attempts to forecast one variable in terms of another known or easily forecast variable.
   c. Makes use, if possible, of autocorrelation or time-lagged variables.
   d. Attempts to weigh the impact of changes in various indicators on general business conditions in a nonmathematical fashion.

---

[1] Other forecasting methods discussed in Sec. 9.E, such as econometric models or the Box-Jenkins technique, can predict turning points, but they are much more complex and expensive to implement.

Answers 9.B

1. a. leading; *b.* lagging; *c.* lagging; *d.* leading; *e.* leading; *f.* coincident; *g.* coincident; *h.* leading   *2. a.* (3); *b.* (2); *c.* (2); *d.* (1)

Section 9.C

Forecasting with Classical Time-Series Analysis— Trend Extrapolation

Learning objective

Your learning objective for this section is to be able to make long-term forecasts using trend extrapolation.

Many business decisions involve long-range forecasts, rather than the intermediate forecasts emphasizing seasonal and cycle, which we just considered. Among these are forecasts of demand (and the forces such as population underlying that demand), the supply of raw materials, the size of necessary production and distribution facilities, and the expected rate of technological advancement.

In such long-term forecasts, the effects of future seasonal, cyclical, and irregular movements are washed out. The best estimate for a long-range forecast is therefore the trend value about which the other components will fluctuate.

To make a long-range forecast by the classical method, you fit what you judge to be the best trend to past data, extrapolate the trend to the year to be forecast, and adjust the Y_c value on the basis of your knowledge about *responsible factors* and *limiting forces*. This is simple mathematically but requires considerable experience and judgment. Fitting trend lines was the subject of Module 6 and will not be reviewed here. Instead the crucial factors of determining which type of trend to fit and how it should be adjusted will be emphasized, as in the following example.

Suppose you're given the task of forecasting United States power consumption for 20 years from now. A common (but not very good) method is to fit a trend to past consumption and extrapolate its rate of change. This method assumes, of course, that both population and consumption per capita will increase in the future as they have in the past and that production will be adequate to meet any demand. (None of these assumptions is actually warranted today.) Among the factors that would have to be considered would be the decline in birth rates and possible changes in

207

demand per capita based on (1) more efficient utilization of power, (2) new power-consuming innovations, and (3) the possible effects of increased costs on the elasticity of demand for power. On the production side, you'd have to consider possible limiting factors such as the effect of nationalistic foreign policies on oil importation, as well as the cost of recovery and water availability for extensive strip mining of Western coal deposits, the environmental effects of heat dispersal in nuclear power plants, and the research and development costs of developing geothermal, oil-shale, tidal, or solar-powered plants.

The choice of the appropriate trend sometimes involves more than deciding what particular form of equation to use for the trend. When there has been a basic change in the variable being forecast, it could be appropriate to separate the data, fitting a new line to the more recent portion.

What type of trend would you fit to the data of Fig. 9.3? Many people say a geometric trend, but closer inspection shows that the series might be described better with two linear trends, the second starting at point L. Comparing the second linear trend to the dotted exponential shows how great a difference there would soon be in forecasts made with the two methods. You might be even more convinced of the appropriateness of using the two linear trends rather than the exponential if (1) you could identify a reason for the dramatic change in the series at point L, such as the addition of a major new product line or (2) you were convinced that limiting factors would prohibit exponential growth in the future.

REVIEW EXERCISE 9.C

1. True or false:
  a. Trend-extrapolation forecasting can make use of least-squares trends.
  b. More than one trend line should never be used to forecast any one time series.

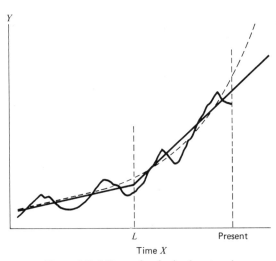

Figure 9.3 / Example of a broken trend.

c. Trend-extrapolation techniques essentially ignore C, S, and I.

d. Trend extrapolation can be used for short, intermediate, or long-run forecasting.

e. Forecasting through trend extrapolation is a purely mechanical process.

f. Consideration of responsible factors and limiting forces is an essential part of forecasting through trend extrapolation.

Answer 9.C

1. a. T; b. F; c. T; d. F; e. F; f. T

Section 9.D

Other Forecasting Methods—Exponential Smoothing

The rest of this module samples forecasting techniques that do not fall in the classical category, including exponential smoothing for short-run forecasting, a variety of large-scale or complex methods used for intermediate forecasting, and a discussion of long-range techniques for technological forecasting.

Although the details of most of these techniques are beyond the scope of this text, you should learn something about them since you'll be hearing of them a lot and will probably want to study them further in the future.

Learning objectives

Your learning objectives for this section are to be able to:

1. Apply single exponential smoothing to make short-run forecasts
2. Explain the uses of double and triple exponential smoothing

---

To understand the rationale for exponential smoothing, let's consider a few models of processes and how their behavior could be forecast.

The first model is simple: it has a constant but unknown mean and particular values vary from that mean at random. How would you forecast the next value in this process? You'd just use the mean of all the past data. The more data you had, the better your forecast would be on the average. You could even calculate the standard deviation to make an estimate of how far off your forecast would be.

Now consider a similar but more complex model. Assume that a process is subject to random variation but has a mean that is changing in an unsystematic way. That is, the mean could be larger or smaller than in the past but is not consistently increasing or decreasing over time. Now you've got a problem. An increase of the current value over the one preceding it could either be a random movement or could have been caused by a change in the process average. If the mean of all the past data were used to predict the next value, you'd consistently underestimate the change (in either direction) in the process average, if in fact one took place. If the immediate past value were used as a predictor of the next, estimates of the next value would be unduly influenced by random movements.

A solution to this paradox is to use a smoothing technique. The simplest such method is to use an unweighted moving average. In that case you'd decide on the length of the moving average, say 10 periods, and then predict the next value as the moving average of the most recent 10 periods, continuously adjusting the average as new data became available.[1] This method really wouldn't be bad, but it does pose a problem. The forecast would gradually approach the new mean of the process, but it would give equal weight to all the past observations. If the process average really had changed, you'd like to give more emphasis to the most recent values. This situation is taken care of by using an *exponentially weighted* moving average. Using this technique, the most recent observation is given the most weight, and although *all* the past values are weighted, the weights diminish exponentially with the age of the observation. This process of weighting is accomplished by the technique of *single exponential smoothing*.

To apply this technique, you'd first decide upon a smoothing constant α, which would give the desired emphasis to the most recent change in observations. You'd then calculate the exponentially smoothed mean and the forecast of the next value as follows, denoting the exponentially smoothed mean by SSM (read "single smoothed mean") to distinguish it from double and triple smoothed means which will be described later:

$$SSM_t = forecast_{t+1} = SSM_{t-1} + \alpha(actual_t - SSM_{t-1})$$
$$= \alpha(actual_t) + (1 - \alpha)SSM_{t-1}$$

This looks more formidable than it really is. It says that the single smoothed mean for period t will be used as a forecast of the process for period $t + 1$. Further, the single smoothed mean for time t will be obtained by adjusting the single smoothed mean for the preceding period, $t - 1$, by an error factor, which is α times the difference between the actual value at the time t and the previous single smoothed mean. This is algebraically the same as multiplying the present actual value by α and the previous single smoothed mean by $1 - \alpha$. Thus, as the process is continued, the most recent observation has a weight of α, the second most recent $\alpha(1 - \alpha)$, the third $\alpha(1 - \alpha)^2$, etc.

---

[1] The moving average would be calculated exactly as described in Module 7, where moving averages were applied in measuring seasonal and cyclical variations.

Table 9.3

(1)	(2) Actual defects per lot	(3)	(4)	(5)
Day		$\alpha(\text{actual})_t$	$(1 - \alpha)\text{SSM}_{t-1}$	$\text{SSM}_t = \text{forecast}_{t+1}$ (3) + (4)
1	11	.3(11)	.7(11)	11.0
2	8	.3(8)	.7(11)	10.1
3	9	.3(9)	.7(10.10)	9.77
4	13	.3(13)	.7(9.77)	10.74
5	9	.3(9)	.7(10.74)	10.22
6	21	.3(21)	.7(10.22)	13.45
7	23	.3(23)	.7(13.45)	16.32
8	18	.3(18)	.7(16.32)	16.82
9	20	.3(20)	.7(16.82)	17.77
10	18	.3(18)	.7(17.77)	17.84

Got it? If you haven't, go on to the example and then come back to this explanation. You'll find it's easier to calculate the values than to understand the description of how to do it.

The example below describes a production process in which the number of defects per lot fluctuates around a mean of 10 through the fifth day. Then on the sixth day the mean rises to 20, and the individual values fluctuate around that value. Starting with the first day, suppose you forecast the number of defects per lot for each succeeding day, using single exponential smoothing with a smoothing constant α equal to 0.3, proceeding as shown in Table 9.3.

To review the process, suppose you're at day 1 and all you know about the process is that there were 11 defectives in that day. To begin the smoothing process, you must assume some value for the previous period's SSM. Since t_1 is the first period and there is no previous information, the most logical stand-in value to use initially for SSM_{t-1} is the current value of 11. Thus,

$$\text{Forecast}_2 = \text{SSM}_1 = \alpha(\text{actual})_1 + (1 - \alpha)\text{SSM}_0$$
$$= .3(11) + .7(11) = 11$$

So the forecast for the second day would be 11. Now if the actual number of defects for the second day turned out to be 8, your forecast for the third day would be

$$\text{Forecast}_3 = \text{SSM}_2 = \alpha(\text{actual})_2 + (1 - \alpha)\text{SSM}_1$$
$$= .3(8) + .7(11) = 10.1$$

If the actual for the third day was 9, the forecast for the fourth day would be

$$\text{Forecast}_4 = \text{SSM}_3 = \alpha(\text{actual})_3 + (1 - \alpha)\text{SSM}_2$$
$$= .3(9) + .7(10.1) = 9.77$$

In this process, the weight given to the actual value for the current time period is .3, to the actual value for the previous time period it is .3(.7), etc. Thus the weight given historical values diminishes exponentially with the age of those values, as shown below:

Time	Weight
-4	$.3(.7^4) = .072$
-3	$.3(.7^3) = .103$
-2	$.3(.7^2) = .147$
-1	$.3(.7) = .21$
0	$.3 = .3$

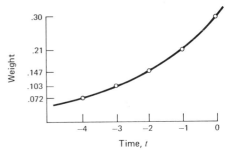

Time, t

Note that if the process average had stayed at 10, as it was for the first 5 days, the forecast would have averaged 10. When the process average increased to 20, the forecast values gradually increased toward 20. If the process had stayed unchanged at 20 thereafter, the mean forecast would eventually have approached 20. The speed at which the forecast approaches 20 depends on the value of the smoothing constant α. The larger α, the more weight is given to the current value and the faster the forecast will reflect a change in the process average. Also, however, the larger α is, the more the forecast will be influenced by random variation in the actual values. Thus choosing a large α results in fast response time but relative instability, while choosing a small α results in more stability but slower response time.

Single exponential smoothing is appropriate when the process mean is changing in an unsystematic way. Now suppose that the process mean is changing according to an *arithmetic* trend but is still subject to random variation. If this were the case, the forecast for the next period using single smoothing would *never* catch up to the ever-changing process mean. Here *double exponential smoothing* would be indicated. A double smoothed exponential mean is achieved simply by smoothing a single smoothed mean. Thus

$$DSM_t = \alpha(SSM_t) + (1 - \alpha)DSM_{t-1}$$

In order to forecast the next value, you'd calculate

$$Forecast_{t+1} = SSM_t + (SSM_t - DSM_{t-1})$$

Using this technique enables the forecast to catch up with the constant increase in the process mean. Further investigation of double smoothing will be afforded in the problems at the end of this module.

Triple exponential smoothing is appropriate when a process mean is changing *exponentially* and the actual values are fluctuating randomly about the exponential trend. As you might expect, a triple smoothed mean is obtained by smoothing a double smoothed mean. Since the work involved in making a forecast becomes complex, triple smoothing will not be used in this book. For future reference, however, you should remember that single smoothing is applied when values fluctuate about a randomly changing mean, double smoothing when the process mean is changing arithmetically, and triple smoothing when it is changing exponentially.

Exponential smoothing is a popular technique for short-run forecasting. By keeping track of the differences between the forecast and actual values, a *tracking signal* can be developed which guides the analyst in changing the smoothing constant or in going to higher-order smoothing. Past information is summarized in a single SSM, making it possible to incorporate much earlier information in a single number and thus saving time and money compared with other methods.

REVIEW EXERCISES 9.D

1. True or false: exponential smoothing:
  a. Is used for short-term forecasting.
  b. Gives weight to *all* past data.
  c. Gives decreasing weight to older data points.
  d. Is usually used to forecast a number of future values at a time.
2. The (larger; smaller) the smoothing constant α, the more quickly the forecast adapts to a real change in the process average but the more it is influenced by random variation.
3. Identify which type of exponential smoothing (single, double, or triple) is appropriate for each of the following circumstances:
  a. The process average is increasing linearly.
  b. The process average is increasing exponentially.
  c. The process average has shifted to a new, steady level.

Answers 9.D

1. a. T; *b.* T; *c.* T; *d.* F   *2.* larger   *3. a.* double; *b.* triple; *c.* single

---

Section 9.E

Other Forecasting Methods —Complex Methods

Learning objectives

Your learning objectives for this section are to be able to identify some large-scale, complex forecasting models including:

  1. Econometric models
  2. Input-output analysis
  3. Systems dynamics
  4. Spectral analysis
  5. The Box-Jenkins method

It may come as a surprise to learn that the forecasting techniques described so far are relatively simple. Only one or a few variables were used in any one technique, and the relationships between variables were conceptually straightforward. Now, five techniques which are assuming increasing importance in government and industry will be described briefly. All are much more complex than those previously studied, and their actual implementation goes considerably beyond the scope of this book.

ECONOMETRIC MODELS

While there are many kinds of econometric models, we're referring here to macro-models involving the simultaneous solution of a complex system of interrelated equations. Most models in use in the United States make intermediate forecasts of the economy, with GNP as the dependent variable and dozens of other variables, many of them time-lagged, being related to GNP and each other through an extensive system of structural equations.

Among the well-known models are the Klein-Goldberger model, the Wharton School model, the Federal Reserve–MIT model, and the Brookings Institute model. These models are composed of from 30 to over 600 structural equations, and their development and maintenance takes years of intensive effort.

To provide some notion of the complexity of these models, consider the mini-macro model by Friend and Faubman,[1] which contains only nine variables that are related through five structural equations and an identity:

$$\Delta C = .86 + .41(\Delta \tilde{Y}_p + \Delta Y_{Dt-1})$$

$$\Delta Y_D = \frac{1.7 + .57(\Delta \tilde{Y} - .10\Delta^2 \tilde{Y})}{1 + t_p} - \frac{\Delta t_p}{1 + t_p} Y_{Dt-1}$$

$$\Delta H = .35 + .06(\Delta \tilde{Y} - Y_{t-1}) + .58\Delta HS_{t-1/2} - .16\Delta PE^e$$
$$\Delta PE = -.82 + .08(\Delta \tilde{Y} + \Delta Y_{t-1}) + .63\Delta PE^e$$
$$\Delta I = 1.51 + .025\Delta S^e - 1.15I_{t-1} + 1.7\Delta PE^e$$
$$\Delta Y = \Delta C + \Delta H + \Delta PE + \Delta I + \Delta G'$$

where
C = consumption expenditures
Y = gross national product
H = residential construction expenditure
HS = housing starts
PE = plant and equipment expenditures
I = nonfarm inventory investment
S = business sales
G' = government expenditures and net exports
Y_D = disposable income
Y_p = average personal tax rate

[1] See Friend and Faubman, *Review of Economics and Statistics*, vol. 44, August 1964, pp. 229–236.

In these equations Δ means "change in," a tilde ($\sim$) means that the variable is forecast, $t - 1$ refers to data from the previous time period, and e is an expected value, analogous to a weighted arithmetic mean.

To forecast the dependent variable in any macromodel, you'd need estimates of all the other variables. Except for time-lagged variables, where past values are known, you'd have to use expectations based on past data or make independent forecasts of the necessary variables. In large models this forecasting problem is a substantial and hazardous undertaking.

In spite of these problems and the necessity for constantly updating both coefficients and structural relationships to keep abreast of changes, the use and accuracy of macromodels is growing.

Needless to say, you're not likely to build a macromodel in your spare time, but you can expect to make use of the forecasts others generate from these models.

INPUT-OUTPUT MODELS

Input-output analysis in essence shows the inputs which are required from various segments of an economy to produce a given output in one sector of that economy. This is accomplished through the use of input-output tables. Probably the most useful input-output table is a *total-requirements* table, which shows both the direct and indirect requirements of each contributing industry required to produce one dollar's worth of goods in a given industry. With such a table it is possible to predict the demands that will be imposed on any industry through changes in any other industry.

Making an input-output analysis is a complex procedure, for it necessitates tracing through all the circuitous paths by which demands for one commodity induce both direct and indirect demands for others. Large-scale models include well over 100,000 possible cross-classifications, and accurate determination of the coefficients requires the collection and analysis of incredible amounts of statistical data.

Macro input-output analysis is used extensively at both the national and regional levels. National studies are used to predict economic growth and forecast sector requirements based on anticipated changes in demand. Regional studies are used to trace the effects of economic inputs, such as new highway construction in the region, or to estimate the region's future needs for water and other resources.

Input-output analysis is also used at the microlevel by industries and individual companies to forecast future production requirements, potential sales, and the availability of raw materials.

Besides the tremendous work involved in preparing an input-output table, there are other problems involved in its use. Coefficients are based on past relationships, and changes in the way the economy operates will not be reflected unless coefficients are updated. Input-output models use as inputs estimates of future requirements and so produce *conditional* forecasts; they state that given certain changes in conditions, certain consequences will follow. The requirements that are used as inputs must be forecast by other means.

215

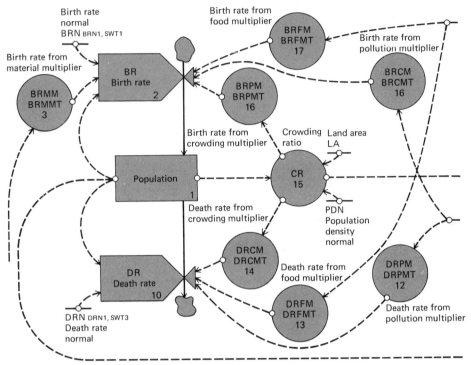

Figure 9.4 / Portion of Forrester's world-dynamics model. *(Reprinted with permission from World Dynamics by J. W. Forrester, Copyright © 1971 Wright-Allen Press, Inc., Cambridge, Mass., p. 20.)*

SYSTEMS DYNAMICS

The concept of systems dynamics relates to *multiloop nonlinear feedback systems,* which describe complex social-technical interactions. Jay W. Forrester, the developer of the method, has applied systems dynamics to industry, urban problems, and the world.[1] To see what a multiloop nonlinear feedback system is, consider a small part of Forrester's model for world dynamics, shown in Fig. 9.4. This diagram relates the level of population, birth rate, and death rate, through a whole series of multipliers. Given parameters for land area and normal population density, the multipliers show the interactions between birth and death rates and food, pollution, material resources, and crowding.

These relationships are nonlinear. A change in one variable does not cause a proportionate change in another variable. Instead its effect depends on its level. Further, there is no one-way sequence of cause and effect, as shown by the many feedback loops, where *A* affects *B*, which affects *C*, which in turn affects *A*.

---

[1] Jay W. Forrester, *Industrial Dynamics*, 1962; *Urban Dynamics*, 1969; and *World Dynamics*, Wright-Allen Press, Cambridge, Mass., 1971.

The effects of inputs into such a system are nonintuitive. A decline in consumption of natural resources, which you might think would lead to less pollution, could increase pollution because of the complex interrelationships in the system. Thus the "obvious" solution to a problem may compound the problem rather than resolve it.

Forrester does not classify systems dynamics as forecasting. The model does not say: This will happen at this time. Its outcomes are conditional; it says: This is what could happen *if* the system were to continue its present course, or: This is what could happen *if* changes were made in the system. Many people view these sorts of conditional statements as part of a normative forecasting process, where the *consequences* of certain acts are forecast, in this case through simulation, and if the consequences are judged to be undesirable, alternative courses of action which could lead to better outcomes, are tested and advocated.

SPECTRAL ANALYSIS

Spectral analysis is a complex, mathematically sophisticated method of analyzing a time series to identify the forces underlying the series and to predict its future behavior. First developed in communications engineering after World War II as an extension of Fourier analysis, its power in analyzing economic time series (and time series in other social sciences) was quickly recognized.

Classical time-series decomposition assumes that time-series data consist essentially of trend, seasonal, cyclical, and irregular movements. This is only one way to view the composition of time series. Fourier analysis, originally developed in astronomy, shows that any series can be described mathematically as a combination of sine waves of various amplitudes and periods. Spectral analysis relaxes the sine-wave constraint and makes the analysis general enough to encompass periodic movements in economic series.

> Speaking very roughly, spectral analysis conceives a time series as a combination of periodic functions each having a similar mathematical form. Spectral methods distribute the variation manifested by a time series among these constituent periodic functions. This process is sometimes referred to as the *decomposition of variance according to frequency*. A spectral variance decomposition reveals the relative weight of the repetitive tendencies inherent within the empirical time series.[1]

Spectral analysis in a sense combines the advantages of regression analysis and classical time-series analyses. Through spectral analysis the time series can be broken down into constitutient periodic functions. The source of these functions—with skill, ingenuity, and cross-spectral analysis—can then be attributed to the effect of certain independent series or variables on the dependent variable. The method can also determine whether the series is autocorrelated or the independent variables are

---

[1] Thomas F. Mayer and William Ray Arney, Spectral Analysis and the Study of Social Change, in Herbert L. Coftner (ed.), *Sociological Methodology*, Jossey Bros., San Francisco, 1974, p. 311.

time-lagged. If seasonals exist, they can easily be identified and measured. Not only can business cycles be identified, but more basic variables underlying the cycle can be identified and the contribution of these variables to specific cycles can be measured. Trends are explained on the basis of combinations of variables whose periods are extremely long.

Like other techniques in this section, spectral analysis is complex, difficult to understand and implement, and expensive. Nevertheless, its use is rapidly gaining popularity, and its influence in the future will undoubtedly be widespread.

THE BOX-JENKINS METHOD

Unlike most forecasting methods, the Box-Jenkins technique of forecasting doesn't assume a particular pattern in the past data of the series to be forecast. Instead it uses an iterative approach of identifying a possible model from a general class of models and then checks that model against the data to see if it satisfactorily describes the series. The criterion for a well-fitting model is that the residuals, or errors between the data points and the forecasting equation, be small, randomly distributed, and independent of each other. If the specified model is satisfactory, it is used for forecasting. If it isn't, the process is repeated using a different tentative model designed to improve on the original model. This process is repeated until satisfactory results are obtained. The flow diagram in Fig. 9.5 illustrates the process.

Among the general classes of models used by Box and Jenkins are moving-average models, autoregressive models, and mixed models which combine the two. The use of autoregression takes advantage of a pervasive characteristic of economic time series. Many other forecasting models, such as regression analysis, are limited, since they are based on the independence of past observations from each other, rather than on their interdependence or autocorrelation.

The Box-Jenkins method, like a regression model but unlike classical time-series decomposition, has the advantage of specifying statistically the confidence you'd have in a forecast. That is, you not only forecast a particular value for the series at some point in the future but can also state a range about that point within which you'd expect the actual value to fall a predetermined percentage of the time.

Advantages of the Box-Jenkins method are that it is very powerful and can be used for a wide variety of problems. Its chief disadvantages are that it requires a relatively large number of data points, is expensive, and is difficult to understand and to explain.

REVIEW EXERCISES 9.E

1. True or false: complex forecasting methods:
   a. Are cheap.
   b. Require extensive data preparation.

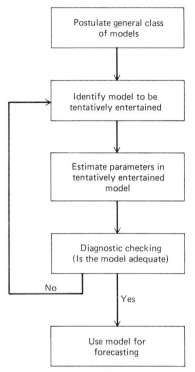

Figure 9.5 / Flow diagram for Box-Jenkins method. (*From G. P. Box and G. M. Jenkins, Time Series Analysis Forecasting and Control, p. 19, Holden-Day, Inc., 1970.*)

   c. Are more likely to be used for short-run forecasting than intermediate forecasting.
   d. Are more likely to be used by an organization than by an individual.
2. Identify which method (econometric methods, input-output, systems dynamics, spectral analysis, Box-Jenkins) is appropriate to each of the following statements:
   a. Describes nonlinear feedback systems.
   b. Breaks a series down into its periodic components.
   c. Uses a system of interrelated structural equations.
   d. Uses a process of successive iterations to find the optimal forecasting equation.
   e. Is often used to predict the effect a given change in one industry will have on another industry.

Answers 9.E

1. a. F; *b.* T; *c.* F; *d.* T   *2. a.* systems dynamics; *b.* spectral analysis; *c.* econometrics; *d.* Box-Jenkins; *e.* input-output

Section 9.F
Other Forecasting Methods—Technological Forecasting

Learning objectives

Your learning objectives for this section are to be able to describe some technological-forecasting techniques to assess long-run futures, including:

1. Envelope curves
2. Morphological analysis
3. The Delphi method
4. Scenario writing

It won't surprise you to learn that technological forecasting is the forecasting of a future state of a technology. People have been playing this game through intuitive methods for a long time. In 1902 H. G. Wells forecast the development of trucks, buses, and private motor carriages. He also said "Imagination refuses to see any sort of submarine doing anything but suffocating its crew and foundering at sea." In 1911 Charles Steinmetz predicted the application of electricity to kitchens, air conditioning, and radio broadcasting. J. B. S. Haldane wrote in 1924 that "In fifty years light will cost about one fiftieth of its present price and there will be no more night in our cities." (He didn't anticipate brownouts and blackouts.) Haldane also anticipated the use of wind, sunlight, and the electrolysis of water and subsequent burning of liquid hydrogen for power. Sir Richard Woolley stated in 1936 that the idea of space flight was "essentially impractical," and upon his appointment as Royal Astronomer in 1956 (a year before Sputnik) said, "Space travel is utter bilge."[1]

So they won a few and lost a few. With the rapid pace of scientific innovation, technological forecasting since 1950 has become more formal and has been applied to make both exploratory and normative forecasts. Exploratory forecasting attempts to answer the question of where it is *possible* to go and what *can* happen. Normative forecasting attempts to assess where society *ought* to go and what *should* happen.

Many techniques applicable in other contexts are also used in technological forecasting. These include trend extrapolation and input-output analysis, discussed

---

[1] These examples and many more can be found in Robert U. Ayres, *Technological Forecasting and Long Range Planning*, McGraw-Hill, New York, 1969.

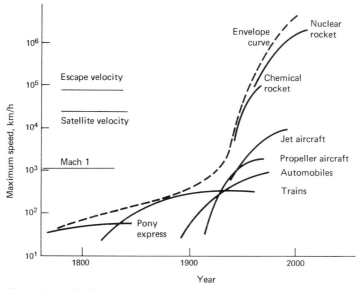

Figure 9.6 / Maximum speed by various transportation methods. (*From Eric Jantsch, Technological Forecasting in Perspective, Organization for Economic Cooperation and Development, Paris, 1967.*)

earlier in this module, hypothesis testing and decision analysis, covered in later modules, and mathematical programming and game theory, not covered in this book. Four techniques will be presented here. They include envelope curves, morphological analysis, the Delphi method, and writing scenarios.

ENVELOPE CURVES

Envelope curves trace the development of many related technologies by measuring a common characteristic over time. Figure 9.6 is an envelope curve which shows the maximum speed attained by various methods of transportation over time. Each method of transportation grew quickly, tapered off, and was followed by another overlapping but higher-reaching technology. If you fitted an envelope (growth) curve over all the technologies, you might be able to predict where new and undeveloped technologies like nuclear rockets might lead and even the path that future technologies presently unknown might take. Further, on the basis of scientific knowledge, you might be able to predict the time in the future when various speeds might be reached and when an ultimate limit such as the speed of light might be approached.

Envelope curves have been successfully applied to many other technologies such as the operating energy of particle accelerators, the speed and memory capacity of computers, and the power generated by various energy sources.

MORPHOLOGICAL ANALYSIS

Morphological analysis is a technique for identifying all the possible solutions to a problem. There are four steps involved in this process:

1. The problem to be solved must be stated as specifically as possible.
2. Characteristic parameters of the process must be identified.
3. Each parameter must be divided into distinguishable states.
4. All paths must be followed and possible paths identified.

This process makes it possible to forecast technological developments by identifying combinations of parameters not previously noted.

This process is not as simple as it seems. Possible combinations of paths (strategies) may number in the millions. Identification of parameters can be difficult and important parameters may be omitted. (The possibilities of nuclear, geothermal, and solar sources of energy were often ignored in past energy forecasts.) Alternatives might be described as possible but not feasible on the basis of limited research. (The rotary automobile engine was considered and discarded as impractical many years ago.)

Morphological analysis can be applied both to exploratory and normative forecasting. An example of exploratory forecasting is Fritz Zwicky's problem of identifying all possible jet engines operating in a pure medium, containing simple elements only, and being activated by chemical energy. (Note how carefully the problem is stated to avoid having too many alternatives to handle.) The parameters are shown in Table 9.4.

Multiplying the possible states for each parameter $(2 \times 2 \times 3 \times 2 \cdots)$ gave 36,864 conceivable alternatives. Further analysis eliminated 11,520 of these combinations as contradictory or impossible. Of the remaining 25,344 configurations, most of which had not been developed, Zwicky identified several with real promise which

Table 9.4

Parameter	Number of states
Intrinsic or extrinsic chemically active mass	2
Internal or external thrust generation	2
Intrinsic, extrinsic, or zero thrust augmentation	3
Internal or external thrust augmentation	2
Positive or negative jet	2
Possible thermal cycles	4
Medium	4
Motion	4
State of propellant	3
Continuous or intermittent operation	2
Self-igniting or non-self-igniting propellant	2

might have been overlooked using other forms of analysis.[1] Thus morphological analysis, by identifying possible inventions, can be used as a research as well as a forecasting tool.

DELPHI FORECASTING

Delphi forecasting, which uses the collective wisdom of a panel of experts, was developed by the Rand Corporation in 1964. A Delphi forecast is distinguished by the way interaction is achieved among participants while minimizing personal influence.

The forecast is made by cycling a panel of experts, numbering anywhere from 10 to 500, through a succession of rounds, usually by mail to avoid the influence of dominant personalities or peer pressure. In the first round participants are asked to identify innovations or breakthroughs that they believe will or should be achieved within a certain lengthy time. These responses are summarized and distributed to the panel in round 2, when the participants are asked to judge the probability of each innovation's occurring, its desirability, and the approximate time it will happen. Subsequent rounds, anywhere from one to perhaps four, give participants a summary of the past round, showing the range and median responses of the panel to each question, and that particular participant's own response. On the basis of this feedback, the respondents either modify their original response or stick with their previous judgment. Respondents are asked to justify their position if their response is significantly different from the rest of the panel, and these minority reports are summarized in later rounds.

After substantial consensus has been obtained or dichotomies solidified, the questioning is stopped and the results summarized to obtain the forecast.

An extensive Delphi forecast of higher education was published by the Western Interstate Commission for Higher Education in 1972. You might want to look it up, both to learn more about Delphi forecasting and to see if you agree with the experts about the future of higher education.[2] (Incidentally, the panel of experts included students, as it should have!)

SCENARIO WRITING

In the literature of forecasting, a *scenario* or alternative *future* is a description of what the future could be like if history took a particular sequence of possible turns. Scenario writing isn't new. Writers like Verne, Wells, Huxley, and Orwell described

---

[1] Fritz Zwicky, *Morphology of Propulsive Power*, Monographs on Morphological Research No. 1, Society for Morphological Research, Pasadena, Calif., 1962.

[2] Vaughn E. Huckfeldt, *A Forecast of Changes in Post Secondary Education*, National Commission for Higher Education Management Systems, Western Interstate Commission for Higher Education, Boulder, Colo., 1972.

alternative futures, sometimes prophetically. More recently, Alvin Toffler[1] popularized scenario writing in *Future Shock*, where he described alternative futures predicated on rapid social and technological changes.

Perceptive scenarios can sometimes identify breakthroughs caused by technological innovation or changes in social and political philosophies which could produce sharp discontinuities with the past and which could not be forecast by any extrapolative techniques. Using this method, businesses or nations can either prepare to take advantage of possible future opportunities or marshall forces to prevent undesirable futures from occurring.

REVIEW EXERCISES 9.F

1. Identify which technological forecasting technique (envelope curve, morphological analysis, Delphi, scenario) is described:
  a. Describes an alternative future that is a consequence of a particular path history might take.
  b. Attempts to achieve a forecast that represents the consensus of a panel of experts.
  c. Traces the pattern over time of successive related technologies.
  d. Enumerates all possible configurations of a product or process.
2. (Exploratory; Normative) forecasts say what will happen while (exploratory; normative) forecasts say what should happen.
3. Technological-forecasting techniques are most appropriate for (short, intermediate, long-term) forecasts.

Answers 9.F

1. a. scenario; *b.* Delphi; *c.* envelope curve; *d.* morphological analysis   *2.* exploratory, normative   *3.* long-term

Questions and Problems

9.1. Using the Survey of Current Business or the Federal Reserve Bulletin, find personal income by categories for the latest reported 3 months.
  a. Using the subcategories of personal income, make a naïve forecast of personal

[1] Alvin Toffler, *Future Shock*, Random House, New York, 1970. Other futuristic books that utilize scenarios are Herman Kahn and B. Bruce-Biggs, *Things to Come: Thinking about the 70s and 80s*, Macmillan, Riverside, N.J., 1972; Donella H. Meadows, Dennis L. Meadows, Jorgen Randers, and William W. Behrens III, *The Limits to Growth*, Universe, New York, 1972; Stuart Chase, *The Most Probable World*, Penguin, Baltimore, 1969; Robert Theobald, *An Alternative Future for America*, Swallow, Chicago, 1968; California Institute of Technology, *The Next Ninety Years: Proceedings of a Conference Held at California Institute of Technology, Pasadena, Calif., March 1967. The Futurist*, a monthly published by the World Future Society, Washington, D.C., contains many scenarios and alternative futures, as well as other future-oriented articles.

income for the latest month. That is, if the months were April, May, and June of the current year, then the forecast for June = [May value + (May value − April value)].

b. What was the amount of error in your forecast, measured in billions of current dollars?

c. What was the percent error in your forecast?

d. Which components of personal income were responsible for most of the error?

9.2. Refer to Prob. 9.1. Make a naïve forecast as described there to forecast GNP for the latest recorded quarter. Answer parts a through d of Prob. 9.1, applied to your forecast of GNP.

9.3. From a current issue of the Survey of Current Business or Business Conditions Digest, compile a list of any five leading and three coincident indicators that are included in the NBER short list of business indicators. Obtain the value of each of these indicators for the three latest available periods. Make up a table showing these indicators and their direction of change (+ or −) over the past two periods. On the basis of this table *and* your knowledge of current affairs, write a few paragraphs describing your view of the present strengths and weaknesses of the economy, and its future in the next quarter.

9.4. From a current issue of Business Conditions Digest, find the diffusion indexes (in Section C, Anticipations and Intentions) made from (1) New orders, manufacturing, (2) Net profits, manufacturing and trade, and (3) Net sales, manufacturing and trade. For each index note:

a. Whether the series would have been useful in anticipating the business cycle turning points that actually occurred.

b. How many times the indexes would have predicted false turning points.

9.5. From a current Historical Chart Book of the Federal Reserve System, find two series where the trend could probably be forecast better by fitting a broken trend, i.e., two different trends to different parts of the data, rather than one single trend to the entire data.

9.6. To study the sensitivity of the value forecast by single exponential smoothing to an *impulse*, forecast the next value for the series 10, 10, 40, 10, 10, 10, 10, 10, 10 using:

a. An α of .1.

b. An α of .3.

c. An α of .5.

d. What conclusions can you reach regarding the size of α and the response to an impulse in the data?

9.7. To study the sensitivity of the value forecast by single exponential smoothing to a *step increase* in the series being forecast, forecast the next value for the series 10, 10, 40, 40, 40, 40, 40, 40, 40 using:

a. An α of .1.

b. An α of .3.

c. An α of .5.

d. What conclusions can you reach regarding the size of α and the response to a step increase in the data?

9.8. You work for a large bakery and must forecast daily demand for various products, including loaves of whole-wheat bread. The production manager tells you that the bakery has kept production records but no records of demand. Judging from memory, though, there has been no identifiable pattern of demand from day to day. Starting today, you record the demand each day, and accumulate the following record of daily demand.

Day	Demand	Day	Demand	Day	Demand	Day	Demand
1	4060	6	3802	11	3878	16	4130
2	3766	7	3906	12	4178	17	3898
3	3888	8	3870	13	4054	18	4070
4	4224	9	3878	14	3850	19	4086
5	4446	10	4084	15	4046	20	3804

a. Forecast the next day's demand using single exponential smoothing with an $\alpha = .10$. (Remember that the data come to you day by day; the second day's demand must be forecast with only the knowledge that the first day's demand was 4060; the third day's demand must be forecast with only the knowledge of the first 2 days' demand, etc.)

b. Calculate your forecast error for each day by subtracting the actual demand from the forecast demand. Do you see any evidence from these errors that single exponential smoothing was or was not appropriate? Explain.

9.9. Double exponential smoothing is used when the values in a series are believed to be fluctuating about a linear trend. To see how double smoothing works:

a. Forecast the next value for a series that is increasing by 2 units per period, starting with a value of 200 and using a smoothing constant of .5.

b. Since there is no random variation in this series, future values should be forecast perfectly if enough iterations are made. How many iterations are required to obtain perfect forecasts for this series?

c. An $\alpha = .5$ is extremely large. What would the effect have been if a more realistic α of, say, .1 had been used? Would there be any advantage to using an $\alpha = .1$ for a real series?

9.10. Envelope curves trace the path of technological progress over a succession of products or methods. If, for example, you traced the contribution of particular drugs to the total profit of a pharmaceutical company, you'd find that the profit contribution of established drugs would be taken over by a succession of new drugs. From your general knowledge or from a search of current business literature identify three companies where an envelope curve for total profits could be made by tracing the leveling off of the sales of old products and the development of new, *related* products that represent higher orders of technology. List the succession of products for each company.

9.11. Find an article dealing with technological forecasting from a current issue of a periodical such as *Technology Review* (MIT), *The Futurist* (The World Future Society), *Business Week*, *Fortune*, or the *Harvard Business Review*.

a. Briefly summarize the article.

b. State whether the forecast is exploratory or normative and how you know.

9.12. From sources like those listed in Prob. 9.11 find a scenario or alternative future related to business.

a. Describe the scenario.

b. How does the scenario differ from fiction about the future?

c. How can scenarios be helpful in business planning?

9.13. In the discussion of association in this module, an illustration was used which involved the short-run relationship between the price and quantity of green peas. In that discussion it was stated that:

a. The correlation between price and quantity unadjusted for trend was $+.90$.

b. The short-run relationship between price and quantity when each series was divided by its least-squares linear trend could be expressed as $\Delta P = -.77\Delta Q$.

c. The short-run correlation between price and quantity was $-.87$.

The data from which these observations were made are shown below. Use these data to validate the statements made in parts *a*, *b*, and *c*.

Year	Thousands of tons	Price per lb	Year	Thousands of tons	Price per lb
1957	10	$.06	1966	24	$.20
1958	12	.07	1967	26	.22
1959	16	.07	1968	22	.29
1960	18	.08	1969	27	.27
1961	17	.10	1970	29	.30
1962	16	.14	1971	26	.35
1963	16	.18	1972	28	.34
1964	18	.19	1973	32	.35
1965	21	.20			

9.14. In Jay W. Forrester, *World Dynamics*, read pages 93 to 95 in chap. 5, entitled Obvious Responses Will Not Suffice.

a. In a paragraph, summarize what Forrester means when he says that obvious responses will not suffice.

b. What is the nature of dynamic systems that makes the intuition of many executives fail?

MODULE 10
PROBABILITY CONCEPTS

At the heart of statistics and decision making lies a concept called *probability*. Probability is a pervasive idea that creeps into your everyday life at innumerable points and permeates every scientific enterprise. It can become a determining factor in decisions made by businessmen.

Probability is frequently used in everyday language. We wouldn't be surprised to hear a politician say, "Taxes will probably go up after the election," a banker assert that "The prime rate of interest will probably fall next year," or a student say, "I'll probably pass statistics—after two more semesters."

In the biological, social, and physical sciences the use of probability has become indispensable. We discover in genetics that the occurrence of a specific characteristic, given a cross of plants or animals, is essentially a matter of probability. We find in physics that it is impossible to predict a particle's specific momentum and position except on a probability basis. Virtually all predictions made in the social sciences have measures of probable error attached to them.

Nevertheless, there is disagreement among statisticians, mathematicians, and philosophers about the precise definition of probability. As one noted philosopher pointed out, despite the fact that man has invented probability, he cannot agree on precisely what it is. In this chapter we'll consider two definitions of probability. Although our own preference will doubtless show through, you may choose the point of view that best suits your purposes.

One more introductory comment before you begin your study of probability. At times some of the material in this module may seem to be unrelated to the world of practical affairs. Actually, however, the concepts here provide an important base for your study of sampling, statistical inference, and decision theory, with which the rest of this book is concerned.

General learning objectives

Your general learning objectives for this module are to be able to:

1. Contrast two definitions of probability
2. Define and explain some basic probability concepts
3. State and apply important laws of mathematical probability, including Bayes' rule
4. Describe the nature and use of the binomial probability distribution and compute binomial probabilities
5. Compute the mean and standard deviation of probability distributions

Section 10.A
The Definition of Probability

Learning objectives

Your learning objectives for this section are to be able to:

1. Contrast the objective and subjective interpretations of probability
2. Define probability
3. Explain the use of the mathematical theory of probability

DEFINITION

A *probability* is a number between 0 and 1. To use an everyday term, it represents the *odds* that a particular event will occur. Probabilities do have certain characteristics that distinguish them from other numbers. Among the most important is the fact that the sum of the probabilities of a set of events that are *mutually exclusive* (non-overlapping) and *collectively exhaustive* (enumerate all possibilities) must add to 1. These imposing terms will be explained in detail in the next section. Now, let's examine two different points of view toward probabilities and how they can be determined.

OBJECTIVE PROBABILITY

The objective point of view considers *probability* as the ratio of successful outcomes of an experiment to the total number of outcomes possible, or as the *relative frequency* of successful outcomes. The experiment, whether in the laboratory or in the field, produces facts on which everyone can agree. It is these objective facts which form the basis of the probability statement. For example, out of a particular group of 10,000 people age 30 years, if 9800 survive to age 35, the probability of survival of a member to age 35 equals .98.

We all know that a particular person can't be 98 percent alive at age 35, though some of us might feel that way or worse at times. The person picked will either be alive or dead at 35. The .98 simply means that if we know no more about the person in question than that he is a member of this particular group out of which 9800 will survive, we assign the group's relative frequency of survival to him. Or, if you prefer, we can give a slightly different interpretation to this objective probability and say that 98 to 2 are the best odds we'll give that this person will survive to age 35.

231

SUBJECTIVE PROBABILITY

According to the subjective view, a probability is simply a number representing a degree of belief concerning the occurrence of a future event. The only limitation regarding this number is that it be between 0 and 1. Complete certainty that a particular event *will* occur is equated with a probability of 1. Complete certainty that the event will *not* occur is equated with a probability of 0. Less than complete certainty concerning the event must then be characterized by a probability somewhere between 0 and 1.

A useful way of viewing subjective probabilities is to relate them to betting odds. If you were willing—just barely willing—to give 3 to 1 odds that the Green Bay Packers would win next season's National Football League championship, you implicitly assess the probability that they will win as 3 out of 4, or .75. While the success of the Packers in previous years might be a factor in assessing these odds, it can hardly be the sole determinant. You know very well that neither the Packers nor their opponents will be exactly the same teams next year as in years past, nor will they be meeting under the same conditions.

In much the same way the businessman, on the combined basis of historical record, current conditions, and perhaps hunch, may formulate the probability of success of a business undertaking. A subjectivist would argue that the basis of this probability, called subjective or personal probability, does not lie in an irresponsible subjectivity but in a subjectivity based on a realistic appraisal of the empirical world. Thus in a business context, we might view the basis of subjective probability as "informed business judgment" regardless of the exact source.

OBJECTIVE AND SUBJECTIVE PROBABILITY: A RESOLUTION

Whether these views are contradictory from a philosophical viewpoint has still to be settled. For us, however, the crucial question is whether they are contradictory from the perspective of the decision maker in business. We don't think so. A businessperson who has encountered a particular problem enough times to have available the relative frequencies of past events to use as probabilities of similar events occurring in the future would be foolish not to use them. On the other hand, if no such relative frequencies are available because the situation is new or unique, you must rely on whatever related and general experience you've had in addition to whatever specific observations you can make to formulate the odds of possible outcomes.

THE MATHEMATICAL THEORY OF PROBABILITY

Whether the probabilities are objective or subjective, we'll often need to manipulate them to obtain useful empirical results. For example, if a man bets on horse *A* of race number 2 and horse *D* of race number 3, what's the probability that he has at least one winner? Or consider the plight of a politician who must decide whether or not to run for election before his opponent is determined by an opposing party's primary. He may rightfully believe that his probability of getting elected depends in part on who his opponent is. How's his probability of getting elected related to the various probabilities of success attached to the contestants in the other primary? In a business context, consider a firm's decision about whether or not to market a new product. The firm, through a market survey, gains some new information with respect to attitudes toward the product. How can this new information be combined with the firm's accumulated past experience and judgment in introducing new products to assess the probability of the product's success?

The kind of questions posed above can often be answered by using a type of mathematical calculus called *mathematical probability*. The questions are real in the sense that they have an empirical context. The mathematical structure used to manipulate these empirical probabilities, however, is purely formal. As it turns out, many empirical processes can be described well by this formal mathematical structure. In the remainder of this module we'll develop a few simple but important probability concepts.

REVIEW EXERCISES 10.A

1. A probability is a number _____.
2. The probabilities of a set of _____ and _____ _____ events add to _____.
3. Interpreting probability as the relative frequency of successful outcomes of an experiment represents the _____ view of probability.
4. The subjective view holds that a probability is simply a degree of belief concerning the occurrence of a future event: true or false?
5. Business decisions are often based on:
    a. Relative frequencies from historical data.
    b. Subjective judgment.
    c. Either *a* or *b*.
    d. Neither *a* nor *b*.
6. The mathematical theory of probability:
    a. Is of little interest in statistical decision making.
    b. Is beyond the scope of this book.
    c. Deals with the manipulation of probabilities and the relationships among them.
    d. None of the above.

Answers 10.A

1. between 0 and 1   *2.* mutually exclusive (nonoverlapping); collectively exhaustive (completely enumerated); 1 (one)   *3.* objective   *4.* true   *5. c*   *6. c*

Section 10.B

Some Basic Probability Concepts

Learning objectives

Your learning objectives for this section are to be able to:

1. Define or explain the following terms:
   a. Venn diagram
   b. Frequency table
   c. Mutually exclusive
   d. Marginal probability
   e. Joint probability
   f. Conditional probability
2. Describe the relationship between marginal, joint, and conditional probabilities

VENN DIAGRAMS AND FREQUENCY TABLES

To develop some important notions related to the manipulation of probabilities, consider the following example. A group consists of ten people, four men and six women. Three of the four men smoke, as do two of the six women. In formal terms we can call the group a sample space which includes ten elements. The sample space or universal set U can be broken down into four subsets, men, women, smokers, and nonsmokers. Note that the subsets "men" and "women" are nonintersecting and may be defined as *mutually exclusive;* in practical terms this means that there can be no single element that had both the characteristics "male" and "female." The same is true of the subsets "smoker" and "nonsmoker." However, other subsets such as "male" and "smoker," for example, are *not* mutually exclusive since one person can have both characteristics.

The situation described above can be seen much more readily by drawing a Venn diagram, which shows the relationships between the subsets, or by constructing a table showing the number of people in each category, as in Fig. 10.1 and Table 10.1.

Persons 1, 2, and 3 in the Venn diagram can be identified as the three male smokers counted in the M,S cell of the frequency table. Similarly, person 6 is the one male nonsmoker in the M,NS cell, etc. It is not necessary to identify each element in a Venn diagram with a specific number, but such a procedure will help us identify specific persons in the discussion that follows.

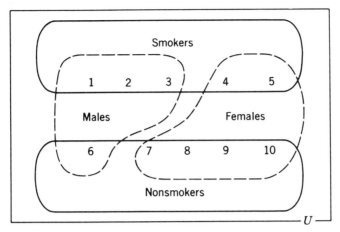

Figure 10.1 / Venn diagram for smoking example.

MARGINAL PROBABILITY

From the frequency table you can easily find, for example, the probability of choosing a male from the group by a method where every person in the group has an equal chance of being chosen. Since four of the ten people are males, the odds would be 4 in 10 that a person so selected would be male. To familiarize you with the symbols that are used in probability calculations, let's summarize the previous sentence as

$$P(M) = \frac{n(M)}{n(U)} = 4$$

Thus the probability of a male is the number of elements in the subset M divided by the number of elements in the universal set U. This probability, and any other one that includes the number of elements in a single category of classification (i.e., male, female, smoker, or nonsmoker) in the numerator of a fraction and the number of elements in the universal set in the denominator, is known as a *marginal probability*. The term "marginal" has nothing at all to do with economic theory—it merely relates

Table 10.1 / Frequency table, smoking example

	Male M	Female F	Total
Smoker S	3	2	5
Nonsmoker NS	1	4	5
Total	4	6	10

to the fact that the numbers in the numerator are to be found at the margins of the frequency table. Other marginal probabilities from the table are therefore:

$$P(F) = \frac{n(F)}{n(U)} = \frac{6}{10}$$

$$P(S) = \frac{n(S)}{n(U)} = \frac{5}{10}$$

$$P(NS) = \frac{n(NS)}{n(U)} = \frac{5}{10}$$

JOINT PROBABILITY

A joint probability is one that relates to more than one category of classification, as the name indicates. The probability of M and S is the number of individuals who are male and smokers divided by the number in the universal set. Since there are three male smokers,

$$P(M \text{ and } S) = \frac{n(M \text{ and } S)}{n(U)} = \frac{3}{10}$$

Similarly,

$$P(F \text{ and } S) = \frac{n(F \text{ and } S)}{n(U)} = \frac{2}{10}$$

$$P(M \text{ and } NS) = \frac{n(M \text{ and } NS)}{n(U)} = \frac{1}{10}$$

$$P(F \text{ and } NS) = \frac{n(F \text{ and } NS)}{n(U)} = \frac{4}{10}$$

Note that whether the expression $n(M$ and $S)$ or $n(S$ and $M)$ is used, we're referring to those three persons who have both the characteristic of being male and that of being a smoker. Therefore,

$$P(M \text{ and } S) = P(S \text{ and } M) = \tfrac{3}{10}$$

CONDITIONAL PROBABILITY

A conditional probability is contingent upon, or conditioned by, prior knowledge. Suppose you picked a person from the group of ten and observed he's a male. What's the probability that he's a nonsmoker? Looking at the frequency table down the Male column, you can observe that only one of the four males is a nonsmoker. Therefore the odds that the person picked is a nonsmoker given that he is male would be

$$P(NS \mid M) = \frac{n(NS \text{ and } M)}{n(M)} = \frac{1}{4}$$

The vertical line dividing NS from M may be read "given." Thus the probability of a nonsmoker given male is equal to the number of elements in the intersection of "nonsmoker" and "male" divided by the number of elements in "male." Similarly,

$$P(NS \mid F) = \frac{n(NS \text{ and } F)}{n(F)} = \frac{4}{6}$$

$$P(M \mid S) = \frac{n(M \text{ and } S)}{n(S)} = \frac{3}{5}$$

RELATIONSHIPS BETWEEN MARGINAL, JOINT, AND CONDITIONAL PROBABILITIES

A conditional probability can be defined solely in terms of the corresponding joint and marginal probabilities. Using the male smoker illustration, the following relationship holds:

$$P(M \mid S) = \frac{P(M \text{ and } S)}{P(S)} = \frac{P(S \text{ and } M)}{P(S)}$$

The proof of this relationship follows from the definition of joint and marginal probabilities. If

$$P(M \text{ and } S) = \frac{n(M \text{ and } S)}{n(U)} \qquad \text{and} \qquad P(S) = \frac{n(S)}{n(U)}$$

then

$$\frac{n(M \text{ and } S)/n(U)}{n(S)/n(U)} = \frac{n(M \text{ and } S)}{n(S)} = P(M \mid S)$$

The formulas we've used so far have all been developed in terms of the smoker-sex example. In more general terms, the relationships can be expressed as follows: for any two categories of classification A and B, consisting of four subsets A_1, A_2, B_1, and B_2,

$$P(A_1) = \frac{n(A_1)}{n(U)}$$

$$P(B_2) = \frac{n(B_2)}{n(U)}$$

marginal probabilities

. . . .

$$P(A_1 \text{ and } B_1) = \frac{n(A_1 \text{ and } B_1)}{n(U)}$$

$$P(A_1 \text{ and } B_2) = \frac{n(A_1 \text{ and } B_2)}{n(U)}$$

joint probabilities

. . . .

$$P(A_1 \mid B_1) = \frac{n(A_1 \text{ and } B_1)}{n(B_1)} = \frac{P(A_1 \text{ and } B_1)}{P(B_1)}$$

$$P(A_1 \mid B_2) = \frac{n(A_1 \text{ and } B_2)}{n(B_2)} = \frac{P(A_1 \text{ and } B_2)}{P(B_2)}$$

conditional probabilities

. . . .

REVIEW EXERCISES 10.B

1. A diagram which shows the relationship between subsets is called a _____ _____.

2. The term "mutually exclusive" applied to two subsets means that each element in one subset is also a member of the other subset: true or false?

3. The same basic information is contained (in different form) in a Venn diagram as in a frequency table: true or false?

4. A probability contingent on prior knowledge or other characteristics is called a _____ probability; a probability that relates to a single category or classification is called a _____ probability; while a probability that relates to more than one category is called a _____ probability.

5. Write a formula that expresses a conditional probability in terms of related joint and marginal probabilities and identify each type of probability in the formula.

Answers 10.B

1. Venn diagram   *2.* False; it means that no element is a member of both subsets
3. true   *4.* conditional; marginal; joint

5.
$$P(A \mid B) = \frac{\overset{\text{joint}}{P(A \text{ and } B)}}{\underset{\text{marginal}}{P(B)}}$$
$\underset{\text{conditional}}{}$

Section 10.C
Manipulating Probabilities: Laws of Multiplication and Addition

Learning objectives

Your learning objectives for this section are to be able to:

1. State and apply:
   a. The law of multiplication, including the special case for independent events
   b. The law of addition, including the special case for mutually exclusive events
2. Define the concept of statistical independence

THE GENERAL LAW OF MULTIPLICATION

The law of multiplication is simply a restatement of the definition of conditional probability. Defining conditional probability as

$$P(A \mid B) = \frac{P(A \text{ and } B)}{P(B)}$$

we can multiply both sides of the equation by $P(B)$, obtaining the relationship called the *law of multiplication*:

$$P(A \text{ and } B) = P(B)P(A \mid B) \qquad (10.1)$$

It also follows that

$$P(A \text{ and } B) = P(A)P(B \mid A) \qquad (10.2)$$

This law says that the joint probability of two subsets is the product of the conditional probability of those subsets times the marginal probability of the subset which is given as the condition.

While you may think of the law of multiplication as an unfamiliar symbolic generalization, you've probably used it many times unknowingly. Some simple examples should illustrate this fact. The probability of drawing two aces in succession from a well-shuffled deck of cards is

$$P(A_1 \text{ and } A_2) \quad = \quad P(A_1) \quad \times \quad P(A_2 \mid A_1)$$

$$\begin{pmatrix} \text{Probability of an} \\ \text{ace on draw 1} \\ \text{and draw 2} \end{pmatrix} = \begin{pmatrix} \text{Probability of an} \\ \text{ace on draw 1} \end{pmatrix} \times \begin{pmatrix} \text{Probability of an} \\ \text{ace on draw 2} \\ \textit{given} \text{ an ace} \\ \text{on draw 1} \end{pmatrix}$$

$$= \quad \frac{4}{52} \quad \times \quad \frac{3}{51} = \frac{12}{2652}$$

The marginal probability of an ace on the first draw is 4/52 since there are 4 aces in the deck of 52 cards. The conditional probability of an ace on the second draw *given* an ace on the first is 3/51 since there are 3 aces left among the 51 remaining cards.

Similarly, the probability of drawing four aces in succession is
$P(A_1 \text{ and } A_2 \text{ and } A_3 \text{ and } A_4)$

$$= P(A_1) \times P(A_2 \mid A_1) \times P(A_3 \mid A_1 \text{ and } A_2) \times P(A_4 \mid A_1 \text{ and } A_2 \text{ and } A_3)$$

$$= \frac{4}{52} \times \frac{3}{51} \times \frac{2}{50} \times \frac{1}{49}$$

$$= \frac{24}{6,497,400}$$

239

The probability of being dealt a royal flush (A, K, Q, J, 10 in any one suit in any order) in a five-card poker hand is

$$\frac{20}{52} \times \frac{4}{51} \times \frac{3}{50} \times \frac{2}{49} \times \frac{1}{48} = \frac{480}{311,875,200}$$

where 20/52 is the *marginal* probability of drawing an A, K, Q, J, or 10 in any suit out of the 52 cards, 4/51 is the *conditional* probability of drawing any 1 of the 4 necessary cards in the suit established by the first draw from the 51 remaining cards, etc.

THE SPECIAL LAW OF MULTIPLICATION: INDEPENDENT EVENTS

An event B is said to be *independent* of an event A if $P(B \mid A) = P(B)$. This situation occurs when event A has no effect whatsoever on event B, in which case knowing that event A has occurred gives you no edge in predicting the occurrence of event B. You may have learned from hard experience that since slot machines have no memory and therefore don't run hot and cold (only the players have memories and emotions which run hot and cold), the probability of a payoff given a payoff on the preceding trial is exactly the same as the overall (marginal) probability of a payoff.

In the case of statistical independence, the law of multiplication

$$P(A \text{ and } B) = P(A \mid B)P(B)$$

reduces to

$$P(A \text{ and } B) = P(A)P(B) \qquad (10.3)$$

since by the definition of independence $P(A \mid B) = P(A)$ for this case.

To solidify the notion of statistical independence, consider again the frequency matrix classifying smokers by sex shown in Table 10.1.

Converting to a probability table by dividing each element by the sum of all the elements, we obtain joint probabilities in each cell and marginal probabilities at each margin, as shown in Table 10.2.

From Table 10.2 it is evident that status as a smoker is *not* independent of sex. If it were, the product of the marginals would equal the corresponding joint probabilities. In Table 10.2 the product of the marginals "smoker" and "male," (.5)(.4), does *not* equal the joint probability of "smoker and male" of .3, and so on.

Table 10.1 (Repeated) / Frequency table, smoking example

	Male M	Female F	Total
Smoker S	3	2	5
Nonsmoker NS	1	4	5
Total	4	6	10

Table 10.2 / Probability table, smoking example

	Male M	Female F	Total
Smoker S	.3	.2	.5
Nonsmoker NS	.1	.4	.5
Total	.4	.6	1.0

Table 10.3 / Probability table, smoking example with independent events

	Male M	Female F	Total
Smoker S	.2	.3	.5
Nonsmoker NS	.2	.3	.5
Total	.4	.6	1.0

If the propensity to smoke were in fact independent of sex, the proportion of male smokers to total males would be the same as the proportion of female smokers to total females, as in Table 10.3.

In this case, the product of each pair of marginals is equal to the corresponding joint probability, proving independence. Thus the knowledge of a person's sex would be of no value in determining the probability that the person smoked since $P(S \mid M) = P(S \mid F) = P(S)$.

THE GENERAL LAW OF ADDITION

The *law of addition* is used to calculate the probability that a number of events will occur, either separately *or* jointly. Thus $P(S$ or $M)$ means the probability that a person selected at random is a smoker *or* a male *or* both. Referring to the Venn diagram presented earlier (repeated here as Fig. 10.2), the probability that a person is a smoker *or* a male is equal to $n(S$ or $M)/n(U) = 6/10$. The specific persons in either of the subsets "smoker" and "male" are those numbered 1, 2, 3, 6, 4, and 5 in the shaded area of the Venn diagram.

For more complex problems it is convenient to calculate this probability using probabilities already calculated. If you look carefully at the Venn diagram, you'll discover that this can be accomplished as follows:

$$P(S \text{ or } M) = P(S) + P(M) - P(S \text{ and } M)$$
$$= \frac{n(S)}{n(U)} + \frac{n(M)}{n(U)} - \frac{n(S \text{ and } M)}{n(U)}$$
$$= \tfrac{5}{10} + \tfrac{4}{10} - \tfrac{3}{10} = \tfrac{6}{10}$$

241

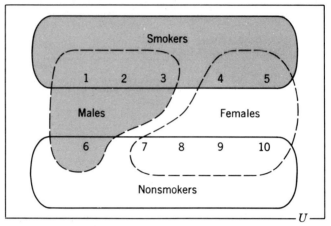

Figure 10.2 / Venn diagram for smoking example.

This equality is known as the law of addition. You must *subtract* $P(S \text{ and } M)$ from the sum of $P(S)$ and $P(M)$ to avoid double counting. If you added the number of smokers to the number of males, you'd count the three persons who are *both* smokers and males twice.

In general, the law of addition for two events A and B is

$$P(A \text{ or } B) = P(A) + P(B) - P(A \text{ and } B) \qquad (10.4)$$

THE SPECIAL LAW OF ADDITION: MUTUALLY EXCLUSIVE EVENTS

If two events are mutually exclusive, there are no elements common to both events. In such a case $P(A \text{ and } B) = 0$, and the general law of addition reduces to the special case,

$$P(A \text{ or } B) = P(A) + P(B) \qquad (10.5)$$

Application of this special case can be demonstrated in relation to the smoking example. Suppose you calculated $P(S \text{ or } NS)$. Obviously one cannot be both a smoker and a nonsmoker (at least at the same time), and $P(S \text{ and } NS) = 0$. Therefore

$$P(S \text{ or } NS) = P(S) + P(NS) = \tfrac{5}{10} + \tfrac{5}{10} = 1$$

(When there are more than two mutually exclusive categories in a particular problem, the either-or probabilities of any two won't, of course, add to 1, as they do for the example here.)

242

REVIEW EXERCISES 10.C

1. If $P(B \mid A) = P(B)$, the events A and B are said to be mutually exclusive (true or false).
2. If $P(A \text{ and } B) = 0$, the events A and B are _____.
3. The general law of multiplication is _____, which, in the special case of independent events, reduces to _____.
4. The general law of addition is _____, which, in the special case of mutually exclusive events, reduces to _____.
5. To calculate that events A or B will occur, either separately or jointly, you'd use:
   a. The law of multiplication.
   b. The law of addition.
   c. The definition of statistical independence.
   d. None of the above.
6. If two cards are dealt from a well-shuffled deck of ordinary playing cards, calculate the probability that:
   a. They are both black aces.
   b. They are either both black or both aces.

Answers 10.C

1. False; this means the events A and B are statistically independent.
2. mutually exclusive
3. $P(A \text{ and } B) = P(A \mid B)P(B)$; $P(A \text{ and } B) = P(A)P(B)$
4. $P(A \text{ or } B) = P(A) + P(B) - P(A \text{ and } B)$; in the case of mutually exclusive events: $P(A \text{ or } B) = P(A) + P(B)$
5. b
6. a. $P(\text{black ace and black ace}) = \frac{2}{52}(\frac{1}{51}) = .00075$
   b. $P(\text{black and black}) = \frac{26}{52}(\frac{25}{51}) = .24510$; $P(\text{ace and ace}) = \frac{4}{52}(\frac{3}{51}) = .00452$
   Therefore, from the law of addition

$$P(BB \text{ or } AA) = P(BB) + P(AA) - P(BB \text{ and } AA)$$
$$= .24510 + .00452 - .00075 = .24887$$

Section 10.D

Bayes' Rule

Learning objectives

Your learning objectives for this section are to be able to apply Bayes' rule and explain its purpose.

REVERSING CONDITIONAL PROBABILITIES: AN EXAMPLE

In the eighteenth century the Reverend Thomas Bayes manipulated the laws of addition and multiplication of probabilities to formulate a rule which has become the cornerstone of modern decision theory. Bayes' rule makes it possible to "reverse the direction" of a conditional probability, i.e., to determine a conditional probability like $P(A \mid B)$ in terms of the reverse, $P(B \mid A)$, and the relevant marginal probabilities. Let's consider an example to illustrate what is involved.

Suppose you're asked to determine which of two apparently identical dice is loaded. One is known to be "fair" (with a probability of a one-spot equal to $\frac{1}{6}$), but the other is loaded to make the probability of a one-spot $\frac{1}{4}$. You choose one die and examine its physical characteristics closely, but you can detect nothing. At this point, as far as you are concerned, the probability that the die is fair is simply $\frac{1}{2}$. Suppose further, however, that you are allowed to test the die by rolling it just once. You do so and obtain a one-spot on the roll. Now how do you feel about the probability that the die is fair?

In symbolic terms, you are trying to determine $P(F \mid O)$, the probability that the die is fair *given* that a one-spot has been rolled. You know the "reverse" conditional probability, $P(O \mid F)$. (The probability of a one-spot, given that the die is fair, is $\frac{1}{6}$). You also know the probability of a one-spot given that the die is unfair, $P(O \mid U) = \frac{1}{4}$, and the marginal probabilities, $P(F) = \frac{1}{2}$ and $P(U) = \frac{1}{2}$. The problem is to determine $P(F \mid O)$ in terms of these known probabilities. Let's muddle through.

From the general definition of a conditional probability

$$P(F \mid O) = \frac{P(F \text{ and } O)}{P(O)}$$

Getting the numerator $P(F \text{ and } O)$ is straightforward. From the law of multiplication,

$$P(F \text{ and } O) = P(O \mid F)P(F)$$

(Note that we have used the conditional probability in the reverse direction, since that is the one that is known.) For our example

$$P(F \text{ and } O) = \tfrac{1}{6} \times \tfrac{1}{2} = \tfrac{1}{12}$$

The tricky part is determining the probability in the denominator, $P(O)$. This is a marginal probability, involving the single event one-spot. The way we can obtain it is to add all the mutually exclusive joint probabilities that include the event. In our example, these are the probabilities $P(F \text{ and } O)$ plus $P(U \text{ and } O)$:

$$P(U \text{ and } O) = P(O \mid U)P(U) = \tfrac{1}{4} \times \tfrac{1}{2} = \tfrac{1}{8}$$

and $\quad P(O) = P(F \text{ and } O) + P(U \text{ and } O) = \tfrac{1}{12} + \tfrac{1}{8} = \tfrac{2}{24} + \tfrac{3}{24} = \tfrac{5}{24}$

244

We're finally ready to use the equation we started with:

$$P(F \mid O) = \frac{P(F \text{ and } O)}{P(O)} = \frac{\frac{1}{12}}{\frac{5}{24}} = \frac{\frac{2}{24}}{\frac{5}{24}} = \frac{2}{5} = 0.4$$

Thus, the odds that the die we rolled is fair have been lowered. Before rolling it, you'd have bet with even odds that the die was fair. After the one-roll experiment, you'd be less sure and could bet with odds of only 2 out of 5, or 0.4.

What we've really done in this example is to revise a set of probabilities to reflect the outcome of an experiment. This revision process will prove extremely useful later as we incorporate the evidence from samples (experiments) into our decision problems.

FORMAL STATEMENT OF BAYES' RULE

In reasoning through the loaded-die illustration, in the context of the example, we've actually derived Bayes' rule. A formal statement of it (using the symbols from our example) might appear as follows:

$$P(F \mid O) = \frac{P(O \mid F)P(F)}{P(O \mid F)P(F) + P(O \mid U)P(U)} \tag{10.6}$$

You'll have occasion to use this rule at several points later in this book.

REVIEW EXERCISES 10.D

1. Consider the example used in previous sections concerning sex vs. smoking habits. Use Bayes' rule to determine the probability that a person chosen at random is a smoker, given that he is male, that is, $P(S \mid M)$. Recall that

$$P(M \mid S) = \tfrac{3}{5} \qquad P(M \mid NS) = \tfrac{1}{5} \qquad P(S) = \tfrac{5}{10} \qquad P(NS) = \tfrac{5}{10}$$

After you have used Bayes' rule to obtain $P(S \mid M)$, you may want to check it by referring to the original frequency table.
2. Bayes' rule can be applied only in situations where a complete frequency table is available to determine relevant probabilities (true or false).

Answers 10.D

1. For this example, the version of Bayes' rule needed is:

$$P(S \mid M) = \frac{P(M \mid S)P(S)}{P(M \mid S)P(S) + P(M \mid NS)P(NS)}$$

245

Substituting the known values gives

$$P(S \mid M) = \frac{(\frac{3}{5})(\frac{5}{10})}{(\frac{3}{5})(\frac{5}{10}) + (\frac{1}{5})(\frac{5}{10})} = \frac{3}{4}$$

You can check these results with the original frequency table by noting that

$$P(S \mid M) = \frac{P(S \text{ and } M)}{P(M)} = \frac{\frac{3}{10}}{\frac{4}{10}} = \frac{3}{4}$$

2. False; Bayes' rule will have greatest usefulness in situations where a complete frequency table is unavailable and certain of the conditional, joint, and marginal probabilities are not known or apparent. (The smoking example is used here primarily to illustrate the mechanics of the rule in a familiar context.)

Section 10.E
Binomial Probabilities

Learning objectives

Your learning objectives for this section are to be able to:

1. Define:
   a. Bernoulli trials
   b. Binomial probabilities
2. Describe the binomial probability distribution
3. Calculate binomial probabilities
4. Use the binomial table to obtain binomial probabilities

BERNOULLI TRIALS

In the dice problem of the previous section, suppose you'd been permitted *two* tosses of the die to help determine whether it is fair. To make use of the experimental information that would result you'd need to be able to compute probabilities for outcomes such as 1 one-spot in 2 tosses of a fair die. This is a *binomial probability*, defined as such because of the following characteristics:

1. The experiment could be viewed as a sequence of separate and distinct *trials* (in this case the two successive tosses of the die).
2. Each trial could result in either of two possible outcomes, which, for convenience, are referred to as *success* and *failure*. (The outcome one-spot may be

arbitrarily defined as success, and the outcome non-one as failure. It makes no difference which is which as long as we are consistent.)

3. The probability of success on any given trial remains constant throughout the sequence of trials. (The probability of obtaining a one-spot is $\frac{1}{6}$ on each toss.)

4. The trials are statistically independent; i.e., the outcome of any given trial does not depend on the outcome of other trials in the sequence. (The outcome of the second toss of the die is unaffected by the outcome of the first toss. The die has no memory!)

Trials which meet the conditions set forth in conditions 2 to 4 are referred to as *Bernoulli trials*. Binomial probabilities measure the probability of obtaining a given number of successes in a given number of Bernoulli trials. Successive tosses of a particular coin, or even simultaneous tosses of identical coins, represent Bernoulli trials, and the probability of obtaining 7 heads out of 10 tosses is a binomial probability.

Examples of Bernoulli processes and the use of binomial probabilities are by no means limited to dice- and coin-tossing experiments. Many empirical processes of importance to business decision makers can be described by classifying a series of distinct elements on an either-or, "go or no-go" basis. Each unit of a product coming off an assembly line might be classified as defective or not defective. Persons comprising the potential market for a particular product might be classified as buyers or nonbuyers. Vouchers examined by an auditor may be viewed as correct or in error.

In many business-related illustrations such as these, the conditions described above for a Bernoulli process may not be met precisely. The probability of a defective output from a manufacturing process may change over time (violating condition 3) as a result of mechanical wear on a machine. Errors in invoices may occur in clusters (violating condition 4) because of the effect of fatigue on clerical employees. Very often, however, the effect of departures from theoretical conditions on the solutions of practical problems is minor, and the assumption of Bernoulli processes may make difficult problems tractable. In any case, the uses of binomial probabilities are so widespread as to justify some particular attention to their calculation.

THE CALCULATION OF BINOMIAL PROBABILITIES

To illustrate the calculation of binomial probabilities, let's expand our dice-tossing experiment to include four successive tosses. Assuming that the die is fair, i.e., that the probability of a one-spot on any roll is $\frac{1}{6}$, what is the probability of obtaining exactly two one-spots (successes) on four tosses (trials)?

Now if these two successes were to occur on the first two tosses, to be followed by two failures, i.e., *SSFF*, we could easily calculate the probability of occurrence according to the law of multiplication for independent events.

$$P(SSFF) = \frac{1}{6} \times \frac{1}{6} \times \frac{5}{6} \times \frac{5}{6} = \frac{25}{1296}$$

Usually, however, we are not concerned about the ordering of the outcomes but only the likelihood of two successes out of four trials in any order. All in all, we must consider all the following possible orderings:

$$
\begin{array}{ll}
SSFF & FFSS \\
SFSF & FSFS \\
SFFS & FSSF
\end{array}
$$

In total, there are *six* possible orders in which the two successes (coupled with two failures) can occur. Each of these orderings has a probability of occurrence of 25/1296, obtained as the product of two factors of $\frac{1}{6}$ and two factors of $\frac{5}{6}$ in some order. Since they are mutually exclusive, the probabilities are additive, and

$$
P(2S, 2F, \text{ in any order}) = 6 \times \frac{25}{1296} = \frac{150}{1296}
$$

In order to eliminate the rather clumsy notation used so far, we can formalize it. Let

$$
\begin{aligned}
n &= \text{number of trials} \\
r &= \text{number of successes in } n \text{ trials} \\
n - r &= \text{number of failures in } n \text{ trials} \\
p &= \text{probability of success in any trial} \\
(1 - p) &= \text{probability of failure in any trial}
\end{aligned}
$$

The probability of r successes in n trials in a particular order is

$$
(p)^r (1 - p)^{n-r}
$$

The number of possible orderings of successes and failures is given by the combinatorial formula for the combination of n elements taken r at a time:

$$
C(n,r) = \frac{n!}{r!(n - r)!}
$$

The ! symbol stands for *factorial*. For $n = 4$, $n!$ means $4 \times 3 \times 2 \times 1$. Note that the number of orderings of two successes in four trials, as given by this formula, is

$$
C(4,2) = \frac{4!}{2!(4 - 2)!} = \frac{4!}{(2!)(2!)} = \frac{4 \times 3 \times 2 \times 1}{(2 \times 1)(2 \times 1)} = \frac{24}{4} = 6
$$

This checks with the result we obtained by enumeration or brute force.

The generalized formula for a binomial probability can now be written by combining the term describing the probability of the desired outcome in a particular order with the combinatorial term which "counts" the number of possible orderings:

$$
P(r \mid n,p) = \frac{n!}{r!(n - r)!} p^r (1 - p)^{n-r} \tag{10.7}
$$

This is read as the binomial probability of r successes, given n trials and probability of success p on any given trial.

To demonstrate the use of this formula, let's consider some further examples.

EXAMPLE 1

What is the probability of obtaining exactly 8 heads out of 10 tosses, assuming a fair coin?

$$P(r = 8 \mid n = 10, p = .5)\frac{10!}{8!2!}\left(\frac{1}{2}\right)^8\left(\frac{1}{2}\right)^2 = .0440$$

EXAMPLE 2

For an assembly-line product past experience indicates that 5 percent of the product is defective. If 15 units are drawn from the assembly line, what is the probability that exactly 2 are defective?

$$P(r = 2 \mid n = 15, p = .05) = \frac{15!}{2!13!}(.05^2)(.95^{13}) = .1348$$

THE BINOMIAL DISTRIBUTION

Actually, the general binomial distribution is a family of probability distributions describing the probabilities of the possible experimental outcomes for all possible combinations of n and p. Since n can be any positive integer and p any value between 0 and 1, the size of the family is unlimited. The values n and p which determine a particular binomial distribution are called *parameters* of the distribution. For purposes of explanation, let us calculate the binomial probabilities for a particular member of this family with parameters $n = 4$ and $p = \frac{1}{6}$, the combination describing the four tosses of our fair die.

$$P(r = 0 \mid n = 4, p = \tfrac{1}{6}) = \frac{4!}{0!4!}\left(\frac{1}{6}\right)^0\left(\frac{5}{6}\right)^4 = 1(\tfrac{625}{1296}) = \tfrac{625}{1296}$$

(You may need to recall that $0! = 1$, by definition, and $k^0 = 1$.)

$$P(r = 1 \mid n = 4, p = \tfrac{1}{6}) = \frac{4!}{1!3!}\left(\frac{1}{6}\right)^1\left(\frac{5}{6}\right)^3 = 4(\tfrac{125}{1296}) = \tfrac{500}{1296}$$

$$P(r = 2 \mid n = 4, p = \tfrac{1}{6}) = \frac{4!}{2!2!}\left(\frac{1}{6}\right)^2\left(\frac{5}{6}\right)^2 = 6(\tfrac{25}{1296}) = \tfrac{150}{1296}$$

$$P(r = 3 \mid n = 4, p = \tfrac{1}{6}) = \frac{4!}{3!1!}\left(\frac{1}{6}\right)^3\left(\frac{5}{6}\right)^1 = 4(\tfrac{5}{1296}) = \tfrac{20}{1296}$$

$$P(r = 4 \mid n = 4, p = \tfrac{1}{6}) = \frac{4!}{4!0!}\left(\frac{1}{6}\right)^4\left(\frac{5}{6}\right)^0 = 1(\tfrac{1}{1296}) = \tfrac{1}{1296}$$

Table 10.4 / Binomial probability distribution for $n = 4$, $p = \frac{1}{6}$

Number of successes r	Probability
0	$\frac{625}{1296} = .482$
1	$\frac{500}{1296} = .386$
2	$\frac{150}{1296} = .116$
3	$\frac{20}{1296} = .015$
4	$\frac{1}{1296} = .001$
	$\frac{1296}{1296}\quad 1.000$

Specifically, it is the summarization of these results for all possible outcomes $r = 0$ through $r = 4$ given in Table 10.4 that is called a binomial probability distribution. Note that since the listed outcomes are mutually exclusive and collectively exhaustive, the sum of the probabilities is equal to 1.0. This is characteristic of all probability distributions, about which you'll learn more in subsequent modules.

BINOMIAL TABLES

Fortunately, a great many binomial probabilities have been calculated for various values of p and n and published in tables. These tables conserve considerable effort, for even though the computation of binomial probabilities is conceptually straightforward, the sheer arithmetic involved in many practical problems could be overwhelming.

The calculation problem is even more formidable when questions concerning *cumulative* probabilities are asked. For example, the probability that *at least* 3 people out of 20 have birthdays on a particular day is a cumulative probability. "At least three people" means three or more, so that we should be forced to calculate not only $P(3)$, but $P(4)$, $P(5)$, . . . , $P(20)$ and to sum over all these terms. Or, a relevant question might be: What is the probability that *fewer than* two defectives appear in a sample of 10 with a given p?

All questions of this sort can be answered by summing over the relevant individual, or point probabilities. In the case of the birthdays it would be easier to calculate $P(0)$, $P(1)$, and $P(2)$ and then to subtract their sum from 1 to get $P(3$ or more). However, in the case of the two defectives it appears that the quickest and easiest procedure to get $P(\text{less than } 2)$ is to calculate $P(0)$ and $P(1)$ and then add them. At any rate, to answer these questions, at least some, and sometimes many individual probabilities would have to be calculated. For this reason most published binomial tables give cumulative probabilities, from which the individual point probabilities can be easily determined. Appendix Table A.1 is such a table.

A few comments are in order concerning this table. First, you must remember that the binomial distribution is really a family of distributions for various combinations of values for p and n. The table in this book considers only n values of 10, 20, 50, and 100. For each n given, you can find probabilities for p values from .02 to .98 at increments of .02.

Also, remember that the table is *cumulative*. It deals with the *upper* end of the distribution for $p \leq .50$ and the *lower* end of the distribution for $p > .50$. For example, with $n = 50$ and $p = .4$, the probability that r is equal to 19 *or more* is given as .6644. Remember that by r we mean the number of successes in a given number of trials. Thus, for this illustration, $P(r \geq 19 \mid n = 50, p = .4) = .6644$. The .6644 is the sum of the point probabilities for all the values of r from 19 through 50.

To determine a point probability, i.e., the probability of exactly r, we merely need to subtract two successive cumulative probabilities. For example, with $n = 20$ and $p = .3$, the probability of $r \geq 5 = .7625$. Given the same n and p, the probability of $r \geq 6 = .5836$. Some reflection will show that $(r \geq 5) - (r \geq 6)$ defines $r = 5$. Thus the point probability that r is the integer 5 is $.7625 - .5836 = .1789$. To get the probability that r is less than some particular number Y at a given n and p combination simply involves subtracting $P(r \geq Y)$ from 1. Although you'd do well to practice a bit with these tables at this point, we'll have occasion to illustrate their use at numerous points as we go along.

REVIEW EXERCISES 10.E

1. Which items are characteristics of Bernoulli trials?
   a. Each trial can result in any of several outcomes.
   b. Each trial can result in either of only two possible outcomes.
   c. The probability of a successful outcome remains constant from trial to trial.
   d. The probability of success changes with the number of trials.
   e. The outcome of a given trial depends on the outcome of previous trials in the sequence.
   f. The trials are statistically independent.
2. Bernoulli trials are generally applicable in games of chance but have little application in business decision problems: true or false?
3. Calculate the binomial probability of obtaining exactly 2 one-spots out of 3 rolls of a fair die.
4. The binomial probability distribution:
   a. Is really a family of distributions.
   b. Has a large number of parameters.
   c. Does not apply to situations involving Bernoulli trials.
   d. None of the above.
5. Parameters of the binomial distribution are _____ and

_____.
6. Use the binomial table in Appendix A.1 to determine:
   a. $P(r \geq 20 \mid n = 50, p = .4)$.
   b. $P(r = 20 \mid n = 50, p = .4)$.
   c. $P(r < 20 \mid n = 50, p = .4)$.
   d. $P(r \geq 35 \mid n = 50, p = .66)$.

Answers 10.E

1. b, c, and f 2. false

3. $P(r = 2 \mid n = 3, p = \frac{1}{6}) = \dfrac{3!}{2! \, 1!} \left(\dfrac{1}{6}\right)^2 \left(\dfrac{5}{6}\right)^1$

$$= 3(\tfrac{1}{36})(\tfrac{5}{6}) = \tfrac{15}{216}$$

4. a

5. n, the number of trials, and p, the probability of success on any given trial

6. a. $P(r \geq 20 \mid n = 50, p = .4) = .5535$ (read directly from the table)

   b. $P(r = 20 \mid n = 50, p = .4) = P(r \geq 20 \mid n = 50, p = .4)$

   $ - P(r \geq 21 \mid n = 50, p = .4)$

   $ = .5535 - .4390 = .1145$

   c. $P(r < 20 \mid n = 50, p = .4) = 1 - P(r \geq 20 \mid n = 50, p = .4)$

   $\phantom{c. P(r < 20 \mid n = 50, p = .4)} = 1 - .5535 = .4465$

   d. Since $p > .5$, the table must be entered from the right, using $1 - p$.

   If $p = .66$, $1 - p = .34$.

   $P(r \geq 35 \mid n = 50, p = .66) = 1 - P(r \leq 34 \mid n = 50, p = .66) = 1 - .6679 = .3321$

Section 10.F

Some Characteristics of Probability Distributions

Learning objectives

Your learning objectives for this section are to be able to:

1. Define and explain the nature of:
   a. A random variable
   b. Expected values
2. Compute the mean and standard deviation of a probability distribution

---

RANDOM VARIABLES

A *random variable* is defined as a quantity that has a definite value for each possible event (or state of nature). These values may be thought of as the outcomes of a probability experiment, or random generating process. Although the values of the random variable are unknown prior to the outcome of the experiment, the *probability* that the random variable will take on specific values may be known in advance.

This definition is perhaps better understood by reference to an earlier illustration. In the die-tossing example, the number of one-spots appearing in four tosses of a fair die is a random variable. Although we cannot say with certainty how many one-spots will appear in any particular experiment (set of four tosses), the binomial probability distribution constructed earlier does give us the likelihood that the random variable will take on the specific values 0, 1, 2, 3, and 4. To generalize, the number of successes r is the random variable of any binomial probability distribution. Recall that n, the number of trials, and p, the probability of success on any given trial, are parameters, or characteristics, of the distribution which serve to determine the probabilities of various outcomes, or values of the random variable.

The concept of a random variable is not restricted to binomial probability distributions. In fact, *any* listing of all the possible values of a random variable together with the probability of each is called a *probability distribution*. Other probability distributions which we'll consider later simply describe a different functional relationship between a random variable and a set of probabilities than that given by the binomial formula.

Random variables and their associated probability distributions can be *discrete* or *continuous*. A variable is discrete if it can take on only a restricted set of values. The random variable r in the die-tossing example is discrete since it can take on integer values, 0, 1, 2, 3, 4. A continuous variable, on the other hand, is capable of assuming *any* value within a given interval. More will be said about them later.

Concern regarding random variables is also appropriate to a discussion involving business decision theory because it is lack of certainty regarding the value of a random variable that characterizes many business problems. For example, the correct quantity of a good to stock would be easy to determine if demand, measured in terms of units that might be sold, were known with certainty. If demand can take on a number of possible values and thus be considered a random variable, the problem of how many to stock becomes a significant one of decision making under uncertainty.

The quantitative nature of values of random variables is a distinguishing characteristic. There is a definite value or number such as demand of 1, 10, 25, etc., that characterizes each state of nature or event. Events described in qualitative, rather than quantitative, terms cannot be random variables, e.g., sweater size would not be a random variable if the sizes were small, medium, and large. (However, if sizes were measured according to inches such as 36, 38, 40, 42, etc., sweater size could be considered a random variable.) This quantitative characteristic is important for it allows for the summarization of distributions of random variables through the use of expectations, or expected values.

EXPECTED VALUES

An *expected value*, or expectation, is obtained by multiplying each possible value of a discrete random variable by the probability of that value, and then adding all the weighted values. In general, an expected value is denoted by the symbol E followed by the random variable in question in parenthesis. Thus if X is a random variable, its expected value is

$$E(X) = \sum XP(X) \tag{10.8}$$

where X is a particular value of random variable, $P(X)$ is its probability, and $\sum$ means the summation of the $XP(X)$ values for all the values of X. You'll learn more about the meaning and interpretation of expected values in later modules.

THE MEAN OF A PROBABILITY DISTRIBUTION

The mean of a probability distribution is equivalent to the expected value of the distribution. Since a probability distribution, by definition, gives the probability of *all* possible values of a random variable, its mean is a population mean, to which we assign the symbol μ_X. Thus, for a probability distribution

$$\mu_X = E(X) = \sum XP(X) \tag{10.9}$$

THE VARIANCE AND STANDARD DEVIATION OF A PROBABILITY DISTRIBUTION

Similarly, the variance of a probability distribution is given the symbol σ_X^2. It is equal to the expected value of the squared deviations of the values of the random variable X from their mean:

$$\sigma_X^2 = E[(X - \mu_X)^2] = \sum (X - \mu_X)^2 P(X) \tag{10.10}$$

It follows that the standard deviation for a probability distribution is given by

$$\sigma_X = \sqrt{\sum (X - \mu_X)^2 P(X)} \tag{10.11}$$

COMPUTING DESCRIPTIVE MEASURES FOR A PROBABILITY DISTRIBUTION

Let's use a simple example to illustrate the concepts discussed above. Assume that four lots of a certain product were sold to a particular industrial user over a period of time to fulfill a contract. The four lots constitute the population—the entire number of lots sold under the contract. Recall that the size of a *population* is denoted by N; therefore in this problem $N = 4$. Now assume that each of these lots was examined for defectives, and it was found that two lots had no defectives, one lot had one defective, and one lot had three defectives. The number of defects per lot is considered here as a random variable.

The probability distribution of defectives per lot is summarized in the first two columns of Table 10.5. The remaining columns are used in the calculation of the population mean and standard deviation. Note that the population mean could also

Table 10.5 / Probability distribution for defectives per lot

Number of defectives per lot X	Probability $P(X)$	$XP(X)$	$X - \mu_X$	$(X - \mu_X)^2$	$(X - \mu_X)^2 P(X)$
0	.50	0	−1.0	1.0	.50
1	.25	.25	0	0	0
3	.25	.75	2.0	4.0	1.00
	1.00	1.00			1.50

$$\mu_X = E(X) = \sum XP(X) = 1.00$$
$$\sigma_X = \sqrt{\sum (X - \mu_X)^2 P(X)} = \sqrt{1.50} \approx 1.22$$

have been obtained by $\sum X/N$; $(0 + 0 + 1 + 3)/4 = 1.00$. The population standard deviation could have been calculated by using

$$\sqrt{\frac{\sum (X - \mu_X)^2}{N}} = \sqrt{\frac{(0 - 1)^2 + (0 - 1)^2 + (1 - 1)^2 + (1 - 3)^2}{4}} \approx 1.22$$

The value of N rather than $N - 1$ is used in the denominator because we are finding the population standard deviation from the entire population; we are not estimating the population standard deviation from a sample.

REVIEW EXERCISES 10.F

1. A random variable has a definite value for each event (or possible outcome) of a random generating process: true or false?
2. The expected value of a random variable:
   a. Is a weighted average of its possible values.
   b. Is equal to $\sum XP(X)$, where X is the random variable.
   c. Is equivalent to the mean of its probability distribution.
   d. All the above.
3. The following is the probability distribution for a random variable X, where X is the number of heads that will be obtained in a simultaneous toss of two fair coins:

No. of heads X	Probability $P(X)$
0	$\frac{1}{4}$
1	$\frac{1}{2}$
2	$\frac{1}{4}$
	1.0

   a. Compute the mean of this probability distribution.
   b. Compute the standard deviation of this probability distribution.
   c. Compute the expected value of the random variable.

Answers 10.F

1. true   *2. d*
3.

X	$P(X)$	$XP(X)$	$X - \mu_X$	$(X - \mu_X)^2$	$(X - \mu_X)^2 P(X)$
0	$\frac{1}{4}$	0	-1	1	.25
1	$\frac{1}{2}$	.5	0	0	0
2	$\frac{1}{4}$	.5	$+1$	1	.25
		1.0			.50

a. $\mu_X = E(X) = \sum XP(X) = 1.0$
b. $\sigma_X = \sqrt{\sum (X - \mu_X)^2 P(X)} = \sqrt{.50} = .71$
c. $E(X) = 1.0$ (the same as the mean)

Questions and Problems

10.1. Give two definitions of the word "probability."
10.2. Give three examples of situations in which the assessment of a probability might be expected to affect a business decision. Do not use situations described in this module.
10.3. You work for a car dealer and are interested in the relationship between the sex of the buyer and the color of the car. Tabulation of past sales results in the following table:

	Sex		
Car color	Male	Female	Total
Dark	100	40	140
Light	100	60	160
Total	200	100	300

a. Determine the marginal probability of light.
b. Determine the joint probability of male and dark.
c. Determine the conditional probability of dark given female.
d. Is color of car independent of sex? Prove your answer numerically.
10.4. Assume that you have determined the following relationships between income level and number of TV sets owned by families:

	Number of TV sets			
Family income	0	1	2 or more	Total
< $5000	40	240	20	300
$5000–$10,000	50	400	50	500
> $10,000	10	160	30	200
	100	800	100	1000

a. Find the marginal probability of less than $5000 income, $P(<5000)$.

b. Find the conditional probability of 0 sets given less than $5000 income, $P(0 \mid <5000)$.

c. Find the probability of the joint occurrence of 0 sets and less than $5000 income, $P(0, <5000)$, using appropriate numbers from the table.

d. Find $P(0, <5000)$ as in part *c*, but using the general law of multiplication and your results from parts *a* and *b*.

e. Is TV ownership independent of income? Prove your answer using appropriate numbers.

10.5. Assume that you carry insurance on your house, your car, and your health. The probability of your filing a claim in any one year on your house is .05, on your car is .20, and on your health is .80.

a. If these three types of claims are independent of each other, find:

(1) The probability of filing a health claim *and* a car claim but not a house claim in 1 year.

(2) The probability of filing either a health claim *or* a car claim or both but not a house claim in 1 year.

(3) The probability of filing all three types of claims in 1 year.

b. Why is the assumption of independence made in part *a* not likely to be completely justified?

10.6. An appliance dealer has kept careful records on sales vs. prospects for washers and dryers. (A prospect is a person who enters the store and asks a salesman about an appliance.) After some time he finds that the probability that a prospect will buy a washer is .10, the probability that a prospect will buy a dryer is .05, and the probability that a person will buy a matching washer and a dryer is .02.

a. What is the probability that a prospect will buy either a washer or a dryer (but not a matching pair)?

b. What is the probability that a prospect will buy a matching dryer, having bought a washer?

c. What is the probability that a prospect will buy a matching washer, having bought a dryer?

d. Is the buying of dryers independent of the buying of washers? Explain.

10.7. The women voters in a particular precinct are all married, and 90 percent of them invariably vote *differently* from their husbands.

a. If 60 percent of the male voters are known to favor Miss Bubbles Cash for mayor over the alternate candidate, what percentage of the female votes can Bubbles expect to receive?

b. In what percentage of the families will husband and wife cast their vote for Bubbles?

Hint: A frequency matrix, expressed in percent, like the one on page 235 may be helpful in solving this problem.

10.8. The New York Mets are leading in the World Series three games to two. The odds are 4 out of 10 that they will clinch the Series by winning the sixth game. Even if they lose the sixth game, there is a 3 out of 10 chance that they will win the seventh and deciding game. What are the odds that the Mets will win the World Series (best four out of seven games)?

10.9. In poker a *flush* is a reasonably good hand. It consists of any five cards of the same suit.

a. What are the odds of drawing five straight spades in the original deal?

b. Suppose the original deal gave you three spades, a heart, and a club, with no numerical combinations of any interest. What are your chances of obtaining two spades on a draw of two cards?

c. In part b, did you need to make an assumption about the number of players in the game? Why?

10.10. To test your ability to manipulate probabilities calculate:

a. The probability of drawing a straight in five cards, i.e., any numerical sequence, regardless of suit, such as 2, 3, 4, 5, 6 or 8, 9, 10, J, Q.

b. The probability of drawing a full house, i.e., three of a kind plus two of a kind, such as 3 nines and 2 sevens, in five cards.

(You should now be able to complete a table of probabilities for all poker hands or for the likelihood of filling certain hands by replacing discards with a draw.)

10.11. Over a cup of coffee after class, a friend of yours claims that he can control the toss of a coin if allowed to spin it with his thumb, catch it in his hand, and flip it on the back of his other hand in the usual manner. In fact, he claims that he can obtain heads 9 times out of 10. You don't think he can and offer him 4 to 1 odds that he can't get 5 heads in a row. (This is equivalent to saying that your prior probability that he can't control the toss is .8.) He flips the coin 5 times and obtains 5 heads. At what odds would you be willing to bet that he can't do it again?

10.12. You know from comments made in class that your professor has two children and that at least one of them is a boy. When you deliver a term paper to his home, the door is answered by a small boy, who admits to being his son. What is the probability that his other child is also a boy?

10.13. Suppose a card game is played with a deck consisting of only the ace of spades, ace of clubs, deuce of spades, and deuce of clubs. The cards are shuffled, and two cards are dealt to an opponent. We are interested in the odds that he has both aces.

a. Given no other information, what are the odds that he has both aces?

b. Suppose we obtain a peek at one of the opponent's cards, noting that it is an ace (although we are unable to determine the suit). What is the probability that his hand contains both aces?

c. If our peek discloses that one of his cards is the ace of spades, what is the probability that the opponent's hand contains both aces?

10.14. A salesman has a long history of making sales on about 60 percent of the calls he makes.

a. What are the chances that on a particular day he will sell more than 6 of the 10 customers he visits?

b. Did you assume statistical independence in part a? Specifically, what does this assumption mean here? Is it a valid assumption? If not, is your answer to part a too high or too low? Why?

c. What are the chances that he will sell exactly 6 out of 10 (assuming independence)?

d. What are the chances that he will sell 4 or less out of 10?

10.15. Give some examples, drawn from a business context, of situations which could be considered as Bernoulli processes. Distinguish between cases where the trials involved meet the theoretical requirements and those where the Bernoulli assumption would represent a good approximation for practical purposes.

10.16. For each of the following binomial probabilities, make a simple sketch showing enough of the binomial distribution to illustrate the probability in question. Then find the probability, using the binomial tables.

a. $P_b(r \geq 12 \mid 20, .3)$ b. $P_b(r = 12 \mid 20, .3)$

c. $P_b(r < 12 \mid 20, .3)$
e. $P_b(r \geq 1 \mid 10, .4)$
g. $P_b(r = 55 \mid 100, .6)$

d. $P_b(r = 0 \mid 10, .4)$
f. $P_b(r \geq 55 \mid 100, .6)$
h. $P_b(r \leq 45 \mid 100, .6)$

10.17. a. Assuming a Bernoulli process, *calculate* the probability of obtaining 4 defective parts from a sample of 10 parts if the proportion of defectives in the population is .2.

b. *Calculate* the probability of obtaining 1 or fewer defective parts from a sample of 10 parts if the proportion of defectives in the population is .2.

c. Check your answer to part *a*, using the binomial tables.

d. Check your answer to part *b*, using the binomial tables.

10.18. A component for an assembly is purchased from companies A, B, and C, which supply the following percentages of the total, with the probability of a defective component shown:

Company	Percent of total	Probability of defective component
A	50	.01
B	30	.03
C	20	.05

Since the parts all look exactly alike and have no company identification, it is impossible to identify a component after the assembly is completed. Upon final assembly one of the parts is found to fail because of a defect in the component subcontracted. What is the probability that the defective part was produced by Company A? Company B? Company C?

MODULE 11
STATISTICAL INFERENCE AND SOME USES OF SAMPLES

Much of the remainder of this book involves, in one way or another, the process of *statistical inference*, the process which enables a decision maker to infer what is true about a *population* of items based on the results of a *sample* drawn from it. Usually, precise statistical statements, or *inferences*, are made with respect to a particular characteristic, called a *parameter*, of the population. In this module, we'll confine ourselves to inferences regarding the *proportion* of items in a population that possess a certain attribute. Specifically, we'll consider the kinds of statements that can be made regarding a population proportion from a knowledge of the sample proportion bearing a particular characteristic. In Module 12, you'll learn some basic concepts of statistical decision theory applied to problems involving population proportions.

Then, in Modules 13 and 14, you'll extend your knowledge of inference and statistical decision theory to problems involving other characteristics of populations.

General learning objectives

Your general learning objectives for this module are to be able to:

1. Define some terms commonly used in sampling and statistical inference
2. Explain the concepts of sampling error and sampling distribution
3. Make point and interval estimates of a population proportion and interpret them

Section 11.A

Basic Concepts of Statistical Inference

Learning objectives

Your learning objectives for this section are to be able to define and explain the following terms with reference to statistical inference:

1. Population
2. Sample
3. Judgment sample
4. Simple random sample
5. Census
6. Sampling error

POPULATIONS

Population, as the term is used in statistical inference, may be defined simply as *all* the elements in a set under consideration; a *sample* is merely a subset of the population. Populations may be finite (containing a definite number of elements) or infinite. The concept of an infinite population derives from the notion of a process that may be expected to continue indefinitely, thereby producing an infinite series of population elements. The output of parts from a production process might be considered an infinite population if no termination of the process itself is in sight.

Note that a population may be defined in any way that best suits the needs of a particular decision problem, identifying only those elements of interest. A population could be defined as all college students in the United States, all students attending a particular university, all students enrolled in a statistics course, or all students patronizing a local pizza parlor, depending on the problem at hand. Likewise, next year's output of manufactured parts, the next shipment, or any other subset of parts produced from a process may be defined arbitrarily as a population. Thus the definition may take any form that is convenient or meaningful as long as consistency is maintained.

SAMPLING

There are many ways in which a sample from which inferences are to be made can be selected. A decision maker could select a sample of items which he considered to be representative of the population on the basis of his own judgment. Certainly items purposefully selected by a knowledgeable individual can make up a sample that yields a considerable amount of useful information. Unfortunately, however, precise statistical inferences cannot be made from *judgment* samples subjectively selected in this manner. The considerable body of statistical theory that has been developed to enable one to make statistical inferences depends on the assumption that the sample in question has been selected *at random*.

Now "random" has a very special meaning in statistics that is quite different from its use in common language. In ordinary terms, "random" often means "without thinking" or "haphazard." In statistics a *simple random sample* is a sample obtained by a process such that each possible combination of items that could make up a given size sample has an equal chance of being selected. To get a better feel for the meaning of this definition observe that a necessary (but not sufficient) condition of simple random sampling is that *every item in the population has an equal chance of being included in the sample*.[1] Although statisticians have developed a variety of more complicated sampling plans that also rely on the concept of randomness, random sampling in this text will refer to simple random samplings as defined above.

To obtain a simple random sample requires a great deal of care. Data cannot be grabbed because they are convenient. Some systematic device such as a table of random numbers must be used to ensure that every possible combination of items in the sample does in fact have an equal chance of being selected. This process of randomization prevents bias from entering into the selection of the items in a sample. Moreover, as mentioned earlier, all the theory relating to statistical inference is predicated on the fact that the samples have been taken at random.

SAMPLE VERSUS CENSUS

Considering the problems involved in selecting a random sample and the sometimes formidable difficulties of mastering the theory and concepts of statistical inference, one might reasonably raise the question: Why take a sample? If indeed a knowledge of some population characteristic is necessary to make a decision, why not take a *census* of the population? One answer is that a census, meaning a complete enumeration of the characteristics of every item in the population, may be impossible or at least prohibitively expensive.

If a manufacturer of flashbulbs wants to know the proportion of defective bulbs in his production process, he can hardly resort to testing every one of them. In this case the testing process is destructive and a complete census would use up the population, leaving no bulbs to sell. In other cases, although a census may not be destructive,

---

[1] The reason this is not a *sufficient* condition to define simple random sampling can best be explained by an example. Suppose it is required to sample 1 percent of the names in a telephone book. A sample could be obtained by selecting every hundredth name. If the starting point were randomly selected from the first 100 names in the book, every name in the book would have, before the selection begins, an equal chance of appearing in the final sample. However, this would not be a simple random sample, as defined here, since a sample combination involving say the fiftieth and fifty-first names would have *no* chance of being selected. From a practical point of view such a departure from the ideal of simple random sampling *might* be desirable, but we make no attempt to deal with such considerations here.

obtaining the necessary information on an item-by-item basis may be extremely costly. Under these circumstances, it may be economical to resort to sampling.

SAMPLING ERROR

You'll probably recognize intuitively, even in the absence of any formal knowledge of statistical inference, that any time a sample is used to estimate a population characteristic the possibility of an estimating error is introduced. Of course, if all items in the population are identical, e.g., if the flashbulbs are all good or all bad, different samples will also have identical characteristics and there will be no sampling error. Usually, however, variability abounds, and population items are not identical. A production run of flashbulbs will contain some good and some bad bulbs, and different random samples drawn from the same process will contain different proportions of good and bad, leading to different statistical inferences about the population. Thus, any time we infer from a particular sample something about the population, we must recognize that the sample will not, in general, be exactly representative of the population. No sample is a microcosm of the population from which it was drawn, and the fact of sampling error must be reckoned with in any problem of statistical inference.[1] Fortunately, the problem is not hopeless, for a variety of procedures for analyzing and dealing with sampling error have been developed. Indeed, in later modules we'll incorporate the dollar costs associated with sampling error directly into the decision process.

REVIEW EXERCISES 11.A

1. A *population* is generally defined:
   a. To include not less than 10 items.
   b. So that all items are alike.
   c. In any way that best suits the needs of a particular decision problem.
   d. None of the above.
2. The principal *disadvantage* of judgment samples is that they:
   a. Don't form the basis for precise statistical statements, or inferences.
   b. Are more difficult to construct than random samples.
   c. Are rarely representative of the population from which they are selected.
   d. All the above.
3. A random sample is a sample selected so that:
   a. Items are included in a haphazard fashion.
   b. Each possible combination of items that could make up the given size sample has an equal chance of being selected.

---

[1] Actually, sampling errors may or may not be more serious than other sources of error in an estimation problem. In some cases, measurement errors may render a census less accurate than a sample estimate. If, for example, you wanted to know the number of e's in the text, a total count might be less accurate than an estimate based on a careful count of the number of e's on one randomly selected page multiplied by the number of pages in the text (because of the clerical errors you're almost certain to make in attempting a complete enumeration).

c. The most convenient items are selected first.

d. None of the above.

4. In a simple random sample, every item in the population has an equal chance of being selected: true or false?

5. A census is:

    a. The same as a random sample.

    b. A complete enumeration of items in the population.

    c. Usually easier to obtain than a sample.

    d. None of the above.

6. Sampling error refers to mistakes made in recording sample information: true or false?

7. Sampling error must be reckoned with in statistical inference because:

    a. Population items are usually identical.

    b. Different random samples drawn from the same population will have different characteristics.

    c. It is impossible to eliminate subjective judgment from the sampling process.

    d. None of the above.

Answers 11.A

1. c   *2. a*   *3. b*   *4.* true   *5. b*

6. False; sampling error refers to the possible estimating error that is introduced any time a sample is used to estimate a population characteristic.

7. b

Section 11.B

Sampling Distributions Involving Population Proportions

Learning objectives

Your learning objectives for this section are to be able to:

1. Explain the use of the following sampling distributions:
    a. Binomial
    b. Hypergeometric
2. Construct a sampling distribution for a simple case

Table 11.1 / Binomial probability distribution for $n = 4$, $p = \frac{1}{6}$

Number of successes r	Probability
0	$\frac{625}{1296} = .482$
1	$\frac{500}{1296} = .386$
2	$\frac{150}{1296} = .116$
3	$\frac{20}{1296} = .015$
4	$\frac{1}{1296} = .001$
	$\frac{1296}{1296} = 1.000$

THE BINOMIAL SAMPLING DISTRIBUTION

A *sampling distribution* is a listing of all possible sample outcomes (from a random sampling process) together with their respective probabilities of occurrence. The *binomial* sampling distribution results when the sampling is binomial or whenever each sample may be considered to represent a number of trials in a Bernoulli process. You'll recall from the previous module that a Bernoulli process has (1) only two possible outcomes on each trial, (2) a constant probability of success on each trial, and (3) statistically independent trials.

Actually, examples of binomial sampling have already been discussed. In the loaded-die example in Module 10, we were allowed to roll the die in question once to assist in deciding whether or not it was loaded. This may be considered a sample of 1 from a Bernoulli process, i.e., a binomial sample of size 1. Later in Module 10 we computed the probability of various possible outcomes of rolling a fair die four times using the binomial formula. This is equivalent to a binomial sample of size 4. We then calculated the binomial probability distribution for the die-rolling problem for $n = 4$ and $p = \frac{1}{6}$ which is repeated as Table 11.1. Since this is a listing of all the possible outcomes of samples together with their respective probabilities of occurrence, it is an example of a *sampling distribution*.

The binomial distribution was applicable in the case of tossing a die four times because each toss could be regarded as a "draw" from a potentially infinite sequence of trials. Many business processes, e.g., the one which produced flashbulbs mentioned earlier, can likewise be usefully regarded as infinite sequences. If the other two conditions prerequisite to a Bernoulli process are also met, i.e., that one of only two possible states must occur and that the probability of a success is constant throughout the process, then the binomial sampling distribution can be used to make statistical inferences for these processes.

SAMPLING FROM A FINITE POPULATION: THE HYPERGEOMETRIC DISTRIBUTION

Many other types of business problems deal with the occurrence of one of two states, success or failure, but involve finite rather than infinite populations. In a market research investigation, the customers in a particular trade area may be classified as buyers or nonbuyers. Similarly, a flashbulb from a shipment of 10,000 bulbs can be good or defective, orders can be filled or unfilled, employees may be male or female, etc. In any of these cases a decision maker may be concerned with the proportion of successes, p, or failures, $1 - p$, in a sample and with how this proportion relates to the proportion in the population.

Strictly speaking, the binomial distribution does not describe the sampling in these examples because the populations are not infinite. This means that removal of one item from the population, such as one flashbulb from a shipment, changes the proportion of defectives in the bulbs remaining. Of course, if the population is reasonably large, the removal of one item is not going to change the probability of success on the next draw, or trial, very much. Still, you'll recall that a requirement of binomial sampling (from a Bernoulli process) is that the probability of success remains constant from trial to trial and that the trials be statistically independent. If sampling takes place *without replacement*, i.e., by removing items selected for the sample so that there is no chance of their reselection, the requirement is violated and the binomial distribution does not apply theoretically. For example, if three consecutive black cards are drawn from an ordinary deck without replacement, the probability of a black card on the next draw is not $\frac{1}{2}$, but $\frac{23}{49}$.

The sampling distribution that *is* theoretically applicable in the situation of sampling without replacement from a finite population is called the *hypergeometric distribution*. Hypergeometric probabilities can be derived in a straightforward manner using the law of multiplication for probabilities and the rules of counting developed earlier in conjunction with the binomial.

For example, the probability of drawing three black cards from a well-shuffled deck without replacement is

$$P(B,B,B) = \tfrac{26}{52}(\tfrac{25}{51})(\tfrac{24}{50})$$

Similarly, the probability of two black and one red (in that order) is

$$P(B,B,R) = \tfrac{26}{52}(\tfrac{25}{51})(\tfrac{26}{50})$$

If we are not concerned about where the one red card falls in the sequence, we recognize that there are three possible sequences (*BBR*, *BRB*, and *RBB*), so that

$$P(2 \text{ black and 1 red, any order}) = 3(\tfrac{26}{52})(\tfrac{25}{51})(\tfrac{26}{50})$$

In the same way, the probability of one black and zero black cards in three draws could be derived, giving the complete sampling distribution for three draws without replacement from an ordinary deck of cards, which is shown in Table 11.2.

The formula for the hypergeometric probability of exactly r successes in n trials is given by

$$P_H(r \mid n) = \frac{C(Np,r)C(Nq, n - r)}{C(N,n)} \tag{11.1}$$

where r = number of successes
      n = number of trials
      N = size of population
      p = proportion of successes in population
      q = proportion of failures = $1 - p$

Table 11.2 / Hypergeometric sampling distribution for the occurrence of black cards in three draws without replacement from an ordinary deck of cards

Event	Probability
3 black, 0 red	$1\left(\frac{26}{52}\right)\left(\frac{25}{51}\right)\left(\frac{24}{50}\right) = .1176$
2 black, 1 red	$3\left(\frac{26}{52}\right)\left(\frac{25}{51}\right)\left(\frac{26}{50}\right) = .3824$
1 black, 2 red	$3\left(\frac{26}{52}\right)\left(\frac{26}{51}\right)\left(\frac{25}{50}\right) = .3824$
0 black, 3 red	$1\left(\frac{26}{52}\right)\left(\frac{25}{51}\right)\left(\frac{24}{50}\right) = .1176$
	1.0000

Although the hypergeometric distribution has been tabulated for certain values, the tables required are much more extensive than for the binomial because there is a different hypergeometric distribution for every combination of sample size, *population size*, and number of successes in the population, whereas the binomial sampling distribution involves only the two parameters n, sample size, and p, proportion of successes.

Fortunately, we do not need to use the hypergeometric in most practical problems since the more manageable binomial provides a very adequate approximation. In fact, unless a sample from a finite population is a substantial proportion of that population—a useful rule of thumb is 20 percent—the assumption of binomial sampling introduces only insignificant errors in the decision process and is justified on the basis of greater simplicity. Somewhat paradoxically, *most* applications of the binomial sampling distribution in this text and in practice occur where the distribution is not theoretically applicable but is a good approximation.

REVIEW EXERCISES 11.B

1. Define a sampling distribution.
2. A binomial sampling distribution will result from:
  a. Samples which consist of a number of trials in a Bernoulli process.
  b. Samples drawn from a finite population.
  c. Either *a* or *b.*
  d. Neither *a* nor *b.*
3. Characteristics of a Bernoulli process include:
  a. Statistically independent trials.
  b. Only two possible outcomes on each trial.
  c. A constant probability of success on each trial.
  d. All the above.
4. The sampling distribution that is theoretically applicable in the situation of sampling without replacement from a finite population is called the _____ _____.
5. Whereas with binomial sampling the probability of success remains constant from trial to trial, with the hypergeometric distribution the probability of success will change from trial to trial: true or false?

6. The binomial distribution is often used to approximate the hypergeometric distribution:
   a. When the sample size is less than 20 percent of the population size.
   b. Because binomial tables are simpler and more readily available.
   c. Both a and b.
   d. Neither a nor b.
7. Suppose you perform a series of experiments in which three "fair" coins are tossed simultaneously, recording in each case the number of heads obtained. Construct the sampling distribution which describes the possible outcomes of this experiment and their probabilities of occurrence.
8. Refer to Exercise 7. What is the true population of heads that will be obtained for this process? In which of the possible sample outcomes will the sample proportion of heads equal the true population proportion?

Answers 11.B

1. a listing of all possible outcomes of samples together with their respective probabilities of occurrence
2. a   3. d   4. hypergeometric distribution   5. true   6. c

7.

Possible outcomes (number of heads)	Probability of occurrence	Event
0	$\frac{1}{8}$	TTT
1	$\frac{3}{8}$	HTT, THT, TTH
2	$\frac{3}{8}$	HHT, HTH, THH
3	$\frac{1}{8}$	HHH
	1	

This listing of possible sampling outcomes ($n = 3$, $p = .5$) from an infinite population, together with their respective probabilities of occurrence, is called the *sampling distribution*.

8. $p = \frac{1}{2}$; *none* of the sample outcomes gives this proportion. (Does this help you understand the concept of sampling error and why sample proportions do not necessarily correspond to population proportions?)

Section 11.C
Estimation

Learning objectives

Your learning objectives for this section are to be able to:

1. Define and explain the use of the following terms and concepts:
   a. Point estimate
   b. Interval estimate
   c. Confidence interval
   d. Confidence coefficient
2. Make point and interval estimates of a population proportion

ESTIMATION OF A POPULATION PROPORTION

Having developed the concept of the binomial as a sampling distribution, let's apply it to a specific problem in statistical inference suggested earlier: the estimation of the proportion of successes in a population p from the proportion of successes in a sample r/n. Suppose, for one reason or another, that the flashbulb manufacturers wished to estimate the proportion of defective bulbs in the production process. We saw earlier that a census was impractical in such a situation; instead the estimate might be based on the testing of 100 bulbs selected at random from the process.

Assume that 7 of the sample of 100 bulbs tested proved defective. What can be inferred about the proportion defective in the population?

POINT ESTIMATES

Naturally, it is by no means certain that the population p is the same as the proportion defective in the sample, 7/100, or .07. Different random samples of 100 would yield different proportions defective, no one of which was necessarily equal to the true p for the population. Nevertheless, in the absence of any additional evidence, .07 is the *best* estimate of p that we can make. There is certainly no incentive to place a higher likelihood on, say, .04 or .09 or any other value. An estimate equal to the sample proportion r/n (for which we use the symbol $\bar{p}$), is called a *point estimate* of p. Note that it consists of a single value with no accompanying information to indicate the reliability of the estimate.[1]

---

[1] This particular estimate of p has the desirable statistical property of being *unbiased*, which technically means that if the estimating procedure were repeated a very large number of times, the mean of the estimates so obtained would equal the true p.

INTERVAL ESTIMATES

It is quite likely that a statistician or anyone else recognizing the possibility of sampling error will wish to hedge his point estimate of p. The statistician, at least, would typically prefer to express his estimate as an *interval*, containing the point estimate but allowing for error on either side. A statement to the effect that the true proportion of defective bulbs in the population is *between* say .05 and .09 would represent an *interval estimate*.

Now if a statistician estimating p were to assert that "p is between 0 and 1," he'd be very safe indeed. In fact, we could say that he is 100 percent *confident* that his interval estimate contains the true value of p. Of course, such an estimate really says nothing that isn't obvious and is of little use to anyone. A much more useful statement would instead establish an interval that was *reasonably* sure to contain the true value of p. With 7 percent defective bulbs in the sample, for instance, your intuition should tell you that the true p for the population is not likely to be as high as 90 or 50, or even 25 percent. The interval estimate need not contain these values. It turns out that it is possible to ascertain specifically how wide the interval must be to provide us with any stated level of confidence that the true p is contained within it.

Suppose we construct what is called a 95 percent *confidence interval* for estimating p. This means that we shall find an interval that we are 95 percent confident contains the true p. It follows that there is a 5 percent chance that it does not. The customary procedure is to split this 5 percent equally and to assume that there is a 2.5 percent chance that the stated interval is too high to include the true p and a 2.5 percent chance that it is too low.

The problem is to find the limits of such an interval. This can be accomplished by using the binomial tables in a reverse fashion. For example, to find the *lower limit* of the confidence interval, we must use the binomial tables (in reverse) to locate a p value such that

$$P(r \geq 7 \mid n = 100, p) = .0250 \qquad \text{or} \qquad 2.5\%$$

Ideally, if we had a complete enough set of binomial tables, we could find a column heading (p value) for which the probability of 7 or more successes out of a sample of 100 would be exactly .0250. Using the tables in this book, we must be satisfied with the p column in which the probability is closest to *but smaller than* .0250 (since we generally wish to be conservative in estimating and obtain a confidence level of *at least* 95 percent). In this case, such a probability is .0041, which appears in the $r \geq 7$ row under the column $p = .02$. Thus $p = .02$ is the lower limit of our confidence interval.

For the *upper limit*, we need to find a p such that

$$P(r \leq 7 \mid n = 100, p) = .0250$$

This gets even trickier, since (as you may recall from the previous module) in order to get $P(r \leq 7)$ from the binomial tables, we must actually take $1 - P(r \geq 8)$. Thus, in the tables we must identify a p such that

$$P(r \geq 8 \mid n = 100, p) = 1 - .0250 = .9750$$

By searching the $r \geq 8$ row of our binomial tables for a probability that is closest to *but greater than* .9750, we find such a value, .9766, in the column for $p = .14$. Thus the upper limit of the confidence interval is $p = .14$.

We're finally prepared to state that based on the observed sample result, the 95 percent confidence interval for the population proportion defective p is .02 to .14.

SOME GENERALIZATIONS CONCERNING INTERVAL ESTIMATES

You're probably painfully aware at this point that the mechanics (if not the reasoning) involved in constructing confidence intervals for a population proportion are tortuous. This is so even though no attempt was made here to prove that the interval constructed is actually 95 percent reliable in estimating p. Of course, more complete binomial tables could have made the job considerably easier, and the most important matter at this point is that you understand the *concepts* involved in constructing a confidence interval. We'll return to this matter of confidence intervals in Module 13, when you'll have a few more statistical tools in your kit, and discuss methods for obtaining approximate confidence interval estimates for p (without using binomial tables) as well as for other population parameters. In the remainder of this section, we'll examine some generalizations about interval estimation that may shed some light on the entire process of statistical inference.

First, let's review the semantics involved in the estimation problem. The sample proportion defective, .07, is called a *point* estimate of p. The range .02 to .14 is a *confidence interval;* and the .95, or 95 percent, may be referred to as a confidence level or *confidence coefficient*. The confidence interval, confidence coefficient, and sample size are intimately related. Their relationship is worth generalizing. For any given sample size, the confidence interval will widen as the confidence coefficient increases. Therefore, if we want a very high level of confidence that p is included in the estimating interval, we must accept a relatively wide interval. If we construct a narrow interval estimate, our confidence that the interval really contains p must be relatively low. The only way to have our cake and eat it, too, in this situation is to increase the size of the sample, which in practice can be done only at an increased cost.

A little experimenting with binomial probabilities—and the problems at the end of this module may force you to do just that—will show that increases in sample size do not provide *proportional* decreases in the confidence interval or proportional increases in the confidence coefficient. For now, a good rule to remember is that to cut a confidence interval in half (with the confidence coefficient remaining the same) generally requires increasing the sample size about fourfold.

It is also worth remembering that unless the sample itself represents a substantial (more than 20 percent fraction of the population, it is the *absolute* size of the sample that matters, rather than its size relative to the population or the percentage of the population that is covered. These somewhat surprising results will be demonstrated with specific examples in Module 13. Let's turn here to some relevant questions concerning the interpretation of confidence intervals.

INTERPRETATION OF THE CONFIDENCE INTERVAL

A strict interpretation of the type of confidence interval constructed above would be as follows. If a very large number of interval estimates were constructed on the basis of successive samples, at least 95 percent of these intervals would contain the true value of p; the other 5 percent (or less) would fail to include it.[1] Now it would be much less cumbersome to interpret the interval as simply meaning that we are 95 percent certain (or the probability is .95) that the true p value falls somewhere between .02 and .14. Although this latter statement is intuitively appealing, classical statisticians frequently object to it on the grounds that it is simply not proper to make probability statements about p, a population parameter. Putting it roughly, they argue that p is what it is and that a statement giving the probability that it is more or less than some limit is meaningless. While it is quite all right to talk of the probability of obtaining a given *sample* result via some sampling procedure, the population p, even if unknown, is fixed.

This argument hits close to the issues raised earlier in connection with objective vs. subjective interpretation of probabilities in Module 10. It certainly may be useful to the business decision maker to view unknown population parameters such as p as if they were random variables, even if they are in fact already fixed or determined.

A homely illustration may serve to sharpen the issues involved in the argument. Suppose a friend tosses a presumably fair coin onto a table and covers it with his hand without allowing you to observe the outcome. If this friend now asks: What is the probability that the coin shows tails? Would you answer one-half? From a strictly objective point of view, the outcome is already determined and the question is meaningless or at best trivial. The probability of a tail is either 0 or 1 depending on the predetermined outcome. However, from your own subjective point of view, it seems perfectly reasonable to assess the *odds* that the coin is tails as 50-50, even if you know the outcome is already determined. This is a little like betting on a videotape rerun of last year's Rose Bowl game. If two people had no knowledge of the outcome, there is no reason they couldn't engage in some spirited wagering, complete with cheering on their favorites. At many points later on in this book, we shall proceed to treat population parameters as if they were random variables, adopting the subjective view of the decision maker.

INTERVAL ESTIMATES AND DECISION MAKING

To the business manager, the probability or odds that some key decision variable lies within specified limits *is* a meaningful concept. The confidence interval—at least the subjective interpretation of it—is a convenient way of summarizing the state of

---

[1] No effort is made here to prove that the method used here to obtain a confidence interval gives these results. A readable but involved discussion is given in Robert Schlaifer, *Introduction to Statistics for Business Decisions*, pp. 217–219, McGraw-Hill, New York, 1961.

available knowledge concerning an unknown quantity. However, its direct usefulness in *decision* problems is not so well established. In the first place, it is not clear what part of the interval is to be used in the decision process: The point estimate or "best guess" within the interval, the limits, or some value in between. Certainly a decision would be based on the point estimate from a particular sample only in the total absence of any other information pertinent to the decision. One would hardly conclude, for example, that an associate was dishonest if he won, say, 7 out of 10 times in an apparently "even" coin-tossing game. An interval estimate, which also fails to incorporate the previous knowledge of the decision maker, has limits which depend on the choice of a level of confidence. This choice is essentially arbitrary, and arbitrary inputs are certainly to be avoided in decision making.

We conclude this section on confidence intervals with the observation that they are useful and widely used in conveying a certain kind of information, but per se they are of little value in the decision-making process. This is not to say that sample information has no use in decision making. A further development of the concepts of statistical inference will show quite the contrary.

REVIEW EXERCISES 11.C

1. A *point estimate* of the proportion of successes in a population:
   a. Consists of a single value.
   b. Is usually taken as the proportion of successes found in the sample.
   c. Is a kind of best guess.
   d. All the above.

2. An *interval estimate:*
   a. Will always contain the true population proportion in the interval.
   b. Will generally contain the point estimate but allow for error on either side.
   c. Is easier to determine statistically than a point estimate.
   d. All the above.

3. The width of a confidence interval:
   a. Is related to the confidence coefficient.
   b. Is related to the sample size.
   c. Both *a* and *b*.
   d. Neither *a* nor *b*.

4. For a given size sample, the width of the confidence interval increases as the confidence coefficient is increased: true or false?

5. For a given level of confidence, we must decrease the sample size in order to obtain a narrower interval estimate: true or false?

6. In sampling from very large populations, it is the size of the sample that determines the accuracy of estimates from it, not the size of the population: true or false?

7. If a very large number of 95 percent confidence interval estimates were constructed on the basis of successive samples from a given population, at least 95 percent of these intervals would contain the true value of the population proportion being estimated: true or false?

8. Confidence interval estimates form the usual basis for making business decisions: true or false?

9. Suppose a die whose fairness is suspected is tossed 50 times and 12 sixes result. Use this sample evidence to construct a 90 percent interval estimate of the true proportion of sixes this die will produce in the long run.

10. Refer to Exercise 9. Make a point estimate of the population proportion.

Answers 11.C

1. *d*   2. *b*   3. *c*
4. True; the estimating interval must become wider if it is to be more likely to contain the true population proportion.
5. False; the sample size must be increased to narrow the estimate. A general rule is that for a given level of confidence (confidence coefficient) the sample size must be increased fourfold to cut the interval in half.
6. true
7. True; this is the strict interpretation of a confidence interval estimate.
8. False; confidence intervals, as such, have limited usefulness as a basis for decision making. However, other forms of statistical inference are most useful, as you'll learn in later modules.
9. For a 90 percent confidence interval there is a 5 percent chance the interval is too high and a 5 percent chance it is too low. To get the lower limit, find a p value such that $P(r \geq 12 \mid n = 50, p) = .0500$. Use the binomial tables (Appendix Table A.1). In the $r \geq 12$ row, the probability closest to but smaller than .0500 is .0402, found in the column for $p = .14$. To get the upper limit, find a p value such that $P(r \leq 12 \mid n = 50, p) = .0500$; or, in order to use the tables

$$P(r \geq 13 \mid n = 50, p) = 1 - .0500 = .9500$$

In the $r \geq 13$ row, the probability closest to but greater than .9500 is .9505, found in the column for $p = .36$. Therefore, the 90 percent confidence interval estimate of p, the proportion of sixes obtained from this die in the long run is .14 to .36.

10. The point estimate of the population proportion, p, would be given by the sample proportion, $12/50 = .24$.

Questions and Problems

11.1. You wish to estimate the proportion of your firm's six employees who carry their own health insurance. The situation is actually as shown in the following table:

Employee	A	B	C	D	E	F
Insurance?	Yes	No	Yes	No	No	No

You select a random sample of two employees on which to base your estimate.
a. What is the probability that your sample will contain 100 percent successes, i.e., employees who *do* carry their own insurance?
b. What is the probability that your sample will contain 50 percent successes?

  c. What is the probability that your sample will contain 0 percent successes?

  d. Tabulate your answers to parts *a* through *c.* What is this tabulation called?

  e. What is the probability that your sample proportion will differ from the true population proportion by more than .25?

  f. Can you use the binomial distribution (or binomial tables) to answer the preceding questions? Why or why not? Would it make any difference if you were sampling from a population of 6000 employees?

11.2. Obtain the sampling distribution of the proportion of employees having health insurance in samples of size 3, drawn from the population in Prob. 11.1.

11.3. Define statistical inference. Give several examples of situations in which a decision maker might want to make an interval estimate for a population proportion. For each example, would the decision maker be more interested in the lower limit or the upper limit of the interval estimate? Why?

11.4. If an interval estimate made for a population proportion proves to be too large to be of practical use, what alternatives do you have to reduce it?

11.5. *a.* About how many heads would you expect to get on tossing a *fair* coin 100 times?

  b. How likely is it that you would get 60 or more heads?

  c. The probability is .95, that is, you can be 95 percent confident, that the proportion of heads will be between _____ and _____.

  d. Will the answer to part *c*, stated in proportions, be the same if the coin is tossed 1000 times? If not, how will it differ? (You should be able to answer this question qualitatively even though you don't have binomial tables for $n = 1000$.)

11.6. Testing of a random sample of 50 flashbulbs reveals 3 defectives.

  a. Make a point estimate of the process (population) fraction defective.

  b. Make an interval estimate of the process fraction defective.

  c. Why is there no *single* correct answer to part *b*?

11.7. Suppose you decide to test 5 parts from a Bernoulli process. Derive the sampling distribution for the proportion of defectives in the sample if the population proportion of defectives is .4.

11.8. Suppose there are 10 persons qualified for a certain job, 4 men and 6 women. A random sample of 5 persons is selected. Derive the sampling distribution for the proportion of men in the sample.

11.9. Why does the distribution in Prob. 11.7 differ from that in 11.8?

11.10. Suppose that you test 10 parts from Bernoulli process and find 4 defectives.

  a. Make a point estimate of the proportion of defectives in the population.

  b. Make an interval estimate for the proportion of defectives in the population, using a 90 percent confidence coefficient.

11.11. Suppose that you test 20 parts from a Bernoulli process and find 8 defectives.

  a. Make a point estimate of the proportion of defectives in the population.

  b. Make an interval estimate for the proportion of defectives in the population, using a 90 percent confidence coefficient.

11.12. Suppose that you test 50 parts from a Bernoulli process, and find 20 defectives.

  a. Make a point estimate of the proportion of defectives in the population.

  b. Make an interval estimate for the proportion of defectives in the population, using a 90 percent confidence coefficient.

11.13. Summarize your answers to Probs. 11.10 through 11.12, and show that the accuracy of the interval estimate is inversely related to the square root of the size of the sample.

11.14. Analyze the following statement: I don't see how we can tell much about how 50 million people are going to vote just from interviewing 750 of them.

11.15. When 100 of a city's registered voters are selected at random to assess their preferences regarding a proposed stadium-financing plan, 58 of those interviewed express disfavor of the plan; the other 42 favor it.

    a. Make an interval estimate of the proportion of voters favoring the plan.

    b. If you had to bet on the outcome of the election concerning the proposed plan, which way would you bet?

    c. What odds could you afford to give and still have a "good bet"?

11.16. You need to know the proportion of homes in a particular area that house teenage children. You hope to estimate this proportion to within .02 with 95 percent confidence but have only a $50 budget. A market research organization gives you an estimate of 75 cents per home to obtain this information by sampling. Can your $50 provide the desired estimate? (State any assumptions you make in solving this problem.)

MODULE 12
CLASSICAL STATISTICAL
DECISION THEORY

You learned in the previous module that point and interval estimates, while useful in some applications, are of little use in the decision-making process. In this module, we'll explore some different ways in which the decision maker can utilize sample information: in *tests of a hypothesis* and in formulation of *statistical decision rules*. Once again, we'll confine this initial discussion to problems involving a population proportion. These concepts and techniques are extended to cover inferences and decision making with respect to other population characteristics in Module 14.

General learning objectives

Your general learning objectives for this module are to be able to:

1. Explain various concepts involved in testing a hypothesis regarding a population proportion
2. Classify and describe the types of errors that are involved in accepting or rejecting a hypothesis based on sample evidence
3. Compute the error characteristics of statistical decision rules and use graphs to describe them
4. Describe the factors involved in choosing among alternative decision rules

---

Section 12.A
Hypothesis Testing

Learning objectives

Your learning objectives for this section are to be able to:

1. Explain the reasoning involved in testing a hypothesis
2. Test a hypothesis concerning a population proportion
3. Explain the term significance level and describe how it is established
4. Explain how a hypothesis is usually selected for testing
5. Distinguish between:
    a. A null hypothesis and an alternative hypothesis
    b. One-tailed and two-tailed tests
    c. Type I and Type II errors

TESTS OF HYPOTHESES

A procedure of classical statistical inference which does incorporate sampling in the decision process is known as *hypothesis testing*. Actually, the test of a hypothesis involves a particular type of decision situation in which there are three alternative decisions or courses of action which can be followed: (1) to *accept* the hypothesis in question, (2) to reject it as inconsistent with the evidence, or (3) to postpone judgment pending collection of additional information. The third alternative is considered in subsequent modules. Here we shall confine the discussion to situations where an immediate selection between the first two alternatives, acceptance or rejection, must be made.

The hypothesis to be tested may be any unambiguous statement concerning a population characteristic. Here again, as in the previous module, discussion will concern only hypotheses about a population proportion p. For example, a manufacturer might hypothesize that a new product will capture at least 30 percent of the existing market for similar items, i.e., that $p \geq .30$. Such a hypothesis might be tested by a sampling from a carefully conceived test market. The flashbulb distributor of Module 11 might use sample evidence to test the hypothesis that the fraction of defective bulbs in a shipment is no greater than .05, that is, $p \leq .05$. A hypothesis of this type, by its nature, is either right or wrong. Note that if we reject it, i.e., conclude that it is wrong, we implicitly *accept* an alternative hypothesis. Rejection of the hypothesis that $p \leq .05$ *implies* that we believe that $p > .05$.

281

Acceptance or rejection of the hypothesis in question depends upon whether the particular sample results observed are consistent with the hypothesis that has been advanced. If, in a coin-tossing experiment, 52 heads were obtained out of 100 tosses of a coin, you'd probably agree that these sample results are consistent with the hypothesis that the coin is fair, that $p = .5$. After all, it's rather unlikely that even a perfectly fair coin would produce *exactly* 50 heads in 100 tosses.[1] On the other hand, obtaining 97 heads out of 100 tosses of a different coin would cause almost anyone to reject the hypothesis of fairness. These results do *not* appear consistent with the hypothesis.

But what is really meant by a statement that a sample result is consistent with a hypothesis or that it isn't? Although the conclusions seemed obvious in the coin-tossing examples, can the intuitive process by which one arrives at these conclusions be formalized?

It can be, by proceeding as follows. Assuming that the hypothesis *is* true, calculate the probability that the sample result actually observed or any "even more extreme" sample result could occur. Obviously, if this probability is very small, we'd be justified in labeling the hypothesis as inconsistent with the sample result and rejecting it. The probability of obtaining 97 *or more* heads out of 100 tosses of a *fair* coin, $P_b(r \geq 97 \mid n = 100, p = .5)$ is so small that it doesn't even appear in the binomial table. (That is, rounded to the fourth decimal place, the probability is .0000.) While 97 out of 100 heads *could* occur with a fair coin, it is so unlikely that the hypothesis that the coin was fair loses credibility.

Conversely, if the probability of obtaining a value equal to or more extreme than the sample result is "reasonably large," the disparity between the sample result and the hypothesis is attributed to chance and the hypothesis is accepted. If 52 heads were observed rather than 97, one would be likely to accept the hypothesis that the coin was fair since the probability of tossing 52 or more heads using a fair coin is

$$P_b(r \geq 52 \mid n = 100, p = .5) = .3822$$

More will be said shortly about how one decides what "reasonably large" means in this context.

Perhaps you can get a better feel for the sort of reasoning involved here from the following example. Several years ago in a Western city a large bakery chain was sued by a customer who claimed that he had bitten into a piece of bread baked by that bakery, had struck a bolt, and had broken a tooth. The jury examined the evidence and established the facts that the tooth had indeed been broken, that the bolt was of a type used in the baking machinery, and that there was a small but finite probability that such a bolt could have fallen into a batch of dough and subsequently been embedded in a loaf of bread offered for sale. On the basis of its deliberations the jury awarded the plaintiff damages.

---

[1] You can use the binomial table to verify that $P_b(r = 50 \mid n = 100, p = .5) = .5398 - .4602 = .0796$.

A month later a rather strange coincidence occurred. Another bakery was sued on exactly the same grounds. This case never got to court. It happened that the same insurance company insured both bakeries, and an insurance adjuster had noticed that the victim of the second accident was also the plaintiff in the former case.

The insurance company figured that the odds of a bolt being embedded in a loaf of bread were probably no greater than 1 in 100,000. However, this could mean that perhaps once out of every 100,000 loaves on the average some unfortunate consumer would get more iron in his bread than would be healthy and the jury was not being unrealistic when it awarded damages to the plaintiff. But how likely would it be that one person would get two such loaves in a relatively short time? Assuming independence and that the person in question bought 15 loaves a month, the binomial probability of getting 2 bad loaves in his sample of 15 *by chance* would be $105(1/100,000)^2 (99,999/100,000)^{13}$ which is about 1 in 100 million.

The important point of this example is that while it would be possible for a sample like this to occur by chance, it is *very* unlikely. The hypothesis that this consumer's situation was the result of plain bad luck was simply not tenable. The insurance company concluded that these events happened not by chance but by cause. Either someone was salting our victim's loaves of bread with bolts or he was onto what he thought was a profitable though painful way of making money. When confronted with the insurance adjustor's calculations, our hard-bitten hero confessed to the latter.

So far, the examples considered all represent extreme situations. The case for rejection or acceptance of the hypothesis is clear-cut, and the decision is intuitively obvious. But what of the gray area in between? Suppose a coin gives 59 heads in 100 tosses. Would this result be consistent with the fair-coin hypothesis? The binomial table shows $P_b(r \geq 59 \mid n = 100, p = .5) = .0443$. Remember that this means that about $4\frac{1}{2}$ percent of the time, or roughly 1 time in 23, a coin that really *is* fair would fall heads 59 or more times in 100 tosses *just as a result of pure chance or sampling error*.

Now in the bread-baking example, the 1 in 100 million odds were viewed as too long, and the chance hypothesis was rejected. Should 1 in 23 odds also be regarded as long odds, or should we accept the fair-coin hypothesis on the grounds that the sample results could very well have occurred "by chance"? The answer to this question involves some very subjective consideration. Different persons might answer differently depending on the circumstances and even, to some extent, on their personality characteristics.

A good way to determine where you yourself would draw the line is to imagine that you're playing what you consider to be a fair game of chance. (To keep it simple, suppose a coin is being tossed to determine who buys coffee.) Two or three successive losses at this sort of game would not be surprising. Even four straight losses might not result in any great distrust of one's opponent. After all, the probability of four losses in four plays of a *fair* game is $(\frac{1}{2})^4 = \frac{1}{16}$, so you'd expect to be this unlucky every so often. But how about five straight losses, $P = \frac{1}{32}$, or six, $P = \frac{1}{64}$, or 10, $P = \frac{1}{1024}$! The point is that although anyone can be unlucky, even very unlucky, there is some point at which he is no longer willing to attribute his misfortune to Lady Luck. The odds connected with this point may be relatively great or very small depending on the circumstances.

SIGNIFICANCE LEVELS

In formal hypothesis testing, the point at which the sample results will be considered inconsistent with the hypothesis is identified *in advance* of obtaining the sample. It is actually a probability level, referred to as the *level of significance* at which the hypothesis is tested. The hypothesis will be accepted as long as the probability of obtaining the observed sample result, given that the hypothesis *is* true, is *greater* than the level of significance selected. It is rejected if the probability that the sample result occurred by chance is *less* than the significance level. For example, testing a hypothesis at a 5 percent or .05 level of significance means that the hypothesis will be rejected only if there is a 5 percent chance or less that results as extreme as those in the sample could have occurred as a result of sampling error. Note that 59 heads out of 100 would lead to rejection of the fair-coin hypothesis at the 5 percent level of significance, since $P(r \geq 59) = .0443 \leq .05$, but *acceptance* at the 2 percent, 1 percent, or other lower levels.

Thus it is clear that whether a particular hypothesis is accepted depends not only on the results of a sample but also on the significance level chosen for the test. This level of significance, customarily represented in statistical notation as the Greek letter alpha, α, is most often taken as .05, .01, or .001. Often, a sample result which leads to rejection at the .05 level, that is, $\alpha = .05$, is called significant evidence against a hypothesis; rejection with $\alpha = .01$ would imply highly significant and with $\alpha = .001$ very highly significant evidence. These terms, like the selection of the α levels themselves, are of course arbitrary.

SELECTION OF THE APPROPRIATE HYPOTHESIS FOR A TEST

If a hypothesis is typically tested at α levels such as .05 or .01, the burden of proof is put on rejecting it. That is, the hypothesis is accepted unless relatively strong evidence against it appears. For this reason, if the traditional procedures are to be applied, some care must be taken in selecting the hypothesis for the test. Remember that acceptance of a hypothesis implies rejection of an alternate, converse hypothesis. Since the deck is stacked in favor of the hypothesis being tested, it is customary to choose that hypothesis in such a way that it represents the accepted norm or the status quo. This kind of hypothesis is called a *null hypothesis*; the other hypothesis whose acceptance is implied by rejection of the null is simply referred to as the *alternate hypothesis*.

In the coin-tossing examples, the null hypothesis would be the accepted norm, namely, that the coin was fair; in this case the alternative conflicts with the generally held view that an ordinary coin is fair.

Because the sample proportion was .59 in the specific coin-tossing experiment discussed, we found an *upper-tail* area corresponding to $P_b(r \geq 59 \mid n = 100, p = .5)$ to test the null hypothesis that the coin was fair. At the 5 percent level of significance, we conclude that the coin diverged from fairness in the direction of producing *more* heads than a fair coin would. If we had observed, say, 45 heads, we would have tested the null hypothesis that the coin was fair by finding the *lower-tail* area corresponding to $P_b(r \leq 45 \mid n = 100, p = .5)$. If this probability turned out to be less than the level of significance we chose for the problem, we should conclude that the coin diverged from fairness in the direction of producing *fewer* heads than a fair coin.

Tests of this kind are called *one-tailed tests* because only one end of the cumulative binomial distribution is used. The tests were concerned with departures in only one direction from the accepted norm.

Before an experiment begins, one might very well be interested in departures by the sample proportion from the expected value in *either* direction. Too many heads *or* too many tails might lead to rejection of the hypothesis that the coin was fair (or that $p = .5$ exactly). Here a *two-tailed test* could be used, with the only real difference being that the significance level α is split in two before comparing it with the probability of the sample result. The null hypothesis would be rejected if the probability of obtaining the actual sample result or one farther from .5 in the direction observed in the sample were less than $\frac{1}{2}\alpha$.

A two-tail test is thus like a one-tail test in concept and operation except for a difference in the way the significance level is interpreted. The difference, however, is a subtle one, and even statisticians do not always agree on one- vs. two-tailed interpretations. Fortunately, we needn't be concerned here with these subtleties and theoretical issues since for purposes of decision making *one-tailed tests* are nearly always appropriate. Even though the decision maker may be interested in deviations in both directions from a norm, any decision leading to action is almost certain to be based on deviations in one direction *or* the other.

For example, an advertiser may be interested in knowing whether or not a new series of ads produced a change in sales, but before he could act, he'd need to know whether the change increased sales or decreased them. The specific act might be to put more money into the new series if an increase were observed or to drop the new agency if a decrease were observed. Because of their greater applicability to decision problems, one-tailed tests will be emphasized in this book.

Let's consider the application of a one-tailed test of a hypothesis to a specific business problem. Returning to the flashbulb example, suppose that for economic reasons the distributor would find the shipment of bulbs acceptable if he were convinced that it contained no more than 4 percent defective bulbs. If his experience with previous shipments had been favorable, he might formulate the hypothesis that $p \leq .04$ and test it against sample evidence. Taking the sample result discussed earlier, 7 defectives out of a sample of 100 bulbs, let us subject this hypothesis to a test of significance at, say, an α level of .05.

Now if the hypothesis were indeed true, with an actual fraction defective in the *population* of exactly .04, the probability of 7 defectives or more in a sample of 100 would be $P_b(r \geq 7 \mid n = 100, p = .04) = .1064$. Since this probability is considerably greater than .05, the hypothesis that $p \leq .04$ should be accepted. Although 7 percent of the *sample* bulbs are defective, this is not sufficient evidence to reject the hypothesis and refuse the shipment. Based on the prescribed test, the bulbs would be rated as acceptable.

285

ERRORS IN HYPOTHESIS TESTING

It should be clear that nothing is ever proved (in the literal or mathematical sense of the word) by a statistical test of a hypothesis. The test described in the previous paragraph does not *prove* that the hypothesis is true and that the true proportion of defective bulbs in the population is $\leq .04$. In fact the 7 out of 100 defectives in the sample points in the opposite direction. Thus the sample results do not confirm the null hypothesis in a positive way in this case, they are just insufficiently strong to negate it. Even in cases where the sample evidence does lead to rejection, it doesn't prove that the hypothesis is false. It merely establishes the falsity beyond some reasonable doubt.

Samples can lead to incorrect inferences, and sampling error can lead us to wrong decisions regarding the acceptance or rejection of hypotheses. It's worth observing that the errors that can be made are of two distinct kinds. We can (1) erroneously *reject* a null hypothesis that is in fact *true* or (2) erroneously *accept* a null hypothesis that is in fact *false*. In standard statistical nomenclature these are referred to as Type I and Type II errors, respectively. The situation is perhaps clarified by examining the four possibilities in a hypothesis test in the form of a 2×2 table (see Table 12.1). Accepting a null hypothesis that is in fact true or rejecting a false one are of course correct decisions. It is the other combination of possibilities that produces incorrect decisions. The maximum risk α of a Type I error has already been identified as the level of significance in the test of a hypothesis. The risk of a Type II error is known as the beta risk, β.

This analysis shouldn't lead you to infer that the two types of error are in any sense equivalent or that they are equally likely to occur. Since tests at the customarily low level of significance α require relatively strong evidence against a hypothesis to reject it, Type I errors occur relatively infrequently. In fact one way to choose the null hypothesis from the alternate when the choice is not obvious is to assign the null in such a way that the most serious or expensive potential errors are made Type I errors and therefore involve an incorrect rejection of the null hypothesis. For example, it might be appropriate to call the hypothesis that a medicine was *not* of acceptable quality the null hypothesis and to test with a low level of significance α. This would be logical because the consequences of accepting the medicine if it were really not up to quality standards could result in the death of persons taking it, making the cost of this type of error very large. Assessment of the risks of the two kinds of error and the means for adjusting these risks are considered in the next section.

Table 12.1

Decision is made to:	Null hypothesis is in fact:	
	True	False
Accept	Correct decision	Type II error
Reject	Type I error	Correct decision

REVIEW EXERCISES 12.A

1. Sample evidence will lead to rejection of a hypothesis:
   a. Only if it is impossible for the hypothesis to be true.
   b. If there is less than a 50 percent chance that the hypothesis is true.
   c. If the sample result is unlikely to have occurred if the hypothesis was true.
   d. None of the above.
2. Suppose you toss a coin 4 times and it comes up heads each time. Is this result inconsistent with the hypothesis that the coin is fair? Explain.
3. Refer to Exercise 2. If you obtained 10 heads out of 10 tosses, would this be inconsistent with the hypothesis that the coin is fair? Explain.
4. In hypothesis testing, the *significance level:*
   a. Is identified or selected in advance of sampling.
   b. Is actually a probability level.
   c. Represents the point at which sample results will be considered inconsistent with the hypothesis being tested.
   d. All the above.
5. A hypothesis will be accepted as long as the probability of obtaining the observed sample result, given that the hypothesis is true, is less than the level of significance: true or false?
6. The *null* hypothesis which is tested is usually associated with an accepted norm, or the status quo: true or false?
7. Two-tailed tests are usually more relevant in business decision problems than one-tailed tests: true or false?
8. A Type I error is made when a null hypothesis is _____ when it is in fact _____.
9. A Type II error is made when a null hypothesis is _____ when it is in fact _____.
10. Type I errors and Type II errors are generally:
   a. Equally serious.
   b. Equally likely to occur.
   c. Both easily avoided by an appropriately designed test.
   d. None of the above.
11. The maximum risk of a Type I error:
   a. Is equal to the significance level.
   b. Is generally greater than the maximum risk of a Type II error.
   c. Can be determined only after the sample is actually taken.
   d. All the above.
12. In Exercise 9 of Sec. 11.C a die whose fairness was suspected was tossed 50 times and 12 sixes were obtained. Use this as sample evidence to test the hypothesis that the die was fair. (A fair die would produce $\frac{1}{6}$ sixes in the long run; as a close approximation, use the binomial tables for $n = 50, p = .16$.) Use whatever level of significance you think is appropriate.

Answers 12.A

1. c
2. If the coin were fair ($p = .50$), the probability of this result would be $(\frac{1}{2})^4 = \frac{1}{16}$, or

.0625. Therefore at a 5 percent level of significance (or at any lower significance level) the hypothesis that the coin is fair would still be accepted. In other words, this sample result is not sufficiently inconsistent with the hypothesis to cause its rejection at the levels of significance usually employed in such tests. Of course, where you'd establish the level of significance in an actual situation is a subjective matter.

3. The probability of this result is $(\frac{1}{2})^{10} = \frac{1}{1024} = .00098$. These results *are* significant at even very low significance levels (say $\alpha = .001$). Therefore, this sample result is inconsistent with the hypothesis that the coin is fair, and the hypothesis would be rejected.

4. *d*

5. False; it'll be accepted as long as the probability is *greater* than the level of significance.

6. true

7. False; since actions are more likely to be taken based on deviations in one given direction or the other, *one-tailed tests* are usually more appropriate.

8. rejected; true   9. accepted; false   *10. d*   *11. a*

12. $P(r \geq 12 \mid n = 50, p = .16) = .0929$. Therefore, unless you tested the hypothesis at an unusually high significance level (say $\alpha = .10$ or higher) the hypothesis would be accepted; i.e., the die would still be considered to be fair.

Section 12.B

Decision Rules

Learning objectives

Your learning objectives for this section are to be able to:

1. Describe a statistical decision rule
2. Compute the probability that a decision rule will lead to acceptance or rejection of a hypothesis for given values of the population proportion
3. Represent a decision rule graphically by constructing each of the following:
   a. Power curve
   b. Operating-characteristic (OC) curve
   c. Error curve
4. Define and determine the maximum risk of Type I error for a decision rule

---

STATISTICAL DECISION RULES

A *statistical decision rule* is nothing more or less than a procedure for testing a hypothesis where the accept-reject decision has been determined in advance for all possible sample outcomes. For example, in the flashbulb-testing problem, a decision rule might be formulated as follows: Take a simple random sample of 100 bulbs; if 8 or more bulbs are defective, reject the shipment; otherwise, accept the shipment.

Notice that the decision rule leaves nothing to judgment. Once such a rule had been formulated, anyone could carry out the instructions provided without knowledge of statistical inference. Formulation of the proper rule, however, is a more difficult matter. The statistician or the decision maker must be concerned with the *error characteristics* of the rule, which requires an assessment of how likely it is that the rule will lead to rejection of a good shipment of bulbs (a Type I error) or acceptance of a bad shipment (a Type II error).

The likelihood that use of the rule will lead to a particular error depends on the true fraction of defective bulbs in the population. Recall that the null hypothesis being tested was that the shipment contained no more than 4 percent defective bulbs, that is, $p \leq .04$. If p were really greater than .04, the null hypothesis would be false and there'd be *no* chance of making a Type I error since we'd *correctly* reject the null hypothesis. The null hypothesis (and the shipment) could be incorrectly accepted, but this would be a Type II error.

Thus the type of error that can be made as well as the probability of an error depend on the true p for the population. A thorough study of the error characteristics of a decision rule must therefore consider all possible values for the parameter p. Let's begin the analysis by determining the probability that the null hypothesis $p \leq .04$ will be rejected for various values of p. These probabilities can be obtained from the binomial table.

Suppose $p = .02$. Then the probability that the decision rule stated earlier (based on 8 or more defectives) will lead to rejection is

$$P_b(r \geq 8 \mid n = 100, p = .02) = .0009$$

This result agrees with the intuitive observation that a sample of 100 drawn from a "good" population containing only 2 percent defectives is very unlikely to contain 8 or more defective bulbs.

You may find it helpful to examine the actual sampling distribution for samples of size 100 drawn from a population whose proportion defective is .02. This sampling distribution is shown and related to the decision rule "reject if $r \geq 8$" in Fig. 12.1.

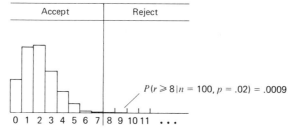

Figure 12.1 / Sampling distribution for $n = 100, p = .02$, related to the decision rule "reject if $r \geq 8$."

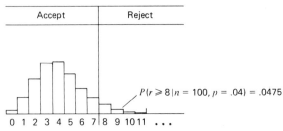

Figure 12.2 / Sampling distribution for $n = 100$, $p = .04$ related to the decision rule "reject if $r \geq 8$."

Notice that when the true population proportion defective is .02, probabilities of sample outcomes such as 0, 1, 2, or 3 are more likely to occur. Indeed, with $p = .02$, there is very little chance that as many as 8 defectives will occur in a sample of 100, which would cause the shipment to be rejected.

Now suppose the true population proportion defective were $p = .04$. The sampling distribution would appear differently, as shown in Fig. 12.2. As you might expect, the most likely sample outcome is now 4 defectives out of 100, and the total of the probabilities to the right of our criterion of 8 or more has now increased to .0475 (which could be read directly from the binomial tables).

Figure 12.3 shows the sampling distributions for other values of the population proportion p related to the decision rule. As p increases, of course, so does the probability that the shipment will be rejected, i.e., the area to the right of the criterion line.

GRAPHICAL REPRESENTATION OF DECISION RULES

A convenient way to represent all this information, as well as that for other values of p not listed, is to graph the probability of rejecting the null hypothesis vs. possible values of the population parameter p. Such a graph is called a *power curve*. The S-shaped curve shown in Fig. 12.4 is characteristic in problems where the area of rejection is an upper tail. However, it should be noted that in problems where the rejection of the null hypothesis involved a lower-tail area, the curve would descend from left to right.

A similarly derived curve that gives the probability of *accepting* the null hypothesis rather than rejecting it is called an *operating-characteristic curve*, or simply OC curve (see Fig. 12.5). Since the probability of accepting the null hypothesis for any assumed value of p is 1 minus the probability of rejecting, the OC curve is a sort of upside-down mirror image of the power curve. Obviously, both curves provide essentially the same information regarding the decision rule they describe.

Actually, neither the power nor the OC curve is as useful as a third curve which combines them, showing the probability of a *wrong decision* for any value of p. It is called, appropriately, an *error curve*. It consists of that portion of the power curve (the probability of rejecting the null) in the range where *rejection* is a wrong decision

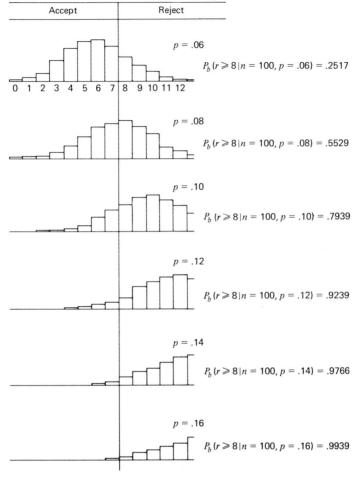

Figure 12.3 / Sampling distributions for various values of p related to the decision rule "reject if $r \geq 8$."

and that portion of the OC curve (the probability of accepting the null) where *acceptance* is a wrong decision. The error curve for the decision rule under discussion is given in Fig. 12.6. Notice that the lower left-hand tail of the curve is identical to the power curve in Fig. 12.4, up to $p = .04$, since if the true proportion is really .04 or less, rejection of the null hypothesis is a Type I error. For p values greater than .04, it is the *acceptance* of the null hypothesis (a Type II error) that represents a wrong decision. Thus each point in the right-hand portion of the curve is 1.0 *minus* the corresponding ordinate on the power curve, making the curve beyond $p = .04$ identical to that portion of the OC curve shown in Fig. 12.5.

291

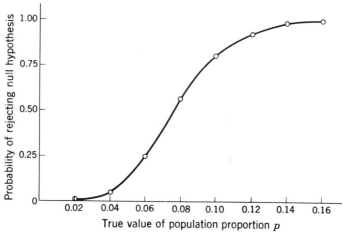

Figure 12.4 / Power curve for the decision rule $n = 100$ (if $r \geq 8$, reject; if $r < 8$, accept). ($H_N: p \leq .04$.)

MAXIMUM RISK OF A TYPE I ERROR

It is common to characterize the entire error curve on the basis of the maximum risk of a Type I error. This maximum risk or probability of a Type I error will occur when a true hypothesis is just on the borderline of becoming false. One would be more likely to conclude in error that a shipment of flashbulbs is of poor quality if the proportion of defectives in the population were .04, the highest proportion of defectives that is acceptable, than if the population proportion defective were smaller than .04. Note that if p, the proportion of defectives in the population, were .02, the risk of a Type I error as calculated on page 289 would be .0009, whereas if p were

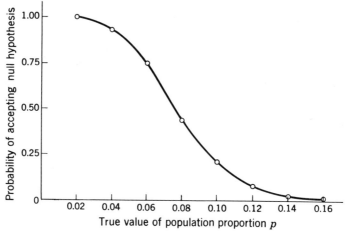

Figure 12.5 / OC curve for the decision rule $n = 100$ (if $r \geq 8$, reject; if $r < 8$, accept). ($H_N: p \leq .04$.)

292

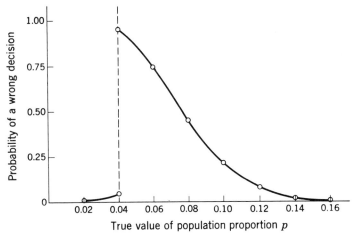

Figure 12.6 / Error curve for the decision rule $n = 100$ (if $r \geq 8$, reject; if $r < 8$, accept). ($H_N: p \leq .04$.)

.04, the α risk would be .0475. If the proportion of defectives in the population were any value greater than .04, it would no longer be possible to make a Type I error in interpreting sample results since the hypothesis is in fact false and rejecting the shipment would be a correct decision. Therefore, this risk for this decision rule, which is also called the level of significance, is .0475.

Conversely, the maximum risk of a Type II error would occur for a p value just barely past .04. This is the case because if the true proportion of defectives in the population were greater than .04, the shipment should be rejected and the only error that could be made would be to accept the shipment, which is a Type II error. The larger the proportion of defectives in the population, the less likely the decision rule would lead one to make a Type II error. For practical purposes, therefore, we can say that the maximum risk of a Type II error is $1 - .0475 = .9525$.

REVIEW EXERCISES 12.B

1. A statistical decision rule is a procedure for testing a hypothesis where the accept-reject criterion is established in advance: true or false?
2. Once established, a decision rule depends heavily upon the use of good judgment by the user: true or false?
3. The use of an appropriate decision rule will prevent the occurrence of:
   a. Type I errors.
   b. Type II errors.
   c. Both a and b.
   d. Neither a nor b.
4. The probability that a decision rule will lead to rejection of a given hypothesis will change for different assumed values of a true population proportion: true or false?
5. An operating-characteristic curve (OC curve) shows the probability of rejecting the null hypothesis for various true values of the population proportion: true or false?

6. The probability that a given decision rule will lead to a wrong decision, given any value of the true population proportion, can be read directly from:
   a. A power curve.
   b. An OC curve.
   c. An error curve.
   d. Any of the above.
7. A power curve, error curve, and OC curve for a given decision rule all contain essentially the same information: true or false?
8. The maximum risk of a Type I error occurs:
   a. At the point where the risk of Type II error is .05.
   b. Where the population proportion equals the proportion indicated in the sample.
   c. At several different points for any given decision rule.
   d. None of the above.
9. For any given value of the population proportion, the risk of making a Type I error is 1 minus the risk of making a Type II error: true or false?

Answers 12.B

1. true
2. False; once established, the decision rule operates mechanically, and leaves nothing to judgment.
3. d   *4.* true
5. False; a power curve shows this; an OC curve shows the probability of *accepting* the null hypothesis for various values of the true population proportion.
6. c.   While it can be *determined* from a power curve or an OC curve, it can be read directly only from an error curve.
7. true
8. d.   The maximum risk of a Type I error occurs at the value of the population proportion specified in the hypothesis.
9. False; generally, for a given value of the population proportion there is only one type of error that can be made. However, it is true that near the value of *p* specified in the hypothesis, the maximum risk of both Type I and Type II errors will occur; the *maximum* risk of a Type I error *is* equal to 1 minus the *maximum* risk of a Type II error.

Section 12.C
Choosing Among Alternative Decision Rules

Learning objectives

Your learning objectives for this section are to be able to:

1. Describe the changes in the error characteristics of decision rules for changes in:
   a. Criterion number
   b. Sample size
2. Define producer's risk and consumer's risk
3. State the principle involved in selecting a "best" decision rule

ERROR CURVES FOR OTHER DECISION RULES

So far we have examined but one particular decision rule, making no value judgments as to its merits. One of the important uses of error curves is to study the error characteristics of *different* decision rules that test the null hypothesis (hereafter denoted as H_N) for the purpose of choosing among them. This study is facilitated by adopting some shorter notation. For example, the rule studied earlier (rejection based on 8 or more defectives) could be written in symbolic form as

$$H_N: p \leq .04 \qquad \text{If } r \geq 8, \text{ reject } H_N$$
$$n = 100 \qquad \text{If } r < 8, \text{ accept } H_N$$

The number 8, on which the action to be taken depends, is called the *criterion number c*. The rule can be written in still shorter form simply as ($n = 100$, $c = 8$).

Effect of changes in the criterion number. Consider first the alternative of leaving the sample size fixed at $n = 100$ and changing the criterion number c. What will be the error characteristics of, say, the rule ($n = 100$, $c = 6$), where rejection is based on only 6 or more defectives? Figure 12.7 shows the error curve for ($n = 100$, $c = 6$) superimposed on the ($n = 100$, $c = 8$) curve given in Fig. 12.6. At this stage, you should be able to validate points on the new curve.

Some observations concerning Fig. 12.7 are in order. While the probability of a Type I error is *higher* for any given level of p using the $c = 6$ rule with an α risk of .2116, it gives a *lower* probability of Type II errors over the entire relevant range of p. This observation can be generalized as follows. For any given sample size changes

295

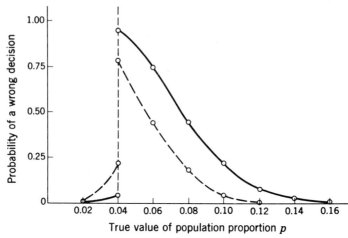

Figure 12.7 / Comparison of error characteristics for decision rules ($n = 100$, $c = 8$), indicated by solid line and ($n = 100$, $c = 6$) indicated by dashed line. ($H_N: p \leq .04$.)

in the criterion number can only reduce the risk of one kind of error at the expense of the other; a change in c alone cannot simultaneously reduce the risks of both types of error.

Effect of changes in the sample size.   The only way both error risks *can* be simultaneously reduced is by increasing the size of the sample. Since this book does not contain a binomial table for sample sizes larger than 100, let's consider the effect of a change in the opposite direction, say, cutting the sample to $n = 50$. The error curve from the ($n = 100$, $c = 8$) rule (Fig. 12.6) is reproduced in Fig. 12.8 to contrast with a

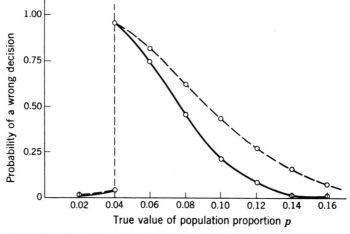

Figure 12.8 / Comparison of error characteristics for decision rules ($n = 100$, $c = 8$) indicated by solid line and ($n = 50$, $c = 5$) indicated by dashed line. ($H_n: p \leq .04$.)

comparable rule for the smaller sample ($n = 50$, $c = 5$). The criterion number $c = 5$ is chosen as comparable with $c = 8$ for the larger sample because it provides approximately the same maximum risk of Type I error (.0490 vs. .0475).

Note that the risks of Type I *and* Type II errors are generally larger for the smaller sample over all ranges of p. We can generalize to the effect that a decision rule can be made more efficient, in the sense that both types of error risk are reduced, by increasing the size of the sample. Of course larger samples are available in practice only at higher costs, so that the increased efficiency of the rule must be balanced against the increased costs of employing it.

THE PROBLEM OF SELECTING THE "BEST" DECISION RULE

To this point you've studied only the error characteristics of alternative decision rules, avoiding the question of which rule should be used in a given decision situation. We'll consider first the problem of how to select the best criterion number c for a given sample size. It's been observed that with n fixed, changes in c merely trade off one type of error risk for another. Let's examine the specific implications of this fact in the context of the flashbulb-testing problem.

It was assumed earlier that the distributor would regard the shipment of bulbs as acceptable if the proportion of defective bulbs were no greater than 4 percent, that is, $p \le .04$. Now if whatever decision rule used leads to rejection of the shipment, there is still some chance that a truly acceptable shipment has been mistakenly rejected and perhaps returned to the manufacturer. It isn't surprising that the risk of this kind of mistake (a Type I error) is often referred to as *producer's risk*. Conversely, the risk of the mistaken acceptance of a truly bad lot (a Type II error) is called *consumer's risk*, based on the notion it is the purchaser who suffers from this mistake. Increases in the c value will make rejection less likely, decreasing the producer's risk but increasing consumer's risk; decreases in c will have just the opposite effect.

The problem of selecting the "best" decision criterion or c value to use is then a problem of deciding on an appropriate balancing of the risks involved. This balance is often determined on an essentially arbitrary basis, generally by specifying the maximum allowable risk of a Type I error (producer's risk) or, equivalently, the significance level α. This risk, or α level, is often set at .05, .01, or some other relatively low level.

Setting α relatively low is consistent with establishing the null hypothesis so that Type I errors are more serious. However, since the specification is often arbitrary, no explicit effort is made to determine how *much* more serious a Type I error really is.

For some types of problems where dollar costs are not available or are extremely difficult to quantify, the decision regarding an appropriate level of Type I and Type II errors must be subjective and in a sense arbitrary. However, even in these cases an effort should be made to appraise the relative seriousness of the errors before the selection of a decision rule. Then the appropriate sample size and decision rule can be determined by considering the α and β risks desired. These techniques will be considered in more detail in Module 14.

For a wide range of important business problems it *is* possible to measure the dollar costs which are associated with Type I and Type II errors, not only for the maximum risks of these errors but for the entire continuum over which the errors can occur. These costs can then be used, together with the cost of sampling, to arrive at the optimal sample size and decision rule. Furthermore, it will also be possible to incorporate information obtained prior to the sample as well as the costs associated with the sample in question into the analysis. Within this framework, one can then decide whether or not to sample at all, how large a sample to take if sampling is desirable, and how to structure an optimal decision rule to interpret the sample results. The nature of this analysis is the subject of the last four modules in this book.

REVIEW EXERCISES 12.C

1. In the specification of a statistical decision rule, the number of items in a sample on which the action to be taken depends is called the _____.
2. For any given sample size, changes in the criterion number:
   a. Generally have no effect.
   b. Can only reduce the risk of one type of error at the expense of increasing the risk of the other type of error.
   c. Can often reduce the risk of both types of error.
   d. None of the above.
3. The risk of both Type I and Type II error can be reduced by increasing the size of the sample: true or false?
4. The risk of a Type I error is often referred to as consumer's risk: true or false?
5. In selecting among alternative decision rules:
   a. A balancing of risks is required.
   b. The relative seriousness of Type I and Type II errors should be considered.
   c. The costs of errors and costs of sampling should be considered where possible.
   d. All the above.

Answers 12.C

1. criterion number *c*   *2. b*   *3.* true
4. False; the risk of a Type I error is referred to as *producer's* risk, since it relates to the idea that a shipment of product that is in fact of good quality will be mistakenly rejected as a result of a decision rule based on a sampling procedure.
5. d

Questions and Problems

12.1.   After extensive remodeling a supermarket takes a simple random sample of size 100 and determines that the proportion of residents in the sample who shop at their store is .08. The population of residents in their market area is very large.

    a. Make an interval estimate for the proportion of customers in the population, using a 90 percent confidence coefficient.

    b. Assume that before the store was remodeled, the management knew that the proportion of customers in the population who shopped there was .06. Test the hypothesis that the proportion of customers in the population has not increased since remodeling. Use a level of significance of .05.

    c. Discuss the relationship between your answers to parts *a* and *b*. Does your interval estimate in part *a* confirm your test in part *b*? Explain.

12.2. You are requested to perform a survey to determine the percentage of time that your company's engineers and scientists spend in oral communication with their colleagues. In order to make the disruptive effect as small as possible, you institute a procedure known as "work sampling," whereby you observe the activities of randomly selected personnel at random times.

    a. You make 100 work sampling checks, finding your subjects engaged in oral communication in 24 cases. Is the percentage of time spent in oral communication significantly greater than 20 percent?

    b. Make an interval estimate of the percentage of time spent in oral communication, using a 90 percent confidence level.

    c. If you had answered part *b* first, could you have then answered part *a* without additional calculations? Explain.

    d. Generalize the relationship between confidence intervals and hypothesis testing.

12.3. Instant Wealth, an investment advisory service, recommends a list of 20 common stocks each quarter which are selected to "outperform the market." In the last quarter, 8 of their selected stocks rose in price, while 12 declined. Of the 500 stocks constituting "Standard and Poor's 500," a list widely accepted as being representative of the market, 140 advanced and 360 declined over the period.

    a. Test the hypothesis that the Instant Wealth service does no better than you could do by throwing darts at the S. and P. 500 list, an investment technique recommended by many finance professors. Use a 5 percent level of significance for the test.

    b. On the basis of part *a*, would you spend $1000 per year for the Instant Wealth service? Why or why not?

12.4. Suppose a friend of yours claims to possess powers of extrasensory perception (ESP) which can be used to detect the color (black or red) of ordinary playing cards as they are drawn from a shuffled deck in an adjacent room.

    a. Design a test of hypothesis to confirm or deny his claim. (To make it simple, assume that after each card is drawn and checked against his "call" it is replaced and the deck reshuffled prior to the next draw. Also, use a sample size for which you have binomial tables.)

    b. On what basis did you choose the null hypothesis in part *a*? Did your choice have anything to do with your prior beliefs concerning ESP?

12.5. In the flashbulb testing problem in this module, suppose a distributor is willing to increase the consumer's risk by increasing to .20 the maximum risk of a Type I error (accepting a shipment of bulbs with a fraction defective of more than .04). Formulate the appropriate decision criterion for sample sizes of:

    a. $n = 100$

    b. $n = 50$

    c. $n = 20$

12.6. Define a power curve, an OC curve, and an error curve, and explain how they are related.

12.7. The point that distinguishes acceptable from nonacceptable performance is always the point at which the maximum risk of a Type I error occurs and is also the point that separates Type I from Type II errors. Explain why this is true.

12.8. Assume that a large lot of flashbulbs is considered acceptable if .04 or fewer are defective. Plot (*a*) the power curve, (*b*) the OC curve, and (*c*) the error curve for the decision rule: Take a simple random sample of 20 bulbs and test them. If 2 or more are defective, reject the lot, otherwise accept it. Use values of the population proportion *p* of .02, .04, .06, .08, .10, .14, and .20.

12.9. Repeat Prob. 12.8 with the following decision rule. Take a simple random sample of 50 bulbs, and test them. If 5 or more are defective, reject the lot, otherwise accept it. Plot the curves on the same grids as the corresponding curves for Prob. 12.8.

12.10. Compare the error curves for Probs. 12.8 and 12.9. How would you summarize the effect of increasing the sample size from 20 to 50?

12.11. A Norwegian classmate is considering importing and selling hand-knit ski sweaters. He's decided to concentrate his selling efforts on sororities and calculates that if he can sell .05 of the girls, he can break even, including a reasonable return for time spent selling. He asks you to set up a sampling plan for him to test the market. You decide to investigate the characteristics of the following decision rule. Take a simple random sample of size 20. If the number of sales in the sample is greater than or equal to 1, get in the business, otherwise don't.

    a. Determine the ordinates of the error curve for the decision rule above for values of *p* of .02, .04, .06, .08, .10, .14, and .20. Graph the error curve.

    b. What is the maximum risk of a Type I error for this decision rule? For what value of *p* does it occur?

    c. What is the maximum risk of a Type II error for this decision rule? For what value of *p* does it occur?

12.12. Repeat Prob. 12.11, using an action limit, i.e., a criterion number, of 2 rather than 1, with everything else in the problem the same. Graph the error curve on the same grid as that for Prob. 12.11.

12.13. Compare the error curves for Probs. 12.11 and 12.12. What has been the effect of increasing the action limit from 1 to 2? Which of these two decision rules do you feel would be better for this problem?

12.14. If the probability of committing a Type I error is fixed at a certain level and the sample size is decreased, what is the effect on the risk of committing Type II errors?

12.15. Given the error curve for a decision rule, state the general effects of:

    a. Altering the criterion number (action limit), leaving the sampling size fixed.

    b. Increasing the sample size, and increasing the criterion number to maintain the same maximum risk of Type I error.

    Illustrate your answers with rough sketches, identifying the regions of Type I and Type II errors.

MODULE 13

THE NORMAL DISTRIBUTION AND PROBLEMS OF ESTIMATION FOR CONTINUOUS DISTRIBUTIONS

You're now ready to undertake a study of the *normal probability distribution*, the most important distribution in statistics. Its importance derives from three sources: (1) It provides a useful means of approximating the binomial distribution, which was seen to be useful in business problems but somewhat cumbersome in certain applications; (2) many real-world variables and processes are accurately described by the normal distribution; i.e., many variables are themselves normally distributed; (3) most important by far is the use of the normal distribution in sampling theory. As you'll see, a variety of useful *sampling distributions* conform to the normal, making it a cornerstone in the study of statistical inference.

General learning objectives

Your general learning objectives for this module are to be able to:

1. Describe the nature and use of:
   a. The normal distribution
   b. The sampling distribution of the mean
   c. The distribution of the difference between sample means
   d. Student's *t* distribution
2. Use the above distributions to make confidence interval estimates for continuous variables

Section 13.A
The Normal Distribution

Learning objectives

Your learning objectives for this section are to be able to:

1. Describe the nature and use of the normal distribution
2. Use tables to compute normal probabilities

THE NORMAL DISTRIBUTION AS AN APPROXIMATION TO THE BINOMIAL DISTRIBUTION

You've had enough experience with the binomial distribution to remember that its calculation becomes rather tedious as n becomes larger. To refresh your memory, let's calculate and graph the binomial distribution for coin-tossing experiments where $p = .5$ and $n = 2, 5,$ and 10. We'll also connect the midpoints of successive bars with a dotted line (see Fig. 13.1).

Obviously, as n becomes larger, the width of the bars becomes smaller and the dotted straight line between the midpoints begins to look like one continuous curve. Furthermore, the area under the dotted line comes very close to equaling the sum of the areas of the bars.

If this process were repeated with larger and larger n's, we'd find distinction between the bars and the dotted line becoming less and less obvious. If n were infinite, the bars would have no width and the dotted lines would become a continuous curve, as shown in Fig. 13.2. This curve is known as the *gaussian* or *normal curve*. The probability corresponding to any given value X can be found by using the expression

$$P_N = \frac{1}{\sigma_X \sqrt{2\pi}} e^{-(X-\mu_X)^2/2\sigma_X^2}$$

where P_N = normal probability
σ_X = standard deviation of distribution of X values
μ_X = mean of distribution of X values
$\pi = 3.14159$
$e = 2.71828$

303

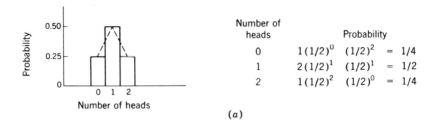

Number of heads	Probability		
0	$1(1/2)^0$	$(1/2)^2$	= 1/4
1	$2(1/2)^1$	$(1/2)^1$	= 1/2
2	$1(1/2)^2$	$(1/2)^0$	= 1/4

(a)

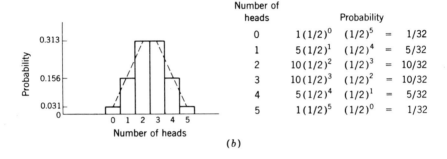

Number of heads	Probability		
0	$1(1/2)^0$	$(1/2)^5$	= 1/32
1	$5(1/2)^1$	$(1/2)^4$	= 5/32
2	$10(1/2)^2$	$(1/2)^3$	= 10/32
3	$10(1/2)^3$	$(1/2)^2$	= 10/32
4	$5(1/2)^4$	$(1/2)^1$	= 5/32
5	$1(1/2)^5$	$(1/2)^0$	= 1/32

(b)

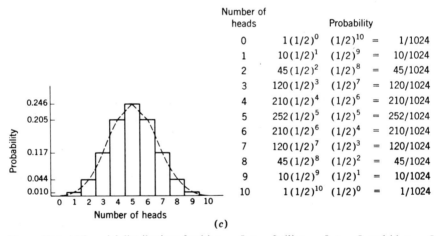

Number of heads	Probability		
0	$1(1/2)^0$	$(1/2)^{10}$	= 1/1024
1	$10(1/2)^1$	$(1/2)^9$	= 10/1024
2	$45(1/2)^2$	$(1/2)^8$	= 45/1024
3	$120(1/2)^3$	$(1/2)^7$	= 120/1024
4	$210(1/2)^4$	$(1/2)^6$	= 210/1024
5	$252(1/2)^5$	$(1/2)^5$	= 252/1024
6	$210(1/2)^6$	$(1/2)^4$	= 210/1024
7	$120(1/2)^7$	$(1/2)^3$	= 120/1024
8	$45(1/2)^8$	$(1/2)^2$	= 45/1024
9	$10(1/2)^9$	$(1/2)^1$	= 10/1024
10	$1(1/2)^{10}$	$(1/2)^0$	= 1/1024

(c)

Figure 13.1 / Binomial distributions for (a) $p = .5, n = 2$, (b) $p = .5, n = 5$, and (c) $p = .5$, $n = 10$.

A little investigation will show that this curve tails off to plus and minus infinity and that its highest value occurs where $X = \mu_X$, at which point P_N becomes equal to $1/\sigma_X \sqrt{2\pi}$. Further investigation would prove that the two points of inflection on the curve occur at distances of $-\sigma_X$ and $+\sigma_X$ from μ_X.

Carl Friedrich Gauss, a nineteenth-century astronomer, didn't arrive at this formula by tossing an infinite number of coins. His problem was one of measurement. He was trying to find the exact orbit of a planet, but successive measurements all had

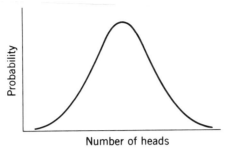

Number of heads

Figure 13.2 / Binomial distribution where $n =$ infinity, the normal distribution.

different values. His theory was that there was a "normal" curve of error distributed around the true value, and he used the formula above to represent this distribution of error.[1] While his normal curve is by no means universally applicable, it does prove extremely useful in all sorts of problems involving measurement. You'll run into a variety of these situations as you develop your ability to use the normal curve.

USE OF NORMAL PROBABILITIES: STANDARDIZED NORMAL DEVIATES

The area under the normal curve between any two limits is equal to the probability that a variable chosen from the distribution at random will fall within these limits. To find such an area, you could substitute the values of the mean and the standard deviation in the formula for the normal curve and integrate between the limits in question. This might be a good exercise in mathematics, but tedious (if not impossible). Moreover, if you had another problem involving a normal distribution with a different mean and standard deviation and different limits, you'd have to repeat the same difficult process again. The necessity of repeated integrations to find specific areas for particular normal distributions is obviated by the use of a *standardized normal distribution* having a mean of 0 and a standard deviation of 1. The areas under various portions of the standardized normal distribution are available in tables such as Appendix Table A.2.

To illustrate the use of such a distribution, suppose that a test had been administered to a very large population and it was found that the distribution of raw scores was normal, with a mean of 100 and a standard deviation of 20. What is the probability that a person chosen at random would have a score of 140 or more? The desired area is shown as the dark shaded area in Fig. 13.3.

---

[1] The normal distribution was discovered by Abraham Demoivre but was first applied by Gauss.

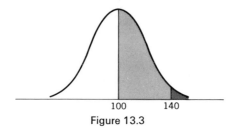

Figure 13.3

The standardized normal deviate z is found by expressing the distance between the mean and the limit in terms of standard deviations. Thus

$$z = \frac{140 - 100}{20} = +2.00$$

Looking up a value of 2.00 in the $(X - \mu_X)/\sigma_X$ column in Appendix Table A.2 you find that .4772 of the total area under the curve falls between the mean and $+2.00$ standard deviations or, in terms of this problem, between 100 and 140 (the light shaded area in the diagram). Therefore .4772 is the probability that a person selected at random would have a score between 100 and 140. Since the normal distribution is symmetrical, 50 percent of the area falls above the mean. Therefore the probability that a person would have a score of 140 or *more* is equal to .5000 − .4772, or .0228.

In using the normal table to find probabilities, you must always be sure that the standardized value you are using is related to the mean of the distribution. Only areas adjacent to the mean of the distribution can be found directly in the table. Other areas must be calculated by adding or subtracting areas that *are* adjacent to the mean. For example, consider the problem of finding the probability that a person would have a score between 120 and 140, area B in Fig. 13.4. Area B can only be found from the standardized table by subtracting area A from area $A + B$ since any area in the table must have the mean as one of the limits. The solution is shown below.

$$z_{140} = \frac{140 - 100}{20} = +2.00 \rightarrow .4772 = \text{area } A + B$$

$$z_{120} = \frac{120 - 100}{20} = +1.00 \rightarrow \underline{.3413 = \text{area } A}$$
$$.1359 = \text{area } B$$

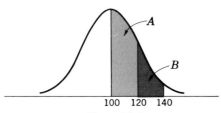

Figure 13.4

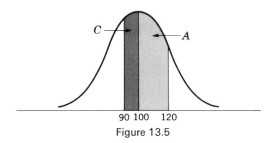

Figure 13.5

In the expressions above, z_{140} refers to the standardized normal deviate corresponding to a score of 140, and the arrow can be read "which leads to an area (or probability) of."

Similarly, to find area $A + C$ in Fig. 13.5, you would have to add area A to area C:

$$z_{90} = \frac{90 - 100}{20} = -.50 \rightarrow .1915 = \text{area } C$$

$$z_{120} = \frac{120 - 100}{20} = +1.00 \rightarrow \underline{.3413 = \text{area } A}$$
$$.5328 = \text{area } A + C$$

In the problems above, you found an area or probability between two limits, given the mean, the standard deviation, and the limits in question. Other types of problems arise in which the probability is known and the unknown is either the limit, the mean, or the standard deviation. Let's work an example of each of these problems.

EXAMPLE 1

Suppose you want to establish limits for letter grades for the same distribution of test scores used above, which had a mean of 100 and a standard deviation of 20. Further, suppose that you want to give 10 percent A's, 25 percent B's, 40 percent C's, 15 percent D's, and 10 percent F's. What test scores represent the limits to such a grade distribution? The problem can be sketched as in Fig. 13.6. Starting with the right tail, you can determine that $(A - 100)/20 = z_{.40}$, where A refers to the lower limit

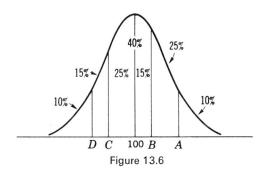

Figure 13.6

307

of the grade A, since 40 percent of the scores are between the mean and the lower limit of 10 percent A's. Since $z_{.40} = 1.28$ from the area table (looking for the z value corresponding to the area closest to .40),

$$\frac{A - 100}{20} = 1.28 \quad \text{and} \quad A = 1.28(20) + 100 = 125.6 \approx 126$$

Similarly, $(B - 100)/20 = z_{.15}$ since 15 percent of the scores must be between the mean and the lower limit of the B's if there are to be 25 percent B's and 10 percent A's. Thus

$$z_{.15} = .39 \quad \text{and} \quad \frac{B - 100}{20} = .39$$

$$B = .39(20) + 100 = 107.8 \approx 108$$

Therefore the lower limit of the B's would be 108 and the upper limit 125.

By using the same computations, you can determine that the C's would fall between 87 and 107, the D's between 74 and 86, and the F's below 74.

EXAMPLE 2

Suppose that you own an Alaskan cannery which packs king crab meat in cans that say "6 oz, drained weight" on the label. Further, suppose that the machine that packs the meat cannot pack every can with exactly the same weight, the weights being normally distributed with a standard deviation of .04 oz. (The standard deviation is a function of the accuracy of the machine. While the mean can be adjusted up or down by setting the machine, the standard deviation is fixed in the short run. It will increase only gradually as the machine wears out and can be decreased only by repairing the machine. Assume that the standard deviation of .04 oz will hold throughout this season's pack.)

It would be unrealistic for any regulatory authority to expect that every single can would have a drained weight of 6 ounces or more because such a rule could be enforced only by opening every can and weighing it, which would leave none to sell. Actually, regulations would be set up in terms of permitting some small percentage of cans to fall below the 6-oz limit. This would enable the regulatory authorities to test cans on a sampling basis, using methods which will be developed in the next chapter. Now suppose that these specifications say that no more than 0.3 percent of the cans can have a drained weight of less than 6 oz. The management question then is at what level to set the mean to be assured that it will meet specifications and at the same time put no more meat in the cans than is necessary (Fig. 13.7). Stated in this way, the problem is simply solved.

$$\frac{\text{Limit} - \mu_X}{\sigma_X} = z_{.003}$$

$$\frac{6.00 - \mu_X}{.04} = -2.75$$

$$\mu_X = 6.110$$

Therefore the mean would be set at 6.110 oz.

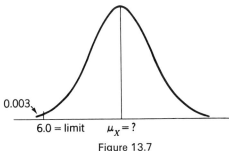

0.003

6.0 = limit $\mu_X = ?$

Figure 13.7

EXAMPLE 3

For the situation described in Example 2, assume that the manufacturer of the packing machine claims that he can repair your machine at a cost of $6000 and reduce its standard deviation to .03 oz. You want to determine whether or not this is a good deal for you. The crab meat costs you 45 cents per ounce. The season's pack is 400,000 cans.

While the manufacturer's representative is still on the phone, you whip out your pocket calculator and a normal table, and perform the following calculations:

If σ_X were .03, the mean could be set at $6.000 + 2.75(.03) = 6.0825$.
Savings per can would be $6.110 - 6.0825 = 0.0275$ oz.
Savings per 400,000 cans $= 400,000(.0275) = 11,000$ oz.
11,000 oz at 45 cents per oz $= \$4950 =$ net savings for a reduction in standard deviation from .04 to .03 (or for any reduction in the standard deviation of .01).

Your response is that $6000 is too much to pay for the repair if the guarantee is for a standard deviation of .03. However, you *would* take the deal if they would guarantee a σ_X of .02 oz [in fact, a guarantee of .02 oz would be worth $4950(2) = \$9900$, well over the $6000 cost].

REVIEW EXERCISES 13.A

1. The normal distribution can be described as an approximation to the _____
   distribution with $p =$ _____ as n _____.
2. The normal distribution is often used:
   a. To approximate the binomial distribution.
   b. To describe measured variables.
   c. Both *a* and *b*.
   d. Neither *a* nor *b*.
3. Light bulbs that are manufactured by a particular process have a mean life of 540 hours. Assuming that the bulb life is a normally distributed variable with a standard deviation of 50 hours, calculate:
   a. The fraction of bulbs manufactured by this process that have a life of less than 500 hours.

  b. The fraction of bulbs with a life between 500 and 600 hours.

  c. The probability that a bulb will last between 450 and 500 hours.

4. Refer to Exercise 3. The worst 10 percent of the bulbs produced will have a life of less than what number of hours?

5. Refer to Exercise 3. Suppose the standard deviation associated with the manufacturing process can be reduced to 25 hours. In such a case, what fraction of the bulbs produced would have a life of less than 500 hours. Compare your answer to that for Exercise 3, part a.

Answers 13.A

1. binomial, .5, as n becomes very large (increases without limit)   2. c

3. a. Standard normal deviate $z = \dfrac{\text{limit} - \mu_X}{\sigma_X}$

$$z_{500} = \frac{500 - 540}{50} = -0.8. \rightarrow \text{area} = .2881$$

Area *below* 500 = .5000 − .2881 = .2119

Remember that the table shows areas *adjacent* to the mean, on either side.

b. $z_{600} = \dfrac{600 - 540}{50} = +1.2 \rightarrow \text{area} = .3849$

Area between 500 and 600 = .3849 + .2881 = .6730

c. $z_{450} = \dfrac{450 - 540}{50} = -1.8 \rightarrow \text{area} = .4641$

$P(450 \le X \le 500)$ = area between 450 and 500 = .4641 − .2881 = .1760

4. You need to find a *limit* such that the lower-tail area is 10 percent, or such that the area adjacent to the mean is 40 percent. Using the normal area table backwards, the area closest to 40 percent (.3997) corresponds to a z value of 1.28. Therefore:

$$z = -1.28 = \frac{\text{limit} - 540}{50}$$

$$\text{Limit} = 540 + (-1.28)(50) = 540 - 64 = 476$$

5. $z_{500} = \dfrac{500 - 540}{25} = -1.6 \rightarrow \text{area} = .4452$

Area below 500 = .5000 − .4452 = .0548

With a standard deviation only half as large (25 as compared with 50), the area below 500 (fraction of bulbs with a life less than 500 hours) is only about one-fourth as large (.0548 as compared with .2119).

Section 13.B

Confidence Intervals for Discrete Distributions Using the Normal Approximation

Learning objectives

Your learning objectives for this section are to be able to use the normal approximation to construct confidence interval estimates based on:

1. Binomial sampling
2. Hypergeometric sampling

NORMAL APPROXIMATION TO AN INTERVAL ESTIMATE FOR A POPULATION PROPORTION: INFINITE POPULATION, LARGE SAMPLE

Now that you've learned how to use the normal table to solve some simple but practical problems where the variables involved were normally distributed, let's return to the use of the normal table as an approximation to the binomial and its use in making statistical inferences about a population proportion.

In Module 11, you learned how to make an interval estimate for a population proportion using the binomial tables. The specific example involved observing 7 defective flashbulbs in a sample of 100 bulbs taken at random from a production process that could be viewed as infinite.

If we knew the *true* proportion of defective bulbs in the population, we could derive the entire sampling distribution for the number of defective bulbs in the sample by using binomial tables. That is, we could specify all the possible outcomes of sampling 100 bulbs, together with the probability of each. Since there are 101 possible outcomes (from 0 defectives to 100 defectives inclusive), such a listing would be very time-consuming. For illustrative purposes, we list a few of the possible outcomes together with their probabilities in Table 13.1.

Having made the entire distribution, we could find its mean and its standard deviation, using the techniques described in Module 10. If we did, we'd find that the mean of the distribution of sample proportions would be equal to the true proportion of successes in the population p and that the standard deviation of the distribution of

311

Table 13.1

Possible outcome (proportion defective)	Probability
0	$P_b(r - 0 \mid n = 100, p)$
.01	$P_b(r = 1 \mid n = 100, p)$
.02	$P_b(r = 2 \mid n = 100, p)$
.03	$P_b(r = 3 \mid n = 100, p)$
. . . .	. . . .
1.0	$P_b(r = 100 \mid n = 100, p)$

sample proportions, denoted by $\sigma_{\bar{p}}$, would be equal to $\sqrt{p(1 - p)}/\sqrt{n}$. These results are extremely important to the discussion that follows and should be kept firmly in mind. Formal proofs that the sample proportions, for which we use the symbol $\bar{p}$, have a mean of p and that $\sigma_{\bar{p}} = \sqrt{p(1 - p)}/\sqrt{n}$ are more appropriate for a course in mathematical statistics and will not be given here. However, the problems at the end of this module should give you ample opportunity to prove them to your own satisfaction.

Since the true proportion is not known, we'll have to estimate it by using the proportion that we observed in the sample, $\bar{p} = .07$. Thus our point estimate of p is .07, and our best estimate of $\sigma_{\bar{p}}$ is $s_{\bar{p}}$, the estimate of the standard deviation of the distribution of sample proportions based on sample information, which is equal to

$$s_{\bar{p}} = \frac{\sqrt{\bar{p}(1 - \bar{p})}}{\sqrt{n - 1}} = \sqrt{\frac{.07(.93)}{99}} = .0255$$

Note that we use $n - 1$ rather than n in the denominator when calculating $s_{\bar{p}}$ since we are estimating a population standard deviation from sample information.

Now the process for making an interval estimate for p becomes much simpler than it was when we used the binomial table. The interval estimate of p is $\bar{p} \pm z(s_{\bar{p}})$. If we choose to use a 95 percent confidence coefficient, as we did earlier in Module 11, in Appendix Table A.2 we look up the z value corresponding to a tail area of .025, obtaining a z value of 1.96. Then the interval estimate for $p = .07 \pm 1.96(.0255) = .07 \pm .05$, or .02 to .12. Note that these values correspond closely to those of .02 and .14 obtained for the same problem in Module 11 by using the more tedious procedure involving the binomial table.

The normal approximation described here gives an adequate approximation of binomial probabilities when np and $n(1 - p)$ are both equal to or greater than 5 and where $n \geq 30$. In other cases (involving small samples or small p or both) the approximation to true binomial probabilities becomes very rough.

NORMAL APPROXIMATION TO AN INTERVAL ESTIMATE FOR A POPULATION PROPORTION: FINITE POPULATION, LARGE SAMPLE

Populations can be assumed to be infinite when the sample is taken from an ongoing process or when the sampling is done with replacement. If the population size is finite and sampling is done without replacement, the assumption of independence essential to a Bernoulli process is violated and the general law of multiplication must be used rather than the special law in determining the number of possible combinations of a given outcome. In these cases the appropriate distribution is the hypergeometric rather than the binomial.

The mean of a hypergeometric sampling distribution is equal to the population proportion, as it was for the binomial. However, the standard deviation of the hypergeometric sampling distribution differs from that of the binomial by a fraction called the *finite correction factor*, which takes into account the relationship between the size of the population and that of the sample. Thus for the hypergeometric distribution

$$s_{\bar{p}} = \sqrt{\frac{N-n}{N-1}} \sqrt{\frac{\bar{p}(1-\bar{p})}{n-1}}$$

where $\sqrt{(N-n)/(N-1)}$ is called the finite correction factor. Inspection of the terms in the finite correction factor shows the relationship between the binomial and the hypergeometric distribution. As the size of the sample n becomes smaller in relation to the size of the population N, the finite correction factor approaches a value of 1 and the hypergeometric approaches the binomial distribution.

Let's change the flashbulb example slightly to illustrate the use of the normal approximation for the hypergeometric distribution. Assume that instead of having the manufacturer sample from a process, the sampling is done by a large distributor of flashbulbs, who tests a random sample of 100 bulbs from a shipment of 1000 and finds that 7 are defective. (Since the cost of sampling is very expensive for a destructive process, it would be unusual to take a sample this large in actual practice.)

In this case $\bar{p} = .07$ is used as a point estimate of p, and $\sigma_{\bar{p}}$, the standard deviation of the sampling distribution of the proportion defective, is estimated by

$$s_{\bar{p}} = \sqrt{\frac{1000-100}{999}} \sqrt{\frac{.07(.93)}{99}} = .024$$

and the interval estimate for p using a 95 percent confidence coefficient is

$$.07 \pm 1.96(.024) = .07 \pm .047 = .023 \text{ to } .117$$

This answer is close to that provided by the binomial distribution since the finite correction factor was .95. In cases where the sample size is a large fraction of the population the difference would be more pronounced.

REVIEW EXERCISES 13.B

1. Suppose you wish to make a 95 percent confidence interval estimate of the proportion of persons in a community of 50,000 who favor a proposed bond issue. A random sample of 50 shows 10 persons in favor.

a. Do you need to use the finite correction factor in this problem? Why or why not?

b. Construct a 95 percent confidence interval for estimating the population proportion in favor.

2. Refer to Exercise 1. Suppose the sample of 50 had been selected entirely from one precinct containing only 200 voters. If you made a 95 percent confidence interval estimate of the proportion of persons in that precinct favoring the issue:

a. Would you need to compute the finite correction factor? Explain.

b. Would the confidence interval obtained in this case be wider or narrower than the interval obtained in part *b* of Exercise 1? Explain.

3. Give the formula for the finite correction factor.

4. The principal advantage of using the normal approximation to estimate confidence intervals in problems involving discrete sampling distributions is that:

a. The normal area table is more accurate than the binomial table.

b. It is generally much simpler.

c. The same interval can be obtained with a smaller sample.

d. None of the above.

5. As long as the sample is reasonably large, the normal approximation can be used to construct confidence intervals based on binomial sampling without serious loss of accuracy: true or false?

Answers 13.B

1. a. No; although (theoretically) sampling without replacement from a finite population is involved, the size of the population is so large relative to the size of the sample that the finite correction factor is unnecessary.

b. $s_{\bar{p}} = \sqrt{\dfrac{\bar{p}(1-\bar{p})}{n-1}} = \sqrt{\dfrac{(.2)(.8)}{49}} = .057$

For a confidence level of 95 percent (.0250 in each tail of the normal curve), the z value is 1.96, and the 95 per cent confidence interval is

$$.20 \pm 1.96(.057) = .20 \pm .11, \text{ or from } .09 \text{ to } .31$$

2. a. Yes; here the sample size is relatively large compared to the size of the population of 200.

b. The interval would be narrower. The finite correction factor will always be less than 1, reducing $s_{\bar{p}}$ and hence the width of the interval.

3. Finite correction factor $= \sqrt{\dfrac{N-n}{N-1}}$

where N = number of items in population

n = number in sample

4. b   *5.* true

Section 13.C

Interval Estimates for Continuous Distributions

Learning objectives

Your learning objectives for this section are to be able to:

1. Describe the sampling distribution of the mean
2. Define the standard error of the mean
3. Make interval estimates based on samples drawn from continuous distributions
4. Determine the sample size necessary to obtain a given precision and confidence level in an interval estimate of the population mean

THE SAMPLING DISTRIBUTION OF THE MEAN

A sampling distribution can be generated for any sample statistic whether it is based on a count, as in the case of the proportion defective, or measurement. The most common statistic that is used to summarize measurements is the simple average, or mean. The sampling distribution of the mean is a listing of all the possible sample means that could be obtained from random samples of a given size taken from the population in question, together with the probability associated with each sample mean. See if you can develop an intuitive feeling for the meaning of the expression "sampling distribution of the mean" from the following example.

Suppose that there are 25,000 men stationed at a large army base. Furthermore, suppose that you have records showing the weight of each man. From these data you calculate a mean weight, μ_X, of 170 lb and a standard deviation, σ_X, of 20 lb. (The distribution of these weights is not normal since there are more people who are greatly overweight than greatly underweight.) The men are housed in barracks that contain 100 men each. Assume that the assignment of a man to a barrack is at random with respect to his weight. If this is the case, each barrack can be considered a random sample of 100 men. You could now find the arithmetic mean of the weights of men in each barrack and would have 250 different sample means.

Now conceptualize an experiment in which every *possible* combination of 100 individual weights (rather than just the 250 described above) were calculated. If the mean of each possible random sample of size 100 were calculated and summarized in a probability distribution by determining the relative frequency associated with each mean, the result would be called the *sampling distribution of the mean.* What characteristics do you think this distribution would have?

The first observation you might make is that the mean of all the sample means would be the same as the mean of the population. This observation is correct and can be generalized. The mean of the distribution of sample means will *always* be equal to the overall mean of the population.

Although this concept is simple enough and the result intuitively obvious, notice that the language is already somewhat confusing. In the discussion which follows you should keep firmly in mind the distinction between (1) the distribution of items (weights of individuals) within a particular sample (one barrack) and (2) the distribution of sample means (the set of average weights for every barrack) around the overall mean for the population (all the men on the base).

Your second observation would probably be that the standard deviation of this distribution of sample means should be considerably smaller than the standard deviation of the population from which the samples were drawn. After all, you must reason, the smallest average weight for any group of 100 men couldn't be as low as the weight of the lightest man on the base, nor could the highest average weight for a barrack be as high as the weight of the heaviest man. If pressed further about the problem of the dispersion of the distribution of mean weights, you just might see that the standard deviation of this distribution would have to be a function of (1) the standard deviation of the *population*, and (2) the size of the *sample*. If the men all weighed the same, the standard deviation of the population would be 0 and the sample means would also show no variation. Furthermore, the smaller the sample size, the greater the variation you would expect in the distribution of sample means. If each man lived in his own one-man tent rather than a barrack of 100 men and were therefore considered a sample of one, the standard deviation of the sample means would be the same as the standard deviation of the population. As more and more men were grouped in a sample, you should expect less and less variation in the means of these samples from the mean of the population.

These observations can be generalized in the statement that the standard deviation of the sampling distribution of the mean is directly related to the standard deviation of the population and inversely related to the size of the sample. To be exact $\sigma_{\bar{X}}$, used to represent the standard deviation of the sampling distribution of the mean, is equal to $\sigma_X/\sqrt{n}$, the standard deviation of the population divided by the *square root* of the size of the sample.[1] To avoid some of the confusing language encountered above, $\sigma_{\bar{X}}$ is often referred to as the *standard error of the mean.*

Your third observation—if you had any strength left after the second and if you were really a mathematician at heart—might be that the distribution of sample means would be likely to resemble a normal distribution more closely than did the

---

[1] This is strictly true only if the population is infinite or if the sampling is done with replacement. In this illustration we should use the finite correction factor $\sqrt{(N - n)/(N - 1)}$ as we did earlier in making interval estimates for a population proportion for a finite population. However, the finite correction factor in this case is $\sqrt{24,900/24,999} = .998$ and so close to 1 that it is ignored.

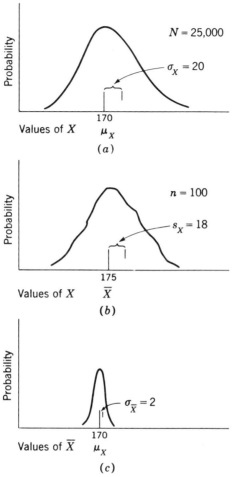

Figure 13.8 / (*a*) Population values; (*b*) values from one sample; (*c*) all sample means.

original population. This observation has been generalized by statisticians as the *central-limit theorem,* which states that for a wide variety of sample statistics (including the sample mean) the *sampling distribution* of the statistic approaches normality as the size of the sample is increased. This fact is one of the prime reasons for the wide use of the normal distribution in statistics and decision theory.

The discussion above can be illustrated by the three diagrams in Fig. 13.8. The first of these illustrates the population. It is asymmetrical and has a mean of 170 lb and a standard deviation of 20 lb. The second illustrates the distribution of weights we might find in one barrack. The mean in this case is, say, 175 lb, and the standard deviation is 18 lb. Other barracks, of course, would have other means and standard deviations. The third curve represents the distribution of all the sample means. It is normal, its mean is 170 lb and its standard deviation is $20/\sqrt{100} = 2$ lb. Note that in the first two cases values of X, or individual weights, are graphed on the X axis about their means. In the third case, sample means $\overline{X}$'s are graphed on the X axis.

Let us summarize what we have tried to show intuitively in the example above.

1. The mean of the sampling distribution of the mean is equal to the mean of the population.
2. The standard deviation of the sampling distribution of the mean is equal to the standard deviation of the population divided by the square root of the size of the sample, for an infinite population.
3. The sampling distribution of the mean approaches normality as the sample size is increased.

You should note the similarity between these statements about the sampling distribution of the mean and those in previous sections regarding the sampling distribution of a proportion.

INTERVAL ESTIMATE FOR THE POPULATION MEAN: INFINITE POPULATION, LARGE SAMPLE

Suppose that you work in a district office of a life insurance company. The general agent in charge of the office asks you to take a sample of records from your files to determine the average size of policy held by individuals. You remember that way back in your college days some professor kept insisting that if you were to make estimates of population parameters based on sample statistics you should take a random sample. That being about all you remember, you proceed to take a random sample of 25 policies and find from them that the sample mean $\overline{X}$ is $9200. You also make an estimate of the population standard deviation based on the sample, obtaining a value of s_X of $5000.

At this point you refer to an old text and find that you can make an interval estimate for the population mean through the following process if the sample size is less than 5 percent of the population:[1]

$$\text{Interval estimate for } \mu_X = \overline{X} \pm zs_{\overline{X}}$$

where z is the standard normal deviate for the desired confidence coefficient and $s_{\overline{X}}$ is the estimate of the standard error of the mean $\sigma_{\overline{X}}$ that is based on sample data. That is,

$$s_{\overline{X}} = \frac{s_X}{\sqrt{n}}$$

---

[1] If the sample were more than 5 percent of the population, the finite correction factor should be taken into account. This is explained on p. 313.

Deciding upon a 90 percent confidence coefficient, you look up the z value corresponding to a tail area of 5 percent (remembering that there are two such tails associated with a 90 percent confidence coefficient) and find that it is 1.645. Therefore, you proceed as follows:

$$\text{Interval estimate} = \$9200 \pm 1.645 \frac{\$5000}{5} = \$9200 \pm 1645 = \$7555 \text{ to } \$10,845$$

Your boss is impressed by your adeptness at statistics but is a bit confused about the meaning of the 90 percent confidence coefficient. You explain that the most simple interpretation of the confidence coefficient is that while you cannot guarantee that the true mean will lie between these limits, you would be willing to bet with odds of 9 to 1 that it does. Further, you explain that you feel confident that these are proper odds because if you were to take a large number of sample means of size 25 and make an interval estimate like this for each sample, you would get different means, standard deviations and intervals, but you know from statistical theory that 9 times out of every 10 (on the average) the interval described would include the true mean. You even make a sketch showing how successive estimates might look (Fig. 13.9).

He says that this is fine, but what if the estimate you just gave him is that shown in Fig. 13.9 for sample 4, the one that did *not* include the true mean. Your response is that in that case you simply would have made an error due to random variation in your sample. You hasten to explain that if he is not willing to take a 1 in 10 chance of making this kind of error, you can recalculate the estimate using whatever confidence coefficient he feels is desirable.

He says that a 9 in 10 chance seems about right to him, but the thing that does bother him is the spread of the interval—it is too large to be of a great deal of use. In fact, he would feel much better if you could produce an interval that would have a spread of about $1000 and still retain the 90 percent confidence coefficient. At this point you remember something else that your professor said—that you should have asked your boss to tell you the confidence coefficient and the approximate size of the interval that would be meaningful to him *before* you determined the sample size.

DETERMINATION OF SAMPLE SIZE FOR AN INTERVAL ESTIMATE OF THE POPULATION MEAN

To cope with the problem above, you reason as follows. To have an interval estimate that spans $1000 means that the interval would spread $\pm\$500$ from the sample mean. Therefore the upper limit L_u could be determined using the following expression

$$L_u = \bar{X} + z \frac{s_X}{\sqrt{n}}$$

Therefore

$$L_u - \bar{X} = z \frac{s_X}{\sqrt{n}}$$

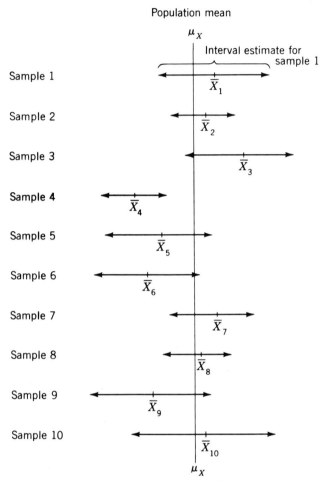

Figure 13.9 / Interval estimates of true population mean for 10 successive samples.

Substituting the desired quantities in the expression above and using the estimate of the population standard deviation derived from your first sample, you could solve for n.

$$500 = 1.645 \frac{5000}{\sqrt{n}}$$

$$\sqrt{n} = \frac{1.645(5000)}{500} = 16.45$$

$$n = 271$$

The same result could be achieved by using the lower limit since

$$L_1 = \bar{X} - z \frac{s_X}{\sqrt{n}}$$

$$L_1 - \bar{X} = -z \frac{s_X}{\sqrt{n}}$$

$$-500 = -1.645 \frac{5000}{\sqrt{n}}$$

$$n = 271$$

To satisfy your boss, you therefore take a random sample of 271. Let us assume that this size of sample is still not an appreciable part of the population and that you obtained a sample mean of \$9300 and a standard deviation of \$4700. The interval estimate for the population mean would then be

$$\bar{X} \pm z \frac{s_X}{\sqrt{n}} = 9300 \pm 1.645 \frac{4700}{\sqrt{271}} = 9300 \pm 469 = \$8831 \text{ to } \$9769$$

This estimate meets the criteria asked by your boss. The confidence coefficient is 90 percent, and the interval is \$938. The interval is not exactly \$1000 because the standard deviation estimated from the sample of 271 turned out to be a little smaller than that estimated from the sample of 25. Note that it was necessary to have an estimate of the standard deviation of the population in order to determine the necessary sample size. If such an estimate were not available from past experience, it would have to be obtained from a small "pilot" sample.

INTERVAL ESTIMATE FOR THE POPULATION MEAN: FINITE POPULATION, LARGE SAMPLE

In the illustration used above, we have assumed that the population was so large that it could for practical purposes be considered infinite. In situations where the population is finite *and* the sample size is an appreciable proportion of the population, the finite correction factor would have to be applied, just as it was for interval estimates made for the population proportion in the preceding section. To be sure that the mechanics of this process are understood, we shall recalculate the interval estimate made for the insurance example above, assuming now that the population size was 600.

The proper sample size would be found as follows (assuming a confidence coefficient of 90 percent, a desired interval of \$1000, and an approximate standard deviation of \$5000):

$$L_u - = \bar{X} + z \sqrt{\frac{N-n}{N-1}} \frac{s_X}{\sqrt{n}}$$

Since n appears in the expression two times, it is a bit more difficult to solve.

$$500 = 1.645 \sqrt{\frac{600 - n}{599}} \frac{5000}{\sqrt{n}} = \frac{1.645(5000)}{\sqrt{599}} \sqrt{\frac{600 - n}{n}} = 335.7 \sqrt{\frac{600 - n}{n}}$$

$$\left(\frac{500}{335.7}\right)^2 = \frac{600 - n}{n}$$

$$2.218 = \frac{600}{n} - 1$$

$$n = \frac{600}{3.218} = 187$$

Note that when we assumed an infinite population, the sample size necessary for an interval estimate spanning $1000 was 271. The calculations above show that if the population size is 600 rather than infinite, the same accuracy could be attained with a smaller sample size. This is as we might expect since the larger the sample is in relation to the population, the more closely it should reflect the characteristics of the population. Therefore, for the same accuracy, we could use a smaller sample size if that sample were an appreciable part of the population. Remember, however, that if the sample isn't an appreciable portion of the population—say, more than 5 percent—it's the absolute size of the sample, rather than its size relative to the population that determines the accuracy of the estimate.

Assume that a sample of size 187 was taken and that $\bar{X}$ was found to be $9250 with s_X equal to $4800. The standard deviation of the sampling distribution of the mean $s_{\bar{X}}$ would then be

$$\sqrt{\frac{N - n}{N - 1}} \frac{s_X}{\sqrt{n}} = \sqrt{\frac{600 - 187}{599}} \frac{4800}{\sqrt{187}} = \$291$$

The interval estimate for μ_X would be calculated as before. With a 90 percent confidence coefficient,

$$\mu_X = \bar{X} \pm z_{.90} s_{\bar{X}} = 9250 \pm 1.645(291) = \$8771 \text{ to } \$9729$$

Again, the interval estimate is not exactly $1000 as planned because the approximate standard deviation used to plan the sample size didn't turn out to be the same as the standard deviation estimated from the sample.

REVIEW EXERCISES 13.C

1. The distribution of sample means:
   a. Has a mean equal to _____.
   b. Has a standard deviation equal to _____.
   c. Approaches the form of a _____ distribution as the sample size is increased.

2. The standard error of the mean:
   - *a.* Is equal to the standard deviation of the population from which samples are drawn.
   - *b.* Is the estimate of the population standard deviation computed from sample data.
   - *c.* Is the standard deviation of the distribution of sample means.
   - *d.* None of the above.
3. A magazine editor wants to know the average family income of its readers. A random sample of 36 readers yields income data with a mean of $13,500 and an estimate of the population standard deviation of $2400. Construct a 90 percent confidence interval estimate of the population mean.
4. Refer to Exercise 3. Suppose you want to estimate the mean income of readers to within $100 with 95 percent confidence. How large a sample would be required?
5. In order to determine the sample size necessary to provide an interval estimate with given precision and confidence level, it is necessary to know the population standard deviation or have an estimate of it: true or false?

Answers 13.C

1. *a.* the mean of the population from which the samples were drawn, $\mu_{\bar{X}} = \mu_X$
   - *b.* the population standard deviation divided by the square root of the sample size,

   $$\sigma_{\bar{X}} = \sigma_X / \sqrt{n}$$

   - *c.* normal

2. *c*

3. $s_{\bar{X}} = \dfrac{s_X}{\sqrt{n}} = \dfrac{2400}{\sqrt{36}} = 400$

For 90 percent confidence, the z value (corresponding to .4500) is 1.64. Confidence interval $= \bar{X} \pm z(s_{\bar{X}}) = \$13,500 \pm (1.64)(400) = \$13,500 \pm 656$

4. For a 95 percent confidence interval, $z = 1.96$.

$$z = 1.96 = \frac{\frac{1}{2} \text{ confidence interval}}{s_{\bar{X}}} = \frac{\frac{1}{2} \text{ confidence interval}}{s_X / \sqrt{n}} = \frac{100}{2400 / \sqrt{n}}$$

$$\sqrt{n} = \frac{1.96(2400)}{100} = 47.04$$

$$n = 47.04^2 = 2213$$

5. True; in a sampling situation, the population standard deviation is rarely known, but it must be estimated based on previous experience, judgment, or a pilot sample.

Section 13.D
Other Sampling Distributions

Learning objectives

Your learning objectives for this section are to be able to:

1. Describe the nature and use of:
   a. The distribution of the difference between sample means
   b. The distribution of the difference between sample proportions
   c. The Student's *t* distribution
2. Use each of the above distributions in constructing confidence intervals

INTERVAL ESTIMATE FOR THE DIFFERENCE BETWEEN TWO POPULATION MEANS: LARGE SAMPLES

There are many situations in business in which you want to make a judgment relative to the similarity or dissimilarity between two population means. One such example could be that of a tire company that has developed a new process which it hopes will increase the mean length of life of tires (as measured by tread wear). In order to find out whether the new process really does produce tires with a greater mean life than those from the old process, the company proposes sampling tires from each process and comparing their mean life. (Both the populations of new and old tires can be considered infinite since they are results of processes.)

The problem now becomes one of deciding whether or not the *population* means are different on the basis of an observed difference between *sample* means. Even if there were no difference whatsoever between the mean length of life produced by the two processes, we should still expect random variation among samples. For example, we might obtain the pairs of sample means shown in Table 13.2.

If a very large number of differences between paired sample means such as those in Table 13.2 were observed, we could construct a distribution of *differences* between sample means. The theoretical distribution corresponding to this experimentally derived distribution is called the sampling distribution of the *difference between sample means*. It would look like the distribution sketched in Fig. 13.10. Upon investigating the properties of this sampling distribution you'd discover three important characteristics. (1) The distribution would approach normality as the size of the sample was increased. (The sampling distribution of the difference between

Table 13.2 / Example of differences between sample means for two processes

Sample pair	(1) Mean, new process, mi	(2) Mean, old process, mi	(3) Difference, mi (1) − (2)
1	19,780	19,600	+180
2	17,960	18,250	−290
3	19,320	19,230	+90
4	18,480	18,520	−40
n	18,465	18,440	+25

sample means is one of the distributions that approaches normality under the central-limit theorem.) (2) The mean of the sampling distribution would be 0. This is intuitively appealing since if the population means were identical, we'd expect that the sum of the differences between paired sample means for the new and the old processes would average 0. (3) The standard deviation of the sampling distribution, estimated from the standard deviation of the samples, would be

$$s_{\bar{X}_1 - \bar{X}_2} = \sqrt{s_{\bar{X}_1}^2 + s_{\bar{X}_2}^2}$$

This equation expresses the standard deviation of the sampling distribution of the difference between sample means as a function of the estimates of the standard error of the mean obtained from each of the two samples.

Fortunately, you don't have to derive the complete sampling distribution in order to make an interval estimate for the difference between the population means. You simply need to take one set of paired sample means and use the relationship

$$\text{Interval estimate, } \mu_{X_1} - \mu_{X_2} = (\bar{X}_1 - \bar{X}_2) \pm z(s_{\bar{X}_1 - \bar{X}_2})$$

where $\bar{X}_1 - \bar{X}_2$ = observed difference between sample means
z = standardized normal deviate corresponding to desired confidence coefficient

$$s_{\bar{X}_1 - \bar{X}_2} = \sqrt{s_{\bar{X}_1}^2 + s_{\bar{X}_2}^2}$$

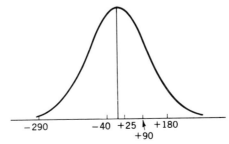

Figure 13.10 / Distribution of differences between sample means (mean, old − mean, new).

For the tire problem, let's assume that we took random samples of size 60 from both the old and the new process, obtaining a sample mean for the new tires of 19,780 mi, with an estimate of the standard deviation of 3000 mi, and a sample mean for the old tires of 19,600, with an estimate of the standard deviation of 2900 mi. Then, with a 90 percent confidence coefficient, the interval estimate would be

$$\mu_{\text{new}} - \mu_{\text{old}} = (19{,}780 - 19{,}600) \pm 1.645 \sqrt{\left(\frac{3000}{\sqrt{60}}\right)^2 + \left(\frac{2900}{\sqrt{60}}\right)^2}$$

$$= +180 \pm 1.645\,(539)$$

$$= -707 \text{ to } +1067$$

This result is interpreted by saying that we are 90 percent sure that the difference between the population means for the new and the old processes will not be more than -707 to $+1067$ mi. The negative sign before the 707 is very important since it indicates that the population mean for the new process might well be as much as 707 mi *less* than that for the old. Obviously the manufacturer's hopes for producing a tire with a higher average life are not substantiated by the results of the sampling. You wouldn't be convinced that the new process was better until the entire range of the interval estimate was positive.

The formula used above to make the interval estimate is strictly valid only under the circumstances listed below:

1. The samples must be equal in size.
2. The samples must have been taken independently of one another.
3. The variances $(s_X)^2$ estimated from the two samples must be nearly the same.

If any of these conditions is not met, techniques must be used which are beyond the scope of this book.

INTERVAL ESTIMATE FOR THE DIFFERENCE BETWEEN TWO POPULATION PROPORTIONS: LARGE SAMPLES

It was shown earlier in this module that techniques for making interval estimates are similar for means and proportions. The method for making an interval estimate for differences between population *proportions* is indeed perfectly analogous to that used for differences between population *means*.

$$\text{Interval estimate, } p_1 - p_2 = (\bar{p}_1 - \bar{p}_2) \pm z s_{\bar{p}_1 - \bar{p}_2}$$

where $p_1 - p_2$ = difference between two population proportions
$\bar{p}_1 - \bar{p}_2$ = observed difference between two sample proportions
z = standardized normal deviate for the desired confidence coefficient

and

$$s_{\bar{p}_1 - \bar{p}_2} = \sqrt{s_{\bar{p}_1}{}^2 + s_{\bar{p}_2}{}^2} = \sqrt{\frac{\bar{p}_1(1 - \bar{p}_1)}{n_1 - 1} + \frac{\bar{p}_2(1 - \bar{p}_2)}{n_2 - 1}}$$

Practice involving the use of this formula can be obtained in the problems at the end of this module.

SMALL SAMPLES: THE *t* DISTRIBUTION

You may have noticed by now that every time we have used the normal distribution to make an interval estimate, we've stated that the sample size must be reasonably large, meaning at least 30. The reason for this proviso is that whenever the standard deviation of the population is *estimated from a sample* (as it usually will be), the normal distribution is only an approximation to the correct sampling distribution. The accuracy of that approximation is good only if the sample size is large.

The distribution that theoretically should be used whenever the standard deviation of the population is estimated from a sample is called the *t distribution* (also known as Student's distribution, not in honor of all struggling statistics students, but because "Student" was the pseudonym used by W. S. Gosset, who formulated it in 1908).[1] Actually, there is not just one standardized *t* distribution but an entire family of them, one for each degree of freedom. In the estimation of a population standard deviation from a sample, the number of degrees of freedom is always $n - 1$, the size of the sample minus 1. The *t* distribution rapidly approaches the normal distribution as the number of degrees of freedom increases. In Fig. 13.11 the *t* distributions for 2, 5, and 20 degrees of freedom are compared with the normal distribution.

From Fig. 13.11 it is obvious that appreciable errors, especially in the calculation of tail areas, could result if the normal distribution were used to approximate the *t* distribution for small samples. Since a separate table similar to the normal area table is necessary for each degree of freedom, tables for the *t* distribution are usually condensed, showing only the standardized deviates corresponding to a limited number of two-tailed areas for a number of degrees of freedom. Such an abbreviated *t* table is found in Appendix Table A.3.

To clarify the difference between interval estimates made with the *t* distribution and the approximation made using the normal distribution, we'll redo the interval estimate for the insurance policy example that appeared earlier in the module and then show the more accurate calculations using the *t* distribution for sample sizes of 25 and 10 (Table 13.3).

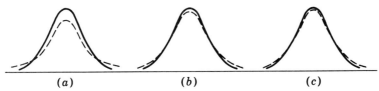

(a)	*(b)*	*(c)*

Figure 13.11 / Comparison of normal (*solid line*) and *t* (*dashed line*) distributions for *(a)* 2 degrees of freedom, *(b)* 5 degrees of freedom, and *(c)* 20 degrees of freedom.

---

[1] Actually, the *t* distribution is theoretically applicable only when the *parent* population from which the sample is drawn is normal. As a practical matter, however, it works reasonably well for problems involving a variety of nonnormal parent distributions where the departure from normality is not too severe.

Table 13.3 / Insurance example, interval estimate for the population mean: infinite population ($X = \$9200$; $s_X = 5000$)

	$s_{\bar{X}} = \dfrac{s_X}{\sqrt{n}}$	Standardized deviate for 90% confidence coefficient	Interval estimate
Sample size 25:			
Normal approximation	1000	$z = 1.645*$	$\bar{X} \pm z(s_{\bar{X}}) = \$9200 \pm \$1645$
t distribution	1000	$t = 1.7111\dagger$	$\bar{X} \pm t(s_{\bar{X}}) = \$9200 \pm \$1711$
Sample size 10:			
Normal approximation	$\dfrac{5000}{3.16} = 1582$	$z = 1.645*$	$\bar{X} \pm z(s_{\bar{X}}) = \$9200 \pm \$2602$
t distribution	$\dfrac{5000}{3.16} = 1582$	$t = 1.8333\ddagger$	$\bar{X} \pm t(s_{\bar{X}}) = \$9200 \pm \$2900$

*From normal table
†From t table for 24 degrees of freedom and a two-tailed probability of .10
‡From t table for 9 degrees of freedom and a two-tailed probability of .10

Note that in our solution to the problem using the normal approximation and a sample size of 25, we *underestimated* the width of the interval by $\$1711 - \$1645 = \$66$ or approximately 4 percent. If we'd used the normal approximation with the sample size of 10, we'd have obtained an interval estimate of $\$9200 \pm \$2602$ rather than the correct value of $\$9200 \pm \$2900$. This error of $\$2900 - \$2602 = \$298$ is greater than 10 percent and would be unacceptable for most problems. The magnitude of the error, then, becomes larger in both absolute and relative terms as the sample size is decreased. This is the reason that the normal distribution is used only for "large" samples, those greater than or equal to 30.

In summary, the t distribution should always be used in making interval estimates when the true standard deviation of the population is unknown and is estimated using s_X, the standard deviation estimated from the sample. The magnitude of the error involved in using the normal approximation rather than t varies with the size of the sample, becoming smaller as the sample size is increased. In most cases the error becomes negligible if the sample size is greater than or equal to 30.

REVIEW EXERCISES 13.D

1. The distribution of the difference between sample means:
  a. Is used in estimating the difference between population means.
  b. Is close to normal for reasonably large samples.
  c. Both *a* and *b.*
  d. Neither *a* nor *b.*

2. The variance of the distribution of the difference between sample means is obtained by adding the variances computed from a pair of samples: true or false?

3. If the confidence interval estimate of the difference between two population means contains the value 0, this implies that the two samples could have come from the same population: true or false?

4. Interval estimates for the difference between two population proportions utilize the same sampling distribution as such estimates for the difference between population means: true or false?
5. The t distribution:
  a. Is sometimes called Student's distribution.
  b. Is used in statistical inference involving large samples.
  c. Both a and b.
  d. Neither a nor b.
6. Theoretically, a sampling distribution will take the form of the t distribution rather than normal whenever:
  a. Proportions are involved rather than sample means.
  b. The population from which samples are drawn is nonnormal.
  c. The standard deviation of the population is estimated from sample data.
  d. None of the above.
7. The t distribution is really a family of distributions, one for each degree of freedom: true or false?
8. The t distribution is seldom used with large samples because:
  a. Tables for the t distribution are generally unavailable.
  b. Serious errors would be produced.
  c. It is impossible to calculate the degrees of freedom.
  d. None of the above.

Answers 13.D

1. c
2. False; the variance of this distribution is estimated as the sum of the squares of the standard errors of the mean as estimated by each sample:

$$s_{\bar{X}_1 - \bar{X}_2}^2 = s_{\bar{X}_1}^2 + s_{\bar{X}_2}^2 = \frac{s_{X_1}^2}{n_1} + \frac{s_{X_2}^2}{n_2}$$

3. true
4. False; while the procedures are analogous, the parameters of the sampling distributions are determined with different formulas.
5. a 6. c 7. true
8. d.   For large samples (say $n = 30$ or more), the t distribution is closely approximated by the normal, which is more convenient to use.

Questions and Problems

13.1.   The discussion of Example 1 in this chapter concludes: by using the same computations, you can determine that the C's would fall between 87 and 107, the D's between 74 and 86, and the F's below 74. Prove that the limits specified in this sentence are correct.
13.2.   A men's sportswear manufacturer is coming out with a new line of golf shirts. Because of the nature of the shirt, a customer's required size can be determined from his weight, as follows:

Weight, lb	Shirt size
Under 140	Small
140–170	Medium
170–200	Large
Over 200	Extra large

If men's weights are (approximately) normally distributed with a mean of 165 lbs and a standard deviation of 20 lbs, how many of each size should a lot of 1000 shirts contain?

13.3. The Neversell Co. pays its salesmen a fixed bonus if they produce over $100,000 in business in any calendar month. Analysis of monthly sales records of three of their crack salesmen yields the following results.

Salesman	Mean monthly sales	Standard deviation of monthly sales
Xavier	$90,000	$ 5,000
Young	80,000	10,000
Zimmer	75,000	20,000

a. How often does each salesman receive a bonus?

b. Is the bonus plan a good one from the company's point of view? Discuss.

13.4. One of the lathes in your auto parts manufacturing company bores the inside diameter of piston rings to their finished dimension. The rings are usable if their inside diameter is between 1.980 and 2.020 in.; however, in order to use them, they must be sorted by size. If the machine is set to produce a mean diameter of 2.000 in., the standard deviation of the machine is 0.0085 in., and the distribution of diameters is normal, what proportion of the rings will

a. Fall below the lower limit?

b. Fall between 1.980 and 1.990 in.?

c. Fall between 1.990 and 2.010 in.?

d. Fall between 2.010 and 2.020 in.?

e. Fall above the upper limit?

13.5. If the rings in Prob. 13.4 are made with too large an inside diameter (greater than 2.020), they must be scrapped at a cost of 27 cents per ring. If they are made with too small an inside diameter, they can be rerun at a cost of 3 cents per ring. The setting of 2.000 used in Prob. 13.4, equalizes the number of scrap and rework pieces. (You realize that the best setting for the mean will be one that would equalize the *cost* of scrap and rework pieces.) At what mean should you set the machine in order to minimize the cost of scrap and rework? *Hint:* Cost is a function of the cost per unit times the proportion too large or too small. Use successive approximations to find the mean that will make the proportion reworked equal 9 times the proportion of scrap. Assume that a 5 standard deviation spread covers the range of all possible values. Also assume that the mean can be set to $\frac{1}{10000}$ in.

13.6. Assume that a population consists of the dollar value of purchases made in a supermarket on successive Thursdays in September by a typical housewife and that these purchases were $3, $12, $9, $22, and $6.

a. Find the mean and the standard deviation of this population. Now assume that we take samples of size 2 at random from this population.

b. Calculate the mean and standard deviation of the sampling distribution of the mean. Do this by listing all the possible combinations obtainable for samples of size 2 taken from the population without replacement. After you have listed all the combinations, summarize them, and calculate the sample mean for each combination, together with the relative frequency of each. Then find the mean and standard deviation of the resulting sampling distribution. For example, some of the combinations are 3 and 12, 3 and 9, 3 and 22, 3 and 6, 12 and 9, 12 and 22, etc. There are 10 such combinations.

c. You should observe from parts a and b that (1) the mean of the sampling distribution is equal to the mean of the population; (2) the standard deviation of the sampling distribution is equal to the standard deviation of the population divided by the square root of the size of the sample times the finite correction factor. That is,

$$\sigma_{\bar{X}} = \frac{\sigma_X}{\sqrt{n}} \sqrt{\frac{N-n}{N-1}}$$

Perform these calculations and prove the relationships stated.

13.7. Assume that the sampling in Prob. 13.6 was done *with* replacement. Answer parts b and c of Prob. 13.6, assuming replacement. *Note:* Your calculations for part b will be different from those of Prob. 13.6 because combinations such as 3 and 3 are now possible. There will be 25 different combinations. Your calculations for part c should show that the mean of the sampling distribution is still equal to the mean of the population but that $\sigma_{\bar{X}}$ is now equal to $\sigma_X/\sqrt{n}$. (The finite correction factor becomes equal to 1 because the population size is now in effect infinite.)

13.8. Explain the differences and relationships between:
a. The standard deviation of a sample.
b. The standard deviation of a distribution of sample means.
c. The standard deviation of a population.

13.9. The Plushtone Carpet Company selected a sample of 101 rolls of carpet from its production process in order to estimate the mean number of defects per roll. Careful examination of the rolls yielded the following data:

Number of defects found in roll	Number of rolls
0	50
1	21
2	15
3	10
4	5
Total	101

a. Make a point estimate of the mean and standard deviation of number of defects per roll for this process.
b. Make an interval estimate of the mean number of defects per roll, using a 98 percent confidence interval.

c. Is the variable "number of defects per roll" normally distributed? How does this affect your answer to parts *a* and *b*?

13.10. As general agent for a life insurance company you are interested in the average size of policy sold under a special program for graduating seniors. You have your secretary take a simple random sample of 100 of this year's sales, and she presents you with the following distribution:

Policy size, thousands $	Number of sales
$ 0– 5	20
5–10	40
10–15	25
15–20	10
20–25	5

a. Estimate the standard deviation of the population.
b. Make an interval estimate for the population mean, using a 90 percent confidence coefficient.

13.11. The following data are collected by an alumni office, showing the annual income (in thousands of dollars) of a random sample of 101 business school graduates four years after graduation. Assume that the size of the population is 10,000.

Income, thousands $	Number
$10–12	31
12–14	44
14–16	18
16–18	7
18–20	1
	101

a. Make a point estimate of the population mean.
b. Make a point estimate of the population standard deviation.
c. Make an interval estimate of the population mean, with a 90 percent confidence coefficient.

13.12. A company that manufactures light bulbs wishes to estimate the mean life of the bulbs produced. A sample of 20 bulbs is tested, giving a mean life of 186.6 hours and a standard deviation of 24.2 hours. Construct a 95 percent confidence interval estimate of the process mean life.

13.13. Demonstrate the effect of sample size in an interval estimate for a population mean by assuming that you take random samples of the sizes indicated below and that in *each* case you obtain an $\bar{X} = 26.0$ and an $s_{\bar{X}} = 3.5$. Make an interval estimate for μ_X for:

a. $n = 2$ *b.* $n = 5$ *c.* $n = 10$
d. $n = 15$ *e.* $n = 20$ *f.* $n = 30$
g. $n = 500$

13.14. Using the normal approximation of the binomial distribution, compute the probability that in 100 tosses of a fair coin you will obtain

a. Exactly 50 heads. *Hint:* Since you are using a continuous distribution to represent one that is actually discrete, you must break up the continuous distribution into discrete chunks. Here, for example, obtain the normal probability that the sample proportion of heads is between .495 and .505, given $p = .50$ and $\sigma_{\bar{p}} = \sqrt{p(1 - p)/n}$.

b. At least 50 heads.

c. Less than 40 heads.

Compare your answers with results obtained from the binomial tables. What explains any differences?

13.15. Assume that a manufacturer of inexpensive bicycle tires produces tires with a proportion of defectives of .01. You buy two of these tires (presumably selected at random from the process).

a. Derive the sampling distribution for p, the proportion of defectives.

b. Find the mean and the standard deviation of the sampling distribution.

c. Find the mean and the standard deviation of the *population*. *Hint:* The population is specified in the following table, where an occurrence has a value of 1 and a nonoccurrence a value of 0.

Occurrences (defectives)	1	0
Probability of occurrence	.01	.99

d. Show that the mean of the sampling distribution is equal to the mean of the population, which is equal to p, and that the standard deviation of the sampling distribution $\sigma_{\bar{p}}$ is equal to the standard deviation of the population divided by the square root of the size of the sample, $\sigma_p/\sqrt{n}$, where $\sigma_p = \sqrt{pq}$.

13.16. Assume that you bought two bicycle tires in a small store that carried a stock of 10 tires, two of which were defective. Assume also that you chose the tires by a random process.

a. Derive the sampling distribution for p, the proportion of defectives.

b. Find the mean and the standard deviation of the sampling distribution.

c. Find the mean and standard deviation of the population. *Hint:* This is the same as the distribution in Prob. 13.15 except for the values of probability p.

d. Show that the mean of the sampling distribution is equal to the mean of the population, which is equal to p, and that the standard deviation of the sampling distribution is equal to the standard deviation of the population $\sqrt{pq}$ divided by the square root of the sample size, times the finite correction factor:

That is,
$$\sigma_{\bar{p}} = \frac{\sigma_p}{\sqrt{n}} \sqrt{\frac{N - n}{N - 1}}$$

$$= \sqrt{\frac{pq}{n}} \sqrt{\frac{N - n}{N - 1}}$$

13.17. a. For the distribution of sample proportions in Prob. 11.1, compute the mean of the sample proportions and the standard deviation of the sample proportions. Use the frontal approach, i.e., use the formulas of Module 3 to compute these descriptive measures for this sampling distribution.

b. Obtain the mean and standard deviation of the sampling distribution by use of the theoretical relationships given in this module.

c. Are the results in parts a and b the same? Will they always be the same?

13.18. How large a sample would be needed to determine the proportion of voters favoring the Republican candidate in a hotly contested election to within .01?

13.19. A company wishes to estimate the effects of a training program that is provided for some of its first-year salespeople. A random sample of 100 salespeople is selected for observation, of which 50 were exposed to the training program, and 50 were not. First-year commissions earned by the two groups were as follows:

	With training	Without training
Average commissions	$10,100	$9950
Standard deviation s_X	1,800	2100

a. Make a point estimate of the net effect of the training program.

b. Make an interval estimate of the effect, using a 98 percent confidence coefficient.

c. What would you recommend to management regarding continuation of the program? Explain.

13.20. A large department store chain in studying its credit sales took random samples of size 65 in each of two stores, one located on the East Coast and one in the Midwest. They found that .56 of the customers in the East used charge accounts, while .67 of the customers in the Midwest did. Make an interval estimate for the difference between population proportions for the two areas using a 95 percent confidence coefficient. Do you think that the difference between the two sample proportions indicates a real difference in the proportion of customers using charge accounts? Why?

13.21. a. Under what circumstances does the precision of a sample estimate depend only on the absolute size of the sample?

b. Under what circumstances does it depend on the relative size of the sample, i.e., the size of the sample as a percentage of the population?

c. Give some illustrations of cases in which you think nonstatisticians are overly concerned about *relative* sample size when they should not be.

MODULE 14
STATISTICAL DECISION RULES AND TESTS OF HYPOTHESES FOR CONTINUOUS DISTRIBUTIONS

This module will provide you with an opportunity to reinforce certain concepts of classical statistical inference. In particular, it extends the study of the various continuous distributions (for which interval estimates were made in the previous module) to the areas of hypothesis testing and formulation of decision rules. In one sense, there is little that is new here. Although the specific methods applicable to continuous distribution problems and the examples used to illustrate them will be different, the basic concepts involved have all been explored earlier. The fundamental notions of statistical inference, hypothesis tests, decision rules, error characteristics, etc., have been explained at length in Modules 11 and 12.

General learning objectives

Your general learning objectives for this module are to be able to:

1. Construct decision rules and tests of hypotheses for problems involving continuous variables and the normal approximation to discrete variables
2. Analyze the error characteristics of these decision rules

Section 14.A

Decision Rules and Hypothesis Testing for a Population Mean

Learning objectives

Your learning objectives for this section are to be able to construct a decision rule and test a hypothesis for a problem involving a continuous variable.

AN EXAMPLE

Assume that you are a large contractor working on the interstate highway system in a midwestern state. In a particular area you need a great deal of dirt for fill that is not available from the right-of-way. You contract with a local gravel-pit operator for 200,000 tons of dirt to be delivered over the road in 20-ton trucks. You have reason to believe that the pit operator might short-weight you if he had the opportunity. At the same time, you can hardly afford to check each truck. You therefore set up a system for spot checking the trucks by weighing a random sample of 64 trucks. If you are willing to take no more than a 1 percent chance of making a Type I error (in this case concluding that you are being shorted when in fact you are not), what should your decision rule be? Assume that from past experience you know that the net weight of dirt carried will vary from truck to truck and that this variation can be described by a standard deviation of about 1 ton, $\sigma_X = 1$.

As you learned in Module 11, the maximum risk of a Type I error, which is 1 percent for this problem, occurs at the point where the pit operator is just barely meeting the standard of a mean weight of 20 tons per truck. If μ_X was 20 tons and you concluded that you were being short-weighted, you would be making a Type I error. However, if the true mean weight per truck was *less* than 20 tons, you would *in fact* be short-weighted, and such a conclusion would be a correct decision rather than an error.

You can find the action limit for the decision rule by assuming that μ_X is exactly 20 and by locating the limit so that the lower-tail probability is 1 percent. This provides

337

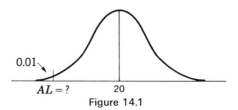

Figure 14.1

a 1 percent chance of the sample mean $\overline{X}$ falling below the action limit when the standard is just being met. The limit is determined as follows (see Fig. 14.1):

$$\sigma_X = 1 \text{ ton} \qquad \sigma_{\overline{X}} = \frac{1}{\sqrt{64}} = .125 \text{ ton}$$

$$-z_{.49} = -2.33 \qquad \frac{AL - 20}{\sigma_{\overline{X}}} = -z_{.49}$$

$$AL = 20 - 2.33(.125) = 19.71 \text{ tons}$$

Thus the decision rule is as follows: Take a simple random sample of size 64 and observe $\overline{X}$, the sample mean. If $\overline{X} \geq 19.71$ tons, conclude that the true mean weight per truck is 20 tons or more and that the total tonnage meets requirements. If $\overline{X} < 19.71$, conclude that the true mean weight per truck is less than 20 tons and that the total tonnage requirement is not being met.

The ordinates for the error curve for this decision rule can be determined easily by sketching the sampling distribution of the mean for various possible values of μ_X and finding the areas that represent the probability of an error (see Fig. 14.2).

The error curve is obtained by plotting probabilities of error against various possible values for μ_X (see Fig. 14.3).

TWO WAYS OF TESTING HYPOTHESES

In the analysis of the preceding paragraphs we tested a hypothesis by formulating an appropriate decision rule and then sampling. To be precise, we first found the appropriate action limit for the decision rule by using the desired level of significance, and then we compared the sample mean with the action limit to see whether the hypothesis should be rejected or accepted. In the dirt-fill problem, for example, we found that the action limit corresponding to an α of .01 was 19.71. If our sample mean had been, say, 19.65, we should reject the null hypothesis that the weight was acceptable.

338

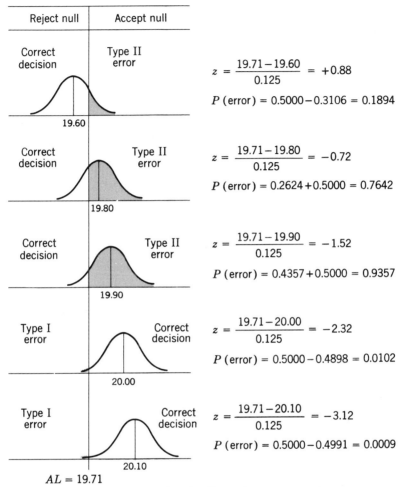

Reject null	Accept null

Correct decision — Type II error

$$z = \frac{19.71 - 19.60}{0.125} = +0.88$$

$$P \text{ (error)} = 0.5000 - 0.3106 = 0.1894$$

19.60

Correct decision — Type II error

$$z = \frac{19.71 - 19.80}{0.125} = -0.72$$

$$P \text{ (error)} = 0.2624 + 0.5000 = 0.7642$$

19.80

Correct decision — Type II error

$$z = \frac{19.71 - 19.90}{0.125} = -1.52$$

$$P \text{ (error)} = 0.4357 + 0.5000 = 0.9357$$

19.90

Type I error — Correct decision

$$z = \frac{19.71 - 20.00}{0.125} = -2.32$$

$$P \text{ (error)} = 0.5000 - 0.4898 = 0.0102$$

20.00

Type I error — Correct decision

$$z = \frac{19.71 - 20.10}{0.125} = -3.12$$

$$P \text{ (error)} = 0.5000 - 0.4991 = 0.0009$$

20.10

$AL = 19.71$

Figure 14.2 / Determination of probabilities of error for the dirt-fill problem.

Exactly the same test could be made, after the sample was taken, by finding what proportion of the sample means could be expected to fall below the sample mean actually obtained if the true mean were 20. If that proportion was less than the level of significance, we should not attribute the difference between the sample mean and the population mean to chance and should therefore reject the null hypothesis. Thus, for the sample mean of 19.65 we should find the left-tail area to be less than .01, as in Fig. 14.4. We should therefore reject the null hypothesis and conclude that the population from which the sample was drawn could not have a mean greater than or equal to 20.

339

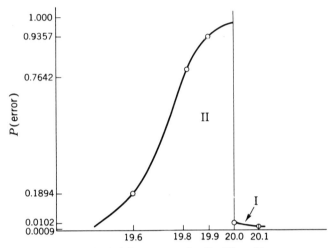

Figure 14.3 / Error curve for dirt-fill problem.

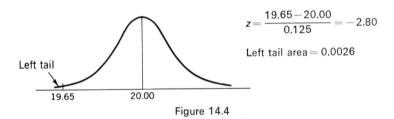

$$z = \frac{19.65 - 20.00}{0.125} = -2.80$$

Left tail area $= 0.0026$

Figure 14.4

REVIEW EXERCISES 14.A

1. Suppose, for the dirt-fill problem described in this section, you're willing to increase your maximum risk of Type I error to 5 percent. Construct a decision rule for a sample of size 100.

2. If instead of constructing the decision rule in Exercise 1 you first obtained a sample of 100 and used the result to test the hypothesis that the population mean is at least 20, using a 5 percent level of significance, would your conclusions regarding the shipments be the same? Why?

3. Except for the difference in the way the probability of given sample results are calculated, the procedures for constructing decision rules and error curves are the same as those outlined earlier for discrete distributions: true or false?

Answers 14.A

1. $\sigma_X = 1$ ton $\qquad \sigma_{\bar{X}} = \dfrac{1}{\sqrt{100}} = .1$

The z value corresponding to a 5 percent tail area (.4500 in the table) is 1.64.

$$z = -1.64 = \frac{AL - 20}{\sigma_{\bar{X}}} = \frac{AL - 20}{.1}$$
$$AL = 20 - 1.64(.1) = 20 - .164 = 19.836$$

The decision rule is as follows. Take a random sample of 100; if $\bar{X} \geq 19.836$, conclude that the truck tonnage meets requirements; otherwise, conclude that it does not.

2. Yes, the conclusions would be the same. A statistical decision rule is really a test of hypothesis where the sample outcomes that will cause you to accept or reject the hypothesis are specified in advance.

3. true

Section 14.B

Error Characteristics of Alternative Decision Rules

Learning objectives

Your learning objectives for this section are to be able to:

1. Describe the changes in error characteristics of a decision rule for changes in action limit and sample size
2. Determine the sample size and action limit necessary to conform to specified error levels

---

EFFECT OF A CHANGE IN THE ACTION LIMIT

The effect of a change in the action limit is easy to see for a continuous distribution. For a lower-tail test such as the dirt-fill example, the action limit would be lowered if we wanted to reduce the level of significance (the maximum risk of a Type I error) and raised if we wanted to increase the level of significance. To make this point more clear, let's chart the sampling distributions for various possible values of the true mean and identify the action limits appropriate for: (1) an α level of .01, (2) an α level of .05, and (3) an α level of .25 (see Fig. 14.5). We'll also graph the error characteristics for each action limit (see Fig. 14.6). We're assuming, as before, that the true standard

341

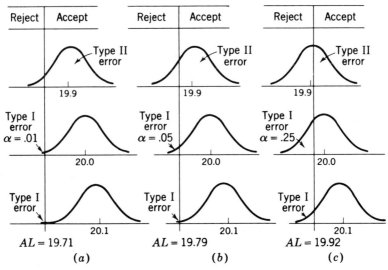

Figure 14.5 / Effect of a change in the action limit. (a) AL = 19.71, α = .01; (b) AL = 19.79, α = .05; (c) AL = 19.92, α = .25.

deviation of the weights of trucks is 1 ton and that the sample size is 64, so that $\sigma_{\bar{x}} = 1/\sqrt{64} = .125$.

Note that the action limit is found in every case from the knowledge that α occurs when the value for the true mean is the lowest *acceptable* value, in this case 20 tons. If the level of significance is .01, the action limit is low and the risks of Type II errors are very large. As the level of significance is raised, the action limit also goes up. This increases the risk of a Type I error wherever $\mu_X \geq 20$ but decreases the risk of a Type II error wherever $\mu_X < 20$. It is important to note that *for a given sample size* we can only trade off the risks of Type I errors for their Type II counterparts; there is no way to reduce both risks simultaneously.

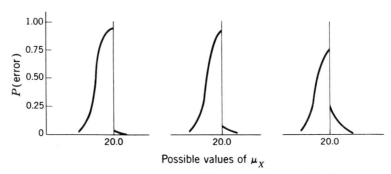

Figure 14.6 / Error curves corresponding to (a), (b), and (c) in Fig. 14.5.

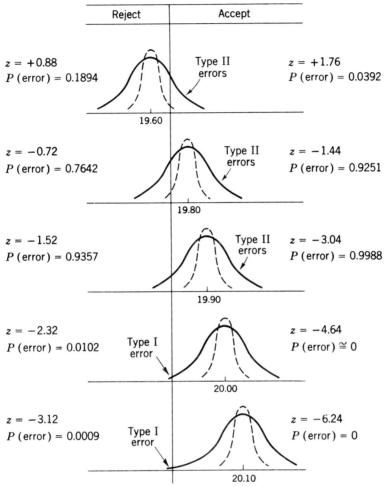

Figure 14.7 / Effect of a change in the sample size. Solid line: $n = 64$; dashed line: $n = 256$.

EFFECT OF A CHANGE IN THE SIZE OF THE SAMPLE

We know that the dispersion of the distribution of sample means is reduced as the sample size is increased, as measured by $\sigma_{\bar{X}} = \sigma_X/\sqrt{n}$. For the dirt-fill problem the standard deviation of the weights of the trucks was 1 ton. Therefore for a sample size of 64 the standard deviation of the sampling distribution of the mean $\sigma_{\bar{X}}$ was $1/\sqrt{64} = 1/8 = .125$. If we wanted to *double* the accuracy of our tests, we should need to cut $\sigma_{\bar{X}}$ in half. This could be accomplished by *quadrupling* the sample size to 256, since $1/\sqrt{256} = 1/16 = .0625$. Calculation of the size of errors for various values

343

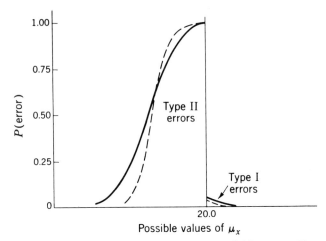

Figure 14.8 / Error curves for Fig. 14.7. Solid line: $n = 64$; dashed line: $n = 256$.

of μ_x and the error curve for the decision rule with an action limit of 19.71 are shown in Figs. 14.7 and 14.8 for sample sizes of 64 and 256. The curves for $n = 64$ are, of course, exactly the same as those shown in Figs. 14.2 and 14.3.

Note that where the value of μ_x is between the action limit (19.71) and the standard (20.0), the risk of a Type II error is increased with an increase in the sample size but that both Type I and Type II errors are decreased with an increased sample size for all other possible values of μ_x.

It might be worthwhile to note specifically what is meant by doubling the accuracy by quadrupling the sample size. With a sample size of 64 it was necessary to set the action limit at 19.71 to achieve a level of significance α of .01. With $\sigma_{\bar{x}}$ only half as large for a sample of 256, it would be necessary only to go half as far from the minimum acceptable value of 20 to achieve this same accuracy, as the calculations in Fig. 14.9 show.

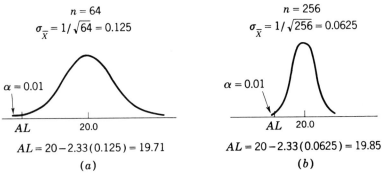

Figure 14.9 / Calculation of action limit of $\alpha = .01$ where $\sigma_x = 1.00$.

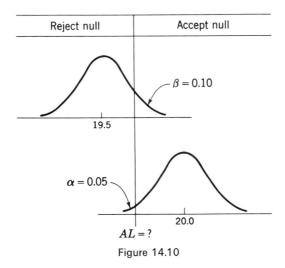

Figure 14.10

DETERMINATION OF SAMPLE SIZE

In problems where the relative costs of Type I and Type II errors cannot be quantified or where there is not time to engage in such a process, the decision with respect to the appropriate sample size is often made by considering the maximum permissible risk of a Type I error, α and a desirable level of risk of a Type II error, β. For the dirt-fill problem the α risk, as noted previously, will occur when $\mu_X = 20$, but the β risk must be defined relative to some *particular value of* μ_X. For example, suppose that prior to sampling in the dirt-fill problem, we decided that we should be satisfied with no more than a 5 percent chance of making a Type I error and no more than a 10 percent chance of making a Type II error *if* the true mean were actually 19.5 tons. We shall assume that from previous studies we were sure that the standard deviation of the population was very close to 1 ton. The problem can be sketched as in Fig. 14.10.

Remember that if the true mean is in fact 19.5, we are being short-weighted. We want to take no more than a 10 percent chance of concluding that the tonnage is acceptable if in fact the true mean is 19.5. On the other hand, we are willing to take at most a 5 percent chance of concluding that the tonnage is short when it really is not. This α risk will always occur at the *smallest* acceptable mean, namely, 20 tons. We find that we can develop two equations to find the action limit:

$$AL = 19.5 + z_{.40}\sigma_{\bar{X}} \quad \text{and} \quad AL = 20.0 - z_{.45}\sigma_{\bar{X}}$$

Since there is but one action limit and we know $z_{.40}$, $z_{.45}$ and σ_X, we can set the two expressions on the right of the equations equal to each other. When we do, we find that the only unknown is n, the necessary sample size:

$$19.5 + 1.28\,\frac{1}{\sqrt{n}} = 20.0 - 1.645\,\frac{1}{\sqrt{n}}$$

345

Solving for n gives

$$\sqrt{n} = \frac{2.925}{.5}$$
$$n = 35$$

(The value of n is 34.22 to the nearest hundredth. In order to achieve at least the accuracy we desire, we must round *up* to the nearest whole number of 35.)

Having found the sample size, we can substitute its value in either of the original equations to determine the appropriate action limit:

$$AL = 19.5 + 1.28 \frac{1}{\sqrt{35}} = 19.72$$

Thus the decision rule is stated as follows. Take a simple random sample of size 35 and obtain $\overline{X}$, the sample mean. If the sample mean is greater than or equal to 19.72, conclude that the tonnage is acceptable. If the sample mean is less than 19.72, conclude that we're being short-weighted.

It must be emphasized that this technique should be used *only* in cases where it is not possible to obtain the functions which show the cost of both types of errors over the entire range of the decision problem. Techniques for developing and using such cost functions in designing decision rules are the subject of Modules 20 to 23.

REVIEW EXERCISES 14.B

1. For a given sample size, a change in the action limit for a decision rule will:
   a. Change the maximum level of Type I error.
   b. Increase the risks of Type I and Type II errors over all values of the population mean.
   c. Both *a* and *b*.
   d. Neither *a* nor *b*.
2. Increases in sample size will generally produce proportional decreases in the risks that a rule will lead to a wrong decision: true or false?
3. Refer again to the dirt-fill problem discussed in the text. Suppose you wished to specify a decision rule such that the maximum risk of Type I error was .02, with a risk of no more than .05 of making a Type II error if the true mean were actually 19.6 tons. What sample size and action limit should be used?
4. Where possible, error specifications such as those in the previous question should be based on _____.

Answers 14.B

1. a
2. False; while increases in sample size will simultaneously reduce the risks of both Type I and Type II errors, such reductions are not generally proportional to the size of the increase.

3. The two equations specifying the action limit are

$$AL = 19.6 + z_{.45}\sigma_{\bar{X}} \qquad AL = 20.0 - z_{.48}\sigma_{\bar{X}}$$

Setting the two expressions equal gives

$$19.6 + 1.64\,\frac{1}{\sqrt{n}} = 20.0 - 2.05\,\frac{1}{\sqrt{n}}$$

$$3.69\,\frac{1}{\sqrt{n}} = 20.0 - 19.6 = 0.4$$

$$\sqrt{n} = \frac{3.69}{0.4} = 9.225$$

$$n = 85$$

The action limit would be

$$AL = 19.6 + 1.64\,\frac{1}{9.225} = 19.6 + .18 = 19.78$$

4. the costs of errors (of each type and size)

Section 14.C

Other Tests of Hypotheses and Decision Rules

Learning objectives

Your learning objectives for this section are to be able to test hypotheses and construct decision rules concerning:

1. A population proportion
2. The difference between population means
3. The difference between population proportions

DECISION RULES FOR POPULATION PROPORTIONS

In Module 13, you learned to make an interval estimate for a population proportion by using the normal approximation to the binomial. In this section, we'll use the same normal approximation to test hypotheses and construct decision rules concerning a population proportion.

To illustrate, suppose that a food company is thinking of redesigning the package in which its leading consumer product is sold. Since the proposed new package is considerably more expensive than the old, the company wants to be relatively sure that customers actually prefer the new package before they adopt it. Therefore, the company samples 144 of its customers at random to test the hypothesis that the proportion of customers favoring the new package over the old is no greater than .5. (Remember, it is common to set up the null hypothesis to represent the status quo, especially when rejection of it involves a substantial cost of some kind.) Because of the cost involved in rejecting this hypothesis and switching to the new package, the company decides to test at a level of significance α of .02. The action limit for the decision rule could be found as follows (see Fig. 14.11):

$$\frac{AL - p}{\sigma_{\bar{p}}} = z_{.48}$$

$$AL = p + z_{.48}\sigma_{\bar{p}} = .5 + 2.05 \sqrt{\frac{.5(.5)}{144}}$$

$$= .5 + 2.05(.0417)$$
$$= .5855 \approx .59 \qquad \text{rounding to the nearest hundredth}$$

The decision rule could be stated as follows. Take a random sample of 144 customers and observe the proportion of favorable responses. If that proportion is .59 or more, conclude that the new package is superior to the old. If the proportion in the sample is less than .59, conclude that the new package is no better than the old.

Now, suppose that such a sample of 144 yields 79 customers who prefer the new package. This is a sample proportion of $79/144 = .55$. Therefore, the hypothesis *can't* be rejected, and it can't be concluded that new package is superior to the old.

If this sample had been taken before the decision rule was formulated, the hypothesis could have been tested directly using the alternative procedure you learned previously. We simply find the area of the upper tail beyond .55, assuming that the true p was .5, and then compare this probability with the level of significance α. The z value is $(.55 - .5)/.0417 = 1.20$, and the probability equals $.5000 - .3849 = .1151$.

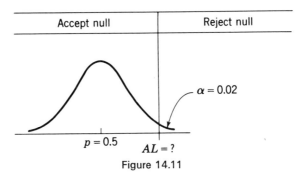

Figure 14.11

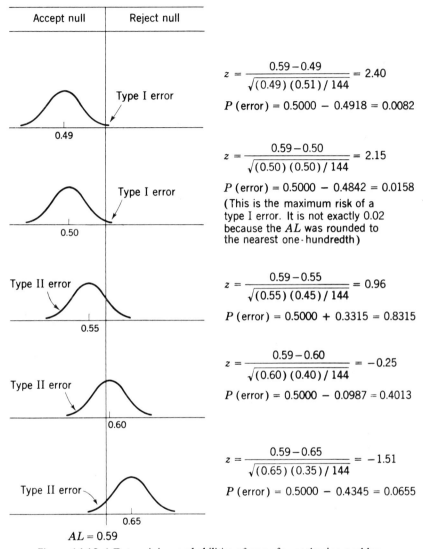

$AL = 0.59$

Figure 14.12 / Determining probabilities of error for packaging problem.

Since this area is *larger* than the level of significance, we'd conclude that the observed difference occurred by chance and that the true population proportion was not greater than .5.

Since this decision rule involves an upper-tail test (the region of rejection of the null hypothesis is the upper tail), it may be instructive to calculate a few points on the error curve and graph them as in Figs. 14.12 and 14.13. Notice that Type I errors can occur only if the true proportion has a value *equal to or less than* .5. If $p \leq .5$, the null hypothesis should be accepted and a Type I error would be to reject the null

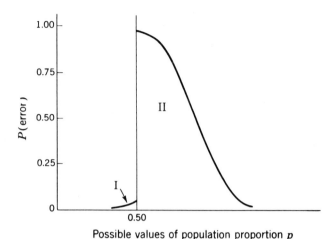

Figure 14.13 / Error curve for packaging problem.

falsely. This type of error would be made if the sample proportion happened by chance to fall *above* the action limit when $p \leq .5$. Similarly, Type II errors can occur only if the true proportion has a value greater than .5. If $p > .5$, the null hypothesis *should* be rejected. An error would be to accept the null falsely. This type of error would be made if the sample proportion happened by chance to fall *below* the action limit when $p > .5$.

Comparing this error curve with any of those for the dirt-fill example, you should note that the regions identifying Type I and Type II errors are reversed. This, of course, is caused by the fact that the dirt-fill problem involved a lower-tail test (Type I errors occurred in the lower tail of the sampling distribution), while this problem involved an upper-tail test (Type I errors occurred in the upper tail of the sampling distribution).

DECISION RULES INVOLVING THE DIFFERENCE BETWEEN POPULATION MEANS

We'll illustrate the formulation of decision rules for the difference between population means using a problem very similar to the tire-testing problem of Module 13. Suppose you decided to test two samples of tires, one from an established process and one from a new process, to see whether you'd be justified in concluding that the tires from the new process produced a higher mean length of life. You decide to take a maximum risk of no more than .10 of concluding that the new tires are better if in fact they are not. At the same time, you're willing to take at most a .20 risk of concluding that the new tires are not superior if in fact the difference between the population means is as much as +1000 mi, where the plus sign indicates superiority of the new tires over the old. Assume that from past experience you can estimate that the standard deviation

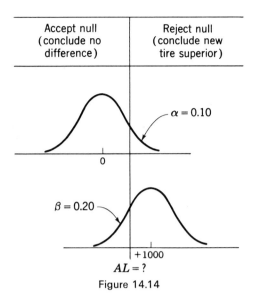

Figure 14.14

of each of the two processes is 3000 mi. We want to find the size of samples appropriate for this test, with $n_1 = n_2$, and to find the appropriate decision rule.[1]

The sampling distribution and the relevant information are illustrated in Fig. 14.14. The appropriate sample size is found as follows:

$$AL = 0 + z_{.40}\sigma_{X_1-X_2} = 1000 - z_{.30}\sigma_{X_1-X_2}$$
$$0 + 1.28\sigma_{X_1-X_2} = 1000 - .84\sigma_{X_1-X_2}$$
$$2.12\sigma_{X_1-X_2} = 1000$$
$$\sigma_{X_1-X_2} = \frac{1000}{2.12} = 472$$

but

$$\sigma_{X_1-X_2} = \sqrt{\sigma_{X_1}{}^2 + \sigma_{X_2}{}^2} = \sqrt{\frac{\sigma_{X_1}{}^2}{n_1} + \frac{\sigma_{X_2}{}^2}{n_2}}$$

since

$$\sigma_{X_1} = \sigma_{X_2} = 3000 \quad \text{and} \quad n_1 = n_2$$
$$\sigma_{X_1-X_2} = \sqrt{\frac{3000^2}{n} + \frac{3000^2}{n}} = \sqrt{\frac{18,000,000}{n}}$$

Therefore

$$\sqrt{\frac{18,000,000}{n}} = 472$$
$$\frac{18,000,000}{n} = 472^2 = 222,784$$
$$n = \frac{18,000,000}{222,784} = 81$$

---

[1] The assumptions of independence, equal sample size, and comparable variances mentioned in Module 13 relative to the use of the formula for $\sigma_{X_1} - {}_{X_2}$ also apply here.

When the sample size has been determined, the action limit is determined by solving

$$AL = 0 + 1.28 \sqrt{\frac{18,000,000}{81}} = 0 + 1.28 \frac{4243}{9} = 604$$

The decision rule can then be stated as follows. Take simple random samples of 81 old tires and 81 new tires, and observe the difference between the sample means. If the difference is equal to or less than $+604$, conclude that there is no difference in the process means. If the difference is greater than $+604$, conclude that the mean for the new tires is higher than for the old.

After having formulated this rule, you could test the hypothesis that the new tires had a higher mean life than the old simply by obtaining the difference between the sample means and comparing it with $+604$. For example, if $\overline{X}_{old} = 19,450$ and $\overline{X}_{new} = 20,095$, you'd observe that the difference of $+645$ was greater than $+604$ and you'd therefore conclude that the new tires in fact have a higher population mean. This test was made, of course, at a .10 level of significance.

If the standard deviation calculated from the samples diverged from the estimate of 3000 used to calculate n, the level of significance would be altered, becoming larger if 3000 were an underestimate of the population standard deviation and smaller if it were an overestimate.

Calculation of the ordinates for the error curve for this decision rule is left for a problem at the end of this module.

TEST OF A HYPOTHESIS INVOLVING THE DIFFERENCE BETWEEN POPULATION PROPORTIONS

It should come as no surprise at this point that the process for formulating decision rules about differences between population proportions is analogous to that just described for differences between population means. To illustrate the process without excessive repetition, let's develop an example in which the sample size is small but an appreciable part of the population and in which the samples are independent. This will necessitate the use of the finite correction factor and the t distribution.

Assume that we need to produce 200 complex parts using a turret lathe. Two operators are assigned to the job. If each produces the same proportion of defectives, as we originally hypothesize, we'd prefer to let each operator produce 100 parts in order to cut production time by one-half. However, after each man has produced 26 parts, we find that operator A has produced 8 defectives and that operator B has produced 11. The question now is whether our original hypothesis that operators A and B are equally good is still valid and S, the difference in their defective rate, is caused by chance or whether operator A is really better than operator B. If we conclude the latter, we'll assign the remaining parts entirely to operator A in order to cut down the defective rate (even though the production time would be increased). Therefore, we decide to test the hypothesis that the difference between the population proportion defective produced by operators A and B is 0, using a level of significance of .05.

We'd proceed as follows:

$$\text{Operator } A\text{'s proportion of defects} = \frac{8}{26} = .308 = \bar{p}_A$$

$$\text{Operator } B\text{'s proportion of defects} = \frac{11}{26} = .423 = \bar{p}_B$$

We want to compare the probability that a difference between sample proportions as great as $.423 - .308$, or $+ .115$, could happen by chance if the true difference between population proportions were 0 with the level of significance of .05. This can be done by determining t from the expression

$$\frac{(\bar{p}_A - \bar{p}_B) - 0}{s_{\bar{p}_A - \bar{p}_B}} = t$$

and using the t table.

However, we must first find the value of $s_{\bar{p}_A - \bar{p}_B}$, the estimate of the standard deviation of the sampling distribution of the difference between population proportions. Since the size of the sample is an appreciable part of the population, we must incorporate the finite correction factor in the formula for $s_{\bar{p}_A - \bar{p}_B}$:

$$
\begin{aligned}
s_{\bar{p}_A - \bar{p}_B} &= \sqrt{s_{\bar{p}_A}^{\,2} + s_{\bar{p}_B}^{\,2}} \\
&= \sqrt{\frac{\bar{p}_A(1 - \bar{p}_A)}{n_A - 1}\frac{N - n_A}{N - 1} + \frac{\bar{p}_B(1 - \bar{p}_B)}{n_B - 1}\frac{N - n_B}{N - 1}} \\
&= \sqrt{\frac{.308(.692)}{25}\frac{74}{99} + \frac{.423(.577)}{25}\frac{74}{99}} = .117
\end{aligned}
$$

Therefore
$$t = \frac{(\bar{p}_A - \bar{p}_B) - 0}{s_{\bar{p}_A - \bar{p}_B}} = \frac{.115}{.117} = .983$$

For 50 degrees of freedom $(n_1 + n_2 - 2)$, the value of t corresponding to a one-tailed level of significance of .05 is approximately 1.680 (interpolating between 30 and ∞ for a two-tailed area of .10). Therefore, the one-tailed probability for $t = .983$ would be considerably *greater* than .05 and the hypothesis that there is no difference between the population proportions is substantiated. We therefore conclude that the two operators' population proportion of defects is the same, and we should proceed with the production run using *both* operators.

INCORPORATION OF COSTS OF ERRORS INTO DECISION RULES

In this module we have assumed that the specific costs of Type I and Type II errors for various values of the population parameter were either impossible to determine or that their determination was prohibitively expensive. If it is possible to determine these costs, they should be incorporated into the process of formulating decision rules. The method of accomplishing this for continuous distributions is the subject of Modules 22 to 23.

REVIEW EXERCISES 14.C

1. It is argued that women score higher on a particular clerical aptitude test than men. A random sample of 30 women taking the test gives a mean score of 275 and an s_X of 90. A similar random sample of 30 men taking the test resulted in a mean score of 251 and an s_X of 93. Would you agree that women consistently score higher on this test?
   a. What hypothesis should be tested to answer this question?
   b. Test the hypothesis at a significance level of .05. What is your conclusion?
2. Similar tests of hypotheses can be made using the normal distribution for:
   a. A population proportion.
   b. The difference between population proportions.
   c. Both *a* and *b*.
   d. Neither *a* nor *b*.

Answers 14.C

1. a. Test the hypothesis that there is no difference between the population means (test scores achieved by women and test scores achieved by men).

b. $s_{\bar{X}_1 - \bar{X}_2} = \sqrt{\dfrac{s_{X_1}^2}{n_1} + \dfrac{s_{X_2}^2}{n_2}} = \sqrt{\dfrac{90^2}{30} + \dfrac{93^2}{30}} = \sqrt{270 + 288.3} = \sqrt{558.3}$

$= 23.6$

$z = \dfrac{\bar{X}_1 - \bar{X}_2}{s_{\bar{X}_1 - \bar{X}_2}} = \dfrac{275 - 251}{23.6} = 1.02 \rightarrow \text{area} = .3461$

Therefore, the probability that a difference this great (or greater) would occur by chance even if there is no difference between population means is

$$.5000 - .3461 = .1539$$

Since this is greater than the significance level of .05 chosen for the test, the null hypothesis should *not* be rejected. We should accept the hypothesis that the population means (test scores achieved by men and women) are the same.

2. c

Questions and Problems

14.1. An airline company you work for decides to check the mean weight of luggage checked by passengers since weight restrictions were lifted. They know that when weight regulations were in force, the mean weight per piece of luggage in December was 20.5 lbs, with a standard deviation of 6 lbs. They ask you to set up a simple sampling plan to check on the current December mean. You ask the management within what tolerance they want to measure the true mean and what degree of confidence they want. They say that they want to estimate the true mean weight within ± 1 lb, with 96 percent confidence. What size random sample will you take to meet their specifications?

14.2. For Prob. 14.1, you should have determined that the required simple random sample size was 151. You set up a sampling plan using a table of random numbers and arrive at the following distribution of weights.

Weight, lb	f	Weight, lb	f
<10	0	30–34	16
10–14	24	35–39	5
15–19	40	40–44	3
20–24	33	>44	0
25–29	30		

a. What is the best point estimate you can make for the population mean?

b. What is the best point estimate you can make for the population standard deviation?

c. Assuming that the true standard deviation is the value you obtained in part b, test the hypothesis that the true mean is still equal to or less than 20.5 lb, using a .01 level of significance.

14.3. Professors at a certain institution have developed an extensive set of programmed learning materials for their introductory business statistics course. In order to determine whether the materials help the students, a large statistics class of 130 students is divided into halves, using a random process. One-half of the students are given the usual instructional materials and problems in the statistics lab. The other half are given the programmed learning material. The students attend the same lecture and are given the same tests. At the end of the semester the students' grades are analyzed with the following results:

	Regular	PL
n	65	65
Mean grade	62	68
Standard deviation of grades	18	19

a. Do you think that the PL labs enable the students to earn better grades? Use a 2 percent, one-tailed level of significance.

b. What are the two kinds of errors one might make in interpreting these data? Which type of error is more likely for this problem?

c. What is the probability of concluding in error that PL does not enable the students to earn better grades if the average gain of students using the PL lab over the regular lab is really 5 grade points?

14.4. A manufacturer of TV color tubes was disturbed by reports from the field that a new, "improved" tube being manufactured had a shorter service life than the tubes made formerly. It found that its research division was already testing a random sample of 20 TV sets for component failures by plugging them in and letting them run continuously until failures occurred. The manufacturer ordered that records be kept on tube life and that the sets be operated until tube failure. It was known from past experience that the mean length of life for "old process" tubes was 9000 hours. After considerable time the test was completed, with the following results: $n = 20$, mean life = 8700 hours, standard deviation = 1200 hours. Test the hypothesis that the new tubes have a true mean length of life equal to or greater than 9000 hours. Use a 10 percent level of significance.

14.5. A company is concerned about the amount of time required for clerical personnel to file a certain kind of record. A sample of 225 observations of the filing operation gives $\bar{X} = 58.2$ seconds, $s_X = 18$ seconds. Test the hypothesis that the true mean time required is 60 seconds or more. Use a level of significance of 5 percent.

14.6. Suppose the company in Prob. 14.5 is also concerned that the proportion of records filed incorrectly is greater than the 1 percent level considered satisfactory. A check of the sample observations in the previous problem shows that 5 of the records were incorrectly filed.

a. Could this error rate be considered satisfactory?

b. Suppose all the filings were performed by one employee. Could his performance be considered satisfactory? What would you recommend with respect to this employee?

c. Discuss any differences in the way you answered parts a and b.

14.7. Refer to the Plushtone Carpet Company (Prob. 13.9). These data can be used in the construction of a statistical decision rule that will tell the company when its process is out of control, e., producing more defects per roll than considered tolerable. Assume that the company considers one defect per roll tolerable. Because a costly shutdown and inspection is made when the process is judged to be out of control, the company wishes to take only 1 chance in 20 of concluding it is out of control when in fact it is operating satisfactorily.

a. What is the appropriate decision rule for a sample of 50 rolls?

b. Plot a power curve for this decision rule.

c. Plot an error curve for this decision rule, identifying the regions of Type I and Type II errors.

14.8. Repeat parts a and b of Prob. 12.2 using the normal approximation of the binomial distribution.

14.9. The standard set for the proportion of defective items involving a complicated assembly in a production process is .20. The company has an order for 500 items. Upon testing the first 100 items, they find 25 defective assemblies. Test the hypothesis that the true proportion of defectives for the lot is less than or equal to .20. Use the normal approximation, with a level of significance of .05.

14.10. In an effort to improve its brand image, the Perkup Coffee Company has retained a marketing research consultant specializing in motivational research. Among the consultant's first recommendations is one that the company change from its traditional blue coffee can to a bright red one with a different design. To substantiate this recommendation, the consultant conducts an interview study in which he examines the purchasing motivation of 80 consumers. His findings are that 46 of the 80, or 57.5 percent prefer the red can. What action do you believe management should take in this situation? Why?

14.11. a. In order to calculate the ordinates of a power curve (or OC or error curve) for a statistical decision rule involving a sample mean, you must have an estimate of σ_X, the population standard deviation. Why?

b. How would the estimate of σ_X usually be obtained?

c. To calculate the points for a power curve for a statistical decision rule involving a sample proportion (using the normal approximation), what parameter must be estimated?

d. Why are the *calculations* referred to in part c more cumbersome than those referred to in part a?

14.12. Does the specification of the maximum risk of Type I error determine the sample size to be used in statistical decision procedure? Explain.

14.13. For the tire example in this module concerning the difference between population means,

a. Calculate the ordinates for the error curve for $(\bar{X}_1 - \bar{X}_2) - 0$ values of -500, -200, 0, $+200$, $+500$, and $+1,000$ for the following decision rule. Take a simple random sample of 81 old tires and 81 new tires and observe the sample means. If the difference between the sample means is less than or equal to $+604$, conclude that there is no difference in the process means. If the difference is greater than $+604$, conclude that the mean for the new tires is higher than for the old.

b. Assume that when you took the samples of 81 of each kind of tire, you found that your preliminary estimate of 3000 mi for the standard deviation of tire life for each type of tire was evidently in error since you got an $s_X = 2500$ from both the samples. Calculate the level of significance for the decision rule in part a, using 2500 as the estimate of the population standard deviation for each type of tire.

14.14. You have doubtless noticed by now that regardless of the parameter under consideration, the formulation of a decision rule always involves the same relationship between z or t value corresponding to the level of significance, the action limit (which is one particular value of the sample statistic making up the sampling distribution), the mean of the sampling distribution, and the standard deviation of the sampling distribution. This relation can be expressed as

z or $t_{\text{level of significance}}$

$$= \frac{\text{sample statistic that is action limit} - \text{mean of sampling distribution}}{\text{standard deviation of sampling distribution}}$$

For example, assuming an infinite population and a large sample size, when formulating decision rules about a *population mean* we use the expression

$$z_{\text{level of significance}} = \frac{\bar{X}_{AL} - \mu_X}{s_X} = \frac{\bar{X}_{AL} - \mu_X}{s_X/\sqrt{n}}$$

Using the appropriate symbols and still assuming an infinite population and a large sample size, specify the same relationship for decision rules concerning:

a. The difference between population means.

b. The population proportion.

c. The difference between population proportions.

MODULE 15
BIVARIATE REGRESSION ANALYSIS

Before introducing the subject of this module, it might be wise to define the two terms used in its title. *Bivariate* means that only two variables are involved, one independent and one dependent. (Multivariate analysis, involving more than one independent variable, is the subject of Module 16.) The expression *regression equation* is often used when speaking of a *least-squares estimating equation*, and the whole subject of estimating one variable in terms of other variables is known as *regression analysis*.[1]

Once it has been decided that there is a linear relationship between two variables in a population, there are two ways to determine an appropriate regression equation and measure the extent of the relationship. One is to use *all* the population data to determine the regression equation and related measures. The other way is to take a *random sample* of the population data and make statistical inferences about the population parameters based on that sample.

Using population data is straightforward. All the techniques for measuring association described in Module 8 could be used to calculate the least-squares regression equation, the standard error of estimate, the coefficient of determination, and other related measures of the relationship. The only (often insurmountable) obstacle to using population data is their cost in both time and money. Most populations dealt with in business are large, and data are difficult to obtain. Even with computers, direct calculation of population parameters is usually prohibitively expensive.

Therefore, regression studies are almost always made using samples. This immediately raises all the problems about statistical inference discussed in Modules 11 to 14. Before studying this module, then, you should be thoroughly familiar with the concepts discussed in Module 8 and Modules 11 to 14.

General learning objectives

Your general learning objectives for this module are to be able to:

1. Test hypotheses concerning populations, using the linear, bivariate regression model
2. Interpret the results of bivariate regression analysis
3. Judge the validity of the model through the analysis of residual errors

---

[1] The term came about because of a historical accident involving Sir Francis Galton, who used these techniques in the study of biological regression (the tendency for progeny to revert or *regress* to historical norms). Galton's theory of regressive traits proved to be wrong, but the name nevertheless became attached to the method of analysis he used.

Section 15.A

The Linear Bivariate Regression Model

Learning objectives

Your learning objectives for this section are to be able to:

1. State the general equations for the linear bivariate model and for the regression equation for population data
2. Identify the three major reasons for the inclusion of an error term in the model
3. State the assumptions made concerning the error terms

Assume you believe that in general there is a linear relationship between company assets and company sales for *all* companies in the United States. This belief can be expressed by the equation

$$\mu_{Y \cdot X} = \alpha + \beta X$$

where X = independent variable, assets

$\mu_{Y \cdot X}$ = conditional mean of sales given a particular level of assets

The Greek letters alpha α and beta β are *population parameters*, referring to the Y intercept and the slope of the line fitted to *all* of the companies in the United States.

Not all the data points would be expected to fall exactly on this line, of course. Since there would be variation about the line, you'd represent any single observation by the model

$$Y = \alpha + \beta X + \varepsilon$$

where the Greek epsilon (ε) represents the errors or deviations from the hypothesized estimating equation.

There are three major reasons such errors can exist:

1. The possibility of errors in measurement. If for some reason you couldn't measure Y exactly, there'd be errors or deviations around the true measurement.
2. The model may not be an exact statement of individual measurements but a statement about average behavior. Not all companies with a certain level of assets would be expected to have exactly the same sales. There would be a *distribution* of sales about each conditional mean.

361

3. There may be an inherent randomness in all behavior, so that even if you knew all of the factors involved, there'd be some variation.

For the regression formulas used in this book to be valid, the error terms must meet three conditions:

1. They must be independent; there can be no relationship between successive error terms.
2. The conditional variance of the error terms $\sigma^2_{Y \cdot X}$ must be the same for all of the conditional distributions.
3. The error terms must be normally distributed about their conditional means.

REVIEW EXERCISES 15.A

1. a. What is the equation for the linear bivariate model?
  b. What is the equation for an estimating (regression) equation for population data for this model?
2. What is the definition of each of the following terms in the estimating equation for a population?
  a. α
  b. β
  c. $\mu_{Y \cdot X}$
3. What are three reasons for including an error term ε in a regression model?
4. What three conditions must be true with respect to the error terms?

Answers 15.A

1. a. $Y = \alpha + \beta X + \varepsilon$
  b. $\mu_{Y \cdot X} = \alpha + \beta X$
2. a. $\alpha = Y$ intercept at origin
  b. $\beta =$ slope
  c. $\mu_{Y \cdot X} =$ a conditional mean for a given value of X
3. measurement error, variation about average behavior, inherent randomness
4. error terms are independent of each other, constant variance of conditional distributions, normal conditional distributions

Section 15.B

The Sample Least-Squares Regression Line as a Maximum-Likelihood Estimator

Learning objectives

Your learning objectives for this section are to be able to:

1. Explain how sampling is used to estimate the regression line
2. Describe the maximum-likelihood approach to estimating

The parameters α and β in the regression equation $\mu_{Y \cdot X} = \alpha + \beta X$ can be calculated from population data using the least-squares criterion. The appropriate normal equations are

$$\sum Y = N\alpha + \beta \sum X$$
$$\sum XY = \alpha \sum X + \beta \sum X^2$$

When using *sample* data to estimate the relationship between two variables in a population, the least-squares regression equation is

$$\overline{Y}_X = a + bX$$

and the normal equations are

$$\sum Y = na + b \sum X$$
$$\sum XY = a \sum X + b \sum X^2$$

In these equations, $\overline{Y}_X$ is an estimator of $\mu_{Y \cdot X}$, and a and b are estimators of α and β.

In fact, given that the error terms are normally distributed, the least-squares line $\overline{Y}_X = a + bX$ is a *maximum likelihood estimator* of the population regression line $\mu_{Y \cdot X} = \alpha + \beta X$. This means that it is more likely (probable) that you'd get the particular a and b values you got through the least-squares solution if the parameters α and β were equal to a and b than if they were any other values.

This concept is illustrated in Fig. 15.1, which shows the scatter diagram from a random sample and some hypothetical *population* regression lines. Do you think it is more likely that this particular scatter of points came from a population whose

363

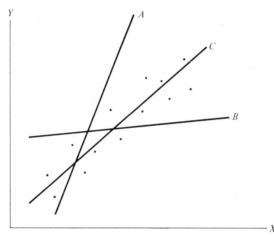

Figure 15.1 / Determining the maximum-likelihood regression line visually.

regression line $\mu_{Y \cdot X} = \alpha + \beta X$ was line A, line B, or line C? If the population regression line were A, you'd expect the sample data points to lie *around* line A. It is clear that of the three candidates, it is *more likely* that the data points came from a population whose regression line is C rather than A or B. If you fit the line $\overline{Y}_X = a + bX$ to the data points, it is more likely that that line will fall on the population line than on any other. Conversely, then, the sample line would be more likely to have come from the population line whose α and β values are equal to a and b than from any other line. This makes the line $\overline{Y}_X = a + bX$ the maximum-likelihood estimator of the line $\mu_{Y \cdot X} = \alpha + \beta X$.

To be sure that you get the idea, let's digress to a simpler case, that of sampling from a Bernoulli process. Suppose you sampled 100 items at random and found 6 of them defective. Your point estimate of the population proportion p would be the sample proportion, $\bar{p} = .06$. The calculations in Table 15.1 show that $\bar{p}$ is in fact the maximum-likelihood estimator of the population proportion p, because it is *more probable* that you'd get 6 defectives in a sample of 100 *if the true p value were .06* than if it were any other value.

Table 15.1

Possible population proportion defective p	Probability of sample outcome $P_b(r = 6 \mid n = 100, p)$
.03	.0496
.04	.1052
.05	.1500
.06	**.1657**
.07	.1429
.08	.1333

REVIEW EXERCISES 15.B

1. A *population* regression line is defined as _____, while the *estimate* of the population regression line from a *sample* is _____.

2. Give the normal equations for a least-squares regression line calculated from a sample.

3. Upon sampling 20 parts from a Bernoulli process, if you find 1 defective, the maximum-likelihood estimate of the proportion of defectives in the population is _____.

4. The maximum-likelihood estimator of the regression line $\mu_{Y \cdot X} = \alpha + \beta X$ is the line _____.

Answers 15.B

1. $\mu_{Y \cdot X} = \alpha + \beta X$, $\bar{Y}_X = a + bX$ *2.* $\sum Y = na + b \sum X$, $\sum XY = a \sum X + b \sum X^2$
3. .05   *4.* $\bar{Y}_X = a + bX$

Section 15.C
Tests of Hypotheses about α and β

Learning objectives

Your learning objectives for this section are to be able to:

1. Describe sampling distributions for a and b, the sample regression coefficients
2. Make interval estimates for α and β
3. Use the standard error of b to judge the usefulness of the regression equation

---

Now that you know how to estimate the population regression line from a sample and have made some assumptions about error terms and their distribution, you can learn to state hypotheses about the population regression line and to test these hypotheses using sample regression estimates.

First, you need to estimate the conditional variance around the regression line, which was minimized by the least-squares criterion. For a population, the conditional variance is

$$\sigma^2_{Y \cdot X} = \frac{\sum (Y - \mu_{Y \cdot X})^2}{N}$$

Here we'll use the sample results to estimate this conditional variance

$$s_{Y \cdot X}^2 = \frac{\sum (Y - \bar{Y}_X)^2}{n - 2}$$

This sample measure is an unbiased estimator of $\sigma_{Y \cdot X}^2$, the population variance around the regression line.[1] How does this relate to testing hypotheses about the regression coefficients? The mathematics is too involved to develop here, but the following statements can be made about the sampling distributions of the regression coefficients a and b:

1. The sampling distributions of a and b are normal if errors around the regression line are normal.
2. The expected value of a is α, and the expected value of b is β. That is, if you found all possible samples of points for a particular sample size n, the mean of all the a's and all the b's would be α and β, respectively, the true population values.
3. The variance of the sampling distribution of a would be

$$\sigma_a^2 = \frac{\sigma_{Y \cdot X}^2 \sum X^2}{n \sum (X - \bar{X})^2}$$

4. The variance of the sampling distribution of b would be

$$\sigma_b^2 = \frac{\sigma_{Y \cdot X}^2}{\sum (X - \bar{X})^2}$$

Since we don't know the population values, we must estimate the variances of these sampling distributions from sample data. When $s_{Y \cdot X}^2$ is used as an estimator of $\sigma_{Y \cdot X}^2$, the formulas become

$$s_a^2 = \frac{s_{Y \cdot X}^2 \sum X^2}{n \sum (X - \bar{X})^2} \qquad \text{and} \qquad s_b^2 = \frac{s_{Y \cdot X}^2}{\sum (X - \bar{X})^2}$$

To refresh your memory about sampling distributions, consider taking all possible samples of size 100 from a large population where the true value of β is 3.5, and finding b for each sample. Very few sample b values would be exactly 3.5. However, most of the sample results would cluster around 3.5, and values farther and farther away would become less likely. Also, if you increased the sample size to 200 or 400, you'd find the b values would cluster around 3.5 more closely and values farther away from 3.5 would become even less likely. Figure 15.2 will help you to understand this concept.

---

[1] See footnote p. 47 for a discussion of degrees of freedom. Here we're estimating two parameters, α and β, from the sample data, so we lose 2 degrees of freedom and the devisor is $n - 2$ rather than n.

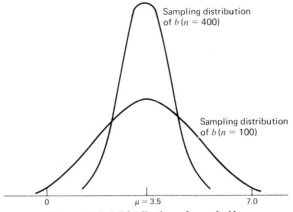

Figure 15.2 / Distribution of sample b's.

EXAMPLE

Suppose you believed there was a linear relationship between income and personal consumption for goods and services, and you wanted to find the slope and intercept of this line. You know that even with zero income, there must be some spending, so you don't expect a to be zero.

Assume that you take a random sample of 20 people and measure their income and expenditure as shown in Table 15.2. From these data you can obtain the values

$$n = 20 \qquad \sum X = 191,200 \qquad \sum Y = 175,300$$
$$\sum X^2 = 2,165,180,000 \qquad \sum XY = 1,973,670,000$$

Substituting these values in the normal equations, you obtain the estimating equation[1]

$$\bar{Y}_X = 325 + .883X$$

Substituting the X values from Table 15.2 in this equation, you can solve for all of the conditional means and calculate the sum of the squared errors around the regression line

$$\sum (Y - \bar{Y}_X)^2 = 14,102,500$$

Now, having estimated α by finding that $a = 325$ and β by finding that $b = .883$, how confident can you be of these estimates? Is it likely that α could be as low as

---

[1] In this and the following module, examples have been solved using a computer program and the results have been rounded for presentation. Since results depend upon when and how rounding takes place in a problem solution, you should not expect to obtain exactly these results should you attempt to solve the problem by hand or by using a small calculator.

Table 15.2 / Income and expenditures data

Person	Income X	Expenditure Y	$Y - \bar{Y}_X$
1	16,300	15,600	884.40
2	6,800	6,400	71.74
3	8,600	9,200	1282.56
4	15,300	14,900	1067.28
5	8,700	7,200	− 805.72
6	7,800	7,600	388.87
7	7,300	7,200	430.31
8	8,300	7,200	− 452.57
9	9,400	7,900	− 723.74
10	10,800	8,800	− 1059.77
11	18,600	15,400	− 1346.22
12	5,100	4,100	− 727.36
13	11,600	11,100	533.93
14	2,700	2,400	− 308.45
15	11,800	11,500	757.35
16	4,600	4,200	− 185.92
17	5,400	6,700	1607.77
18	12,900	12,100	386.19
19	13,300	11,100	− 966.97
20	5,900	4,700	− 833.66

225 or as high as 425? Could β be as low as .80 or as high as .95? The answers to these and other similar questions can be found using the standard deviations of the sampling distributions of a and b. The formulas are[1]

$$s_a^2 = \frac{s_{Y \cdot X}^2 \sum X^2}{n \sum (X - \bar{X})^2} = \frac{783,472(2,165,180,000)}{20(337,308,000)} = 251,455$$

$$s_a = \sqrt{s_a^2} = \sqrt{251,455} = 501$$

$$s_b^2 = \frac{s_{Y \cdot X}^2}{\sum (X - \bar{X})^2} = \frac{783,472}{337,308,000} = .00232$$

$$s_b = \sqrt{s_b^2} = \sqrt{.00232} = .0482$$

The sampling distribution for b is shown in Fig. 15.3. Note that it is assumed to be normal, with mean .883 (the maximum-likelihood estimate of the unknown β) and standard error .0482 (the square root of the variance of b). How can you make

---

[1] If you are trying to check the calculations, remember that $s_{Y \cdot X}^2 = \sum (Y - \bar{Y}_X)^2/(n - 2)$ and (from Module 3) that $\sum (X - \bar{X})^2 = \sum X^2 - (\sum X)^2/n$.

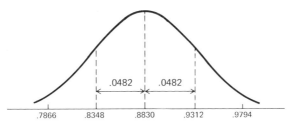

Figure 15.3 / Sampling distribution for b; $b = .883$, $s_b = .0482$.

use of this information to compute confidence intervals or test hypotheses? To make an interval estimate for α using a 95 percent confidence coefficient, you'd calculate

$$\text{Interval estimate for } \alpha = a \pm t_{.95}s_a$$

Remember that since $\sigma_{Y \cdot X}^2$ was estimated from $s_{Y \cdot X}^2$, the t distribution for $n - 2$ degrees of freedom must be used rather than the normal distribution. Since for 95 percent confidence and 18 degrees of freedom, $t = 2.10$, the interval estimate for α is

$$325 \pm 2.10(501) = 325 \pm 1052$$

Similarly, a 95 percent confidence interval estimate for β is

$$\text{Interval estimate for } \beta = b \pm t_{.95}s_b$$
$$= .883 \pm 2.10(.0482)$$
$$= .883 \pm .101 = .782 \text{ to } .984$$

It is particularly important to note that this interval does not contain zero; both its lower and upper limits are positive. If an interval estimate for β *did* include zero, it would mean that you couldn't even be sure if the sign of β were positive or negative. In that case, using the regression equation to make predictions would be meaningless.

Hypotheses about α or β would be made in the manner familiar from similar tests made for means or proportions in Module 14. For example, if you wanted to test the hypothesis that β is equal to or less than zero, you'd calculate

$$t = \frac{b - \beta}{s_b} = \frac{.883 - 0}{.0482} = 18.32$$

Since t for a 1 percent one-tailed level of significance at 18 degrees of freedom $= 2.55$, you'd reject the hypothesis that β could be zero or less.

REVIEW EXERCISES 15.C

1. The formula for an estimate of the standard deviation of the sampling distribution of a is _____.
2. The formula for an estimate of the standard deviation of the sampling distribution of b is _____.
3. Assume that you obtained the following statistics for a sample of size 15:

$$a = 87 \qquad s_a = 37.8 \qquad b = 7 \qquad s_b = 5.65$$

Make interval estimates for α and β, using a 90 percent confidence coefficient.
4. From the results of Exercise 3 you should be convinced that the regression equation from which a and b come is useful: true or false?

Answers 15.C

1. $s_a = \sqrt{\dfrac{s_{Y \cdot X}^2 \sum X^2}{n \sum (X - \bar{X})^2}}$ 2. $s_b = \sqrt{\dfrac{s_{Y \cdot X}^2}{\sum (X - \bar{X})^2}}$

3. Interval estimate for $\alpha = 87 \pm 67$
   Interval estimate for $\beta = 7 \pm 10$
   (Remember that there are 13 degrees of freedom, so $t = 1.771$.)
4. False; the interval estimate for β includes zero, so the regression equation is useless.

Section 15.D

Prediction Using the Regression Equation

Learning objectives

Your learning objective for this section is to be able to make predictions using regression equations:

1. For conditional means of Y, given X
2. For individual values of Y, given X

POINT ESTIMATES FROM A REGRESSION EQUATION

There are two sorts of point estimates you might want to make using a regression equation: predicting a *conditional mean* of Y given a particular value of X or predicting a *single value* of Y given a particular value of X.

Point estimates in either of these situations are made simply by substituting the appropriate value of X in the regression equation. Thus, for the income-expenditure example,

$$\overline{Y}_X = 325 + .883X$$

and for an income level of, say, $11,700,

$$\overline{Y}_X = 325 + .883(11,700) = \$10,656$$

This figure, $10,656, is the best point (single) estimate you could make of the *mean* expenditure of *all* persons having incomes of $11,700. It is also the best point estimate you could make of the expenditures of a *particular person* picked at random from the group of all persons having incomes of $11,700.

INTERVAL ESTIMATES FROM A REGRESSION EQUATION

While point estimates, either for a conditional mean or an individual value, are easily made from a regression equation, interval estimation is more difficult because you must take account both of the error terms inherent in the population and of additional errors that can come about when estimating α and β from a sample. The error terms inherent in the population are no problem; they have been estimated before using the standard error of estimate, $s_{Y \cdot X}$.

Estimation of the errors involved in using a and b as estimators of α and β have not been considered before. Figure 15.4 shows estimates of possible population regression lines which might be obtained from different samples. The lines are all different, of course, because of sampling errors and the effect of these errors in calculating intercepts and slopes. Errors in measuring the slope are of particular importance because as values of X to be used in the prediction diverge from the mean

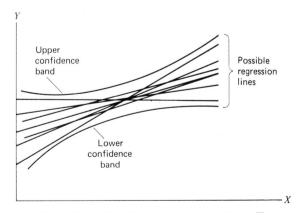

Figure 15.4 / Confidence band for predicting $\overline{Y}$.

371

of X, any errors involved in measuring b will become magnified. Thus any confidence interval made from a sample regression equation will form a *curved* confidence band; as predicted values diverge from the mean, the band becomes wider. Just how wide the band is depends on the confidence coefficient and whether the estimate is being made for a *conditional mean* or for a *single* conditional value.

Interval estimates for a conditional mean. Remember that in Module 13 interval estimates were made for the mean of a single variable using $s_{\bar{X}}$, the estimate of the standard deviation of the sampling distribution of the mean. When the population was large in relation to the sample, or when sampling was made with replacement, this standard deviation was calculated by dividing s_X, the estimate of the population standard deviation, by the square root of n

$$s_{\bar{X}} = \frac{s_X}{\sqrt{n}}$$

The scatter of points about a *conditional* mean is also affected by the inherent variation in the population and the size of the sample. In addition, the scatter is affected by the errors in measuring a and b, as noted before. The formula for the standard deviation of the sampling distribution of a conditional mean, which is called the *standard error of the conditional mean*, is

$$s_{\bar{Y} \cdot X} = \frac{s_{Y \cdot X}}{\sqrt{n}} + s_{Y \cdot X} \sqrt{\frac{(X - \bar{X})^2}{\sum (X - \bar{X})^2}}$$

or, equivalently,

$$s_{\bar{Y} \cdot X} = s_{Y \cdot X} \sqrt{\frac{1}{n} + \frac{(X - \bar{X})^2}{\sum (X - \bar{X})^2}}$$

Note that $s_{\bar{Y} \cdot X}$ represents the standard error of the *conditional* mean, as opposed to $s_{Y \cdot X}$, which is the standard error of estimate.

The term $\sqrt{(X - \bar{X})^2 / \sum (X - \bar{X})^2}$ is the statistic necessary to correct for the distance that the X value to be estimated lies from the mean of X. This term becomes zero if the value of X substituted in the estimating equation is equal to the mean of X, and as the X value diverges farther and farther from the mean of X, the correction term gets larger and larger.

An interval estimate for a conditional mean is made in the usual fashion:

$$\text{Interval estimate for a conditional mean} = \bar{Y}_X \pm t s_{\bar{Y} \cdot X}$$

For the income-expenditure problem, a 95 percent confidence interval estimate for the conditional mean when $X = \$11,700$ is easily calculated using statistics developed in the previous sections:

$$\bar{Y}_X = \$10,656 \qquad\qquad \bar{X} = 9560$$
$$t_{18} = 2.10 \qquad\qquad \sum (X - \bar{X})^2 = 337,308,000$$
$$s^2_{Y \cdot X} = 783,475 \qquad\qquad s_{Y \cdot X} = 885.1$$

372

The interval estimate is then

$$\bar{Y}_X \pm t s_{Y \cdot X} \sqrt{\frac{1}{n} + \frac{(X - \bar{X})^2}{\sum (X - \bar{X})^2}} = 10,656 \pm 2.10(885.1) \sqrt{\frac{1}{20} + \frac{(11,700 - 9560)^2}{337,308,000}}$$

$$= 10,656 \pm 468.7$$

Interval estimate for an individual value. If an entire population was available, an interval estimate for an *individual value* of Y given a value of X would be based solely on the error term around the estimating equation. Thus for a *population*,

$$\text{Interval estimate for } Y \text{ given } X = \mu_{Y \cdot X} \pm t \sigma_{Y \cdot X}$$

To make an interval estimate for a single value of Y given a value of X *from a sample*, you must take account of the error involved in estimating the regression line as well as the variation inherent in the population.

Since these two sources of error are independent, the variances are additive and the combined error terms are measured by

$$s_{Y_p \cdot X} = \sqrt{s_{\bar{Y} \cdot X}^2 + s_{\hat{Y} \cdot X}^2}$$

or, equivalently,

$$s_{Y_p \cdot X} = s_{Y \cdot X} \sqrt{1 + \frac{1}{n} + \frac{(X - \bar{X})^2}{\sum (X - \bar{X})^2}}$$

where $s_{Y_p \cdot X}$ refers to the standard error of estimate for a *particular* value of Y given a value of X.

For the income-expenditure problem, a 95 percent confidence interval estimate for an *individual's* expenditures, given an income of \$11,700, would be

Interval estimate for Y given X

$$= \bar{Y}_X \pm t s_{Y \cdot X} \sqrt{1 + \frac{1}{n} + \frac{(X - \bar{X})^2}{\sum (X - \bar{X})^2}}$$

$$= 10,656 \pm 2.10(885.1) \sqrt{1 + \frac{1}{20} + \frac{(11,700 - 9560)^2}{337,308,000}}$$

$$= 10,656 \pm 1916.9$$

Naturally, for the same level of confidence, the confidence interval for an estimate of an *individual* conditional value will be larger than that for a conditional *mean*,

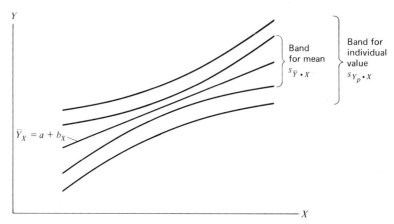

Figure 15.5 / Confidence bands for predicting mean and individual values.

for any value of X. Figure 15.5 illustrates the relationship between the two confidence bands.

REVIEW EXERCISES 15.D

1. The confidence band for predicting an individual value is larger than that for predicting a conditional mean because:
   a. The $(X - \bar{X})^2$ term gets bigger as X diverges from $\bar{X}$.
   b. Both error terms involved in estimating the coefficients a and b and those inherent in the population must be considered.
   c. The value of t is larger in the case of predicting individual values.
2. Assume the following values:
   $\bar{Y}_X = 120 + 2X$ $s_{Y \cdot X} = 13$ $n = 25$ $\sum (X - \bar{X})^2 = 1000$ $\bar{X} = 50$
   a. Make an interval estimate (with a 95 percent confidence coefficient) for the *conditional mean* of Y when $X = 60$.
   b. Make an interval estimate (with a 95 percent confidence coefficient) for an *individual value* of Y when $X = 60$.

Answers 15.D

1. b

2. a. $240 \pm 2.069(13) \sqrt{\frac{1}{25} + \frac{100}{1000}} = 240 \pm 10$

   b. $240 \pm 2.069(13) \sqrt{1 + \frac{1}{25} + \frac{100}{1000}} = 240 \pm 29$

Section 15.E
The Correlation Coefficient

Learning objective

Your learning objective for this section is to be able to test hypotheses concerning the correlation coefficient

In Module 8, the correlation coefficient was defined as

$$r = \sqrt{\frac{\text{explained variation}}{\text{total variation}}}$$

Let's now treat its determination as a sampling problem. There is a true value of correlation in the population, but any given sample is unlikely to produce exactly that same correlation coefficient.

If the population correlation coefficient is in fact zero, then the sampling distribution will be symmetric around a zero mean. You can test the hypothesis that ρ (rho), the population correlation coefficient, equals 0 by using the test statistic

$$t = \frac{r\sqrt{n-2}}{\sqrt{1-r^2}}$$

The computed value is compared with the critical value from the t tables with $n-2$ degrees of freedom. If it is greater than the critical value, you'll reject the hypothesis that the population correlation coefficient is zero.

If the correlation coefficient in the population is not zero, the sampling distribution becomes rather complex. While it is possible to make transformations on r in order to test hypotheses, tests on correlations other than the hypothesis that $\rho = 0$ are seldom of interest. The details of such transformations can be found in advanced texts on statistics if you ever need to test such a hypothesis.

EXAMPLE

The correlation coefficient computed for the income-expenditure example of the previous section is $+.9742$. Testing the hypothesis that this value is significantly different from zero, you'd calculate

$$t = \frac{r\sqrt{n-2}}{\sqrt{1-r^2}} = \frac{.9742\sqrt{18}}{\sqrt{1-.9742^2}} = 18.32$$

Since this value is much greater than the value of t at the .01 (two-tailed) level for 18 degrees of freedom, which is 2.878, you can be confident that the correlation coefficient is significantly different from zero. Thus there *is* a significant linear relationship between the variables.

It can be shown that if the correlation coefficient is zero, β will also be zero. This means that significance tests of ρ and β related to zero are tests for the same thing, the significance of the linear relationship between the variables. Look at the test for $\beta = 0$ on page 369. The t value of 18.32 is exactly the same as that calculated above.

REVIEW EXERCISES 15.E

1. The statistic $r\sqrt{n-2}/\sqrt{1-r^2}$ is:
 a. The standard deviation of the sampling distribution of r.
 b. The value of t for testing the significance of r.
2. Given that $n = 10$ and $r = .7$, test the hypothesis that ρ, the population coefficient of correlation, is $= 0$. Use a 95 percent, two-tailed test.

Answers 15.E

1. b

2. $t = \dfrac{r\sqrt{n-2}}{\sqrt{1-r^2}} = \dfrac{.7\sqrt{8}}{\sqrt{1-.7^2}} = 2.77$

since t for 95 percent confidence at 8 degrees of freedom $= 2.306$, conclude that ρ is significantly different from zero.

Section 15.F
Analysis of Residual Error

Learning objectives

Your learning objectives for this section are to be able to:

1. Define and explain residual error
2. Use residual errors to evaluate subjectively the validity of the regression model

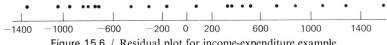

Figure 15.6 / Residual plot for income-expenditure example.

It was stated in Section A that the error terms had to meet three conditions or assumptions of the model before the regression model to be developed would be valid:

1. The error terms are independent of each other.
2. The error terms are normally distributed.
3. The variance of the error terms about their conditional means is a constant.

After completion of a regression analysis, the error terms, or *residuals*, measured by $Y - \bar{Y}_X$, should be examined to see whether the conditions assumed in the model have been met. The three plots of the residuals described below not only provide such a check but also give some clues to what may be wrong if the conditions are not met. Each of these plots will then be used to check the validity of the model for the income-expenditure example.

A SIMPLE RESIDUAL PLOT

A simple plot of residuals consists of locating each $Y - \bar{Y}_X$ value on a horizontal line. The least-squares criterion assures that the mean of the residuals will be zero. If they are in fact normally distributed, the residuals will form a symmetrical distribution around the mean of zero. Most of the points will be clustered near the mean, with the number of points decreasing as the distance from the mean increases.

The 20 residuals for the income-expenditure example are plotted in Fig. 15.6. It is evident that they meet the normality condition quite well. Figure 15.7 shows how residual plots might look if the normality criterion were not met. In Fig. 15.7a, the points are spread uniformly along the line, instead of clustering near the mean. In Fig. 15.7b, the distribution of residuals is skewed rather than symmetrical.

Figure 15.7 / Residual plots indicating assumptions violated: (a) uniform distribution of residuals, (b) skewed distribution of residuals.

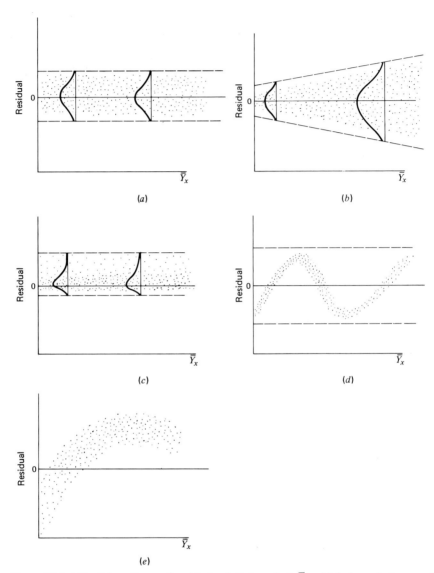

Figure 15.8 / Possible patterns of residuals plotted against $\overline{\overline{Y}}_x$: (a) independent, normal, constant variance; (b) nonconstant variance; (c) nonnormal; (d) nonindependent; (e) inadequate model.

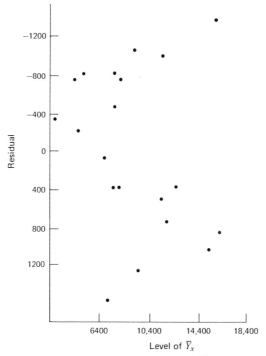

Figure 15.9 / Plot of residuals against $\bar{Y}_x$ for example problem.

PLOTTING RESIDUALS AGAINST $\bar{Y}_x$

It is also useful to plot the residuals on a graph as a function of $\bar{Y}_x$, the predicted value. Figure 15.8 shows five such plots, illustrating that:

a. Independence, normality, and constant variance conditions are met.
b. Constant variance condition is violated.
c. Normality condition is violated.
d. Independence condition is violated.
e. The model is inadequately defined.

The only plot requiring additional comment is Fig. 15.8*e*, inadequate model definition. Such a plot could occur because a nonlinear regression should have been used, some transformation should have been made in the data before fitting the regression equation, or more independent variables need to be added to explain the dependent variable. The last of these cases is the topic of the next module.

Figure 15.9 is the plot of the residuals for the income-expenditure example. Its pattern indicates that all of the conditions of independence, constant variance, and normality are fairly well met.

379

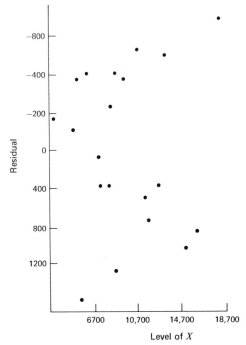

Figure 15.10 / Plot of residuals against X for example problem.

PLOTTING RESIDUALS AGAINST X

A third basic plot is that of the residuals as a function of X, the independent variable. The basic forms this plot can take and their causes are exactly like those illustrated by plotting the residuals against $\bar{Y}_X$, so they won't be repeated here.

Figure 15.10 shows this plot for the residuals of the income-expenditure example. Again, the plot indicates that all the conditions are fairly well met in this example.

REVIEW EXERCISES 15.F

1. In a valid analysis of regression, the error terms should:
  a. Be independent of each other.
  b. Be insignificant.
  c. Have a constant variance.
  d. Be normally distributed.
  e. Be larger than the $Y - \bar{Y}_X$ values.
2. Identify the probable cause for plots of residuals like those below.

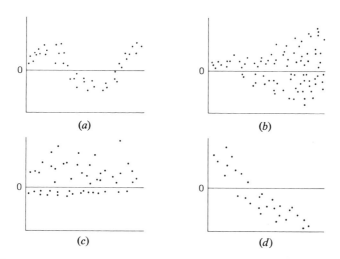

(a)   (b)

(c)   (d)

Answers 15.F

1. a, c, d   *2. a.* lack of independence; *b.* variance not constant; *c.* distribution not normal; *d.* inadequate model

Questions and Problems

15.1. For the data of Prob. 8.1:

    a. Calculate the regression equation for estimating error rate on the basis of machine speed.

    b. Make interval estimates for the population regression coefficients α and β, using a 90 percent confidence coefficient. On the basis of these estimates, are you justified in using the regression equation to predict errors? Why or why not?

    c. Make an interval estimate of the error rate when the machine is run at an output of 175 pieces per hour. Use a 95 percent confidence coefficient.

    d. Plot the residuals from the linear regression equation as a function of the predicted value of the dependent variable, error rate. Does this plot indicate that the assumptions on which the regression model was predicated are being met?

15.2. For the data of Prob. 8.2:

    a. Calculate the linear regression equation for estimating the time it takes to perform the task through a knowledge of noise level.

    b. Find the coefficient of correlation and test the hypothesis that it is not significantly different from zero, using a 5 percent level of significance. Interpret the meaning of this test.

    c. Make an interval estimate for the time it would take to perform the task if the noise level at the work station were 30 decibels. Use a 90 percent confidence coefficient.

15.3. For the data of Prob. 8.3:

    a. Calculate the coefficients of determination and correlation.

  b. Test the hypothesis that the correlation coefficient is not significantly different from zero, using a 5 percent level of significance. Interpret the meaning of this test.

  c. Make an interval estimate, using a 95 percent confidence coefficient, for the *average* servicing cost you'd expect for companies with a 30,000-name mailing list.

  d. Make an interval estimate, using a 95 percent confidence coefficient, for the servicing cost for a *particular company* that had a mailing list of 30,000 names.

  e. Explain why the interval estimates in parts *c* and *d* differ.

15.4. For the data of Prob. 8.4:

  a. Calculate the regression equation you'd use to estimate the maximum number of servings through a knowledge of the number of registrants.

  b. Make interval estimates for the population regression coefficients α and β, using a 90 percent confidence coefficient. On the basis of these estimates, can you say that a knowledge of the number of registrants is helpful in predicting the number of servings?

  c. Make an interval estimate for the maximum number of servings to plan on for a conference that has 525 registrants. Use an 80 percent confidence coefficient.

  d. Plot the residuals from the linear regression equation as a function of the independent variable, number of registrants. On the basis of this plot, do you believe the assumptions of the regression model are being met?

15.5. For the data of Prob. 8.5:

  a. Calculate the linear regression equation for estimating appeal on the basis of income.

  b. Calculate the linear regression equation for estimating income on the basis of appeal.

  c. Calculate the coefficients of determination and correlation.

  d. Test the hypothesis that the coefficient of correlation isn't significantly different from zero. Use a 5 percent level of significance.

  e. Make an interval estimate for the income of a person who gave the bank a rating of 4. Use a 90 percent confidence coefficient.

  f. Make an interval estimate for the rating an individual can expect to give the bank if their income is $19,000. Use a 90 percent confidence coefficient.

15.6. Assume that the data of Prob. 8.6 constitute a random sample.

  a. Calculate the linear regression equation for predicting store sales from the regional forecast.

  b. Make an interval estimate for the population regression coefficients α and β, using a 90 percent level of confidence. On the basis of these estimates, do you believe the regression equation should be used to make estimates of sales?

  c. Make an interval estimate for the store's sales when the wholesaler's forecast is 2980, using an 80 percent confidence coefficient.

  d. Make an interval estimate for the store's sales when the wholesaler's forecast is 3050, using an 80 percent confidence coefficient.

To assist in calculating measures for Probs. 7 to 12 see the note preceding Prob. 8.7. Note that in those formulas s_x^2 and s_y^2 are not adjusted for degrees of freedom (their divisor is n, not n − 1).

15.7. For the data of Prob. 8.7:

  a. Calculate the coefficients of determination and correlation and explain what they mean.

  b. Test the hypothesis that the correlation coefficient is not significantly different from zero, using a 5 percent level of significance.

c. Determine the linear regression equation that you'd use to estimate work performance on the basis of training.

d. Make an interval estimate with a 90 percent confidence coefficient for the work performance of an employee having 8 months of training.

15.8. For the data of Prob. 8.8:

a. Fit a linear regression line with building permits as the independent variable and sales as the dependent variable.

b. Make an interval estimate for the population regression coefficients, using a 98 percent confidence coefficient. Interpret the significance of the estimate for β.

c. Make an interval estimate for the sales you'd expect when 85 building permits were issued 4 months earlier. Use a 98 percent confidence coefficient.

15.9. For the data of Prob. 8.9:

a. Calculate the regression equation you'd use to estimate profitability based on sales volume.

b. Make an interval estimate for the population regression coefficients, using a 90 percent confidence coefficient. On the basis of the estimate for β, what can you say about the usefulness of the regression equation?

c. Make an interval estimate for profitability next year if next year's sales are estimated at 200 million dollars. Use a 95 percent confidence coefficient.

15.10. For the data of Prob. 8.10:

a. Calculate the regression equation used to estimate sales on the basis of test scores.

b. Make an interval estimate for the population regression coefficients, using a 90 percent confidence coefficient. Do you believe that the test is useful in predicting sales? Why or why not?

c. Make an interval estimate, using a 95 percent confidence coefficient, for the sales generated by a person who scored 70 on the test.

d. Make an interval estimate, using a 95 percent confidence coefficient, for the sales generated by a person who scored 90 on the test.

e. Explain why the interval calculated in part *d* is larger than that for part *c*.

15.11. For the data of Prob. 8.11:

a. Calculate the coefficients of determination and correlation for this relationship.

b. Test the hypothesis that the coefficient of correlation is not significantly different from zero. Explain the significance of this test.

c. Calculate the linear regression equation for estimating actual running time based on estimated running time.

d. Compute a 90 percent confidence interval estimate for the *average* actual running time of jobs which are estimated to take 30 seconds.

e. Compute a 90 percent confidence interval estimate for the actual running time of a job submitted by an individual who estimated the time to be 30 seconds.

f. Explain the reason that the estimate made in part *d* was smaller than that made in part *e* even though the same confidence coefficient was used.

15.12. For the data of Prob. 8.12:

a. Calculate the coefficients of determination and correlation for this problem.

b. Test the hypothesis that the coefficient of correlation is not significantly different from zero. Do you believe that the voltage at which the part is operated affects its life? Why?

c. Compute the regression equation for estimating length of life based on the voltage at which the equipment is operated.

d. Make an interval estimate, using a 95 percent confidence coefficient, for the length of life you would expect, *on the average*, from equipment operated at 30 volts.

15.13. Explain the meaning of maximum-likelihood estimation. Use regression analysis a your model and use graphs to illustrate your major points.

15.14. Explain why $s^2_{\bar{Y} \cdot X}$, the variance of the conditional mean, becomes larger as you move away from $\bar{X}$, the mean of X.

15.15. What does it mean to say that b is an estimate of β? Include in your discussion the concepts of sampling, expected value, and confidence intervals.

15.16. Prove mathematically that the t test to see whether the correlation coefficient is significantly different from zero is exactly the same as the t test to see whether b is significantly different from zero. Both formulas are given in the book.

MODULE 16
MULTIVARIATE REGRESSION ANALYSIS

General learning objectives

Your general learning objectives for this module are to be able to:

1. Solve for the coefficients of a linear multiple regression equation, and test their significance
2. Use the multiple regression equation to make estimates of the dependent variable
3. Calculate the coefficients of multiple determination and correlation
4. Measure the importance of each independent variable in predicting the dependent variable by calculating coefficients of partial determination

Section 16.A

The Multivariate Linear Model

Learning objectives

Your learning objectives for this section are to be able to:

1. Formulate a linear multiple regression model
2. Use the least-squares method to estimate the parameters of the model using sample data
3. State the assumptions required in using multivariate linear regression analysis

In bivariate regression, there was only one independent and one dependent variable. Data points could be plotted in two-dimensional space, forming the familiar scatter diagram. The least-squares criterion was then used to fit a regression *line* through these data points.

In three-variable multivariate regression, there are *two* independent variables and one dependent variable. Data points would have to be plotted in three-dimensional space. The regression procedure fits a two-dimensional *plane* through the points, as shown in Fig. 16.1. Imagine this illustration as a box with the top tilted *at a strange angle*. The top of the box forms the *regression plane* that cuts through the data points.

The multivariate regression model is a simple extension of the bivariate model. The only difference is that other independent variables are added. The population model for a regression model with two independent variables is

$$Y = \alpha + \beta_1 X_1 + \beta_2 X_2 + \varepsilon$$

The equation for the population regression line is

$$\mu_{Y \cdot X_1 X_2} = \alpha + \beta_1 X_1 + \beta_2 X_2$$

For *sample* data, the model is defined as

$$Y = a + b_1 X_1 + b_2 X_2 + e$$

The equation for the sample regression line is

$$\overline{Y}_{X_1 X_2} = a + b_1 X_1 + b_2 X_2$$

387

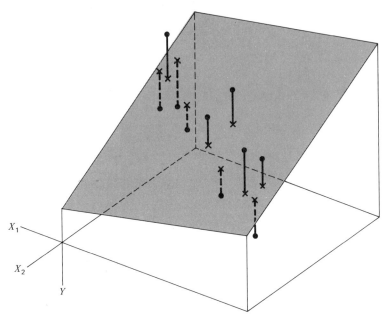

Figure 16.1 / Schematic of multiple regression with two independent variables.

The symbols for the multivariate model are a little more complex than for the bivariate model because they must clearly identify the number of variables in the model. Thus $\mu_{Y \cdot X_1 X_2}$ is the conditional mean of Y *given* values of *both* X_1 and X_2, β_1 is the slope of the regression plane viewed, say, from the *front* of the box in Fig. 16.1, while β_2 is the slope of the same regression plane viewed from the *side* of the box.

The familiar least-squares criterion is used to fit the regression plane. Using sample data, the equation for a particular point is

$$Y = a + b_1 X_1 + b_2 X_2 + e$$

The sum of the squared errors would then be

$$\sum (e^2) = \sum [Y - (a + b_1 X_1 + b_2 X_2)]^2$$

Since $\bar{Y}_{X_1 X_2} = a + b_1 X_1 + b_2 X_2$, it can be substituted in the equation for $\sum (e^2)$:

$$\sum (e^2) = \sum (Y - \bar{Y}_{X_1 X_2})^2$$

The least-squares solution that minimizes these squared errors produces the following three normal equations:

$$\sum Y = na + b_1 \sum X_1 + b_2 \sum X_2$$
$$\sum X_1 Y = a \sum X_1 + b_1 \sum X_1^2 + b_2 \sum X_1 X_2$$
$$\sum X_2 Y = a \sum X_2 + b_1 \sum X_1 X_2 + b_2 \sum X_2^2$$

These equations can then be solved simultaneously to obtain the least-squares estimates of a, b_1, and b_2.

EXAMPLE

As an example, consider the Module 15 data on the relationship between income and expenditures. It seems possible that additional explanatory power for expenditures would come from knowing household size as well as income. The original data are reproduced in Table 16.1, along with the information on household size.

To solve the normal equations, the following computations are required:

$$n = 20 \qquad \sum X_1^2 = 2,165,180,000$$

$$\sum X_1 = 191,200 \qquad \sum X_2^2 = 136$$

$$\sum X_2 = 48 \qquad \sum X_1 X_2 = 497,400$$

$$\sum Y = 175,300 \qquad \sum Y^2 = 1,813,530,000$$

$$\sum X_1 Y = 1,973,670,000$$

$$\sum X_2 Y = 465,000$$

Table 16.1 / Household income, size, and expenditures

Household	Expenditures Y	Income X_1	Size of household X_2
1	$15,600	$16,300	4
2	6,400	6,800	2
3	9,200	8,600	4
4	14,900	15,300	2
5	7,200	8,700	2
6	7,600	7,800	3
7	7,200	7,300	2
8	7,200	8,300	1
9	7,900	9,400	1
10	8,800	10,800	2
11	15,400	18,600	3
12	4,100	5,100	2
13	11,100	11,600	4
14	2,400	2,700	1
15	11,500	11,800	4
16	4,200	4,600	2
17	6,700	5,400	3
18	12,100	12,900	3
19	11,100	13,300	2
20	4,700	5,900	1

Inserting these values into the normal equations gives

$$175,300 = 20a + 191,200b_1 + 48b_2$$

$$1,973,670,000 = 191,200a + 2,165,180,000b_1 + 497,400b_2$$

$$465,000 = 48a + 497,400b_1 + 136b_2$$

Solving this set of equations yields[1]

$$a = -495 \qquad b_1 = .8114 \qquad b_2 = 626$$

The least-squares estimating equation is

$$\bar{Y}_{X_1 X_2} = -495 + .8114X_1 + 626X_2$$

This equation is interpreted as follows. For each dollar increase in income, expenditures will go up by 81 cents, *at any fixed level of family size*. Also, for a unit increase in family size, expenditures will go up by $626, *at any fixed level of income*. The concept of holding all other variables at a fixed level in interpreting a coefficient is very important. In effect, each b is interpreted as a conditional coefficient, where the condition is that all other independent variables are fixed at a given level.

REVIEW EXERCISES 16.A

1. How many normal equations would you have in a model with four independent variables?
2. What criterion is used to find the normal equations in a multivariate regression model?
3. In a three-variable model (two independent variables), the effects of a unit change in X_2 depend upon the level of X_1 (true or false).

Answers 16.A

1. Five; there are five unknowns (a and four b_i), and there would then be five simultaneous equations, the normal equations.
2. The criterion used is least squares, finding the plane that minimizes the sum of the squared deviations.
3. False; the effects of a unit change in X_2 are b_2, and this is true at any and all levels of X_1.

---

[1] Do not forget that results have been rounded from computer output and you should not expect to obtain exactly these results should you solve the problem by hand.

Section 16.B

Testing the Significance of Multiple Regression Coefficients

Learning objectives

Your learning objectives for this section are to be able to:

1. Calculate explained, unexplained, and total variation in a multivariate regression problem
2. Test hypotheses on the coefficients of a multivariate regression equation

---

Before using a multiple regression equation developed from sample data to predict values of the dependent variable, you need to know if the population coefficients differ significantly from zero. That is, you need to know that the relationship among the variables is statistically significant.

The procedure for making these tests is completely analogous to those used in Module 15 for bivariate analysis. Before testing the multivariate equation, then, we'll review the bivariate model and use it to develop some new relationships.

TESTING THE BIVARIATE MODEL

Back in Module 8 there was a discussion of the partitioning of the total variation about the mean of the dependent variable into two components, the variation explained by the independent variable and the residual, or unexplained, variation. The relationship was

$$\sum (Y - \overline{Y})^2 = \sum (\overline{Y}_X - \overline{Y})^2 + \sum (Y - \overline{Y}_X)^2$$

or

Total variation = explained variation + unexplained variation

The unexplained variation, or residual error, was then used to calculate the standard error of estimate $s_{Y \cdot X}$, which measured the standard deviation of the Y values around

391

the estimating equation. The formula for $s_{Y \cdot X}$, correcting for degrees of freedom as in Module 15, was

$$s_{Y \cdot X} = \sqrt{\frac{\sum (Y - \bar{Y}_X)^2}{n - 2}}$$

The square of this statistic, $s_{Y \cdot X}^2$, called the unexplained *variance*, was then used to make a t test to find if β, the slope of the population equation, was significantly different from zero. The formula developed in Module 15 for this test was

$$t = \frac{b - 0}{s_b} = \frac{b}{\sqrt{s_{Y \cdot X}^2 / \sum (X - \bar{X})^2}}$$

For the bivariate income-expenditure example,

$$t = \frac{b}{\sqrt{s_{Y \cdot X}^2 / \sum (X - \bar{X})^2}} = \frac{.883}{\sqrt{783,472/337,308,000}} = 18.32$$

Since the critical value of t at the .05 level of significance with 18 degrees of freedom was found to be 2.10, β was judged significantly different from zero and the regression line could therefore be used to make estimates of the dependent variable.

Now let's consider an alternative way of looking at this significance problem. For the bivariate income-expenditure problem, we found

$$\text{Total variation} = \sum (Y - \bar{Y})^2 = 277,025,500$$
$$\text{Unexplained variation} = \sum (Y - \bar{Y}_X)^2 = 14,102,500$$
$$\text{Explained variation} = \sum (\bar{Y}_X - \bar{Y})^2 = 262,923,000$$

The explained variation, 262,923,000, is the *change in squared error due to using an explanatory variable X*. Now, without explanation, we define

$$t = \sqrt{\frac{\text{explained variation}}{s_{Y \cdot X}^2}} = \sqrt{\frac{\text{explained variation}}{\text{unexplained variation/degrees of freedom}}}$$

For the bivariate income-expenditure problem, then,

$$t = \sqrt{\frac{\text{variation explained by } X}{\text{unexplained variation/degrees of freedom}}} = \sqrt{\frac{262,923,000}{783,472}} = 18.32$$

This, of course, is the same value that was obtained using the formulas from Module 15. You can now see that β is significantly different from zero, *because of the ability of the independent variable X to explain a great deal of the squared error of the original Y values about their mean.*

TESTING THE SIGNIFICANCE OF AN ADDITIONAL VARIABLE

Having formulated a multivariate problem by adding another independent variable, household size, to the income-expenditure problem, you'd want to test the slope of the *new* variable, b_2, to find if β_2, the population coefficient for household size, is significantly different from zero.

Calculating the variations for the new regression equation

$$\bar{Y}_{X_1 X_2} = -495 + .8114 X_1 + 626 X_2$$

you'd find

$$\text{Total variation} = \sum (Y - \bar{Y})^2 = 277{,}025{,}500$$
$$\text{Unexplained variation} = \sum (Y - \bar{Y}_{X_1 X_2})^2 = 7{,}669{,}749$$
$$\text{Explained variation} = \sum (\bar{Y}_{X_1 X_2} - \bar{Y})^2 = 269{,}355{,}751$$

However, not all of the explained error can be attributed to the newly added variable "household size." Remember that with income alone in the bivariate equation, the explained variation was 262,923,000. Therefore, only the *difference* between the explained variation with the *two* independent variables and the explained variation with *one* independent variable can be attributed to the second independent variable. For our problem, then, only the difference of

$$269{,}355{,}751 - 262{,}923{,}000 = 6{,}432{,}751$$

can be attributed to the new variable, "household size."

Now we can compute[1]

$$t = \sqrt{\frac{\text{variation explained by addition of } X_2}{\text{unexplained variation/degrees of freedom}}} = \sqrt{\frac{6{,}432{,}751}{7{,}669{,}749/17}} = 3.78$$

Looking in the t table, we find that the contribution of the new variable, household size, is significant because the critical level of t at the .05 level of significance with 17 degrees of freedom is 2.11.[2]

---

[1] In general, 1 degree of freedom is lost for every constant in the regression equation. Therefore, for this problem, 3 degrees of freedom are lost, leaving 17.

[2] The statistical test developed here uses the t distribution for significance testing. Many computer programs for regression analysis will print a value called F for testing the significance of an additional variable. The relationship between t and F when testing for the addition of a new explanatory variable is $t = \sqrt{F}$. In advanced statistics texts you'll find other uses for the F distribution where the above relationship does not hold.

393

ADDITIONAL COMMENTS

In the analysis we've been dealing with, involving income, expenditures, and household size, there are three different possible regression equations (one of which has not yet been discussed):

$$\bar{Y}_{X_1} = 324 + .883(\text{income})$$
$$\bar{Y}_{X_1X_2} = -495 + .8114(\text{income}) + 626(\text{size})$$
$$\bar{Y}_{X_2} = 3656 + 2129(\text{size})$$

This last equation deals with predicting expenditures on the basis of *household size alone*. While this equation turns out to be a fair predictor of expenditures, it isn't as good as income alone, or as good (as would be expected) as the two independent variables together in a multivariate equation.

Look at the first two equations above. You should note that when the second independent variable, "size" was entered in the equation, the values of the coefficients changed from the first equation. You should now realize that you can't simply compute all possible bivariate regression equations and put them together. The multivariate equation will be entirely different.

What caused the "income" coefficient to drop from .883 to .8114 when the variable "size" entered the equation? It can be shown that

$$b_1' = b_1 - b_2'(b_{X_2X_1})$$

where the primes indicate the coefficients of the new multivariate equation and $b_{X_2X_1}$ is a regression coefficient predicting variable X_2 from variable X_1. What the equation says is that the new coefficient for X_1 is the old coefficient (b_1) *adjusted* for the predictive ability of X_2 (as measured by b_2) and the joint relationship between X_1 and X_2 (as measured by $b_{X_2X_1}$). The equation becomes more complicated as more variables enter, but you should see that any b coefficient in a multivariate model reflects not only the relationship between that variable and the dependent variable Y but the joint relationship between all independent variables.

REVIEW EXERCISES 16.B

1. In a six-variable regression model (five independent variables) what would be the degrees of freedom for computing the variance around the regression plane, assuming the sample size was 50?

2. Associate each formula with its name.
   a. $\sum (Y - \bar{Y}_X)^2$ (1) Residual or unexplained variation
   b. $\sum (Y - \bar{Y})^2$ (2) Explained variation
   c. $\sum (\bar{Y}_X - \bar{Y})^2$ (3) Total variation

3. What would the following formula be used to test?

$$\sqrt{\frac{\text{Change in explained variation}}{\text{Unexplained variation/degrees of freedom}}}$$

4. To compute a multivariate regression equation, all you have to do is compute all the simple bivariate regression equations and use the respective b coefficients (true or false).
5. What is a fairly standard test on b coefficients?

Answers 16.B

1. 44; it would be $n - m$, where m represents the six coefficients estimated in the model and n is the sample size.
2. a. 1; b. 3; c. 2
3. It would be a t test to see if the β coefficient of the variable that caused the change in explained variation was significantly different from zero. The change in variation is the increase in explained variation (or the decrease in unexplained variation, since both are the same) found by looking at the models with and without the new variable and comparing them.
4. false
5. A fairly standard test is the one performed in Exercise 3, that is, a test to determine whether β is significantly different from zero.

Section 16.C

Prediction

Learning objective

Your learning objective for this section is to be able to make interval estimates for the dependent variable using a multiple regression equation

---

Prediction in the multivariate case is exactly like prediction in the bivariate regression, except for having multiple independent variables. For a particular prediction, you simply insert the values of the independent variables in the regression equation and find the corresponding value of the dependent variable. Using the income-expenditure–household size problem, suppose you wanted to estimate the expenditures for a family of three with an income of $12,000. The point estimate is

$$\bar{Y}_{X_1 X_2} = -495 + .8114(12,000) + 626(3) = \$11,120$$

How confident are you in this estimate? Again you have the problem of whether you are attempting to predict the *average* expenditures for *all* families of size 3 with incomes of $12,000 or the expenditures of *a particular* family with these characteristics.

In predicting *mean* values, you've only to concern yourself with uncertainty about the coefficients of the estimated equation. For multiple regression the equation becomes rather complicated. However, an approximation that is relatively good for larger values of n is[1]

$$s^2_{\bar{Y} \cdot X_1 X_2} = \frac{s^2_{Y \cdot X_1 X_2}}{n} = \frac{451{,}162}{20} = 22{,}558$$

If you wanted to construct a 95 percent confidence interval, you'd first look in the t table with 17 degrees of freedom to find that the critical value is 2.11 and then construct the interval

$$\text{Interval estimate} = \bar{Y}_{X_1 X_2} \pm t \sqrt{s^2_{\bar{Y} \cdot X_1 X_2}}$$
$$= 11{,}120 \pm 2.11 \sqrt{22{,}558}$$
$$= 11{,}120 \pm 317$$

You're more confident in this prediction than you would've been in a prediction based on income alone, thanks to the added predictive power in knowing family size in addition to income.

If you're trying to predict family expenditures for *a particular* family, you'd be less confident in your answer because of the added variability around the regression plane in addition to the variability of your estimates of the regression plane. Again, the equation is an approximation to the true equation. The variance of a particular point is

$$s^2_{Y_p \cdot X_1 X_2} = s^2_{\bar{Y} \cdot X_1 X_2} + s^2_{Y \cdot X_1 X_2} = 22{,}558 + 451{,}162 = 473{,}720$$

To construct a 95 percent confidence interval, compute

$$\text{Interval estimate} = \bar{Y}_{X_1 X_2} \pm t \sqrt{s^2_{Y_p \cdot X_1 X_2}}$$
$$= 11{,}120 \pm 2.10 \sqrt{473{,}720}$$
$$= 11{,}120 \pm 1452$$

REVIEW EXERCISES 16.C

1. What is $s^2_{\bar{Y} X_1 X_2}$ called?
2. How does $s^2_{Y_p \cdot X_1 X_2}$ differ from $s^2_{\bar{Y} X_1 X_2}$?
3. What do you use as the degrees of freedom when using the t table for making confidence intervals?

---

[1] Using values computed in Section B

$$s^2_{\bar{Y} \cdot X_1 X_2} = \frac{\text{unexplained variation}}{\text{degrees of freedom}} = \frac{7{,}669{,}749}{17} = 451{,}162$$

Answers 16.C

1. $s^2_{\hat{Y}_{X_1 X_2}}$ is the variance of the estimated regression plane. It reflects uncertainty in the estimates of the regression coefficients.
2. $s^2_{Y_p \cdot X_1 X_2}$ is the variance of predicting a Y value for *particular* values of X_1 and X_2. It contains uncertainty about the parameters of the regression plane $(s^2_{\hat{Y} \cdot X_1 X_2})$ as well as the additional uncertainty concerning variation of points around the regression plane $(s^2_{Y \cdot X_1 X_2})$ and is the sum of the two variances.
3. The degrees of freedom will always be $n - m$, the sample size minus the number of parameters estimated by the regression equation.

Section 16.D

Multiple and Partial Determination and Correlation

Learning objectives

Your learning objectives for this section are to be able to:

1. Calculate and interpret the coefficients of multiple determination and correlation
2. Calculate and interpret the coefficients of partial determination and correlation
3. Explain the concept of stepwise regression

THE COEFFICIENTS OF MULTIPLE DETERMINATION AND CORRELATION

The coefficient of determination r^2 was defined in Module 8 as

$$r^2 = \frac{\text{explained variation}}{\text{total variation}}$$

Its square root r was called the coefficient of correlation.

The ratio of explained to total variation, we said, showed the improvement in predicting ability achieved by using the variable X to predict Y values, rather than using the mean of Y. Another way of saying the same thing is that r^2 is the ratio of the variation *explained* by the variable X to the *unexplained* variation *before* the variable X was introduced; i.e.,

$$r^2 = \frac{\text{variation explained by } X}{\text{unexplained variation before introducing } X}$$

Exactly the same definition applies in multiple regression. Here R^2, the *coefficient of multiple determination*, measures the improvement in predicting ability gained through the use of *all* the independent variables, over the use of the mean of Y. R, the coefficient of multiple correlation, measures the relationship between the independent variables and the dependent variable on a scale ranging from 1 (perfect correlation) to 0 (no correlation). Since different b's could have different signs, R does not have a sign. Thus, introducing appropriate subscripts for a problem with two independent variables,

$$R^2 = \frac{\text{variation explained by } X_1 \text{ and } X_2}{\text{unexplained variation before introducing } X_1 \text{ and } X_2}$$

For the income-expenditure problem, you found earlier that

$$r^2 = \frac{\text{explained by } X_1}{\text{unexplained before } X_1} = \frac{262,923,000}{277,025,500} = .95$$

Upon introducing the additional variable, household size, the coefficient of determination becomes

$$R^2_{Y \cdot X_1 X_2} = \frac{\text{explained by } X_1 \text{ and } X_2}{\text{unexplained before } X_1 \text{ and } X_2} = \frac{269,355,751}{277,025,500} = .97$$

The interpretation of these two measures, r^2 and R^2, is straightforward. The introduction of X_1 into the problem enabled you to explain 95 percent of the original squared error. The introduction of *both* X_1 and X_2 enabled you to explain 97 percent of the original squared error.

Don't jump to the conclusion, though, that the variable X_2 alone would explain only 2 percent of the total variation. In fact, if X_1 were excluded completely and you used X_2 alone to estimate Y, you'd find that X_2 (household size) would explain 34 percent of the original squared error.

How could X_1 by itself explain 95 percent, X_2 by itself explain 34 percent, and X_1 and X_2 together explain 97 percent? The answer lies in the relationship *between* X_1 and X_2. The separate r^2 values add to the multiple R^2 value only if the independent variables are completely independent. In this problem, though, there is a fairly strong correlation between the variables X_1 (income) and X_2 (household size), so adding the second variable didn't improve the overall predicting ability a great deal. The problem of correlation between independent variables is known as *multicol-*

linearity. While this subject won't be developed further here, you should be aware that its existence poses problems both in the calculation and interpretation of multiple regression measures.

THE COEFFICIENTS OF PARTIAL DETERMINATION AND CORRELATION

You'll remember that in the multiple regression equation

$$\overline{Y}_{X_1 X_2} = a + b_1 X_1 + b_2 X_2$$

the coefficient b_2, for example, showed the change in Y per unit change in X_2 when X_1 was *held constant.* Using squared errors, it is possible to develop an analogous measure to show how much of the variation in the dependent variable is explained by any particular independent variable when all the other independent variables are *held constant.* Such a measure is called a *coefficient of partial determination.* Its square root, with the sign of the corresponding regression coefficient, is called a *coefficient of partial correlation.*

The coefficient of partial determination is obtained exactly like other coefficients of determination. For two independent variables, for example, the coefficient of partial determination for X_2 is found by comparing the variation *explained by the addition of X_2* with the *unexplained variation before the addition of X_2.* Thus,

$$r^2_{YX_2 \cdot X_1} = \frac{\text{variation explained by addition of } X_2}{\text{unexplained variation before addition of } X_2}$$

The subscripts in the expression $r^2_{YX_2 \cdot X_1}$ indicate the coefficient of partial determination between Y and X_2 when X_1 is held constant.

For the income-expenditure–household size problem we calculated

$$\text{Variation explained by } X_1 = 262{,}923{,}000$$
$$\text{Variation explained by } X_1 \text{ and } X_2 = 269{,}355{,}751$$

The difference between these values, 6,432,751, must then be the variation explained by the *addition* of X_2.

The unexplained variation before the introduction of X_2 is the unexplained variation remaining *after* the use of X_1, namely 14,102,500. Therefore,

$$r^2_{YX_2 \cdot X_1} = \frac{\text{variation explained by addition of } X_2}{\text{unexplained variation before addition of } X_2} = \frac{6{,}432{,}751}{14{,}102{,}500} = .46$$

Thus, while the variable "household size" X_2 explained 34 percent of the variation in expenditures Y when income X_1 was *ignored*, it explains 46 percent of the variation in expenditure when income is *held constant*. This is equivalent to saying that "household size" would explain 46 percent of the variation in expenditures for a population in which all families had the same income. In the social sciences it is very difficult, if not impossible, to hold some variables constant *physically* while studying the interrelationships of others. The use of partial coefficients enables you to hold variables constant *statistically* while studying the interaction of other variables.

STEPWISE REGRESSION

Stepwise regression is often used as an exploratory procedure in business research. If you wanted to develop a multiple regression to predict some variable, you'd want to include the most relevant independent variables. In stepwise regression, a likely single independent variable is related to the dependent variable through a regression equation. Then other independent variables are added, one at a time. If their partial coefficients or t tests show that they make a significant contribution, they're kept in the equation; if not, they're dropped and new independent variables are tested.

To illustrate this procedure, consider the income-expenditure–size problem once more. Let's say that the first variable you tested was income, and you found

$$\bar{Y}_{X_1} = 325 + .883X_1$$

where Y = expenditures
   X_1 = income

Upon testing for significance, you find that for the variable X_1

$$r^2_{YX_1} = .95 \quad \text{and} \quad t_{X_1} = 18.32$$

These both indicate that the variable X_1 is very useful in predicting Y. Now you might add variable X_2 (household size). When you do, you get

$$\bar{Y}_{X_1X_2} = -495 + .8114X_1 + 626X_2$$
$$r^2_{YX_2 \cdot X_1} = .46 \quad t_{X_2} = 3.78$$

Since r^2 is fairly large and t is still significant at the .05 level, you could keep household size in the equation (even though the multiple R^2 of .97 is not much larger than the bivariate r^2 of .95). Now you could add other variables, such as savings or miles driven to work, one at a time, to see if they were worth incorporating in the model.

Sooner or later, the gain in predicting ability will no longer equal the cost of collecting and processing the new variable, and you'd terminate the process. While for most purposes little is to be gained by using more than 10 or so independent variables, in some business applications up to 40 or 50 independent variables have been included in a regression equation.

REVIEW EXERCISES 16.D

1. Match the following:

a. $\bar{Y}_{X_1X_2}$

(1) $\dfrac{\text{Variation explained by } X_1}{\text{Unexplained variation before } X_1}$

b. $r^2_{YX_2 \cdot X_1}$

(2) $\dfrac{\text{Variation explained by addition of } X_2}{\text{Unexplained variation before addition of } X_2}$

c. $R^2_{Y \cdot X_1X_2}$

(3) $a + b_1X_1 + b_2X_2$

d. $r^2_{YX_1}$

(4) $\dfrac{\text{Variation explained by } X_1 \text{ and } X_2}{\text{Unexplained variation before } X_1 \text{ and } X_2}$

(5) Coefficient of partial determination for X_2, holding X_1 constant

(6) Coefficient of multiple determination for X_1 and X_2

2. In stepwise regression:
   a. Variables are added one at a time.
   b. Variables are kept in the regression equation only if they prove to be significant.
   c. You'd keep adding significant variables as long as you could find them.
   d. All the above.

Answers 16.D

1. a. 3; *b.* 2, 5; *c.* 4, 6; *d.* 1   *2. a* and *b*

Questions and Problems

16.1. Refer to Prob. 8.2, which involves the relationship between noise at a work station and the time required to perform a task. After analyzing the problem in the original context, you discover that you haven't accounted for the *experience* of the individuals. Even though they could all perform the task equally well, a person with more experience might be less distracted by noise. You revise your data set to include years on the job:

Noise X_1, decibels	Time Y, min	Experience X_2, years on the job	Noise X_1, decibels	Time Y, min	Experience X_2, years on the job
0	11.5	4	0	9.5	7
20	12.5	3	20	13.0	2
40	14.0	11	40	16.0	8
60	20.0	5	60	19.5	7
80	28.5	8	80	27.5	10

   a. Solve for the *bivariate* regression equation with noise as the independent variable and calculate the total variation and the explained variation. (You may already have done some of this work in Prob. 8.2.)

b. Solve for the *multiple* regression equation with both noise and experience as independent variables.

c. Make a *t* test to see if the addition of the second independent variable, experience, was significant. Use a 5 percent level of significance.

d. Find the coefficient of multiple determination and the coefficients of partial correlation for the variables X_1 and X_2. Explain the meaning of these statistics.

e. Make an interval estimate for the time required by a supervisor with 8 years experience who was placed in a work situation with 35 decibels of noise, using a 95 percent confidence coefficient.

16.2.   In Prob. 8.4 you made estimates of the number of servings at any one meal, based on the number of people attending conferences. You now believe that the weather during the conference also affects the number of meals served. You knew the weather during the past conferences, and added this information to your previous data, measuring weather on a 5-point scale from 1 (very bad) to 5 (excellent).

Registrants X_1	Maximum servings at any one meal Y	Weather X_2	Registrants X_1	Maximum servings at any one meal Y	Weather X_2
289	235	3	358	275	4
339	315	2	160	158	3
391	355	3	365	345	1
479	399	2	319	305	2
482	475	1	561	522	1
500	441	2	331	225	5

a. Solve for the multiple regression equation with registrants and weather as independent variables.

b. Make an interval estimate using a 90 percent confidence coefficient for the maximum number of servings on the average, when there is excellent weather (5) during a conference with 173 people.

c. Make an interval estimate for the maximum number of servings at a *particular* meal for the same conference as in part b, also with a 90 percent confidence coefficient.

d. Explain the difference between the two interval estimates in parts b and c.

16.3.   In Prob. 8.5 a bank studied the relationship between customer's perceptions of their services and customer's income. Now they decide to include level of education in the analysis, since that question was also solicited on the questionnaire. The data are:

Annual income X_1	Appeal score Y	Education X_2, years	Annual income X_1	Appeal score Y	Education X_2, years
$14,700	2	12	$15,300	6	12
15,300	4	13	13,300	5	15
16,500	6	16	21,400	9	17
19,900	7	15	17,900	1	12
18,400	9	14	15,300	4	14
8,300	8	16	18,300	9	16
16,900	4	15	16,100	4	13
9,600	1	12			

a. Calculate the multiple regression equation for predicting appeal on the basis of income and education.

b. Calculate the coefficient of multiple determination and explain its meaning.

c. Find the coefficients of partial determination for each of the two independent variables and explain their meaning.

d. Make a point estimate of the bank's appeal to persons with 14 years of education and incomes of $17,000.

16.4. In addition to using a wholesaler's regional forecast to predict toy sales, as in Prob. 8.6, you decide to include the money spent on promotion by your store as well. The data are then:

Regional forecast X_1, thousands	Store sales Y, thousands	Store promotion X_2	Regional forecast X_1, thousands	Store sales Y, thousands	Store promotion X_2
$2940	$144	$4280	$3050	$235	$6710
2970	175	4700	2980	166	5890
3000	200	6010	2880	114	3620
3040	220	5700	2980	196	3770
3040	246	4930	2960	190	4950

a. Fit two separate bivariate regression lines, one with the regional forecast as the independent variable and the other with store promotion as the independent variable.

b. Using the two equations above, make appropriate t tests to determine which of the independent variables contributes most in predicting store sales.

c. Find the multiple regression equation and test to see if the second (least important) independent variable contributes significantly to the equation's explanatory power.

d. Compute the coefficients of multiple determination and correlation for the multivariate equation.

e. Make an interval estimate, with a 90 percent confidence coefficient, for next year's sales if the regional forecast is 3.1 million dollars and the advertising budget is $6000.

In the following problems, related to Probs. 8.7 to 8.12, you won't be able to compute residual errors directly because the original data points are not provided. However, the following formulas can be used to calculate partial and multiple correlation coefficients from simple bivariate coefficients:

$$r_{X_1Y} = \frac{n\sum X_1Y - \sum X_1 \sum Y}{\sqrt{[n\sum X_1^2 - (\sum X_1)^2][n\sum Y^2 - (\sum Y)^2]}}$$

= simple correlation coefficient

$$r_{X_2Y \cdot X_1} = \frac{r_{X_2Y} - r_{X_1Y}r_{X_1X_2}}{\sqrt{1 - r_{X_1Y}^2}\sqrt{1 - r_{X_1X_2}^2}}$$

= partial correlation coefficient (between X_2 and Y, holding X_1 constant)

$$R_{Y \cdot X_1X_2}^2 = \frac{r_{X_1Y}^2 + r_{X_2Y}^2 - 2r_{X_1Y}r_{X_2Y}r_{X_1X_2}}{1 - r_{X_1X_2}^2}$$

= coefficient of multiple determination

16.5. In evaluating a firm's training program, you're interested in the relationship between a measure of work performance on a 9 point scale Y, the length of the employee's training program in months X_1, and the employee's age X_2. The following data are generated from a simple random sample of 20 employees:

$$\sum X_1 = 191 \qquad \sum X_1^2 = 2107$$
$$\sum X_2 = 719 \qquad \sum X_2^2 = 26{,}020$$
$$\sum Y = 94 \qquad \sum Y^2 = 530$$
$$\sum X_1 X_2 = 6912 \qquad \sum X_1 Y = 1026$$
$$n = 20 \qquad \sum X_2 Y = 3392$$

a. Calculate the multiple regression equation for estimating work performance through knowledge of an employee's training and age.
b. Calculate and interpret the coefficients of partial determination $r^2_{X_2 Y \cdot X_1}$ and $r^2_{X_1 Y \cdot X_2}$.
c. Compute and interpret the value of the coefficient of determination.
d. Make a point estimate of the work performance rating of an employee who was 30 years old and had 12 months of training.

16.6. You are interested in forecasting sod sales for a local nursery. During the growing months, the yards of newly built houses are usually ready to sod about 4 months after the issuance of a building permit. Further, you know that many people who have recently moved to town and bought older houses have had their yards sodded within 2 months of their move. You gather data from a random sample of past jobs you have done and obtain the following statistics, where Y is sod sales in thousands of dollars, X_1 is the number of building permits 4 months earlier, and X_2 is the number of new residents 2 months earlier.

$$\sum X_1 = 4762 \qquad \sum X_1^2 = 394{,}909$$
$$\sum X_2 = 9096 \qquad \sum X_2^2 = 1{,}431{,}789$$
$$\sum Y = 242 \qquad \sum Y^2 = 1058$$
$$\sum X_1 X_2 = 726{,}391 \qquad \sum X_1 Y = 20{,}094$$
$$n = 60 \qquad \sum X_2 Y = 37{,}613$$

a. Find the multiple regression equation for estimating sod sales on the basis of building permits and new residents.
b. Calculate a measure which shows how much better you can predict, on the average, through the use of the regression equation than using the mean of past sales.
c. Calculate and interpret measures which show the relative importance of the two independent variables.

16.7. The large company for which you work has had increasing sales but declining profitability. You feel that the employee overhead required to coordinate a larger company may more than offset increasing sales, so you gather sample data on profitability as a percent of sales Y, sales in tens of thousands of dollars X_1, and the number of employees X_2. These data are summarized below:

$$\sum X_1 = 5{,}024{,}269 \qquad \sum X_1^2 = 1{,}270{,}580{,}000{,}000$$
$$\sum X_2 = 63{,}190 \qquad \sum X_2^2 = 207{,}280{,}300$$
$$\sum Y = 233 \qquad \sum Y^2 = 2853$$
$$\sum X_1 X_2 = 16{,}043{,}500{,}000 \qquad \sum X_1 Y = 57{,}989{,}330$$
$$n = 20 \qquad \sum X_2 Y = 707{,}480$$

a. Compute the multiple regression equation for estimating profitability from sales and number of employees.

b. Interpret the meaning of the coefficients of net regression, b_1 and b_2, in the context of this problem.

c. What would be the effect on profitability if yearly sales of 280 million dollars could be generated with 3200 employees?

d. Calculate and interpret the coefficient of correlation and the two coefficients of partial correlation.

16.8. You're studying the relationships between insurance salespersons' sales per year in tens of thousands of dollars Y, their years of experience X_2, and their scores on a test which measures sales ability X_1. You obtain the following information from a simple random sample of 80 salespersons:

$$\sum X_1 = 5662 \qquad \sum X_1^2 = 406{,}472$$
$$\sum X_2 = 569 \qquad \sum X_2^2 = 4329$$
$$\sum Y = 4044 \qquad \sum Y^2 = 242{,}344$$
$$\sum X_1 X_2 = 40{,}499 \qquad \sum X_1 Y = 290{,}701$$
$$n = 90 \qquad \sum X_2 Y = 30{,}679$$

a. Calculate the multiple regression equation for estimating sales based on the test score and years of experience.

b. Calculate the coefficients of partial determination and explain their meaning.

c. Make a point estimate of the sales generated by a person who had 4 years of experience and scored 85 on the test.

d. Compute the coefficient of multiple correlation and explain its meaning.

16.9. Data from a random sample of 100 student jobs at a computer center were analyzed with respect to the actual running time Y, the running time estimated by the student X_1, and the core storage requested by the student X_2. Statistics summarizing these data are

$$\sum X_1 = 7109 \qquad \sum X_1^2 = 517{,}314$$
$$\sum X_2 = 15{,}191 \qquad \sum X_2^2 = 2{,}344{,}739$$
$$\sum Y = 3060 \qquad \sum Y^2 = 99{,}529$$
$$\sum X_1 X_2 = 1{,}090{,}530 \qquad \sum X_1 Y = 222{,}562$$
$$n = 100 \qquad \sum X_2 Y = 463{,}587$$

a. Calculate (1) the bivariate regression equation for predicting actual running time based on estimated running time and (2) the associated coefficient of correlation.

b. Calculate (1) the bivariate regression equation for predicting actual running time based on the requested core storage and (2) the associated coefficient of correlation.

c. Calculate (1) the multiple regression equation using all three variables, with actual running time as the dependent variable, and (2) the associated coefficient of multiple regression.

d. Write a paragraph summarizing what you have learned from performing the calculations above.

16.10. An electronics firm studied the relationship between time to failure Y, operating voltage X_1, and room temperature X_2 for a piece of equipment advertised to be completely reliable at any operating voltage between 5 and 50 volts. They tested a simple random sample of 30 pieces of equipment, with the following results:

$$\sum X_1 = 776 \qquad \sum X_1{}^2 = 22{,}421$$
$$\sum X_2 = 2197 \qquad \sum X_2{}^2 = 170{,}562$$
$$\sum Y = 2150 \qquad \sum Y^2 = 173{,}949$$
$$\sum X_1 X_2 = 56{,}722 \qquad \sum X_1 Y = 50{,}496$$
$$n = 30 \qquad \sum X_2 Y = 163{,}006$$

a. Solve for the multiple regression equation with time to failure as the dependent variable.

b. Calculate the coefficients of partial determination, $r^2_{X_1 Y \cdot X_2}$ and $r^2_{X_2 Y \cdot X_1}$, and explain their meaning.

c. How much better can time to failure be predicted through using the multiple regression equation than if only the mean time to failure were used to predict the next failure, disregarding operating voltage and room temperature?

d. Make a point estimate of the time to failure for a piece of equipment operated at 45 volts and 80°F.

16.11. Discuss the relationship between the t test for entering a new variable in the equation and the partial correlation for that variable in terms of explained and unexplained variation.

16.12. In the confidence interval for predicting the conditional mean, we suggested that an approximate formula for the variance of the conditional mean is

$$s^2_{\bar{Y}_{x_1 x_2}} = \frac{s^2_{Y \cdot x_1 x_2}}{n}$$

When would this formula be exact, and why do you suppose it is a good approximation when n is large? *Hint:* It may help to return to the discussion of the exact formula with one independent variable in Sec. 15.C.

MODULE 17
NONPARAMETRIC STATISTICS

Over the past seven modules you've been studying statistical inference. Inferences were made about population parameters based on sample statistics; confidence statements were made about the range within which a population parameter was likely to lie. In order to make these inferences and confidence statements, you had to know the distribution of the population being sampled. Samples were assumed to be taken from a Bernoulli process, for example, or from a normal distribution. In this module you'll learn about applying the concepts of statistical inference using *distribution-free* tests. In these tests, no assumptions need be made about the distribution of the population.

Such tests would be appropriate, for example, where small samples were taken from skewed populations and the sampling distribution of the statistic to be tested would not normalize under the central-limit theorem. Distribution-free tests are also appropriate for ordinal or categorical data, where measurements are ranked according to size or placed in categories, such as occupational classifications.

Inferences based on a knowledge of the distribution of the population are called *parametric tests*, and the process is referred to as *classical statistical inference*. Inferences based on distribution-free methods are called *nonparametric tests*.

General learning objectives

Your general learning objectives for this module are to:

1. Describe the difference in assumptions between the classical tests made in previous modules and the nonparametric tests made in this module
2. Make nonparametric tests on single variables, tests for comparing two samples, and tests of dependence

Section 17.A
An Introduction to Nonparametric Statistics

Learning objectives

Your learning objectives for this section are to be able to:

1. Describe a typical problem where the normal distribution assumption cannot be used and apply the sign test to this problem
2. Use Fisher's rank-randomization test to compare two population measures
3. Contrast parametric tests with nonparametric tests and explain how the distribution-free methods are developed

Suppose a nonquantitative friend came to see you about a statistical problem he had in writing a paper and said, "Here's a list of the ages of 10 students randomly drawn from the population of students on campus. Can you test the hypothesis that the median age of our students is 23 years?" What would you do? Could you help him? Suppose the list of ages he hands you is

$$18, 18, 18, 19, 20, 20, 22, 25, 28, 35$$

A couple of things you might want to do based on your previous knowledge is to compute the mean and the variance of the ages. If you did, you'd find

$$\bar{X} = 22.3 \text{ years} \qquad s^2 = 27.81 \qquad s = 5.27$$

You then tell your friend that, assuming normality, approximately 68 percent of the population of students are between 17 and 27.6 years old (the mean plus or minus 1 standard deviation). He says that's ridiculous because he knows that very few students are under 17, yet you seem to indicate that 16 percent of the students have ages lower than 17. You now see some of the problems in interpreting *skewed* distributions as *normal* distributions. Such interpretations may be misleading or even meaningless.

Suppose your friend reminds you that he's not interested in the mean anyway but in the median. The median of the sample is 20, since half of the students have an age less than or equal to 20 and half have an age greater than or equal to 20. Though the difference between the sample median of 20 and your friend's hypothesized median of 23 seems large, it might be due to sampling error. The hypothesis that the true median is 23 can be tested using the *sign test*.

409

THE SIGN TEST

Assume for the moment that the hypothesis that the median age is 23 is true. Also assume that when we say 23 years, we mean *exactly* 23 years, to the day, hour, and second, and that no one in the population is *exactly* 23 years old in this sense. (The reason for this assumption will be discussed later.) Given these conditions, the probability that you'd draw a person at random from the population whose age was greater than 23 would be .5, as would the probability that any person would be less than 23.

Now go back to the sample data and assign a plus sign to each age above 23, and a minus sign to each age below 23. Your data list would now look like this:

$$18, 18, 18, 19, 20, 20, 22, 25, 28, 35$$
$$- \quad - \quad - \quad - \quad - \quad - \quad - \quad + \quad + \quad +$$

If the hypothesis that the population median is 23 is true, the probability of obtaining the seven minus and three plus signs we got is P_b ($r = 7 \mid 10, .5$) $= .1172$. However, in testing this hypothesis we're not interested in just the obtained result but in the probability of obtaining a result as extreme *or more* extreme than that obtained.[1] From the binomial tables, we find that P_b ($r \geq 7 \mid 10, .5$) $= .1719$. Further, since we're testing to find if the population median is *exactly* 23 (not $\geq$ 23 or $\leq$ 23), results of seven pluses and three minuses would be just as damaging to the hypothesis as seven minuses and three pluses. (Technically, this is called a *two-tailed* test.) Therefore, the required probability to test the hypothesis that the population median is 23, based on the sample outcome we observed, is P_b ($r \leq 3$ or $r \geq 7 \mid 10, .5$) $= .3438$. Since this probability is greater than any level of significance we're likely to use, the hypothesis that the true median's 23 should be accepted.

The test just completed is the *sign test* for the median of a population, and it is a distribution-free method. No assumptions were made about the form of the *population* distribution. In fact, it was the knowledge that the distribution of ages was not normal that made us turn to a distribution-free statistic to test the hypothesis. It should be noted that we *did* know the distribution of the *observation characteristic* and the *test statistic*. In this case the observation characteristic, or the sample observations, were merely pluses and minuses, and the test statistic, used to test the unusualness of the sample, was the binomial distribution.

FISHER'S RANK-RANDOMIZATION TEST

As a second example of a distribution-free statistic, suppose your friend said, "In addition, I have a sample of the ages of 10 students randomly drawn from the

---

[1] You may want to refresh your memory on this point by reviewing Module 11, p. 272.

population of students at another university in our state. These ages are 18, 19, 21, 21, 24, 27, 31, 33, 34, and 37. I'd like to know if the distributions of ages are the same in the two schools. Can you tell me?"

How might you approach this problem? You might compute the significance of the difference between means using the *t* test, but you know this is incorrect since the population is not normal and the sample size is so small that you can't appeal to the central-limit theorem.

Before conducting any test, let's replace each observation in the two sets with a number expressing its rank order in the *total* set of 20 numbers, as if they all came from the same population. If several observations have the same value, each is replaced by the average of their ranks. Thus, the lowest age is 18 and there are four such ages, taking up ranks 1 through 4. The average of 1, 2, 3, and 4 is 2.5, so each age 18 is replaced by rank 2.5. The original age distributions and the new rankings are then as shown in Table 17.1.

Table 17.1

Ages:										
Your school	18	18	18	19	20	20	22	25	28	35
Other school	18	19	21	21	24	27	31	33	34	37

Rank order:										
Your school	2.5	2.5	2.5	5.5	7.5	7.5	11	13	15	19
Other school	2.5	5.5	9.5	9.5	12	14	16	17	18	20

Now, let's use the *difference between mean ranks* as a measure of the differences between the schools. The mean rank for your school is 8.6 and for the other 12.4, making the difference between mean ranks 3.8. The question is whether the difference of 3.8 in mean rank is large enough to say that the age distribution is different between the two schools.

Before making the test, we need to know how many ways the 20 ages in the two samples could have been distributed between the two schools *by chance*. Using the techniques discussed in Module 10, it can be found that there are 184,756 such ways, all equally likely.[1] One of these ways, for example, would be:

Your school	11	12	13	14	15	16	17	18	19	20
Other school	2.5	2.5	2.5	2.5	5.5	5.5	7.5	7.5	9.5	9.5

which produces a difference in average ranks of 10.

The hypothesis of no difference is tested by calculating in how many of the 184,756 possible combinations the difference in mean rank would *by chance* be greater than

---

[1] The combination of 20 things 10 at a time is

$$\frac{N!}{r!(N-r)!} = \frac{20!}{10!(10!)} = 184{,}756$$

3.8, the observed value. (Tedious, but rewarding!) Using a computer, it was found that 29,210 of the possible arrangements have absolute differences in average ranks that are greater than or equal to the observed 3.8. Therefore, the probability of obtaining a value of 3.8 or greater by chance is equal to $29,210/184,756 = .1581$. Testing the hypothesis at, say, a .05 level, you'd accept the null hypothesis that there was no difference between ages in the two schools.

In this problem we didn't make any assumptions about the form of the population distributions. The form of the sample characteristic was the rank order in the set of all possible obtained ages. What about the distribution of the test statistic? Its distribution was based on the *randomization distribution* of all equally likely outcomes under the hypothesis, a very important concept in many distribution-free statistics. We chose an arbitrary statistic which would be sensitive to differences in the two obtained distributions, and in this case we chose one that is particularly sensitive to differences in central tendency. We then computed this statistic for all possible random assignments of the obtained age ranks. We then asked: How unusual is the obtained sample outcome relative to all possible random outcomes? The answer to this question is the p value (or probability value) that is compared with the desired level of significance (α level) to decide whether to accept or reject the hypothesis.

INTERPRETATION AND ADDITIONAL COMMENTS

The two examples used in this section bring out several important points. First, there was no need to make assumptions about the distribution of the population values, and the distributions of the sample characteristic and of the test statistic can be made explicit.

Second, two relatively common problems were presented where it was clear that parametric statistics would be inappropriate because the distributions were clearly not normal. Many researchers would have used parametric statistics anyway, but you now know that alternative methods exist.

Third, two very different procedures for distribution-free statistics have been presented. The first was a procedure based on a known distribution for the observation characteristic. In this case it was the binomial distribution, but many other methods are based on the hypergeometric and other distributions. The second procedure was based on Fisher's method of randomization, where all possible arrangements of the data are obtained and the test statistic computed for each such arrangement. Neither of these procedures relies on assumptions about the population to develop an approximate distribution for the test statistic: they rely only on information from the obtained sample. This is again in contrast to the parametric procedures.

Two major considerations aren't brought out directly by the examples. The first is that the observations must be independent. That is, each succeeding observation does not depend on any of the preceding or following observations. This same assumption is generally also needed for parametric statistics. This requirement is under the control of the experimenter, since the process of drawing observations is specified by the experimenter, who can generally ensure independent observations.

The second new consideration concerns the assumption of a continuous distribution of observations in the population (nothing is said about the form of the distribution, only that it is continuous). From probability theory you know that this means that the probability of a sample's containing equal observations is zero. What do you do when equal observations appear, and why might they occur? Equal observations might occur because of imprecise measuring instruments. For example, when we asked for ages we rounded to the nearest year, but if we had included months, days, hours, etc., we'd have arrived at a continuous distribution with a very small probability of any two ages matching. In the second example, where ages were ranked, we handled this problem by assigning an average rank to each matching observation. This is the procedure generally used, but it does lend a bias to the results. While we used the combinatorial formula and computed exactly the number of arrangements that exceeded the difference of 3.8, it's possible to use tables that have precomputed significance levels for various possible outcomes or the possible outcomes necessary for certain significance levels. These tables are constructed on the assumption that there aren't any tied observations, and using them with tied observations will produce slightly incorrect results.

In the first example (the sign test), what would you have done if some of the observations equaled the hypothesized median of 23? Again, this is an impossible situation under the assumption of continuity. Bradley recommends two ways of handling this problem.[1] (1) Drop any observations that equal the median and work the test with the reduced sample size. While this procedure is technically correct, it does reduce the power of the test to reject a false hypothesis because of the reduced sample size. (2) Assign the ties first in such a way as to maximize the possibility of rejecting the hypothesis and second in such a way as to minimize this possibility. You then have two significance levels and can report that

$$p_{min} \leq P_h \leq p_{max}$$

or that the probability of rejecting a true hypothesis lies between these two values. If both values lie below the required level of significance, you won't reject the hypothesis, and if both are above the required level of significance you will reject the hypothesis. If the required level of significance lies between these maximum and minimum values, the test is inconclusive.

EXAMPLE

Suppose the sampled ages were

$$18, 19, 21, 23, 23, 25, 26, 27, 29, 33$$

and the hypothesis is still that the median age is 23. You now have two values of 23 and have to decide what to do with them when signs are assigned to the data. The

---

[1] James V. Bradley, *Distribution Free Statistical Tests*, Prentice-Hall, Englewood Cliffs, N.J., 1968.

413

first way would be to assign them minus signs and the second to assign them plus signs. The results using the first method are

The probability of obtaining exactly five plus signs and five minus signs under the hypothesis that the probability of a plus or a minus is .5 is .2461. Assigning the probability of exactly .5 equally to both tails means that the probability of obtaining a result of five or more pluses or five or fewer pluses is 1.0. For the second method, the results would be

$$- - - + + + + + + +$$

The probability of obtaining this pattern of observations is .1172, and the probability of obtaining a pattern as unusual or more unusual than this is .3438. Since both these values lie above a significance level of .05, you wouldn't reject the null hypothesis.

REVIEW EXERCISES 17.A

1. Why was a classical hypothesis test not appropriate for the distribution of ages in a college?
2. True or false: In Fisher's rank-randomization test:
   a. You must consider all possible sample outcomes from the population.
   b. The significance test would have been the same whether ranks or the original data had been used.
   c. Using the difference between mean ranks as the test statistic made it no different from the normal parametric test.
3. In both the sign test and the rank-randomization test, it was assumed that the population was continuous: true or false?
4. In handling observations equal to the hypothesized median using the sign test, the most conservative procedure (the one making rejection the most difficult) is a sound procedure: true or false?

Answers 17.A

1. The distribution was not normal.
2. a. False; you considered all possible combinations of the obtained sample but did not consider other sample values that might have been obtained.
   b. False; using raw data would have given extreme values more weight in the analysis and could have changed the results.
   c. False; using mean rank differences was merely an indicator of central tendency. Any characteristic could have been used that would be sensitive to differences in central tendency.
3. true
4. True; the procedure discussed in the book is to assign values equal to the hypothesized median both plus and minus signs, compute the significance both ways, and determine

the range of significance. This conservative approach is good because you generally want to have strong evidence against a hypothesis before you reject it, and if it can be rejected by using a conservative procedure, you'll have more subjective confidence in the rejection.

Section 17.B
Tests on Single Variables

Learning objectives

Your learning objectives for this section are to be able to:

1. Describe the general distribution-free tests available for testing distributions of single variables
2. Utilize two tests for comparing a single distribution to a hypothesized distribution: the chi-square (χ^2) test, and the Kolmogorov-Smirnov test

---

There are three major kinds of tests that can be performed when a single measure has been obtained. These are tests for location or central tendency, tests for dispersion, and tests for goodness of fit to a hypothesized distribution. We'll discuss only the first and last of these because there is little general interest in tests for dispersion.

SIGN TEST OF LOCATION

The location parameter referred to in most distribution-free tests is the median, for which the appropriate test is the sign test discussed in the previous section. In the sign test, each observation is coded according to whether it falls above or below the hypothesized median, and the binomial probability of obtaining such an arrangement or a more extreme arrangement is computed. This probability can then be used to judge the significance of the results obtained.

The rationale for this test can be extended to percentiles other than the median (which is the fiftieth percentile). You could test the hypothesis that the twenty-fifth percentile (first quartile) was some particular value and code all observations falling below the hypothesized value as minus and all observations above as plus. The logic of the test would be the same as for the median, except that the probability of a minus would be .25 and the probability of a plus .75. The likelihood of the observed values or more extreme results could be computed and compared to the level of significance. This test could be constructed as either a one- or a two-tailed test.

415

THE CHI-SQUARE (χ^2) TEST

Suppose you're the personnel director in the regional offices of a large food chain. You receive a directive from corporate headquarters requesting a progress report on the implementation of the company's equal opportunity program. One of the goals of the program is to have the same proportion of supervisory personnel by racial group as there is in the population of the region. To check your progress, you tabulate census statistics on the percentage by racial group in the population and compare these with a random sample of 500 supervisory employees in the region. The statistics are given in Table 17.2.

Table 17.2

Racial group	Obtained in sample		Population	
	Number	%	Expected number	%
White	395	79	300	60
Chicano	50	10	100	20
Black	40	8	50	10
Indian	5	1	25	5
Other	10	2	25	5
	500	100	500	100

The numbers in the Expected number column were obtained by multiplying the sample size by the population percentages, so they represent the numbers you'd theoretically expect in 500 employees if the equal opportunity goal were met.

The question you want to answer is whether there is a significant difference between the theoretical and the observed frequencies, and the null hypothesis is that there is no significant difference.

The probability of obtaining this particular sample outcome *by chance*, if there were in fact the same proportion of supervisors by racial group in your stores as people in the general population, is the multinomial probability

$$\frac{500!}{(395!)(50!)(40!)(5!)(10!)} (.60^{395})(.20^{50})(.10^{40})(.05^{5})(.05^{10})$$

This would be hard enough to calculate, but what's really needed isn't just this probability, but this probability plus those of any samples more extreme than this! Fortunately, a distribution known as *chi-square* (χ^2) can be used as a test of significance in cases like these, where theoretical and observed frequencies are being compared. The *chi-square* statistic is

$$\chi^2 = \sum \frac{(O - E)^2}{E}$$

where O = observed (sample) frequencies
E = expected (theoretical) frequencies

416

For this problem, then,

$$\chi^2 = \frac{(395 - 300)^2}{300} + \cdots + \frac{(10 - 25)^2}{25} = 82.08$$

One of the parameters for the χ^2 distribution is the number of degrees of freedom, which for this kind of problem is 1 less than the number of *categories*, in this case 4. To test this value against a level of significance, turn to the χ^2 table, Appendix Table A.4.

From the table, you find that χ^2 for 4 degrees of freedom is 13.277 at the .01 level of significance and 18.465 at the .001 level. Since your value is much larger than these, the observed difference is highly unlikely to have occurred by chance, and *the null hypothesis should be rejected.* Now all you have to do is tell headquarters the bad news and prepare yourself for their reaction.

Note the similarity between this test and the sign test you learned earlier. In both you used a probability distribution for the obtained results based on some hypothesized probabilities. In the sign test you used the binomial probability distribution and in this test you used the multinomial distribution. Since the multinomial distribution is burdensome to compute (especially where you want to compute the probability of more extreme results) you used a χ^2 distribution *as an approximation* to the multinomial. The exact derivation of the χ^2 approximation is not important for our purposes, but it's important for you to understand how to use the χ^2 table in order to test hypotheses about the fit of an obtained distribution to a hypothetical distribution.

One major point you should note is how large the sample size should be in order to use the χ^2 test. While there is little agreement on this point, a generally accepted rule of thumb is that the expected frequency in any cell should be at least 5. For our example the expected percentage for the "Indian" category was 5 percent, so in order to arrive at an expected frequency of 5, the sample size would have to be 100. Our actual sample of 500 was then sufficient for the test to be valid.

The χ^2 test is particularly valuable when used with *nominal* data, as in our example, where there is categorical classification with no implied order. The χ^2 test is often used to compare interval data as well, particularly in comparing sample observations with theoretical probability distributions. A much better test for this sort of data is the Kolmogorov-Smirnov test, which follows.

KOLMOGOROV-SMIRNOV TEST FOR GOODNESS OF FIT

Continuing the personnel manager game, suppose you're interested in comparing your region with the national statistics for your company concerning the age of employees when they are first hired. You take a random sample of 200 employees in your region and compare the results with the national statistics in Table 17.3.

The rationale for the Kolmogorov-Smirnov test is complicated, but its application is easy. The only necessary statistic is the maximum deviation between the actual

Table 17.3 / Data for Kolmogorov-Smirnov test, sample data vs. national

Age category	Actual (sample)			National (expected)			Actual − national
	No.	%	Cumulative proportion	No.	%	Cumulative proportion	Difference, cumulative proportion
18–20	116	58	.58	84	42	.42	.16
21–23	52	26	.84	62	31	.73	.11
24–26	28	14	.98	34	17	.90	.08
27–29	2	1	.99	12	6	.96	.03
30–32	2	1	1.00	8	4	1.00	.00
	200	100		200	100		

and expected cumulative proportions. For the problem being considered, the maximum deviation is .16, which occurs in the first age category. To test for significance, you must use the Kolmogorov-Smirnov table, Appendix Table A.6. At a .05 level of significance, the critical value of D (the maximum deviation) is $1.36/\sqrt{N}$, where N is the sample size. Since the maximum deviation of .16 is greater than the critical value of .096, you'd reject the hypothesis of equal expected and actual distributions and conclude that the entry age distribution in your region was different from the national distribution.

You'd have come to this same conclusion if you'd applied the χ^2 test to this problem. However, the Kolmogorov-Smirnov test is much easier to apply and is a more powerful test (more likely to reject a false hypothesis) than the χ^2 test.

As a second example of the use of the Kolmogorov-Smirnov test, consider the hypothesis that the entry age distribution obtained from the sample of 200 came from a *normally distributed* population, rather than conforming to the national distribution.

The normal distribution to which you compare the observed values should have the same mean and standard deviation as the observed values, so your first step is to calculate those measures.[1] You'd find that

$$\bar{X} = 20.83 \quad \text{and} \quad s_X = 2.5062$$

A normal distribution is fitted to these statistics by calculating the left-tail probabilities of the normal distribution from minus infinity to the *upper limit of each age category*. Since the data are discrete, you have to split the difference at the boundaries of the classes, making the successive upper limits 20.5, 23.5, etc. Then, by calculating the difference between each of these limits and the mean of 20.83 and dividing this difference by the standard deviation of 2.5062, you can find z, the number of standard deviations each upper limit is from the mean. You can then use the normal tables to

---

[1] You'd apply the grouped data formulas developed in Module 3 to calculate these measures.

Table 17.4 / Application of Kolmogorov-Smirnov test for goodness of fit to a normal distribution

Age category	Upper limit	Deviation, upper limit − mean	Deviation Standard deviation z	Cumulative normal probability $-\infty$ to z	Cumulative probability actual data	Difference, cumulative actual − cumulative normal
18–20	20.5	−.33	−.13	.4483	.58	.1317
21–23	23.5	+2.67	+1.07	.8577	.84	−.0177
24–26	26.5	+5.67	+2.26	.9881	.98	−.0081
27–29	29.5	+8.67	+3.46	.9997	.99	−.0097
30–32	32.5	+11.67	+4.66	1.0000	1.00	.0000

find successive left-tail cumulative probabilities. These calculations are summarized in Table 17.4, together with the calculation of the maximum deviation.

Using the Kolmogorov-Smirnov table as in the previous test, you compare the maximum deviation of .1317 with the critical value of D (again $1.36/\sqrt{N} = .096$). The test indicates that the hypothesis that the sample age distribution came from a normal population should be rejected.

REVIEW EXERCISES 17.B

1. The sign test can only be used to test the median: true or false?
2. The basic distribution of the sign test is the hypergeometric: true or false?
3. In the χ^2 test for goodness of fit, the χ^2 distribution is used only as an approximation to a cumulative multinomial probability, which is the distribution of the observation characteristic: true or false?
4. In the Kolmogorov-Smirnov test, the test statistic is the smallest deviation between the expected and actual cumulative distributions: true or false?
5. Use the χ^2 test to decide if a certain magazine is purchased equally by men and women, based on a sample of 100, in which 60 purchasers were men and 40 were women. Test at a .05 level of significance.
6. A national survey shows that of families owning cars, 80 percent have one car, 15 percent have two, and 5 percent have three. You take a random sample of 50 families in your community and find that 36 own one car, 8 own two, and 6 own three. Test the hypothesis that car ownership in your community is not significantly different from the national ownership. Use the Kolmogorov-Smirnov test, with a .05 level of significance.

Answers 17.B

1. False; it can be used to test any percentile.
2. False; it is the binomial.
3. true
4. False; the test statistic is the maximum deviation between the expected and actual cumulative distributions.

5.

	Observed		Theoretical	
	No.	%	No.	%
Men	60	60	50	50
Women	40	40	50	50
	100	100	100	100

$$\chi^2 = \sum \frac{(O - E)^2}{E}$$

$$= \frac{10^2}{50} + \frac{10^2}{50} = 4$$

For 1 degree of freedom, .05 significance level, $\chi^2 = 3.841$. Therefore the magazine is not purchased equally by men and women.

6.

No. of cars	Observed		Cumulative probability	Theoretical	Cumulative probability	Difference cumulative
	No.	%		%		
1	36	72	.72	80	.80	.08
2	8	16	.88	15	.95	.07
3	6	12	1.00	5	1.00	.00
	50	100		100		

Maximum difference $= .08$ critical value of $D = \dfrac{1.36}{\sqrt{N}} = .192$

Community ownership is not significantly different from the national standard.

Section 17.C

Tests Comparing Two Samples

Learning objectives

Your learning objectives for this section are to be able to:

1. Differentiate between matched and independent samples
2. Use two tests for comparing the location of matched samples, the sign test and the Wilcoxon test
3. Use two tests for comparing the location of independent samples, the Mann-Whitney U test, and the Westenberg-Mood test

Three kinds of tests can be made which involve data from two samples, comparisons of location or central tendency, comparisons of dispersion, and comparisons of the dependence between the variables. This section will focus on comparisons of location, while tests of dependence will be discussed in the next section. Comparisons of dispersion again won't be considered because of their limited application.[1]

In comparing two variables, the method of collecting the data must be considered. As in the single-variable case, sampling is considered to be random. However, it is possible to collect *independent* samples from two different populations, and it is also possible to collect what are called *matched* samples. This last case typically occurs when subjects are randomly assigned to two different experimental treatments but are matched on other characteristics (like age, sex, etc.), where the purpose is to determine whether there is any difference in experimental treatments.

Sign test on equal location—matched samples. Suppose you ran an experiment where matched pairs of subjects were randomly assigned to an experimental and a control group. This could be done by selecting families and asking them a series of questions. Some of the questions, such as family income, size of family, etc., are used for matching purposes, while another relates to the standard brand of household detergent used. All the families are given an unmarked box of detergent which they

---

[1] Combinations of tests can be made which employ a comparison of dispersion. For example, if two distributions are known to have the same location, then a test comparing the goodness of fit of the distributions to each other becomes in fact a comparison of dispersion.

are asked to use and evaluate (it is supposedly a new brand). However, half of the matched sample is just given their regular detergent in the unmarked box, while the other half is really given a new detergent. At the end of the experiment, all are asked to evaluate the detergent relative to their regular brand, on a 7-point scale going from much worse to much better. Suppose 20 families participated in the experiment, and their responses at the end of the experiment were as shown in Table 17.5. Is there a significant difference between the responses of those who actually were using their old brand and those using the new brand?

Consider the hypothesis that the two distributions are equal. Then each response is a random draw from the distributions and, for example, the scores of 5 and 3 for the first pair of subjects could just as easily have been 3 and 5. Now list the signs of the differences between the paired responses. The list below is calculated by taking new brand — old brand, but it wouldn't matter if old brand — new brand were used instead:

$$+ \; + \; - \; - \; + \; + \; - \; - \; + \; +$$

Under the hypothesis that these are random draws from equal distributions, plus and minus signs have equal probability. Therefore you can again use the binomial probability distribution to test the hypothesis that the obtained number of plus signs arose by chance. In this case, the probability of a result as extreme or more extreme than the one obtained is

$$P_b \, (r \geq 6 \text{ or } \leq 4 \mid 10, .5) = .7540$$

and at any ordinarily used level of significance, you can't reject the hypothesis of equal distributions. You'd then conclude that the families judged the new brand to be no different from their old brand.

For this test, the actual hypothesis being tested is that the difference score distribution has a median of zero. This will occur if the distributions are equal for the two test situations or if they are symmetric and have equal medians. Thus, it would be possible to have two distributions with the same median, but because of different shapes, the median of the difference score distribution won't be zero and the hypothesis would be rejected. Therefore, the alternative hypothesis in this case is that there is

Table 17.5

Matched pair no.	New-brand response	Old-brand response	Matched pair no.	New-brand response	Old-brand response
1	5	3	6	6	1
2	7	2	7	3	4
3	5	6	8	1	3
4	3	5	9	6	2
5	4	3	10	7	6

some difference in the distributions. If you can assume equal shapes, or symmetry, the test becomes a test of the equality of the medians of the individual distributions.

In this example, it would probably have been better to test the *one-tailed* hypothesis that the new brand was not *better* than the old. Calculating the upper-tail probability $P_b (r \geq 6 \mid 10, .5) = .3770$, you'd conclude that the signs could have been assigned by chance and that the new brand was not judged to be better than the old.

Wilcoxon test on equal location—matched samples. One of the problems with the sign test used above is that it doesn't consider the *magnitude* of the differences in paired samples and so ignores some useful information. The Wilcoxon test considers both the sign and the magnitude of the differences.

To calculate the statistics used in the Wilcoxon test, first list the sign and magnitude of the paired differences, then convert the *absolute* differences (disregarding signs) to rank order, and then append the sign of the original differences to the rank order. For the soap-test example, the calculations are:

Paired difference	+2	+5	−1	−2	+1	+5	−1	−2	+4	+1
Rank order	6	9.5	2.5	6	2.5	9.5	2.5	6	8	2.5
Signed rank	6	9.5	−2.5	−6	2.5	9.5	−2.5	−6	8	2.5

In applying the Wilcoxon test, the above difference between responses is considered as fixed, but the sign of the differences, under the hypothesis that chance alone was operating, is considered to be randomly assigned. Therefore only sample results are used, and no assumptions are made about the population distribution.

The next step in the test is to calculate *all* possible ways that signs could be assigned to each of the ranked differences. (This concept of randomization was applied in Fisher's rank-randomization test in Sec. 17.A.) There are 2^n such possible arrangements, all equally likely, making $2^{10} = 1024$ for the soap problem.

For each of these possible arrangements it is possible to calculate some statistic that reflects differences between the original ranked observations. The Wilcoxon test uses the *mean of the signed rank differences* as the appropriate measure. For the soap problem, this mean is

$$\frac{6 + 9.5 - 2.5 - 6 + 2.5 + 9.5 - 2.5 - 6 + 8 + 2.5}{10} = \frac{21}{10} = 2.10$$

The test could now be made (the hard way) by calculating all possible assignments of signs to the rankings, calculating the mean signed ranked difference for each, and then finding what proportion of all of these ways produced means as large or larger than the one observed. Fortunately, a table for the Wilcoxon test, Appendix Table A.7, is available. Entering this table with the sample size of 10 paired differences, we find that the observed mean rank difference must be greater than 3.9 to be significant at the .05 level. It can be seen that the hypothesis of equal distributions cannot be rejected at that level of significance because our mean difference is only 2.10. Again, it appears that families can't distinguish between the new brand of soap and their old brand.

Mann-Whitney U test on equal location—independent samples. In many problems, samples are not matched by pairs but are independent. For example, suppose that you wanted to make a quick test on the mileage delivered by two grades of gasoline your company used for its maintenance fleet, which consisted of 12 pickups, all used for local calls. Records show that yesterday 5 of those trucks had used grade 1 gas while 5 had used grade 2 and that the mileages delivered were as follows:

Grade 1	13.7	13.2	15.7	12.3	14.7		
Grade 2	14.3	12.5	15.2	14.5	13.9	15.1	14.9

You decide to test the hypothesis that the grades of gasoline deliver the same mileages, using the Mann-Whitney test.

As usual, the first step is to replace each observation by its rank in the total of the 12 samples:

Grade 1	4	3	12	1	8		
Grade 2	6	2	11	7	5	10	9

The Mann-Whitney test is very similar to Fisher's rank-randomization test, studied in Sec. 17.A. However, instead of using the difference between mean ranks as the test statistic, the Mann-Whitney test uses the sum of the ranks in either category. Using the grade 1 category for this problem, that sum is $4 + 3 + 12 + 1 + 8 = 28$.

Now, having this sum, you must compute

$$U = n_1 n_2 + \frac{n_1(n_1 + 1)}{2} - \sum R_1$$

where $\sum R_1 = $ sum of ranks in group 1
$n_1, n_2 = $ respective sample sizes

If the resulting number is larger than $n_1 n_2 / 2$, you must compute

$$U' = n_1 n_2 - U$$

For your problem, then,

$$U = 5(7) + \frac{5(5 + 1)}{2} - 28 = 22$$

and
$$U' = 5(7) - 22 = 13$$

424

Instead of having to compute the different sums of ranks that could be obtained in 12!/7!(5!) orderings of the test data and finding how many of them are equal to or greater than 28, you're rescued again by a table, this time Appendix Table A.8, which relates the statistics of U and U' calculated above to significance levels. Referring to this table, you find that the difference is not significant at the .05 level, and you conclude that mileages delivered by the two grades of gas are not different.

The Westenberg-Mood test on equal location—independent samples. As a final test of location, we'll consider the Westenberg-Mood median test. Here the hypothesis is that the medians of the populations from which the samples are drawn are equal. This test is very sensitive to violations of this hypothesis and insensitive to other differences in the distributions.

Using the gasoline-mileage data again, you'd begin this test by estimating the median mileage from the total sample data of 12 observations. This median is 14.4 mi/gal, exactly halfway between the sixth and seventh of the mileage observations when they are ranked by size.

Grade	1	2	1	1	2	2	2	1	2	2	2	1
Mileage	12.3	12.5	13.2	13.7	13.9	14.3	14.5	14.7	14.9	15.1	15.2	15.7

$$Md \overset{\downarrow}{=} 14.4$$

Now construct a table giving the number of values in each sample that fall above and below the combined median.

	> Md	< Md	
Grade 1	2	3	5
Grade 2	4	3	7
	6	6	12

Consider the total sample size of 12 and assume this is drawn from a single population or two identical populations. How many ways can this sample be arranged so that 5 items appear in the grade 1 group and 7 items appear in the grade 2 group? This is equivalent to asking how many different samples of 5 (the grade 1 group) can be drawn from the miniature population of 12 without replacement. It is the number of combinations of 12 things taken 5 at a time. Of these different samples or combinations, how many result in exactly 2 items greater than the median and 3 items less than the median? The number of ways of getting 2 above the median is simply the number of combinations of 6 things taken 2 at a time, and for each of these there are many ways of drawing the remaining 3 below the median from the total of 6 below the median (again a combinatorial problem).

Given this information, what's the probability of having the arrangement in the table occur? It is

$$P \text{ (obtained table)} = \frac{C(6, 2)C(6, 3)}{C(12, 5)} = .009$$

However, you're interested not simply in the point probability of the obtained table but in the probability of the obtained table or anything more extreme. For a one-tailed test, you'd have to compute

$$\frac{C(6, 2)C(6, 3)}{C(12, 5)} + \frac{C(6, 1)C(6, 4)}{C(12, 5)} + \frac{C(6, 0)C(6, 5)}{C(12, 5)}$$

For a two-tailed test, you'd also have to compute extreme values in the opposite direction. It turns out that this probability is exactly the same as the first, so it's necessary to compute only one tail (as in the above formula) and double the obtained value for a two-tailed test.

Fortunately, tables for the Westenberg-Mood test have been computed for many small sample sizes and are given in Appendix Table A.9. The use of this table requires some notation, so the information from the example above will be converted to algebraic notation as follows:

	$>$ Md	$<$ Md	
Group 1	b	$B - b$	B
Group 2	a	$A - a$	A

The letters are assigned to numbers on the basis of the following rules:

1. The A row is the group with the larger sample size.
2. a and b are in the same column, and the choice of column is made on the basis of the criterion that

$$aB > bA$$

Table A.9 is then entered with the values A, B, and a, and the table gives the critical value of b that causes rejection of the hypothesis of equal medians for the two populations. For the above numerical example, when the table is entered with

$$A = 7 \qquad B = 5 \qquad a = 4$$

the critical value of b can't be found. This means that there is *no* value for b that is small enough to cause rejection of the hypothesis at the .05 level. This is an indication that the small sample size doesn't provide enough power to reject false hypotheses.

REVIEW EXERCISES 17.C

1. In the sign test for location for matched samples, what is the basic hypothesis being tested?

2. In the Wilcoxon test for location for matched samples, the method of randomization is applied to the signs of the matched differences: true or false?

3. In computing a U statistic for independent samples, you're effectively using Fisher's method of rank randomization mentioned in Sec. 17.A: true or false?

4. The difference between the sign test and the Wilcoxon test for matched samples is that the sign test considers the magnitude of the difference between matched observations: true or false?
5. The Westenberg-Mood test is based on the principle of randomization: true or false?

Answers 17.C

1. The basic hypothesis is that the median of the difference distribution is zero.
2. true
3. true
4. False; the Wilcoxon test considers the magnitude of the difference between matched observations.
5. true

Section 17.D
Tests of Dependence

Learning objective

Your learning objective for this section is to be able to compute measures of association for:

1. Ordinal data
2. Categorical data

When variables are continuous and have an interval scale, it's possible to compute the correlation coefficient between them. It isn't necessary to make the normality assumption unless statistical tests are to be made on the correlation coefficient. However, if the data are strictly ordinal or categorical, then distribution-free methods *must* be used to measure correlation.

KENDALL'S COEFFICIENT OF RANK CORRELATION

Suppose two raters evaluated and rank-ordered 10 candidates for a job opening, and you want to determine the relationship (or correlation) between the two raters' evaluations. The data you have are:

Candidate	1	2	3	4	5	6	7	8	9	10
Rater 1	9	2	7	8	10	1	3	4	6	5
Rater 2	8	4	6	10	9	2	1	5	7	3

427

First, choose one of the raters, say rater 1, and order the candidates from 1 through 10. Then place the corresponding rater 2 ratings in the same order. This results in:

Rater 1	1	2	3	4	5	6	7	8	9	10
Rater 2	2	4	1	5	3	7	6	10	8	9

If there were a perfect *positive* relationship between the two raters, rater 2 ratings would also go sequentially from 1 through 10. If there were a perfect *negative* relationship, rater 2 ratings would go from 10 to 1. If there were no relationship, then rater 2 rankings would be randomly distributed. Therefore, some statistic needs to be found which will give a large positive number for perfect positive correlation and a large negative number for perfect negative correlation.

Look at the rankings for rater 2 (with rater 1 rankings in the correct sequential order). How many times does a smaller ranking follow a larger ranking, and how many times does a larger ranking follow a smaller ranking? Look at the first ranking of 2. There is one smaller rank following, namely, the rank of 1. The next rank is 4, and there are two smaller rankings following it, namely, 1 and 3. Continuing with this pattern, you'll find a total of seven smaller rankings following a larger one. Call this number S; that is, $S = 7$. Now do this for the total number of times a larger ranking follows a smaller one. This number is 38, and we'll call it L; that is, $L = 38$. You can check your counting because the total number of comparisons is $n(n - 1)/2$, which is the sum of S and L. Now compute the value $L - S = V$ and consider how V behaves under various conditions. If rater 2 values were in the exact sequential order from 1 to 10, then L would equal 45, S would equal 0, and V would equal 45. The number 45 would indicate perfect correlation. If rater 2 values were in the exact inverse sequential order from 10 to 1, L would equal 0, S would equal 45, and V would equal -45. The number -45 would indicate perfect negative correlation. For the rater's evaluation example, $L = 38$, $S = 7$, and $V = 31$, indicating some positive correlation.

The *significance* of this answer of 31 depends on the randomization distribution across all possible arrangements of rater 2 rankings. How many arrangements are there? It would be the number of permutations of 10 things taken 10 at a time, or $10! = 3,628,800$. Since it would be difficult to compute all possible values of V to determine whether the hypothesis of randomness should be rejected, appropriate tables have been prepared. From Appendix Table A.10, you find that the obtained value of 31 is significant at the .05 level since it exceeds the critical value of 21. In fact, it is significant beyond the .005 level, so you'd reject the two-tailed hypothesis of no relationship and accept the alternative that there is a relationship between the two sets of rankings.

The value V can be converted to a number that's similar to the correlation coefficient. Note that the maximum value of V will be $n(n - 1)/2$, so if V is divided by this maximum value, a number results that lies between -1 and $+1$. For our example,

$$\tau = \frac{31}{45} = .69$$

where τ (lowercase Greek tau) is Kendall's coefficient of rank correlation.

Table 17.6 / Observed frequencies

	Laborer	Clerical	Managerial	Total
Own home	5	12	15	32
Rent home	12	7	12	31
Rent apartment	23	9	7	39
Own trailer	7	5	4	16
Rent trailer	4	2	3	9
Total	51	35	41	127

While this example used rankings given by individual raters, it would be possible to take paired measurements, i.e., height and weight, of individuals, rank-order the respective variables, and compute the rank-order correlation coefficient. This would be especially useful if the variables of interest were ordinal data.

CHI-SQUARE TEST OF ASSOCIATION

In many instances, data are not ordered but are categorical. The chi-square distribution can be used to test association in such data.

For example, suppose you wanted to find out whether there's any relationship between a person's occupation and type of residence. You might take a sample of subjects and *cross-classify* them as in Table 17.6, where the numbers represent the number of subjects fitting that category combination. Does there appear to be any relationship between occupation and residence type? In order to answer this question, you first need to calculate the numbers you'd expect in each cell if there were no relationship. Now if ownership and residence type were *independent*, the probability of their joint occurrence would be equal to the product of the marginal probabilities of their separate occurrences:

$$P(\text{occupation and residence}) = P(\text{occupation})P(\text{residence})[1]$$

For any particular joint occurrence, then, such as a laborer owning his own home,

$$P(\text{laborer and own home}) = P(\text{laborer})P(\text{own home}) = \frac{51}{127}\frac{32}{127} = .1011$$

Applying this probability to the total number in the sample, you can determine that *if* membership were independent of occupation, the number of laborers owning their own homes in the sample would be .1011(127) = 12.85.

This process can be repeated to give the table of *expected* values (Table 17.7) under the assumption of independence.

---

[1] This is the special law of multiplication for independent events, which was developed in Module 10.

Table 17.7 / Expected frequencies

	Laborer	Clerical	Managerial
Own home	12.85	8.82	10.33
Rent home	12.45	8.54	10.01
Rent apartment	15.66	10.75	12.59
Own trailer	6.43	4.41	5.16
Rent trailer	3.61	2.48	2.91

The significance of the difference between these theoretical (or expected) frequencies and the actual frequencies can be tested using χ^2. The value of χ^2 is calculated by squaring the difference between the actual and expected frequencies in each cell, dividing by the expected frequency, and summing this statistic over all the cells:

$$\chi^2 = \sum \frac{(O_{ij} - E_{ij})^2}{E_{ij}}$$

where E_{ij} = expected value in the ith row, jth column
O_{ij} = observed value in the ith row, jth column

The resulting figure is distributed as χ^2, with

$$(m - 1)(n - 1) \text{ degrees of freedom}$$

where m = number of rows
n = number of columns

For this problem, the computed value of χ^2 is 15.4775, with 8 degrees of freedom $[(5 - 1)(3 - 1)]$. Checking the χ^2 table, Appendix Table A.5, you find that this value is significant at the .05 level, so you'd reject the hypothesis of independence and conclude that ownership and occupation are related. Note that the greater the deviation between the observed and expected values, the larger the χ^2 value and the higher the probability that the hypothesis of no difference would be rejected.

Although χ^2 can be used to determine the significance of the relationship between two categorical variables, it doesn't directly give a measure of the degree of the relationship. A measure that has been proposed is ρ, which ranges in value from 0 to 1. It is computed as

$$\rho = \sqrt{\frac{\chi^2}{N(C - 1)}}$$

where C = smaller of row or column size (minimum of m or n)
N = total sample size
For the numerical example above,

$$\rho = \sqrt{\frac{15.4775}{127(2)}} = \sqrt{.0609} = .247$$

430

If there's no relationship between the variables, the value of ρ will be 0. If there's perfect relationship, the value of ρ will be 1, so ρ is a measure similar to the correlation coefficient. For this problem, it can be seen that though there is a significant correlation between occupation and ownership, it isn't very strong.

REVIEW EXERCISES 17.D

1. In the following list, how many times does a smaller ranking follow a larger ranking?
$$1, 4, 2, 6, 3, 5$$
2. The significance of Kendall's τ depends upon a randomization distribution: true or false?
3. In a χ^2 test of association, the expected number of observations in a cell is computed by assuming there is no relationship between the variables: true or false?
4. The formula for the χ^2 is:
$$\chi^2 = \sum \frac{(\text{observed} - \text{expected})^2}{\text{observed}}$$
true or false?

Answers 17.D

1. Four; 2 and 3 follow 4, 3 and 5 follow 6.
2. true   3. true
4. False; the denominator should be the expected frequency.

Questions and Problems

17.1. The quality control department in a manufacturing firm wanted to make a quick check of a machine to see if it was running within tolerance. They took a sample of 10 items from the process and measured the following deviations from standard:

$-.07$	.04	.01	.02	.10
.03	$-.02$	.04	.01	.05

a. Using the sign test, determine if the median is significantly different from zero (at a 1 percent level of significance).
b. Test the tolerance to see if the seventy-fifth percentile is .06.

17.2. A researcher sampled 15 families from a city to determine median income and obtained the following data:

5,400	14,800	17,800
13,800	12,600	12,600
15,500	11,500	31,500
8,700	25,200	10,700
11,800	17,400	7,300

a. Using the sign test, test the hypothesis that the median income is $10,500 at the 10 percent level of significance.

b. Test the hypothesis that the ninetieth percentile for income is $20,000.

17.3. An administrator in a small university was interested in finding the median grade-point average (GPA) of the junior class. A sample of 10 students produced:

3.65	2.58	2.33	2.40	3.00
2.48	2.07	2.54	2.33	2.68

a. Test the hypothesis that the median GPA is 2.4 using the sign test at the 20 percent level of significance.

b. Since the top 20 percent of the class receive special awards, the administrator wants to choose a cutoff GPA. Test the hypothesis that the eightieth percentile is 3.3 at the 1 percent level of significance.

17.4. In Prob. 17.1, assume you wanted to test the hypothesis that the distribution of errors was normal with a mean of zero and a variance of $.03^2$.

a. Use the Kolmogorov-Smirnov test to determine if your hypothesis is true.

b. You took some additional observations and classified the errors into the following groups. Using both the Kolmogorov-Smirnov test and the chi-square test, determine if the normality assumption is true.

Error	Frequency	Error	Frequency
$-.10$ to $-.08$	4	.02 to .04	23
$-.07$ to $-.05$	10	.05 to .07	14
$-.04$ to $-.02$	19	.08 to .10	7
$-.01$ to .01	28		

17.5. In Prob. 17.2, assume you wanted to test the hypothesis that the logs of income followed a normal distribution with mean 4.1 and variance $.1^2$. The reason for taking logs is that income itself is a skewed right distribution, and taking logs pulls the distribution in and makes it more normal in shape. Using the Kolmogorov-Smirnov test, determine if the hypothesis is true.

17.6. In Prob. 17.3, the administrator hypothesized that the distribution of grades was normal with mean of 2.4 and variance of $.4^2$. Using the Kolmogorov-Smirnov test, determine if the hypothesis is true.

17.7. A researcher had taken a survey concerning attitudes and wanted to determine if the sample characteristics were representative of the United States adult population. One of the characteristics of interest was age. Sample results and information on the population were:

Age group	Sample	Population %	Age group	Sample	Population %
18–20	8	6.1	45–54	28	17.8
21–24	18	7.5	55–64	26	13.6
25–34	57	19.8	65 and over	23	14.3
35–44	40	20.9			

a. Using the chi-square test, determine if the sample matches the population at the 5 percent level of significance.

b. Using the Kolmogorov-Smirnov test, determine if the sample matches the population.

17.8. In the previous questions, you used the Kolmogorov-Smirnov test on both single and grouped data. Discuss the effects of grouping on the test. It might help to draw a graph of single data compared to the hypothesized distribution, and then see what happens if you group the data in different ways.

17.9. In previous questions you used the chi-square test where there was a predetermined hypothesis concerning the mean and variance of the distribution. Sometimes you may want to estimate these from the sample data and simply test the hypothesis that the distribution is normal (or some other theoretical distribution). What effect do you think this'll have on the chi-square test? What adjustments have to be made in the test when you do this?

17.10. In an experiment, 20 people were matched and assigned to two different test groups. In one of the test groups, a discussion was held concerning how each person could contribute to the betterment of race relations. The second group simply saw a film telling them what they could do to improve race relations. Each group then responded on a 9-point scale concerning how involved they would become in a human relations project (where a 1 is very involved and a 9 is not involved at all). The matched responses were:

Pair	1	2	3	4	5	6	7	8	9	10
Discussion	1	4	3	3	1	5	2	2	4	3
Movie	3	5	5	4	4	8	5	3	9	5

a. Using the sign test, determine if the two groups were significantly different at the 20 percent level of significance.

b. Using the Wilcoxon test, determine if the two groups were significantly different at the 20 percent level of significance.

17.11. An industrial psychologist interested in the effects of work situation on performance, chose 30 workers and matched them according to background and experience. They were then assigned to two different work situations and their performance measured in terms of productivity. The results were:

Pair	1	2	3	4	5	6	7	8	9	10	11	12	13	14	15
Situation 1	1	4	3	8	2	7	9	3	4	11	9	3	1	2	5
Situation 2	2	6	2	8	4	11	9	4	3	8	11	7	3	1	7

a. Using the sign test, determine if there is any effect of situation on productivity at the 10 percent level of significance.

b. Using the Wilcoxon test, determine if the two groups were significantly different at the 10 percent level of significance.

17.12. In Prob. 17.10, assume that there was not a matching of subjects, so the 20 were just randomly assigned to the groups but the results were the same.

a. Use the Mann-Whitney *U* test to determine if responses are significantly different between groups at the 1 percent level of significance.

b. Use the Westenberg-Mood test to determine if the responses are significantly different at the 1 percent level.

c. Compare your answers to those obtained when the samples were matched.

17.13. In Prob. 17.11, assume there wasn't matching of workers and that they were simply randomly assigned to work situations.
  a. Use the Mann-Whitney U test to determine if productivity is significantly different at the 10 percent level of significance.
  b. Use the Westenberg-Mood test to determine if productivity is significantly different at the 10 percent level of significance.
  c. Compare your answers to those obtained when the samples were matched.

17.14. An instructor had a class participate in a group project. At the end of the project, the instructor rank-ordered the participants in terms of their contribution to the project, and the group leader also ranked each of the participants. What is the rank-order correlation between the instructor and the group leader?

Student	1	2	3	4	5	6	7	8	9	10
Group-leader ranking	4	7	1	6	2	9	8	3	10	5
Instructor ranking	4	5	3	7	1	10	8	2	9	6

17.15. The supervisor of a work group was asked to rank-order subordinates in terms of promotion potential. The boss of the supervisor also rank-ordered the same people. What is the rank-order correlation between the supervisor and the boss?

Worker	1	2	3	4	5	6	7	8	9	10	11	12
Supervisor rank order	6	1	5	2	9	8	11	3	7	10	4	12
Boss rank order	3	4	1	2	7	5	8	9	12	6	10	11

17.16. A researcher wanted to determine if there was any relationship between the area of town in which people lived and the area of town in which they worked. The following information was obtained from a sample of 271 residents:

Home area	Work area				
	NE	NW	SE	SW	Central
NE	8	13	7	8	20
NW	8	10	14	7	13
SE	14	8	13	21	7
SW	7	10	7	13	8
Central	5	8	7	10	25

  a. Using the table values, find the proportion of people living in each area of town, and the proportion of people working in each area of town. These are called the *marginal distributions*.
  b. Is there a relationship between work area and living area? Use the chi-square test with a 10 percent level of significance.
  c. What is the strength of the relationship?
  d. Describe the relationship in words.

17.17. The director of a conference facility wanted to know if there was any relationship between the size of a conference and the opinion of the people attending about the quality of the service. A sample of participants from each conference always filled out a questionnaire in which one of the questions dealt with the service quality (good, indifferent, poor). The following data were collected:

Size	Evaluation		
	Good	Indifferent	Poor
0–49	13	20	8
50–99	11	13	12
100–199	45	13	7
200–399	55	70	42
400 and over	58	83	114

a. Is there a relationship between conference size and evaluation? Use the chi-square test at a 20 percent level of significance.
b. What is the strength of the relationship?
c. Describe in words the nature of the relationship. What comments do you have for the director based on this evaluation?
d. Do the observations meet the assumption of independence?

MODULE 18
SURVEY SAMPLING

The last eight modules dealt with problems in statistical inference, where samples were taken, measurements made, and sample results generalized as tests of significance or confidence statements about population parameters. Little has yet been said about the process of taking the sample and gathering information, except that simple random sampling was used. However, there are other procedures available for sampling which may be better in terms of the cost of sampling or in giving smaller confidence intervals for a given sample size. Two of these alternative sampling plans, stratified and cluster samples, are discussed in this module.

In addition many samples on which decisions are based are designed to collect information from people rather than making measurements on inanimate objects. This means that some sort of questionnaire must be designed to gather the information. Some general rules for designing such questionnaires are discussed in Sec. 18.C.

Finally, besides sampling error, there are other kinds of errors that can come about in gathering and interpreting statistics, such as nonresponse to surveys or interviewer bias. In many real-world situations, these sources of error may be more important than the sampling error. Section 18.D discusses the subjective evaluation of surveys and some possible ways to account and adjust for these additional sources of error.

General learning objectives

Your general learning objectives for this module are to be able to:

1. Define terms used in sampling
2. Differentiate between and describe:
   a. Simple random sampling
   b. Stratified sampling
   c. Cluster sampling
3. Identify problems involved in obtaining information from respondents using questionnaires
4. Describe the sources of error in surveys, such as sampling error, nonresponse bias, and improper questioning

Section 18.A
The Sampling Process

Learning objectives

Your learning objectives for this section are to be able to:

1. Distinguish between probability and nonprobability samples
2. Define probability samples and simple random samples
3. Use a table of random numbers
4. Define the following terms used in sampling:
   a. Frame
   b. Population
   c. Element
   d. Sampling unit
   e. Sample

PROBABILITY AND NONPROBABILITY SAMPLES

There are two basic types of samples, probability samples and nonprobability samples. Probability (random) samples are samples taken in such a way that laws of probability (or chance) dictate the composition of the sample. When used as an adjective, as in random sample, the word "random" is synonomous with the word "probability." In a way, the term "random sample" is unfortunate, because it is often misinterpreted as haphazard. The process through which probability samples are taken is called *randomization*. This process is far from being haphazard; in fact, it requires great care.

However, probability samples are usually worth the extra effort, because *only* if sampling is done at random can statistical inferences be made about populations based on sample statistics. In order to make statistical inferences, you must know the shape and standard deviation of the appropriate sampling distribution. You can determine these characteristics of the sampling distribution *only* if the sampling is random.

Three types of probability samples will be discussed with reference to survey sampling in Sec. 18.B, namely, simple random samples, stratified samples, and cluster samples.

Nonprobability samples are all those which don't make use of the process of randomization. From this it follows that statistical inferences can't be made from these samples. In fact, it would be rather nice if some term, such as "chunk" were applied to this process rather than the term "sample," just to distinguish clearly between the two.

439

Nonprobability samples may be very useful or worthless. If they are selected by just grabbing the nearest bodies without thinking, their results would probably be more misleading than helpful. If you just grabbed the first 10 people you met to survey public opinion on a particular topic, you'd be very likely to get a biased sample—all students, perhaps, if you were in a classroom, all businesspersons going to work if you were downtown at 8 A.M., or all shoppers if you were downtown at 2 P.M.

Other kinds of nonprobability samples, such as judgment or quota samples, can be very useful and are in fact widely used. *Judgment samples* are samples chosen not by a randomizing process but on the basis of careful subjective judgment. For example, it might be impossible to identify, choose at random, locate, and interview in depth a sample of top executives in the oil industry. However, it might be perfectly feasible and very informative to interview a carefully selected sample of oil-industry executives (taking care not to interpret their statements through the use of statistical inferences, of course).

Quota samples are judgment samples but are taken using some systematic method to avoid bias. For example, you might assign reporters to interview a certain number of oil company executives, a certain number of technical experts, and a certain number of representatives of oil-producing countries.

RANDOMIZATION

You already know that probability samples are necessary for making statistical inferences and how to make those inferences. How to assure that a sample is random has not yet been discussed.

A probability (random) sample is a sample obtained by a process such that each possible combination of items that could make up a given size sample has a *known* chance of being selected. A *simple random sample* is a random sample taken in such a way that each possible sample combination has an *equal* chance of being selected.[1] This definition assumes that sampling is *without* replacement: once an item is selected from the population, it can't be returned. Sampling with replacement is seldom used. All the sampling schemes in this book refer to sampling without replacement.

A simple random sample is obtained by choosing successive items from the population in such a way that after each selection, every element remaining in the population has an equal probability of being chosen. This process can be approximated through physical simulation, the use of tables of random digits, or by a computer simulation.

You've surely participated in local lotteries where random sampling was physically approximated by putting tickets in a box, stirring thoroughly, and selecting the winning ticket without looking. This sort of process only approximates a theoretical random process, of course, since it's unlikely that the stirring process is completely thorough.

---

[1] See Module 11, p. 264, for elaboration and an example.

Much more elaborate physical devices have been used for such serious purposes a selecting draft numbers.

Tables of random digits are very useful for obtaining random samples, particularly if the sample size is small. The most common form of table is one that lists up to 100,000 or more uniformly distributed random digits. The term *uniformly distributed* means that one-tenth of the digits are 0s, one-tenth are 1s, etc. The arrangement of these digits in the table is random, having been generated either by a physical mixing process (in older tables) or by a computer (in more recent tables). An abbreviated section of a table of random numbers is shown in Table 18.1.

To illustrate the use of a random-number table, suppose you wanted to take a simple random sample of 100 employees from a computer tape that listed each of the company's 5000 employees. You don't care at all about the order in which they're listed, as long as each employee is identified and retrievable. Before using the table of random digits, you'd have to decide on a system for its use, from which you won't deviate. That system could be to flip through the pages of the random table, stop somewhere without looking, and place a pencil on a number without looking. Assuming that you haven't stabbed yourself or otherwise missed the page, you'd then start the selection process on the page with the number on which your pencil fell. (You don't want to start at the beginning of the table every time, or you run the risk of repeating random samples you took before.) Then, you'd decide to select random digits on that page by, say, reading digits down the rightmost column, and reading the digits from left to right. (Every time you sampled, you would designate a different system, reading numbers from bottom to top, diagonally, or in any other way, as long as you designate the system *in advance.*)

Having done all this, suppose that the page segment on which you'll start is that of Table 18.1. Starting at the left of the sequence of five digits in the right column, the first number to be included in your sample would be employee number 2061. (You only need the first four digits because the population size is 5000, a four-digit number.) The second employee would be number 1726, and the third, 4975. (You can't use the numbers 5181 or 8364, since they're bigger than the population size of 5000.) You'd proceed down the column, and then down the next, selecting the numbers 1244, 4180, 2207, etc., until you had filled your quota of 100 employees.

Random numbers can be generated on a computer by writing a program, but

Table 18.1 / Abbreviated section of a table of random digits

65144	20617
59602	17265
91790	51812
91360	83646
41808	49758
68445	70269
22079	57195
19008	82150
14042	99431
60644	12446

nowadays most computer systems have random generating functions you can call upon. The only thing you must be careful about is that you understand exactly what'll happen when that function is used. Sometimes uniform digits will be generated; sometimes, perhaps, they'll be normally distributed random digits. If you don't use the system properly, you can keep generating the same set of random digits as you sampled repeatedly in the same program, or you could generate a new set every time the instruction was encountered. Your system user's manual provides you with the information to select the function you need.

DEFINITIONS

In order to discuss sampling in the context of taking surveys, several new terms must be defined.

Population. A collection of elements about which inferences are made.

For example, you might want to make some inferences about characteristics of people living in Boulder, Colorado. Then, all persons living within the city limits of Boulder constitute the population. The population must be carefully defined since it places boundaries on the sample. You might really be interested not in the people living within the city limits of Boulder but in Boulder County or metropolitan Boulder. You might really be interested only in the *adult* population and would then have to define not only geographical limits but also the characteristics of an adult (perhaps simply age).

Element. The object on which measurements are made.

An element is an *individual item* of the population. It is the unit of interest on which measurements are made. It could be individuals, or households, for example. If you're interested in the mean income of *adults* in Boulder, the element is adults. If you're interested in the mean *household* income, the element is households.

Sampling unit. A nonoverlapping collection of elements.

Suppose that the element of interest were the individual in Boulder. You could draw a sample of individuals from the population, but it might be more convenient to group elements into *sampling units* such as households. It may be easier to get a list of households and draw the sample from that list, even though you were interested in individuals. Each sampling unit then might contain one, two, or even more elements. If each sampling unit contains only one element, sampling units and elements refer to the same thing. Note how this differs from defining households as the elements. If you're interested in household income, the household is the element, not the individuals within the household.

Frame. The list of sampling units from which the sample is drawn.

You usually need a list of some kind from which to draw the sample. This list is the *frame*. There is seldom a one-to-one correspondence between the population and the frame. If you wanted to sample households in Boulder, you could get a list from the Post Office or use the telephone directory. The Post Office list would probably be a week or more old. It would contain nonexistent households and wouldn't contain new households. The telephone directory would be even worse, since many households do not have phones and some may have unlisted numbers. In fact, the Denver-Boulder metropolitan directory contains less than 80 percent of the households in the area.

Sample. A collection of sampling units drawn from the frame.

Measurements are made on the sample, and inferences are made about the population of interest on the basis of those measurements.

REVIEW EXERCISES 18.A

1. Classify each type of sample below with respect to whether it is a probability (P) or a nonprobability (NP) sample.
   a. Judgment sample.
   b. Simple random sample.
   c. Cluster sample.
   d. Quota sample.
   e. Stratified sample.
2. Statistical inferences cannot be made when using nonprobability samples: true or false?
3. In a probability sample, each possible combination of items that could make up a sample has a _____ chance of being selected, while in a simple random sample, each possible combination of items that could make up a sample has an _____ chance of being selected.
4. In using a table of random numbers, exactly the same system should be followed each time a sample is taken: true or false?
5. Match the statements with the appropriate terms:
   a. Frame   (1) a Nonoverlapping collection of elements
   b. Population   (2) a Collection of elements about which inferences are made
   c. Element   (3) One of the authors of this book
   d. Sampling unit   (4) a Collection of sample units drawn from the frame
   e. Sample   (5) Object on which measurements are made
                       (6) List of sampling units from which the sample is drawn

Answers 18.A

1. a. NP; *b.* P; *c.* P; *d.* NP; *e.* P   *2.* true   *3.* known, equal   *4.* false
5. a. 3, 6; *b.* 2; *c.* 5; *d.* 1; *e.* 4

Section 18.B
Examples of Probability Samples and Their Uses

Learning objectives

Your learning objectives for this section are to be able to define and use:

1. Simple random sampling[1]
2. Stratified sampling
3. Cluster sampling

SIMPLE RANDOM SAMPLING (REVIEW)

A simple random sample has been defined as a sample taken in such a way that every possible combination of items that could make up a given size sample has an equal chance of being selected.

When a simple random sample has been taken, it's possible to test hypotheses and estimate parameters for many types of problems, including tests involving proportions, means, differences between proportions, and differences between means, and for predicted values using a regression equation. The mechanics of these procedures will be summarized using a simple example involving an interval estimate for a population mean.

Assume that you want to make an interval estimate for the true mean labor cost of producing handcrafted musical instruments. Labor costs are a function of both the time spent on the product and the wages paid the workers. Since many instruments are produced, the population can be considered infinite. You take a simple random sample of size 100, and find that the sample mean labor cost $\bar{X}$ is \$600 per instrument, with an estimated population standard deviation s equal to \$100. You want to make an interval estimate of the population mean μ using a 98 percent confidence coefficient.

The fact that a simple random sample has been taken enables you to estimate the standard deviation of the sampling distribution of the mean as $s_{\bar{X}} = s_X/\sqrt{n} = 100/\sqrt{100} = 10$. This statistic measures the variation about the true mean that you'd expect from sample means taken from samples of size 100.

---

[1] This is a review of previous material.

444

Since a simple random sample was used, you can also be assured that this sampling distribution will be approximately normal for a sample size as large as 100. Finding from the normal tables that the z value for 98 percent confidence is 2.33, the interval estimate is then

$$\overline{X} \pm z s_{\overline{X}} = 600 \pm 2.33(10) = \$577 - \$623$$

The theory involved in the use of simple random sampling is relatively straightforward, and the calculations are easy. However, simple random sampling is often inefficient and expensive. For example, simple random sampling of the inhabitants of the United States could include interviewing single citizens in cities scattered all the way from Miami to Ketchikan. The expense of collecting such a sample could well be prohibitive.

For these reasons, many more *efficient* sampling plans have been devised. These plans are all based on probability sampling. Though more complex both in theory and application than simple random sampling, they are more powerful because they enable the researcher to obtain more precision for the same amount of money or a stated level of precision for less money. Two plans widely used in survey sampling, stratified sampling and cluster sampling, will be discussed here.

STRATIFIED SAMPLING

In stratified sampling, the frame is subdivided into *strata* according to some population characteristic, and techniques of simple random sampling are applied to samples from each strata. Estimates for the population can then be made by combining the information obtained from the subsamples.

Stratified sampling is effective any time the variances of the subcategories are smaller than the variance of the entire population. Estimates of people's weights, for example, can be made more efficiently by stratifying the population by sex, since the weights of women are more uniformly distributed about the mean weight for women and the weights of men around their mean than the weights of the entire population are about the population mean. This situation is illustrated in Fig. 18.1.

Let's use a numerical example to illustrate the entire process. We'll first consider a stratified sample and then compare its results to a simple random sample composed of the same values.

Suppose you're interested in finding out how much per week families in a certain community would be willing to pay for cable television. You might believe that willingness to pay is related to family income, with higher-income families being willing to pay more for cable TV. Suppose you could divide your frame (a list of families in the community) into high- and low-income groups, or *strata*. You do so and find that one-third of the families fall in the high-income group and two-thirds in the low-income group.

Realizing that sampling error is a function of sample size, and trying to make that sampling error as small as possible, you decide to allocate a sample of 100 in proportion to the relative sizes of the strata. You therefore take a simple random sample of

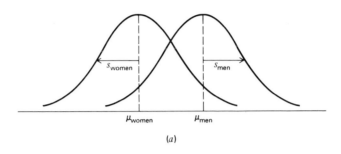

(a)

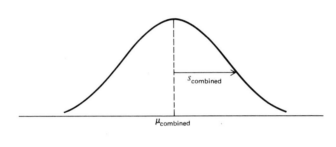

(b)

Figure 18.1 / Comparison of weight distributions of a population with weight distributions of substrata: (a) substrata distributions; (b) population distribution.

size 33 from the high-income group and one of size 67 from the low-income group. From these samples, you calculate the statistics in Table 18.2 in order to make interval estimates for the population mean of each stratum.

You now calculate separate interval estimates for the strata as follows, using a 95 percent confidence coefficient. (The sample sizes are large enough to permit you to use the normal table as a substitute for the t table.)

$$\text{Interval estimate, high} = \bar{X}_H \pm z s_{\bar{X}_H}$$
$$= 12.24 \pm 1.96(.54) = 12.24 \pm 1.06$$
$$= \$11.18 \text{ to } \$13.30$$
$$\text{Interval estimate, low} = \bar{X}_L \pm z s_{\bar{X}_L}$$
$$= 2.75 \pm 1.96(.30) = 2.75 \pm .59$$
$$= \$2.16 \text{ to } \$3.34$$

You can combine these separate estimates into an estimate for the entire population by weighting each stratum mean by the proportion of the *population* in that

446

Table 18.2

Stratum	Proportion of population	Sample size	Mean $\bar{X}$	Variance $s_X{}^2$	$s_{\bar{X}}$*
High income	$\frac{1}{3}$	33	12.24	9.5	.54
Low income	$\frac{2}{3}$	67	2.75	6.2	.30

*Remember that $s_{\bar{X}}$ is an estimate of the standard deviation of the sampling distribution of the mean and is equal to $s_X/\sqrt{n}$, assuming, as we do here, that the population is large compared with the sample and the finite correction factor is not necessary.

stratum and each stratum sampling distribution variance by the *square* of the proportion of the population in that stratum:

$$\text{Combined } \bar{X} = P_H(\bar{X}_H) + P_L(\bar{X}_L)$$
$$= \tfrac{1}{3}(12.24) + \tfrac{2}{3}(2.75) = 5.91$$
$$\text{Combined } s_{\bar{X}}{}^2 = (P_H)^2(s_{\bar{X}_H})^2 + (P_L)^2(s_{\bar{X}_L})^2$$
$$= (\tfrac{1}{3})^2(.54^2) + (\tfrac{2}{3})^2(.30^2) = .072$$

The interval estimate using combined data is

$$\text{Interval estimate population} = \bar{X}_C \pm zs_{\bar{X}_C}$$
$$= 5.91 \pm 1.96\sqrt{.072} = 5.91 \pm .53$$
$$= \$5.38 \text{ to } \$6.44$$

Now, to see the advantages of stratifying, let's calculate an interval estimate for the whole sample of 100, as we'd have done before learning about stratified sampling. Since you don't have the original data, you can't check this, but if you'd estimated the mean and variance from the entire sample of 100, you'd have found:

Sample size	Mean $\bar{X}$	Variance $s_X{}^2$	$s_{\bar{X}}$
100	5.91	27.20	.52

The interval estimate would have been

$$\text{Interval estimate, simple random sampling} = \bar{X} \pm zs_{\bar{X}} = 5.91 \pm 1.96(.52)$$
$$= 5.91 \pm 1.02 = \$4.89 \text{ to } \$6.93$$

You can see that stratifying paid off. It reduced the range for 95 percent confidence from $\pm\$1.02$ to $\pm\$0.53$. This was possible because the variances of the subgroups were much smaller than the variance of the combined group. If they had *not* been smaller, it would have indicated that the categories on which you were stratifying were not well chosen.

One further point. If you'd had estimates of the variances of the subgroups *before* subdividing, you could have made the sample sizes proportional to *both* the population proportions in the strata and the strata variances. This would have increased the power of the stratification still more. In your example, this wasn't possible because, as it often happens, you had no prior knowledge of the necessary variances.

CLUSTER SAMPLING

An important problem in either simple random sampling or stratified sampling is the cost of gathering the information, especially where the sampled population is scattered. Also, in many cases it is impossible to obtain a frame of the population (a list of members) that is required for both of these sampling methods.

One way to solve these problems is to use *cluster sampling*. In cluster sampling:

1. The population is divided into *clusters* of elements.
2. The clusters are randomly sampled.
3. All the elements in the sampled clusters are examined.

For example, in the problem about how much families in a community would be willing to pay for cable TV, either a simple random sample or a stratified sample would have required a frame, and the interviewers would have to travel to all parts of the community to gather information. In cluster sampling, the community would be divided into blocks, a random sample of those blocks would be chosen, and the attitude of *each* family living in the block would be measured.

The purpose in cluster sampling is to divide the population into subpopulations, each one representative of the whole population. Presumably if you were completely successful, you'd have to enumerate only one of the clusters, since it would be a perfect representation of the entire population. Note that this is the opposite of the purpose in stratified sampling. Here we want each subpopulation (cluster) to be as heterogeneous (varied) as the entire population, and we want no variation between cluster means, since each one should be representative of the entire population.

To estimate the mean and variance of a population from cluster sampling the following formulas are used:

$$\bar{X} = \frac{\sum \bar{X}_C}{m}$$

$$s_{\bar{X}}^2 = \frac{M - m}{M} \frac{\sum (\bar{X}_C - \bar{X})^2}{m(m - 1)}$$

where $\bar{X}_C$ = mean of cluster
M = number of clusters in population
m = number of clusters in sample

In these formulas, it is assumed that the number of elements in each cluster is the same or close to the same.[1]

---

[1] If the differences in cluster size are large, more complicated formulas must be used. These formulas are found in most books on sampling theory.

Table 18.3 / Results of cluster sampling, cable TV problem

Cluster	Mean $\bar{X}_C$	$\bar{X}_C - \bar{X}$	$(\bar{X}_C - \bar{X})^2$
1	$6.50	6.50 − 6.26	.0576
2	5.95	5.95 − 6.26	.0961
3	6.30	6.30 − 6.26	.0016
4	6.15	6.15 − 6.26	.0121
5	6.40	6.40 − 6.26	.0196
	31.30		.1870

$$\bar{X} = \frac{\sum \bar{X}_C}{m} = \frac{31.30}{5} = 6.26$$

$$s_{\bar{x}}^2 = \frac{M - m}{M} \frac{\sum (\bar{X}_C - \bar{X})^2}{m(m - 1)} = \frac{30 - 5}{30} \frac{.1870}{5(5 - 1)} = .0078$$

The first formula indicates that the estimate of the population mean is simply the average of the cluster means. The second formula can be explained by an analogy. Look at each cluster as if it were an individual, and the cluster mean as an observation on that individual. Then the total population size is the number of clusters in the population, and the formula gives the variance of this estimate.

To illustrate the use of these formulas, assume that in the cable TV problem, the community was divided into 30 blocks and 5 of those blocks were chosen at random. All families in each cluster were then interviewed, and the statistics on what they were willing to pay were compiled and analyzed in Table 18.3.

The confidence interval estimate (with a 95 percent confidence coefficient) is then

$$\text{Interval estimate, population mean} = \bar{X} \pm zs_{\bar{x}}$$
$$= 6.26 \pm 1.96\sqrt{.0078} = 6.26 \pm .17$$
$$= \$6.09 \text{ to } \$6.43$$

SYSTEMATIC SAMPLING

A special form of cluster sampling is called *systematic sampling*. To illustrate, suppose you wanted to sample a list of accounts receivable for a company. One way would be to take a simple random sample, but then you'd need a list of all of the accounts and randomly draw from that list. An alternative method would be to randomly draw one account from the first K accounts, and then use every Kth account thereafter to compromise a systematic sample.

To illustrate the point using a tiny example, suppose the company had 12 accounts receivable, and you wanted to draw a systematic sample of 3 accounts. K would then equal $12/3 = 4$, and you'd randomly draw 1 of the first 4 accounts and then every fourth account thereafter. If the accounts were coded by the letters A through L, and when you sampled from the first four accounts you drew the third, the sequence of accounts you'd sample would be:

A   B   C   D   E   F   G   H   I   J   K   L
          ↑   ↑   ↑

The accounts (C, G, K) are a randomly chosen cluster of the four possible clusters (A, E, I), (B, F, J), (C, G, K) and (D, H, L).

Since you've drawn only one cluster, you can't use the formulas above that were used when a number of clusters were evaluated. Instead, you must assume that the mean and variance of the cluster that was chosen are representative of the population mean and variance, and you then consider the cluster to be equivalent to a simple random sample. You'd then use the formulas for simple random sampling to make interval estimates or tests of significance.

You must be careful never to take systematic samples where the interval between samples is equal to a *periodic tendency* in the population. For example, in sampling daily receipts from a supermarket, you'd never choose a K value equal to 7. If you did, every item in the sample would be for the same day of the week. Instead of having a random sample of days, you'd have, say, a sample of all Tuesdays or one of all Saturdays, neither of which would be representative of the entire week.

EFFICIENCY OF CLUSTER SAMPLING

The strength of cluster sampling lies more in its economy than its power. If the variation between cluster means is consistent or uniform, cluster sampling will produce the same accuracy as simple random sampling at far less cost, or, alternatively, the sample size could be increased over simple random sampling and more accuracy could be achieved at the same cost. However, if there is wide variation in the uniformity between clusters, reliable estimates cannot be made with cluster sampling.

REVIEW EXERCISES 18.B

1. Stratification is done to:
    a. Make each stratum as homogeneous as possible and the variance between strata as large as possible.
    b. Make the strata as heterogeneous as possible.
    c. Try to make strata means as similar as possible.
2. In estimating the population mean from a stratified sample, a weighted average of stratum means is used, where the weights are the proportion that the sample within the stratum is of the total sample size: true or false?
3. The weights used in estimating the variance of the sampling distribution of means are the same as the weights used in estimating the mean itself: true or false?
4. One of the objectives of cluster sampling is to make the variance between clusters as large as possible and have the clusters as homogeneous as possible: true or false?

5. Cluster sampling can be viewed as simple random sampling, where the elements are clusters and the observations are the cluster means: true or false?

6. When observations within clusters are correlated, i.e., people on the same block giving similar responses, cluster sampling will be more precise than simple random sampling: true or false?

7. If you had a population of 200 items and wanted a systematic sample of size 10, you'd randomly choose one of the first 10 items and then choose every tenth one thereafter: true or false?

8. The chief advantage of stratified or cluster sampling over simple random sampling is greater accuracy for the same cost or the same accuracy for less cost: true or false?

Answers 18.B

1. *a*
2. False; the correct weights to use are the proportion that each stratum size is of the total population size. The weights are based on the population, not the sample.
3. False; the weights are the squares of the weights used in estimating the mean.
4. False; ideally, you want the clusters to be as heterogeneous as the population with no variation between cluster means.
5. true
6. False; cluster sampling will be less precise than simple random sampling because repeated observations within a cluster add very little information (they are correlated).
7. False; you'd choose an item out of the first 20 and then choose every twentieth thereafter.
8. true

Section 18.C
Questionnaire Design

In Module 2, the concepts of primary and secondary data and problems related to the accuracy of data were introduced. Most of that discussion centered around secondary data (data collected by others that you want to use), and much related to problems of measurement. The focus of this section will be on obtaining primary data (data that you collect) through the use of questionnaires.

Learning objectives

Your learning objectives for this section are to be able to:

1. Describe alternative methods of asking questions of respondents
2. List some general rules for designing questionnaires

QUESTIONNAIRE CONSTRUCTION

Purpose

The first step in any research project is to define the problem. Presumably you have some reason for sampling and asking questions of respondents. You must determine what information you want and how that information is going to help you solve the problem. Simply asking a bunch of questions and hoping you'll find something useful is rarely successful.

For example, deciding that you want to conduct a sample survey to find out why people use toothpaste is an inadequate statement of purpose. Presumably most people use toothpaste to clean their teeth, and you can afford to forget about the few (excluding babies) who eat it, those who use it for glue, or those who use it as a pop art medium. A better definition of purpose might be, To determine why people prefer a particular brand of toothpaste and how the reasons they give are related to specific measurable characteristics (like age, sex, or income), in order to determine the most productive advertising appeals for particular markets.

Method of Analysis

Most students in market research classes seem to make up questionnaires and gather responses with no notion of how they intend to analyze the data. As a consequence, they sometimes end up with reams of computer output which no one can understand, that attempts to relate every response to all other responses, sometimes involving tens of thousands of multiple cross-classifications with related statistical measures.

A student once called a professor he didn't even have for the class, at home on a Sunday morning, and confronted him with the following problem. He had a question on a questionnaire that required the respondent to rank 12 characteristics of a product, giving weights of 1 to 10 to the importance of each characteristic. Not knowing what to do with the responses, he'd decided to run a multiple regression using the 12 response values as independent variables. The trouble was that he didn't have a dependent variable, so he used the total of the 12 responses as the dependent variable. The computer had dutifully ground out some answers, and he was calling to see how to interpret them. When asked what such a remarkable procedure had to do with what he wanted to find out, he couldn't even verbalize the purpose of the questionnaire!

Another student asked professional skiers to rank their preference for each of some 25 brands of skis sold in the United States. He then tried to figure out ways to use all these data, not realizing that once the respondent got down past perhaps his third or fourth preference, the ratings given to the other brands had little significance.

Never include a question if you don't know how you are going to analyze the response and relate it to the problem you're trying to solve.

The Order of Questions

The order of questions on a questionnaire is also important. Always start with questions that are easy to answer and that arouse the respondents' interest. (This is easy to prescribe but difficult to do in practice.) In conducting an interview questionnaire for the toothpaste problem mentioned earlier, you might start with the question: How many brands of toothpaste do you think are on the market? Such a question might arouse the interest of the respondent, like a guessing game. You might even then provide the answer and continue with further questions.

The major and more difficult questions should occur at the middle of the interview. Sensitive questions should always be last. If you began an interview by asking the respondent's income, she might quit answering immediately. The subject may be more willing to answer the same question at the end of the interview. Also, such questions may be a minor part of the interview, being used for relatively unimportant purposes of classification. If that is the case and the question is asked last, you already have the important responses and haven't lost much if the interview is terminated.

METHODS OF ASKING QUESTIONS

There are three different ways that responses to questions can be solicited, through:

1. Open-ended responses
2. Checking categories
3. Scaling responses

Open-ended questions permit respondents to formulate their own answers. This has both advantages and disadvantages. Respondents have the opportunity to say exactly how they feel and may express their opinions clearly. On the other hand, they may have definite opinions but fail to communicate them in their responses. In order to analyze open-ended responses, they must be categorized by the analyst. Much valuable information could be lost in this process if the analyst were not careful about structuring categories or interpreting statements.

Open-ended questions must be carefully constructed. For example, consider the question: do you believe your state should fund public transportation out of general tax revenue? A yes answer to this question is clear, but a no answer is ambiguous. A person might mean that the state should not fund public transportation at all or that it should fund public transportation but not out of general tax revenue. The question could have been broken down into two questions:

1. Do you believe your state should fund a public transportation system?
2. If your answer to question 1 was yes, do you believe that such funding should come from general tax revenues of the state?

Another example might be the question: What are the most attractive features of the car you now own? This is pretty bad. A respondent may own several cars and not know which one to talk about. The question could solicit responses such as "The fact that it's paid for," which is a perfectly legitimate answer but may not be what you meant by feature. A respondent might write a beautiful paragraph listing dozens of features, which would be impossible to analyze. The question might be better if it were stated as: What is the most attractive feature of the last car you bought? That would be great, unless the last car someone bought was in 1914, and the most attractive feature was that it had rubber tires.

Questions which enable the respondent to *check categories* are more structured than open-ended questions. For example, the car question above might be handled by asking two questions:

1. How old is your most recently purchased car?
   ___ 1 year or less
   ___ 2 to 4 years
   ___ 5 years or more
2. The most attractive feature of your most recently purchased car is:
   ___ its mileage
   ___ its dependability
   ___ its style
   ___ other (list)

Questions which require the checking of categories can be easily analyzed if only one answer is permitted. Then, for example, an analyst might find that 45 percent of the owners rated mileage as most important, while only 10 percent listed style. Assuming that the sampling was random, tests discussed in other modules could be applied to see if such responses were statistically significant. When respondents can check more than one answer, the analysis and interpretation of the responses often pose very difficult statistical questions. Avoid questions like this whenever possible.

When attitudes are measured, *scales* are often used rather than open-ended or categorical questions. Examples of scaled questions are:

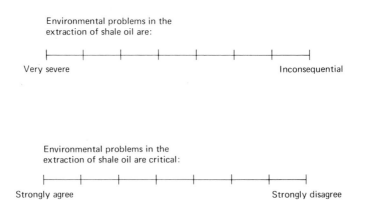

Many other versions of such questions exist. The analysis of responses usually consists of assigning numbers to the scale points (such as "very severe" = 7 and "inconsequential" = 1). Statistical measures can then be calculated from the coded responses. How responses to scaled questions should be coded and interpreted, however, is a complex subject about which experts disagree.

In all the types of questions mentioned above, great care should be taken to prevent bias and misunderstanding. In the middle Watergate period, pollsters soliciting public opinion on whether President Nixon should be impeached found that many people erroneously thought that "impeach" meant "found guilty and removed from office." In the questions about public transportation discussed earlier, some respondents may have thought the question was about support for a national public transportation system rather than a system within the state. Others may even have thought the question had something to do with school busing.

There are obviously biased ways of phrasing questions that should be avoided, such as: Do you agree that your state should not spend general tax revenues for public transportation?

There are also many other more subtle forms of bias that can exist in both questionnaires and interviews. Some of these may be racial or cultural biases. A word may have different meanings in Brooklyn and San Diego, or between groups of teenagers and senior citizens. It is well known that whether the race of an interviewer is the same or different from that of the interviewee affects many responses, usually in the direction of giving answers which the respondent thinks the interviewer will favor.

In order to remove as many of these sorts of defects as possible and to be sure that the method of analysis to be used is fully understood, questionnaires should always be *pretested* on as representative a group of people as possible.

REVIEW EXERCISES 18.C

1. True or false:
   a. Well-constructed questionnaires usually attempt to cover the waterfront and should be as broad as possible.
   b. It is easy to figure out an appropriate method for analyzing responses after the questionnaires have been returned.
   c. Difficult questions should be put at the beginning of a questionnaire or interview, while the person is fresh and ready to answer.
   d. Open-ended questions usually are converted into categorical classifications for purposes of analysis.
   e. Categorical questions that permit multiple responses should be avoided if possible because they are difficult to analyze.
   f. Interpreting scaled responses is difficult because different respondents might interpret the scale in different ways.
   g. Errors of bias are usually simple to find and compensate for.

Answers 18.C

1. a. F; *b.* F; *c.* F; *d.* T; *e.* T; *f.* T; *g.* F

Section 18.D

Measuring Errors in Research

Learning objectives

Your learning objectives for this section are to be able to:

1. Specify the major sources of error in sampling for research purposes
2. Explain why sampling errors may be a small part of the total error in a large research project
3. Explain why a decision-making approach to research requires subjective modifications of sample results
4. Apply error-ratio analysis to the problem of nonsampling errors

There are three major sources of error in any research project:

1. Sampling error
2. Nonresponse error
3. Measurement error

The first of these, sampling error, has been discussed extensively throughout previous modules. It forms the basis of the statistical sampling distributions and formulas that were developed.

In many scientific studies where measurements are made on objects, sampling error may be the only error present. Whenever an item is chosen to be in the sample, a measurement can be made on it (it does not refuse to cooperate) with an instrument that has a high degree of accuracy (no measurement problems). However, when a survey is conducted with people as the subjects and they are asked questions, they may refuse to respond (nonresponse error) or their response to the questions may be inaccurate (measurement error).

In order to specify these errors, we'll use the following definitions:

t = true value of variable under study
r = research result of measuring variable
p = true value of variable in planned sample
a = true value of variable in final sample

The ratio that's most important, and the one we'd like to be able to estimate is

$$\frac{t}{r} = \text{ratio of true to research result}$$

Since any estimate of this value must lie outside of the research itself, it must be estimated subjectively.

You already know that sampling error results from a difference between the true value in the population and the true value in the planned sample. Therefore,

$$\frac{t}{p} = \text{sampling error ratio}$$

There might be situations where you knew, a priori, that the planned sample was biased. Going back to the cable TV example of Sec. 18.A, you might know of certain parts of town where the incidence of television sets was low and where those who had them could not possibly afford the costs of cable TV. Therefore, on the basis of cost efficiency, you decide to eliminate those areas. In terms of the whole town, your sample is now biased upward. In response to the question: Would you be interested in cable TV? you might decide that the true proportion in the population will only be 85 percent of what you obtain with your sample, so for this example,

$$\frac{t}{p} = \text{sampling error ratio} = .85$$

Out of the planned sample, some of the respondents will refuse to cooperate. You might easily assume that those who refuse are probably not interested in cable television (especially if the introduction to the questionnaire indicates what it is about), so again those who respond have an upward bias. What is being measured here is the difference between the true value in the planned sample and the true value in the final sample. You might guess in this case that the proportion interested in the planned sample would be 90 percent of the proportion interested in the actual sample obtained. Therefore,

$$\frac{p}{a} = \text{nonresponse error ratio} = .9$$

Finally, you have the problem of the question itself and any bias it may introduce. When asked whether or not they are interested in a topic, those who are interested will generally say so, but many people who aren't really interested will say they are. Therefore, you can assume that there's some upward bias in response to the question and that the true value in the obtained sample will be less than the measured value in the obtained sample because of the upward bias. Let's assume that this ratio is also 90 percent, so that

$$\frac{a}{r} = \text{measurement error ratio} = .9$$

You can now form the product

$$\frac{t}{p}\frac{p}{a}\frac{a}{r} = \frac{t}{r}$$
$$.85(.9)(.9) = .69$$

If you believe all of the estimates of bias indicated, you're really saying that the true measure of interest in the *population* will only be 69 percent of the measured value in the *sample*. That's quite a jump, and it would be very important to any company interested in cable TV to know just how biased any estimate of interest was.

Remember that none of this was based on statistical theory but is subjective in nature. Although the pure researcher would simply report his sample result along with a confidence interval, the decision maker would certainly be interested in this analysis of bias. When dealing with human subjects, the errors due to nonresponse and measurement may easily be greater than the error due to sampling.

REVIEW EXERCISES 18.D

1. Name the three major sources of error in any research project.
2. With a well planned sample, the sampling error ratio could be less than 1.00: true or false?
3. It is possible for a measurement error ratio to be greater than 1.0: true or false?
4. A nonresponse error ratio of .20 for the question: Are you interested in investing in the commodities market? would mean that the interest on the part of the general public to investing in the commodities market was:
  a. High.
  b. Low.
5. You'd be likely to use error-ratio analysis if you were sampling the output of a production line: true or false?

Answers 18.D

1. sampling error, measurement error, and nonresponse error
2. True; you may selectively eliminate a part of the potential population on the basis of prior knowledge.
3. True; self-reporting of any behavior that might be considered socially unacceptable, for example, will usually be downward-biased, making the measurement error ratio greater than 1.0.
4. low
5. False; since you'd be measuring things rather than people's attitudes, you wouldn't have any refusals, your measurements would very likely be accurate, and your samples would be unbiased, so the sampling error ratio could be presumed to be 1.0.

Questions and Problems

18.1. Describe the difference between a probability and a nonprobability sample. What are some specific types of each?
18.2. Assume that you wanted to take a sample of size 10 from a population of 90 items (randomly numbered from 1 to 90). Define a procedure for drawing this sample

using a table of random numbers. Using Table 18.1 (or any other random-number table), carry this procedure through and indicate the specific elements you'd sample.

18.3. Describe the difference between a population and a frame. Also, describe the difference between an element and a sampling unit. Use a specific example to illustrate these concepts.

18.4. A simple random sample has been defined as a sample taken in such a way that each possible sample (combination of items) has an equal chance of being selected. Describe what this means. Why isn't this true of stratified or cluster sampling?

18.5. Someone came to you, as the local statistician, with the following set of data which represents the response to a 9-point scale concerning using gasoline tax money to fund urban mass transit (where 1 is very favorable and 9 is very unfavorable in opinion):

1, 3, 6, 4, 2, 1, 5, 4, 7, 3, 9, 7, 6, 9, 7

a. What is the estimate of the mean response, and what is the 95 percent confidence interval under the assumption of simple random sampling?

b. The person now tells you that the first 10 responses came from urban areas in the state and the remainder from rural areas and that it was a stratified sample where the population was two-thirds urban and one-third rural. What is your estimate of the mean and 95 percent confidence interval now?

c. Explain any differences between your answers to parts *a* and *b*. Also explain any similarities.

18.6. Determine a current social or political problem in your community. Choose one where a decision will ultimately be made, and assume that the decision makers want to find out how the community feels about the issue.

a. Define the problem carefully. Include the boundaries of the problem; i.e., what are you going to exclude from the study?

b. Define the relevant factors of the problem. What are the important factors that will affect the decision to be made?

c. Define the information needed from the population to include the substantive (problem-related) information and descriptors of the population that might affect how you interpret responses (income, age, etc.).

d. Construct a questionnaire to obtain the information.

e. Decide on a sampling plan. Will you use simple random sampling, cluster sampling, or what? Justify your choice.

18.7. You work for a soft drink bottling company and want to establish a sampling plan for quality control purposes. Five different batches of ingredients are mixed daily. Each batch produces 100 gross of bottles (a gross is 144 bottles). The quality from the bottom to the top of the vat containing the batch may vary due to improper mixing, and the vat is emptied into bottles from the bottom. The bottles are packed 24 to a carton, and the cartons packed 10 to a case.

a. Determine a sampling procedure to examine the quality of the drink. Remember that when a bottle is opened, the product is destroyed, so you can't conduct a 100 percent sample. You could sample bottles (randomly or systematically), sample cases, or cartons (cluster sampling), and you clearly must stratify to be sure you check each batch.

b. Assume that it costs 4 cents to produce a bottle and they sell for 25 cents each. How much is your sampling plan going to cost?

c. Describe the decision procedure inherent in your sampling plan; i.e., what do you do when you find a bad bottle? Assuming that you are going to throw some away, what is your modified sampling plan during the throwaway process, and how do you decide to begin accepting bottles again?

18.8. You work for a large chain of retail stores and are interested in sampling to find the operating characteristics of these stores. You suspect that many of these characteristics will be related to the size of the store (in sales volume), so you decide to take a stratified sample. One of the characteristics you measure is profitability (as a percent of sales), and you obtain the following results:

Store size	Population size (no. of stores)	Sample size	Mean % profit	Variance of profits
Small	150	20	8.0	1.5
Medium	100	25	9.5	2.5
Large	50	20	7.0	2.0

a. What is your estimate of the mean percentage profit and what is your 95 percent confidence interval on the mean? *Hint:* The sample is not proportional to the population, so be sure you use the correct weights.

b. What can you see in the problem that indicates why the largest sample was taken in medium-sized stores? What does taking a larger sample size there do in terms of the confidence interval?

18.9. You want to take a sample from a metropolitan area to determine the average income of the area. It is a five-county area with half of the population living in one county (the major city of the area) and the remaining half spread among the other four counties. You guess that income will be different for the two areas, so you stratify your sample and obtain the following:

Area	Size	Sample size	Mean income	Variance of income
City	250,000	100	$ 9,500	4,000,000
Other	250,000	100	12,500	12,250,000

What's your estimate of the mean income in the area, and what is your 90 percent confidence interval?

18.10. In Prob. 18.9, suppose your sample sizes had been 75 for the city and 125 for other areas.

a. What's your estimate of the mean income in the area and what's your 90 percent confidence interval?

b. Compare this answer to that obtained when the sample sizes were equal. What caused the difference? What rule of thumb can you develop from this?

18.11. Suppose, in Prob. 18.9, that the cost of sampling in the two different areas has to be considered, because you have a total budget of $5000. The cost of sampling in the city is $5 per interview (because the area is compact) but the cost of sampling in the remaining four-county area is $7.50 per interview.

a. You decide to sample in proportion to size (take half of the interviews in each area). How many interviews would you take? Assuming the sample means and variances are as shown in Prob. 18.9, what's your estimate of the mean with a 90 percent confidence interval?

b. Now suppose you decide to take only one-third of your interviews in the city and the remaining in the four-county area. How many interviews would you take in each area? Assuming the same sample means and variances, what's your estimate of the mean with a 90 percent confidence interval?

c. Compare your answers to parts *a* and *b* and indicate the reasons for the differences. What rule of thumb might you develop from this?

18.12. One rule that has been developed for minimizing the cost for a given confidence interval (or minimizing the confidence interval for a given cost) is to sample directly in proportion to population size, directly in proportion to the standard deviations in the strata, and inversely in proportion to the square root of the costs in the strata. Using this rule, what would be the optimum proportions to sample in each stratum in Prob. 18.11?

18.13. Suppose you're interested in the average age of the population in a city. The elements are then defined as individuals. You decide to use cluster sampling, where the city has been broken into blocks of approximately equal size. There are 1000 blocks. You randomly choose 10 of them and find the age of each person living in the block:

Block	Mean age	Block	Mean age
1	28.3	6	33.5
2	24.5	7	29.5
3	34.7	8	43.2
4	31.2	9	29.8
5	36.4	10	32.1

What's your estimate of the mean age of the population and your 99 percent confidence interval for that estimate?

18.14. You're an inspector for quality control in a manufacturing operation, and you want to determine the proportion of defective items coming off the line. The items are packed 50 to a carton, and 1000 cartons are produced daily. You decide to use cluster sampling of cartons, and at the beginning of the day you decide which 10 of the cartons will be chosen for inspection. On one particular day you found the following:

Carton	Defective	Carton	Defective
1	2	6	5
2	1	7	3
3	3	8	1
4	2	9	2
5	3	10	1

a. What's your estimate of the mean number of defectives and the 50 percent confidence interval for that mean?

b. You want to be 90 percent certain that the proportion of defectives is less than 5 percent. From this sample, are you?

18.15. You're examining the accounts receivable for your company and want to find the average outstanding balance. There are 10,000 accounts alphabetically arranged, and you decide on a sample of 100.

a. Define the exact procedure you'd use for systematic sampling.

b. Assume that the mean of the 100 accounts was $134 and the variance was $950. What's your estimate of the mean balance and your 90 percent confidence interval for that estimate?

18.16. You want to know the mean grade-point average for graduating seniors in your school, but you don't have time to check every record. You do have a list of seniors arranged in grade-point-average sequence, and you decide on a sample of 20 out of the 500 seniors.

a. Define your sampling procedure.

b. The mean you calculated was 2.9, and the variance was .09. What's your 75 percent confidence interval for the mean?

c. Since you're estimating grade-point average and the list is arranged by that average, you might question your results. How do you think this affects your answer?

18.17. You want to examine the daily sales of a store during a 56-week period and decide on a sample of 14 days. Describe the sampling plan you'd use for this problem.

18.18. Look at Prob. 18.9 as a decision problem, where you must have an excellent estimate of the income in the five-county region. In the city about 10 percent of the people failed to respond, and you believe that they have incomes of less than $3000. Maybe your mean is biased upward and if they'd responded, your mean would have gone down by 5 percent. You also feel that those who responded may have overstated their incomes and that the true income of the respondents is about 90 percent of the stated income. On the other hand, in the remaining four counties, nonrespondents would probably have much higher income, so that estimate would really be 110 percent of the obtained value. Additionally, those responding probably understated income, and you feel the actual income is 105 percent of the stated income. Since you used random sampling, you don't feel there is any sampling bias. What is your estimate of the mean income under these conditions?

18.19. In Prob. 18.5, the researcher now tells you that one-fourth of the population wasn't sampled since their responses were sure to be very unfavorable (9). Also, a number of people failed to respond (about 20 percent of those asked). They probably have no opinion and so could be counted in the middle of the scale (5). Considering this as a simple random sample of 15, that is, ignoring the information in part *b* of Prob. 18.5, what is your estimate of the mean attitude now? There's no exact answer to this, so justify your conclusion verbally.

MODULE 19
DECISION MAKING
UNDER UNCERTAINTY
WITHOUT SAMPLING

Confronted with the problem of decision making under uncertainty, the unsophisticated person usually reacts in a remarkably sophisticated way. A statistician might say that the decision maker should consider alternative courses of action and choose the act that maximizes his expected utility. The decision maker himself has a simpler explanation. He'd say that he considers the possibilities and chooses the one that's the "best bet." In the rest of this module we shall attempt to show that the decision maker's best bet and the statistician's maximization of expected utility are in fact very similar, the main difference being that the statistician's method is more systematic.

General learning objectives

Your general learning objectives for this module are to be able to:

1. Construct a payoff table for analyzing a decision problem under uncertainty
2. Calculate the expected monetary value and expected opportunity loss of alternative decision strategies to select the best strategy
3. Determine the cost of uncertainty, the expected value of perfect information, and other measures useful for analyzing decision problems

Section 19.A
Payoff Tables and Expected Values

Learning objectives

Your learning objectives for this section are to be able to:

1. Describe the construction and use of a payoff table for a decision problem
2. Distinguish between acts and events
3. Define expected monetary value (EMV) and explain its use
4. Explain the meaning and importance of a decision maker's utility for money

PAYOFF TABLES

Much of modern decision theory had its beginnings at the gambling table some 300 years ago. The elements in a gambling situation are closely analogous to those involved in many current business decisions. Therefore an initial illustration using a game of chance is appropriate both historically and practically. Suppose that you're offered the opportunity to play a version of an old carnival game called chuck-a-luck. You pay $1 for the opportunity to roll two dice. If you roll 2 sixes, you get your $1 back plus $2. If you roll a six and a "not-six," you get the $1 back plus $1. If you roll 2 not-sixes, you lose your original entry fee.

Before you play, you clearly have two alternatives—either to accept the conditions of the game and play or to choose not to play. But which of these alternatives is the best bet *before* the dice are rolled?

One point should be made here. The decision to play or not to play obviously has to be made before the dice are thrown. This is what is meant by decision making under uncertainty. If you could roll the dice and then decide after looking at them whether or not to play, the decision would be pretty simple.

Most business problems also contain an element of uncertainty and decisions must be made *before* this uncertainty is resolved. Therefore one of our major concerns will be to formulate systematic procedures to help decide what course of action is the best bet before the outcome is known. There is little reward in business for being a good Monday morning quarterback.

Back to our decision problem. We can summarize the situation thus far by constructing a *payoff table*. This table lists the net profit that will be made for every

465

Table 19.1 / Payoff table for chuck-a-luck

Event, sixes	Act	
	Play	Not play
2	$ 2	$0
1	1	0
0	−1	0

possible combination of *acts* and *events*. In our case the acts are to play or not to play, and the events are the outcomes of the roll. The payoff table is shown in Table 19.1.

Using this table, we can formulate several sorts of rules that may help us come to a decision. If we're pessimistic and assume the worst will happen to us regardless of the act we choose, we observe that the worst outcome (no sixes) if we choose to play will result in a loss of $1, while the worst result if we choose *not* to play will be no loss (and no profit). Following the reasoning of choosing the act that will minimize our maximum loss would result in our preference for the act "not play." This rule is known as a *minimax rule:* choosing the best act, assuming that the least favorable event will occur. If we were optimistic rather than pessimistic, we might formulate a *maximax rule:* assuming that the most favorable event will occur and choosing the act that maximizes profit given this event. For the problem at hand the maximax rule would lead us to play since the best outcome is a $2 profit, given that we play and roll 2 sixes.

While rules of this sort are useful for certain types of decision problems, it is apparent that they are not very satisfactory here since neither rule takes into consideration how *likely* the various events are. If the odds were overwhelmingly in favor of at least 1 six occurring, most of us would not hesitate to play. On the other hand, if the odds of no sixes were very high, most of us would figure that the odds were too much against us to warrant playing.

The next problem, then, is to find the odds of the various outcomes. One tedious but precise method of evaluating the odds is to list all the possible combinations of faces that might turn up. This enumeration is shown in Table 19.2.

Note that there are 36 possible combinations, only one of which results in two

Table 19.2 / Combinations of faces that can be obtained in rolling two dice

Die 1	Die 2	Die 1	Die 2	Die 1	Die 2	Die 1	Die 2	Die 1	Die 2	Die 1	Die 2
1	1	1	2	1	3	1	4	1	5	1	6
2	1	2	2	2	3	2	4	2	5	2	6
3	1	3	2	3	3	3	4	3	5	3	6
4	1	4	2	4	3	4	4	4	5	4	6
5	1	5	2	5	3	5	4	5	5	5	6
6	1	6	2	6	3	6	4	6	5	6	6

Table 19.3 / Calculation of expected profit, chuck-a-luck

Event, sixes	Odds	Act			
		Play		Not play	
		Payoff	Weighted payoff	Payoff	Weighted payoff
2	$\frac{1}{36}$	$\$+2$	$\$+\frac{2}{36}$	$\$0$	$\$0$
1	$\frac{10}{36}$	$+1$	$+\frac{10}{36}$	0	0
0	$\frac{25}{36}$	-1	$-\frac{25}{36}$	0	0
		Weighted average $= -\frac{13}{36}$			0

sixes, so the odds of two sixes are 1/36. Similarly, there are 10 ways of obtaining one six and one not-six for odds of 10/36, while the odds of obtaining no sixes are 25/36.[1]

Although an assessment of these odds is helpful, they alone aren't enough to form an adequate basis for a decision any more than the payoffs alone were. Even though the odds of two sixes are only $\frac{1}{36}$, the game would have considerable appeal if the payoff for two sixes were $200 rather than $2.

It seems that a realistic decision rule must somehow consider both the odds and the payoffs. The most satisfactory method of combining odds and payoffs is simply to weight each payoff by the odds that it will occur, add the weighted payoffs for each act, and choose the act that has the highest weighted average. This process is carried out in Table 19.3.

We have finally arrived at a rule that will guide us to rational decisions under uncertainty. In the case of chuck-a-luck with two dice the weighted average or expected value of not playing ($0) is greater than the weighted average of playing ($-\$13/36$ or approximately $-\$.36$), and the better decision is to choose *not* to play.

EXPECTED MONETARY VALUE

Of course, you know that what we have called odds up to this point could also be termed probabilities. Therefore, the weighted averages obtained for each act are really *expected values*. Remember that in Module 10 we defined expected value as $\sum XP(X)$, where X is the value of a discrete random variable and $P(X)$ is its probability. Here, the X is the payoff for a particular act-event combination, $P(X)$ is the probability of the event, and $\sum XP(X)$, is the sum of the weighted conditional values for a particular act. Instead of calling this simply the weighted payoff for an act, we'll refer to it in the remainder of this book as the *expected monetary value* (EMV) of an act.

---

[1] These odds could also be calculated using the formulas for binomial probabilities you learned in Module 10. For example, to get the odds of rolling 1 six

$$P(r = 1 \mid n = 2, p = \tfrac{1}{6}) = \frac{2!}{1!(1!)} \left(\frac{1}{6}\right)^1 \left(\frac{5}{6}\right)^1 = \frac{10}{36}$$

UTILITY FOR MONEY

You may have had some reservations about the statement that the "best" decision in the chuck-a-luck problem was *not* to play. You might well decide to play such a game if you felt the pleasure involved in playing was sufficient to compensate for the unfavorable (negative) EMV. If, on this basis, you decided to play, it would mean that your utilities are not linear with money.

To understand what is meant by the phrase "utility is not linear with money," let's consider the attitude several different people might have toward the risk of losing or gaining various amounts of money.

First consider the person with limited means and his reaction to a situation in which he had to choose between accepting or rejecting a business deal in which the odds of gaining $10,000 were 6 in 10 and the odds of losing $10,000 were 4 in 10

We can calculate the EMV for accepting or rejecting the deal as we did for the chuck-a-luck problem, by weighting the payoff for each event by its probability and adding all the weighted payoffs for all the events. For the act accept the deal, the EMV is .6(10,000) + .4(−10,000) = $2000. The EMV for rejecting the deal (doing nothing) is $0.

In spite of the fact that the EMV of accepting the deal is higher than that of rejecting it, this person, like most of us, would probably reject the opportunity because the loss of $10,000 would hurt him more than the gain of $10,000 would help him.

If we plotted the utility for various amounts of money against the dollar value of money for such a person, we'd get a curve concave to the X axis as in Fig. 19.1. Note that a gain of $10,000 produces a gain in utility of Δ_1, which is considerably smaller than the loss in utility suffered from a loss of $10,000, or Δ_2.

Now let's consider how a person in different circumstances might react to a slightly different opportunity. Assume that this person has to pay a creditor $10,000 by tomorrow and must declare bankruptcy if he doesn't. He's confronted with another deal, where the probability of gaining $10,000 is .4 and the probability of losing $10,000 is .6. The EMV of accepting is .4(10,000) + .6(−10,000) = −$2000, while the EMV of rejecting is 0. It is very likely that this person would accept the deal in

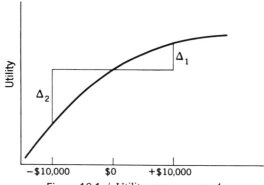

Figure 19.1 / Utility-money curve *A*.

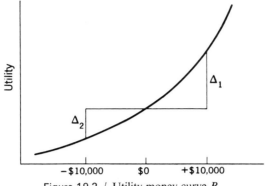

Figure 19.2 / Utility-money curve *B*.

spite of the fact that the EMV of accepting is lower than that of rejecting because the loss of $10,000 would hurt him less than the gain of $10,000 would help him.

The utility-vs.-money curve for this person would be convex to the X axis, as shown in Fig. 19.2. For this person the gain in utility of a gain of $10,000, or Δ_1, is greater than the loss in utility of a loss of $10,000, or Δ_2.

The third person is one for whom a loss of $10,000 would be undesirable but not fatal and for whom a gain of $10,000 would be nice but would please him no more than the equivalent loss would have hurt him. Such a person's utility for money curve would be linear. (This expression is often abbreviated by saying that the person's utility is linear with money.) The appropriate curve is shown in Fig. 19.3.

At any point on the curve, $\Delta_1 = \Delta_2$, that is, a gain of $10,000 gives him as much pleasure (gain in utility of Δ_1) as a loss of $10,000 hurts him (loss in utility of Δ_2). Such a person, if he wants to be consistent with his utilities, will always choose the act with the highest EMV.

Since most business decisions involve dollar amounts small enough (relative to the size of the business) to represent neither a bonanza nor a catastrophe, the utility for money curve for such decisions may generally be considered linear. Therefore, we'll

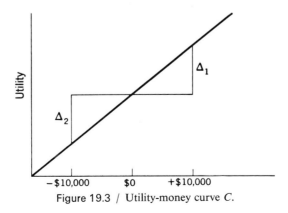

Figure 19.3 / Utility-money curve *C*.

accept the criterion of maximization of expected monetary values as a valid guide to decision making under uncertainty throughout the remainder of the book.

In some business decisions, e.g., a small firm drilling for oil, the dollar amounts may be very large (relatively), and utility may not be linear with money. To properly analyze such a problem, you'd have to determine your specific utility for money curve,[1] convert dollar values to utilities, and choose the act which maximized expected utility rather than expected monetary value. While this process could be difficult, it is by no means impossible.

REVIEW EXERCISES 19.A

1. A payoff table lists the net profit that will occur for each possible combination of _____ and _____.

2. An *event* is a strategy or choice available to the decision maker in a decision problem: true or false?

3. Generally, the payoffs associated with various act-event combinations are all that is necessary to select the best alternative in a decision situation: true or false?

4. Expected monetary values are usually computed for each possible event in a decision problem: true or false?

5. An expected monetary value is the weighted average payoff of following a particular course of action: true or false?

6. The weights used in computing monetary values are _____.

7. EMV is *not* a good guide to action when:
  a. Probabilities used to compute it are based on relative frequencies.
  b. The decision maker's utility for money is not linear.
  c. Dollar amounts involved are relatively small.
  d. None of the above.

8. For many business decisions, where the dollar amounts involved are not extremely large relative to the size of the business, the utility for money may be assumed linear and EMV considered a good guide to action: true or false?

Answers 19.A

1. acts, events

2. False; an *event* is a condition or outcome that is generally beyond the decision maker's control (sometimes referred to as a "state of nature"). The strategies or choices available to the decision maker are called *acts.*

3. False; it is also necessary to know (or be able to estimate) the probabilities of the various possible events that may occur.

4. False; EMV is computed for each possible act under consideration, using the conditional outcome for each event weighted by the probability of its occurrence.

5. true

6. The probabilities (or odds) that various events will occur.

7. b   *8.* true

---

[1] This can be achieved through a process called the *standard gamble technique,* devised by Von Neumann and Morgenstern.

Section 19.B

Analysis of a Decision Problem

Learning objectives

Your learning objectives for this section are to be able to:

1. Determine for a given decision problem:
   a. Conditional profits
   b. Conditional opportunity losses
   c. Expected monetary values (EMV)
   d. Expected opportunity losses (EOL)
   e. The optimal act
2. Explain the meaning and use of the concept of opportunity loss

A DECISION PROBLEM

In order to investigate the calculation of EMV and related statistics in greater detail, let's consider a simple but reasonably realistic business decision problem. The owner of the small sporting goods store can take advantage of a special opportunity to buy skis. If he buys in lots of 20 pairs, he can get the skis for $60 per pair rather than his usual cost of $80. The retail price for the skis is $120. However, if he overstocks, he'll have to clear his inventory at the end of the season by selling the skis at $50 per pair, at which price all leftover skis will be sold. If he understocks, he can order skis as he needs them at his regular cost of $80 a pair. Let's assume that his best estimate of the demand for skis at the regular price is as follows:

Demand, pairs	Probability
20	.2
40	.4
60	.3
80	.1

In other words, he figures that the odds of selling 20 pairs are 2 in 10, 40 pairs 4 in 10, 60 pairs 3 in 10, and 80 pairs 1 in 10 and that there is no chance that the demand will be less than 20 or more than 80. For convenience, we've assumed that demand will be in whole lots of 20. The question, of course, is how many skis the dealer should order.

DETERMINATION OF CONDITIONAL PROFITS

The first step in analyzing a problem of this sort is to determine entries in the payoff table, i.e. the profits realized for every combination of stock and demand. These profits are, of course, dependent or conditional on the level of demand and on the level of stock and are called conditional profits. Table 19.4 shows the calculation of conditional profits for the payoff table in question.

Although the calculations in Table 19.4 are straightforward, it might help to review them briefly and suggest a generalization. In any case where stock and demand are equal, the conditional profits will equal the number of pairs of skis stocked times the net profit per pair. This relationship could be expressed either as $CP = D(120 - 60) = 60D$ or as $CP = S(120 - 60) = 60S$. If stock is greater than demand, an overstocking exists. In all these cases (labeled "overstocked" in the Stocking State column) the conditional profits are equal to $60 per pair of skis stocked initially, minus the loss suffered in selling the overstocked skis late in the season. The appropriate equation if $S > D$ (when stock is greater than demand) is

$$CP = D(120 - 60) + (S - D)(50 - 60) = 70D - 10S$$

The conditional profit of the entries marked "overstocked" can be determined by substituting appropriate levels of D and S in the equation above.

If $S < D$, the stock is less than the amount demanded and the dealer is understocked (labeled "understocked" in the Stocking State column). This necessitates the dealer's buying skis during the season at a higher cost, and the resulting conditional profit can be determined through the relationship

$$CP = S(120 - 60) + (D - S)(120 - 80) = 20S + 40D$$

Table 19.4 / Determination of conditional profits for ski problem

Demand D	Stock S	Stocking state	Conditional profit	
20	20	$D = S$	$20(120 - 60)$	$= \$1200$
20	40	Overstocked	$20(120 - 60) + 20(50 - 60)$	$= 1000$
20	60	Overstocked	$20(120 - 60) + 40(50 - 60)$	$= 800$
20	80	Overstocked	$20(120 - 60) + 60(50 - 60)$	$= 600$
40	20	Understocked	$20(120 - 60) + 20(120 - 80)$	$= 2000$
40	40	$D = S$	$40(120 - 60)$	$= 2400$
40	60	Overstocked	$40(120 - 60) + 20(50 - 60)$	$= 2200$
40	80	Overstocked	$40(120 - 60) + 40(50 - 60)$	$= 2000$
60	20	Understocked	$20(120 - 60) + 40(120 - 80)$	$= 2800$
60	40	Understocked	$40(120 - 60) + 20(120 - 80)$	$= 3200$
60	60	$D = S$	$60(120 - 60)$	$= 3600$
60	80	Overstocked	$60(120 - 60) + 20(50 - 60)$	$= 3400$
80	20	Understocked	$20(120 - 60) + 60(120 - 80)$	$= 3600$
80	40	Understocked	$40(120 - 60) + 40(120 - 80)$	$= 4000$
80	60	Understocked	$60(120 - 60) + 20(120 - 80)$	$= 4400$
80	80	$D = S$	$80(120 - 60)$	$= 4800$

Note that if demand equals stock, both the CP equations for overstocking and for understocking reduce to $60 times the number of skis involved. Thus all the entries in the payoff table could have been determined by using the following equations:

$$CP = 70D - 10S \quad \text{if } S \geq D \quad\quad (19.1)$$
$$CP = 20S + 40D \quad \text{if } S < D \quad\quad (19.2)$$

Equations like these will be called *conditional profit functions.* As you'll see in later modules, it's often advantageous in more complex problems to derive the equations from the conditions of the problem and then determine the conditional profits from these functions.

Now that all the conditional profits can be determined, we can arrive at the optimal number of skis to stock by weighting the conditional profits for each act by the probabilities attached to each level of demand and adding all the products for each act, just as we did for the chuck-a-luck example. The weighting is shown in Table 19.5.

The optimal act (marked with an asterisk) is to stock 60 pairs since such an act produces the highest combination of probabilities times payoffs. Since the calculation is in terms of money, as opposed to units of utility, the expected values are called expected monetary values, and EMV*, that is, $2560, is known as the expected monetary value of the optimal act.

OPPORTUNITY LOSSES

Sometimes it is simpler to determine optimal acts through the use of *conditional opportunity losses* (COL) rather than conditional profits. An *opportunity loss* is defined as the difference between the conditional profit of the optimal act, *given a particular event*, and the conditional profit of any other act, given the same event.

The meaning of opportunity loss can most easily be illustrated by converting a table of conditional profits into a table of conditional opportunity losses. The first

Table 19.5 / Determination of optimal act, ski problem

Event demand, pairs	Probability of event (weight)	Stock 20 pairs		Stock 40 pairs		Stock 60 pairs		Stock 80 pairs	
		CP	CP × prob- ability	CP	CP × prob- ability	CP	CP × prob- ability	CP	CP × prob- ability
20	.2	$1200	$ 240	$1000	$ 200	$ 800	$ 160	$ 600	$ 120
40	.4	2000	800	2400	960	2200	880	2000	800
60	.3	2800	840	3200	960	3600	1080	3400	1020
80	.1	3600	360	4000	400	4400	440	4800	480
EMV			$2240		$2520		$2560*		$2420

Table 19.6 / Optimal conditional profit for each event, ski problem

Event: demand, pairs	Act			
	Stock 20 pairs	Stock 40 pairs	Stock 60 pairs	Stock 80 pairs
20	$1200*	$1000	$ 800	$ 600
40	2000	2400*	2200	2000
60	2800	3200	3600*	3400
80	3600	4000	4400	4800*

step is to examine the conditional profits to determine the optimal act for each event. Table 19.6 shows the conditional profits from Table 19.5, with the optimal act for each event marked with an asterisk. Note that the highest conditional profit for any level of demand occurs, as we'd expect, where the amount stocked is equal to the amount demanded.

The table of conditional opportunity losses can be obtained by subtracting the CP for the act in question from the optimal CP for that event. Thus the first row of the COL table (COL for demand 20) is obtained by subtracting each entry for that row from $1200. The complete COL table is shown in Table 19.7.

Two observations can be made regarding the entries in Table 19.7. First, the conditional opportunity losses form a pattern. For every 20 pairs that the dealer is overstocked, the opportunity loss grows by increments of $200, while for every 20 pairs he is understocked, the opportunity loss grows by increments of $400. These relationships can be determined directly from the facts of the problem in the form of equations, instead of deriving the COL table from a table of conditional profits. These relationships are

$$COL = 10(S - D) \qquad \text{if } S > D$$

(The dealer loses $10 on each pair of skis that is overstocked.)

$$COL = 20(D - S) \qquad \text{if } S < D$$

(The dealer loses the opportunity to increase his profit by $20 for each pair of skis understocked.)

$$COL = 0 \qquad \text{if } S = D$$

Table 19.7 / COL table, ski problem

Event: demand, pairs	Act			
	Stock 20 pairs	Stock 40 pairs	Stock 60 pairs	Stock 80 pairs
20	$ 0	$200	$400	$600
40	400	0	200	400
60	800	400	0	200
80	1200	800	400	0

Table 19.8 / Calculation of expected opportunity losses, ski problem

Event: demand, pairs	Prob- ability of event (weight)	Stock 20 pairs		Stock 40 pairs		Stock 60 pairs		Stock 80 pairs	
		COL	COL × prob- ability	COL	COL × prob- ability	COL	COL × prob- ability	COL	COL × prob- ability
20	.2	$ 0	$ 0	$200	$ 40	$400	$ 80	$600	$120
40	.4	400	160	0	0	200	80	400	160
60	.3	800	240	400	120	0	0	200	60
80	.1	1200	120	800	80	400	40	0	0
EOL			$520		$240		$200*		$340

(The dealer has optimized his profits.) These equations can be summarized as

$$\text{COL} = 10(S - D) \quad \text{if } S \geq D \quad (19.3)$$
$$\text{COL} = 20(D - S) \quad \text{if } S < D \quad (19.4)$$

Second, the equations and the COL table illustrate the fact that opportunity losses measure either the regret of suffering an out-of-pocket loss (for overstocking) or the regret of not taking advantage of an opportunity for gain (for understocking). Opportunity losses always measure positive amounts of regret and can *never* be negative. If you act optimally, you suffer no regret; if you don't act optimally, you suffer a positive amount of regret. (The conditional profit of the optimal act *minus* the conditional profit of any other act for the same event can never be negative.)

As you might expect the optimal act can be identified by minimizing expected opportunity losses as well as by maximizing expected profits. Calculation of the optimal act through minimizing expected opportunity loss is shown in Table 19.8. The optimal act is to stock 60 pairs, with an expected opportunity loss of $200.

REVIEW EXERCISES 19.B

1. A garden shop sells a certain tropical plant which has only a limited demand and can be purchased only at the beginning of the Christmas season. These plants cost the shop $60 each and are sold to customers for $100 each. Any plants unsold at the end of the season must be sacrificed at a price of $30. The owner estimates the Christmas demand for the plant as follows:

Demand	Probability
0	.2
1	.3
2	.4
3	.1
	1.0

Construct a table which shows the conditional profits involved in stocking 0, 1, 2, and 3 tropical plants.

2. Refer to Exercise 1. Calculate the EMV for each act and select the optimum act.

3. Refer to Exercise 1. Construct a table showing conditional opportunity losses for the various acts and calculate EOL for each act.

4. The act with the highest EMV in a decision problem will always have the lowest EOL: true or false?

5. For any given event, the conditional opportunity loss involved in a particular act selected by a decision maker is the difference between _____ and

_____.

6. Conditional opportunity losses:
   a. Are positive only for the optimal act.
   b. Are never negative.
   c. Are never zero.
   d. None of the above.

Answers 19.B

1.

		Act: Stock			
Demand	Probability	0	1	2	3
0	.2	0	$-30	$-60	$-90
1	.3	0	+40	+10	-20
2	.4	0	+40	+80	+50
3	.1	0	+40	+80	+120

Note that if $S \geq D$, $CP = 40D - 30(S - D) = 70D - 30S$; and if $S < D$, $CP = 40S$.

2.

		Act: Stock			
Demand	Probability	0	1	2	3
0	.2	0	$-6	$-12	$-18
1	.3	0	+12	+3	-6
2	.4	0	+16	+32	+20
3	.1	0	+4	+8	+12
EMV		0	$+26	$+31	$+8

The optimum act is stock 2 plants.

3.

		Act: Stock			
Demand	Probability	0	1	2	3
0	.2	0 (0)	$30 (6)	$60 (12)	$90 (18)
1	.3	$ 40 (12)	0 (0)	30 (9)	60 (18)
2	.4	80 (32)	40 (16)	0 (0)	30 (12)
3	.1	120 (12)	80 (8)	40 (4)	0 (0)
EOL		$56	$30	$25	$48

4. true
5. the conditional profit (for that act-event combination); the conditional profit of the *best* act given that event
6. *b*

Section 19.C
Some Further Concepts

Learning objectives

Your learning objectives for this section are to be able to:

1. Define the following concepts:
    a. Cost of uncertainty
    b. Expected value of perfect information (EVPI)
    c. Cost of irrationality
    d. Expected profit under certainty
2. Compute the above measures for a given decision problem and explain their meaning
3. Distinguish between expected values and realized values in a decision situation

---

COST OF UNCERTAINTY

The expected opportunity loss of the optimal act, EOL*, is called the *cost of uncertainty*. If you had a perfect forecasting device, you'd always know what event would occur. You'd then choose the best act for that event, and your opportunity losses would be 0. Therefore the EOL* is the price you have to pay for having to make a decision in the face of uncertainty, and it is called the cost of uncertainty.

EXPECTED VALUE OF PERFECT INFORMATION

If you could buy the perfect forecasting device mentioned in the preceding paragraph, how much would it be worth? Since a perfect forecast would reduce expected opportunity loss to 0, it would be logical to pay any amount up to EOL* for the forecasting service but no more. Thus EOL* provides a measure of what perfect information would be worth, and can also be called the expected value of perfect information (EVPI).

COST OF IRRATIONALITY

Faced with uncertainty, a person who wants to be rational will choose the optimal act. If he chooses another act instead, he's acting irrationally. This, of course, is his option, but the difference between EOL* and the larger EOL for the act he chooses measures the cost of his irrationality. The difference between EOL* and the EOL of any other act is the same as the difference between EMV* and the EMV for that same act except that the sign is reversed.

EXPECTED PROFIT UNDER CERTAINTY

Assume that a forecasting service could tell the ski dealer any time he was confronted with the opportunity to make a special purchase of skis what the demand would be for that season. If the forecaster said the demand would be for 20 pairs of skis the dealer would stock 20 pairs, with a profit equal to the conditional profit for the act-event combination demand 20, stock 20, namely, $1200. If the forecast was for 40 skis, he'd stock 40, sell them all, and make a profit of $2400, and so on, for all levels of demand. These values could be called profits under certainty. They're the conditional profits marked with asterisks (to denote optimum profit) you saw earlier.

Now if the dealer used this forecaster's services every time he was confronted with this opportunity, and if the odds of the various demands were as originally stated, he could calculate his average profit by weighting the profits under certainty by the odds of their occurring. This calculation, performed in Table 19.9, produces a measure called the expected profit under certainty (EPC).

Under conditions of certainty the EOL, as mentioned previously, would be 0, and the sum of EPC and EOL under certainty would be equal to $2760 + 0 = $2760. Note that this same value can always be obtained for profit under certainty by adding the EMV for the act in question and the EOL for that same act.

In the ski problem, the EMV for the act stock 20, for example, was $2240 (Table 19.5), and the EOL for that act was $520 (Table 19.8). Their sum is $2760, the EPC. This value of $2760 could thus be obtained by adding the EMV for *any* act to the EOL for that same act.

Table 19.9 / Calculation of expected profit under certainty, ski problem

Event: demand, pairs	Probability of event (weight)	CP of optimal act, given demand	CP × probability
20	.2	$1200	$ 240
40	.4	2400	960
60	.3	3600	1080
80	.1	4800	480
EPC			$2760

EXPECTED VALUES VS. REALIZED VALUES

We began this module defining an optimal decision as one that looks like the best bet *before* action is taken. We saw that there were two elements to what made a particular act the best bet, namely, the payoffs associated with all the act-event combinations and how likely the events were to occur. We defined the act having the greatest weighted payoff, i.e., the highest expected value, as the optimal act or best bet.

You should realize, however, that while the act with the highest expected value identifies the act with the most promise before the fact, the amount of EMV* is *not* how much we'll make if we take that course of action. Once an act is taken, profits are no longer conditional, they are determined. In the chuck-a-luck problem, for example, the only possible monetary outcomes of playing the game once are $-\$1$, $+\$1$, or $+\$2$. The expected monetary value is the amount we can expect to average if we play the game a large number of times. What we are saying, then, is that *the act that maximizes the average profit over a large number of trials is the best act to choose before the fact, regardless of the number of times we'll be confronted with the situation.*

Expected opportunity losses are interpreted the same as other expected values. Thus, the expected opportunity loss of the optimal act is not the amount of money (or utility) a person will lose on taking the optimal act. The expected opportunity loss of the optimal act shows, on the average, the amount the decision maker pays for having to make his decision under uncertainty.

It should be emphasized again that maximization of expected value is not the only guide to action. However, it's a guide for making decisions under uncertainty which when followed will lead the decision maker to act in a manner consistent with his beliefs about the situation. Thus, procedures followed in this module constitute a systematic way of bringing to bear on the decision all the information the decision maker has about the situation. We have assumed in this module that the decision maker doesn't have the opportunity to sample in order to secure more information about the problem before having to make a decision. How sampling procedures can be used to reduce the cost of uncertainty in decision problems will be discussed at length in the next four modules.

REVIEW EXERCISES 19.C

1. The cost of uncertainty is defined as _____.
2. The expected value of perfect information:
    a. Is equal to the cost of uncertainty.
    b. Tells what a perfect forecast would be worth in the given decision situation.
    c. Both *a* and *b*.
    d. Neither *a* nor *b*.
3. For a given act chosen by a decision maker, the cost of irrationality measures the difference between the EMV of that act and _____.
4. The expected profit under certainty (EPC) can be obtained by taking the weighted average of the highest (best) conditional profits for each event, using the probabilities of the various events as weights: true or false?

479

5. Refer to Exercise 1 in Sec. 19.B. Determine:
   a. The cost of uncertainty.
   b. EVPI.
   c. The cost of irrationality if three plants are stocked.
   d. The expected profit under certainty.
6. Refer to Exercise 5. The profit that will actually be made on these plants in a given season will be equal to:
   a. The EMV of the act selected.
   b. The EMV of the best act.
   c. The expected profit under certainty.
   d. None of the above.
7. The expected opportunity loss of the optimal act is the average amount of money that will be lost if that act is selected: true or false?

Answers 19.C

1. EOL of the optimal act   2. c   3. EMV of the optimal (best) act
4. True; it may also be obtained by adding the EMV and EOL for *any* of the acts under consideration; this sum should be the same for each act.
5. a. $25; the EOL of the optimal act (stock 2)
   b. $25; by definition, the same as the cost of uncertainty; i.e., the EOL of the optimal act
   c. $48 − $25 = $23 or $31 − $8 = $23
   d. $56. This amount can be obtained by adding the EMV and EOL for any act, or as follows:

Demand	Probability	CP of optimal act, given demand	CP × weight
0	.2	$ 0	0
1	.3	40	12
2	.4	80	32
3	.1	120	12
			$56

6. d. EMV of the act that is chosen is only an expectation, not the actual amount that will be earned in any given season. (It should be, of course, the average amount earned over a large number of similar seasons.)
7. False; it is the amount (on the average) that the decision maker pays for having to make the decision under uncertainty.

Questions and Problems

19.1. a. Define each of the following:
         (1) Conditional profit   (2) Expected profit (EMV)
         (3) EMV*   (4) Opportunity loss

(5) Expected opportunity loss   (6) EOL*

(7) EVPI   (8) Expected profit under certainty

(9) Cost of uncertainty   (10) Cost of irrationality

    b. Show, wherever you can, the identities or relationships that exist between the terms in part *a* and explain them in your own words.

19.2. Assume that you are given the following payoff table:

Event	Conditional profit		
	Act 1	Act 2	Act 3
A	$20	$10	$ 0
B	35	40	30
C	50	55	60

You are told that the probability of events *A*, *B*, and *C* are .5, .3, and .2, respectively.

    a. Calculate the EMV for each act, and identify the optimal act.

    b. Draw up a table of conditional opportunity losses, calculate the EOL for each act, and identify the optimal act.

    c. Calculate the expected profit under certainty.

    d. Calculate the cost of irrationality for each of the nonoptimal acts.

    e. What is the cost of uncertainty?

    f. What is the expected value of perfect information?

19.3. Suppose the newsboy in Prob. 1.8 attaches the following probability weights to various levels of demand for newspapers on a particular day:

Demand, number of papers	18	19	20	21	22	23
Probability	.1	.1	.2	.3	.2	.1

Assuming that unsold newspapers are worthless,

    a. How many papers should he purchase?

    b. How much does he expect to make on the day in question?

    c. If he believed the demand situation would stay the same, how much would he expect to make in 30 days?

    d. How much could he afford to pay for a perfect forecast of demand?

19.4. You run a concession at football games in a small town. A question you must resolve is how many hot dogs to stock on a typical night. You can buy buns for 48 cents per dozen and weiners for 60 cents per dozen. If they are not sold, the weiners are a total loss, but the buns can be returned, in which case you receive 12 cents per dozen for them. Catsup, mustard, etc., average 2 cents a hot dog (24 cents per dozen) for hot dogs *sold*. Hot dogs sell for 20 cents *each*. Assume that the only possible levels of demand are 10, 20, and 30 dozen, and that these levels have probabilities of .2, .5, and .3 respectively.

    a. Determine the conditional profit functions.

    b. Make a table of conditional profits.

    c. Determine the optimal number to stock, using conditional profits.

    d. Determine the opportunity loss functions.

     e. Make an opportunity loss table from the conditional profit table.

     f. Check the opportunity loss table using the conditional opportunity loss functions.

     g. Determine the optimal number to stock, using the opportunity loss table.

     h. Determine the cost of uncertainty.

     i. Determine the expected value of perfect information.

     j. Determine the expected profit under certainty.

19.5. Do you think *your* utility for money curve over the range of $-\$1000$ to $+\$1000$ looks like that in Fig. 19.1, 19.2, or 19.3? Why do you feel that way? If you received a windfall profit of $10,000 tomorrow, might your utility for money curve change? Explain.

19.6. Occasionally, corporations or individuals may decide to self-insure against certain kinds of risks. A large chain store, for example, might self-insure against the risks of fire and theft, although an independent (one store) operator would be very reluctant to do so.

     a. On a per store basis, are the expected losses as a result of these risks different in the two situations?

     b. Why else might the decision makers' optimal acts be different in the two situations?

19.7. Would you rather play the chuck-a-luck game (with two dice) described in the text once with a $1000 bet or 1000 times making a $1 bet each time? Why? Does your answer have any relationship to part *b* of Prob. 19.6?

19.8. You have a part-time job in a shoe department and have a chance to show off your knowledge of statistics by solving the following problem. Children's shoe boots (size 5B) cost you $5 each ($60 per dozen); they sell for $8 each ($96 per dozen) during the winter but must be marked down to $3 each ($36 per dozen) in the spring to clear the stock. You have determined the following distribution of demand:

Dozen	10	20	30
Probability	.5	.3	.2

Determine the optimal number of boots to stock using a table of conditional profits.

19.9. Kostplus Corporation, a manufacturer of aerospace subsystems, is under government contract to produce 5000 assemblies, each of which requires a delicate component that must meet rigid specifications. These components can be purchased in any quantity from a subcontractor, who will guarantee that their quality meets the specifications, at a cost of $15.80 each. Company engineers estimate that the components could be produced internally at a lower cost, but the nature of the production process is such that a high proportion—perhaps as high as 50 percent—of the components will not meet specifications. From previous experience with processes involving similar technology, the following estimates are made:

Fraction of parts not meeting specifications	Probability	Fraction of parts not meeting specifications	Probability
0	.05	0.30	.15
0.10	.40	0.40	.10
0.20	.25	0.50	.05

The fixed setup cost involved in the production process is $20,000, and the variable costs are $10 per unit. Defective components can be discovered, reworked, and replaced in the course of the assembly operation at a cost of $8 each.

    a. What is the expected cost of supplying the 5000 components internally (including the cost of defectives)?

    b. What are the anticipated savings (or losses) from producing vs. purchasing the 5000 components?

    c. What is the cost of uncertainty in this decision problem?

    d. Are your answers to parts *b* and *c* the same? Explain why or why not.

    e. What is the EVPI?

    f. Are your answers to *c* and *e* the same? Explain why or why not.

    g. Interpret the meaning of the EVPI in this problem.

19.10. Suppose, in the situation described in Prob. 19.9, that Kostplus discovers that it is not possible to rework defective components to meet the necessary specifications. Components can be tested at a cost of 20 cents each, but any component found defective must be considered worthless and must be replaced by a new one. This implies that a decision to produce might involve more than 5000 units and/or that some components might be purchased to supplement the internal production. Units in excess of the 5000 acceptable components required have a net resale value of $6 each.

    a. What are the possible acts (decision strategies) under these conditions?

    b. Write a generalized conditional payoff equation for this problem.

    c. Should Kostplus produce any components? If so, how many?

    d. Is the cost of uncertainty higher or lower than in part *c* of Prob. 19.9? Rationalize this difference.

19.11. Suppose defensive common stocks return an average 7 percent in years of economic expansion and 4 percent in recession years. Growth stocks return 30 percent in expansion years but may be expected to lose 40 percent in value in recession years. Of the last 25 years 7 have been recession years, as the term is used here.

    a. Over the long term, would you expect growth stocks or defensive stocks to perform better? (Assume, for purposes of this problem, that there is no particular pattern to the spacing of the recession years over the period.)

    b. How sure would you have to be that a recession was going to occur in the coming year to warrant shifting a portfolio from growth stocks to defensive stocks?

19.12. A man has the opportunity to buy $30,000 of term life insurance covering a 1-year period. The probability that he will survive the year is .995. His utility is linear with money.

    a. Draw up a payoff table showing the conditional profits of each act-event combination.

    b. What is the maximum amount he would be willing to pay for such a policy?

19.13. You are given the opportunity to play chuck-a-luck with three dice. The rules of the game are as follows:

    You pay $1 to play.
    You roll the dice once.
    If you roll 3 sixes, you get $3 and your $1 back.
    If you roll 2 sixes, you get $2 and your $1 back.
    If you roll 1 six, you get $1 and your $1 back.
    If you get 0 sixes, you lose your $1 entry fee.

a. Draw up a table of conditional profits. Be sure to show all the act-event combinations.

b. Calculate the expected monetary values for the acts play and don't play.

c. If your utility were linear with money, would you play the game or not? Explain.

19.14. The E. Z. Pay Co. has annual fixed costs of 1 million dollars, variable costs of $10 per unit of product, and a selling price of $25 per unit. The company has an opportunity to make additional credit sales without increasing its fixed costs of operation, but the potential customers are poor credit risks. Some of the proposed accounts could be collected in a reasonable time, but many could not be collected at all. Unfortunately, the company has no adequate means for predicting in advance which customers will pay and which will default.

a. What percentage of the proposed credit sales must create collectible accounts in order to make the additional sales profitable?

b. Does your answer to part a suggest any generalization about credit policy and its relationship to the utilization of productive capacity?

c. According to generally accepted accounting procedures, the net accounts receivable figure shown on a firm's balance sheet is actually an expected value. Explain.

MODULE 20
THE ECONOMICS OF
DECISION RULES AND
SAMPLING

In the previous module, you learned how to choose between alternative decision strategies in the face of uncertainty. Now, let's consider another possibility: *to take no action* based on the available information, delaying any action *until additional information is available.* Conceptually, the strategy "buy additional information before making a final decision" should always be added to the list of strategies (or acts) in a decision problem, unless timing is such that an immediate final decision must be made. This is true because additional information, in the form of a sample, will generally reduce the cost of uncertainty inherent in the decision situation. If this cost can be reduced by more than the cost of obtaining the information, it's economically desirable to sample before making a final decision.

Statistical decision rules, which you studied at length in previous modules, do provide the means for basing a decision on sample results. Until now, however, we haven't attempted to evaluate the economic consequences of utilizing samples and decision rules in business situations. In this module, we'll examine these matters for situations in which the sampling is binomial. Module 23 will extend the discussion to include a continuous (normal) distribution. The first three sections of this module will deal with the selection of the *best* action limit or criterion number to use with a particular size sample in a business decision problem. The final section will consider the broader questions of the economics of sampling: whether information (a sample) should be purchased and, if so, how much (how large a sample) should be obtained.

General learning objectives

Your general learning objectives for this module are to be able to:

1. Differentiate between classical hypothesis testing and business decision making
2. For a given business decision problem select:
   a. The optimum decision criterion to use with particular sample information
   b. The optimum size sample to take before making a decision

Section 20.A

Statistical Decision Rules in Business Situations

Learning objectives

Your learning objectives for this section are to be able to:

1. Describe the basis for selecting decision rules in classical hypothesis testing
2. Explain why such a basis is inadequate for business decision making
3. Describe the factors involved in selecting a decision rule for making a business decision

The error curves you studied in Module 12 provided a graphic analysis of the properties of decision rules. One such curve, reproduced here as Fig. 20.1, shows the probability of making a wrong decision for given values of the process parameter p, when using a (100, 8) rule for accepting a shipment of flashbulbs when .04 is the highest acceptable level of defectives.[1] You'll, recall however, that when you compared the

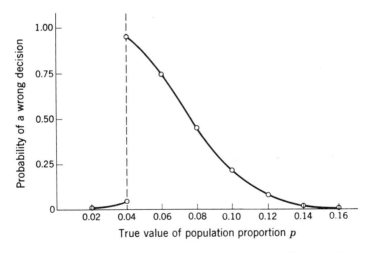

Figure 20.1 / Error curve for the decision rule $n = 100$ (if $r \geq 8$, reject; if $r < 8$, accept). ($H_N : p \leq .04$.)

---

[1] This curve is developed on pp. 289–293 of Module 12. You might want to review that process before continuing.

error curves for several alternative decision rules, there wasn't any sure way to select the "best" rule from among them. It was suggested that decision rules are often selected so that the maximum risk of Type I error is set arbitrarily at, say, 5 percent. Such a decision rule admittedly stacks the deck in favor of accepting the null hypothesis being tested. No justification was offered except that the null hypothesis selected for a test either represented (in some sense) the status quo or was strongly preferred on the basis of accumulated experience.

In some cases such a method of selecting a hypothesis may be well founded. Under our judicial system a person accused of a crime is assumed innocent and must be proved guilty beyond all reasonable doubt. For moral and social reasons, we consider it justifiable to establish a hypothesis of innocence and to test it via legal proceedings in a manner that ensures that the risks of a Type I error are relatively small. We do this because we believe the *costs* of making a Type I error (sending an innocent person to jail) are relatively greater than the costs of making a Type II error (allowing a guilty man to go free). Even though in this example the costs are intangible, it is clear that cost considerations provide the appropriate basis for selecting and testing a hypothesis.

Likewise, in designing classical tests of hypotheses, the risk of a Type I error is usually specified at a low level such as .05. This seemingly arbitrary specification may be appropriate for certain types of scientific work, where we purposely wish to put the burden of proof on a new scientific theory which contradicts established doctrines. Orderly scientific progress requires that new ideas bear the burden of proof.

But the same does not hold for most business decision-making situations where there is no a priori reason for minimizing errors of one kind at the expense of making errors of the other. The classical approach can be justified only on the basis of *cost* considerations, where the costs of one kind of error are quite different from the costs of the other kind. There are many business problems in which Type I errors are no more serious than Type II.

Whenever possible we'll incorporate the economic consequences of the two kinds of wrong decisions in the procedure for selecting an appropriate decision rule. Of course, the business decision maker is concerned not only with the probability of making a wrong decision but also with the magnitude of the loss resulting from a wrong decision. Thus, it's really the *expected loss* resulting from use of a particular decision rule that's important to the selection process.

Unfortunately, the computation of this expected loss isn't a simple matter. As you've seen from your earlier study, there is no *one* risk of a Type I or a Type II error. These risks depend upon the true value of the population parameter p. Likewise, there is no such thing as *the* cost of a Type I or of a Type II error. Generally these costs will also depend upon the value of the parameter p.

For purposes of making business decisions, you'll not only be concerned with the question of whether a particular hypothesis is true or false, i.e., whether p is more or less than some specified value, but also with how far the true value of p may deviate from some economic break-even point. Suppose, for example, that the proportion of p of a particular market that'll buy a new product represents the source of uncertainty (the random variable) in a decision problem. It's potentially far more serious if actual sales fall far below the break-even level of profitability than if the sales are slightly below. On the other hand, you wouldn't be very concerned about failing to undertake the production of a new product whose sales would have been only slightly above the break-even level, but you'd be very much concerned about passing up a high-volume item.

Thus in assessing the merits of a decision rule to apply to a business situation, i.e., computing the expected opportunity loss resulting from its use, you must consider:

1. The probability that the particular decision rule will lead to an incorrect decision *for every given level of p*. These probabilities have been referred to earlier as the probabilities of Type I or Type II errors, and they have been shown by the error curve or (indirectly) by the power curve or the OC curve for the rule.
2. The opportunity loss that would result from a wrong decision *for every given level of p*.

Note that the probability of an incorrect decision and the loss from a wrong decision are both conditional upon a given level of p. That is to say, this probability and loss will generally be different for each value of p considered. A complication in assessing the expected loss resulting from the use of a decision rule arises from the fact that various values of the parameter p generally won't be equally likely. Therefore, in addition to the two factors listed above, you must consider a third:

3. The probability that various levels of p (states of nature) will occur.

You'll see specifically how these three factors enter into the selection of a decision rule in the next section, where we consider a particular business decision situation.

REVIEW EXERCISES 20.A

1. In classical hypothesis testing, the statistical decision rule is normally designed so that:
   a. The null hypothesis being tested is likely to be rejected.
   b. Economic consequences of a wrong decision are considered.
   c. The risk of making a Type I error is low.
   d. None of the above.
2. Classical hypothesis testing is appropriate for scientific work, where the burden of proof is placed on new theories which contradict established doctrines: true or false?
3. In business decision situations, the cost (as well as the probability) of making wrong decisions should be explicitly considered: true or false?
4. In business decision problems, the cost of making a wrong decision is generally the same for all values of the "process parameter" (or true state of nature), even though the risk of making the wrong decision will vary: true or false?
5. The expected loss resulting from the use of a particular business decision rule will depend on:
   a. The probability that the decision rule will lead to a wrong decision for each possible value of the population parameter.
   b. The opportunity loss resulting from a wrong decision for each possible value of the population parameter.

c. The probability of each possible value of the population parameter occurring.

d. All the above.

Answers 20.A

1. c   2. true   *3.* true

4. False; both the cost of a wrong decision and the probability of making it will be different for different values of *p*.

5. *d.*   All these functions are included in the computations (illustrated in the next section).

Section 20.B

Break-Even Analysis for a Business Decision Problem

Learning objectives

Your learning objectives for this section are to be able to calculate for a given business decision problem:

1. The economic break-even value of *p*
2. The conditional opportunity losses (COL) for different values of *p*
3. The expected opportunity loss (EOL) for an immediate decision without sampling[1]

A BUSINESS DECISION PROBLEM: NEW PRODUCT DEVELOPMENT

Suppose a firm selling to 20,000 industrial accounts is considering adding a new product to its line. Management is somewhat reluctant to make this proposed addition because its development costs are high. It is estimated that $500,000 would be required for full-scale development. Further, the management believes the proposed product to be a one-shot item, having virtually no possibility of repeat sales to the same customer. It is unique, so its addition can be expected to have no effect, either positive or negative, on sales of the existing line.

---

[1] This is a review of an objective covered in the previous module.

Table 20.1 / Probability distribution for new product

Proportion purchasing	Probability
.02	.1
.04	.3
.06	.3
.08	.2
.10	.1
	1.0

The product would add nothing to existing overhead expenses (above the $500,000 development costs) and could be produced at a variable cost of $1200 per unit. Variable selling expense would be approximately $300 per unit. Because of the nature of the item, it can be produced to order, so no inventory need be carried.

As a result of previous experience with similar products and interviews with company salesmen, the market research department believes the product could be most profitably priced at $2000. They are able to assign the probability distribution in Table 20.1 to the proportion of customers who'll actually purchase the new product.

CALCULATION OF AN ECONOMIC BREAK-EVEN POINT AND CONDITIONAL OPPORTUNITY LOSSES

A useful first step in the analysis of this type of problem is to calculate the economic break-even value of p, the proportion of the total population of customers purchasing the product. This calculation will involve no use of statistical analysis, only simple business arithmetic. In general, you must simply compute

$$\text{Contribution margin} = \text{selling price} - \text{variable cost}$$

and
$$\text{Break-even volume} = \frac{\text{fixed cost}}{\text{contribution margin per unit}}$$

Here, the selling price is $2000 per unit and the total of variable costs is $1500 (or $1200 + $300). Contribution margin is therefore $500 per unit and

$$\text{Break-even volume} = \frac{\$500,000}{\$500} = 1000 \text{ units}$$

Since 1,000 out of the firm's 20,000 customers must buy the product in order for the firm to break even, the *break-even proportion* (BEP) is 1000/20,000 = .05.

If the true proportion of customers who'd ultimately purchase the product is less than .05, the firm will experience an out-of-pocket loss if the product is produced; i.e., the total contribution to profit and overhead won't be sufficient to cover the

491

Table 20.2 / Conditional-opportunity-loss functions

	Develop	Don't develop
If $p < .05$	COL = \$500,000 − \$500p(20,000) = \$10,000,000(.05 − p)	COL = 0
If $p > .05$	COL = 0	COL = \$500p(20,000) − \$500,000 = \$10,000,000(p − .05)

fixed development costs incurred. On the other hand, if p is greater than .05, an opportunity loss will be incurred if the product is *not* produced, as a result of the lost profit opportunity.

Of course, if $p \geq .05$ and the firm decides to produce, or if $p \leq .05$ and the firm decides not to produce, a correct decision will have been made and the firm won't incur any opportunity loss. The conditional opportunity loss (COL) functions for these four possibilities are shown in Table 20.2.

To be sure that the equations are understood, let's talk our way through the equation in the cell "Develop if $p < .05$." If the decision is made to develop, a cost of \$500,000 will be incurred for development. Some of this cost will be recovered by selling units at a profit of \$500 each to a certain proportion of the population p. The gross profit will be \$500p(20,000). However, if $p < .05$, the profit will not cover the development cost, and a measure of our regret would be the net cost

$$\$500,000 - \$500p(20,000) = \$10,000,000(.05 - p)$$

In order to calculate the COL for any act-event combination, you only have to substitute the desired value of p in the appropriate equation in Table 20.2. For example, for the act "develop" and the event $p = .02$, COL = \$10,000,000(.05 − .02) = \$300,000. In a similar manner you could find all the other COLs shown in Table 20.3.

EXPECTED OPPORTUNITY LOSS FOR AN IMMEDIATE DECISION WITHOUT SAMPLING

Now if you must make an immediate decision whether to develop the product or not, you could proceed as before to calculate the expected opportunity losses (EOLs) of the two decisions using as weights the probabilities of Table 20.1. This procedure is carried out in Table 20.4. The EOL of the decision to develop the product is \$60,000,

Table 20.3 / Opportunity loss table

p	Develop	Don't develop
.02	\$300,000	\$ 0
.04	100,000	0
.06	0	100,000
.08	0	300,000
.10	0	500,000

Table 20.4 / Analysis of intermediate decision (without sampling)

Event			Act		
		Develop		Don't develop	
Proportion buying p	$P(p)$	COL	Weight × COL	COL	Weight × COL
.02	.1	$300,000	$30,000	$ 0	$ 0
.04	.3	100,000	30,000	0	0
.06	.3	0	0	100,000	30,000
.08	.2	0	0	300,000	60,000
.10	.1	0	0	500,000	50,000
EOL			$60,000		$140,000

compared with an EOL of $140,000 for the decision not to develop. If no other information were available, you should decide to develop the product since that act has the lower EOL.

REVIEW EXERCISES 20.B

Suppose that in the product-development problem described in this section, variable cost estimates are revised upward to $1250 per unit (instead of $1200) and fixed development costs are estimated at $540,000 (instead of $500,000). Variable selling expenses are still estimated at $300 per unit, and the selling price of $2000 still produces the same probability distribution of customers who'll buy the new product:

Proportion purchasing	Probability
.02	.1
.04	.3
.06	.3
.08	.2
.10	.1
	1.0

1. Compute the economic break-even value of p given these changes in cost estimates.
2. Compute COLs for the decisions develop and don't develop to fill in the table below.

Opportunity loss table

p	Develop	Don't develop
.02	_____	_____
.04	_____	_____
.06	_____	_____
.08	_____	_____
.10	_____	_____

3. Compute the EOL of an immediate decision without sampling:

p	Develop	Don't develop
.02		
.04		
.06		
.08		
.10		

4. In the text of this section it was shown that the correct decision without sampling was to develop the product. Have the slightly higher cost estimates here changed this decision? Why?

Answers 20.B

1. Contribution to profit and overhead = \$2000 − (\$1250 + \$300) = \$450

$$\text{Break-even volume} = \frac{\text{fixed costs}}{\text{contribution/unit}} = \frac{\$540,000}{\$450/\text{unit}} = 1200 \text{ units}$$

Since there are 20,000 potential customers,

$$\text{BEP} = \frac{1200}{20,000} = .06$$

2. Conditional opportunity loss functions would be:

	Develop	Don't develop
If $p < .06$	COL = \$540,000 − \$450p(20,000) = \$9,000,000(.06 − p)	COL = 0
If $p > .06$	COL = 0	COL = \$450p(20,000) − \$540,000 = \$9,000,000(p − .06)

and the opportunity loss tables would appear as follows:

Opportunity loss table

p	Develop	Don't develop
.02	\$360,000	\$ 0
.04	180,000	0
.06	0	0
.08	0	180,000
.10	0	360,000

3.

		Develop		Don't develop	
p	$P(p)$	COL	Wt. × COL	COL	Wt. × COL
.02	.1	$360,000	$36,000	$ 0	$ 0
.04	.3	180,000	54,000	0	0
.06	.3	0	0	0	0
.08	.2	0	0	180,000	36,000
.10	.1	0	0	360,000	36,000
EOL			$90,000		$72,000

4. Yes; the decision should now be *don't develop*, because the EOL without sampling is lower ($72,000 compared with $90,000).

Section 20.C

Selecting the Best Decision Criterion for a Particular Sample

Learning objectives

Your learning objectives for this section are to be able to:

1. Compute for a given decision rule, sample size, and criterion number:
   a. The probability that the rule will lead to a wrong decision
   b. The EOL from using the rule
2. Select the optimum criterion to use with a particular sample size

---

EOL WITH SAMPLING

Because of the sizable losses that can be incurred, an alert management might desire additional information before making a decision. Continuing the product-development example, suppose that the firm's marketing research manager recommends an intensive survey of a random sample of customers to determine whether they'd purchase the item in question. Since such a survey would be relatively expensive if definite commitments were to be obtained from the customers contacted, let's assume that the sampling is limited to 20 customers.

Deferring for the moment all questions about the economic desirability of sampling or the particular sample size of 20 that was chosen, let's address the problem of what

495

the optimal decision rule should be. It's this rule that tells you how to use the sample results once they're obtained.

We want to specify a rule of the form: If some number c or more out of the 20 prospective purchasers buy the product in question, go ahead with development; if less than c express an interest, don't develop the product.

The selection of an appropriate value of c should involve consideration of all three of the elements listed earlier on page 489. The immediate decision without sampling involved only two of those elements, namely, the costs (or opportunity losses) of wrong decisions and the probabilities of various states of nature (values of p). In introducing the use of a decision rule utilizing sample evidence, you must consider the remaining element, the probabilities that the use of the decision rule will lead to an incorrect decision.

The probability of a wrong decision. The probability that use of a particular decision rule will lead to a wrong decision, for any value of p, can be obtained from binomial tables. Consider, for example, the case of a decision rule ($n = 20$, $c = 1$). This rule says that if one or more of the prospective purchasers interviewed wants to buy the product, you should develop it. The probability that this decision rule will lead to error, and even the nature of the error itself, depends upon the true value of p. Let's evaluate the probability of an error for each value of p using Fig. 20.2 as an aid to understanding.

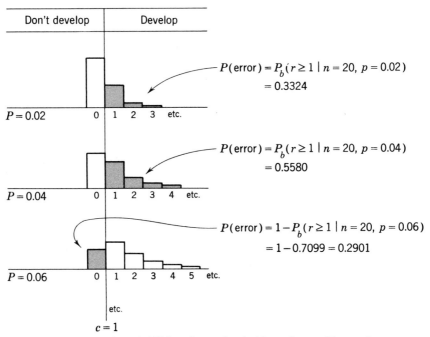

Figure 20.2 / Probabilities of error for decision rule $n = 20$, $c = 1$.

If $p = .02$, the probability that the decision rule $n = 20$, $c = 1$ will lead to a wrong decision is given by the binomial probability $P_b(r \geq 1 \mid n = 20, p = .02)$. This value, .3324, can be obtained directly from the binomial table. If $p = .04$, the probability of a wrong decision from the decision rule will be given by $P_b(r \geq 1 \mid n = 20, p = .04)$. This probability, from the table, is .5580. Notice that as soon as p is more than .05 (the break-even point), you can no longer obtain the probability that the decision rule will lead to an incorrect decision directly from the binomial table. The reason for this is that for p values greater than .05, the wrong decision is not to develop but to fail to develop the product.

If, for example, $p = .10$, the firm can make a substantial profit by developing the product. The only way that the decision rule could lead to the *wrong* decision (not to develop the product) is if the sample contains no positive responses (since any number of responses of one or more will lead to development, a *correct* decision). Given $p = .10$, the probability of no favorable responses in the sample can be obtained indirectly from the binomial table, as 1 minus the probability of one or more favorable responses, or $1 - .8784 = .1216$. In each case the probabilities in Table 20.5 represent the probability of making a wrong decision for a given level of p. Remember, however, that the character of the wrong decision changes from one side to the other as you pass over the break-even value of p. While the numbers in the upper part of the table are read directly from the binomial table, those in the lower portion (for values of p greater than .05) are obtained by *subtracting* the probability read in the binomial table from 1.

Note that for this particular decision rule ($n = 20$, $c = 1$) the action limit of 1 in 20 is equal to the break-even value of .05. This won't be the case for other possible decision rules, so don't confuse the action limit (which tells you how to interpret the sample) with the break-even value (which tells you which tail of the distribution represents the probability of an error).

EOL for a particular decision rule. We can now proceed with the computation of the EOL resulting from the use of the decision rule $n = 20$, $c = 1$. For each of the given values of p there is a certain opportunity loss associated with a wrong decision. These losses are the nonzero entries in Table 20.3, calculated earlier.

Since each of these losses is a conditional loss, you need to know the probability that it will be incurred in order to compute the *expected* (or weighted average)

Table 20.5 / Conditional probabilities of a wrong decision from the decision rule $n = 20$, $c = 1$ for various values of p

p	Probability of a wrong decision, given p	Source
.02	.3324	Read directly
.04	.5580	Read directly
.06	.2901	$1 - .7099$
.08	.1887	$1 - .8113$
.10	.1216	$1 - .8784$

opportunity loss. The probability in question is actually a *joint* probability. Specifically, it's the probability of the joint event that a particular value of p (state of nature) occurs *and* that the decision rule employed ($n = 20$, $c = 1$) leads to a wrong decision. This is best illustrated by a specific example.

We calculated earlier that if $p = .02$, a decision to develop (in that case a wrong decision) will result in an opportunity loss of $300,000. Note that this loss will actually be incurred only in the case where $p = .02$ *and* a wrong decision is made. The probability of the joint event $p = .02$ *and* wrong decision can be obtained by a straightforward application of the multiplication rule for probabilities, that is,

$$P(p \text{ and wrong decision}) = P(\text{wrong decision} \mid p) \times P(p)$$

The probability of a wrong decision *given* that $p = .02$ is .3324, from Table 20.5. The marginal probability that $p = .02$ from the subjective management estimate given in Table 20.1 is .1. Therefore, the *joint* probability of incurring an opportunity loss of $300,000 because of a wrong decision to develop is .3324(.1) or .03324. The probabilities of joint events involving other levels of p, calculated in a similar manner, are shown in column 4 of Table 20.6.

The sum of these joint probabilities, .33757, represents the *marginal* probability of a wrong decision from using the decision rule. That is, the chances that use of the rule $n = 20$, $c = 1$ will lead to a wrong decision are about 34 in 100, or 1 in 3. However, it isn't this overall probability of a wrong decision which is of primary concern. In order to compute the EOL for our decision rule, you must weight the conditional opportunity losses of a wrong decision (from Table 20.3) by the probabilities that they will be incurred (the joint probabilities from column 4 of Table 20.6). This procedure is carried out in Table 20.7.

We seem to be utilizing a set of probability weights which add to .33757 rather than 1, which would be inconsistent with the earlier method of computing expected value. This inconsistency is apparent rather than real. Omitted from the calculations in Table 20.7 is the fact that about two-thirds of the time (.66243), you'd be incurring an opportunity loss of 0 as a result of making the *correct* decision.

We'll designate the final figure in Table 20.7, $52,817, as EOL ($n = 20$, $c = 1$), the EOL resulting from the procedure of employing a sample of 20 and a criterion number of 1 to make the decision.

Table 20.6 / Computation of probability weights for computing EOL, resulting from the use of the decision rule $n = 20$, $c = 1$

(1) p	(2) $P(p)$	(3) $P(\text{wrong decision} \mid p)$	(4) $P(\text{wrong decision and } p)$
.02	.1	.3324	.03324
.04	.3	.5580	.16740
.06	.3	.2901	.08703
.08	.2	.1887	.03774
.10	.1	.1216	.01216
$P(\text{wrong decision})$			.33757

Table 20.7 / Calculation of EOL using the decision rule $n = 20$, $c = 1$

(1) p	(2) COL of a wrong decision	(3) Probability of incurring loss	(4) = (2) × (3)
.02	$300,000	.03324	$ 9,972
.04	100,000	.16740	16,740
.06	100,000	.08703	8,703
.08	300,000	.03774	11,322
.10	500,000	.01216	6,080
EOL ($n = 20$, $c = 1$)			$52,817

EOL for different criterion numbers. You can compute the EOL of other decision rules in a similar fashion. For example, taking the sample size of 20 as fixed, you may consider other values of c that may lead to superior results, i.e., lower EOLs. Evaluation of the EOL for the rule $n = 20$, $c = 2$, is carried out in Tables 20.8 and 20.9. The value of $77,902 obtained for EOL ($n = 20$, $c = 2$) is substantially greater than that for EOL ($n = 20$, $c = 1$), demonstrating the superiority of the use of $c = 1$ as the criterion number for a sample of 20. Higher c values, $c = 3, 4, 5 \ldots$, will give progressively worse results (larger EOLs), and of course $c = 0$ is meaningless as a criterion. (Zero or more favorable responses will always be found in any sample, rendering this sampling procedure useless.) Note that in the general case where some value of c other than 1 is optimal, you must obtain a higher EOL for a c value on each side of it to be sure it's the best.

A c value of 1 is thus the optimal decision criterion for use with a sample of size 20 in this problem. If the suggested survey of 20 of the firm's customers is made, development of the product should be undertaken if one or more of the customers "buys" it. Only if there are *no* favorable responses out of the sample of 20 should the firm decide not to develop the product.

Alternative methods of computation. Before leaving the mechanics of computing the EOLs resulting from the use of particular decision rules, you should note that alternative computational schemes are available. Each of the figures in the final

Table 20.8 / Computation of probability weights for computing EOL for the decision rule $n = 20$, $c = 2$

(1) p	(2) $P(p)$	(3) $P(\text{wrong decision} \mid p)$	(4) $P(\text{wrong decision and } p)$
.02	.1	.0599	.00599
.04	.3	.1897	.05691
.06	.3	.6605	.19815
.08	.2	.5169	.10338
.10	.1	.3917	.03917
$P(\text{wrong decision})$			.40360

499

Table 20.9 / Computation of EOL for the decision rule $n = 20$, $c = 2$

(1) p	(2) COL of a wrong decision	(3) Probability of incurring loss	(4) = (2) × (3)
.02	$300,000	.00599	$ 1,797
.04	100,000	.05691	5,691
.06	100,000	.19815	19,815
.08	300,000	.10338	31,014
.10	500,000	.03917	19,585
EOL ($n = 20$, $c = 2$)			$77,902

column of the computations of Table 20.7 or 20.9 is obtained as the product of the three factors considered earlier: (1) the conditional cost of a wrong decision, given p, (2) the probability of a wrong decision, given p, and (3) the probability of occurrence of a given level of p. As in any case where multiplying three figures together, the end result doesn't depend on the *order* of multiplication. For purposes of explanation, we chose to multiply the probabilities first and then the joint probability obtained by the conditional costs. We might have chosen to multiply the conditional costs by the conditional probabilities of error first, obtaining a set of expected loss figures which are still conditional on various values of p and which must finally be weighted by the $P(p)$ values. A third alternative is perhaps best of all for computational purposes. Since the conditional probabilities of a wrong decision, $P(\text{wrong decision} \mid p)$ are the only numbers which change for different decision rules, it might be advantageous to multiply the other two constant factors [conditional cost × $P(p)$] first, saving the changing conditional probabilities for the last step. This will result in only one *new* set of multiplications for each EOL (n, c) evaluation, rather than two sets.

REVIEW EXERCISES 20.C

1. Refer to the development problem in the text (break-even $p = .05$). For the decision rule "take a sample of size 50, and if 1 or more customers sampled buy the product, develop" ($n = 50$, $c = 1$), give the probability of a wrong decision for each level of p indicated.

p	Probability of a wrong decision, given p
.02	_____
.04	_____
.06	_____
.08	_____
.10	_____

2. Calculate the probability weights for computing the EOL of the decision rule ($n = 50$, $c = 1$, that is, the joint probabilities of various given levels of p and a wrong decision:

p			
.02	———	———	———
.04	———	———	———
.06	———	———	———
.08	———	———	———
.10	———	———	———

3. Using the decision rule $n = 50$, $c = 1$ in this problem, what is the overall (marginal) probability of making a wrong decision?
4. Using the COLs computed in the previous section of the text and given below, compute the EOL of the decision rule $n = 50$, $c = 1$:

p	COL of a wrong decision		
.02	$300,000	———	———
.04	100,000	———	———
.06	100,000	———	———
.08	300,000	———	———
.10	500,000	———	———

5. If you computed additional EOLs for different criterion numbers as follows:

$$\text{EOL}(n = 50, c = 2) = \$38,263 \qquad \text{EOL}(n = 50, c = 3) = \$43,682$$

the optimal criterion number for a sample of 50:
a. Is $c = 1$.
b. Is $c = 2$.
c. Is $c = 3$.
d. Cannot be determined without computing the EOL for other higher criterion numbers.

Answers 20.C

1.

p	Probability of a wrong decision, given p
.02	.6358 (read directly)
.04	.8701 (read directly)
.06	$1 - .9547 = .0453$
.08	$1 - .9845 = .0155$
.10	$1 - .9948 = .0052$

2.

(1) p	(2) $P(p)$	(3) $P(\text{wrong decision} \mid p)$	(2) × (3) $P(\text{wrong decision and } p)$
.02	.1	.6358	.06358
.04	.3	.8701	.26103
.06	.3	.0453	.01359
.08	.2	.0155	.00310
.10	.1	.0052	.00052
$P(\text{wrong decision})$			.34182

3. The marginal probability of making a wrong decision is .34182, the sum of the joint probabilities computed in the previous question.

4.

(1) p	(2) COL of a wrong decision	(3) Probability weights (probability of wrong decision and p)	(2) × (3)
.02	$300,000	.06358	$19,074
.04	100,000	.26103	26,103
.06	100,000	.01359	1,359
.08	300,000	.00310	930
.10	500,000	.00052	260
COL ($n = 50$, $c = 1$)			$47,726

5. b. The fact that, for $c = 2$, the COL is lower than for $c = 1$ or $c = 3$ demonstrates that $c = 2$ is the optimal criterion number.

Section 20.D
The Economics of Sampling

Learning objectives

Your learning objectives for this section are to be able, given a business decision problem:

1. To calculate and explain the meaning of:
   a. The expected value of sample information (EVSI)
   b. The net gain from sampling
2. To determine the optimal size sample to take

CALCULATION OF THE EXPECTED VALUE OF SAMPLE INFORMATION

The importance and usefulness of the foregoing analysis extends far beyond selection of the optimal decision criterion for a particular sample size. With the benefit of this analysis you can now consider questions relating to the economics of sampling. Earlier you saw that the expected value of *perfect* information (EVPI), in cases of decision making under uncertainty, is equal to the expected opportunity loss of the optimal act. This EVPI, while it placed an *upper limit* on the amount you should be willing to spend to gain additional information before making a decision, didn't enable you to determine the desirability of obtaining the less than perfect information always provided by a sample. You could say only that if sampling was more costly than the EVPI calculated for the decision problem, the sampling should not be undertaken. However, if the cost of sampling is somewhat less than the EVPI, you're in no position to evaluate the relative desirability of obtaining a sample before a decision is made vs. making an immediate decision without sampling.

In the product development problem considered in this module, the EVPI is $60,000, the EOL of the best act without sampling, which is to develop (see Table 20.4). This figure does place an upper bound on the amount you'd be willing to spend for sample information, which is always less than perfect. Suppose, however, that the sampling of 20 customers proposed by the management could be conducted at a cost of $10,000—not an unreasonable figure for the type of detailed investigation necessary to determine the customer's needs. You know that not more than $60,000 should be spent for sample information, but should you spend $10,000?

To evaluate the desirability of obtaining a sample before a decision is made, you need to know the *expected value of sample information* (EVSI). For any given sample size, the EVSI can be computed as the difference between the EVPI and the EOL resulting from the use of the best decision rule for the sample size in question. Thus, in the product development example, the EVPI is $60,000. From this you must deduct $52,817, the expected opportunity loss resulting from the use of the best decision criterion in conjunction with a sample of size 20, that is, $c = 1$. The difference, $7183, is the EVSI for a sample of size 20.

The EVSI may also be thought of as the reduction in the cost of uncertainty brought about by the use of the sampling procedure. EVPI, as noted earlier, is identical to (in fact another name for) the cost of uncertainty in a decision-making situation. The EOL after sampling is similarly the expected cost of uncertainty after the sample has been taken and the optimal decision criterion applied. It is reasonable that the reduction in the expected cost of uncertainty represents the value of sample information, EVSI. Having obtained this figure, you need only to compare it with the cost of actually obtaining the sample to ascertain the economic feasibility or desirability of sampling. In the present case, the sample of 20 *shouldn't* be taken since its cost, $10,000, is greater than its expected value, $7183.

SELECTION OF AN OPTIMAL SAMPLE SIZE

EVSI for various sample sizes. The above comparison *doesn't* indicate that all possible sampling procedures are undesirable; it says only that a sample of size 20 costs more than its expected value. Other sample sizes may yield expected values in excess of their cost. Therefore, the procedure involved in the calculation of EVSI must be repeated for all possible sample sizes because the reduction in uncertainty resulting from sampling won't necessarily be proportional to the size sample taken.

From the earlier study of sampling distributions, you might suppose that the reduction in uncertainty from increasing sample sizes is somewhat less than proportional to the increase in sample size. Also, the cost of obtaining the sample needn't necessarily be proportional to the sample size. There may be some fixed costs associated with taking any size sample, and generally some variable costs may be directly related to the size of the sample taken. Determination of an optimal sample size can be accomplished only by subtracting the cost of obtaining the sample from the EVSI, obtaining the *net gain* that is achieved with various size samples.

Making this procedure more cumbersome is the fact that the EVSI calculation for each sample size must be based on the use of an *optimal* decision criterion, or c value. Notice, therefore, that the determination of the optimal sample size in a practical case involves many calculations like those in Tables 20.6 to 20.9. Not only must you determine the optimal decision criterion for each given sample size but you must also repeat this calculation for all possible sample sizes. Only then are you in a position to compare the EVSI resulting from the use of various (n, c) combinations to the costs of obtaining the samples and ultimately to determine an optimal arrangement.

Actually, this isn't as complex as it might seem at first sight. The optimal decision criterion number c will change only occasionally and systematically as the sample size increases. For example, suppose it's determined that $c = 1$ represents the optimal criterion number for a given small sample (as it does for $n = 20$ in the example). Then for the next larger size sample ($n = 21$), the optimal c will be either 1 or 2. It can be proved mathematically that if the EOL using the decision rule $n = 21$, $c = 1$ is *less* than the EOL for $n = 20$, $c = 1$, then $c = 1$ *is* an optimum for $n = 21$. If the EOL for $n = 21$, $c = 1$ is greater, then $c = 2$ is the optimum for $n = 21$. Thus usually only one computation of an EOL (n, c) must be made. Even if some sample sizes are skipped, proceeding in a systematic, commonsense fashion will limit the number of computations required.

As a practical matter, it isn't necessary to consider every possible value of n, the sample size. Some very large values for n can be ruled out immediately because the cost of obtaining such a sample would exceed the EVPI in the decision problem. Since sampling information of any sort must necessarily be less than perfect, there wouldn't be any point in considering these sample sizes further.

Also, a rough idea of the optimal sample size might be obtained by considering only certain "round" sample sizes and omitting from consideration the possibilities in between. For example, you might proceed in a problem involving the determination of an optimal sample size to consider n values of 5, 10, 20, 50, 100, 200 .... Before many trials are made, it'll probably be possible to zero in on some number which closely approaches the optimal sample size.

You're further assisted by the fact that generally in sampling-size determinations the total cost curve (represented by the sum of actual sampling costs and the remaining cost of uncertainty after sampling) will be rather flat in the region of the optimum.

That is, you can probably miss the true optimal sample size somewhat without seriously increasing the expected costs. It must be kept in mind that the cost of the time spent in analysis is another element that should be considered. Usually a fairly rough calculation to determine the amount of information that can profitably be purchased before making a decision will prove sufficient.

Net gain from sampling. Let's return to the product-development problem to consider whether the purchase of additional information before making a decision is economically desirable in that case. You saw earlier that the use of the decision rule $n = 20$, $c = 1$ wasn't desirable since the EVSI ($7183) was exceeded by the cost of obtaining the sample, $10,000. Suppose the $10,000 sample cost is composed of a $4000 fixed cost of setting up the sampling procedure and a $300-per-customer variable cost. (In practice, these costs probably wouldn't be known with certainty. However, as elsewhere in the analysis, you may work with the *expected* costs of sampling.) Using the methods of analysis outlined in this chapter, you can compute EVSI, sample cost, and the net gain from sampling for various sample sizes, thus determining the desirability of purchasing various quantities of information in the product-development situation. Results of the computations, which you should verify, are given in Table 20.10 for $n = 10$, 20, 50, and 100.

These results deserve some comment. Notice that for a sample of 10, the EVSI is *negative*, indicating that it is better to make an immediate decision without sampling than employ the decision rule $n = 10$, $c = 1$ even if the sample of 10 is available at no cost. Because of the high probabilities of a wrong decision—not developing a profitable product due to zero successes in the small sample—the EOL ($n = 10$, $c = 1$) is $75,198, which is greater than the $60,000 cost of uncertainty in the decision problem. While a sample of 20 has positive value, this value, as noted earlier, doesn't exceed its cost. The same is true for the sample of size 100. The sample of 50, on the other hand, does promise informational value greater than its cost when utilized with its optimal criterion number. From Table 20.10, it appears that a sample of size 50 represents the optimal sampling arrangement. Although there is probably some other sample size near 50 that would yield even greater net gain, the difference would be slight. If net gain from sampling were plotted against sample size, the net-gain curve would be rather flat between $n = 20$ and $n = 100$. Thus as a practical matter, you might be satisfied to employ the decision rule $n = 50$, $c = 2$.

Table 20.10 / Net gain from sampling for various sample sizes

(1) Sample size n	(2) Optimal criterion number c	(3) EVSI $60,000 - \text{EOL}(n, c)$	(4) Sample costs, $4000 + 300n$	(5) Net gain from sampling (3) − (4)
10	1	$-15,198	7,000	$-22,198
20	1	7,183	10,000	-2,817
50	2	21,737	19,000	+2,737
100	5	32,436	34,000	-1,564

Note that the $2737 gain projected is an *expected* gain. As with other expected values, you have no assurance that this particular gain will be realized or even that the sampling procedure will save you from a wrong decision. Remember, also, that the expected gain is based on possible *opportunity losses* from wrong decisions, which have no necessary relationship with accounting profits. If the sample of 50 advocated by your analysis led to a decision not to develop the product, you'd have nothing to show for your efforts, in an accounting sense, but a $19,000 expense item (the cost of the sample). It doesn't show up on the company's books that the $19,000 investment may have saved it from a substantial loss.

One additional point should be considered. You've seen earlier that where conditional values are large relative to the financial capacity of the decision maker, expected utilities may have to be substituted for expected monetary values as a decision criterion. In the product-development example, the gain expected from purchasing additional information is relatively small (even though it is positive) compared with the cost of obtaining the sample. However, even though the $19,000 sample cost seems to be a large out-of-pocket expense (as opposed to lost opportunity), remember that much larger out-of-pocket losses are possible if a wrong decision to develop the product is made. You can't be sure how the decision to purchase additional information might be changed without a repetition of the analysis using utilities rather than dollars.

REVIEW EXERCISES 20.D

1. The expected value of sample information (EVSI) for a given sample size is the _____ less the _____ for the optimal decision rule.

2. For a given sample size, the net gain from sampling is equal to the _____ less the _____.

3. In the decision problem described in the text of this module, suppose the fixed cost of taking a sample was $10,000 but the variable cost per customer was only $100. Using the information below (from Table 20.10), determine whether a sample size of about 50 is optimal. Explain.

Sample size	EVSI		
10	$-15,198	_____	_____
20	7,183	_____	_____
50	21,737	_____	_____
100	32,436	_____	_____

Answers 20.D

1. EOL* without sampling, optimal EOL (n, c) *2.* EVSI, cost of sampling

3.

Sample size	EVSI	Cost of sampling	Net gain
10	$-15,198	11,000	$-26,198
20	7,183	12,000	-4,817
50	21,737	15,000	+6,737
100	32,436	20,000	+12,436

The increase in fixed cost but decrease in variable cost made the larger sample sizes more desirable. $n =$ about 100 is better.

Questions and Problems

20.1. For the product-development problem in this module, confirm the fact that for a sample of size 50 the optimum criterion number is $c = 2$.

20.2. Prior to formal publication, faculty members at two institutions are using a mimeographed version of a text in their classes. The fixed cost of mimeographing is $800. The variable cost is $1.50 per copy. Their estimate that 300 students will be in the course next semester can be considered an accurate point estimate. The major source of uncertainty is the proportion of students next semester who'll order new texts (as opposed to buying used copies from former students). The authors sold the text last semester at $5 per copy (this does not include the bookstore's markup).

The authors find that information on the proportion of students who might order new books is hard to obtain. After conferring with the bookstore's manager and other knowledgeable persons, they arrive at the following distribution for the proportion of students who will order new texts.

Proportion	.5	.6	.7	.8	.9
Probability	.1	.4	.2	.2	.1

a. Should the authors publish the text next semester, assuming that the price will be $5 per copy and that an immediate decision must be made without sampling?

b. If the correct decision in part a is "not to publish at the same price" and they decide to publish, what price would have to be charged to break-even?

c. Since the authors do not want to lose any money on the venture listed above, and since the probability distribution on the proportion of students buying new texts is quite flat, they devise the following sampling procedure. The second term at one of the institutions, which is on the quarter system, starts about a month before the second term for the second institution, which is on the semester system. The text will be used in a class of 50 students at the first institution. After the class at the first institution starts, students will be given the option to buy new texts at a price of $5. The text won't be used the first week of the course, and the information about the number of students in the class who order the texts can be used to estimate how many will be sold and to determine what price to charge. Assuming that the students at both institutions are alike in their decision to purchase new or used texts and that the class of 50 constitutes a sample from a

Bernoulli process, what (n,c) decision rule should the authors use to interpret the sample (n, of course, is 50)?

20.3. Suppose you've been offered $100 if you can pick a loaded pair of dice from four dice that appear identical. You know only that one pair is fair and that the other is loaded to come up showing a total of seven about 60 percent of the time. You examine each pair carefully but can detect absolutely no apparent difference between them.

    a. How much would you pay for the chance to try to select the loaded pair?

    b. How much would you pay to roll one pair (of your choosing) once before deciding which pair is loaded?

    c. How much would you pay to roll one pair *twice* before deciding?

    d. How much would you pay to roll one pair *four* times before deciding?

    e. What generalization can be drawn from your answers to parts *b* through *d*?

20.4. In the situation described in Prob. 20.3, suppose one pair (call it pair A) of dice "looked" loaded to you. While you are not sure of your choice, you feel the odds are 4 to 1 that A is the loaded pair.

    a. How much would you pay for the chance to try to select the loaded pair?

    b. How much would you pay to roll the A pair once before making a decision?

    c. Compare your answers to part *b* of this problem to part *b* of Prob. 20.3. What generalization is suggested?

    d. What is the EVPI in this problem? How does it compare with EVPI in the previous problem? Does this comparison relate to the comparison in *c*?

20.5. *a.* Confirm the EVSI data given in column 3 of Table 20.10 (for the product-development problem) for $n = 10$, $n = 50$, and $n = 100$.

    b. Explain the meaning of the EVSI for $n = 10$ in this problem.

20.6. Assume that a student has a part-time job in a city about 40 mi from the campus. He also has an old car that is badly in need of a minor repair costing $37.50. Being a fair roadside mechanic, he can always fix the car so that it will get him to his job, but the repair is of a temporary nature, and the car is as likely to break down on the next trip as it ever was. If the car does break down while he is going to work, he'll lose an hour's time, during which he could have made $2.50. He figures that until he graduates, he'll make 300 trips to work, after which he'll sell the car for junk. Being a diligent statistics student, he decides to approach his decision problem— whether or not to repair the car—in a scholarly manner. On the basis of past experience he arrives at the following probability distribution for p, the proportion of times the car will break down.

p	.01	.05	.10
$P(p)$	.2	.5	.3

    a. Calculate the EOLs of the acts repair and don't repair, and identify the optimal act. Assume that the breakdowns occur as a Bernoulli process.

    b. Being cautious as well as diligent, he decides to consider the history of the last 2 weeks (10 trips) as a sample before he makes a decision about a repair. Formulate the optimal decision rule for this sample of 10.

    c. If he had 1 breakdown in the sample of 10, what should he do?

    d. What is the EVSI for the optimal decision rule found in part *b*?

20.7. For a given sample size, the EVSI is equal to the EVPI minus the EOL of the best decision rule for that sample size. Explain the process by which one obtains the EVPI and the EOL of the best decision rule, and explain why it is logical to call the difference between them the EVSI.

20.8.　Explain carefully the process through which the optimal sample size for a particular decision problem is determined.

20.9.　A large computer manufacturer maintains a program to update its customer engineers. In the past they have sent all qualified engineers to a special school that lasts 10 weeks and costs the company $1000 per student. They are now contemplating a two-track program. They propose sending all students to a very intensive one-week program that costs $100 per student. Students who pass this course will be sent to a supplementary school at a cost of $600 per student. Those who fail will be enrolled in the regular $1000 per student course. If the proportion of students who pass the intensive course is large enough, it'll save money, whereas if the proportion is small, it'll lose money. Having no previous experience, the manufacturer places the following probability distribution on the proportion of students who will pass. There are currently 500 engineers that it would ordinarily enroll in the program.

p	.15	.20	.25	.30	.35
$P(p)$	.2	.3	.2	.2	.1

a. If the company is to make an immediate decision without running a pilot sample, should it institute the special program or stay with the regular program?

b. Because of the uncertainty with respect to the distribution of p prior to sampling, the company decides to check on the validity of its decision by taking a random sample of engineers and sending them through the first week of the special program to see how many will pass. The cost of this special school is $100 per student. Determine the optimal (n,c) decision rule. Will it pay to sample? Why or why not?

20.10.　In your plant you have an old machine which performs an operation on a part you are manufacturing. The cost of labor plus material for the work performed by this machine comes to 23 cents per piece. You have an order for 50,000 parts. Before you produce them, you want to consider the possibility of buying a new machine to replace the old one. The new machine costs $1253. You can get $300 scrap value for the old machine. Because of increased speed, the new machine can produce parts at a unit cost of 15 cents. However, there is one drawback to the new machine. With the old machine the proportion of defectives is known to be .05. Since the defective rate is a function of both the operator and the machine, the manufacturer cannot specify the defective rate on the new machine. From his experience and yours, however, you arrive at the following probability distribution for the proportion defective.

p	.05	.07	.09	.11	.13
$P(p)$	.15	.25	.30	.15	.15

Assume that the defectives are generated by a Bernoulli process and that the entire cost of the new machine can be allocated to the 50,000 parts. *Note:* In the questions that follow you'll have to calculate costs on the basis of *good* pieces, i.c., the cost for 50,000 *good* pieces on the old machine, for example, is

$$\$0.23 \frac{50,000}{.95} = \$12,105$$

a. If you must make a decision without sampling, what should that decision be, and what is the EOL of the optimal act?

b. The seller of the machine gives you the opportunity to sample to determine the proportion defective by having your operator run a sample on a new machine owned by another manufacturer in your city. The seller agrees to pay the other manufacturer for the time lost in production due to running your sample, but you have to pay the cost of sampling, which is $\$10 + \$0.15n$. Should you sample? If so, how large a sample should you take, and what criterion number should you use?

20.11. You've probably noted by now that for problems like Prob. 20.10 you can easily calculate the optimal decision rule without sampling by simply finding the expected value of the random variable and comparing it with the break-even point. If this is the case, why is it necessary to calculate the EOL of the possible acts and compare them? Explain fully.

20.12. A distributor of Christmas tree lights is contemplating the purchase of the season's supply of 100,000 bulbs from a foreign manufacturer. This manufacturer claims that the new bulbs are "at least as good" as the domestically produced brand he has purchased in former years, which he knows from experience run about 2 percent defective. However, the distributor is doubtful concerning the quality of the foreign product, subjectively estimating the following probability distribution for fraction defective:

Fraction defective	0.01	0.02	0.05
Probability	.1	.4	.5

The cost of having to replace defective bulbs (including the cost of customer goodwill lost) is estimated at 50 cents per bulb. The foreign bulbs are 1 cent each cheaper to the distributor but can be sold at the same price as the domestic bulbs.

a. From the information above, would you recommend purchase of the foreign-produced bulbs?

b. Suppose an independent testing laboratory will obtain and test a random sample of 100 of the foreign bulbs for a fee of $125. How could such a sample best be utilized?

c. Would you recommend purchase of the sample information?

20.13. ABCO Controls purchases a certain machined part in lots of 4000 for use in a valve assembly it produces. Most of the time only about 1 percent of the purchased parts fail to meet specifications, but occasionally a bad shipment is received that may contain as many as 15 percent defective parts. Although only crude records are available, it appears that about 10 percent of the shipments received have been bad, as defined here.

Currently, incoming shipments are 100 percent inspected for defectives at a cost of $200 per lot. All defectives are found in this way and returned to the manufacturer who replaces them at no cost. If the parts are not inspected, defectives would eventually be discovered in the assembly process. To remove and replace them at this point involves a cost of $3 per defective part.

ABCO is considering the establishment of a sampling procedure to replace the 100 percent inspection. To set up for the sampling procedure each time a lot is received would cost $35, and inspection of a random sample could then be accomplished at a cost of 10 cents per part included. Full (100 percent) inspection of the remaining parts would still cost about $200 after sampling.

a. Should the sampling procedure be instituted? If so, how large a sample should be taken?

b. What decision criterion should be used?

MODULE 21
COMBINING SAMPLE DATA WITH PRIOR INFORMATION

Module 20 was concerned with the economic desirability of sampling, focusing on the question of how much (if any) sample information should be purchased *before* making a final decision. This analysis would, of course, be conducted before any sample was taken. In this module, you learn a means for incorporating sample information into your analysis of a decision problem *after* the sample has been taken and the results are known. You'll see that the procedures considered here duplicate some of the information obtained from the previous analysis. However, there may be situations where a sample was taken without the benefit of the analysis of the previous module. Clearly, you should include such sample information, once obtained, in your analysis, whether or not on an a priori basis it would have been desirable to obtain the sample information in the first place.

General learning objectives

Your general learning objectives for this module are to be able to:

1. Revise a prior probability distribution to incorporate sample results
2. Use revised probabilities to analyze decision alternatives and the purchase of additional information

Section 21.A

Revision of Probability Distributions to Incorporate Sample Data

Learning objectives

Your learning objectives for this section are to be able to:

1. Explain the general procedures for incorporating sample information into a decision analysis
2. Use sample information to revise a prior probability distribution of possible outcomes

THE ANALYSIS OF SAMPLE DATA

To illustrate how sample results are incorporated into a decision analysis, let's return to the product-development example of the previous module. In the circumstances of that example it's entirely reasonable that the decision maker, because of the high development costs involved, might have obtained additional information before making a final decision, even if no formal analysis was performed. For purposes of illustration, suppose that a sample of size 20 *had* been obtained at a cost of $10,000. It's quite clear that no analysis of the economics of sampling had been undertaken by the decision maker before obtaining such a sample, for this analysis, conducted in the last module, showed that a sample of size 20 did not represent a desirable purchase of information; i.e., the cost of information obtained was greater than the resulting reduction in the cost of uncertainty.

Now just because this information is expected to be worth less than its cost, the decision maker can scarcely afford to ignore it. Suppose the sample of 20 customers that had been taken contained no customers who exhibited a desire to buy the product. Intuitively, you'd feel less confident of the decision to develop that would have been made in the absence of sample information. Certainly a final decision at this point should give some weight to the sample results as well as the subjective business judgments on which the probability distribution of possible outcomes was originally based.

Of course, the analysis you learned in the preceding module could always be carried out on an after-the-fact basis once the sample results were known. Recall that the

515

first step of that analysis involved a method for determining the optimum criterion number to use with a given sample size. For the product-development example you found that for a sample of size 20 the optimal criterion number was $c = 1$. That is, if a sample of size 20 was taken before making a final decision, its results should be utilized in the following manner. If one or more of the 20 customers sampled expressed a desire to buy the product, a decision should be made to develop the product. Only if none of the 20 customers expressed a favorable response to the product should its development be forgone.

Since the particular sample considered here actually contained no "buy" responses, you should therefore decide not to develop, reversing the decision that would have been made without the benefit of the sample information. It would be perfectly proper to use this decision rule to interpret the sample results obtained and to make a final decision concerning product development. However, you'll recall that the effort required to determine the optimal criterion number ($c = 1$) was considerable. It required a trial-and-error procedure, and each trial in itself involved a rather lengthy calculation.

As you'll learn in this module, there's a more efficient means of incorporating sample results into the analysis once these results are known. Instead of considering all possible sample outcomes (as the previous analysis did), it requires consideration only of the specific sample outcome actually observed, after the fact. Incorporation of the known sample outcome into the analysis and ultimate selection of a decision alternative will be accomplished by *revising* the probability distribution of the various outcomes, or states of nature, which provided the weights for use in calculating the EOLs (or expected monetary values) of the decision alternatives. Once you've revised the *prior* probability distribution, you can simply recompute the EOLs, using the same COLs as before, changing only the weighting system represented by the probability distribution.

REVISION OF PRIOR PROBABILITIES

To demonstrate the revision procedure, let's revise the subjective probability distribution of the product-development example so that it includes the sample information $n = 20$, $r = 0$. It's obvious that the lack of favorable responses would make you less confident of the decision to develop, perhaps revising the original probability distribution (which favored development) enough to swing your final decision the other way. Let's see just how much the original or prior probability distribution of the possible proportion of customers buying the product would be affected by this specific sample outcome.

Conditional probability of the observed sample outcome. The first step in the revision procedure is to calculate the probability of obtaining the observed sample outcome, given various states of nature. In the problem at hand, this is represented by the probability of getting zero favorable responses in a sample of 20 customers for various possible levels of p, the proportion of customers actually buying the product.

These values obtained are *conditional* probabilities, in that they depend on the value of *p*.

Although they may be assumed to be binomial probabilities, they can't be read directly from a binomial table of the form given in this book because each such probability is discrete, as opposed to the cumulative binomial probabilities of the form $P_b(r \geq R \mid n, p)$ contained in the table. If you look for a value of *r* equal to 0 in the binomial table, you find that such a value doesn't appear. This is, of course, because at least zero successes in a sample of any given size will *always* occur. The probability of *zero or more* successes is simply equal to 1. You are interested instead in the probability of *exactly r* successes out of *n* tries (in this case 0 out of 20), and this probability can be obtained only as the difference between the cumulative probabilities from the table. By subtracting the binomial probability that $r \geq 1$ from the binomial probability that $r \geq 0$ (which is 1.0000), you can obtain the probability that *r* is *exactly* equal to 0.

Thus, given the condition that $p = .02$, the probability of zero successes will be $1.0000 - .3324$ (from the binomial table), or .6676. Similarly, other conditional probabilities, where $p = .04, .06, \ldots$, can be obtained. They are shown in column 3 of Table 21.1.

Reversing the conditional probabilities: the use of Bayes' rule.

Note again that the numbers found in column 3 are *conditional* probabilities of $r = 0$, *given p*. To obtain the revised probability distribution, you must ultimately determine the probability of various levels of *p*, *given* the sample results ($r = 0$). Earlier in this course you learned a method for reversing the direction of conditional probabilities, i.e., a method for determining $P(B \mid A)$ when $P(A \mid B)$ and certain other information was available. The technique involved the use of Bayes' rule. In one form, Bayes' rule simply states that

$$P(B \mid A) = \frac{P(A \text{ and } B)}{P(A)} = \frac{P(A \mid B)P(B)}{P(A)}$$

Modifying these symbols for the problem at hand gives

$$P(p \mid r) = \frac{P(r \text{ and } p)}{P(r)}$$

Table 21.1 / Revision of the prior probability distribution to incorporate the sample results $n = 20, r = 0$

(1) p	(2) Prior $P(p)$	(3) $P(r = 0 \mid p)$	(4) $P(r = 0 \text{ and } p)$	(5) Revised $P(p)$
.02	.1	.6676	.06676	.1985
.04	.3	.4420	.13260	.3943
.06	.3	.2901	.08703	.2588
.08	.2	.1887	.03774	.1122
.10	.1	.1216	.01216	.0362
$P(r = 0)$			.33629	1.0000

The sample size n is of course fixed. Specifically, you want to know

$$P(p \mid r = 0) = \frac{P(r = 0 \text{ and } p)}{P(r = 0)}$$

where $n = 20$.

The joint probabilities of $r = 0$ *and* each level of p can be calculated by simply multiplying the numbers in column 2 (the marginal or prior probability of p) by the numbers in column 3 (the conditional probability of $r = 0$, given p), a straightforward application of the multiplication rule. The remaining need is to find the marginal probability of $r = 0$.

The marginal probability of any event can always be determined (if all else fails) by adding the joint probabilities of *all compound events* in which the event in question is involved. You *could* observe an actual sample outcome $r = 0$ in each of the cases, $p = .02$, $p = .04$, $p = .06$, $p = .08$, and $p = .10$. Adding these joint probabilities together, i.e., summing column 4, you'll obtain the marginal probability that $r = 0$. This number can also be interpreted as the likelihood of the particular sample outcome $r = 0$ occurring, based on your prior probability information (or assumptions) regarding states of nature.

Completing the application of Bayes' rule, you can now determine the conditional probability $P(p \mid r)$ by dividing each of the joint probabilities in column 4 by the marginal probability represented by the total of that column. Put another way, you're simply expressing the numbers in column 4 as a percentage of their total. These conditional probabilities of $(p \mid r)$ appear in column 5, representing the *revised* probability distribution.

REVIEW EXERCISES 21.A

1. In making a decision, information available from a sample should be ignored unless it can be shown that the sample was economically justifiable: true or false?

2. Sample information can be incorporated into a decision analysis by:
   a. Comparing the actual sample data with a predetermined decision rule.
   b. Revising the prior probability distribution of sample outcomes to incorporate the sample data and using the revised distribution to analyze the decision problem.
   c. Either *a* or *b*.
   d. Neither *a* nor *b*.

3. Revising a prior probability distribution to incorporate sample information:
   a. Must be done before the sample is taken.
   b. Involves a use of Bayes' rule.
   c. Is meaningful only if sample results agree with the prior information.
   d. None of the above.

4. The binomial probability of exactly 2 favorable responses out of a sample of 20 (for any given population proportion p):
   a. Cannot be found using the binomial tables in this book.
   b. Can be found by adding probabilities.
   c. Can be found by subtracting one binomial probability from another.
   d. None of the above.

5. Suppose, for the product-development example described in the text, a sample of only 10 had been taken with zero favorable responses by customers who'd buy the product. Determine the probability of obtaining this sample result for each possible level of p indicated below:

P	$P(r = 0 \mid p)$
.02	_____
.04	_____
.06	_____
.08	_____
.10	_____

6. Refer to Exercise 5. Given the prior probability distribution shown below, compute the marginal probability of obtaining zero customers purchasing out of a sample of 10.

P	$P(p)$			
.02	.1	_____	_____	_____
.04	.3	_____	_____	_____
.06	.3	_____	_____	_____
.08	.2	_____	_____	_____
.10	.1	_____	_____	_____

7. Revise the prior probability distribution to incorporate the sample result $n = 10$, $r = 0$. (Approximate computations are sufficient.)

Answers 21.A

1. False; even if a before-the-fact analysis showed that a particular sample shouldn't have been taken, the results of such a sample after the fact shouldn't be ignored. They should be used to revise the prior probability distribution and incorporated into the decision analysis.

2. c   3. b   4. c

5. $P(r = 0 \mid n, p) = 1 - P(r \geq 1 \mid n, p)$; for a sample of size 10:

P	$P(r = 0 \mid p)$
.02	$1 - .1829 = .8171$
.04	$1 - .3352 = .6648$
.06	$1 - .4614 = .5386$
.08	$1 - .5656 = .4344$
.10	$1 - .6513 = .3487$

6.

P	$P(p)$	$P(r = 0 \mid p)$	$P(r = 0 \text{ and } p)$
.02	.1	.8171	.08171
.04	.3	.6648	.19944
.06	.3	.5386	.16158
.18	.2	.4344	.08688
.20	.1	.3487	.03487
Marginal probability that $r = 0$			.56448

7. $P(p \mid r = 0) \text{ [revised]} = \dfrac{P(r = 0 \text{ and } p)}{P(r = 0)}$

$P(p) \text{ [revised]}$

$\dfrac{.08171}{.56448} = .145$

$\dfrac{.19944}{.56448} = .353$

$\dfrac{.16158}{.56448} = .286$

$\dfrac{.08688}{.56448} = .154$

$\dfrac{.03487}{.56448} = .062$

$\overline{}$

1.000

Section 21.B

The Use of Revised Distributions

Learning objectives

Your learning objectives for this section are to be able to:

1. Use a revised probability distribution in decision making
2. Explain how sample information changes the cost of uncertainty

RECOMPUTATION USING REVISED PROBABILITIES

Once revised probabilities have been obtained, they may be used in the same manner as the prior probabilities obtained earlier from subjective management judgments. You could use them, for example, to weight the conditional opportunity losses in the product-development problem, as show in Table 21.2. A comparison of the EOLs computed by using the revised probability distribution shows that the decision "don't develop," now having the lower EOL, represents the superior strategy. The "develop" decision, which was optimal without sampling (see Module 20) is changed as a consequence of incorporating the sample outcome ($n = 20$, $r = 0$) into our probability weights.

This result, of course, is consistent with the result obtained in the last module—that for a sample size of 20, the best criterion number is 1, indicating that the product should be developed only if one or more favorable responses are encountered in the sample. Since zero favorable responses have been encountered, the alternative decision "don't develop" would be made on the basis of an $n = 20$, $c = 1$ decision rule. Thus, to this point, you have done nothing more with the revision-of-probabilities approach than could have been done with the previous analysis of decision rules. The same selection between the decision alternatives would be made using either approach. Notice, however, that the effort involved in the revision is somewhat less. This is because the calculation is a once-through process, rather than the trial-and-error type required to select an optimal criterion number. In general, where sample results are already available, incorporating them into the analysis of the decision can be accomplished more easily by revising the probability distribution and recomputing the EOLs, as described in this module.

THE COST OF UNCERTAINTY USING REVISED PROBABILITIES

Revising the probability distribution will change the weights involved in the computation of expected opportunity losses (EOLs). Therefore, using the revised probability distribution, the EOL of the optimum act, which is the cost of uncertainty, will be a different value from that computed earlier, without sampling, using the prior probability distribution. The EOL based on revised probabilities will also be different from the EOL of a decision rule involving a sample but computed before a sample is

Table 21.2 / Computation of EOLs using revised probability distribution

p	$P(p)$ = revised	Develop		Don't develop	
		Conditional loss	Weighted value	Conditional loss	Weighted value
.02	.1985	$300,000	$59,550	$ 0	$ 0
.04	.3943	100,000	39,430	0	0
.06	.2588	0	0	100,000	25,880
.08	.1122	0	0	300,000	33,660
.10	.0362	0	0	500,000	18,100
EOL			$98,980		$77,640

actually taken, as was done in the previous module to analyze the desirability of sampling.

For example, using the revised probability distribution which incorporated the sample result $n = 20, r = 0$, the EOL of the best act (now "don't develop") is $77,640. On the other hand, you saw from Table 20.7 that the EOL involved in employing the decision rule $n = 20, c = 1$ was $52,817. It is important to realize why these figures are different. The $52,817 obtained earlier represents a result *expected* from sampling and takes into consideration all possible sample outcomes. The $77,640 figure is based on *one particular sample outcome*, $r = 0$, and its incorporation into the analysis.

The fact that the remaining cost of uncertainty *after* this particular sample outcome was higher than that expected *before* sampling (and indeed even higher than the $60,000 cost of uncertainty without sampling) might be considered a result of bad luck. Other sample outcomes would most certainly have lowered the cost of uncertainty in this decision situation. In this particular instance the sample result $n = 20, r = 0$ actually changed the best decision from "develop" to "don't develop." In changing the decision, the sample result also (unfortunately) makes what should be done somewhat less certain. Although your best alternative at this point is "don't develop," you're in a sense less sure of this decision than you were of the opposite decision, which would have been made in the absence of sample information. This is because the sample results essentially contradicted or were (relatively speaking) inconsistent with the subjective prior probability distribution.

A COMPARISON OF METHODS: BEFORE-THE-FACT OR AFTER-THE-FACT ANALYSIS OF SAMPLE RESULTS

This module has focused on an after-the-fact analysis that deals with a situation in which a sample has been taken and the outcome is known. The sample outcome is used to obtain a revised probability distribution, which is then used in the same way as any other probability distribution of possible states of nature in a decision problem. The previous module dealt instead with a before-the-fact, or a priori, analysis designed to determine whether sampling was economically desirable or not.

As for making any final decision after sample results are obtained, the two approaches would result in exactly the same decision. That is, if you apply the optimal decision rule to use with a particular size of sample, determined by means of the analysis described in the previous module, it'll lead to the same decision that would be made by revising the original probability distribution of possible outcomes to incorporate the observed sample results and applying the revised probability distribution as the weighting factors in computation of expected opportunity losses. One advantage of the revision procedure is that it's generally simpler. Perhaps more important, the revision procedure enables you to obtain a revised probability distribution which can form the basis for decisions about purchasing *more* information before making a decision. Although in many circumstances the two procedures may lead to the same result and the choice between them may be based solely on convenience, each has its place and each belongs in the quantitative decision maker's tool kit.

REVIEW EXERCISES 21.B

1. In Exercise 7 of Sec. 21.A you obtained a revised probability distribution that incorporated the sample result $n = 10$, $r = 0$ for the product-development problem. Using this revised distribution and the conditional opportunity losses shown below, determine whether the prior decision to develop (made without benefit of sample information) would be changed:

		Develop		Don't develop	
		Conditional loss	Weighted value	Conditional loss	Weighted value
p	$P(p)$ = revised				
.02	.145	$300,000		$ 0	
.04	.353	100,000		0	
.06	.286	0		100,000	
.08	.154	0		300,000	
.10	.062	0		500,000	

2. Refer to Exercise 1. After incorporating the sample results into the decision analysis, the cost of uncertainty is _____.

3. This cost of uncertainty is actually greater, using the revised probability distribution incorporating the sample results, than the cost of uncertainty (the EOL of the optimum act) without sampling; this increase occurs because:

a. The cost of uncertainty is always greater after sampling.

b. The sample results were invalid.

c. The sample results reversed the decision to be made without sampling.

d. None of the above.

4. A sample result that tended to confirm a decision maker's prior probabilities about various states of nature would generally reduce the cost of uncertainty in the decision situation: true or false?

5. Application of the optimal decision rule for a particular size of sample will often lead to a different decision than using actual sample results to revise probabilities, which are then used as weights in the decision analysis: true or false?

Answers 21.B

1.

		Develop		Don't develop	
		Conditional loss	Weighted value	Conditional loss	Weighted value
p	$P(p)$ = revised				
.02	.145	$300,000	$43,500	$ 0	$ 0
.04	.353	100,000	35,300	0	0
.06	.286	0	0	100,000	28,600
.08	.154	0	0	300,000	46,200
.10	.062	0	0	500,000	31,000
EOL			$78,800		$105,800

The proper decision is still to develop the product; although the EOL of the decision "to develop" increased (from $60,000 to $78,800), it remains less than the EOL of the alternative decision.

2. $78,800   3. *d*   4. true

5. False; the decision would be the same using the analysis (before sampling) described in the previous module or the probability revision procedure (after sample results are known) described in this module.

Section 21.C
Obtaining Additional Information before Making a Decision

Learning objectives

Your learning objectives for this section are to be able to:

1. Use prior and sample information to analyze the purchase of *additional* information before making a decision
2. Distinguish between classical and Bayesian analysis of a decision problem

---

THE POSSIBILITY OF FURTHER SAMPLING

The revised probability distribution obtained in Sec. 21.A (Table 21.1) and used as the set of weights in recalculating the EOLs for decision alternatives in Sec. 21.B (Table 21.2) doesn't necessarily represent the last word. It's in no sense final but could in turn be employed as the *prior* probability distribution in another series of calculations to decide whether it would be profitable to sample still more. Generally, the decision maker retains the alternative of purchasing still more information before making a decision.

An analysis of the economics of further sampling could be undertaken by using procedures identical to those in Module 20, except that the probability distribution of the various states of nature $P(p)$ used would be given by the *revised* probabilities of Table 21.1. Except for the change in these probabilities, the rest of the analysis would be carried out exactly as before.

Thus a full and complete analysis of a decision problem would involve:

1. Deciding what size sample (if any) is desirable
2. Taking the sample in question and observing this sample outcome

3. Deciding on the basis of the sample outcome whether to:
   a. Choose strategy *A*
   b. Choose strategy *B*
   c. Obtain still further sample information before making a decision

The important thing to remember here is that the appropriate set of probability weights at any point in the analysis is obtained from combining the original set of prior probabilities with *all* available sample information. This sample information can be incorporated in one step (by pooling all previous samples) or in a sequence of revisions made as additional information becomes available. If two successive samples are taken in the same problem, the revised probabilities after the first sample become the prior probabilities for the second sample. Notice that the only distinction between prior and revised probabilities is relative to some particular sample. Once the information in a sample has been incorporated into a revised probability distribution, the decision maker can, in essence, forget that a sample has been taken.

In Sec. 21.A we assumed that a sample result $n = 20$, $r = 0$ had been obtained in the product-development problem (even though the before-the-fact analysis of the previous module showed such a sample size to be economically undesirable). Having used this sample outcome to obtain a revised probability distribution, we determined that the best final decision, considering all the information available, was "don't develop." However, the high cost of uncertainty associated with this decision ($77,640 from Table 21.2) suggests that an *additional* purchase of sample information be considered.

To determine whether further sampling is desirable, you must compute the EVSI and the net gain resulting from a second sample for various possible sample sizes. The net gain from sampling results, which you can confirm, are given in Table 21.3.

Note that the $10,000 cost already incurred from taking a sample of 20 plays no part in these calculations. It is in effect a sunk cost and has no relevance in considering whether to make an immediate final decision or to sample further. The net gain from sampling is seen to be positive (and substantially so) for all sample sizes considered,

Table 21.3 / Net gain from further sampling, based on revised probability distribution of possible states of nature

(1) Sample size n	(2) Optimal criterion number c	(3) EVSI $[\$77,640 - \text{EOL}(n, c)]$	(4) Sample costs, $300n*$	(5) Net gain from sampling (3) − (4)
10	1	$18,659	$ 3,000	$15,659
20	2	25,010	6,000	19,010
50	3	39,823	15,000	24,823
100	6	49,871	30,000	19,871

*It is assumed that since one sample has already been taken, the $4000 fixed cost of sampling won't be incurred again. A different assumption can be made without changing the procedure or underlying reasoning.

even though once again 50 appears to be (roughly) the economically optimal size sample to take.

The fact that the prospective net gains from sampling are much higher than they were earlier might be somewhat puzzling. This occurs because you're much more uncertain about the proper decision to make after the first sample of 20 has been taken and the results interpreted. Recall that before any sampling was undertaken, the correct decision would have been to develop the product and the associated EOL (cost of uncertainty) was $60,000.

The results of the first sample changed the proper decision to don't develop and also served to increase the cost of uncertainty to $77,640. Even though $10,000 has previously been spent for sampling, it's now more desirable than ever to purchase additional information. (Of course, if the first sample results had been different, say, $n = 20$, $r = 4$, then the original decision to develop would have been confirmed and the cost of uncertainty would have been lowered. A final decision at that point might have been desirable.)

The calculations in Table 21.3 show that if it's possible in view of the time remaining to make a decision, an *additional* sample of roughly 50 items should be taken. As before, Table 21.3 gives no assurance that exactly 50 represents the optimal sample size; you might wish to consider other sample sizes between $n = 20$ and $n = 100$ as possibilities.

It's interesting to note that the optimal criterion number for a sample size of 50 is no longer $c = 2$. Indeed, even though 50 again represents the best sample size for those considered, $c = 3$ is now the optimal criterion number. This change has occurred because the revised probability distribution was used in place of the prior probability distribution in the EOL (n, c) computations. As indicated in Table 21.3, the optimal criterion number will change for other sample sizes as well.

When the results of a *new* sample of size 50 are obtained, any final decision should be based on the stated decision rule: If 3 or more of the 50 customers interviewed decide to buy the product, develop; if fewer than 3 buy, don't develop. However, once the second sample has been taken and the results are known, you still have available the alternative of buying even more information before making a decision. The analysis summarized in Table 21.3 can be repeated by using a still further revision of the probability distribution. Ordinarily, a large number of stages won't be required since one or two samplings may confirm the proper direction of a final decision and the subsequent analysis of the economics of sampling will indicate that further sampling is not desirable.

CLASSICAL VS. BAYESIAN DECISION ANALYSIS

An important point of separation between classical and Bayesian decision analysis is whether or not a prior probability distribution that may have been subjectively derived is merged with the observed sample information. Classical statistical decision rules essentially assume that before the sample is taken, no prior probability distribution exists (or, more properly, that the prior probability distribution is rectangular, i.e., all possible states of nature are equally likely). The classical statistician would thus argue that statistical decision making must be based not on business judgment but entirely on sample results. The Bayesian, on the other hand, would argue that decision should be based on the *combined* impact of *all* information relevant to the decision problem, including both sample results and whatever prior information is available, whether the prior information is in the form of historical relative frequencies (objective information), businessmen's judgment (subjective information), or some combination.

If it's true, as it may be in many cases, that very little is known about the random variable which is the source of uncertainty in a decision problem, then the prior probability distribution of possible states of nature can properly be represented by a nearly rectangular distribution. In such a situation, the revision procedure will be found to result in giving the sample results prime importance, with very little weight being given to the prior distribution. What's important is that the state of the decision maker's prior knowledge (or lack of it) is made specific. In many business situations, it's tempting for decision makers to say, "I've no idea what the demand will be" or "I've no idea what the fraction defective will be," etc. However, if pinned down, they'll then admit that by saying "I have no idea," they don't really mean that all states of nature are *equally* likely. Forced to do so, they'll attach a probability distribution to possible states of nature that isn't necessarily rectangular, even though it may be rather broad and flat. It seems reasonable that whatever information the decision maker possesses should be incorporated into the analysis in an explicit way. Use of the Bayesian approach outlined in this module makes it possible to combine all information relevant to the decision problem.

REVIEW EXERCISES 21.C

1. Once a sample has been taken and the results have been incorporated into the decision analysis, the decision maker should:
   a. Select the alternative with the lowest EOL.
   b. Consider the desirability of further sampling before making a final decision.
   c. Ignore the revised probability distribution.
   d. None of the above.
2. The economics of further sampling can be analyzed using the procedures described in the previous module to calculate the expected value of sample information (EVSI) and the net gain from sampling: true or false?
3. In analyzing the net gain from further sampling, the probability weights used in the computations should come from:
   a. The decision maker's original prior distribution.
   b. The sampling distribution.
   c. A revised distribution which incorporates the prior distribution and all sample results collected to date.
   d. None of the above.
4. To incorporate the results of a *second* sample into probability weights, you'd apply the revision procedures described in Sec. 21.A to:
   a. The original prior distribution.

b. The revised distribution, which incorporates the results of the first sample.

c. Either *a* or *b*.

d. Neither *a* nor *b*.

5. Bayesian decision analysis combines observed sample data with _____ _____, whereas classical decision analysis is based on _____ _____ only.

6. Prior information employed in Bayesian analysis may be based on:

a. Historical relative frequencies.

b. Business judgment.

c. Either *a* or *b* or both.

d. Neither *a* nor *b*.

7. In Bayesian analysis, it's generally best to ignore prior information that is not based on observable facts or definite opinions: true or false?

Answers 21.C

1. b   2. true   *3. c*   *4. b*   5. prior information; sample data   *6. c*

7. False; the spirit of Bayesian analysis is that the state of the decision maker's prior knowledge, however indefinite it may be and whatever its basis, is incorporated in the analysis in an explicit manner.

Questions and Problems

21.1. A pinochle deck consists of 48 cards, a *double* run from the nine up through the ace of each suit. There are two nines of clubs, two tens of clubs, two jacks of clubs, etc. Suppose you are asked to determine by intuition or sampling or both whether an ordinary-looking package of new cards (with no markings on the package) is a pinochle deck or an ordinary 52-card deck. You aren't allowed to count the cards in the package, but it looks a little thin to you. You therefore assign the following odds:

State of nature	Probability
Pinochle deck	.6
Ordinary deck	.4

Suppose you're allowed to draw two randomly selected cards from the deck. How would you revise the probability that it was a pinochle deck if the cards were:

a. The king of hearts and the 10 of clubs?

b. The queen of spades and the 4 of spades?

c. Both jacks of diamonds?

21.2. Criticize or explain the following statement: The revision of probabilities using Bayes' rule provides a means for combining hunches with hard facts.

21.3. In the product development problem discussed throughout Modules 20 and 21, it was determined that a sample of size 50 should be taken before making a decision (see

Table 20.10). Suppose that such a sample is taken and that 5 of the 50 customers indicate they will buy the product.

a. Test the null hypothesis that the proportion of customers who will buy the product is less than .05 (the break-even value).

b. If time pressures demand an immediate decision (following this sample), what should be done?

c. Did you use your results from part a to answer part b? Explain carefully why or why not.

d. If additional time were available should additional information be collected?

21.4. You're a printer who specializes in photographic mail-order Christmas cards. You're considering a free high-quality enlargement of the picture on the card as an incentive for large-lot purchases. To process the enlargement, you'll have to purchase additional photographic equipment, and you decide to check the market before embarking on the scheme by offering the opportunity to a random sample of customers. (You'll then meet the commitment to them by contracting out the enlargement work.) Before taking the sample, your prior distribution on the proportion of customers who will accept the offer is:

p	.05	.10	.15	.20	.25
$P(p)$	.15	.25	.30	.20	.10

You take the sample of 100 and receive 12 special orders. Revise the prior distribution to take into account the information provided by the sample.

21.5. Refer to Prob. 20.2. Assume that the sample of 50 is taken and that 37 students order the text.

a. Revise the original prior distribution of the proportion of students ordering the text to take into account the information obtained from the sample.

b. Use the revised distribution obtained in part a to arrive at a new break-even price for the text. Fixed and variable printing costs remain the same as originally stated in Prob. 20.2.

21.6. Refer to the computer manufacturer's training problem in Prob. 20.9. Assume that the company took a random sample class of 10 students, conducted the 1-week session, and found that 5 of the students passed.

a. Revise the prior distribution of Prob. 20.9 to take this information into account. Assume that the sampling was binomial.

b. Having taken the first sample, would it pay to take a second sample? If so, what should the optimal decision rule be? If not, prove that it's better to make a final decision after the first sample.

21.7. For the machine purchase of Prob. 20.10, your answer to part b should indicate that sampling is desirable. Assume that you therefore sample with the optimal decision rule and that you observe six defectives in the sample.

a. Revise the prior distribution of Prob. 20.10 to take this new information into account.

b. Having taken the first sample, will it pay to take a second sample? If so, what should the optimal decision rule be? If not, prove that you're better off to make a final decision after having sampled only once.

21.8. After you've performed the calculations for Probs. 20.10 and 21.7, your boss is quite impressed with your facility in decision-theory problems. He's so impressed, in fact, that he asks you to write a concise but complete explanation of the reasoning process you have used so that he can present it to the executive committee at its next meeting. (He'd like to do this himself, but he confesses that he really doesn't understand it.) Write such an explanation.

21.9. Refer to Prob. 20.12. Suppose that the testing laboratory was retained to analyze the foreign-made bulbs and that their report showed 4 defectives out of 100.

    a. Revise management's subjective probabilities regarding these bulbs to reflect the sample information.

    b. Compute the EOL for the decision alternatives using the revised probability distribution.

    c. How much was this sample worth to the distributor (using hindsight)?

    d. Would you recommend that another sample of 100 be analyzed (at the same cost as before)?

21.10. Explain the statement: The revised probability distribution for the random variable from the first sample becomes the prior probability distribution for use in deciding whether or not a second sample is desirable. How does this relate to the statement that the decision maker should make use of *all* the information available to him before making a decision?

21.11. Explain how a decision maker can tell when it is desirable to do no more sampling and to make a decision to act one way or another.

21.12. A large professional association is trying to estimate the percentage of its membership that will attend a convention. The executive committee assigns the following probabilities:

Percent attendance	Probability
0.05	.4
0.10	.3
0.15	.2
0.20	.1
	1.0

    a. In order to make better estimates for planning purposes, it is decided to poll a sample of the association membership by telephone; 10 members are called, and 2 state they'll attend. Revise the probability distribution to account for this information.

    b. Based on the prior probabilities, how likely was it that this particular sample result would be obtained?

    c. Ten more members are called, with no favorable responses. Revise the revised distribution obtained as an answer to part *a* to reflect this new information.

    d. Suppose the two samples of 10 each were pooled before the revision was made. Revise the *original* probability distribution for the result $n = 20$, $r = 2$.

    e. Compare your answers to parts *c* and *d*. Can you generalize regarding successive revisions vs. pooling sample information?

21.13. a. Under what circumstances might sample information actually prove worse than worthless to a decision maker?

    b. Would such a situation indicate that the sample should not have been taken? Explain.

21.14. In Prob. 21.1, assume you're allowed to draw four cards instead of two and that the cards drawn (in order) were queen of spades, four of spades, king of hearts, and ten of clubs.

    a. What is your revised probability that the deck is a pinochle deck?

    b. Suppose the draws are costing you money, say, at the rate of $100 per card. Can you see any advantage to using sequential sampling procedure, i.e., drawing and observing the first card before deciding whether to draw the second, etc?

    c. Can you generalize your answer to part *b* for all sampling situations?

21.15. Explain how you might determine in *advance* of taking the first sample in the product-development problem what sample outcomes might lead you to make a final decision (at that point) and what outcomes would lead you to collect more information before making a decision. (This sort of analysis results in what is called a *sequential* sampling design.) You may wish to assume the availability of a computer to perform the necessary calculations.

MODULE 22

NORMAL PRIOR DISTRIBUTIONS AND THEIR REVISION

In Modules 20 and 21 you saw how sample evidence can be combined with prior information in solving a decision problem. There, the sampling was binomial, and the prior information took the form of a discrete probability distribution. We now wish to extend these concepts to situations where the sampling and prior distributions are continuous. We'll first consider the use of the normal distribution to summarize prior information.

General learning objectives

Your general learning objectives for this module are to be able to:

1. Use a normal distribution to summarize prior information
2. Revise a normal prior distribution to take account of sample information
3. Apply normal distribution analysis to the solution of decision problems and describe its uses and limitations

Section 22.A

The Normal as a Prior Distribution

Learning objectives

Your learning objectives for this section are to be able to:

1. Use a normal distribution to summarize prior information
2. Apply a normal prior distribution to a specific decision situation by:
   a. Calculating the break-even point
   b. Specifying a linear loss function
3. State the conditions under which the decision depends on the mean of the estimating distribution

NORMAL PRIOR PROBABILITIES

The normal distribution has characteristics which are representative of a typical decision maker's prior beliefs in many kinds of decision problems. It works especially well when these beliefs are subjective, i.e., informed business judgments, rather than objectively based on historical relative frequencies or other "hard" facts. You learned for example, that the normal distribution is symmetrical and bell-shaped, implying that the values of a normally distributed variable are equally likely to fall a given distance from either side of the mean and that small deviations from the mean are more likely than large ones. Using the normal as a prior estimating distribution then implies (1) that the decision maker's best guess is as likely to be in error by a given amount in one direction as another and (2) that while various sizes of estimating error are possible, small errors are more likely than large ones. Certainly such statements won't describe the prior distribution in *all* decision situations, but they do seem to describe the nature of most subjective estimates of the random variables that provide the source of uncertainty in decision problems. Generally we *do* feel that our best guess is as apt to be high as low and, however unsure we may be, that it's more apt to be near the true value than far away.

Of course, the use of a normal prior distribution actually involves much more specific assumptions than these. Given the mean μ_o and the standard deviation σ_o of the normal prior distribution, we can state, according to our knowledge of the normal distribution, that the decision maker believes there are about 2 chances out of 3 the true mean μ of the random variable is within σ_o of the estimated mean, μ_o, i.e., that the true μ lies within the range $\mu_o \pm \sigma_o$. Or we could say that the decision maker is about 95 percent sure that μ is within $2\sigma_o$ of the estimated mean.

But where do we obtain the standard deviation σ_o for a prior estimating distribution? A decision maker may willingly give you a best guess (the mean μ_o) of the prior distribution but may claim to be quite unable to provide the σ_o (not having spent the hours you have spent poring over a decision-theory text). Actually, any sort of statement regarding the betting odds of probabilities of estimating errors of a certain size, given the assumption of a normal prior distribution, enables you to compute σ_o. Suppose, for example, that a decision maker is willing to bet even money that the estimate of true mean of some variable is correct to within 10 units. This implies a probability of .5 for the event that μ is within the range $\mu_o \pm 10$. Now recall from our earlier discussion of the normal distribution that about 68 percent of the area under the normal curve is included by a range $\mu_o \pm \sigma_o$. This means that somewhat less than σ_o in either direction would be required to encompass 50 percent of the area (corresponding to the probability of .5) under the normal curve.

In fact, we can use the normal area table to find precisely what distance on either side of the mean (measured in standard-deviation units) would include 50 percent of the total area—25 percent on either side of the mean. Using the normal area table backward, we see that an area of 25 percent on either side would require a distance of somewhere between .67 and $.68\sigma_o$.

This means that the 10-unit estimating error on which our decision maker was willing to give 50-50 odds represents, say, $.67\sigma_o$, or roughly two-thirds of the standard deviation of his prior estimating distribution. Since $.67\sigma_o = 10$,

$$\sigma_o = \frac{10}{.67} = 15$$

and 15 is the σ_o for the normal prior distribution. This technique, of course, is not limited to the use of 50-50 odds. A σ_o could be derived in similar fashion from any probability statement concerning the magnitude of estimating error. Once obtained, the σ_o can be used to derive other probability statements concerning estimating errors, which then can be checked against the decision maker's intuitive feel for these errors.[1]

Now, let's apply the use of a normal prior distribution to a specific decision situation.

A DECISION PROBLEM

Suppose that a mail-order firm with 900 retail outlets is contemplating the installation of a centralized data processing system in its home office with tape input units in each of the retail outlets. The total system including the inputs could be leased from the office equipment manufacturer for a two-year period at a cost of $180,000 per month

---

[1] If a σ_o derived in the above manner produces statements with which the decision maker cannot roughly agree, this simply implies that his prior distribution is not normal, and other methods must be used.

(or $4,320,000 for the entire period). It's designed to provide more efficient accounts receivable and inventory record keeping. Since the firm believes that its current accounting, billing, and inventory control practices are providing satisfactory levels of customer service, economic justification for the facility must be made on the basis of a saving in clerical effort. Management feels that the elimination of clerical labor hours could be accomplished without creating serious personnel problems. Some of these hours are now spent by part-time and temporary employees, and normal attrition of the clerical work force could be expected to take care of the remaining reduction in the work force.

There is, of course, some uncertainty in the dollar savings that will actually be achieved by the computer system. The customer representative for the computer manufacturer has estimated that monthly savings of $250 in clerical costs could be achieved for each retail branch. If so, this would mean total savings for the 900 branches of $900 \times $250 = $225,000$. For the 24-month period of the lease arrangement the estimated savings would be $225,000 \times 24 = $5,400,000$. Since the total leasing costs are $4,320,000, this estimate pictures the installation as quite profitable.[1]

The firm's president has asked his own systems analysis group to study the validity of the manufacturer's estimates. While they agree that $250 per month per branch represents a reasonable best guess as to the clerical cost reductions, including wages, fringe benefits, and reducible overhead, the chief analyst has pointed out the possibility of a sizable error in this estimate. Differences in the operations of the individual branches are apt to produce considerable dispersion among the results actually achieved, and some basic doubts regarding the system's operating effectiveness when integrated with other company procedures makes the cost savings figure subject to uncertainty.

The chief analyst points out that there is *some* chance, although he believes it rather unlikely, that total labor costs could be *increased* as a result of the change. Pressed to provide a "feel" for the underlying uncertainty, he estimates that the chances are about 50-50 that the average cost savings (per branch per month) will actually be between $150 and $350, that is, $250 \pm 100.

The systems group also reports that the 2-year period for which the lease is contemplated represents a reasonable period for decision-making purposes. Changes in the technology of the type of equipment being considered are rapid, and it seems unlikely that the decision made now will have any measurable impact on future decisions in this area.

BREAK-EVEN POINT AND LOSS FUNCTIONS

Under the foregoing circumstances, the company faces a decision problem where the conditional payoffs of the decision to lease depend on the average cost savings

---

[1] The time value of money is not considered here. It could be considered (although this would make the problem more complicated) by appropriate discounting of the cash flows, but the decision-theory analysis wouldn't be altered.

per month per branch for the entire company over the 2-year period. We can, in fact, calculate the value of this average which would allow the firm to break even on the lease. The average savings per branch per month, which we can designate in the problem as μ (the mean of our basic random variable) times 900 branches times 24 months will give the total cost savings resulting from the leased equipment. In order to break even, the firm must have total savings equaling the total lease payments, $4,320,000. Therefore, the break-even value μ_b will be such that

$$\mu_b \times 900 \times 24 = \$4,320,000$$

and
$$\mu_b = \frac{4,320,000}{900 \times 24} = \$200/\text{branch/month}$$

Thus, if the true value of μ turned out to be greater than $200 per branch per month, the lease would prove profitable. However, if μ in fact is less than $200, the decision to lease will prove in retrospect to be an incorrect decision and the firm will incur a loss. A general statement of the potential opportunity losses involved in this decision situation is given in Table 22.1. Notice the *symmetrical* character of the opportunity loss functions. They imply, for example, that a decision to lease with a true μ of $100 (an incorrect decision) results in the same magnitude of opportunity loss ($100 $\times$ 900 $\times$ 24 = $2,160,000) as a decision *not* to lease with a true μ of $300 (also an incorrect decision). Putting this another way, we can say that errors in estimating μ are just as serious in one direction as in the other. It's also true that the size of the opportunity loss is proportional to the size of the estimating error, resulting in a decision situation we describe technically as possessing *linear* loss functions.

Although symmetrical linear loss functions are not characteristic of *all* decision problems, such functions *are* found in many practical applications of business decision theory. In any case, to simplify a discussion that's already rather complex, we'll restrict ourselves to consideration of this type of problem in this module and the next.

This discussion does help emphasize one point that was probably clear in the beginning: the proper decision for the firm to make depends on the value of μ, the average savings per branch per month. The true value of μ is, of course, unknown, even though the firm has collected substantial information relevant to estimating it. This information can be summarized in the form of a normal prior probability distribution. From the previous statement of the problem, the mean of the prior estimating distribution μ_o should be taken as $250. This was regarded as the best estimate of obtainable cost savings. The σ_o for this estimating distribution can be obtained from the statement that the chances are about 50-50 that this average cost

Table 22.1

True value of μ	Correct decision	Incorrect decision	Opportunity loss
$\mu \geq \mu_b$	Lease	Don't lease	$(\mu - \mu_b)(900 \times 24)$
$\mu < \mu_b$	Don't lease	Lease	$(\mu_b - \mu)(900 \times 24)$

savings will be between $150 and $350. You saw on page 536 that 50-50 odds of including the true value in an interval estimate implied about $.67\sigma_o$ each direction from the μ_o. Since $.67\sigma_o = \$100$, for this problem, $\sigma_o = \$100/.67 = \$150$.

DECISION MAKING WITH A NORMAL PRIOR DISTRIBUTION

We are now ready to apply the prior estimating distribution to the actual decision process. Remember that the firm should decide to lease the data processing equipment if $\mu \geq \$200$. Since μ_o, the best estimate of μ, equals $250, which is greater than $200, and since the opportunity losses are symmetrical (equally severe in both directions), there's really no reason *not* to proceed with leasing the equipment. In fact, *in any problem where the opportunity losses are symmetrical in both directions from the break-even value of μ and where the prior distribution is also symmetrical, the decision rests on a simple, common-sense comparison of the mean of the estimating distribution with the break-even value.* Here, since $\mu_o > \mu_b$, the decision (to lease) would be made accordingly.

Note that when the loss functions and the prior distribution are symmetrical, it's only the mean of the estimating distribution that's important in making the decisions. The form of the estimating distribution we've used (in this case, normal) and its other parameters (in this case σ_o) haven't been used in making the decision. Indeed you may find it difficult to see how we've used any statistical decision theory at all, up to this point, to supplement common-sense reasoning. The fact is, we haven't. Statistical theory and the additional information we've obtained relative to the estimating distribution of μ are useful only in the solution of two important related problems:

1. How to combine knowledge or judgment in the form of a prior distribution with information obtained from a sample
2. How to determine the economic desirability of obtaining sample information prior to making a decision

The first of these problems is considered in the following section; the second is reserved for the next module.

REVIEW EXERCISES 22.A

1. Suppose a company is considering the addition of a new product to its line which would require an addition to its fixed costs of $80,000 per year. The selling price of the product would be $100 per unit, and variable costs are estimated at $60 per unit. Management estimates that sales of the product would be 2500 units per year but believes there is about a 10 percent chance that they might run 4000 or higher.

   a. Assuming that management's prior estimate of sales of the product can be represented by a normal distribution, such a distribution would be described by $\mu_o = $ _____ and $\sigma_o = $ _____.

   b. Calculate the break-even level of sales.

   c. Specify the linear loss function for this decision problem.

d. What decision should be made?

e. In a problem like this, the decision depends on a comparison of _____ with _____.

2. Only the *mean* of the estimating distribution is important in making a decision when the loss functions in the decision problem are:
   a. Symmetrical.
   b. Linear.
   c. Both *a* and *b.*
   d. Neither *a* nor *b.*

3. Symmetrical linear loss functions are rarely applicable in actual business problems: true or false?

Answers 22.A

1. a. μ_o = 2500 units (management's best estimate). From the Appendix, Table A.2, $z = 1.28$ corresponds to an area adjacent to the mean of .3997 (or a tail area of .1003, approximately 10 percent). Therefore,

$$z = 1.28 = \frac{4000 - 2500}{\sigma_o} = \frac{1500}{\sigma_o}$$

and

$$\sigma_o = \frac{1500}{1.28} = 1172 \text{ units}$$

b. $\mu_b = \dfrac{\$80,000}{\$100 - \$60} = \dfrac{\$80,000}{\$40} = 2000 \text{ units}$

c. The loss functions are

$$(\mu - 2000)(\$40) \quad \text{and} \quad (2000 - \mu)(\$40)$$

d. Since $\mu_o > \mu_b$, the product should be added to the line

e. μ_o (the mean of the estimating distribution), μ_b (break-even)

2. c

3. False; they are quite common in many types of business decision problems and provide a reasonable approximation in many others.

Section 22.B

Revision of Normal Prior Distributions

Learning objectives

Your learning objectives for this section are to be able to:

1. Revise a normal prior distribution to take account of sample information
2. Describe the characteristics of the revised distribution, including its mean and standard deviation
3. Define and explain the concept of information content
4. Use the revised distribution to make a decision

REVISION OF NORMAL PRIOR PROBABILITIES

A procedure was explained in Module 21 for revising a decision maker's prior estimate of probabilities. This procedure, based on Bayes' rule, provided a means for incorporating sample evidence along with prior beliefs in decision problems, where the values of the random variable—the source of the uncertainty in the decision problem—were discrete or point values. Here a procedure will be developed which enables us to revise prior beliefs that are represented by a continuous probability distribution, namely, the normal, using sample results obtained from a normal sampling distribution. The revised estimating distribution for μ will represent the combined effects of the prior estimating distribution (often subjective) and the sampling distribution (objective).

What are the implications of the requirement that the sampling distribution also be normal? Remember that a particular sample mean $\overline{X}$ is only one of many possible $\overline{X}$ values that would be obtained from different random samples of a given size drawn from a population. Also, recall that these $\overline{X}$ values are approximately normally distributed around the true population mean μ as long as the sample size is reasonably large. The distribution of sample means will likewise be approximately normal for even smaller values of n as long as the population is close to symmetrically distributed.[1] The mean of the sampling distribution will be μ, and its standard deviation will

---

[1] Actually, if the *parent* (not the prior) distribution from which the samples are drawn is normal, the sampling distribution will be normal for even small samples. Recall that if $s_{\overline{x}}$ is used as an estimate of $\sigma_{\overline{x}}$, the t distribution is applicable (see Module 13, pp. 327–328 and Sec. 22.D). Here, for simplicity, we assume normality of the sampling distribution.

541

be $\sigma_{\bar{X}}$, the standard error of the mean, given by the formula $\sigma_{\bar{X}} = \sigma_X/\sqrt{n}$. Where the population standard deviation σ_X is unknown, $s_{\bar{X}}$ can be used to estimate $\sigma_{\bar{X}}$ (as in Modules 13 and 14):

$$s_{\bar{X}} = \frac{s_X}{\sqrt{n}}$$

where s_X is the estimate of the population standard deviation σ_X, based on sample data.

The revised distribution could be obtained by breaking down the prior and sampling distributions into discrete chunks and proceeding exactly as in Module 21, where Bayes' rule was used to revise a discrete prior distribution. However, as you may recall, that procedure was cumbersome. It would be made even more so here by the additional step of first converting a continuous probability distribution into a discrete one. The beauty of using normal distributions to represent the prior distribution and sample evidence is that the computations required to obtain the revised distributions are greatly simplified. In fact with normal prior and sampling distributions *the revised estimating distribution will also be normal*, and its mean and variance can easily be obtained.

INFORMATION CONTENT

To explain the procedures involved in obtaining the characteristics of the revised distribution, we'll first find it useful to define a new concept, *information content* (IC), equal to the reciprocal of the variance of a distribution. For the prior distribution,

$$IC_o = \frac{1}{\sigma_o^2} \tag{22.1}$$

As the formula implies, the greater the variance of a distribution, the less the informational content. A decision maker who is rather unsure of his prior estimates of a variable will represent his beliefs with an estimating distribution with a large variance. It makes sense that such a distribution should be described as having relatively low informational content. Of course the IC value really provides no additional description of the distribution beyond that given by the variance. It is a useful concept primarily because it simplifies the relationships between prior, sampling, and revised distributions, making these relationships intuitively easier to understand.

The information content of a sample, $IC_{\bar{X}}$, will likewise be equal to the reciprocal of the variance of the sampling distribution:

$$IC_{\bar{X}} = \frac{1}{\sigma_{\bar{X}}^2} = \frac{1}{(\sigma_X/\sqrt{n})^2} = \frac{n}{\sigma_X^2} \tag{22.2}$$

Note that the information content of a sample is proportional to its size, logically enough, and inversely proportional to the variance of the population from which the sample is drawn.

CHARACTERISTICS OF THE REVISED DISTRIBUTION

Although we won't attempt to prove it here, you should be aware of the following important result. If the prior estimating distribution is normal, with mean μ_o and information content IC_o, and if the sampling distribution is normal with sample information content $IC_{\bar{X}}$, then the revised distribution is also normal with a mean μ_r given by

$$\mu_r = \frac{IC_o \mu_o + IC_{\bar{X}} \bar{X}}{IC_o + IC_{\bar{X}}} \tag{22.3}$$

Note that this revised mean is really only an ordinary *weighted average* of the prior mean and sample mean, where the weights used are the information contents of the prior distribution and sample, respectively.

An added advantage of the information content concept is that the IC_r for the revised distribution, and hence its variance, can also be obtained simply. As might be expected, the information content in the revised distribution is the sum of information provided by the prior and sampling distributions:

$$IC_r = IC_o + IC_{\bar{X}} \tag{22.4}$$

Or if we wish to know the variance of the revised distribution, this expression can be rewritten as

$$\frac{1}{\sigma_r^2} = \frac{1}{\sigma_o^2} + \frac{1}{\sigma_{\bar{X}}^2} \tag{22.5}$$

(since IC was defined as the reciprocal of the variance). Then,

$$\sigma_r^2 = \frac{\sigma_o^2 \sigma_{\bar{X}}^2}{\sigma_o^2 + \sigma_{\bar{X}}^2} \tag{22.6}$$

A word of caution is in order concerning the use of these formulas. There are three variances involved here—all pertaining to distributions used in *estimating* μ, namely, the prior, sampling, and revised distributions. It's all too easy to get one or more of these variances confused with the population variance σ_X^2, which measures the dispersion of values within the population itself, or with the sample estimate of it, s_X^2, which is based on the dispersion of individual values making up a particular sample. The dispersion or spread among individual values constituting a population or sample is something entirely different from the dispersion of a distribution used to *estimate* the population mean. Essentially σ_o, $\sigma_{\bar{X}}$, and σ_r measure the precision of various estimates of μ; σ_X^2, or its stand-in s_X^2, which measures the dispersion of actual observations, is used in determining $\sigma_{\bar{X}}^2$, but that is the only way it's involved in the revision process. All this may become clearer to you in the context of the examples which follow.

AN EXAMPLE OF THE NORMAL REVISION PROCESS

To illustrate the method of revising a normal distribution, let's use the normal prior distribution of the computer-leasing problem described in Sec. 22.A. There it was determined that the firm should lease the equipment if it produced an average savings of $200 or more per branch for the 900 branches. The prior estimate formulated by company staff was represented by a normal probability distribution with a mean μ_o of $250 (the best guess) and standard deviation of $150.

While this estimate of μ indicates that the company should lease, the relatively large σ_o for the estimating distribution is disquieting. Suppose the company finds it possible to have a month's trial run with a randomly selected sample of 30 of its branches to determine the cost savings available.

Assume that there's no seasonal pattern to savings achieved and that the company can take the information derived from the sample as representative of the entire period of the proposed lease. Then let's assume that the following results are calculated from the 30 individual values of monthly cost savings in the sample:

$$\bar{X} = \$194.20 \qquad s_X = \$251.55$$

From the latter value[1] we can estimate the standard deviation of the sampling distributions as

$$s_{\bar{X}} = \frac{s_X}{\sqrt{n}} = \frac{251.55}{\sqrt{30}} = 45$$

We're now prepared to put together the company's prior estimates and the sample information to obtain a revised estimating distribution. First,

$$\mathrm{IC}_o = \frac{1}{150^2} = \frac{1}{22,500} = .0000444$$

$$\mathrm{IC}_{\bar{X}} = \frac{1}{45^2} = \frac{1}{2025} = .0004938$$

Then the mean of the revised distribution μ_r is obtained from the weighted average

$$\begin{aligned}
\mu_r &= \frac{\mu_o \mathrm{IC}_o + \bar{X} \mathrm{IC}_{\bar{X}}}{\mathrm{IC}_o + \mathrm{IC}_{\bar{X}}} \\
&= \frac{250(.0000444) + 194.20(.0004938)}{.0000444 + .0004938} \\
&= \$198.62
\end{aligned}$$

---

[1] The s_X larger than $\bar{X}$ indicates that the sample probably contains some negative X's, that is, branches where the cost *savings* are negative due to an actual increase in costs.

The revised distribution will have an information content of

$$IC_r = IC_o + IC_{\bar{X}}$$
$$= .0000444 + .0004938$$
$$= .0005382$$

and a standard deviation σ_r of

$$\sigma_r = \sqrt{\frac{1}{IC_r}} = \sqrt{\frac{1}{.0005382}} = \sqrt{1858} = \$43.10$$

DECISION MAKING WITH THE REVISED DISTRIBUTION

We now know that the revised distribution for estimating μ is normal, with a mean of $198.62 and a standard deviation of $43.10. Even though the preceding computations have been rather involved, the revised distribution is used for decision-making purposes in the same common-sense way as the prior distribution. You'll recall that in the absence of sample information the prior mean μ_o was simply compared with the economic break-even point μ_b to determine the proper decision. (Since $\mu_o = \$250$ and $\mu_b = \$200$, estimated savings were sufficient to justify a decision to lease the equipment.)

The *revised* best estimate of cost savings per branch, taking the information obtained from the sample of 30 branches into account, is $198.62. Since this μ_r value is less than μ_b, that is $198.62 < \$200$, the proper decision at this point would be to *reject* the lease arrangement. As before, it's the simple comparison of the *mean* of the revised estimating distribution with the break-even value that governs the decision. The σ_r for the revised distribution is important only in connection with *further* revision in the light of additional sample information.

Now the sample evidence was in this case sufficient to swing the decision from acceptance of the lease arrangement to rejection. Needless to say, this won't always happen. The sample evidence, properly weighted, may fail to pull the revised mean past the break-even point—it just barely did in the illustration—or it may support the prior estimate, causing the decision maker to be surer than ever of his judgments. What is important is that we now have at our disposal a systematic method for combining the results of a sample with subjective prior estimates (business judgments) that can be represented by normal estimating distributions. Since the revised distribution is also normal, further sample evidence can be incorporated as it becomes available by repeating the revision process, treating this revised distribution as if it were a prior distribution, just as you did in Module 21.

REVIEW EXERCISES 22.B

1. The information content of a distribution is defined as:
   a. Its variance.

b. The reciprocal of its variance.

c. The reciprocal of its standard deviation.

d. None of the above.

2. The information content of a revised distribution is equal to the sum of the information content of the prior distribution plus the information content of the sampling distribution: true or false?

3. The variance of a revised distribution is equal to the sum of the variance of the prior and sampling distributions: true or false?

4. The mean of a revised distribution is a weighted average of _____ _____ and _____, where the weights are _____ _____.

5. Refer to the computer-leasing problem described in the text. Instead of the sample results indicated, suppose a sample of 49 had been taken, yielding

$$\bar{X} = \$210 \qquad s_X = \$280$$

a. Based on these sample results, what is the information content of the sampling distribution $IC_{\bar{X}}$?

b. Use these sample data to revise the original prior distribution (with $\mu_o = \$250$, $\sigma_o = \$150$).

c. Based on this revised distribution, what decision should be made?

6. If the prior estimating distribution is normal and a reasonably large sample is taken, the revised distribution:

a. Will be normal.

b. Generally won't be normal.

c. Can't be predicted.

d. None of the above.

7. Additional sample results can be incorporated into a normal estimating distribution by using a revised distribution previously obtained in place of the prior in the estimating process: true or false?

Answers 22.B

1. b   2. true

3. False; although the information contents are additive, the variances aren't [see Eq. (22.6)].

4. Mean of the prior distribution, sample mean, information contents of the prior and sampling distributions, respectively

5. a. $s_{\bar{X}} = \dfrac{s_X}{\sqrt{n}} = \dfrac{\$280.00}{\sqrt{49}} = \$40$

therefore

$$IC_{\bar{X}} = \frac{1}{40^2} = .0006667$$

b. $\mu_r = \dfrac{\mu_o IC_o + \bar{X} IC_{\bar{X}}}{IC_o + IC_{\bar{X}}}$

$= \dfrac{250(.0000444) + 210(.0006667)}{.0000444 + .0006667}$

$= \$212.35$

$IC_r = IC_o + IC_{\bar{X}} = .0000444 + .0006667 = .0007111$

$\sigma_r = \sqrt{\dfrac{1}{IC_r}} = \sqrt{\dfrac{1}{.0007111}} = \sqrt{1406}$

$= \$37.50$

c. The lease arrangement should be accepted, since $\mu_r > \mu_b$.

6. a   7. true

Section 22.C

Other Uses and Limitations of Normal Estimating Distributions

Learning objectives

Your learning objectives for this section are to be able to:

1. Distinguish between classical confidence-interval estimation and Bayesian estimating procedures and explain why they produce different results
2. Describe the limitations of normal distribution estimating procedures because of:
   a. Nonnormal prior distributions
   b. Nonnormal sampling distributions

REVISED DISTRIBUTIONS AND CONFIDENCE INTERVALS

It may prove useful to contrast the more traditional confidence-interval estimating procedure (discussed in Module 13) for normal sampling with the revised estimating distribution of Sec. 22.B. The sample of 30 branches could have been used as the basis for, say, a 95 percent confidence-interval estimate of average cost savings per branch:

$$95\% \text{ confidence interval} = \bar{X} \pm 1.96 s_{\bar{X}} = \bar{X} \pm 1.96 \frac{s_X}{\sqrt{n}} = \$194.20 \pm 1.96(45)$$

$$= \$194.20 \pm \$88.20$$

547

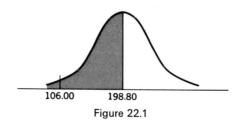

106.00   198.80

Figure 22.1

(To be strictly correct, a t value of 2.045 should have been used in place of $z = 1.96$ since s_X was used to estimate σ_X. However, the normality of the sampling distribution is assumed in obtaining the revised distribution, so it seems more reasonable to base a confidence interval on the same assumption for comparative purposes. For an n as large as 30, the difference is small anyway.)

One interpretation of this interval is that the decision maker can be 95 percent sure that the range $106.00 to $282.40 contains the true value of average savings.

Using the revised estimating distribution, on the other hand, which is normal with $\mu_r = $198.62 and $\sigma_r = $43.10, the decision maker would obtain the probability that μ was in the interval $106 to $282.40 as follows (see Fig. 22.1):

$$z = \frac{\mu - \mu_r}{\sigma_r} = \frac{106.00 - 198.62}{43.10} = -2.15$$

The area from the normal table corresponding to $z = -2.15$ is .4842. Therefore $P(106 < \mu < 198.80) = .4842$. Likewise, for the upper part of the range (Fig. 22.2)

$$z = \frac{\mu - \mu_r}{\sigma_r} = \frac{282.40 - 198.62}{43.10} = 1.94$$

The area from the normal table corresponding to $z = 1.94$ is .4738. Thus, $P(106.00 < \mu < 282.40) = .4842 + .4738 = .9580$, as opposed to the confidence coefficient of .9500.

On the other hand, by using the revised distribution the decision maker could be

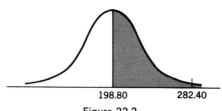

198.80   282.40

Figure 22.2

548

95 percent sure that the true average savings were between \$114.14, or 198.62 − 1.96(43.10), and \$283.10, or 198.62 + 1.96(43.10), compared with the confidence interval of 106.00 to 282.40. What causes the difference in these estimates? Why is the revised probability that μ is within the confidence interval different from the confidence coefficient?

The answer, of course, is that the revised distribution incorporates prior information whereas the confidence-interval estimate doesn't. In fact, the only time that the use of a revised distribution and classical interval estimation will lead to similar results is when absolutely no prior information is available. This means that the decision maker, before sampling, would have to consider *all* possible values of the random variable equally likely, in which case the prior estimating distribution would have infinite variance and zero information content. Under these circumstances, his revised distribution for estimating μ would have a mean equal to $\overline{X}$ and standard deviation equal to $\sigma_{\overline{X}}$, as in Fig. 22.3.

This curve has the exact properties of the distribution of sample means (for samples of size n drawn from a population with mean μ and standard deviation σ_x) with one important conceptual difference. Although it's also normal and has a standard deviation $\sigma_{\overline{X}}$, the mean of the pictured distribution is the sample mean $\overline{X}$, whereas the mean of the sampling distribution is the true population mean μ.

Basically what's happened is that the random variable has been switched. The revised distribution in Fig. 22.3 is an *estimating* distribution constructed for the purpose of estimating the true value of μ, which is treated as if it were a random variable. The best estimate of μ in the absence of any prior information is of course $\overline{X}$, the mean of the sample. The sampling distribution of $\overline{X}$ on the other hand, is an abstraction describing how the values of a random variable $\overline{X}$, which are the means of all possible samples of a given size drawn from a population, are distributed around the true population mean.

Note that the type of distribution appearing in Fig. 22.3, although it incorporates no prior information, wasn't drawn in earlier modules dealing with classical estimation procedures. The reason is the classical objection, discussed at length in Module 11, to the interpretation of a population parameter, such as μ, as a random variable. The Bayesian, who favors such an interpretation, might object to a revised distribution

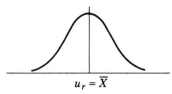

$$u_r = \overline{X}$$

Figure 22.3 / Revised distribution for estimating μ when no prior information is available ($\sigma_o = \infty$; $IC_o = 0$; $\sigma_r = \sigma_{\overline{X}} = \sigma_x/\sqrt{n}$).

549

such as that shown in Fig. 22.3 on other grounds, arguing that situations where absolutely no prior information is available (where all values of a decision variable are equally likely) are very rare. If the prior information is vague and prior estimates are uncertain, the information content of the prior distribution will reflect this. The Bayesian would simply take the position that it isn't necessary to go to the extreme of ignoring prior information altogether.

DEPARTURES FROM NORMALITY

The results of the previous sections rest on the fundamental assumption that both the prior and sampling distributions are normal. What of the situation where this assumption is not valid?

Consider first the effects of a nonnormal prior distribution. If, as is usually the case, the information content of the prior distribution is small relative to that of the sampling distribution, the shape of the prior distribution will have little effect on either the shape of the revised distribution or the numerical values calculated as its parameters. Unless the decision maker's prior estimates are very definite (small σ_o^2 and high IC_o) and quite nonnormal, the formulas developed above for the normal case can be used without a serious loss of accuracy.

The situation is a little more complicated when nonnormal sampling distributions are considered. A distribution of sample means can be nonnormal for either of two reasons. First, the parent population from which the samples are drawn can depart seriously from the normal distribution. Under this circumstance, the sampling distribution will be very close to normal if the sample is large, but it may not be for small samples. Remember that the central-limit theorem promises only an approach to normality as the sample size is increased.

Second, the distribution of sample means can be treated as strictly normal only when the true population standard deviation is known. In almost all practical problems it's necessary to estimate the population standard deviation from the sample standard deviation. Where s_X is used in place of σ (with the appropriate correction for the loss of a degree of freedom), sample means will be distributed according to the t distribution described in Module 13. Here again, however, we may note that the t distribution approaches normality as the sample size increases.

The situation may then be summarized as follows. An adequate approximation to normal sampling distributions will be obtained regardless of other circumstances as long as the sample size is reasonably large—a good rule of thumb here would be $n \geq 30$, although this depends on the nonnormality of the parent distribution. The revision formulas of this module can be used without hesitation for large samples. Although they're often used with smaller samples, you should be aware of the theoretical limitations involved when the prior and sampling distributions are nonnormal. A feel for the magnitude of errors involved can be obtained by a study of Sec. 22.D, where the continuous methods of this module are applied to a problem discussed earlier in which the normality assumptions are less well founded.

REVIEW EXERCISES 22.C

1. Classical confidence-interval estimates generally give the same results as estimates made using revised distributions obtained by the methods described in this module: true or false?

2. The true mean of a population μ is treated as a random variable in:
 a. Classical confidence-interval estimation.
 b. Bayesian estimation using revised distributions.
 c. Both *a* and *b*.
 d. Neither *a* nor *b*.

3. In classical confidence-interval estimation, it is assumed that no prior information exists: true or false?

4. If no prior information exists, it can be said that:
 a. All possible values of a random variable being estimated are equally likely to occur.
 b. The prior distribution has no information content.
 c. The prior distribution has infinite variance.
 d. All the above.

5. If prior information exists concerning a population, the best estimate of the population mean is still the mean of a sample: true or false?

6. An estimating distribution for a random variable will generally have the same characteristics (mean and standard deviation) as a sampling distribution for samples of a given size: true or false?

7. Even though a decision maker's prior estimating distribution is nonnormal, it may still be acceptable to use the revision procedures for normal distributions described in this module: true or false?

8. A distribution of sample means can be nonnormal because:
 a. Small samples may be drawn from nonnormal populations.
 b. The population standard deviation is estimated from sample data.
 c. Either *a* or *b*.
 d. Neither *a* nor *b*.

9. An adequate approximation of normal sampling distributions is generally obtained for sample sizes larger than 30: true or false?

Answers 22.C

1. False; revised distributions generally incorporate prior information, whereas confidence-interval estimates don't. They lead to similar results only if no prior information is available.

2. b   *3.* true   *4. d*

5. False; the best estimate of a population mean is the mean of the revised distribution incorporating both sample data and prior information.

6. False; only if no prior information is available will the estimating distribution for a random variable have the exact characteristics of the sampling distribution.

7. True; generally, the information content of the prior distribution is small relative to that of the sampling distribution, so that the shape of the sampling distribution won't have much effect on the results. (Theoretically, however, the revision methods in this module apply only to normal distributions.)

8. c   *9.* true

Section 22.D

Alternative Methods for Discrete Prior Distributions

Learning objectives

Your learning objectives for this section are to be able to:

1. Apply the normal distribution analysis of this module to problems involving discrete prior distributions
2. Identify the advantages and limitations of this approach

APPLICATION OF NORMAL DISTRIBUTION ANALYSIS TO DECISION PROBLEMS INVOLVING DISCRETE PRIOR DISTRIBUTIONS

Revision of prior distributions for estimating a population proportion using Bayes' rule and binomial tables was described at length in Module 21. The procedure involved, although simple enough in concept, suffers from two drawbacks: (1) the prior and revised distributions used are discrete, implying that only certain specified values of the random variable p are possible; (2) the necessary arithmetic is burdensome and time-consuming.

The purpose of this section is to consider an alternative method of revising discrete prior distributions of p or other random variables which treats them as *continuous* rather than discrete. Specifically, the method explained here converts a prior distribution of p to normal form and then utilizes the normal revision procedure explained in this module. The method is illustrated by applying it to the decision problem (the product-development situation) used earlier to illustrate discrete revision procedures.

AN ALTERNATIVE ANALYSIS OF THE PRODUCT-DEVELOPMENT PROBLEM

In Module 20 and 21 a problem involving a decision whether or not to develop a new product was posed. To reiterate the more important facts of that problem, it was economically desirable to develop the product if gross profits per unit of $500 could more than cover fixed development costs of $500,000. The firm would thus have to

552

sell 1000 units of the product among its 20,000 regular customers. Our previous analysis of this problem, cast in a binomial framework, set up the break-even point in terms of the proportion of customers who would have to buy the product, that is, $p = 1000/20,000 = .05$.

Suppose we now recast the problem in a continuous framework, replacing the proportion of customers buying p, the random variable (and source of uncertainty in the problem), with the *average* dollar profit *per customer* μ. The break-even value of this variable μ_b would be $\$500,000/20,000 = \$25$ per customer.

The subjectively derived prior distribution of the proportion of customers expected to purchase (Table 20.1), repeated on the left, can be recast as shown on the right.

Proportion of customers purchasing	Probability	Average profit per customer	Probability
.02	.1	$10	.1
.04	.3	20	.3
.06	.3	30	.3
.08	.2	40	.2
.10	.1	50	.1

This is simply a different way of expressing the same managerial judgments regarding prospects for the product that were previously expressed in the proportion purchasing distribution. While the new distribution isn't strictly normal, it's symmetrical and bell-shaped enough to reasonably approximate a normal prior distribution. The parameters of this distribution can be calculated as $\mu_o = \$29.00$ and $\sigma_o = \$11.36$. (It may be good practice for you to verify these figures.)

A comparison of the prior mean profit per customer of $29 with the break-even value of $\mu_b = \$25$ indicates that in the absence of any further information, the product *should* be developed. This is the same decision reached earlier in the EOL analysis (without sampling) of Table 20.4.

The real purpose here, however, is to consider the applicability of the normal *revision* process to this problem. Now notice that the distribution of profit *per customer* is *not* normal. Indeed, by the nature of this particular problem, all customers either buy the product, in which case the resulting profit is $500, or don't buy, in which case the profit is 0. Instead of being anywhere near normal, the distribution of profits by customers consists of just the two values 500 and 0, for example,

Customer number	Gross profit realized
1	$ 0
2	0
3	0
4	500
5	0
.....	....
20,000	0

Actually, the nonnormality of this *parent* distribution, or population, in itself doesn't matter. In the revision process described earlier in this module we're concerned with the normality of the prior and *sampling* distributions. Of course, with a parent population as violently nonnormal as the one described above and a sample size as small as 20, the sampling distribution won't be exactly normal. Nevertheless, we'll proceed here to assume that the sampling distribution *is* normal and to carry out the normal analysis of the product-development problem. The results of this analysis can then be compared with the results previously obtained by discrete methods to see what errors are introduced by the normality assumptions. If the errors aren't serious, the normal methods afford a desirable alternative approach because of their relative computational ease.

Since from the prior distribution the expected value of p is .058, we can estimate $\sigma_{\bar{p}}$ as[1]

$$\sigma_{\bar{p}} = \sqrt{\frac{p(1-p)}{n}} = \sqrt{\frac{.058(.942)}{20}} = .0523$$

This can be translated into terms of dollar sales per customer (our continuous variable), giving

$$\sigma_X = \$26.15$$

then

$$\sigma_r = \sqrt{\frac{\sigma_o^2 \sigma_X^2}{\sigma_o^2 + \sigma_X^2}} = \sqrt{\frac{11.36^2(26.15)^2}{11.36^2 + 26.15^2}} = \$10.42$$

Also,

$$IC_o = \frac{1}{11.35^2} = .00775 \quad \text{and} \quad IC_X = \frac{1}{26.15^2} = .00146$$

Now since 0 buyers were actually found in the sample of 20 discussed in Module 21, the sample average profit per customer $\bar{X}$ is also 0, and

$$\mu_r = \frac{IC_o(\mu_o) + IC_X(\bar{X})}{IC_o + IC_X}$$

$$= \frac{.00775(29.00) + .00146(0)}{.00775 + .00146} = \$24.40$$

Thus, using the normal analysis, the sample of $n = 20$, $r = 0$ or $n = 20$, $\bar{X} = 0$ leads to a revised estimating distribution, assumed to be normal, with a mean of \$24.40 and a standard deviation of \$10.42. Using the sample prior distribution and sample data in discrete form in Module 21, we obtained the revised distribution shown on the left, but, as before, we can express proportion purchasing in terms of average profit per customer, as on the right:

---

[1] Estimating $\sigma_{\bar{p}}$ according to the prior best estimate of p is generally superior to using the sample p in the estimate. In the problem under discussion, the sample proportion buying was 0, which would if used in the formula lead to an estimate of $\sigma_{\bar{p}} = 0$, which would in turn cause the entire procedure to break down!

Alternative methods for discrete prior distributions

Proportion purchasing p	$P(p)$ (revised)	Average profit per customer	Probability (revised)
.02	.1985	$10	.1985
.04	.3943	20	.3943
.06	.2588	30	.2588
.08	.1122	40	.1122
.10	.0362	50	.0362

Calculation of the mean and standard deviation of this distribution, on the right, which you can also verify, gives $\mu_r = \$23.93$ (compared with $\mu_r = \$24.40$ using normal methods) and $\sigma_r = \$10.30$ (compared with $\sigma_r = \$10.42$ using normal methods). The difference in results between the normal and discrete revision methods is insignificant, even though the normality assumptions were violated, particularly with repect to the sampling distribution. Of course, this one illustration doesn't in itself prove the adequacy of the normal analysis of seemingly nonnormal discrete problems, and it isn't possible to generalize regarding the accuracy of the approximation obtained. Still, it does seem to provide remarkably close results in many practical decision situations, and its relative simplicity has much to recommend it. Certainly it makes sense to utilize the normal revision methods as a first pass in discrete decision situations. Should the decision prove borderline, the more accurate but more complex discrete methods can then be applied.

REVIEW EXERCISES 22.D

1. An important reason for applying normal distribution analysis to decision problems involving discrete prior distributions is that:
   a. Most discrete distributions closely approximate normal.
   b. It isn't possible to revise discrete distributions otherwise.
   c. Computations are less burdensome.
   d. None of the above.
2. While it isn't possible to generalize regarding the accuracy of normal approximations to discrete distributions, such approximations can prove useful in a variety of decision situations: true or false?
3. A large production run of manufactured parts is estimated to be 20 percent defective by a production manager, who further believes there's 1 chance in 5 that the defective rate is as high as 25 percent. A sample of 100 parts shows 27 defective parts. Use the normal approximation described in this section to obtain a revised estimate of the proportion of defective parts.

Answers 22.D

1. c   2. true
3. Using the proportion defective as the random variable, the mean of the prior estimating distribution μ_o is 20 percent. Since there's 1 chance in 5 that this random variable is

555

greater than 25 percent, $P(\mu \geq 25) = .20$; a tail area of .2000 (internal area of .3000) corresponds to $z = .84$. Therefore,

$$z = .84 = \frac{25\% - 20\%}{\sigma_o} \quad \text{and} \quad \sigma_v = \frac{5\%}{.84} \approx 6\%$$

Also, using the mean of the prior estimating distribution as the best available estimate for the percentage defective gives

$$\sigma_{\bar{p}} = \sqrt{\frac{p(1 - p)}{n}} = \sqrt{\frac{.25(.75)}{100}} = .043 \quad \text{or} \quad \sigma_X = 4.3\%$$

Then
$$IC_o = \frac{1}{6^2} = .027 \quad \text{and} \quad IC_X = \frac{1}{4.3^2} = .053$$

and, since the sample percentage defective is 27/100, or $\bar{X} = 27\%$,

$$\mu_r = \frac{IC_o(\mu_o) + IC_X(\bar{X})}{IC_o + IC_X} = \frac{(.027)(25) + (.053)(27)}{.027 + .053} = 26.3\% \text{ defective}$$

Questions and Problems

22.1. Acme Products is considering the addition of a new product to its line. The product would increase the company's fixed cost by $2000 per year. The selling price is $15 and variable costs are $11 per unit. The market research department estimates that demand will be 600 units per year but that there is a 25 percent chance that sales will fall below the level of break-even profitability.
   a. What is the break-even level of demand?
   b. What are the characteristics of the company's demand estimating distribution? (Assume that a normal distribution is appropriate.)
   c. What decision should the company make?

22.2. Distinguish between the following variances, identifying the distribution for which each measures dispersion:
   a. σ_o^2 b. σ_X^2 c. s_X^2
   d. $\sigma_{\bar{X}}^2$ e. σ_r^2

22.3. A normal prior estimating distribution has $\mu_o = 42$ and $\sigma_o = 1$. A sample of size 49 is taken with $\bar{X} = 41$ and $s_X = 14$. For the revised estimating distribution, compute:
   a. μ_r b. σ_r c. $P(\mu_X \leq 40)$

22.4. a. In Prob. 22.3, how large would an additional sample have to be to reduce the standard deviation of the revised distribution σ_r to .5?
   b. What assumption did you have to make to answer part a?
   c. Can you generalize these results? Is the reduction in σ_r, that is, the improvement in the precision of your estimating distribution, proportional to the increase in sample size?

22.5. Spend 'n Save, a department store chain, wishes to estimate the average size of a charge sale. The credit manager estimates an average of $12, and indicates that he is about 50 percent sure that the average would be between $10 and $14. To supplement his judgment, he draws a random sample of 100 charge slips from last year's records and computes $\bar{X} = \$9.64$ and $s_X = \$3.10$.

a. Construct a 95 percent confidence-interval estimate of μ_X, the mean size of charge sale.

b. Use the credit manager's estimates to construct a prior estimating distribution for μ_X.

c. Revise the estimating distribution to reflect the sample results.

d. From the revised distribution obtained in part c, you can be 95 percent sure that μ_X is between _____ and _____.

e. Compare the answers to parts a and d.

f. What general statement can you make regarding classical and Bayesian estimating procedures?

22.6. D. H. Roberts recently purchased a small manufacturing company. Among the company's assets are accounts receivable carried on the company's balance sheet at $180,000. Roberts has been skeptical regarding the collectibility of these accounts, which represent balances owed by a total of 1440 different customers and many of which are long overdue. He is considering selling the accounts to a factor, who takes full responsibility for collection as well as the risk of noncollectibility. The factor has offered 50 percent of the book value, or $90,000, for the accounts. After carefully looking over the records, Roberts estimates that if he were to attempt to collect these accounts himself, he'd have to spend about $30 per customer in collection expenses. He is uncertain, because of the low credit ratings of many customers and the large number of charges which have apparently been disputed by customers, how much can actually be collected. He estimates that it should run about $120 per customer but could run as low as $50 per customer (about a 10 percent chance).

a. Should Mr. Roberts sell the accounts receivable or try to collect them?

b. The company controller suggests trying to collect a random sample of the accounts before the decision is made. Thirty accounts are selected, with $6010 being collected. Collection expenses for these accounts are $2110. Would these results alter the decision? (If you think you lack some information necessary to analyze this part of the problem, see whether you can make an intelligent guess at the answer.)

22.7. Suppose the sample of 30 accounts in Prob. 22.6 yields net collections (gross amount collected less collection expense) with a mean of $130 per account and $s_X = \$60$.

a. Obtain a revised normal estimating distribution for net collections per account.

b. Should the accounts receivable be sold to a factor?

22.8. A mining company is investigating the desirability of buying and developing an ore body. The ore body is estimated to contain 5 million tons of ore. It will cost 2 million dollars to purchase and develop the field, including the erection of a processing plant on the site. Variable costs of mining and processing are $50 per ton of ore. The selling price of the metal to be recovered is 24 cents per pound. To simplify the problem don't worry about discounting future cash flows, and assume that all the figures used above are certain.

The random variable in the problem is the average grade of the ore (the percent of the metal in the ore). We can assume that all the metal in the ore is recoverable and that there are no by-products of any value.

On the basis of past experience and preliminary site testing, management estimates that the average grade of the ore body $\mu_o = 12$ percent. They also believe that it is reasonable to assume a normal prior distribution, with a 50-50 chance that the grade will be within ± 1.0 percent from μ_o.

Recognizing that there is a fairly large chance that the true mean could be below the break-even value, the management decides to drill 25 test cores in a random pattern into the ore body to check the grade of the ore. When they do, they find that $\bar{X}$, the average ore grade from the 25 cores, is 9.5 percent with $s_X = 2.5$ percent.

Taking into consideration all the evidence they have accumulated up to this point, should they decide to mine the body or not?

22.9.   a. In designing a sampling procedure for a normal prior distribution decision problem (see Module 23) the optimum decision criterion $\bar{X}_{AL}$ is not generally specified in advance of taking the sample. Can you surmise why?

b. How *is* the sample result used in this case to make the decision?

22.10. In the computer-leasing problem discussed in this module, the sample evidence was responsible for changing the decision that would have been made without sampling.

a. What is the lowest value of mean cost savings for the sample that would have left the decision without sampling—to lease the equipment—unchanged?

b. How might a different s_X value for the sample have changed the final decision?

c. How might a similar sample result (same $\bar{X}$ and s_X) from a larger or smaller sample have changed the decision?

22.11. XL Tire and Rubber, Inc., distributes its products through 700 retail outlets. To stimulate slumping sales, the company president is considering a large promotional campaign involving the use of local radio and newspaper advertising and the use of loss leaders. With the golf season at its peak and enthusiasm for the sport running high, the president believes that the sale of high-quality, name-brand golf balls at giveaway prices will attract customers to his retail outlets. He is hopeful, of course, that these customers will buy tires or other products once they are in the store. The golf balls would cost the company $6 per dozen. The proposed plan is to sell the balls at $.99 per package of three on a one-package-to-a-customer basis, with 200 dozen balls being allocated to each retail outlet. This price should be low enough to attract customer traffic and to assure that all the golf balls will be sold during the promotion period. Selling expenses, including inventory carrying costs, shipping, etc., are estimated at 15 cents per package of three. Advertising expenses for the promotion would involve an agency fee of $30,000 to plan the campaign and local expenditures of $1000 for each retail outlet.

a. Assuming the XL gross profit margin (contribution to profit and fixed overhead) averages 25 percent on sales, how much additional merchandise would each golf ball purchaser have to buy (on the average) to make the promotion a success?

b. What specific assumptions did you have to make to answer part a?

c. Formulate *your own* normal prior estimating distribution of average sales per golf-ball purchaser. (You don't have to know anything about the tire business— just base your μ_o on your best estimate as to how this sort of promotion would work out. If you're not sure, this can be reflected by a large σ_o for your estimating distribution.)

d. What decision regarding the promotion would *you* make?

22.12. The Instant Wealth investment advisory service is considering expanding its weekly market letter that is mailed to subscribers to include additional statistical material and recommendations. Since this material is supplementary in nature, there wouldn't be any market for it outside its existing list of subscribers. The Instant Wealth president believes that the new supplement can be sold to about half of the firm's 12,000 subscribers but concedes that there is a 10 percent chance that as few as one-quarter may buy and a 10 percent chance that as many as three-quarters may buy it. These estimates assume pricing the supplement at $50 per year.

The variable cost of producing this supplement is estimated at $30 per subscriber per year, but it would involve initial development costs (including research, purchase of data, computer programming, etc.) of $80,000. The president believes that these development costs must be recovered quickly since competition will copy the supplement, probably forcing him to lower the price to a much less attractive level within 2 years.

    a. Express the president's estimate of the proportion of customers who'll buy the supplement as a normal prior distribution.

    b. Based on the above information alone, what should be done?

22.13. In the problems considered earlier involving work sampling (see Probs. 12.2 and 14.8), 24 employees were observed in written communication out of the 100 spot checks. Management, surprised at these results and aware of similar studies done elsewhere, believes that the true percentage is probably around 20 percent, with only a 10 percent chance that it could run as high as 24 percent (or as low as 16 percent).

    a. Obtain an estimating distribution incorporating both the management estimate and the previous sample results.

    b. What amount of information is contained in the prior estimating distribution? How does it compare with the information content of the sample?

22.14. In Prob. 21.4, the prior distribution assumed for p was a discrete probability distribution.

    a. Do the best you can to represent this prior information by a normal distribution.

    b. Use the normal revision process to incorporate the sample results $n = 100$, $r = 12$.

    c. How does the mean of the revised normal distribution in part *b* compare with the mean of the revised discrete distribution in Prob. 21.4?

    d. Is the normal approximation accurate enough to be useful? Explain.

22.15. Give some examples of practical situations in which you think the normal revision process outlined in this module *wouldn't* be applicable. Indicate in each case whether you think it is the normality assumption concerning the prior distribution or concerning the sampling distribution (or some other assumption) that has been violated.

MODULE 23
THE ECONOMICS OF SAMPLING: THE NORMAL CASE

Whether additional information in the form of a sample should be purchased before making a final decision and, if so, how large a sample should be obtained was considered in Module 20. There, you learned to compute the expected value of sample information (EVSI) for various sizes of samples, which could then be compared with the costs of the various sizes to determine the economic desirability of each in a given decision problem. However, the analysis there was limited to cases where the decision maker's prior probability distribution was discrete and the proposed sampling was binomial, i.e., drawn from a Bernoulli process. In this module, the economic analysis of sampling will be extended to the *normal* case, where the prior and sampling distributions are normal.

General learning objectives

Your general learning objectives for this module are to be able to:

1. Given a decision problem in which the prior distribution is normal, compute:
   a. The cost of uncertainty
   b. The expected value of sample information
2. Identify the factors affecting the value of sample information and determine the optimal sample size
3. Use the normal approximation to analyze the economics of sampling for a discrete (binomial) decision problem

Section 23.A

Loss Functions and Expected Values

Learning objectives

Your learning objectives for this section are to be able, given a normal prior distribution in a decision problem with linear loss functions, to compute:

1. The expected value of perfect information (cost of uncertainty)
2. The expected profit under conditions of absolute certainty
3. The expected monetary value (expected profit) of the optimum decision

EXPECTED VALUE OF PERFECT INFORMATION

As a first step in assessing the value of sample information, let's examine the method for computing the value of *perfect* information (EVPI) where the probability distribution of the random variable is normal. You should recall that the EVPI in a decision problem is equal to the cost of uncertainty, which is in turn defined as the expected opportunity loss (EOL) of the optimal act.

Suppose the decision maker in the computer-leasing problem of the last module, armed with only the prior information (in the form of a normal distribution) supplied by his staff, wishes to know the cost of the uncertainty with which he is faced. Remember that the prior best estimate μ_o of \$250 average savings per branch per month would lead him to decide in favor of leasing the equipment. Let us compute the EOL for this (optimal) decision.

As long as the average savings realized was greater than the economic break-even value μ_b of \$200, the decision to lease would prove correct and no opportunity loss would be experienced. Should the true value of the average savings μ be less than \$200, however, the decision would (in retrospect) be incorrect. It was shown in Module 22 that the dollar magnitude of the opportunity loss under these circumstances is $(\mu_b - \mu)(900)(24)$, or $(200 - \mu)(21,600)$. The entire opportunity loss function for the decision to lease, which is linear with a slope of $-21,600$ for the $\mu < \$200$ portion and which is simply equal to 0 for values of $\mu \geq 200$, is shown in Figure 23.1.

The procedure previously used to evaluate EOLs is to multiply the opportunity loss conditional on each state of nature (or value of the random variable) by the probability that each state of nature will occur. These products are summed over all possible values of the random variable to obtain the EOL for the decision in question. The

563

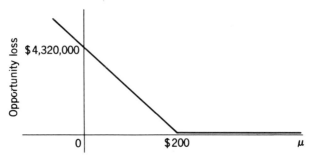

Figure 23.1 / Opportunity loss for the decision to lease.

difficulty in applying this procedure here is that the random variable has an infinite number of possible values. Whereas, before, our analysis was limited to several possible states of nature representing discrete values of the random variable, its distribution is now being regarded as *continuous*. Specifically, it is assumed to be normally distributed, with $\mu_o = 250$ and $\sigma_o = 150$. This distribution is shown superimposed on the opportunity loss function in Fig. 23.2.

AN APPROXIMATION USING THE DISCRETE METHOD

Of course, the EOL could be computed in straightforward fashion by the method previously used if the continuous probability distribution is first broken up into discrete values. This can be accomplished by using discrete values equal to the midpoint of arbitrarily selected intervals to represent the entire interval in the calculations. This is analogous to using the midpoint of each class interval to represent all the values in the class in computing the mean or standard deviation of a frequency distribution (see Appendix Table A). Suppose, for example, that the range of values for μ is broken up into $50 intervals, as shown in Fig. 23.2. Any interval, such as the

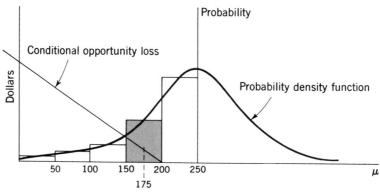

Figure 23.2

Table 23.1 / Approximate computation of expected opportunity loss (EOL) for the decision to lease without sampling

Interval	Midpoint	COL	Probability	COL × probability
$150 < \mu < 200$	175	$ 540,000	.1193	$ 64,422
$100 < \mu < 150$	125	1,620,000	.0927	150,174
$50 < \mu < 100$	75	2,700,000	.0669	180,630
$0 < \mu < 50$	25	3,780,000	.0443	167,454
$-50 < \mu < 0$	-25	4,860,000	.0247	120,042
$-100 < \mu < -50$	-75	5,940,000	.0128	76,032
$-150 < \mu < -100$	-125	7,020,000	.0061	42,822
$-200 < \mu < -150$	-175	8,100,000	.0024	19,440
$-250 < \mu < -200$	-225	9,180,000	.0013	11,934
$-300 < \mu < -250$	-275	10,260,000	.0004	4,104
				$837,054

shaded range from 150 to 200, can be represented by its midpoint, in this case 175. The COL for $\mu = 175$ (it would be $540,000) would then be multiplied by the probability of the range (150 to 200), which the point 175 represents. Probabilities for each interval such as $P(150 < \mu < 200)$ can of course be obtained from the normal area tables and in turn can be multiplied by their respective midpoint COLs. Intervals to the right of $200, the break-even point, can be ignored, since the COL term in the product is 0 for all $\mu \geq \$200$. Likewise, at some point in the left tail of the distribution the probability term for μ falling within a stated interval becomes 0 for practical purposes (even though the normal distribution theoretically extends to infinity). Thus the calculations, as shown in Table 23.1, would have to be made only for μ values less than 200 and greater than, say, -300.

The sum of these products of COL times probability is the EOL of the decision to lease. This figure is of couse an approximation since the procedure used in Table 23.1 was formulated by breaking up the continuum of possible values for μ into a series of intervals and treating them as if they were discrete values. Now this approximation could be made more accurate by using a narrower interval, but the volume of calculations would be correspondingly increased, and it's cumbersome enough for the 50-unit interval used in Table 23.1. As the interval is made narrower and narrower, ultimately approaching the continuous case this procedure is designed to approximate, the arithmetic burden continues to expand.

A CONTINUOUS APPROACH: THE NORMAL LOSS INTEGRAL

Fortunately, mathematics comes to our aid in this situation. The use of calculus makes it possible to circumvent the numerical approximation above and to obtain a theoretically correct result through the use of a simple formula. If the prior estimating distribution is normal and the opportunity loss function is linear, the EOL of the optimal act—also the cost of uncertainty and EVPI—can be determined by the following formula

$$\text{EOL} = L\sigma_o N(D_o) \tag{23.1}$$

where L = absolute slope of the nonzero portion of opportunity loss functions
σ_o = standard deviation of prior distribution

The final factor in the formula, $N(D_o)$, called the *normal loss integral*, has a value which can be determined from Appendix Table A.4. First, the argument D_o is determined:

$$D_o = \frac{|\mu_o - \mu_b|}{\sigma_o} \tag{23.2}$$

Logically enough, the D_o value is based on the *difference* between the economic break-even and best estimate values of μ which determines the relative positions of the normal estimating distribution and the opportunity loss line. This difference is normalized by the customary step, dividing by σ_o, so that it's expressed in terms of a number of standard deviation units. Once obtained, the D_o value is used to look up the value of the function $N(D_o)$ in Appendix Table A.4.

The use of the formula is simplified by the fact that algebraic signs are irrelevant. It is the *absolute value* of the slope of the opportunity loss line L and the absolute difference $|\mu_o - \mu_b|$ that are required. Application to the computer-leasing problem should demonstrate how easy it really is to use this approach. L, the absolute slope of the COL line, is 21,600 [remember that the function was $(200 - \mu)(21,600)$], and σ_o is 150. Also

$$D_o = \frac{|\mu_o - \mu_b|}{\sigma_o} = \frac{|250 - 200|}{150} = .33$$

and from Appendix Table A.4, $N(D_o) = .2555$. Then for the (optimal) decision to lease the equipment, the EOL* is

$$\begin{aligned}
\text{EOL*} &= L\sigma_o(D_o) \\
&= 21,600(150)(.2555) \\
&= \$828,000
\end{aligned}$$

This figure is of course superior to the approximation of about $837,000 obtained by the procedure of Table 23.1

As you've learned, the EOL* can also be interpreted as the *cost of uncertainty* with which the decision maker is faced. More important, it can also be regarded as the EVPI. While *perfect* information is never available in a practical situation, the EVPI figure at least provides an upper limit on the value of prospective sample information. Since

$$\text{EVPI} = \text{EOL*} = \$828,000$$

we at least know that no more than $828,000 should be spend for additional information.

OTHER CALCULATIONS

Now let's reconsider several other concepts used earlier in the light of the normal distribution analysis used here. One concept originally developed in Module 19, the expected profit under conditions of absolute certainty (EPC), can be formulated in the present context as

$$\text{EPC} = L\sigma_o[D_o + N(D_o)] \tag{23.3}$$

which, substituting our leasing problem data, gives

$$\begin{aligned} \text{EPC} &= 21{,}600(150)(.3333 + .2555) \\ &= \$1{,}908{,}000 \end{aligned}$$

This figure, not to be confused with EVPI, describes the amount of profit (in this case, cost savings) the decision maker could expect to realize if he had available a perfect forecast of the uncertain random variable in his decision problem. In the problem at hand, given the uncertainty regarding the cost savings per branch per month, the decision maker's expected profit (savings), or EMV, is

$$\begin{aligned} \text{EMV} &= (900 \text{ branches})(24 \text{ months})(\$250/\text{branch/month}) - \\ &\quad \$4{,}320{,}000 \\ &= \$5{,}400{,}000 - \$4{,}320{,}000 = \$1{,}080{,}000 \end{aligned}$$

As before, EMV + EVPI should equal EPC. That is, the expected profit given uncertainty plus the cost of that uncertainty, EVPI, equals the expected profit under certain conditions. Here

$$\begin{aligned} \text{EMV} + \text{EVPI} &= 1{,}080{,}000 + 828{,}000 \\ &= \$1{,}908{,}000 = \text{EPC} \end{aligned}$$

which checks with our previous result, as it should.

REVIEW EXERCISES 23.A

1. The expected value of perfect information (EVPI) in a decision problem depends on:
   a. The dispersion of the prior estimating distribution.
   b. The difference between the mean of the estimating distribution and the break-even value for the random variable.
   c. The slope (or severity) of the loss function.
   d. All the above.
2. Where the prior distribution is normal and loss functions are linear, the expected profit and the cost of uncertainty can be computed using a simple formula involving the normal loss integral: true or false?
3. For the leasing problem described in the text, assume all facts the same except that the mean of the prior distribution μ_o is 240 (instead of 250) and the standard deviation of the prior, σ_o, is 200 (instead of 150). Compute

   a. The expected value of perfect information.
   b. The cost of uncertainty.
   c. The expected profit from the decision to lease.
   d. The expected profit under conditions of absolute certainty.
4. Use your results to Exercise 3 to prove that EPC = EMV + EVPI.

Answers 23.A

1. d   2. true

3. *a.* $D_o = \dfrac{\mu_o - \mu_b}{\sigma_o} = \dfrac{240 - 200}{200} = .20$

    From the Appendix Table A.4: $N(D_o) = N(.20) = .3069$. Then

$$\text{EVPI} = \text{EOL*} = L\sigma_o N(D_o) = 21,600(200)(.3069) = \$1,326,000$$

   b. The cost of uncertainty = EOL* = \$1,326,000 (the same as EVPI)
   c. EMV = (900 branches)(24 months)(\$240/branch/months) − \$4,320,000
        = \$5,184,000 − \$4,320,000 = \$864,000
   d. EPC = $L\sigma_o[D_o + N(D_o)]$ = 21,600(200)(.20 + .3069)
        = 21,600(200)(.5069) = \$2,190,000
4. EPC = EMV + EVPI = \$864,000 + \$1,326,000 = \$2,190,000 which is equal to EPC
   from part *d* of Exercise 3.

Section 23.B
The Expected Value of Sample Information

Learning objectives

Your learning objectives for this section are to be able to:

   1. Compute the expected value of sample information (EVSI) given a normal prior distribution in a decision problem
   2. Identify the factors affecting EVSI
   3. Distinguish between the expected value and actual value of sample information and explain why they are different

EXPECTED VALUE OF SAMPLE INFORMATION

In Module 20 we defined the expected value of sample information (EVSI) as the difference between EVPI and the EOL resulting from the use of the *best* decision criterion in conjunction with a particular sample size. Another way of putting this is that the value of a sample is reflected in the reduction in the cost of uncertainty that it produces. Although this concept is straightforward enough, the computation of the EVSI for the discrete case (Module 20) was very involved, partly because the minimum EOL for a given sample size was a function of the value of the criterion number c used and partly because each individual point in the discrete probability distribution occupied a distinct place in the computational procedure.

Here also the normal distribution analysis has the advantage of greater simplicity. For a normal prior distribution and normal sampling, i.e., a distribution of sample means which is expected to be normal, EVSI is given by a type of formula now familiar:

$$EVSI = L\sigma_I N(D_I) \tag{23.4}$$

The only difference between this formula and the one for EVPI (or EOL*) is the subscripts on the σ and D terms. The σ_I used here represents the degree of improvement in the estimate (of μ) that is made as a result of the sample information. Specifically, σ_I^2 is defined as the improvement, or *reduction* in variance, between the prior estimating distribution and the revised distribution which takes into account the sample evidence, i.e.,

$$\sigma_I^2 = \sigma_o^2 - \sigma_r^2 \tag{23.5}$$

Of course σ_r^2, the variance of the revised distribution, is not *known* before the sample results are obtained, but it *can* be estimated by using an estimate of $\sigma_{\bar{X}}^2$ and the relationship from Module 22:

$$\sigma_r^2 = \frac{\sigma_{\bar{X}}^2 \sigma_o^2}{\sigma_o^2 + \sigma_{\bar{X}}^2}$$

The $\sigma_{\bar{X}}^2$ estimate in turn requires that the variance of the original population σ_X^2 be estimated, either from earlier sampling, from experience with similar data, or perhaps from pure judgment. Remember that

$$\sigma_{\bar{X}}^2 = \frac{\sigma_X^2}{n}$$

By substitution for σ_r^2, Eq. (22.5) can be rewritten

$$\sigma_I^2 = \sigma_o^2 - \frac{\sigma_{\bar{X}}^2 \sigma_o^2}{\sigma_o^2 + \sigma_{\bar{X}}^2} = \frac{\sigma_o^2 \sigma_o^2}{\sigma_o^2 + \sigma_{\bar{X}}^2} \tag{23.6}$$

Then the σ_I of the EVSI expression [Eq. (23.4)] can be obtained as

$$\sigma_I = \sqrt{\frac{\sigma_o^2 \sigma_o^2}{\sigma_o^2 + \sigma_{\bar{X}}^2}} \tag{23.7}$$

The D_I of Eq. (23.4) is defined like D_o before, with only the substitution of σ_I for σ_o:

$$D_I = \frac{|\mu_o - \mu_b|}{\sigma_I} \tag{23.8}$$

The calculation of EVSI may now be illustrated for the leasing problem. Let us determine the expected value of a sample of branches of size 30 (such as the one actually taken and used to revise the prior distribution in Module 22) on an a priori basis, i.e., *before* any such sample is taken. Values are needed to put into the equation

$$\text{EVSI} = L\sigma_I N(D_I)$$

L is \$21,600, the same value used in the calculation of EVPI. To get σ_I, we must first estimate the population standard deviation σ_X. Remember that this σ_X is a measure of the dispersion or spread of the individual items in the parent population, in this case the cost savings of individual branches. It *isn't* the same as σ_o, which measures the expected accuracy of the estimate of *average* savings. Although in the last chapter σ_X was estimated by the s_X value of \$251.55, the s_X value is calculated directly from the sample data and wouldn't be available *before* the sample is taken. Let's suppose that the company is able to estimate σ_X as \$300 based on the experience of the computer manufacturer or other information, implying that roughly two-thirds of the per branch per month savings will fall within $\pm\$300$ from the average savings. Then

$$\sigma_{\bar{X}} = \frac{\sigma_X}{\sqrt{n}} = \frac{\$300}{\sqrt{30}} = \$54.80$$

$$\sigma_I = \sqrt{\frac{\sigma_o^2 \sigma_o^2}{\sigma_o^2 + \sigma_{\bar{X}}^2}} = \sqrt{\frac{150^2(150^2)}{150^2 + 54.8^2}} = \$141$$

$$D_I = \frac{|\mu_o - \mu_b|}{\sigma_I} = \frac{|250 - 200|}{141} = \frac{50}{141} = .355$$

and from Appendix Table A.4

$$N(D_I) = .2463$$

Finally,

$$\text{EVSI} = L\sigma_I N(D_I) = 21,600(141)(.2463) = \$750,000$$

FACTORS AFFECTING EVSI

The EVSI for a sample of only 30 in the leasing problem was \$750,000, which may seem surprisingly high and close to the EVPI of \$828,000. Why should the value of a modest size sample be so great in this situation? A closer examination of the formula for EVSI provides some clues to the answer. Partially, of course, the large EVSI is due to the relatively large L (the unit increase in opportunity loss per unit decrease in average cost savings). However, L also appears in the formula for EVPI, so this in itself can't explain the size of EVSI relative to EVPI.

The real key to the relatively large EVSI is the σ_I, a measure of the improvement in the prior estimate *expected* to be produced by the sample information. The σ_I enters the formula in two ways: (1) it appears directly as the second factor in the equation, so that the larger the σ_I, the larger the EVSI; (2) it appears in the denominator of the expression for D_I

$$D_I = \frac{|\mu_o - \mu_b|}{\sigma_I}$$

so that the larger the σ_I, the smaller the D_I. However, you can see from an examination of Appendix Table A.4 that $N(D)$ is inversely related to D; $N(D)$ decreases as D increases, so that the larger the σ_I, the *larger* the function $N(D_I)$. Thus, increases in σ_I affect EVSI directly through both the second and third terms in the equation.

The question might then be raised: What produces larger σ_I values? Recall the expression:

$$\sigma_I = \sqrt{\frac{\sigma_o^2 \sigma_o^2}{\sigma_o^2 + \sigma_X^2}}$$

which can also be written

$$\sigma_I = \sqrt{\frac{\sigma_o^2 \sigma_o^2}{\sigma_o^2 + \sigma_X^2/n}}$$

A careful examination of this expression reveals that σ_I is directly related to σ_o, directly related to n, and inversely related to σ_X. That is, the potential or expected value of sample information will be greatest in cases where the prior estimating variance is large (which means that the decision maker has little prior information), the sample size is large (which is logical), and the parent population variance is small (which minimizes sampling errors). These results are all in agreement with what intuition might tell you about the sampling process, which should make the seemingly "mystical" formula for EVSI somewhat less so.

One further point might be noted. D_I depends not only on σ_I but on $|\mu_o - \mu_b|$, the absolute difference between the prior best estimate and the break-even point, as well. The larger this difference, the larger the D_I and the smaller the $N(D_I)$. EVSI will hence be less when the prior best estimate is well above or below the economic break-even point. This again should agree with your intuition. When a decision appears relatively clear-cut, sample information is potentially less valuable than when the decision is borderline.

EXPECTED VS. ACTUAL VALUE OF SAMPLE INFORMATION

The point that the expected value of sample information is not generally equal to its actual value was emphasized in Module 21, but it bears repeating here. The actual value of a sample in a decision problem depends on how much it reduces the cost of uncertainty. The EOL of the best decision, given the revised information, must be compared with the EOL of the best decision that could be made on the basis of prior information. This difference, observed with the benefit of hindsight *isn't* necessarily equal to the value the sample is *expected* to have beforehand. In the leasing example, the cost of uncertainty (also EVPI) based on prior information was $828,000. Using the values from the estimating distribution as *revised* (for the results of the sample of 30 actually obtained) in place of the prior parameters we get

$$\text{Revised cost of uncertainty} = L\sigma_r N(D_r)$$

$$= 21,600(43.10)N \frac{198.62 - 200}{43.10}$$

$$= 21,600(43.10)(.3841)$$
$$= \$358,000$$

Thus the actual reduction in the cost of uncertainty—and hence the value of the sample —once this particular sample was actually taken was $828,000 - 358,000 = \$470,000$. This compares with an *expected* value EVSI of $750,000. The sample simply turned out to be, in retrospect, less valuable than anticipated.

REVIEW EXERCISES 23.B

1. In this section, the EVSI was calculated for a sample of size 30. Using the same prior estimates, calculate EVSI for a sample of 100.
2. Indicate whether each of the following changes would produce an increase (+) or decrease (−) in EVSI. For each case, assume all other factors remain constant:
    a. Increase in the standard deviation of the parent population from which the sample is to be drawn.
    b. Increase in the standard deviation of the prior estimating distribution for the random variable.
    c. Increase between the best estimate of the random variable and its break-even value in the decision problem.
    d. Increase in the sample size.
3. The EVSI is equal to the reduction in the cost of uncertainty that occurs as a result of sampling: true or false?

Answers 23.B

1. $\sigma_{\bar{X}} = \dfrac{\sigma_X}{\sqrt{n}} = \dfrac{\$300}{\sqrt{100}} = \$30$

$$\sigma_I = \sqrt{\frac{\sigma_o^2 \sigma_o^2}{\sigma_o^2 + \sigma_{\bar{X}}^2}}$$

$$= \sqrt{\frac{150^2(150^2)}{150^2 + 30^2}} = \frac{506,250,000}{22,500 + 900} = \frac{506,250,000}{23,400} = 21,635 = \$147$$

$$D_I = \frac{|\mu_o - \mu_b|}{\sigma_I} = \frac{250 - 200}{147} = .34$$

From Appendix Table A.4, $N(.34) = .2518$

$$\text{EVSI} = L\sigma_I N(D_I) = 21,600(147)(.2518) = \$800,000$$

2. *a.* $-$; *b.* $+$; *c.* $-$; *d.* $+$
3. False; the *expected* value of sample information is *not* necessarily the same as the reduction in the cost of uncertainty brought about by incorporating actual sample results into the estimating distribution. Sample results may turn out to be more or less valuable than their expected value as viewed before the sample is taken.

Section 23.C

Optimal Sampling Procedures

Learning objectives

Your learning objectives for this section are, given a normal prior distribution in a decision problem, to be able to:

1. Determine the optimal size sample
2. Specify a decision rule to be used with a given sample

OPTIMAL SAMPLE SIZE

In the previous section, we analyzed the expected benefit of a sample of 30. Although its EVSI was impressively high, the cost of obtaining it was not discussed. There is certainly no assurance that when both values and costs are considered, this particular sample size will be optimal. The optimal sample size can be determined, as in Module 20, by computing the *net gain from sampling* for various possible sample sizes. This net gain, you may recall, is the difference between the EVSI and the actual cost of obtaining the sample information.

Suppose that in the computer-leasing problem the trial run from which sample information is obtained is available at a fixed setup cost of $60,000 and an estimated net cost per branch (or item in the sample) of $2000; i.e.,

$$\text{Sample cost} = 60,000 + 2000n$$

Table 23.2 provides a systematic framework for computing the net gain from sampling. The variance of the sampling distribution σ_X^2 is computed in column 2 for each sample size. These values are entered into the formula for σ_I (along with the prior variance σ_o^2, which is a constant in any given problem) in column 3. D_I is

573

Table 23.2 / Determination of net gain from sampling, computer-leasing problem

(1) Sample size n	(2) $\sigma_{\bar{x}}^2 = \dfrac{300^2}{n}$	(3) $\sigma_I = \sqrt{\dfrac{150^2(150^2)}{150^2 + \sigma_{\bar{x}}^2}}$	(4) $D_I = \dfrac{\|250 - 200\|}{\sigma_I}$	(5) $N(D_I)$	(6) EVSI $= 21{,}600\sigma_I N(D_I)$	(7) Sample cost, $60{,}000 + 2000n$	(8) Net gain from sampling
20	4500	137	.365	.2427	$718,000	$100,000	$618,000
30	3000	141	.355	.2463	750,000	120,000	630,000
40	2250	143	.350	.2481	766,000	140,000	626,000
50	1800	144	.347	.2493	775,000	160,000	615,000

computed in column 4 by dividing the constant $|\mu_o - \mu_b|$ difference by the various σ_I values. $N(D_I)$ is then obtained from the table and EVSI calculated as the product of L (a constant) times σ_I times $N(D_I)$. The final Net Gain from Sampling column is the difference between EVSI (column 6) and the cost of the sample (column 7).

The maximum net gain from sampling does occur at about $n = 30$. Notice, however, that the net gain is relatively insensitive to the sample size. This also implies that the subjective estimate of σ_X that had to be made to carry out the calculations could be somewhat in error without any serious effect in the decision to purchase additional information. For this problem, as is often the case, sampling per se appears very valuable, but the exact size of the sample is not crucial.

SPECIFICATION OF A DECISION RULE IN ADVANCE OF SAMPLING

The sample of 30 branches taken in the leasing-decision problem was used (in Module 22) to revise the prior probability distribution. The decision not to lease was based on a comparison of the mean of the revised estimating distribution with the economic break-even point. Instead of proceeding in this fashion, we could have formulated a statistical decision rule that would have specified in advance the action to be taken as a result of various possible sample outcomes. This would entail using the relationship for revising a prior mean:

$$\mu_r = \frac{\mu_o IC_o + \bar{X} IC_{\bar{X}}}{IC_o + IC_{\bar{X}}}$$

and solving for the sample mean $\bar{X}$ that would make the revised mean just equal to the economic break-even point μ_b. Manipulation of the above equation gives

$$\bar{X} = \frac{\mu_r(IC_o + IC_{\bar{X}}) - \mu_o IC_o}{IC_{\bar{X}}}$$

Substitution of μ_b for μ_r provides an expression for the action limit $\bar{X}_{AL}$ for the sample mean:

$$\bar{X}_{AL} = \frac{\mu_b(IC_o + IC_{\bar{X}}) - \mu_o IC_o}{IC_{\bar{X}}}$$

Notice that one term in this expression, namely, $IC_{\bar{X}}$ is generally unknown before the sample is taken. $IC_{\bar{X}}$, the information content of the sample, is equal to $1/\sigma_{\bar{X}}^2$ or

$1/(\sigma_X^2/n)$. The variance of the population σ_X^2 is generally unknown in sample situations, usually being estimated by the s_X^2 statistic calculated from sample data. Where σ_X *is* known or can be estimated accurately from available data or judgment, a decision rule can be formulated in advance. However, since it's usually more reasonable to estimate σ_X^2 from sample data, and since the revision process for the normal case is relatively straightforward, the actual revision is usually carried out instead for the sample data on an after-the-fact basis, as in Module 22.

REVIEW EXERCISES 23.C

1. The optimal sample size occurs where EVSI is a maximum: true or false?
2. The procedure for determining optimal sample size outlined in this section is the same as the one you studied previously for decision problems involving discrete distributions, except that:
   a. The net gain from sampling is obtained differently.
   b. EVSI is determined differently.
   c. Computations are much more burdensome for normal distributions.
   d. All the above.
3. Specification of a decision rule in advance of sampling:
   a. Requires an estimate of the population variance.
   b. Will lead to different results than decision making based on a revised distribution.
   c. Is impossible where the prior distribution is normal.
   d. None of the above.

Answers 23.C

1. False; the optimal sample size occurs where the *net gain from sampling* (EVSI less the *cost* of sampling) is a maximum (and positive).
2. b   3. a

Section 23.D

Normal Distribution Analysis for Discrete Sampling Problems

Learning objective

Your learning objective for this section is to be able to apply the methods described in this module for analyzing the economics of sampling to a decision problem involving a discrete distribution

---

NORMAL ANALYSIS OF A DISCRETE DECISION PROBLEM

Section 22.D described the use of normal distribution analysis to revise a discrete prior probability distribution to reflect sample information actually obtained through a binomial sampling process. Specifically, this normal analysis was applied to the product-development problem of Modules 20 and 21. Despite the fact that normality assumptions were not strictly valid, the results obtained were extremely close to those obtained by the more cumbersome discrete revision methods described in Module 21.

This section applies the normal analysis to the economics of sampling in binomial type sampling situations. While discrete methods are available (as explained in Module 20) calculation of EVPI and EVSI by the analysis described in this module is much simpler and quicker. Let's re-examine the economics of sampling for the product-development problem using normal analysis.

EXPECTED VALUE OF PERFECT INFORMATION

Where the prior distribution may be assumed normal, you've seen that the EVPI is given by

$$EVPI = L\sigma_o N(D_o)$$

You saw in Sec. 22.D that the decision maker's prior information in the product-development problem can be described by a distribution of average profit per customer that was normal with $u_o = \$29$ and $\sigma_o = \$11.36$. The opportunity loss function is

$$(\mu - \$25)(20{,}000) \qquad \mu \geq \$25$$
$$(\$25 - \mu)(20{,}000) \qquad \mu < \$25$$

since μ represents average sales per customer, $25 is the break-even value of average sales, and the firm has 20,000 customers. L, the absolute slope of this function, is 20,000. Then

$$EVPI = 20{,}000(\$11.36)N\left[\frac{|29 - 25|}{11.36}\right]$$
$$= 20{,}000(\$11.36)(.2474) = \$56{,}200$$

This compares with an EVPI calculated by discrete methods in Module 20 of $60,000. The discrepancy, which is relatively minor, arises because the discrete prior distribution in this problem does depart somewhat from normal.

EXPECTED VALUE OF SAMPLE INFORMATION

You also saw earlier that the *sampling* distribution in this problem *isn't* exactly normal. Nevertheless, let us calculate the EVSI for various sample sizes in the manner of Table 23.2. The only important difference in the procedure is that the expected variance of the sampling distribution σ_X^2 must be obtained by first obtaining $\sigma_{\bar{p}}^2$ for various sample sizes on the assumption that p is .058 (the expected value of p from the prior estimating distribution):

Sample size n	$\sigma_{\bar{p}}^2 = \dfrac{p(1 - p)}{n} = \dfrac{.058(.942)}{n}$
10	.00546
20	.00273
50	.00109
100	.000546

Now the relationship of average profit per customer to proportion of customers buying is

Average profit/customer

$$= \frac{\text{(proportion buying)(20,000 customers)($500 profit/unit)}}{20,000 \text{ customers}}$$

$$= p(\$500)$$

To convert the *variance* of proportion of customers into average profit per customer, we multiply not by 500 but by 500^2; that is,

$$\sigma_X^2 = \sigma_{\bar{p}}^2(250,000)$$

Therefore we estimate:

n	$\sigma_{\bar{X}}^2$
10	.00546(250,000) = 1365
20	.00273(250,000) = 682
50	.00109(250,000) = 272
100	.000546(250,000) = 136

These values are inputs to column 2 of the format in Table 23.3 which is similar to Table 23.2. Taking the sample costs from Table 21.9, we can obtain net gain from sampling as shown in Table 23.4.

Table 23.3 / Normal approximation for EVSI, product-development problem

(1) Sample size	(2) $\sigma_{\bar{X}}^2$	(3) $\sigma_I = \sqrt{\dfrac{11.36^2(11.36^2)}{11.36^2 + \sigma_{\bar{X}}^2}}$	(4) $D_I = \dfrac{29 - 25}{\sigma_I}$	(5) $N(D_I)$	(6) EVSI $= 20,000\sigma_I N(D_I)$
10	1365	.334	1.197	.0561	$ 3,750
20	682	4.53	.883	.1036	9,390
50	272	6.45	.620	.1633	21,070
100	136	7.93	.504	.1966	31,180

Table 23.4 / Normal approximation for net gain from sampling, product-development problem

Sample size n	EVSI	Sample cost	Net gain from sampling
10	$ 3,750	$ 7,000	$ − 3250
20	9,390	10,000	− 610
50	21,070	19,000	+ 2070
100	31,180	34,000	− 2820

This analysis suggests that, of the sample sizes considered, $n = 50$ represents the optimum. This is the same optimal size determined by the discrete analysis in Module 20. The net gain from sampling for $n = 50$ computed here, $2070, compares with an earlier figure of $2737 (Table 20.9). Although the EVSI figures calculated by the two methods are different, the *conclusions* regarding the amount of additional information that should be purchased are the same.

Although it is impossible to generalize as to when the normal analysis will be completely adequate for discrete problems of the type considered here, it will almost always provide a useful starting point. If net gain from sampling is flat in the region of the optimum, i.e., if the gain doesn't appear very sensitive to sample size, the choice of an exact n doesn't matter much anyway. If the net gain does change rapidly with sample size, a complete discrete analysis could be done in the region of the optimum. At least it could save considerable time and effort to use the normal analysis to locate this optimum region.

REVIEW EXERCISES 23.D

1. Normal distribution analysis is sometimes used to determine the optimal sample size in a discrete binomial decision problem because:
  a. It's more exact.
  b. It is often the only feasible method.
  c. It's simpler and quicker.
  d. None of the above.
2. Given a discrete decision problem, the EVSI values calculated using the normal approximation may be somewhat different than using discrete methods but are often close enough for practical purposes: true or false?
3. Even if more exact methods are needed to determine the exact optimal sample size, the normal approximation methods outlined in this section may be useful for locating the region of the optimum: true or false?

Answers 23.D

1. c   *2.* true   *3.* true

Questions and Problems

23.1. Give two examples each where the COL function in a business decision situation is
  a. Linear.
  b. Nonlinear.
  c. In your answers to part *b*, are the departures from linearity serious? Do you think the methods of this module could be used as an approximate means of solving such problems?

23.2. Refer to Prob. 22.1. Suppose the market for the proposed product will last only 1 year.
  a. What is the maximum amount Acme could profitably spend on market research to better ascertain demand?
  b. As a practical matter, would you recommend spending that much? Why?

23.3. Refer to Prob. 22.11. Suppose the advertising agency, in an effort to land the contract to manage the entire golf-ball promotion, offers to conduct a pilot study involving a random sample of 10 of the XL branches for a fee of $10,000. The agency will pay all expenses (including the cost and selling expenses of the golf balls) of the promotion. In addition, it'll maintain and analyze records necessary to determine the amount of additional purchases made by customers who wouldn't have visited the stores without the promotion.
  a. Would you buy the pilot study? *Note:* In Prob. 22.11 you were asked to formulate your own prior distribution. Use it here also.
  b. What is your EVPI?
  c. Do you think a larger pilot study might be desirable? Explain.

23.4. In the computer-leasing problem described in the preceding module, the EVPI was calculated as $828,000. What would the EVPI have been if:
  a. σ_o were $100 instead of $150?
  b. μ_b were $250 instead of $200?
  c. L were $43,200 instead of $21,600?
  Write out generalizations for the type of changes in parts *a* to *c*. For each case, describe the relationship of the variable in question to EVPI.

23.5. Repeat parts *a* to *c* of the previous problem for the effect on EVSI for samples of size 30, 40, and 50. Is $n = 30$ still the optimum size sample to take in each case?

23.6. A computation of the EVSI using the method described in this chapter requires certain data inputs. List these inputs, and state the source from which each would customarily be obtained.

23.7. You are given the task of explaining to an executive who knows no statistics the concept of the value of sample information in a decision situation. Describe, in nonstatistical terms, factors which contribute to a high (or low) EVSI.

23.8. Why is the actual value of sample information that has been obtained different from the EVSI for that sample size?

23.9. Churn & Churn, a stock brokerage firm, is contemplating a change in their commission charges on convertible bond transactions. Currently, they are charging $5.00 per bond. Their controller has estimated that their out-of-pocket costs on such transactions are $12 fixed cost (regardless of the size of the order) plus $2.50 per bond. Clearly, they are not even breaking even on one or two bond orders. They are considering raising the minimum charge on bond orders to $20. Although they believe that many customers will no longer place one or two bond orders with the firm, they aren't concerned about losing this business since it is unprofitable anyway. The real concern is that these customers will direct *other* brokerage business, which is profitable, elsewhere.

A check of customer accounts reveals that about 4000 of the firm's customers had convertible-bond transactions during the last year. The firm's partners were called together to make estimates of the amount of *net* revenues that would be gained or lost because of the changes. The consensus was that about $20 per convertible-bond customer would be *gained* in net revenues in the coming year. Specifically, 8 of the firm's 12 partners felt that the net effect would be between 0 and $40 per customer for this year. It was agreed that by the end of the coming year, competing firms would have to make similar changes, so that the situation would have to be reappraised at that time. For this reason and because of the turnover in customer accounts the partners didn't attempt to forecast any longer-run effects.

One of the younger partners, a recent business school graduate by the name of Churn, suggests that a *sample* of the customers involved should be studied through a combination of detailed analyses of accounts records and personal interviews.

Perusal of the records could show bond and nonbond commissions generated by the customer and a careful interview with him could reveal his attitude toward the proposed change and his intentions regarding the future conduct of his investment affairs. Measurement could thus be made of the net effect on the firm's revenues for each customer sampled.

Churn believes that he can get one of his former professors to perform such a study at a cost of $2000 plus $40 per customer contained in the sample.

The professor agrees to the terms but warns the partners not to expect too much since a preliminary examination of customer accounts convinces him that there will be considerable variability in the net revenue effect from customer to customer. He is heard to mumble, "Population standard deviation must be at least $100."

What should Churn & Churn do?

23.10. Refer to Prob. 22.12. The president of Instant Wealth is having second thoughts about making the initial outlay necessary to produce the new supplement. One of his junior executives has suggested including an advertisement of the supplement and an invitation to purchase it in the current mailing to all subscribers. The president is reluctant to do this, however, since he feels it would destroy the firm's well-established image if the response from subscribers wasn't sufficiently favorable and the supplement had to be cancelled. After some discussion, he does agree to including the advertising in a mailing to a sample of 200 subscribers. How much can Instant Wealth afford to spend on development of promotional materials, etc., for the sample of 200?

23.11. Refer to Prob. 23.10. Suppose the cost of sampling is $2000 plus $6 per customer included. Would some other size sample be more desirable than the 200 to which the Instant Wealth president has agreed? How would you convince him to change his mind?

23.12. In the computer-leasing problem described in the preceding modules, a sample of 30 branches was taken, and the prior distribution was revised accordingly (see Module 22). The best decision at that point was to reject the leasing arrangement. Suppose a *further* sample was being considered before making a decision. If the cost of obtaining this sample was $60,000 + 2000n$, how large an additional sample would you recommend? *Hint:* The revised distribution obtained in Module 22 should be used in place of the original prior distribution in the leasing problem.

23.13. For the mining problem presented in Prob. 22.8, find:

    a. The expected opportunity loss of the optimal act without sampling.

    b. The expected profit under certainty.

    c. The expected monetary value of the optimal act.

    Note: You should be able to check your answers for parts *a* to *c* by using the relationship EMV + EOL = EPC.

23.14. For the data of Prob. 22.8 and 23.13, assume that before any sample is taken, management's best estimate of σ_x is .03. Find the optimal sample size for this problem, assuming that the cost of sampling is $10,000 + 4000n$.

23.15. Why might the method used in this module to determine the optimum sample size in a decision situation give an answer that is only approximately correct? Is the departure from the true optimum serious? Explain.

23.16. The prior distribution in Prob. 20.10 only very roughly resembles a normal distribution. Represent this prior distribution as best you can by a normal distribution, and use normal methods to determine the optimal size sample to take. For purposes of comparison with the earlier results, use only n values of 10, 20, 50, and 100.

23.17. *a.* What are the advantages of using the "normal" methods of Module 23 to determine optimal sample size as compared to the discrete methods of Module 20?

    b. Under what circumstances would you feel justified in using the normal methods to approximate the optimum sample size for a discrete problem?

APPENDIX A
Tables

Table A.1 lists cumulative binomial probabilities for values of p (by increments of .01) for values of n of 10, 20, 50, and 100. For values of $p \leq .50$, the table shows the probability of *r or more* successes in n trials. For values of $p > .50$, the same table can be used to find the probability of *r or fewer* successes in n trials.

Table A.1 / Cumulative binomial probabilities

	If $p \leq .50$	If $p > .50$
	Use these r values to find the probability of r or more successes in n trials $\sum_r^n C(n,r)_p{}^r(1-p)^{n-r}$	Use these r values to find the probability of r or fewer successes in n trials $\sum_o^r C(n,r)_p{}^r(1-p)^{n-r}$

r					$n = 10$						r
	$p = 01$	02	03	04	05	06	07	08	09	10 $= (1-p)$	
1	0956	1829	2626	3352	4013	4614	5160	5656	6106	6513	9
2	0043	0162	0345	0582	0861	1176	1517	1879	2254	2639	8
3	0001	0009	0028	0062	0115	0188	0283	0401	0540	0702	7
4			0001	0004	0010	0020	0036	0058	0088	0128	6
5					0001	0002	0003	0006	0010	0016	5
6									0001	0001	4
	$p = 11$	12	13	14	15	16	17	18	19	20 $= (1-p)$	
1	6882	7215	7516	7787	8031	8251	8448	8626	8784	8926	9
2	3028	3417	3804	4184	4557	4920	5270	5608	5932	6242	8
3	0884	1087	1308	1545	1798	2064	2341	2628	2922	3222	7
4	0178	0239	0313	0400	0500	0614	0741	0883	1039	1209	6
5	0025	0037	0053	0073	0099	0130	0168	0213	0266	0328	5
6	0003	0004	0006	0010	0014	0020	0027	0037	0049	0064	4
7			0001	0001	0001	0002	0003	0004	0006	0009	3
8									0001	0001	2
	$p = 21$	22	23	24	25	26	27	28	29	30 $= (1-p)$	
1	9053	9166	9267	9357	9437	9508	9570	9626	9674	9718	9
2	6536	6815	7079	7327	7560	7778	7981	8170	8345	8507	8
3	3526	3831	4137	4442	4744	5042	5335	5622	5901	6172	7
4	1391	1587	1794	2012	2241	2479	2726	2979	3239	3504	6
5	0399	0479	0569	0670	0781	0904	1037	1181	1337	1503	5
6	0082	0104	0130	0161	0197	0239	0287	0342	0404	0473	4
7	0012	0016	0021	0027	0035	0045	0056	0070	0087	0106	3
8	0001	0002	0002	0003	0004	0006	0007	0010	0012	0016	2
9								0001	0001	0001	0001	1
	$p = 31$	32	33	34	35	36	37	38	39	40 $= (1-p)$	
1	9755	9789	9818	9843	9865	9885	9902	9916	9929	9940	9
2	8656	8794	8920	9035	9140	9236	9323	9402	9473	9536	8
3	6434	6687	6930	7162	7384	7595	7794	7983	8160	8327	7
4	3772	4044	4316	4589	4862	5132	5400	5664	5923	6177	6
5	1679	1867	2064	2270	2485	2708	2939	3177	3420	3669	5
6	0551	0637	0732	0836	0949	1072	1205	1348	1500	1662	4
7	0129	0155	0185	0220	0260	0305	0356	0413	0477	0548	3
8	0020	0025	0032	0039	0048	0059	0071	0086	0103	0123	2
9	0002	0003	0003	0004	0005	0007	0009	0011	0014	0017	1
10								0001	0001	0001	0
	$p = 41$	42	43	44	45	46	47	48	49	50 $= (1-p)$	
1	9949	9957	9964	9970	9975	9979	9983	9986	9988	9990	9
2	9594	9645	9691	9731	9767	9799	9827	9852	9874	9893	8
3	8483	8628	8764	8889	9004	9111	9209	9298	9379	9453	7
4	6425	6665	6898	7123	7340	7547	7745	7933	8112	8281	6
5	3922	4178	4436	4696	4956	5216	5474	5730	5982	6230	5
6	1834	2016	2207	2407	2616	2832	3057	3288	3526	3770	4
7	0626	0712	0806	0908	1020	1141	1271	1410	1560	1719	3
8	0146	0172	0202	0236	0274	0317	0366	0420	0480	0547	2
9	0021	0025	0031	0037	0045	0054	0065	0077	0091	0107	1
10	0001	0002	0002	0003	0003	0004	0005	0006	0008	0010	0

Table A.1 / *(continued)*

r					n = 20						r
	p = 01	02	03	04	05	06	07	08	09	10 = (1 − p)	
1	1821	3324	4562	5580	6415	7099	7658	8113	8484	8784	19
2	0169	0599	1198	1897	2642	3395	4131	4831	5484	6083	18
3	0010	0071	0210	0439	0755	1150	1610	2121	2666	3231	17
4		0006	0027	0074	0159	0290	0471	0706	0993	1330	16
5			0003	0010	0026	0056	0107	0183	0290	0432	15
6				0001	0003	0009	0019	0038	0068	0113	14
7						0001	0003	0006	0013	0024	13
8								0001	0002	0004	12
9										0001	11
	p = 11	12	13	14	15	16	17	18	19	20 = (1 − p)	
1	9028	9224	9383	9510	9612	9694	9759	9811	9852	9885	19
2	6624	7109	7539	7916	8244	8529	8773	8982	9159	9308	18
3	3802	4369	4920	5450	5951	6420	6854	7252	7614	7939	17
4	1710	2127	2573	3041	3523	4010	4496	4974	5439	5886	16
5	0610	0827	1083	1375	1702	2059	2443	2849	3271	3704	15
6	0175	0260	0370	0507	0673	0870	1098	1356	1643	1958	14
7	0041	0067	0103	0153	0219	0304	0409	0537	0689	0867	13
8	0008	0014	0024	0038	0059	0088	0127	0177	0241	0321	12
9	0001	0002	0005	0008	0013	0021	0033	0049	0071	0100	11
10			0001	0001	0002	0004	0007	0011	0017	0026	10
11							0001	0001	0002	0004	0006	9
12									0001	0001	8
	p = 21	22	23	24	25	26	27	28	29	30 = (1 − p)	
1	9910	9931	9946	9959	9968	9976	9982	9986	9989	9992	19
2	9434	9539	9626	9698	9757	9805	9845	9877	9903	9924	18
3	8230	8488	8716	8915	9087	9237	9365	9474	9567	9645	17
4	6310	6711	7085	7431	7748	8038	8300	8534	8744	8929	16
5	4142	4580	5014	5439	5852	6248	6625	6981	7315	7625	15
6	2297	2657	3035	3427	3828	4235	4643	5048	5447	5836	14
7	1071	1301	1557	1838	2142	2467	2810	3169	3540	3920	13
8	0419	0536	0675	0835	1018	1225	1455	1707	1982	2277	12
9	0138	0186	0246	0320	0409	0515	0640	0784	0948	1133	11
10	0038	0054	0075	0103	0139	0183	0238	0305	0385	0480	10
11	0009	0013	0019	0028	0039	0055	0074	0100	0132	0171	9
12	0002	0003	0004	0006	0009	0014	0019	0027	0038	0051	8
13			0001	0001	0002	0003	0004	0006	0009	0013	7
14							0001	0001	0002	0003	6

Table A.1 / *(continued)*

r					$n = 20$	*(Continued)*					r
	$p = 31$	32	33	34	35	36	37	38	39	$40 = (1 - p)$	
1	9994	9996	9997	9998	9998	9999	9999	9999	9999	10000	19
2	9940	9953	9964	9972	9979	9984	9988	9991	9993	9995	18
3	9711	9765	9811	9848	9879	9904	9924	9940	9953	9964	17
4	9092	9235	9358	9465	9556	9634	9700	9755	9802	9840	16
5	7911	8173	8411	8626	8818	8989	9141	9274	9390	9490	15
6	6213	6574	6917	7242	7546	7829	8090	8329	8547	8744	14
7	4305	4693	5079	5460	5834	6197	6547	6882	7200	7500	13
8	2591	2922	3268	3624	3990	4361	4735	5108	5478	5841	12
9	1340	1568	1818	2087	2376	2683	3005	3341	3688	4044	11
10	0591	0719	0866	1032	1218	1424	1650	1897	2163	2447	10
11	0220	0279	0350	0434	0532	0645	0775	0923	1090	1275	9
12	0069	0091	0119	0154	0196	0247	0308	0381	0466	0565	8
13	0018	0025	0034	0045	0060	0079	0102	0132	0167	0210	7
14	0004	0006	0008	0011	0015	0021	0028	0037	0049	0065	6
15	0001	0001	0001	0002	0003	0004	0006	0009	0012	0016	5
16						0001	0001	0002	0002	0003	4
	$p = 41$	42	43	44	45	46	47	48	49	$50 = (1 - p)$	
1	10000	10000	10000	10000	10000	10000	10000	10000	10000	10000	19
2	9996	9997	9998	9998	9999	9999	9999	10000	10000	10000	18
3	9972	9979	9984	9988	9991	9993	9995	9996	9997	9998	17
4	9872	9898	9920	9937	9951	9962	9971	9977	9983	9987	16
5	9577	9651	9714	9767	9811	9848	9879	9904	9924	9941	15
6	8921	9078	9217	9340	9447	9539	9619	9687	9745	9793	14
7	7780	8041	8281	8501	8701	8881	9042	9186	9312	9423	13
8	6196	6539	6868	7183	7480	7759	8020	8261	8482	8684	12
9	4406	4771	5136	5499	5857	6207	6546	6873	7186	7483	11
10	2748	3064	3394	3736	4086	4443	4804	5166	5525	5881	10
11	1480	1705	1949	2212	2493	2791	3104	3432	3771	4119	9
12	0679	0810	0958	1123	1308	1511	1734	1977	2238	2517	8
13	0262	0324	0397	0482	0580	0694	0823	0969	1133	1316	7
14	0084	0107	0136	0172	0214	0265	0326	0397	0480	0577	6
15	0022	0029	0038	0050	0064	0083	0105	0133	0166	0207	5
16	0004	0006	0008	0011	0015	0020	0027	0035	0046	0059	4
17	0001	0001	0001	0002	0003	0004	0005	0007	0010	0013	3
18						0001	0001	0001	0001	0002	2

Table A.1 / *(continued)*

r					$n = 50$						r
	$p = 01$	02	03	04	05	06	07	08	09	$10 = (1-p)$	
1	3950	6358	7819	8701	9231	9547	9734	9845	9910	9948	49
2	0894	2642	4447	5995	7206	8100	8735	9173	9468	9662	48
3	0138	0784	1892	3233	4595	5838	6892	7740	8395	8883	47
4	0016	0178	0628	1391	2396	3527	4673	5747	6697	7497	46
5	0001	0032	0168	0490	1036	1794	2710	3710	4723	5688	45
6		0005	0037	0144	0378	0776	1350	2081	2928	3839	44
7		0001	0007	0036	0118	0289	0583	1019	1596	2298	43
8			0001	0008	0032	0094	0220	0438	0768	1221	42
9				0001	0008	0027	0073	0167	0328	0579	41
10					0002	0007	0022	0056	0125	0245	40
11						0002	0006	0017	0043	0094	39
12							0001	0005	0013	0032	38
13								0001	0004	0010	37
14									0001	0003	36
15										0001	35
	$p = 11$	12	13	14	15	16	17	18	19	$20 = (1-p)$	
1	9971	9983	9991	9995	9997	9998	9999	10000	10000	10000	49
2	9788	9869	9920	9951	9971	9983	9990	9994	9997	9998	48
3	9237	9487	9661	9779	9858	9910	9944	9965	9979	9987	47
4	8146	8655	9042	9330	9540	9688	9792	9863	9912	9943	46
5	6562	7320	7956	8472	8879	9192	9428	9601	9726	9815	45
6	4760	5647	6463	7186	7806	8323	8741	9071	9327	9520	44
7	3091	3935	4789	5616	6387	7081	7686	8199	8624	8966	43
8	1793	2467	3217	4010	4812	5594	6328	6996	7587	8096	42
9	0932	1392	1955	2605	3319	4071	4832	5576	6280	6927	41
10	0435	0708	1074	1537	2089	2718	3403	4122	4849	5563	40
11	0183	0325	0535	0824	1199	1661	2203	2813	3473	4164	39
12	0069	0135	0242	0402	0628	0929	1309	1768	2300	2893	38
13	0024	0051	0100	0179	0301	0475	0714	1022	1405	1861	37
14	0008	0018	0037	0073	0132	0223	0357	0544	0791	1106	36
15	0002	0006	0013	0027	0053	0096	0164	0266	0411	0607	35
16	0001	0002	0004	0009	0019	0038	0070	0120	0197	0308	34
17			0001	0003	0007	0014	0027	0050	0087	0144	33
18				0001	0002	0005	0010	0019	0036	0063	32
19					0001	0001	0003	0007	0013	0025	31
20							0001	0002	0005	0009	30
21								0001	0002	0003	29
22										0001	28

Table A.1 / *(continued)*

r	p = 21	22	23	24	25	26	27	28	29	30 = (1 − p)	r
					n = 50 *(Continued)*						
1	10000	10000	10000	10000	10000	10000	10000	10000	10000	10000	49
2	9999	9999	10000	10000	10000	10000	10000	10000	10000	10000	48
3	9992	9995	9997	9998	9999	10000	10000	10000	10000	10000	47
4	9964	9978	9986	9992	9995	9997	9998	9999	9999	10000	46
5	9877	9919	9948	9967	9979	9987	9992	9995	9997	9998	45
6	9663	9767	9841	9893	9930	9954	9970	9981	9988	9993	44
7	9236	9445	9603	9720	9806	9868	9911	9941	9961	9975	43
8	8523	8874	9156	9377	9547	9676	9772	9842	9892	9927	42
9	7505	8009	8437	8794	9084	9316	9497	9635	9740	9817	41
10	6241	6870	7436	7934	8363	8724	9021	9260	9450	9598	40
11	4864	5552	6210	6822	7378	7871	8299	8663	8965	9211	39
12	3533	4201	4878	5544	6184	6782	7329	7817	8244	8610	38
13	2383	2963	3585	4233	4890	5539	6163	6749	7287	7771	37
14	1490	1942	2456	3023	3630	4261	4901	5534	6145	6721	36
15	0862	1181	1565	2013	2519	3075	3669	4286	4912	5532	35
16	0462	0665	0926	1247	1631	2075	2575	3121	3703	4308	34
17	0229	0347	0508	0718	0983	1306	1689	2130	2623	3161	33
18	0105	0168	0259	0384	0551	0766	1034	1359	1741	2178	32
19	0045	0075	0122	0191	0287	0418	0590	0809	1080	1406	31
20	0018	0031	0054	0088	0139	0212	0314	0449	0626	0848	30
21	0006	0012	0022	0038	0063	0100	0155	0232	0338	0478	29
22	0002	0004	0008	0015	0026	0044	0071	0112	0170	0251	28
23	0001	0001	0003	0006	0010	0018	0031	0050	0080	0123	27
24			0001	0002	0004	0007	0012	0021	0035	0056	26
25				0001	0001	0002	0004	0008	0014	0024	25
26						0001	0002	0003	0005	0009	24
27							0001	0002	0003	23	
28									0001	0001	22

r	p = 31	32	33	34	35	36	37	38	39	40 = (1 − p)	r
1	10000	10000	10000	10000	10000	10000	10000	10000	10000	10000	49
2	10000	10000	10000	10000	10000	10000	10000	10000	10000	10000	48
3	10000	10000	10000	10000	10000	10000	10000	10000	10000	10000	47
4	10000	10000	10000	10000	10000	10000	10000	10000	10000	10000	46
5	9999	9999	10000	10000	10000	10000	10000	10000	10000	10000	45
6	9996	9997	9998	9999	9999	10000	10000	10000	10000	10000	44
7	9984	9990	9994	9996	9998	9999	9999	10000	10000	10000	43
8	9952	9969	9980	9987	9992	9995	9997	9998	9999	9999	42
9	9874	9914	9942	9962	9975	9984	9990	9994	9996	9998	41
10	9710	9794	9856	9901	9933	9955	9971	9981	9988	9992	40
11	9409	9563	9683	9773	9840	9889	9924	9949	9966	9978	39
12	8916	9168	9371	9533	9658	9753	9825	9878	9916	9943	38
13	8197	8564	8873	9130	9339	9505	9635	9736	9811	9867	37
14	7253	7732	8157	8524	8837	9097	9310	9481	9616	9720	36
15	6131	6698	7223	7699	8122	8491	8805	9069	9286	9460	35

Table A.1 / *(continued)*

r					$n = 50$ *(Continued)*						r
	$p = 31$	32	33	34	35	36	37	38	39	$40 = (1 - p)$	
16	4922	5530	6120	6679	7199	7672	8094	8462	8779	9045	34
17	3734	4328	4931	5530	6111	6664	7179	7649	8070	8439	33
18	2666	3197	3760	4346	4940	5531	6105	6653	7164	7631	32
19	1786	2220	2703	3227	3784	4362	4949	5533	6101	6644	31
20	1121	1447	1826	2257	2736	3255	3805	4376	4957	5535	30
21	0657	0882	1156	1482	1861	2289	2764	3278	3824	4390	29
22	0360	0503	0685	0912	1187	1513	1890	2317	2788	3299	28
23	0184	0267	0379	0525	0710	0938	1214	1540	1916	2340	27
24	0087	0133	0196	0282	0396	0544	0730	0960	1236	1562	26
25	0039	0061	0094	0141	0207	0295	0411	0560	0748	0978	25
26	0016	0026	0042	0066	0100	0149	0216	0305	0423	0573	24
27	0006	0011	0018	0029	0045	0070	0106	0155	0223	0314	23
28	0002	0004	0007	0012	0019	0031	0048	0074	0110	0160	22
29	0001	0001	0002	0004	0007	0012	0020	0032	0050	0076	21
30			0001	0002	0003	0005	0008	0013	0021	0034	20
31					0001	0002	0003	0005	0008	0014	19
32						0001	0001	0002	0003	0005	18
33								0001	0001	0002	17
34										0001	16

	$p = 41$	42	43	44	45	46	47	48	49	$50 = (1 - p)$	
1	10000	10000	10000	10000	10000	10000	10000	10000	10000	10000	49
2	10000	10000	10000	10000	10000	10000	10000	10000	10000	10000	48
3	10000	10000	10000	10000	10000	10000	10000	10000	10000	10000	47
4	10000	10000	10000	10000	10000	10000	10000	10000	10000	10000	46
5	10000	10000	10000	10000	10000	10000	10000	10000	10000	10000	45
6	10000	10000	10000	10000	10000	10000	10000	10000	10000	10000	44
7	10000	10000	10000	10000	10000	10000	10000	10000	10000	10000	43
8	10000	10000	10000	10000	10000	10000	10000	10000	10000	10000	42
9	9999	9999	10000	10000	10000	10000	10000	10000	10000	10000	41
10	9995	9997	9998	9999	9999	10000	10000	10000	10000	10000	40
11	9986	9991	9994	9997	9998	9999	9999	10000	10000	10000	39
12	9962	9975	9984	9990	9994	9996	9998	9999	9999	10000	38
13	9908	9938	9958	9973	9982	9989	9993	9996	9997	9998	37
14	9799	9858	9902	9933	9955	9970	9981	9988	9992	9995	36
15	9599	9707	9789	9851	9896	9929	9952	9968	9980	9987	35
16	9265	9443	9585	9696	9780	9844	9892	9926	9950	9967	34
17	8757	9025	9248	9429	9573	9687	9774	9839	9888	9923	33
18	8051	8421	8740	9010	9235	9418	9565	9680	9769	9836	32
19	7152	7617	8037	8406	8727	8998	9225	9410	9559	9675	31
20	6099	6638	7143	7608	8026	8396	8718	8991	9219	9405	30
21	4965	5539	6099	6635	7138	7602	8020	8391	8713	8987	29
22	3840	4402	4973	5543	6100	6634	7137	7599	8018	8389	28
23	2809	3316	3854	4412	4981	5548	6104	6636	7138	7601	27
24	1936	2359	2826	3331	3866	4422	4989	5554	6109	6641	26
25	1255	1580	1953	2375	2840	3343	3876	4431	4996	5561	25

Table A.1 / *(continued)*

r						$n = 50$ (*Continued*)					r
	$p = 41$	42	43	44	45	46	47	48	49	$50 = (1-p)$	
26	0762	0992	1269	1593	1966	2386	2850	3352	3885	4439	24
27	0432	0584	0772	1003	1279	1603	1975	2395	2858	3359	23
28	0229	0320	0439	0591	0780	1010	1286	1609	1981	2399	22
29	0113	0164	0233	0325	0444	0595	0784	1013	1289	1611	21
30	0052	0078	0115	0166	0235	0327	0446	0596	0784	1013	20
31	0022	0034	0053	0079	0116	0167	0236	0327	0445	0595	19
32	0009	0014	0022	0035	0053	0079	0116	0166	0234	0325	18
33	0003	0005	0009	0014	0022	0035	0053	0078	0114	0164	17
34	0001	0002	0003	0005	0009	0014	0022	0034	0052	0077	16
35		0001	0001	0002	0003	0005	0008	0014	0021	0033	15
36				0001	0001	0002	0003	0005	0008	0013	14
37						0001	0001	0002	0003	0005	13
38								0001	0001	0002	12

r						$n = 100$					r
	$p = 01$	02	03	04	05	06	07	08	09	$10 = (1-p)$	
1	6340	8674	9524	9831	9941	9979	9993	9998	9999	10000	99
2	2642	5967	8054	9128	9629	9848	9940	9977	9991	9997	98
3	0794	3233	5802	7679	8817	9434	9742	9887	9952	9981	97
4	0184	1410	3528	5705	7422	8570	9256	9633	9827	9922	96
5	0034	0508	1821	3711	5640	7232	8368	9097	9526	9763	95
6	0005	0155	0808	2116	3840	5593	7086	8201	8955	9424	94
7	0001	0041	0312	1064	2340	3936	5557	6968	8060	8828	93
8		0009	0106	0475	1280	2517	4012	5529	6872	7939	92
9		0002	0032	0190	0631	1463	2660	4074	5506	6791	91
10			0009	0068	0282	0775	1620	2780	4125	5487	90
11			0002	0022	0115	0376	0908	1757	2882	4168	89
12				0007	0043	0168	0469	1028	1876	2970	88
13				0002	0015	0069	0224	0559	1138	1982	87
14					0005	0026	0099	0282	0645	1239	86
15					0001	0009	0041	0133	0341	0726	85
16						0003	0016	0058	0169	0399	84
17						0001	0006	0024	0078	0206	83
18							0002	0009	0034	0100	82
19							0001	0003	0014	0046	81
20								0001	0005	0020	80
21									0002	0008	79
22									0001	0003	78
23										0001	77

Table A.1 / *(continued)*

r	$n = 100$ *(Continued)*										r
	$p = 11$	12	13	14	15	16	17	18	19	$20 = (1 - p)$	
1	10000	10000	10000	10000	10000	10000	10000	10000	10000	10000	99
2	9999	10000	10000	10000	10000	10000	10000	10000	10000	10000	98
3	9992	9997	9999	10000	10000	10000	10000	10000	10000	10000	97
4	9966	9985	9994	9998	9999	10000	10000	10000	10000	10000	96
5	9886	9947	9977	9990	9996	9998	9999	10000	10000	10000	95
6	9698	9848	9926	9966	9984	9993	9997	9999	10000	10000	94
7	9328	9633	9808	9903	9953	9978	9990	9996	9998	9999	93
8	8715	9239	9569	9766	9878	9939	9970	9986	9994	9997	92
9	7835	8614	9155	9508	9725	9853	9924	9962	9982	9991	91
10	6722	7743	8523	9078	9449	9684	9826	9908	9953	9977	90
11	5471	6663	7663	8440	9006	9393	9644	9800	9891	9943	89
12	4206	5458	6611	7591	8365	8939	9340	9605	9773	9874	88
13	3046	4239	5446	6566	7527	8297	8876	9289	9567	9747	87
14	2076	3114	4268	5436	6526	7469	8234	8819	9241	9531	86
15	1330	2160	3173	4294	5428	6490	7417	8177	8765	9196	85
16	0802	1414	2236	3227	4317	5420	6458	7370	8125	8715	84
17	0456	0874	1492	2305	3275	4338	5414	6429	7327	8077	83
18	0244	0511	0942	1563	2367	3319	4357	5408	6403	7288	82
19	0123	0282	0564	1006	1628	2424	3359	4374	5403	6379	81
20	0059	0147	0319	0614	1065	1689	2477	3395	4391	5398	80
21	0026	0073	0172	0356	0663	1121	1745	2525	3429	4405	79
22	0011	0034	0088	0196	0393	0710	1174	1797	2570	3460	78
23	0005	0015	0042	0103	0221	0428	0754	1223	1846	2611	77
24	0002	0006	0020	0051	0119	0246	0462	0796	1270	1891	76
25	0001	0003	0009	0024	0061	0135	0271	0496	0837	1314	75
26		0001	0004	0011	0030	0071	0151	0295	0528	0875	74
27			0001	0005	0014	0035	0081	0168	0318	0558	73
28			0001	0002	0006	0017	0041	0091	0184	0342	72
29				0001	0003	0008	0020	0048	0102	0200	71
30					0001	0003	0009	0024	0054	0112	70
31						0001	0004	0011	0027	0061	69
32						0001	0002	0005	0013	0031	68
33							0001	0002	0006	0016	67
34								0001	0003	0007	66
35									0001	0003	65
36										0001	64
37										0001	63

Table A.1 / *(continued)*

r				$n = 100$ (Continued)							r
	$p = 21$	22	23	24	25	26	27	28	29	$30 = (1 - p)$	
1	10000	10000	10000	10000	10000	10000	10000	10000	10000	10000	99
2	10000	10000	10000	10000	10000	10000	10000	10000	10000	10000	98
3	10000	10000	10000	10000	10000	10000	10000	10000	10000	10000	97
4	10000	10000	10000	10000	10000	10000	10000	10000	10000	10000	96
5	10000	10000	10000	10000	10000	10000	10000	10000	10000	10000	95
6	10000	10000	10000	10000	10000	10000	10000	10000	10000	10000	94
7	10000	10000	10000	10000	10000	10000	10000	10000	10000	10000	93
8	9999	10000	10000	10000	10000	10000	10000	10000	10000	10000	92
9	9996	9998	9999	10000	10000	10000	10000	10000	10000	10000	91
10	9989	9995	9998	9999	10000	10000	10000	10000	10000	10000	90
11	9971	9986	9993	9997	9999	9999	10000	10000	10000	10000	89
12	9933	9965	9983	9992	9996	9998	9999	10000	10000	10000	88
13	9857	9922	9959	9979	9990	9995	9998	9999	10000	10000	87
14	9721	9840	9911	9953	9975	9988	9994	9997	9999	9999	86
15	9496	9695	9823	9900	9946	9972	9986	9993	9997	9998	85
16	9153	9462	9671	9806	9889	9939	9967	9983	9992	9996	84
17	8668	9112	9430	9647	9789	9878	9932	9963	9981	9990	83
18	8032	8625	9074	9399	9624	9773	9867	9925	9959	9978	82
19	7252	7991	8585	9038	9370	9601	9757	9856	9918	9955	81
20	6358	7220	7953	8547	9005	9342	9580	9741	9846	9911	80
21	5394	6338	7189	7918	8512	8973	9316	9560	9726	9835	79
22	4419	5391	6320	7162	7886	8479	8943	9291	9540	9712	78
23	3488	4432	5388	6304	7136	7856	8448	8915	9267	9521	77
24	2649	3514	4444	5386	6289	7113	7828	8420	8889	9245	76
25	1933	2684	3539	4455	5383	6276	7091	7802	8393	8864	75
26	1355	1972	2717	3561	4465	5381	6263	7071	7778	8369	74
27	0911	1393	2009	2748	3583	4475	5380	6252	7053	7756	73
28	0588	0945	1429	2043	2776	3602	4484	5378	6242	7036	72
29	0364	0616	0978	1463	2075	2803	3621	4493	5377	6232	71
30	0216	0386	0643	1009	1495	2105	2828	3638	4501	5377	70
31	0123	0232	0406	0669	1038	1526	2134	2851	3654	4509	69
32	0067	0134	0247	0427	0693	1065	1554	2160	2873	3669	68
33	0035	0074	0144	0262	0446	0717	1091	1580	2184	2893	67
34	0018	0039	0081	0154	0276	0465	0739	1116	1605	2207	66
35	0009	0020	0044	0087	0164	0290	0482	0760	1139	1629	65
36	0004	0010	0023	0048	0094	0174	0303	0499	0780	1161	64
37	0002	0005	0011	0025	0052	0101	0183	0316	0515	0799	63
38	0001	0002	0005	0013	0027	0056	0107	0193	0328	0530	62
39		0001	0002	0006	0014	0030	0060	0113	0201	0340	61
40			0001	0003	0007	0015	0032	0064	0119	0210	60
41				0001	0003	0008	0017	0035	0068	0125	59
42				0001	0001	0004	0008	0018	0037	0072	58
43					0001	0002	0004	0009	0020	0040	57
44						0001	0002	0005	0010	0021	56
45							0001	0002	0005	0011	55
46								0001	0002	0005	54
47									0001	0003	53
48										0001	52
49										0001	51

Table A.1 / *(continued)*

r	$n = 100$ *(Continued)*										r
	$p = 31$	32	33	34	35	36	37	38	39	$40 = (1 - p)$	
1	10000	10000	10000	10000	10000	10000	10000	10000	10000	10000	99
2	10000	10000	10000	10000	10000	10000	10000	10000	10000	10000	98
3	10000	10000	10000	10000	10000	10000	10000	10000	10000	10000	97
4	10000	10000	10000	10000	10000	10000	10000	10000	10000	10000	96
5	10000	10000	10000	10000	10000	10000	10000	10000	10000	10000	95
6	10000	10000	10000	10000	10000	10000	10000	10000	10000	10000	94
7	10000	10000	10000	10000	10000	10000	10000	10000	10000	10000	93
8	10000	10000	10000	10000	10000	10000	10000	10000	10000	10000	92
9	10000	10000	10000	10000	10000	10000	10000	10000	10000	10000	91
10	10000	10000	10000	10000	10000	10000	10000	10000	10000	10000	90
11	10000	10000	10000	10000	10000	10000	10000	10000	10000	10000	89
12	10000	10000	10000	10000	10000	10000	10000	10000	10000	10000	88
13	10000	10000	10000	10000	10000	10000	10000	10000	10000	10000	87
14	10000	10000	10000	10000	10000	10000	10000	10000	10000	10000	86
15	9999	10000	10000	10000	10000	10000	10000	10000	10000	10000	85
16	9998	9999	10000	10000	10000	10000	10000	10000	10000	10000	84
17	9995	9998	9999	10000	10000	10000	10000	10000	10000	10000	83
18	9989	9995	9997	9999	9999	10000	10000	10000	10000	10000	82
19	9976	9988	9994	9997	9999	9999	10000	10000	10000	10000	81
20	9950	9973	9986	9993	9997	9998	9999	10000	10000	10000	80
21	9904	9946	9971	9985	9992	9996	9998	9999	10000	10000	79
22	9825	9898	9942	9968	9983	9991	9996	9998	9999	10000	78
23	9698	9816	9891	9938	9966	9982	9991	9995	9998	9999	77
·24	9504	9685	9806	9885	9934	9963	9980	9990	9995	9997	76
25	9224	9487	9672	9797	9879	9930	9961	9979	9989	9994	75
26	8841	9204	9471	9660	9789	9873	9926	9958	9977	9988	74
27	8346	8820	9185	9456	9649	9780	9867	9922	9956	9976	73
28	7736	8325	8800	9168	9442	9638	9773	9862	9919	9954	72
29	7021	7717	8305	8781	9152	9429	9628	9765	9857	9916	71
30	6224	7007	7699	8287	8764	9137	9417	9618	9759	9852	70
31	5376	6216	6994	7684	8270	8748	9123	9405	9610	9752	69
32	4516	5376	6209	6982	7669	8254	8733	9110	9395	9602	68
33	3683	4523	5375	6203	6971	7656	8240	8720	9098	9385	67
34	2912	3696	4530	5375	6197	6961	7643	8227	8708	9087	66
35	2229	2929	3708	4536	5376	6192	6953	7632	8216	8697	65
36	1650	2249	2946	3720	4542	5376	6188	6945	7623	8205	64
37	1181	1671	2268	2961	3731	4547	5377	6184	6938	7614	63
38	0816	1200	1690	2285	2976	3741	4553	5377	6181	6932	62
39	0545	0833	1218	1708	2301	2989	3750	4558	5378	6178	61
40	0351	0558	0849	1235	1724	2316	3001	3759	4562	5379	60
41	0218	0361	0571	0863	1250	1739	2330	3012	3767	4567	59
42	0131	0226	0371	0583	0877	1265	1753	2343	3023	3775	58
43	0075	0136	0233	0380	0594	0889	1278	1766	2355	3033	57
44	0042	0079	0141	0240	0389	0605	0901	1290	1778	2365	56
45	0023	0044	0082	0146	0246	0397	0614	0911	1301	1789	55

Table A.1 / *(continued)*

r					$n = 100$ *(Continued)*						r
	$p = 31$	32	33	34	35	36	37	38	39	$40 = (1-p)$	
46	0012	0024	0046	0085	0150	0252	0405	0623	0921	1311	54
47	0006	0012	0025	0048	0088	0154	0257	0411	0631	0930	53
48	0003	0006	0013	0026	0050	0091	0158	0262	0417	0638	52
49	0001	0003	0007	0014	0027	0052	0094	0162	0267	0423	51
50	0001	0001	0003	0007	0015	0029	0054	0096	0165	0271	50
51		0001	0002	0003	0007	0015	0030	0055	0098	0168	49
52			0001	0002	0004	0008	0016	0030	0056	0100	48
53				0001	0002	0004	0008	0016	0031	0058	47
54					0001	0002	0004	0008	0017	0032	46
55						0001	0002	0004	0009	0017	45
56							0001	0002	0004	0009	44
57								0001	0002	0004	43
58									0001	0002	42
59										0001	41
	$p = 41$	42	43	44	45	46	47	48	49	$50 = (1-p)$	
1	10000	10000	10000	10000	10000	10000	10000	10000	10000	10000	99
2	10000	10000	10000	10000	10000	10000	10000	10000	10000	10000	98
3	10000	10000	10000	10000	10000	10000	10000	10000	10000	10000	97
4	10000	10000	10000	10000	10000	10000	10000	10000	10000	10000	96
5	10000	10000	10000	10000	10000	10000	10000	10000	10000	10000	95
6	10000	10000	10000	10000	10000	10000	10000	10000	10000	10000	94
7	10000	10000	10000	10000	10000	10000	10000	10000	10000	10000	93
8	10000	10000	10000	10000	10000	10000	10000	10000	10000	10000	92
9	10000	10000	10000	10000	10000	10000	10000	10000	10000	10000	91
10	10000	10000	10000	10000	10000	10000	10000	10000	10000	10000	90
11	10000	10000	10000	10000	10000	10000	10000	10000	10000	10000	89
12	10000	10000	10000	10000	10000	10000	10000	10000	10000	10000	88
13	10000	10000	10000	10000	10000	10000	10000	10000	10000	10000	87
14	10000	10000	10000	10000	10000	10000	10000	10000	10000	10000	86
15	10000	10000	10000	10000	10000	10000	10000	10000	10000	10000	85
16	10000	10000	10000	10000	10000	10000	10000	10000	10000	10000	84
17	10000	10000	10000	10000	10000	10000	10000	10000	10000	10000	83
18	10000	10000	10000	10000	10000	10000	10000	10000	10000	10000	82
19	10000	10000	10000	10000	10000	10000	10000	10000	10000	10000	81
20	10000	10000	10000	10000	10000	10000	10000	10000	10000	10000	80
21	10000	10000	10000	10000	10000	10000	10000	10000	10000	10000	79
22	10000	10000	10000	10000	10000	10000	10000	10000	10000	10000	78
23	10000	10000	10000	10000	10000	10000	10000	10000	10000	10000	77
24	9999	9999	10000	10000	10000	10000	10000	10000	10000	10000	76
25	9997	9999	9999	10000	10000	10000	10000	10000	10000	10000	75

Table A.1 / *(continued)*

r	$n = 100$ *(Continued)*										r
	$p = 41$	42	43	44	45	46	47	48	49	$50 = (1-p)$	
26	9994	9997	9999	9999	10000	10000	10000	10000	10000	10000	74
27	9987	9994	9997	9998	9999	10000	10000	10000	10000	10000	73
28	9975	9987	9993	9997	9998	9999	10000	10000	10000	10000	72
29	9952	9974	9986	9993	9996	9998	9999	10000	10000	10000	71
30	9913	9950	9972	9985	9992	9996	9998	9999	10000	10000	70
31	9848	9910	9848	9971	9985	9992	9996	9998	9999	10000	69
32	9746	9844	9907	9947	9970	9984	9992	9996	9998	9999	68
33	9594	9741	9840	9905	9945	9969	9984	9991	9996	9998	67
34	9376	9587	9736	9837	9902	9944	9969	9983	9991	9996	66
35	9078	9368	9581	9732	9834	9900	9942	9968	9983	9991	65
36	8687	9069	9361	9576	9728	9831	9899	9941	9967	9982	64
37	8196	8678	9061	9355	9571	9724	9829	9897	9941	9967	63
38	7606	8188	8670	9054	9349	9567	9721	9827	9896	9940	62
39	6927	7599	8181	8663	9049	9345	9563	9719	9825	9895	61
40	6176	6922	7594	8174	8657	9044	9341	9561	9717	9824	60
41	5380	6174	6919	7589	8169	8653	9040	9338	9558	9716	59
42	4571	5382	6173	6916	7585	8165	8649	9037	9335	9557	58
43	3782	4576	5383	6173	6913	7582	8162	8646	9035	9334	57
44	3041	3788	4580	5385	6172	6912	7580	8160	8645	9033	56
45	2375	3049	3794	4583	5387	6173	6911	7579	8159	8644	55
46	1799	2384	3057	3799	4587	5389	6173	6911	7579	8159	54
47	1320	1807	2391	3063	3804	4590	5391	6174	6912	7579	53
48	0938	1328	1815	2398	3069	3809	4593	5393	6176	6914	52
49	0644	0944	1335	1822	2404	3074	3813	4596	5395	6178	51
50	0428	0650	0950	1341	1827	2409	3078	3816	4599	5398	50
51	0275	0432	0655	0955	1346	1832	2413	3082	3819	4602	49
52	0170	0278	0436	0659	0960	1350	1836	2417	3084	3822	48
53	0102	0172	0280	0439	0662	0963	1353	1838	2419	3086	47
54	0059	0103	0174	0282	0441	0664	0965	1355	1840	2421	46
55	0033	0059	0104	0175	0284	0443	0666	0967	1356	1841	45
56	0017	0033	0060	0105	0176	0285	0444	0667	0967	1356	44
57	0009	0018	0034	0061	0106	0177	0286	0444	0667	0967	43
58	0004	0009	0018	0034	0061	0106	0177	0286	0444	0666	42
59	0002	0005	0009	0018	0034	0061	0106	0177	0285	0443	41
60	0001	0002	0005	0009	0018	0034	0061	0106	0177	0284	40
61		0001	0002	0005	0009	0018	0034	0061	0106	0176	39
62			0001	0002	0005	0009	0018	0034	0061	0105	38
63				0001	0002	0005	0009	0018	0034	0060	37
64					0001	0002	0005	0009	0018	0033	36
65						0001	0002	0005	0009	0018	35
66							0001	0002	0004	0009	34
67								0001	0002	0004	33
68									0001	0002	32
69										0001	31

Table A.2 / Table of areas for standardized normal probability distribution

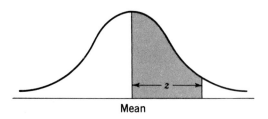

Mean

Example: For $z = 1.64$, the shaded area is .4495 out of a total area under the curve of 1.

z	.00	.01	.02	.03	.04	.05	.06	.07	.08	.09
0.0	.0000	.0040	.0080	.0120	.0160	.0199	.0239	.0279	.0319	.0359
0.1	.0398	.0438	.0478	.0517	.0557	.0596	.0636	.0675	.0714	.0753
0.2	.0793	.0832	.0871	.0910	.0948	.0987	.1026	.1064	.1103	.1141
0.3	.1179	.1217	.1255	.1293	.1331	.1368	.1406	.1443	.1480	.1517
0.4	.1554	.1591	.1628	.1664	.1700	.1736	.1772	.1808	.1844	.1879
0.5	.1915	.1950	.1985	.2019	.2054	.2088	.2123	.2157	.2190	.2224
0.6	.2257	.2291	.2324	.2357	.2389	.2422	.2454	.2486	.2518	.2549
0.7	.2580	.2612	.2642	.2673	.2704	.2734	.2764	.2794	.2823	.2852
0.8	.2881	.2910	.2939	.2967	.2995	.3023	.3051	.3078	.3106	.3133
0.9	.3159	.3186	.3212	.3238	.3264	.3289	.3315	.3340	.3365	.3389
1.0	.3413	.3438	.3461	.3485	.3508	.3531	.3554	.3577	.3599	.3621
1.1	.3643	.3665	.3686	.3708	.3729	.3749	.3770	.3790	.3810	.3830
1.2	.3849	.3869	.3888	.3907	.3925	.3944	.3962	.3980	.3997	.4015
1.3	.4032	.4049	.4066	.4082	.4099	.4115	.4131	.4147	.4162	.4177
1.4	.4192	.4207	.4222	.4236	.4251	.4265	.4279	.4292	.4306	.4319
1.5	.4332	.4345	.4357	.4370	.4382	.4394	.4406	.4418	.4429	.4441
1.6	.4452	.4463	.4474	.4484	.4495	.4505	.4515	.4525	.4535	.4545
1.7	.4554	.4564	.4573	.4582	.4591	.4599	.4608	.4616	.4625	.4633
1.8	.4641	.4649	.4656	.4664	.4671	.4678	.4686	.4693	.4699	.4706
1.9	.4713	.4719	.4726	.4732	.4738	.4744	.4750	.4756	.4761	.4767
2.0	.4772	.4778	.4783	.4788	.4793	.4798	.4803	.4808	.4812	.4817
2.1	.4821	.4826	.4830	.4834	.4838	.4842	.4846	.4850	.4854	.4857
2.2	.4861	.4864	.4868	.4871	.4875	.4878	.4881	.4884	.4887	.4890
2.3	.4893	.4896	.4898	.4901	.4904	.4906	.4909	.4911	.4913	.4916
2.4	.4918	.4920	.4922	.4925	.4927	.4929	.4931	.4932	.4934	.4936
2.5	.4938	.4940	.4941	.4943	.4945	.4946	.4948	.4949	.4951	.4952
2.6	.4953	.4955	.4956	.4957	.4959	.4960	.4961	.4962	.4963	.4964
2.7	.4965	.4966	.4967	.4968	.4969	.4970	.4971	.4972	.4973	.4974
2.8	.4974	.4975	.4976	.4977	.4977	.4978	.4979	.4979	.4980	.4981
2.9	.4981	.4982	.4982	.4983	.4984	.4984	.4985	.4985	.4986	.4986
3.0	.49865	.4987	.4987	.4988	.4988	.4989	.4989	.4989	.4990	.4990
4.0	.4999683									

Table A.3 / Percentage points for the sampling distribution of t

Values in the heading refer to two-tailed probabilities corresponding to t values found in the body. (For one-tailed probabilities, divide by 2.) For example, for 9 degrees of freedom and $t = 1.833$, the two-tailed probability is .10, and for 9 degrees of freedom and $t = 3.05$, the two-tailed probability is between .01 and .02.

Degrees of freedom	Probability P				
	.20	.10	.05	.02	.01
1	3.078	6.314	12.706	31.821	63.657
2	1.886	2.920	4.303	6.965	9.925
3	1.638	2.353	3.182	4.541	5.841
4	1.533	2.132	2.776	3.747	4.604
5	1.476	2.015	2.571	3.365	4.032
6	1.440	1.943	2.447	3.143	3.707
7	1.415	1.895	2.365	2.998	3.499
8	1.397	1.860	2.306	2.896	3.355
9	1.383	1.833	2.262	2.821	3.250
10	1.372	1.812	2.228	2.764	3.169
11	1.363	1.796	2.201	2.178	3.106
12	1.356	1.782	2.179	2.681	3.055
13	1.350	1.771	2.160	2.650	3.012
14	1.345	1.761	2.145	2.624	2.977
15	1.341	1.753	2.131	2.602	2.947
16	1.337	1.746	2.120	2.583	2.921
17	1.333	1.740	2.110	2.567	2.898
18	1.330	1.734	2.101	2.552	2.878
19	1.328	1.729	2.093	2.539	2.861
20	1.325	1.725	2.086	2.528	2.845
21	1.323	1.721	2.080	2.518	2.831
22	1.321	1.717	2.074	2.508	2.819
23	1.319	1.714	2.069	2.500	2.807
24	1.318	1.711	2.064	2.492	2.797
25	1.316	1.708	2.060	2.485	2.787
26	1.315	1.706	2.056	2.479	2.779
27	1.314	1.703	2.052	2.473	2.771
28	1.313	1.701	2.048	2.467	2.763
29	1.311	1.699	2.045	2.462	2.756
30	1.310	1.697	2.042	2.457	2.750
∞	1.28155	1.64485	1.95996	2.32634	2.57582

Source: R. A. Fisher, "Statistical Methods for Research Workers," (14th Edn.) Copyright © 1972 by Hafner Press, A division of Macmillan Publishing Co., Inc., by permission of the author and publishers.

Table A.4 / Unit normal loss integral

The values in the body of the table $N(D)$ are expected opportunity losses for linear loss functions and a normal distribution with a mean of 0 and a standard deviation of 1. The value D represents the standardized deviation of the break-even value from μ. For example, given $\mu_o = 250$, $\mu_b = 200$ and $\sigma = 150$,

$$D = \left| \frac{\mu_o - \mu_b}{\sigma} \right| = .33 \quad \text{and} \quad N(D) = .2555$$

D	.00	.01	.02	.03	.04	.05	.06	.07	.08	.09
.0	.3989	.3940	.3890	.3841	.3793	.3744	.3697	.3649	.3602	.3556
.1	.3509	.3464	.3418	.3373	.3328	.3284	.3240	.3197	.3154	.3111
.2	.3069	.3027	.2986	.2944	.2904	.2863	.2824	.2784	.2745	.2706
.3	.2668	.2630	.2592	.2555	.2518	.2481	.2445	.2409	.2374	.2339
.4	.2304	.2270	.2236	.2203	.2169	.2137	.2104	.2072	.2040	.2009
.5	.1978	.1947	.1917	.1887	.1857	.1828	.1799	.1771	.1742	.1714
.6	.1687	.1659	.1633	.1606	.1580	.1554	.1528	.1503	.1478	.1453
.7	.1429	.1405	.1381	.1358	.1334	.1312	.1289	.1267	.1245	.1223
.8	.1202	.1181	.1160	.1140	.1120	.1100	.1080	.1061	.1042	.1023
.9	.1004	.09860	.09680	.09503	.09328	.09156	.08986	.08819	.08654	.08491
1.0	.08332	.08174	.08019	.07866	.07716	.07568	.07422	.07279	.07138	.06999
1.1	.06862	.06727	.06595	.06465	.06336	.06210	.06086	.05964	.05844	.05726
1.2	.05610	.05496	.05384	.05274	.05165	.05059	.04954	.04851	.04750	.04650
1.3	.04553	.04457	.04363	.04270	.04179	.04090	.04002	.03916	.03831	.03748
1.4	.03667	.03587	.03508	.03431	.03356	.03281	.03208	.03137	.03067	.02998
1.5	.02931	.02865	.02800	.02736	.02674	.02612	.02552	.02494	.02436	.02380
1.6	.02324	.02270	.02217	.02165	.02114	.02064	.02015	.01967	.01920	.01874
1.7	.01829	.01785	.01742	.01699	.01658	.01617	.01578	.01539	.01501	.01464
1.8	.01428	.01392	.01357	.01323	.01290	.01257	.01226	.01195	.01164	.01134
1.9	.01105	.01077	.01049	.01022	$.0^2 9957$	$.0^2 9698$	$.0^2 9445$	$.0^2 9198$	$.0^2 8957$	$.0^2 8721$
2.0	$.0^2 8491$	$.0^2 8266$	$.0^2 8046$	$.0^2 7832$	$.0^2 7623$	$.0^2 7418$	$.0^2 7219$	$.0^2 7024$	$.0^2 6835$	$.0^2 6649$
2.1	$.0^2 6468$	$.0^2 6292$	$.0^2 6120$	$.0^2 5952$	$.0^2 5788$	$.0^2 5628$	$.0^2 5472$	$.0^2 5320$	$.0^2 5172$	$.0^2 5028$
2.2	$.0^2 4887$	$.0^2 4750$	$.0^2 4616$	$.0^2 4486$	$.0^2 4358$	$.0^2 4235$	$.0^2 4114$	$.0^2 3996$	$.0^2 3882$	$.0^2 3770$
2.3	$.0^2 3662$	$.0^2 3556$	$.0^2 3453$	$.0^2 3352$	$.0^2 3255$	$.0^2 3159$	$.0^2 3067$	$.0^2 2977$	$.0^2 2889$	$.0^2 2804$
2.4	$.0^2 2720$	$.0^2 2640$	$.0^2 2561$	$.0^2 2484$	$.0^2 2410$	$.0^2 2337$	$.0^2 2267$	$.0^2 2199$	$.0^2 2132$	$.0^2 2067$
2.5	$.0^2 2004$	$.0^2 1943$	$.0^2 1883$	$.0^2 1826$	$.0^2 1769$	$.0^2 1715$	$.0^2 1662$	$.0^2 1610$	$.0^2 1560$	$.0^2 1511$
3.0	$.0^3 3822$	$.0^3 3689$	$.0^3 3560$	$.0^3 3436$	$.0^3 3316$	$.0^3 3199$	$.0^3 3087$	$.0^3 2978$	$.0^3 2873$	$.0^3 2771$
3.5	$.0^4 5848$	$.0^4 5620$	$.0^4 5400$	$.0^4 5188$	$.0^4 4984$	$.0^4 4788$	$.0^4 4599$	$.0^4 4417$	$.0^4 4242$	$.0^4 4073$
4.0	$.0^5 7145$	$.0^5 6835$	$.0^5 6538$	$.0^5 6253$	$.0^5 5980$	$.0^5 5718$	$.0^5 5468$	$.0^5 5227$	$.0^5 4997$	$.0^5 4777$

Source: Reproduced by permission of the President and Fellows of Harvard College, from Robert Schlaifer, "Introduction to Statistics for Business Decisions," pp. 370–371, McGraw-Hill Book Company, New York, 1961.

Table A.5 / Chi-square distribution

This table contains critical chi-square values for upper-tail probabilities Q. At any given degrees of freedom v an obtained value of χ^2 larger than the tabled value will cause a rejection of the null hypothesis.

v	Q					
	.100	.050	.025	.010	.005	.001
1	2.70554	3.84146	5.02389	6.63490	7.87944	10.828
2	4.60517	5.99147	7.37776	9.21034	10.5966	13.816
3	6.25139	7.81473	9.34840	11.3449	12.8381	16.266
4	7.77944	9.48773	11.1433	13.2767	14.8602	18.467
5	9.23635	11.0705	12.8325	15.0863	16.7496	20.515
6	10.6446	12.5916	14.4494	16.8119	18.5476	22.458
7	12.0170	14.0671	16.0128	18.4753	20.2777	24.322
8	13.3616	15.5073	17.5346	20.0902	21.9550	26.125
9	14.6837	16.9190	19.0228	21.6660	23.5893	27.877
10	15.9871	18.3070	20.4831	23.2093	25.1882	29.588
11	17.2750	19.6751	21.9200	24.7250	26.7569	31.264
12	18.5494	21.0261	23.3367	26.2170	28.2995	32.909
13	19.8119	22.3621	24.7356	27.6883	29.8194	34.528
14	21.0642	23.6848	26.1190	29.1413	31.3193	36.123
15	22.3072	24.9958	27.4884	30.5779	32.8013	37.697
16	23.5418	26.2962	28.8454	31.9999	34.2672	39.252
17	24.7690	27.5871	30.1910	33.4087	35.7185	40.790
18	25.9894	28.8693	31.5264	34.8053	37.1564	42.312
19	27.2036	30.1435	32.8523	36.1908	38.5822	43.820
20	28.4120	31.4104	34.1696	37.5662	39.9968	45.315
21	29.6151	32.6705	35.4789	38.9321	41.4010	46.797
22	30.8133	33.9244	36.7807	40.2894	42.7956	48.268
23	32.0069	35.1725	38.0757	41.6384	44.1813	49.728
24	33.1963	36.4151	39.3641	42.9798	45.5585	51.179
25	34.3816	37.6525	40.6465	44.3141	46.9278	52.620
26	35.5631	38.8852	41.9232	45.6417	48.2899	54.052
27	36.7412	40.1133	43.1944	46.9630	49.6449	55.476
28	37.9159	41.3372	44.4607	48.2782	50.9933	56.892
29	39.0875	42.5569	45.7222	49.5879	52.3356	58.302
30	40.2560	43.7729	46.9792	50.8922	53.6720	59.703
40	51.8050	55.7585	59.3417	63.6907	66.7659	73.402
50	63.1671	67.5048	71.4202	76.1539	79.4900	86.661
60	74.3970	79.0819	83.2976	88.3794	91.9517	99.607
70	85.5271	90.5312	95.0231	100.425	104.215	112.317
80	96.5782	101.879	106.629	112.329	116.321	124.839
90	107.565	113.145	118.136	124.116	128.299	137.208
100	118.498	124.342	129.561	135.807	140.169	149.449
z_Q	$+1.2816$	$+1.6449$	$+1.9600$	$+2.3263$	$+2.5758$	$+3.0902$

Source: E. S. Pearson and H. O. Hartley, eds., *Biometrika Tables for Statisticians*, vol. 1 (1st ed.), table 8. Reproduced with the kind permission of E. S. Pearson and the trustees of *Biometrika*.

Table A.6 / Upper percentage points of D in the Kolmogorov-Smirnov one-sample test

The critical values of the maximum absolute deviation in the Kolmogorov-Smirnov test are shown in this table. Any deviation *larger* than the tabled value for a given sample size will cause a rejection of the hypothesis of equal distribution.

N	Q		
	.10	.05	.01
1	.950	.975	.995
2	.776	.842	.929
3	.642	.708	.828
4	.564	.624	.733
5	.510	.565	.669
6	.470	.521	.618
7	.438	.486	.577
8	.411	.457	.543
9	.388	.432	.514
10	.368	.410	.490
11	.352	.391	.468
12	.338	.375	.450
13	.325	.361	.433
14	.314	.349	.418
15	.304	.338	.404
16	.295	.328	.392
17	.280	.318	.381
18	.278	.309	.371
19	.272	.301	.363
20	.264	.294	.356
25	.24	.27	.32
30	.22	.24	.29
35	.21	.23	.27
Over 35	$\dfrac{1.22}{\sqrt{N}}$	$\dfrac{1.36}{\sqrt{N}}$	$\dfrac{1.63}{\sqrt{N}}$

Source: Adapted from F. J. Massey, "The Kolmogorov-Smirnov Test for Goodness of Fit," *Journal of the American Statistical Association*, vol. 46, 1951, p. 70. Reproduced by permission.

Table A.7 / Critical values of the Wilcoxon test for two samples

This table gives critical values for the Wilcoxon test for mean rank differences. If the difference (absolute) is larger than the tabled value, reject the hypothesis of equal central tendencies and accept the alternative that there is a difference. If the obtained difference (absolute) is smaller than the tabled value, you can't reject the hypothesis. If n is larger than 40, use the normal approximation

$$z = \frac{S - \dfrac{n(n+1)}{4}}{\sqrt{\dfrac{n(n+1)(2n+1)}{24}}}$$

where S is the sum of the positive values, or the absolute value of the sum of the negative values, whichever is smaller. The value of z is then referred to the two-tailed normal distribution.

	Significance level		
n	.1	.05	.01
6	2.834		
7	3.143	3.429	
8	3.250	3.750	
9	3.223	3.889	4.778
10	3.500	3.900	4.900
11	3.637	4.182	5.091
12	3.667	4.334	5.334
13	3.770	4.385	5.616
14	3.929	4.500	5.786
15	4.000	4.667	6.000
16	4.125	4.875	6.125
17	4.177	5.000	6.295
18	4.278	5.056	6.500
19	4.422	5.158	6.632
20	4.500	5.300	6.800
21	4.620	5.477	7.000
22	4.682	5.591	7.137
23	4.783	5.653	7.305
24	4.917	5.750	7.417
25	5.000	5.880	7.560
26	5.039	5.962	7.731
27	5.186	6.075	7.852
28	5.215	6.215	8.000
29	5.345	6.311	8.104
30	5.434	6.367	8.234
31	5.484	6.517	8.388
32	5.563	6.563	8.500
33	5.667	6.697	8.637
34	5.736	6.795	8.795
35	5.829	6.858	8.915
36	5.889	6.945	9.000
37	5.973	7.055	9.163
38	6.027	7.132	9.290
39	6.103	7.231	9.385
40	6.200	7.300	9.500

Table A.8 / Critical values for the Mann-Whitney U test

The critical values of the Mann-Whitney U test that are just significant are shown in this table. If U is larger than the tabled value, don't reject the hypothesis of equal central tendencies. If it's equal to or smaller than the tabled value, reject that hypothesis and accept the alternative that there's a difference. If $U > n_1 n_2/2$, you must use $U' = n_1 n_2 - U$ to test the hypothesis. Note that this is a two-tailed test. If n_2 is greater than 10, use the normal approximation

$$z = \frac{U - n_1 n_2/2}{\sqrt{n_1 n_2 (n_1 + n_2 + 1)/12}}$$

Larger sample size n_1	Smaller sample size n_2	Level of significance		
		.10	.05	.01
5	1			
	2	0		
	3	1	0	
	4	2	1	
	5	4	2	0
6	1			
	2	0	0	
	3	2	1	
	4	3	2	0
	5	5	3	1
	6	7	5	2
7	1			
	2	0	0	
	3	2	1	0
	4	4	3	1
	5	6	5	2
	6	8	6	3
	7	11	8	4
8	1	0		
	2	1	0	
	3	3	2	0
	4	5	4	1
	5	8	6	2
	6	10	8	4
	7	13	10	6
	8	15	13	7
9	1	0		
	2	1	0	
	3	4	2	0
	4	6	4	1
	5	9	7	3
	6	12	10	5
	7	15	12	7
	8	18	15	9
	9	21	18	11

Table A.8 / *(continued)*

Larger sample size n_1	Smaller sample size n_2	Level of significance		
		.10	.05	.01
10	1	0		
	2	1	0	
	3	4	3	0
	4	7	5	2
	5	11	8	4
	6	14	11	6
	7	17	14	9
	8	20	17	11
	9	24	20	14
	10	27	23	16

Table A.9 / Critical values for the median test

This table is used to find the significance of the difference between the medians of two populations. The 2 × 2 table is

a	$A - a$	A
b	$B - b$	B
$a + b$		$A + B$

where A is the largest sample size and a and b are in the same column and are chosen such that $aB \geq bA$. The table contains the largest values of b, for given A, B, and a combinations, such that you can just reject the hypothesis of equal medians. If the obtained b from the sample is less than or equal to the tabled value, you can reject the hypothesis, but if it is greater than the tabled value, you can't reject the hypothesis. This is a two-tailed test, and these tables are applicable to any 2 × 2 table where either the row totals are equal or the column totals are equal, and this condition is true in the median test.

A	B	a	.10	.05	.01	A	B	a	.10	.05	.01
3	3	3	0			7	5	7	2	1	0
4	4	4	0	0				6	1	0	
	3	4	0					5	0		
5	5	5	1	1	0		4	7	1	1	0
		4	0	0				6	0	0	
	4	5	1	0				5	0		
		4	0				3	7	0	0	
	3	5	0	0				6	0		
	2	5	0				2	7	0		
6	6	6	2	1	0	8	8	8	4	3	2
		5	1	0				7	2	2	0
		4	0					6	1	1	0
	5	6	1	1	0			5	0	0	
		5	0	0				4	0		
		4	0				7	8	3	2	1
	4	6	1	0	0			7	2	1	0
		5	0	0				6	1	0	
	3	6	0	0				5	0	0	
		5	0				6	8	2	2	1
	2	6	0					7	1	1	0
7	7	7	3	2	1			6	0	0	
		6	1	1	0			5	0		
		5	0	0			5	8	2	1	0
		4	0					7	1	0	0
	6	7	2	2	1			6	0	0	
		6	1	0	0			5	0		
		5	0	0			4	8	1	1	0
		4	0					7	0	0	
								6	0		
							3	8	0	0	

Table A.9 / (continued)

A	B	a	.10	.05	.01
8	3	7	0	0	
	2	8	0	0	
9	9	9	5	4	3
		8	3	3	1
		7	2	1	0
		6	1	1	0
		5	0	0	
		4	0		
	8	9	4	3	2
		8	3	2	1
		7	2	1	0
		6	1	0	
		5	0	0	
	7	9	3	3	2
		8	2	2	0
		7	1	1	0
		6	0	0	
		5	0		
	6	9	3	2	1
		8	2	1	0
		7	1	0	
		6	0	0	
		5	0		
9	5	9	2	1	1
		8	1	1	0
		7	0	0	
		6	0		
	4	9	1	1	0
		8	0	0	
		7	0	0	
		6	0		
	3	9	1	0	0
		8	0	0	
		7	0		
	2	9	0	0	
10	10	10	6	5	3
		9	4	3	2
		8	3	2	1
		7	2	1	0

A	B	a	.10	.05	.01
10	10	6	1	0	
		5	0	0	
		4	0		
	9	10	5	4	3
		9	4	3	2
		8	2	2	1
		7	1	1	0
		6	1	0	
		5	0	0	
	8	10	4	4	2
		9	3	2	1
		8	2	1	0
		7	1	1	0
		6	0	0	
		5	0		
	7	10	3	3	2
		9	2	2	1
		8	1	1	0
		7	1	0	
		6	0	0	
		5	0		
	6	10	3	2	1
		9	2	1	0
		8	1	1	0
		7	0	0	
		6	0		
	5	10	2	2	1
		9	1	1	0
		8	1	0	
		7	0	0	
		6	0		
	4	10	1	1	0
		9	1	0	0
		8	0	0	
		7	0		
	3	10	1	0	0
		9	0	0	
		8	0		
	2	10	0	0	
		9	0		

Table A.10 / Critical values for the rank-correlation test

This table gives the critical values of $|V|$ for the rank-order correlation test. For example, if you had a sample of 12 and $|V| = 35$, you'd enter the table and find that the critical value at .01 level of significance was 38 and at .05 was 30. You would conclude that the correlation was significantly different from zero at the .05 level of significance but not at the .01 level. If n is larger than 40, use the normal approximation

$$z = \frac{V}{\sqrt{n(n-1)(2n+5)/18}}$$

Variations of this formula exist which account for tied observations and corrections for continuity. They can be found in advanced texts on distribution-free methods.

	Smallest value of V_0 for which $P(V \geq V_0) \leq \alpha$				Smallest value of V_0 for which $P(V \geq V_0) \leq \alpha$		
n	.10	.05	.01	n	.10	.05	.01
4	6			23	65	75	99
				24	68	80	104
5	8	10					
6	11	13	15	25	72	86	110
7	13	15	19	26	77	91	117
8	16	18	22	27	81	95	125
9	18	20	26	28	86	100	130
				29	90	106	138
10	21	23	29				
11	23	27	33	30	95	111	145
12	26	30	38	31	99	117	151
13	28	34	44	32	104	122	160
14	33	37	47	33	108	128	166
				34	113	133	175
15	35	41	53				
16	38	46	58	35	117	139	181
17	42	50	64	36	122	146	190
18	45	53	69	37	128	152	198
19	49	57	75	38	133	157	205
				39	139	163	213
20	52	62	80				
21	56	66	86	40	144	170	222
22	61	71	91				

Source: L. Kaarsemaker and A. van Wijngaarden, Tables for Use in Rank Correlation, *Statistica Neerlandica*, vol. 7, pp. 41–54, table III, 1953 (reproduced as Report R73 of the Computation Department of the Mathematical Centre, Amsterdam), with permission of the authors, the Mathematical Centre, and the editor of *Statistica Neerlandica*.

Table A.11 / Table of Logarithms to Base 10

N	0	1	2	3	4	5	6	7	8	9
10	0000	0043	0086	0128	0170	0212	0253	0294	0334	0374
11	0414	0453	0492	0531	0569	0607	0645	0682	0719	0755
12	0792	0828	0864	0899	0934	0969	1004	1038	1072	1106
13	1139	1173	1206	1239	1271	1303	1335	1367	1399	1430
14	1461	1492	1523	1553	1584	1614	1644	1673	1703	1732
15	1761	1790	1818	1847	1875	1903	1931	1959	1987	2014
16	2041	2068	2095	2122	2148	2175	2201	2227	2253	2279
17	2304	2330	2355	2380	2405	2430	2455	2480	2504	2529
18	2553	2577	2601	2625	2648	2672	2695	2718	2742	2765
19	2788	2810	2833	2856	2878	2900	2923	2945	2967	2989
20	3010	3032	3054	3075	3096	3118	3139	3160	3181	3201
21	3222	3243	3263	3284	3304	3324	3345	3365	3385	3404
22	3424	3444	3464	3483	3502	3522	3541	3560	3579	3598
23	3617	3636	3655	3674	3692	3711	3729	3747	3766	3784
24	3802	3820	3838	3856	3874	3892	3909	3927	3945	3962
25	3979	3997	4014	4031	4048	4065	4082	4099	4116	4133
26	4150	4166	4183	4200	4216	4232	4249	4265	4281	4298
27	4314	4330	4346	4362	4378	4393	4409	4425	4440	4456
28	4472	4487	4502	4518	4533	4548	4564	4579	4594	4609
29	4624	4639	4654	4669	4683	4698	4713	4728	4742	4757
30	4771	4786	4800	4814	4829	4843	4857	4871	4886	4900
31	4914	4928	4942	4955	4969	4983	4997	5011	5024	5038
32	5051	5065	5079	5092	5105	5119	5132	5145	5159	5172
33	5185	5198	5211	5224	5237	5250	5263	5276	5289	5302
34	5315	5328	5340	5353	5366	5378	5391	5403	5416	5428
35	5441	5453	5465	5478	5490	5502	5514	5527	5539	5551
36	5563	5575	5587	5599	5611	5623	5635	5647	5658	5670
37	5682	5694	5705	5717	5729	5740	5752	5763	5775	5786
38	5798	5809	5821	5832	5843	5855	5866	5877	5888	5899
39	5911	5922	5933	5944	5955	5966	5977	5988	5999	6010
40	6021	6031	6042	6053	6064	6075	6085	6096	6107	6117
41	6128	6138	6149	6160	6170	6180	6191	6201	6212	6222
42	6232	6243	6253	6263	6274	6284	6294	6304	6314	6325
43	6336	6345	6355	6365	6375	6385	6395	6405	6415	6425
44	6435	6444	6454	6464	6474	6484	6493	6503	6513	6522
45	6532	6542	6551	6561	6571	6580	6590	6599	6609	6618
46	6628	6637	6646	6656	6665	6675	6684	6693	6702	6712
47	6721	6730	6739	6749	6758	6767	6776	6785	6794	6803
48	6812	6821	6830	6839	6848	6857	6866	6875	6884	6893
49	6902	6911	6920	6928	6937	6946	6955	6964	6972	6981
50	6990	6998	7007	7016	7024	7033	7042	7050	7059	7067
51	7076	7084	7093	7101	7110	7118	7126	7135	7143	7152
52	7160	7168	7177	7185	7193	7202	7210	7218	7226	7235
53	7243	7251	7259	7267	7275	7284	7292	7300	7308	7316
54	7324	7332	7340	7348	7356	7364	7372	7380	7388	7396

Table A.11 / *(continued)*

N	0	1	2	3	4	5	6	7	8	9
55	7404	7412	7419	7427	7435	7443	7451	7459	7466	7474
56	7482	7490	7497	7505	7513	7520	7528	7536	7543	7551
57	7559	7566	7574	7582	7589	7597	7604	7612	7619	7627
58	7634	7642	7649	7657	7664	7672	7679	7686	7694	7701
59	7709	7716	7723	7731	7738	7745	7752	7760	7767	7774
60	7782	7789	7796	7803	7810	7818	7825	7832	7839	7846
61	7853	7860	7868	7875	7882	7889	7896	7903	7910	7917
62	7924	7931	7938	7945	7952	7959	7966	7973	7980	7987
63	7993	8000	8007	8014	8021	8028	8035	8041	8048	8055
64	8062	8069	8075	8082	8089	8096	8102	8109	8116	8122
65	8129	8136	8142	8149	8156	8162	8169	8176	8182	8189
66	8195	8202	8209	8215	8222	8228	8235	8241	8248	8254
67	8261	8267	8274	8280	8287	8293	8299	8306	8312	8319
68	8325	8331	8338	8344	8351	8357	8363	8370	8376	8382
69	8388	8395	8401	8407	8414	8420	8426	8432	8439	8445
70	8451	8457	8463	8470	8476	8482	8488	8494	8500	8506
71	8513	8519	8525	8531	8537	8543	8549	8555	8561	8567
72	8573	8579	8585	8591	8597	8603	8609	8615	8621	8627
73	8633	8639	8645	8651	8657	8663	8669	8675	8681	8686
74	8692	8698	8704	8710	8716	8722	8727	8733	8739	8745
75	8751	8756	8762	8768	8774	8779	8785	8791	8797	8802
76	8808	8814	8820	8825	8831	8837	8842	8848	8854	8859
77	8865	8871	8876	8882	8887	8893	8899	8904	8910	8915
78	8921	8927	8932	8938	8943	8949	8954	8960	8965	8971
79	8976	8982	8987	8993	8998	9004	9009	9015	9020	9025
80	9031	9036	9042	9047	9053	9058	9063	9069	9074	9079
81	9085	9090	9096	9101	9106	9112	9117	9122	9128	9133
82	9138	9143	9149	9154	9159	9165	9170	9175	9180	9186
83	9191	9196	9201	9206	9212	9217	9222	9227	9232	9238
84	9243	9248	9253	9258	9263	9269	9274	9279	9284	9289
85	9294	9299	9304	9309	9315	9320	9325	9330	9335	9340
86	9345	9350	9355	9360	9365	9370	9375	9380	9385	9390
87	9395	9400	9405	9410	9415	9420	9425	9430	9435	9440
88	9445	9450	9455	9460	9465	9469	9474	9479	9484	9489
89	9494	9499	9504	9509	9513	9518	9523	9528	9533	9538
90	9542	9547	9552	9557	9562	9566	9571	9576	9581	9586
91	9590	9595	9600	9605	9609	9614	9619	9624	9628	9633
92	9638	9643	9647	9652	9657	9661	9666	9671	9675	9680
93	9685	9689	9694	9699	9703	9708	9713	9717	9722	9727
94	9731	9736	9741	9745	9750	9754	9759	9763	9768	9773
95	9777	9782	9786	9791	9795	9800	9805	9809	9814	9818
96	9823	9827	9832	9836	9841	9845	9850	9854	9859	9863
97	9868	9872	9877	9881	9886	9890	9894	9899	9903	9908
98	9912	9917	9921	9926	9930	9934	9939	9943	9948	9952
99	9956	9961	9965	9969	9974	9978	9983	9987	9991	9996

APPENDIX B
Glossary of Symbols and Abbreviations

$<$	Less than
$\leq$	Less than or equal to
$>$	Greater than
$\geq$	Greater than or equal to
$!$	Factorial
$\lvert\ \rvert$	Absolute value of
$\approx$	Approximately equals
$\mid$	Given
α	Lowercase alpha—(1) Y intercept at the origin for a population estimating equation; (2) exponential smoothing constant; (3) level of significance, maximum risk of a Type I error
a	Y intercept at the origin for a trend line or sample estimating equation
AL	Action limit
β	Lowercase beta—(1) Slope of a population estimating equation; (2) risk of a Type II error
b	(1) Slope; change in Y per unit change in X; (2) ratio of one value to preceding value in an exponential equation
c	(1) Constant of X^2 term in parabolic equation; (2) criterion number; action limit for a hypothesis concerning a proportion
C	Cyclical component in time-series decomposition
χ^2	(Lowercase chi squared) Chi-square statistic
$C(n,r)$	Combination of n things r at a time
COL	Conditional opportunity loss
CP	Conditional profit
d	Coded midvalue; deviation from an assumed mean in class interval units
D	(1) Maximum deviation in Kolmogorov-Smirnov test; (2) standardized deviation used in determining unit normal loss integral
DSM	Double smoothed exponential mean
ε	(Lowercase epsilon) The error term in regression analysis for a population
e	(1) The constant $2.71828\cdots$; (2) the error term in analysis of association for a sample
E	Expectation; expected value; employment
EM	Estimated mean
EMV	Expected monetary value
EMV*	Expected monetary value of the optimal act
EOL	Expected opportunity loss
EOL*	Expected opportunity loss of the optimal act
EPC	Expected profit under certainty
EVPI	Expected value of perfect information
EVSI	Expected value of sample information
f	Frequency; number of items in a class
i	Class interval, partially smoothed irregular variation in time series

I	Irregular or random variation in time-series decomposition
IC	Information content
K	Asymptote of a growth curve
L	Absolute slope of conditional opportunity loss function
L_{Md}	Lower limit of the median class
L_{Mo}	Lower limit of the modal class
μ	(Lowercase mu) Arithmetic mean of a population
$\mu_{Y \cdot X}$	Conditional mean of Y given X for a population estimating equation
m	Number of clusters in a sample
M	Number of clusters in a population
Md	Median
Mo	Mode
MV	Midvalue
n	Number of trials; size of a sample
N	Size of a population
$N(D)$	Unit normal loss integral
O	Output
OC	Operating characteristic
π	(Lowercase pi) The constant $3.14159 \cdots$
p	Population proportion; probability of a success in a Bernoulli process
p_n	Given-year price
p_0	Base-year price
P	Probability
P_b	Binomial probability
P_H	Hypergeometric probability
P_N	Normal probability
$\bar{p}$	Sample proportion, r/n
$P(A)$	Marginal probability of A
$P(A \text{ and } B)$	Joint probability of A and B
$P(A \mid B)$	Conditional probability of A given B
q_n	Given-year quantity
q_0	Base-year quantity
r	(1) Number of successes in a sample; (2) coefficient of correlation
r^2	Coefficient of determination
$r_{YX_2 \cdot X_1}$	Coefficient of partial correlation (between Y and X_2 when X_1 is held constant)
$r^2_{YX_2 \cdot X_1}$	Coefficient of partial determination
R	Coefficient of multiple correlation
R^2	Coefficient of multiple determination
σ	(Lowercase sigma) Standard deviation of a population
σ^2	Population variance
$\sigma_{\bar{p}}$	Standard deviation of the sampling distribution of a proportion
$\sigma_{\bar{p}_1 - \bar{p}_2}$	Standard deviation of the sampling distribution of the difference between two population proportions
$\sigma_{\bar{X}}$	Standard deviation of the sampling distribution of the mean
$\sigma_{\bar{X}_1 - \bar{X}_2}$	Standard deviation of the sampling distribution of the difference between two population means
$\sigma_{Y \cdot X}$	Standard deviation of Y given X for a population (standard error of estimate)
$\sum$	(Capital sigma) Summation

$\sum R_1$	Sum of ranks in group 1 for Mann-Whitney test
s	Sample estimate of a population standard deviation
s^2	Sample estimate of a population variance
$s_{\bar{p}}$	Sample estimate of the standard deviation of the sampling distribution of a proportion
$s_{\bar{p}_1-\bar{p}_2}$	Sample estimate of the standard deviation of the sampling distribution of the difference between two population proportions
$s_{\bar{X}}$	Sample estimate of the standard deviation of the sampling distribution of the mean
$s_{\bar{X}_1-\bar{X}_2}$	Sample estimate of the standard deviation of the sampling distribution of the difference between two population means
$s_{Y\cdot X}$	Sample estimate of the standard deviation of Y given X (sample standard error of estimate)
S	Seasonal component in time-series decomposition
Sk	Skewness
SSM	Single smoothed exponential mean
τ	(Lowercase tau) Kendall's coefficient of rank correlation
t	Standardized deviate for Student's t distribution
T	Trend component in time-series decomposition
U	(1) Universal set; (2) statistic for Mann-Whitney test
Var	Variance $=\sigma^2$ or s^2
$\bar{X}$	Arithmetic mean of a sample
Y_c	Calculated ordinate for a trend line
$\bar{Y}_X$	Conditional mean of Y given X for a sample estimating equation
z	Standardized normal deviate

INDEX

INDEX